HERO
CITY

OSPREY
PUBLISHING

DEDICATION
For Bruno

HERO CITY

LENINGRAD 1943–44

PRIT BUTTAR

OSPREY PUBLISHING
Bloomsbury Publishing Plc
Kemp House, Chawley Park, Cumnor Hill, Oxford OX2 9PH, UK
29 Earlsfort Terrace, Dublin 2, Ireland
1385 Broadway, 5th Floor, New York, NY 10018, USA

E-mail: info@ospreypublishing.com

www.ospreypublishing.com

OSPREY is a trademark of Osprey Publishing Ltd

First published in Great Britain in 2024

ISBN: HB 978 1 4728 5661 6; PB 978 1 4728 5662 3; eBook 978 1 4728 5659 3;
ePDF 978 1 4728 5660 9; XML 978 1 4728 5663 0; Audio 978 1 4728 5658 6

24 25 26 27 28   10 9 8 7 6 5 4 3 2 1

Plate section image credits and captions are given in full in the List of Illustrations (pp. 7–9).

Maps by Prit Buttar
Index by Zoe Ross

Typeset by Deanta Global Publishing Services, Chennai, India
Printed and bound in Great Britain by CPI (Group) UK Ltd, Croydon CR0 4YY

Editor's note
For ease of comparison please refer to the following conversion table:
1 mile = 1.6km
1 yd = 0.9m
1 ft = 0.3m
1 in. = 2.54cm/25.4mm
1 lb = 0.45kg

Osprey Publishing supports the Woodland Trust, the UK's leading woodland conservation charity.

To find out more about our authors and books visit www.ospreypublishing.com. Here you will find
extracts, author interviews, details of forthcoming events and the option to sign up for our newsletter.

CONTENTS

LIST OF ILLUSTRATIONS

'Come on, let's dig a trench!' This photograph is part of a collection showing daily life in Leningrad during the siege, and was published in a USSR Information Bulletin in 1943. (Merrill C. Berman Collection)

'The city has carefully covered and camouflaged the statue of Lenin.' Until the Germans were driven back, Leningrad remained under constant threat. (Merrill C. Berman Collection)

A wounded man is evacuated from the battlefield around Leningrad. The flood of casualties overwhelmed hospitals close to the front line, and the wounded were often moved further to the rear. (Photo by Keystone-France\Gamma-Rapho via Getty Images)

A trio of Soviet infantrymen in position, armed with the PPSh-41. It was much-loved due to its reliability even in sub-zero temperatures, so crucial in fighting in the unforgiving winters on the Eastern Front. (Courtesy of the Central Museum of the Armed Forces, Moscow via Stavka)

An artillery position of the Spanish Blue Division in front of Leningrad during the winter of 1942/43. Although the Germans had a low opinion of their martial abilities, the soldiers of the Blue Division generally performed well in combat. (Photo by ullstein bild/ullstein bild via Getty Images)

January 1943: Overcome with emotion, soldiers from Leningrad and Volkhov fronts cheer, wave their hats and embrace heartily. After over a year of encirclement, the siege ring around Leningrad was broken during *Iskra*. (Photo by Keystone/Getty Images)

German grenadiers taking positions in the trenches south of Lake Ladoga, February 1943. In the winter, frostbite regularly caused more casualties than enemy action, and in the summer the mosquitoes and the damp, muddy landscape posed a different set of problems. (Photo by ullstein bild/ullstein bild via Getty Images)

A mother and child walk past the ruins of a building in Leningrad in 1943. Although the siege ring had been broken, the city remained in a vulnerable position. (Photo by B. Kudoyarov/Hulton Archive/Getty Images)

Battle break: German soldiers standing next to a Tiger and a destroyed Soviet KV-1 in September 1943. Much of the terrain in the battles in this region was unsuited to the massed use of tanks. (Photo by ullstein bild/ullstein bild via Getty Images)

A German sign indicates a mine-free path in a minefield near Leningrad. Both sides made use of minefields, making the dense forested country even more difficult to navigate. (Sueddeutsche Zeitung Photo / Alamy Stock Photo)

Two German infantrymen during a snow storm in their trench position, December 1943. Soldiers of both sides struggled through the snow, frozen swamps, and shattered forests of the region, fighting and dying in a manner that was little different from the terrible attritional battles of the First World War. (Photo by ullstein bild/ullstein bild via Getty Images)

A Guards artillery forward observation team calls in target coordinates to its commander. The Red Army placed great expectations on the efficacy of its 'god of war', the massed artillery that was used in every offensive operation, but these were rarely met, in part due to weaknesses in reconnaissance. (From the fonds of the RGAKFD in Krasnogorsk via Stavka)

Keeping watch in a front-line position, this German soldier has grenades to hand and photos of loved ones pinned to the tree. In wooded countryside such as this men had be constantly alert for enemy patrols. (Nik Cornish)

C. Bykova (left) and R. Skrypnikova, two Soviet snipers, are shown in camouflage battle garb, returning from a combat assignment. Successful snipers were treated almost as celebrities by the Soviet Union, with constant newspaper stories about their exploits. (Bettmann/Getty Images)

Soviet troops on a reconnaissance mission on the Leningrad front, January 1944. Such patrols were also tasked with capturing 'tongues' – prisoners who could be interrogated about the German dispositions. (Sovfoto/UIG/Bridgeman Images)

Latvian SS volunteers being briefed. Latvian soldiers fought in the Leningrad sector and the battles that followed the end of the siege, as the Red Army pressed into the Baltic States. (Nik Cornish)

Soviet troops from the 110th Rifle Corps rush into the Catherine Palace in Pushkin on 24 January 1944. The liberation of Pushkin, Krasnoye Selo and the Peterhof effectively marked the end of the siege of Leningrad. (Robert Forczyk collection)

Major General Nikolai Pavlovich Simoniak, the officer who succeeded in breaking the blockade of Leningrad and leading the breakout from Oranienbaum. Simoniak was arguably the best Soviet tactical commander in the siege of Leningrad. (Robert Forczyk collection)

Red Army soldiers lead German prisoners of war through the streets of Leningrad, a city they failed to capture despite a siege lasting 900 days, from 1941 to 1944. (Photo © CORBIS/Corbis via Getty Images)

The Piskarevskoye Cemetery became the site of mass graves during the siege. As Zhdanovism and Stalin's long-standing hostility to Leningrad began to take hold after the war, the site lay neglected until the mid-1950s. (Alexey Ivanov, Flickr, CC BY-SA 2.0, https://creativecommons.org/licenses/by-sa/2.0/)

The long-delayed plans for a formal memorial to the siege of Leningrad were resurrected in the 1960s. The bronze figures of the Monument to the Heroic Defenders of Leningrad depict a variety of people, including both soldiers and civilians. (Author's collection)

These poignant figures are intended to portray the suffering of ordinary people during the siege, although it is clear that there was an unwillingness to portray the true emaciated state of Leningraders during the first winter. (Author's collection)

The museum beneath the monument contains mosaics showing various aspects of the siege. This example shows victory celebrations in 1944. (Author's collection)

The sign on Nevsky Prospekt that reads: 'Citizens! During artillery fire this side of the street is more dangerous'. The notice by the flowers reads: 'This inscription was saved in memory of the heroism and courage of Leningraders during the 900-day blockade of the city'. This is not actually true, as it was erased and later re-created. (Author's collection)

Memorials to historic events reflect the society in which they are created. It is best to see both Piskarevskoye Cemetery and the Monument to the Heroic Defenders of Leningrad in this light. (Author's collection)

LIST OF MAPS

DRAMATIS PERSONAE

GERMANY

Augsberger, Franz – Brigadeführer, commander 20th *Estnische SS-Freiwilligen* Division

Backe, Herbert – State Secretary in the *Reichsministerium für Ernährung und Landwirtschaft* ('Reich Ministry for Food and Agriculture')

Berlin, Wilhelm – General, commander 227th Infantry Division

Boeck-Behrens, Hans, Generalmajor – chief of staff Sixteenth Army

Busch, Ernst – Generaloberst, commander Sixteenth Army

Carius, Otto – junior officer, *Schwere Panzer Abteilung 502*

Erdmannsdorff, Werner von – Generalmajor, commander 18th Motorised Division and eponymous group

Fehn, Gustav – General, temporary commander XXVI Corps

Foertsch, Albert Friedrich – Oberst, chief of staff Eighteenth Army

Friessner, Johannes – General, commander eponymous group, later commander *Armee Abteilung Narwa*

Geerkens, Heinrich – Oberst, commander 9th Field Division

Grase, Martin – General, commander XXVI Corps from January 1944

Hansen, Christian – General, commander X Corps, later commander of Sixteenth Army

Hansen, Erich – General, commander LIV Corps

Hasse, Wilhelm – Generalleutnant, chief of staff Army Group North until 22 January 1943

Herzog, Kurt – General, commander XXXVIII Corps

Hilpert, Carl – General, commander eponymous group and later LIV Corps

Hohnschild, Hermann Friedrich – Korvettenkapitän, commander eponymous battlegroup

Hühner, Werner – Generalleutnant, commander 61st Infantry Division

Jähde, Wilhelm – Major, commander *Schwere Panzer Abteilung 502*

Kinzel, Eberhard – Generalleutnant, chief of staff Army Group North from late January 1943

Kleinhenz, German – Oberstleutnant, commander 401st Grenadier Regiment, 170th Infantry Division

Krosigk, Dedo von – Major, battalion commander 18th Motorised Infantry Division

Küchler, Georg von - Generalfeldmarschall, commander Army Group North

Lamey, Hubert – Generalmajor, commander 28th Jäger Division

Laux, Paul – General, commander II Corps

Leyser, Ernst von – General, commander XXVI Corps

Lindemann, Georg – Generaloberst, commander Eighteenth Army

Loch, Herbert – General, commander XXVIII Corps

Lubbeck, Wilhelm – artillery spotter, 58th Infantry Division

Model, Walter – Generaloberst, commander Army Group North from 1 February 1944

Rosenthal, Wilfried von – Major, operations officer 225th Infantry Division

Sinnhuber, Johann – General, commander of 28th Jäger Division

Sponheimer, Otto – General, commander LIV Corps

Steiner, Felix – Obergruppenführer, commander III SS-Panzer Corps

Usinger, Christian – Generalleutnant, commander 223rd Infantry Division

Wedel, Hermann von – Generalmajor, commander 10th Field Division

Wegener, Wilhelm – General, commander L Corps

Wengler, Maximilian – Oberstleutnant, later Oberst, commander 366th Grenadier Regiment

Zander, Erwin – Generalleutnant, commander 170th Infantry Division

Zeitzler, Kurt – Generaloberst, chief of general staff

Ziegler, Gerhard – Major, commander 374th Grenadier Regiment

SOVIET UNION

Afanasyev, Nikolai Ivanovich – partisan officer

Beregovaya, Lyubov Borisovna – young girl in Leningrad

Berggolts, Olga Fyodorovna – poet

Borshchev, Semen Nikolayevich – Colonel, commander 46th Rifle Division

Burakovsky, Ivan Nikolayevich – Colonel, commander 73rd Naval Rifle Brigade

Dukhanov, Mikhail Pavlovich – Lieutenant General, commander Sixty-Seventh Army

Dushevsky, Iosif Mikhailovich – infantry company commander

Eremenko, Andrei Ivanovich – General, commander 1st Baltic Front

Fedyuninsky, Ivan Ivanovich – Lieutenant General, deputy commander Volkhov Front, later commander Second Shock Army

Galitsky, Kuzma Nikitovich – Lieutenant General, commander Third Shock Army

Govorov, Leonid Aleksandrovich – Colonel General, commander Leningrad Front

Inber, Vera Mikhailovna – poet and diarist

Katukov, Mikhail Yefimovich – Lieutenant General, commander First Tank Army

Kazakov, Mikhail Ilyich – Lieutenant General, commander Tenth Guards Army

Khozin, Mikhail Semenovich – Colonel General, commander eponymous Special Group

Khrushchev, Nikita Sergeyevich – First Secretary of the Communist Party of the Soviet Union 1953–64

Kirov, Sergei Mironovich – First Secretary of the Leningrad Communist Party 1927–34

Korovnikov, Ivan Terentyevich – Lieutenant General, commander Fifty-Ninth Army

Krasnov, Anatoly Andreyevich – Major General, commander 45th Guards Division

Kuznetsov, Aleksei Aleksandrovich – First Secretary of the Leningrad Communist Party 1946

Maslennikov, Ivan Ivanovich – General, commander Forty-Second Army

Meretskov, Kirill Afanasyevich – General, commander Volkhov Front

Morozov, Dmitry Alekseyevich – artillery officer

Odintsov, Georgy Fedorovich – Lieutenant General, artillery commander Leningrad Front

Ovsyannikova, Tamara Rodionovna – signaller

Petrova, Nina Pavlona – sniper

Popov, Markian Mikhailovich – General, commander 2nd Baltic Front

Roginsky, Sergei Vasilyevich – Lieutenant General, commander Fifty-Fourth Army

Romanovsky, Vladimir Zakharovich – Lieutenant General, commander Second Shock Army

Shavrova, Yevgeniya – diarist in Leningrad

Shtemenko, Sergei Matveyevich – Colonel General, Chief of Operations Directorate

Simoniak, Nikolai Pavlovich - Major General, commander 136th Rifle Division

Skoybeda, Vitaly Valerievich – politician, member of *Demokraticheskogo Soyuza*

Sobchak, Anatoly Aleksandrovich – last Communist Party leader in Leningrad, first city mayor

Starikov, Filipp Nikanorovich – Lieutenant General, commander Eighth Army

Sviklin, Teodor-Verner Andreyevich – Major General, deputy commander Fifty-Ninth Army and commander of eponymous group

Sviridov, Vladimir Petrovich – Major General, commander Fifty-Fifth Army, later Sixty-Seventh Army

Sukhomlin, Aleksandr Vasilyevich – Lieutenant General, commander Fifty-Fourth Army, later commander Tenth Guards Army

Timoshenko, Semen Konstantinovich – Marshal, commander Northwest Front

Tolbukhin, Fedor Ivanovich – Lieutenant General, commander Sixty-Eighth Army

Vasilevsky, Aleksandr Mikhailovich – Marshal, chief of general staff and deputy defence minister

Vlasov, Andrei Andreyevich – Lieutenant General, commander Second Shock Army 1942, later commander ROA

Voronov, Nikolai Nikolayevich – General, head of Red Army artillery and deputy defence minister

Voroshilov, Kliment Yefremovich – Marshal, special *Stavka* representative

Zhdanov, Andrei Aleksandrovich – First Secretary of Leningrad Communist Party during the siege

Zhukov, Georgy Konstantinovich – Marshal, Deputy Commander-in-Chief of the Red Army

OTHERS

Bangerskis, Rūdolfs – General, Inspector General of the Latvian Legion (Latvia)

Esteban-Infantes, Emilio – Generalleutnant, commander Blue Division (Spain)

Garcia-Navarro, Antonio – Colonel, commander Spanish Legion (Spain)

Kryssing, Christian Peder – Brigadeführer, commander *Kampfgruppe Küste* (Norway)

Mannerheim, Carl Gustav Emil – Field Marshal, commander-in chief Finnish armed forces, later prime minister (Finland)

Ryti, Risto – Finnish prime minister (Finland)

Veiss, Voldemārs – Obersturmbannführer, battlegroup commander 2nd Latvian Brigade (Latvia)

INTRODUCTION

A Singular City

In 1946, Aleksei Aleksandrovich Kuznetsov, seeking election as First Secretary of the Leningrad Communist Party, gave a speech in which he articulated the special nature of the city in which he had lived and worked throughout the war:

> How is it possible not to love such a city? How do you not love a city into which, since the moment of its foundation, no enemy has stepped foot? ... The first city to stop the enemy, holding out during a 29-month siege ... a city whose glory eclipsed the glory of Troy![1]

It was a statement that would have come as no surprise to Leningraders. They had always seen their city as something special, and for them the events of the great siege were confirmation of their status. Leningrad was a uniquely important city, not just in the Soviet Union but on the entire planet.

Ever since it was founded by Peter the Great, the city on the banks of the Neva River – known first as St Petersburg, then as Petrograd, then as Leningrad and now once more as St Petersburg – was seen both by its residents and by other Russians as different. As a relatively recent creation, deliberately laid out with a grid-like street plan and then embellished by the tsars with a wealth of neo-classical architecture, it had none of the winding streets and narrow alleys of so many other cities. It was deliberately fashioned as Russia's 'window to the west', both as a showcase of the ability of Russia to match any city created by other nations and as a portal via which advanced ideas might flow into what the tsars had always recognised was a country lagging behind its competitors. The cultural embellishments added to it over the years ensured that it was a powerful magnet for artists and writers, and over the decades of its existence many of the books written by its inhabitants reflected a curious truth. Their portrayals of this city in the far north, with its sharp winters and endless daylight in midsummer, created a remarkable two-way effect. In their attempts to describe the city in all its splendour and squalor, authors like Dostoyevsky provided multiple points of reference for the city's inhabitants. Nikolai Pavlovich Antsiferov, who wrote extensively on the cultural history of a city that was still St Petersburg when he was born, remembered how Dostoyevsky's descriptions had helped him when he was an impoverished student: 'All the adversities of Petersburg life are accepted beforehand: literature has made them attractive … I even liked the danger and prospect of hunger … I looked at life through the prism of literature.'[2]

Vladimir Nikolayevich Toporov, a prominent Soviet and Russian philologist, was a native of Moscow but recognised the unusual relationship between St Petersburg and its literature: 'In the most complex and perhaps key cases, it is equally difficult to decide conclusively what in the text is from the city, and – more often – what in the city is from the text.'[3]

It was almost inevitable that the inhabitants of this unusual city with its rich and self-referential literature would come to regard themselves as different from the rest of the Russian Empire. In his great novel *Petersburg*, Andrei Bely referred somewhat disdainfully to other Russian cities as little more than clusters of wooden houses, and other residents of St Petersburg regarded their home city 'as a civilised, cultured, systematically organised, logically rectilinear, harmonious, European city' compared to 'Moscow, a chaotic, disorderly, contrary-to-logic, semi-Asiatic village'. Conversely, many other Russians – particularly those who saw east-looking Moscow as the true centre of Russia rather than west-looking St Petersburg – came to treat the inhabitants of the city in the north as different and the subject of suspicion; they saw St Petersburg as 'soulless, bureaucratic, official, unnaturally regular, abstract, bleak, escheated, [and] un-Russian' whereas Moscow was 'soulful, domestically intimate, patriarchal, cosy, down-to-earth, natural, [and] Russian'.[4] In later years, chief amongst those who disliked and were suspicious of the politically unruly, west-looking, individualistic St Petersburg or Leningrad was Josef Stalin.

St Petersburg became Petrograd and then Leningrad, and almost as if the city was preparing for what lay ahead it endured severe winters and famine during the Russian Civil War. Sergei Mironovich Kirov, First Secretary of the Leningrad Communist Party, was assassinated in December 1934 and it is probable that Stalin had a role in the killing – the *NKVD** had markedly reduced Kirov's personal protection immediately prior to the assassination and although the assassin, Leonid Nikolayev, was arrested entering the Smolny Institute,

---

* *Narodny Komissariat Vnutrennikh Del* or 'People's Commissariat for Internal Affairs', the Soviet Union's internal security force and forerunner of the KGB.

headquarters of the Leningrad Communist Party, in October with a loaded pistol, he was released without charge and his gun was returned to him. Kirov had been hugely popular in Leningrad but was also becoming increasingly popular across the Soviet Union, much to the irritation of others. In the Communist Party Congress of February 1934, he was declared the joint winner with Stalin in a ballot of members for high office, but this result was only because a close supporter of Stalin allegedly destroyed a large number of pro-Kirov ballot papers. With his potential rival removed by the assassin Nikolayev, Stalin used the killing as a trigger for a wave of repression that rolled across all parts of Soviet society in the years that followed. Leningrad, always regarded by Stalin as wayward and difficult to control, was particularly singled out.

Then came the siege of Leningrad, an event without parallel in the Second World War. Other cities – Warsaw, Budapest, Königsberg, even Berlin – endured sieges at various stages of the war, but none lasted remotely as long as the ordeal of Leningrad. The front line ran through the southern suburbs and there was regular contact between citizens and the soldiers fighting to protect them from the Germans, and with all parts of Leningrad within German artillery range, the entire urban area effectively became part of the extended battlefield. This was certain to leave deep scars and memories of unique experiences, and after the war the pre-established special character of Leningrad and its population added to this sense that the city and its people had endured something exceptional. The relatively high proportion of writers and poets who lived in Leningrad added an additional layer to the distinctive manner in which the siege and those who endured it would be remembered. But the combination of the natural desire of people to make sense of their personal experiences, enhanced by these particular features of Leningrad, ran contrary to how Stalin wished the war years to be remembered. The result would be many years of partial truths, large omissions, and deliberate falsehoods.

This is the conclusion of the story that began with an earlier volume that described the coming of the war to Leningrad and the bitter fighting of 1941 and 1942,[5] and covers the battles that first broke the siege ring in 1943 and then a year later drove the Wehrmacht back from Leningrad and into Estonia. It also looks at the post-war legacy of the siege and how in many ways the conflict between the memories of ordinary people and the official, orthodox Soviet view contributed to the growing sense of disillusionment and distrust that eventually swept away the Soviet Union in 1991. The complex past of the city, from the moment of its creation by Peter the Great to recent times, has created a place that continues to be inextricably linked to the literature it has inspired; as was the case in the past, St Petersburg both inspires writers and is in turn inspired by them.

CHAPTER 1

UNFINISHED BUSINESS

In many respects, it seemed as if the year of 1943 commenced with the war in Eastern Europe finely poised. The German Sixth Army was surrounded in Stalingrad and much of the southern sector of the long front line was highly fluid, with Soviet units attempting to push west and southwest to reach the shores of the Sea of Azov or the great bend of the Dnepr River – if they achieved either objective, they would isolate an even greater number of German troops and almost guarantee the rapid collapse of the Wehrmacht. But both logistic constraints and the wear and tear of constant high-tempo operations were beginning to bite, steadily eroding the fighting power of the Red Army's formations. By contrast, the Germans had started the winter fighting in a configuration that was completely unsuited to defending against a major Soviet offensive; through a mixture of forced and voluntary retreats, they were pulling back and reducing their own overstretched supply lines. Together with fresh troops arriving from the west, the armies that the Red Army was striving to destroy were steadily moving into positions from where they would be able to mount a powerful counteroffensive to restore integrity of the front line. It seemed as if much would depend on which side could achieve its objectives first.

Elsewhere on the Eastern Front, the battlefield was far less fluid. The last weeks of 1942 saw bitter fighting around the Rzhev salient to the west of Moscow as the Red Army threw wave after wave of troops at the German lines. The attempts to destroy the salient were predicated upon a belief that it formed a potential starting point for a new German offensive against Moscow, but the Soviet attacks were at least partly driven by the stubborn determination of Marshal Georgy Konstantinovich Zhukov, deputy commander-in-chief of the Red Army, to crush German positions that had repeatedly defied his earlier attacks. Struggling forward through hilly, densely forested terrain, hundreds of thousands of Soviet soldiers perished in repeated, futile assaults on intact German defences.[1]

Further north too, there was a depressing familiarity to the positions occupied by the two sides. The Germans continued to hold a line that ran from the Gulf of Finland past the southern outskirts of Leningrad to the Neva River and on to Lake Ladoga; from here, their lines ran south to the Volkhov River and on to Novgorod in the south. Immediately to the west of Leningrad, on the southern shore of the Gulf of Finland, was the Oranienbaum bridgehead, a small area held by the Red Army and dependent upon seaborne supplies for its survival. Leningrad, the second city of the Soviet Union, had been besieged since the autumn of 1941 when the Wehrmacht first reached Lake Ladoga and cut off contact by land. During the winter of 1941–42, the city's inhabitants and defenders endured almost indescribable suffering in the midst of a bitterly cold winter as the Germans attempted to starve them into submission. Throughout 1942, the Red Army tried in vain to break through to the siege perimeter in order to lift the siege, suffering terrible casualties in the process. To a large extent, the areas where Soviet forces would mount their attacks were easy to predict. The road and rail network of the region was poor, limiting the ability of the Red Army to concentrate the resources needed for a deliberate attack against strong defences, and the positions of the front lines meant that there was no potential for surprise or innovative manoeuvre. Twice in 1942, small breaches in the German defences were achieved and on both occasions the Soviet Second Shock Army was inserted through these gaps in attempts to push on through the depths of the German positions. Each time, the narrowness of the initial penetration was exploited by the Wehrmacht to launch counterattacks that resulted in the isolation and almost complete destruction of Second Shock Army.

But although the front line from Lake Ladoga in the north to the southern limits of the German Army Group Centre seemed to be relatively static, the situation was significantly different from when the siege lines were first established. The heavy fighting of 1942 all along this vast front resulted in major changes in the two armies. The reality was that there was no longer any prospect of the Wehrmacht being able to assert itself and to dictate events in the same manner as before. The losses suffered by German forces through 1942 might have been far smaller than those suffered by the Soviet units facing them, but in many respects they were more serious. In particular, there were two categories of losses that would greatly hamper German operations for the rest of the war.

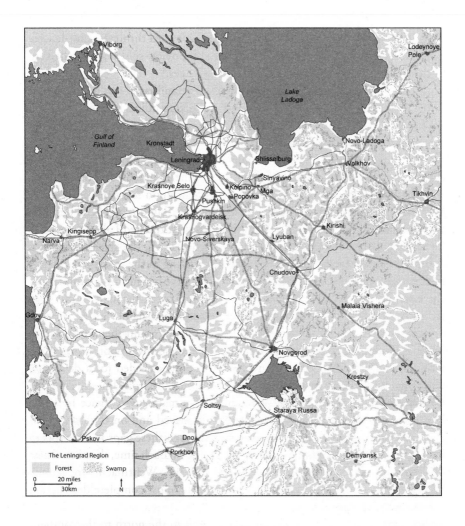

The first was the high casualty rate amongst German non-commissioned officers (NCOs) and officers. These men represented one of the greatest assets of the Wehrmacht at the outset of the war with the Soviet Union – highly experienced soldiers with campaigns against Poland, France, and Britain behind them, men who knew how to fight and survive and equally importantly were able to pass on these skills to the new recruits who reached the front line. As their numbers declined, the flexibility and initiative shown by German command at almost every level also diminished, a trend that was worsened by Hitler's increasing insistence on rigid and inflexible orders imposed from above.

The consequence was that the Germans had far less ability to respond to their numerically superior opponents with the speed and agility that was such a feature of their successes of earlier years.

The second category of German losses that had a huge impact on the performance of the Wehrmacht has barely been covered in the past. Although much has been written about the performance of Germany's panzer divisions – and German propaganda repeatedly highlighted their operations – the bulk of the Wehrmacht was made up of infantry divisions. Unlike their western opponents (and increasingly as the war progressed, their eastern opponents too), Wehrmacht infantry formations were heavily dependent upon horses to move their equipment; the equine establishment of an infantry division ran to over 2,600 animals, which were needed for reconnaissance as well as draught animals.[2] In some cases, the number was even higher. During the winter of 1941–42, the Wehrmacht lost a staggering total of 179,000 horses, far in excess of the number of replacements available.[3] Although German units captured large numbers of cavalry ponies, these were no substitute for the large draught horses that had been lost and the consequence was a major reduction in mobility. Repeatedly in the fighting of the winter of 1941–42, German units were forced to abandon artillery and other equipment simply because they no longer had sufficient horses to retain full mobility. Even units that still had significant numbers of horses then struggled to find fodder for their animals, particularly during the winter. The consequence was either a need to use already overstretched logistic capacity to move fodder, or to send the horses far to the rear, effectively leaving the infantry formations immobile.

A recurring feature of the war was that German infantry units would often be capable of determined resistance when occupying prepared positions, but if they were levered out of those positions they were swiftly forced to abandon so much heavy equipment that their performance declined rapidly, particularly as a major component of German defensive successes in 1942 had been the use of concentrated artillery fire to crush Soviet assault units. There were also growing concerns amongst front-line commanders about the quality of replacement drafts that arrived from Germany. Increasingly, it was necessary to establish training units close to the front line where these recruits could be given intensive teaching about how to fight and survive, and how to use heavy weapons – for example, the men sent to anti-tank units often hadn't even seen the larger-calibre guns in current use, as one officer in the anti-tank battalion of a panzer division in Army Group Centre described:

The replacement drafts from the *Ersatzheer* ['Replacement Army'] were relatively poorly trained. *Panzerjäger-Ersatz- und Ausbildungsabteilung 17*, which was responsible for our battalion, suffered badly from a shortage of weapons and training equipment, particularly in terms of trucks. All the young soldiers were therefore gathered together in the division's newly established *Feldersatzbataillon 82* in Melechovno ...

In addition to general basic training, which covered all types of weapons – infantry training including with machine-guns – the main training [prior to deployment in the east] was with the 37mm anti-tank gun. Training was to a small extent based upon experiences in the Polish and French campaigns, but was inadequate for the circumstances encountered later in Russia as it took too little account of battlefield conditions ... The 50mm anti-tank gun was only available in small numbers and was therefore regarded as something of a *Wunderwaffe* ['wonder weapon'] ... No value was placed at that time on training for night and woodland fighting.[4]

If the Red Army could learn how to force the Germans out of their positions, there was a growing likelihood of success. But acquiring this skill proved to be a costly and painful business.

Like every army in the Second World War, the Red Army discovered at the outset of the conflict that many of its assumptions about warfare were incorrect. In almost every respect – training, leadership, equipment, organisation, and doctrine at strategic, operational and tactical level – it found itself having to learn rapidly whilst at the same time fighting for the very existence of the Soviet Union. In any circumstances, ascending this steep learning curve would have been extremely challenging; in the midst of such a brutal conflict, it was even more difficult. To compound the problem still further, Stalin's purges of the Red Army (and indeed of every part of Soviet society) in the 1930s had left the military leadership in a badly weakened state. So many officers at every level had been detained – and many had then been executed – that commanders in 1941 were often in posts several grades higher than their expertise, experience, and training would have permitted in other circumstances. Others were in senior posts more due to their unwavering loyalty to Stalin than any aptitude or competence. The ongoing climate of fear meant that even after the fighting commenced in the summer of 1941, most officers were reluctant to draw attention to themselves by showing initiative and instead tried to ensure their personal survival by rigid adherence to their orders. The result was a pattern of repetitive attacks with infantry being thrown en masse at strong German defences. Casualties soared all along the front line as a consequence of rigid orders that were enforced and followed with little regard for the death toll.

Nonetheless, there was a general awareness that the Red Army needed to learn from its mistakes if it was to survive and ultimately triumph in its existential struggle with the Wehrmacht. Detailed reports were submitted by commanders after each operation and attempts were then made to identify what changes were needed; indeed, the structured approach adopted by the Soviet Union was in many respects superior to that of many other nations. But such analysis can only result in improvement if certain conditions are fulfilled. The first is that the analysis of reports leads to accurate recognition of the problems that led to failure. The second is that appropriate steps are taken to improve matters in the future.

The quality of the analysis of failures was variable. In many cases, the conclusions that were drawn were accurate, but frequently there was a lack of precision. To use a medical analogy, it is important to distinguish between symptoms and the underlying illness – addressing just the symptoms will often leave the illness itself untreated. Many of the Red Army's reports complained about the costly and futile use of frontal attacks rather than attempting to find weaknesses or to bypass German positions, but failed to recognise that these tactics were the consequence of other problems: poor training of both officers and men at every level; rigid insistence by higher commands that their orders had to be obeyed to the letter; and the continuing fear that failing to follow orders precisely might result in arrest and possible execution.

The solutions that were suggested by reports were also often inadequate. Poor training was frequently identified, but although field service manuals were rewritten, there seems to have been little attempt to alter basic training, or to improve the skill levels of field commanders. The terrible casualty rate that resulted from poor training and doctrine actually made matters even worse – in order to replenish depleted formations, the Soviet Union was often forced to shorten already inadequate basic training still further. It was normal policy for soldiers in the Red Army to reach their units with incomplete training and it was the responsibility of the unit to complete that training, but in the middle of intense fighting it was almost impossible for such steps to be taken. Officers in front-line units took what steps they could, sometimes mixing veterans with new recruits in the hope that the older soldiers would be able to show their new comrades how to fight and survive, but presented with large numbers of poorly trained recruits, officers must have felt that they had no option but to use them in mass attacks.

There was a further weakness in the Red Army, which was also the case in the old armies of the tsars and then persisted in the Soviet Union and the modern

Russian Army. Western armies are highly dependent upon senior NCOs who have long years of military service behind them. In every part of western armies, from front-line units to supply and support services, these veterans represent the 'institutional memory' of the army and are an invaluable pool of knowledge and experience. They can help new recruits learn faster and can reliably take command of units if officers are killed or wounded. As already mentioned, the Wehrmacht at the beginning of 1943 was beginning to suffer from depleted numbers of such men; by contrast, the Red Army entered the conflict with no such tradition. Just like every other level of the army, the NCOs had to learn from costly experience in the middle of battle.

And yet, despite all of these handicaps, there was slow evolution. The equipment of the army improved steadily, with the old tank fleets of the 1930s being replaced by increasing numbers of modern, reliable vehicles like the T-34. Weaknesses in equipment – for example, the lack of radios in tanks and aircraft – were addressed perhaps more easily than training issues. And despite the appalling losses around Rzhev, along the Volkhov River, and around the narrow German corridor that extended to Lake Ladoga at Sinyavino and Shlisselburg, a core of soldiers was emerging who had – often through pure luck – survived the slaughter and were becoming skilled fighters. Casualties would continue to be high, but as in every battle in history, inexperienced men were more likely to be killed or wounded. The veteran survivors of 1941 and 1942 were the nucleus around which the ultimate triumph of the Red Army at a tactical level would be built.

Many of the senior commanders of the Red Army of 1941 were gone by the end of 1942. Some were killed in combat, while others were dismissed (and on occasion executed). Some were captured by the Germans, and a few – Lieutenant General Andrei Andreyevich Vlasov is perhaps the best known example – would ultimately turn against the Soviet Union. Their replacements were of variable quality, but Stalin was now acutely aware that the Soviet state would have to fight with what it had. Further punishment would serve no purpose. And just as the surviving soldiers in the front line were becoming more experienced and skilled, there was similar evolution amongst their senior commanders. The men who would lead the Red Army to victory were now coming to the fore.

Training deficiencies and leadership problems were only part of the constellation of factors that had handicapped the Red Army for the first 18 months of the war. Its organisation and doctrine were also faulty, and these too were slowly changing. Like the armies that Imperial Russia sent to war in 1914, the Red Army had paid too little attention to the lowly but critical functioning of logistics. Pre-war planning had anticipated the need for mass mobilisation of trucks and tractors from civilian use in the event of war, but these vehicles were often not available – those in charge of farm collectives in peacetime, for example, completed their reports more to satisfy their superiors than to give an accurate picture. Consequently, requisitioned trucks and other vehicles were often unusable due to mechanical problems or a lack of spare parts, or simply didn't exist at all. The poor road network of the Soviet Union meant increased reliance on railways, which made the task of the Germans in detecting troop movements – and then interdicting them – far easier. Many of the reports after operations in 1942 identified weaknesses and inadequacies in supply chains, but improvements were slow to appear.

Even in the face of these problems, the Red Army was becoming increasingly able to impose itself on the course of battles. The most striking example of this in late 1942 was around Stalingrad, where Soviet units carried out a sweeping encirclement of the German Sixth Army. Here, the Red Army was able to make the most of the opportunities presented to it: the huge salient extending to Stalingrad; relatively weak defences on the deep flanks of the salient, held by Romanian troops; and open terrain where mechanised units could advance quickly. Elsewhere, the terrain of the main battlefields – around the Rzhev salient and on the approaches to Leningrad – was far less suitable for rapid advances. Dense woodland and swamps were everywhere, and there were few roads and railways. In these sectors, there was as yet little evidence that the Red Army had learned how to unpick the tough German defensive lines and achieve significant gains.

While the Red Army went through the painful process of learning how to fight and win, the people of Leningrad endured almost unimaginable suffering. As German units moved ever closer to Leningrad in the last weeks of 1941, German policy about the city became clearer. Remarkably, no definitive decision had been made before the invasion of the Soviet Union about what precisely would happen when the Wehrmacht captured the city – Hitler identified its capture as an essential objective, citing Leningrad's importance both as a centre of armaments production and as the cradle of the Russian Revolution, but it was only as German troops approached Leningrad that clear decisions were made. Rather than advancing to capture the city – as many field commanders and their troops had expected – the Wehrmacht was ordered to avoid urban fighting. Probably quite correctly, Hitler and others recognised that assaulting an urban area in the face of determined resistance would lead to protracted warfare and a high casualty rate. Instead, the city was to be isolated and starved into defeat.

The surrender of Leningrad to the Germans was explicitly to be rejected: the Germans had no intention of finding themselves in control of an area with a large, hungry urban population.

The intentions of the Germans towards Leningrad encapsulate one of the key truths about the German attack on the Soviet Union. Since the First World War, industrialisation of agriculture in the Soviet Union had been accompanied by a considerable growth in the population, predominantly in urban centres. The Germans never had any intention of being burdened with several million people in Leningrad, Moscow, Kiev, and other large cities who would then need to be fed; instead, the urban population was to be eliminated. This would be through a mixture of artillery and air bombardment, starvation, or expulsion into Siberia (where it was expected they would starve anyway). The mass killing of Jews that followed in the wake of the Wehrmacht in 1941 was merely the prelude to death on a far larger scale. From an early stage, the intention was twofold: firstly, the huge grain production of Ukraine and other fertile regions of the Soviet Union was to be seized for consumption within Europe; secondly, this seizure was expected to result in widespread deaths, thus depopulating the conquered regions and clearing the way for settlement by ethnic Germans.

The quantity of grain to be seized was assessed at a very early stage of planning, and was increased as plans were developed. In February 1941, Herbert Backe, State Secretary in the *Reichsministerium für Ernährung und Landwirtschaft* ('Reich Ministry for Food and Agriculture') reported that there was likely to be an annual shortfall of about 5 million tons of grain in Germany and German-controlled territories, and it was suggested that by reducing grain consumption within the Soviet Union by about 10 per cent, roughly 4 million tons of grain would be made available for transfer to the west, combined with the normal Soviet surplus of about 1 million tons.[5] Given that the figure of 5 million tons was in addition to normal Soviet grain exports, a 10 per cent reduction of grain consumption within the Soviet Union would result in widespread shortages and deaths. But by the end of March 1941, a much larger figure was being discussed. Reducing Soviet consumption by 12 per cent would release nearly 9 million tons of grain.[6] If the original plans would have created severe shortages, these new plans would exacerbate those shortages into fully fledged famine on a huge scale.

As planning for the conquest of the Soviet Union gathered pace and complexity, members of *Wirtschaftsführungsstab Ost* ('Economic Command Staff East') met on 2 May 1941 and discussed the demands that would be placed upon agricultural production in the Soviet Union and the consequences for the population. By this stage, there was no question about the expected (and desired) outcome:

> The war can only continue to be waged if the entire Wehrmacht is fed from Russia during the third year of the war.
>
> As a result, if what is necessary for us is extracted from the land, tens of millions of people will doubtless starve to death.[7]

Backe was the person who was tasked with drawing up the details of what later became known as the Hunger Plan. Later in May, after further input from Backe's ministry, *Wirtschaftsführungsstab Ost* added further clarity on what was expected:

> Many tens of millions of people in this country [the conquered parts of the Soviet Union] will become superfluous and will die or must emigrate to Siberia. Attempts to rescue the population there from death through starvation by obtaining surpluses from the black earth zone [i.e. Ukraine] prevent the possibility of Germany holding out until the end of the war.[8]

Most of the 'surplus' grain would come from Ukraine, and the various German agencies now took a close look at the amount of grain produced compared with what they determined was essential to support the population of Ukraine. Their estimates made no allowances for feeding the residents of Kiev, Kharkov, and the industrial cities of the Donbas region. By eliminating any requirement to feed the urban population of Ukraine and preventing any transfer of food to other urban centres across the Soviet Union, the Germans now calculated that their estimates of how much grain could be appropriated were far higher. The original figure of 5 million tons had already been increased to nearly 9 million tons, but now they concluded that this could be raised still further to 25 to 30 million tons.

Given that mass killing through starvation was therefore an accepted consequence of the war, it is unsurprising that the destruction of the population of Leningrad by starvation was regarded as an appropriate 'solution' to the problem of what to do with such a large number of civilians, and even though the final decision about what to do with Leningrad was made several weeks after the invasion commenced, it was well known that Hitler intended the destruction of all urban centres. On 5 May 1941, an Austrian diplomat attended a meeting with Brigadeführer Franz Walter Stahlecker, who was to command *Einsatzgruppe*

A in the Soviet Union, and noted Hitler's explicit wishes with regard to Russia's urban centres:

> All cities and cultural sites including the Kremlin are to be razed to the ground; Russia is to be reduced to the level of a nation of peasants, from which there is no return.[9]

Nor should the deaths from starvation in Leningrad and elsewhere be regarded as an unfortunate but unavoidable side effect of German policy: from the outset, the intention was explicitly to destroy both the Soviet state and a large proportion of the population. As the commencement of Operation *Barbarossa*, the invasion of the Soviet Union, became imminent, Backe's instructions to the men who would be responsible for agricultural oversight in the conquered territories grew ever more explicit. On 1 June, he wrote:

> The Russian has already endured poverty, hunger, and frugality for centuries. His stomach is elastic, hence [there should be] no false sympathy. Do not attempt to apply the German standard of living as your yardstick to alter the Russian way of life.[10]

If there was any lingering doubt, it was removed in a speech given by Heinrich Himmler to a group of senior SS figures in Wewelsburg Castle. Gruppenführer Erich von dem Bach-Zelewski, who was to be *Höhere SS- und Polizei-Führer* ('Higher SS and Police Commander', often abbreviated to *HSSPF*) in the central region was one of those present and later recalled that Himmler explicitly stated that the purpose of the Russian campaign was the decimation of the Slavic population by 30 million.[11] The needs of Germany and its occupied territories, with their non-Slav populations, were of greater importance than the needs of Russian people. Within the racially layered mindset of Nazi Germany, the logical conclusion was that the inferior Slavs would simply have to die. Alfred Rosenberg, who was head of the *Reichsministerium für die Besetzten Ostgebiete* ('Reich Ministry for the Occupied Eastern Territories', often abbreviated to *Ostministerium*), made this even clearer just two days before the invasion commenced:

> The feeding of the German people stands without doubt at the top of German demands in the east, and here the southern territories [i.e. Ukraine] and northern Caucasus will have to balance out German food requirements. By no means do we acknowledge the obligation to feed the Russian people as well from these

surplus territories. We know that that is a harsh necessity that is beyond any emotion. A very extensive evacuation will without doubt be necessary, and very difficult years will certainly be in store for the Russian people.[12]

The repeated use of euphemisms like 'evacuation' or 'emigration' to describe the forcible expulsion of people from seized territories was another characteristic of the manner in which the Germans wrote and discussed their intentions. It is worth noting though that this ruthless destruction of the people of the European parts of the Soviet Union should not be regarded as the only option available to Germany. Despite his statements, Rosenberg himself regarded the plan effectively to eliminate the Slav population and to replace them with Germans as unworkable, at least in the short to medium term. He proposed instead that as the Wehrmacht advanced, the conquered regions should be turned into a series of puppet states that would help provide manpower for the continuation of the war. Hitler dismissed this out of hand. The inferior Slavs would have to die.

The Hunger Plan was therefore drawn up in detail before the invasion began. Soviet collective farms were widely disliked in many rural areas and had the Germans abolished them, they might have gained considerable support from the population and potentially achieved increases in agricultural production; instead, the Germans fully intended to use the collective system in order to requisition grain. But drawing up statistical plans about quantities of grain that were to be seized and estimating the resulting death toll in Soviet cities was a relatively straightforward exercise. Implementing such a plan was quite a different matter. Stalin's deliberate starvation of Ukraine in 1932–33 – now known as the *Holodomor* – was possible because of the existence of a large police force and other security agencies supported by widespread Communist Party groups, which knew the local population in Ukraine and were completely loyal to Moscow. The Germans eliminated any pre-existing police organisations, and the task of creating new bodies and then using them for rapid implementation of the Hunger Plan was almost impossible. With so many men tied up in protracted fighting against the Red Army, the German military lacked the resources to implement the plan with the same degree of ruthlessness as Stalin's *Holodomor*. The historian Timothy Snyder described the situation succinctly:

[By the autumn of 1941] the classical dilemma of political economy, guns or butter, was supposed to have been resolved in a miraculous way: guns would make butter. But now, three months into the war, the men carrying the guns very much needed the butter. As the war continued beyond the planned twelve weeks, German soldiers were competing with German civilians for limited food supplies. The invasion itself had halted the supply of grain from the Soviet Union. Now three million German soldiers simply had to be fed, without reducing food rations within Germany itself.[13]

The disruption of rural life by the arrival of the Wehrmacht had not been properly anticipated, and there were few or no plans for mitigating the consequences of so many men being absent from the countryside, because they had been drafted into the Red Army or killed by the Germans, or had fled east. In many cases, German attempts to enforce the policies of the Hunger Plan were haphazard, and, aware that the rural population was hiding food from the occupying forces, some local occupation authorities resorted to brutal steps. But when severe measures were taken, the result was increased partisan activity as local people took up arms against the invaders.

Despite these failures, there was widespread hunger in the occupied parts of the Soviet Union. One estimate suggests that the implementation of the Hunger Plan and the deliberate attempt to starve Leningrad to death resulted in the deaths of about 4.2 million Soviet citizens.[14] Many of these deaths were in Ukraine, where just a few years before several million people had starved to death in the *Holodomor*. For the second time in less than a decade, the region suffered deaths from starvation as the result of the measures taken by extremist dictators.

From the first moments that Hitler and his entourage began to draw up their plans, the war in the east was completely different from the fighting in the west. There had been a taste of what was to come in Germany's invasion of Poland, with widespread arbitrary killing of civilians. There was limited outcry from some in the Wehrmacht, but the conduct of the war in the west in 1940 seemed to put most of these concerns to rest. Regardless of this, the constraints of international law were not to apply in the war with the Soviet Union. At a conference with senior Wehrmacht officers at the end of March 1941, Hitler delivered a monologue that lasted over two hours. General Franz Halder, who was chief of the general staff, noted in his diary:

[This will be] a clash of two ideologies. [Hitler delivered] a crushing denunciation of Bolshevism, identified with a social criminality. Communism is an enormous danger for our future. We must forget the concept of comradeship between soldiers. A Communist is no comrade before or after the battle. This is a war of extermination. If we do not grasp this, we shall still beat the enemy, but thirty years later we will again have to fight the Communist foe ...

This war will be very different from the war in the west. In the east, harshness today means lenience in the future. Commanders must make the sacrifice of overcoming their personal scruples.[15]

Neither Halder nor any of the other generals present seemed to regard these instructions as unacceptable. Detailed orders followed, including the 'Jurisdiction order'; this explicitly removed any obligation on commanders to prosecute their soldiers for any crimes against civilians, unless the crime was detrimental to the war effort.[16] With this characterisation of the war against the Soviet Union as a struggle between incompatible systems, the use of almost any measure to achieve the desired end was regarded as acceptable, including mass starvation. A few days before the invasion began, Joseph Goebbels, Germany's propaganda minister, wrote in his diary:

The Führer says whether we are right or wrong, we must win. This is the only way. And it is right, moral and necessary. And once we have won, who will ask us about the methods. In any case, we have so much to account for that we must win; otherwise our whole people – and we in the first place, and all that we love – would be erased.[17]

The importance of this diary entry is its clear recognition that the Nazis had already crossed important legal and ethical boundaries; their conduct in the past could only be justified if they secured their ultimate outcome, and this would require still further boundaries to be transgressed.

Once the siege perimeter was established around Leningrad, it seems that the main concern of the German high command was about the possible effect of such mass deaths on the morale of their soldiers. Anticipating attempts by desperate, starving civilians to flee from Leningrad, instructions were issued for artillery to be used to prevent any such refugees from reaching German lines. Wherever possible, killing was to be done at a distance. Similarly, when he visited the Eastern Front to assess the slaughter of Jews by the SS *Einsatzgruppen*, Himmler expressed concern that murder on such a scale ran the risk of brutalising German personnel to the extent that they might become difficult to integrate back into civilian life. There was no concern whatever for the victims.

Throughout 1942, while the armies of the Soviet Union hurled themselves into bloody fighting in their attempts to break through to Leningrad, the city itself continued to endure the privations of being besieged. The first winter saw horrific conditions in Leningrad and a spiralling death rate from starvation, cold, and German shelling and bombing, but through a mixture of good fortune, ingenuity, and sheer stubbornness, many of the inhabitants of Leningrad survived. The second winter of the siege was milder in terms of weather, and the city itself was better prepared. Large numbers of people had been evacuated across Lake Ladoga and there were extensive preparations to prevent the catastrophic conditions that had prevailed in late 1941 and early 1942. Many damaged buildings were torn down and the salvaged timber either used to make other buildings more weatherproof or stockpiled as firewood. By late 1942, food stockpiles were significantly greater than they had been 12 months before, not least because every available patch of land within the siege perimeter had been cultivated. The fuel situation was also completely transformed. Coal shipments across Lake Ladoga during the summer of 1942 deliberately exceeded consumption in order to ensure that there would be sufficient supplies for both domestic and industrial use in the coming winter, and Soviet engineers laid a fuel pipeline on the lakebed. This allowed an average of 300 tons per day to be delivered to Leningrad, and matters were improved still further when electric cables were also put in place, allowing the damaged but still functioning power station in Volkhov to deliver electricity to the city.[18]

Despite having to divert considerable resources to deal with the repeated Soviet attempts to break the siege of the city, the Germans continued the aerial and artillery bombardment of Leningrad when resources permitted. German guns shelled the city on 246 days, firing a total of more than 50,000 shells. These bombardments killed nearly 900 people and wounded several thousand more, but despite the bombardment and continuing privations – and the effects of starvation from the previous winter, which lingered for months or even years – the factories of Leningrad manufactured impressive quantities of munitions. About 1.7 million artillery shells and mortar bombs and over 1.25 million hand grenades were handed over to the city's garrison from factories where about 80 per cent of the workforce was female – almost all the men had been drafted either into the Red Army or the militia battalions that were raised in haste as the Germans approached the city in late 1941.[19]

The German forces facing both Leningrad and the Soviet units attempting to lift the siege by attacking from the east were under the control of Army Group North, currently commanded by Generalfeldmarschall Georg von Küchler. During the invasion of Poland, he commanded the German Third Army but was dismissed for criticising the manner in which Generaloberst Werner Freiherr von

Fritsch had been removed from his post as commander-in-chief of the Wehrmacht. He was rapidly appointed as commander of Eighteenth Army after the intervention of Fritsch's successor, Generaloberst (later Generalfeldmarschall) Walther von Brauchitsch. He led his new command into the Netherlands in the summer of 1940 and was by now a willing adherent to Hitler's views of how the war should be conducted in order to seize territory for German expansion. After hearing about the manner in which Poles were being oppressed, he wrote in his war diary in August 1940:

> I stress the necessity of ensuring that all soldiers in the army, particularly officers, refrain from any criticism of the struggle being conducted by the *Generalgouvernement* [the title for the German administration in the Polish areas that had not been formally annexed into Germany] against the population, for example in the treatment of Polish minorities, including the Jews and the affairs of the clergy. The ethnic final solution to this struggle of the people, which has been raging on the eastern frontier for centuries, requires particularly strict measures.[20]

As preparations for Operation *Barbarossa* began to take shape, Eighteenth Army was transferred to East Prussia where it was to form one of the three principal formations of Army Group North. In April 1941, Küchler addressed a conference of division commanders:

> We are separated from Russia, ideologically and racially, by a deep abyss. Russia is, if only by the mass of her territory, an Asian state … The Führer does not wish to palm off responsibility for Germany's existence on to a later generation; he has decided to force the dispute with Russia before the year is out. If Germany wishes to live in peace for generations, safe from a threatening danger in the east, this cannot be a case of pushing Russia back a little – or even hundreds of kilometres – but the aim must be to annihilate European Russia, to dissolve the Russian state in Europe.[21]

This was a recurring theme in the manner in which many in the German military attempted to justify the brutal measures that were to be used in the Soviet Union: by acting in such a merciless manner, the Germans would spare their descendants from having to take any such actions. Once the invasion began Küchler continued to follow the same ruthless path. As the German army groups pressed into the Soviet Union, they were followed closely by the *Einsatzgruppen*, SS bodies that were responsible for security behind the front line. In reality, this involved the killing of anyone who was regarded as potentially hostile to the German occupation, particularly the Jews, who were seen throughout the German system as being indistinguishable from Bolsheviks. The *Einsatzgruppen* were also tasked with eliminating other 'undesirable' elements of the population, a task that they carried out without hesitation, and the following example shows both the ruthlessness of the *Einsatzgruppen* and the complicity of Wehrmacht personnel in their actions.

In September 1941, the soldiers of XXVIII Corps, which was part of Küchler's command, advanced towards Leningrad from the south and southeast and captured the former Hermitage of the Assumption in the village of Makarevskaya, which was now being used as a hospital for people with mental illnesses and learning difficulties. A few weeks later, Küchler received a report from the headquarters of XXVIII Corps requesting the elimination of these patients. Two reasons were given for the request. The first was that there was the risk of infectious epidemic that might then spread to German personnel. The second bluntly stated:

> The inmates of the institution are, in the sense of the German viewpoint, objects that have lives that are no longer worth living.[22]

Küchler promptly issued orders for the patients to be handed over to *Einsatzgruppe A*. In his regular reports to Berlin, Stahlecker, commander of *Einsatzgruppe A*, meticulously listed the activities of his men:

> It transpired that a particularly large number of unreliable Russians had been assigned to work on the newly seized railway line in Krasnogvardeisk. In total, 67 persons were executed between 6 November and 20 November. In addition, 855 persons were killed in a *Sonderaktion* ['special action'] on 20 November.[23]

This 'special action' was the killing of patients from the mental hospital. This mass execution was followed by the killing of a further 230 patients shortly before the end of 1941, explicitly at the request of Küchler – the obsession with preventing epidemics was frequently used as justification for mass executions of prisoners and detainees being held in unsanitary conditions.[24] The reality is that by executing such people under whatever excuse was expedient, accommodation was freed up for other uses, an issue that was particularly important with the onset of winter and the need to provide shelter for military personnel. It is also worth noting that the subunit of *Einsatzgruppe A* that was operating in this area – Obersturmbannführer Erich Ehrlinger's *Einsatzkommando 1b* – had only 100 personnel. In order to carry out such mass executions, it relied on personnel from police and military units, who would only be assigned to such tasks with the approval of their commanders. In a manner that was typical of how many people in Nazi Germany dealt with such matters, the language of Küchler's headquarters changed as the killing of the patients proceeded. There was no longer any talk of 'elimination'; instead, reports merely stated that the personnel of *Einsatzkommando 1b* had 'evacuated' the patients. Given the widespread knowledge about the conduct of Stahlecker's *Einsatzgruppe A* – not least because of the extensive cooperation between the Wehrmacht and Stahlecker's men – there can have been no doubt in anyone's mind about the true fate of the patients.

In early 1942, Küchler took command of Army Group North. His old army was now commanded by Generaloberst Georg Lindemann, who led his troops during the bitter defensive fighting along the Volkhov River as the Red Army tried in vain to break through to Leningrad. Despite his successes in stopping the Soviet attacks – and particularly in encircling and destroying Second Shock Army during the summer – he wasn't a popular man with his subordinates. He had a reputation for blaming setbacks on those under his command, earned during his time as a corps commander, but his steady if unspectacular performance as commander of Eighteenth Army was sufficient for now for him to retain his post.

The other main formation of Army Group North was Sixteenth Army, under the command of Generaloberst – later Generalfeldmarschall – Ernst Busch. He had held the post since October 1939, leading his army through the Champagne region of France in 1940 and then into the Soviet Union in 1941, and was another who accepted without question the dark ideology of Nazi Germany. Like many in the late 19th and early 20th centuries, he was a lifelong adherent to the concept of social Darwinism – just as individual life forms competed and the strongest prospered, so the same logic was applied to nations or ethnic groups. Naturally, Busch and most other European social Darwinists regarded white races as superior to all others, and this concept fitted very easily into Nazi ideology. For Busch, the battlefield was the obvious arena on which such racial and nationalistic competition for resources would play out. He saw wars in future as becoming all-encompassing and requiring the full resources of the nation. He wrote in 1937:

> In future, wars will be total conflicts, wars that will extend into three dimensions – land, sea, air – a people's war, with all political, scientific, and spiritual forces …

in future, wars are unthinkable without the involvement of mechanised and motorised formations, or without the use of the engine … The zone of attack, in which infantrymen will shoulder the main burden of the war of the future, is also the zone in which victory or death will reign … Only independent, decisive, tough combatants can meet the demands that will be placed on infantrymen.[25]

Despite these words, Busch – like Lindemann and Küchler – was far removed from the enthusiasts for panzer warfare, men like Guderian, Manstein, Hoth, and Kleist. Throughout his career he remained at heart an infantryman, regarding the use of armoured vehicles as purely limited to supporting infantry operations. To a large extent, this conservative mindset made little difference in the battlefields of the north. Army Group North had very limited armoured assets at its disposal, and the terrain was very unsuitable to the massed use of tanks. Huge forests dominated the largely flat landscape, with innumerable streams and rivers flowing sluggishly towards Lake Ladoga or the Baltic Sea in the north. Swamps were everywhere, and even where the ground was dry, soldiers on both sides complained that any attempt to dig fortifications rapidly hit water. All year round, Soviet and German infantrymen endured some of the worst conditions on the Eastern Front – in the winter, frostbite regularly caused more casualties than enemy action, and in the summer the damp, muddy landscape and the plagues of mosquitoes and midges posed a different set of problems.

The Red Army's units that faced Army Group North came under two commands. In the north was Leningrad Front, currently under the leadership of Leonid Aleksandrovich Govorov who was promoted to colonel general early in 1943. During the Russian Civil War, he fought for the White Russian forces of Admiral Kolchak, only switching to the Bolshevik cause in December 1919 after the general collapse of Kolchak's army in Siberia. Although he then fought with distinction, being wounded twice in 1920, his old allegiance to the White Russian cause inevitably brought him under suspicion during the dark years of Stalin's purges in the 1930s. He was widely thought to have close links to other senior figures who were arrested, charged, and executed during the purges but he somehow survived the era without being placed under arrest. When the Red Army attacked Finland in late 1939 and failed to overcome determined Finnish resistance, he was appointed chief of staff of the artillery of Seventh Army, and the successful penetration of the Finnish defences of the Mannerheim Line owed much to his work.

When war with Germany broke out in the summer of 1941, Govorov held a number of posts before taking command of Fifth Army in October following the wounding of Dmitry Danilovich Lelyushenko, the previous commander. His divisions successfully stopped the final assault of the German Fourth Army just 20 miles southwest of the outskirts of Moscow. He then joined the general Red Army counteroffensive that drove the Wehrmacht back from the Soviet capital, but was hospitalised early in 1942 with appendicitis.

Govorov had served as an artilleryman for much of his military career and when he was assigned to the northern sector at the end of April 1942 – he later became commander of Leningrad Front in June – he prioritised the restructuring of his artillery units. The Leningrad Counter-Battery Artillery Corps was created and made use of the guns of the Baltic Fleet to engage German gun batteries in order to reduce the effect of German bombardments both of Red Army positions and of Leningrad. Under his supervision, the ad hoc defences that had been thrown up in haste and desperation in late 1941 around the southern edge of Leningrad were reorganised and strengthened, creating five distinct lines of defence. He also worked on improving lines of communication and movement within the siege perimeter, allowing the units defending the city to move rapidly from one location to another. In short, the steps that he took made any lingering prospect of a German assault to capture the city an almost impossible undertaking.

The priority for Govorov was not so much to prevent the fall of Leningrad, but to break the siege ring and restore contact overland with the outside world. The narrow German-held corridor that extended to the shore of Lake Ladoga at Shlisselburg was the obvious point at which the Red Army was most likely to make its effort, and the Germans fortified their positions to create a series of lines that were every bit as formidable as the Soviet defences south of Leningrad. Despite repeated failures in this sector, Govorov began planning for another attempt, which would ultimately take place in early 1943.

Outside Leningrad, a small group of Soviet units continued to survive on the Baltic coastline to the west of the city around the town of Oranienbaum. This pocket had been created in late 1941 when German forces pushed north to the very outskirts of Leningrad and reached the coast immediately to the west of the city, and despite drawing up plans to eliminate the 'bridgehead', the Germans were unable to proceed due to other priorities. Backed by the long-range guns of the Baltic Fleet, the soldiers in the bridgehead continued to defy the Germans, tying down two infantry divisions. When the pocket was created, the Soviet units within it were from Eighth Army, but after the headquarters of this army was withdrawn the forces became known as the 'Coastal Operational Group'. For the moment, Govorov was content to leave the bridgehead alone with sufficient forces – at the beginning of 1943, two rifle divisions, separate brigades and battalions amounting to a third division, and a single tank battalion – to defend against any German attack. There was always the option of transferring troops into the bridgehead if the need for stronger defences – or plans for an offensive operation – should require such a move.

In addition to the forces in the Oranienbaum bridgehead, Govorov had four armies in and around Leningrad itself. These armies – particularly Sixty-Seventh Army, commanded by Lieutenant General Mikhail Pavlovich Dukhanov and defending about 12 miles of the Neva River from Lake Ladoga towards the southwest – would be his main resources in the coming attempt to break the German siege ring.

Outside Leningrad, the Red Army's units to the east and then along the line of the Volkhov Front were under the control of Volkhov Front, commanded by General Kirill Afanasyevich Meretskov. The path of his career is in many respects a microcosm of the impact of Stalin's paranoia on the army. Unlike Govorov, Meretskov had revolutionary leanings before the Russian Revolution, becoming an active member of the Bolshevik movement a year before the fall of tsarist rule. He was repeatedly wounded during the Russian Civil War and then ascended the military hierarchy in the years that followed. In the late 1930s, as Stalin's purges began to tear great holes in the leadership of the Red Army, Meretskov rose to the post of deputy chief of the general staff and then became commander of Leningrad Military District. In this role, he was ordered to make preparations for the war with Finland and expressed serious doubts about the practicality of conducting an offensive through the dense forests of the frontier region. Nonetheless, he took command of Seventh Army once hostilities began and eventually led it to success. In the second half of 1940, he became chief of the general staff but was then abruptly removed and replaced by Zhukov; it seems that this was at least partly because Meretskov repeatedly warned about imminent war with Germany and demanded that greater steps be taken to prepare for such a conflict.

When war with Germany broke out in June 1941, Meretskov was sent to Leningrad as a representative of *Stavka* (the Soviet military high command) but was promptly summoned back to Moscow, where he was arrested. The purges of the Red Army were still under way, and several officers who had been arrested had given statements implicating him in anti-Soviet conspiracies. There is no evidence that he was actually involved in any such plots – indeed, nor is there any substantial evidence for the existence of so many groups trying to overthrow Soviet rule. As was the case on so many occasions, prisoners who were being beaten during interrogation attempted to placate their captors by giving names of former colleagues; Stalin chose to use these confessions as clear evidence of multiple conspiracies and therefore as justification for ongoing purges. Meretskov was badly beaten and abused and was apparently forced to sign a confession, but the file relating to his arrest and captivity was later destroyed. He appealed to Stalin to be sent to the front where he could at least make a contribution to the defence of the Soviet Union and was released in September; when he attended a meeting with Stalin and other senior figures shortly after, Zhukov noted that Meretskov was still so weak from mistreatment that he was the only person in the meeting who was permitted to sit.[26]

Despite his poor physical condition, the crises along the front line were so severe that Meretskov was immediately dispatched to take command of his former unit, Seventh Army. He succeeded in stopping a Finnish offensive and then took command of Fourth Army, which successfully defeated the German advance to Tikhvin. Thereafter, he became commander of Volkhov Front and commanded it during the Lyuban Operation of 1942. This was an attempt to force the line of the Volkhov River to the southeast of Leningrad and then to advance on the cities of Lyuban and Chudovo prior to pushing on to Leningrad itself; although the strong German defensive line was breached and Second Shock Army was then inserted through the breach, every attempt to widen the penetration failed and the Germans were eventually able to restore their former front line, isolating and destroying much of Second Shock Army. In the context of his recent arrest and mistreatment, it is perhaps unsurprising that Meretskov assigned blame for the failed operation to his subordinates, particularly Vlasov, commander of Second Shock Army. Vlasov became a prisoner of war and later led a small anti-Soviet army made up of former Red Army prisoners of war; he has been widely vilified as an opportunistic traitor in the years since the war in Soviet and Russian accounts, and he was therefore a convenient scapegoat for the setbacks of Volkhov Front.

Even as the Lyuban Operation was running into difficulties, *Stavka* made major changes to command arrangements. In an attempt to improve coordination between the forces in the Leningrad encirclement and those along the Volkhov River, Volkhov Front was abolished and its armies subordinated to Leningrad Front. Meretskov spent a spell as Zhukov's deputy at the headquarters of Western Front near Moscow and then briefly commanded Thirty-Third Army before returning to the north, where Volkhov Front had been re-established. Still under the continuing scrutiny of Stalin and bearing the stigma of his earlier arrest, he organised another attempt to batter through the German lines at Sinyavino in the late summer and early autumn of 1942. In Soviet historiography, this is known as the Third Sinyavino Operation, but many western accounts do not distinguish between the first two operations (in the winter of 1941–42) and refer to Meretskov's assault as the Second Sinyavino Operation. Operating in terrain that was deeply unsuitable for an offensive operation, Meretskov's armies managed to penetrate over half way to the siege perimeter with the reconstituted Second Shock Army once more in the forefront of the fighting, but once again the initial penetration was too narrow and the Germans were able to pinch off a large group of Soviet units. Although many of the trapped soldiers managed to slip through to safety in the dense forests and swamps of the region, Second Shock Army was effectively destroyed for the second time in just a few months.

On this occasion too, Meretskov escaped punishment for the failed operation. By this stage of the war, Stalin was aware that whatever deficiencies his commanders might have, the Soviet Union was going to have to fight with what it had available and any replacement for Meretskov was unlikely to be a big improvement. Moreover, Meretskov could claim two mitigating factors. Firstly, the very difficult nature of the terrain was now well known to everyone. Secondly, information from prisoner interrogations and intelligence channels had alerted *Stavka* to German plans for a renewed offensive in the Leningrad region, intended either to overrun the city entirely or at least to create a tighter siege perimeter before the onset of winter in late 1942. The operation – codenamed *Nordlicht* – was abandoned largely because of German casualties suffered in stopping Meretskov's attempt to break through to Leningrad, and shortly thereafter the crisis that erupted far to the south with the encirclement of the German Sixth Army in Stalingrad and the collapse of the entire German front line along the Don forced the diversion of all German reinforcements (and an increasing proportion of Germany's logistic efforts) to eastern Ukraine.

As 1942 drew to a close, Meretskov began to draw up plans in collaboration with Govorov for another offensive in the Sinyavino–Shlisselburg area. Volkhov Front had six armies, including Second Shock Army which had once more been reconstituted, and every attempt would be made to learn from the failures of 1942. The Red Army's losses in the northern sector in the war to date were staggeringly high. One estimate is that the fighting around Sinyavino, Shlisselburg, Tikhvin, Lyuban, and Chudovo from September 1941 to the end of 1943 resulted in over 612,000 men killed, wounded or missing.[27] Despite this, the regiments and divisions had been replenished with new drafts and even though most remained below their establishment strength, the forces of Leningrad and Volkhov Fronts had formidable resources at their disposal. Leningrad Front had 22 rifle divisions and eight tank brigades, while Volkhov Front had 34 rifle divisions and 11 tank brigades. In addition, both Fronts had numerous independent rifle brigades and battalions and independent artillery units of up to division size variously equipped with mortars, heavy guns, and anti-tank weaponry. The opposing German forces totalled 40 infantry divisions and a single motorised division, plus numerous corps- and army-level assault gun brigades and artillery units. Like their Soviet opponents, none of these were at full strength and German losses in 1942 had also been high, albeit lower than those of the Red Army. The battles that had resulted in over 612,000 Soviet losses also inflicted about 130,000 casualties from all causes on the Wehrmacht, though accurate comparison of losses is difficult due to different accounting methods and time periods.[28] Numerically at least, the Red Army enjoyed a considerable advantage at the beginning of 1943.

The mood of the soldiers in the front line was very different from the previous winter. At the end of 1941, the German soldiers had felt a general sense of disappointment that they had not finished their victorious march across the Baltic States and into Russia with a crowning victory, i.e. the capture of Leningrad itself. Nonetheless, the impressive advance of Army Group North – and the numerous battles won in the process – were sources of considerable satisfaction, and most believed at the end of 1941 that the final collapse of the Red Army was surely close. In any case, few can have expected Leningrad to survive a winter of starvation, freezing temperatures, and constant bombardment. The capture of the city might not have taken place as the soldiers had expected, but victory seemed purely a matter of time. By the end of 1942, few were thinking in terms of taking Leningrad. Instead of moving closer to the city, the German soldiers had been forced to fight bitter defensive battles against a foe who seemed to have limitless resources. Even though each Soviet assault had been beaten off, German ranks were growing thinner. Wilhelm Lubbeck, an infantryman, noted that his infantry regiment had been renamed as a grenadier regiment:

> This change nominally reflected the augmentation of its overall firepower through an increase in heavy weapons such as machine-guns and large mortars. In reality, any increase in firepower could not fully compensate for the regiment's attrition of manpower that had reduced our overall strength by at least a battalion.[29]

The sense of dissatisfaction that came from not capturing Leningrad at the end of 1941 was in many aspects exacerbated when stories circulated about how close the Soviet defenders had been to collapse. Otto Carius served as a junior officer in *Schwere Panzer Abteilung 502* ('502nd Heavy Tank Battalion'), one of the few armoured assets available to Army Group North, and he described how many such stories originated:

> We discovered from a female medic we had captured that the city had been practically starved out in the winter of 1941–1942. The corpses had been stacked like firewood. (As the driver of a colonel, she had let her vehicle run onto a mine. As punishment, she had to accompany assault parties as a medic.) She said that life in Leningrad had practically normalised itself again. The populace went about its work undisturbed. Where and when the Germans would fire was already known.
>
> Besides, she said, we scarcely had any ammunition. When we then discovered from other prisoner statements that there had scarcely been a soldier in the city in 1941 and that Leningrad had practically already been given up by the Russians, it dawned on even the lowliest mess hall driver that this error could never be rectified.[30]

The latter statement is incorrect. Although the Soviet units that retreated to the Leningrad perimeter in late 1941 had suffered repeated defeats, they were still capable of putting up strong resistance and any attempt by the Germans to penetrate into the urban core of Leningrad would have resulted in bitter streetfighting, the outcome of which would have been far from clear. But the effect of such stories on the men who endured life in the muddy, mosquito-infested trenches of the front line is easy to imagine.

One of the units of Army Group North was 250th Infantry Division, made up of Spanish volunteers and generally known as the *División Azul* or 'Blue Division' on account of the colour of the tab on the shoulders of the division's uniforms. Despite the generally low opinion of the Germans for almost all the nationalities that fought alongside them – particularly after the collapse of Romanian, Italian and Hungarian formations in the southern sector in late 1942 – the soldiers of the Blue Division generally performed as well in combat as most German units. Nonetheless, the experience of long months of warfare in the harsh environment of the northern sector took its toll on these men from a far warmer climate. When two volunteers – with previous service in Franco's forces during the Spanish Civil War – returned to their homes at the end of their deployment in late 1942, many were shocked by the transformation that had taken place:

> Those two and all the others who 'have been there' now look like sleepwalkers. Their conversation is incoherent and missing half the words. They have a sunken,

lost look, without vigour, with a feverish sheen and veiled. They have become horribly thin and are black from gunpowder … One might say the shadow of death, which was so close to them and has repeated its deed so many times before them, still hangs over them.[31]

German soldiers returning home on leave from the Eastern Front made a similar impression upon their families, most of whom were already aware that the war wasn't going well, though the encirclement of the German Sixth Army in Stalingrad wasn't widely known at the beginning of 1943, with only the vaguest hints in German news media. Officers at higher levels would have been aware that reinforcements were being rushed to the south, but few would have known the details of the disaster that was overtaking the Wehrmacht in the city on the Volga. By contrast, Soviet soldiers received triumphant reports about the advances that were being achieved and some of this information made its way across the front line by a variety of routes – signals intercepts, captured documents, prisoner interrogations, and even loudspeaker broadcasts from the Red Army's lines. Many Germans might have found it difficult to believe the increasing rumours of catastrophe, but the impact of this news on the Red Army resulted in a huge boost in morale and confidence. The setback in the failed attack on Sinyavino was rapidly put to one side as detailed preparations began for a new offensive. Dmitry Alekseyevich Morozov, a Red Army artillery officer, later wrote:

The end of autumn and the beginning of winter brought a lot of good news. Reports arrived of major victories of our troops. In the lower Volga region, three Fronts launched an offensive and on 23 November completed the encirclement of a large group of Fascist troops, numbering more than 300,000 men and a huge amount of military equipment. Burakovsky [a comrade of Morozov] went to the army headquarters and returned looking cheerful. He said that there was a lot of talk of an offensive …
According to all reports, the offensive was just around the corner.[32]

The general mood of the soldiers on either side of the front line was therefore markedly different. On the German side, the confidence of previous years was gone. There was no longer the complete belief in imminent and decisive victory; instead, there was a growing realisation that not only was victory no longer guaranteed, but there was an increasing awareness that defeat was a real and growing possibility. The inadequate replacements, the ongoing casualties, and the apparently endless resources of the enemy were all growing indicators that the tide was turning against Germany and the news from other sectors (however it reached the front line) merely added to this sense of gloom, and men returning to the front line from leave brought with them reports of increasing damage to German cities from British and American air raids. But despite the growing evidence of their personal experiences, it seems that belief in Hitler remained strong in the rank and file. A few officers might have been contemplating some form of action against the higher leadership, but they were greatly outnumbered by those who remained loyal, if increasingly pessimistic.

On the Soviet side of the front line, the mood was very different at the end of 1942 from a year before. The grim determination to survive that had dominated in the winter of 1941–42 was replaced by increasing confidence, particularly in light of the news from Stalingrad. The terrible casualties suffered in the failed attacks along the Volkhov River and at Sinyavino, and the frustration and disappointment of the front line being essentially the same as it had been at the beginning of 1942, were of course significant causes of concern, but after the disastrous setbacks of the first six months of the conflict there was increased belief that final victory over the hated Fascist invaders would be achieved, albeit only after the most strenuous efforts. Just as confidence in Hitler remained strong amongst ordinary German soldiers, Soviet troops in the front line also appear to have been sure that their nation would prevail. Their motivation was more than merely survival – there was a growing desire for revenge. Reports from partisans and articles in the various front-line newspapers highlighted the atrocities carried out by the Germans in the occupied parts of the Soviet Union, and for soldiers whose home towns and cities were now under German control, there were particularly strong motivations for achieving victory.

The manner in which ordinary soldiers reconciled themselves to the shockingly high casualty rate amongst Red Army units is also striking. Many memoirs and accounts written after the war make the same point: there was a widespread attitude amongst the troops that they were not going to survive the war. The men who endured the murderous fighting of 1942 knew that in many cases it was purely down to luck that they had lived while so many others had died, and such luck was bound to run out sooner or later. Russian literature has for centuries highlighted the stoic fatalism of ordinary Russians, and this continuing trait combined with the death rate contributed greatly to men simply believing that their personal chances of survival were negligible. But just as the Germans were able to combine a growing sense of pessimism based upon their experiences with their deep-rooted belief in Hitler leading them to triumph, so the Soviet soldiers also managed to reconcile such conflicting points of view. After the war, the

Soviet Union would attempt to define this as a unique virtue of the Soviet system: the ultimate victory of the Soviet people over Nazi Germany was only possible due to the strength of the people, led and guided by the special values of the Communist Party. But in many respects, the determination to win – even if combined with a sense that personal survival was extremely unlikely – owed little to the Communist system. The Germans had left the ordinary people of the Soviet Union with no real choice. If they didn't fight and win, they faced death on a huge scale.

Already, the siege of Leningrad was assuming the characteristics of a legend. It was inevitable that Soviet propaganda would make the most – at home and abroad – of the survival of the city, and Soviet newspapers were full of accounts of the selfless manner in which ordinary citizens had endured unimaginable suffering and privation. During the weeks of bitter fighting in Stalingrad at the opposite end of the long Eastern Front, there were frequent proclamations by local Communist Party officials in both Leningrad and Stalingrad, expressing solidarity with their comrades in the other city. The clear message of the Soviet propaganda was not merely that both cities continued to defy the Germans, but that their ability to do so was due to the Soviet system and Communist Party leadership. In tone and character, these messages were little different from those propagated by Goebbels in Berlin, lauding the heroic nature of the Germans and the values of the Nazi Party in leading them through the war.

Amongst ordinary civilians in Leningrad, the mood had changed just as much during 1942 as it did amongst the soldiers in the city and along the Volkhov River. The fear and widespread sense of doom that had prevailed in Leningrad during the first winter was greatly reduced a year later. In late 1941, the Wehrmacht was threatening not just Leningrad but also Moscow, and in the months that followed it recovered from its setbacks in the Red Army's counteroffensive outside the Soviet capital to sweep across the flat terrain of the southern sector to reach the Don and Volga valleys, and then penetrate into the Caucasus region. But as 1942 drew to a close, the successful encirclement of German forces in Stalingrad and the near-total collapse of German defences along the Don valley lifted spirits across the entire nation. The hated Fascists could be beaten.

CHAPTER 2

ISKRA – PLANNING

As the days grew shorter and colder at the end of 1942 and the two sides licked their wounds following the failure of the latest Soviet attempt to break the siege ring, thoughts turned to the future. A further attack to try to establish firm land contact between Leningrad and Volkhov Fronts was inevitable, and the two armies tooks whatever measures they could – on the Soviet side, to learn from the failed operations of 1942 in order to deliver better results in 1943, and on the German side, to defend with the same tenacity as before regardless of what the Red Army tried to do.

The terrain was singularly difficult for offensive operations. The German advance through the region in 1941 had only been possible because the Wehrmacht was pursuing a defeated opponent – the broken divisions of the Red Army were in no state to stop the German advance or even to establish a continuous front line. Having secured a foothold on the shore of Lake Ladoga, the Wehrmacht took full advantage of the terrain to establish a formidable array of defensive positions. The generally flat region between the Neva River in the west and the Volkhov River in the east was crossed by a number of streams and small rivers, each with areas of marshland on either bank. There were numerous areas of woodland, particularly further south, and many of these remained relatively intact despite the heavy shelling and fighting of the preceding year. The only significant high ground was immediately to the west of Sinyavino, the so-called Sinyavino Heights; in any other landscape, such a modest area of high ground would have been utterly insignificant, but in this region the Sinyavino Heights represented a key position, giving the occupier the ability to oversee the entire stretch of land held by the Germans. Control of the heights was therefore recognised by both sides as critical in the coming battles.

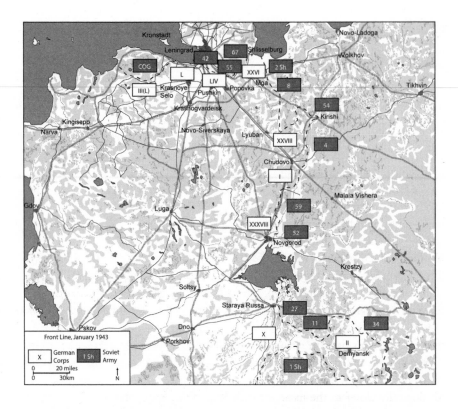

Front Line, January 1943

| X | German Corps | 1 Sh | Soviet Army |

0   20 miles
0   30km   N

The German lines between Leningrad and Volkhov Fronts were held by Lindemann's Eighteenth Army. To the west, facing the Soviet defences south of Leningrad and along the Neva, was III Luftwaffe Field Corps with L Corps immediately to the east; their formations would play little part in the fighting of January. The eastern neighbour of L Corps was LIV Corps commanded by General Erich Hansen, deployed from the town of Pushkin in the west to the most southern point of the Neva River; in this sector of just 13 miles, there were three German divisions – the Spanish Blue Division in the west, *SS-Polizei* in the centre, and 5th Mountain Division in the east. Hansen was about to leave his post in order to become head of the German military mission in Romania; his replacement was to be General Carl Hilpert, who had spent the first half of the winter of 1942 defending the northwest face of the Rzhev salient with XXIII Corps, and he would take up his new post on 20 January.

SS-Polizei had been created in October 1939 as *Polizei-Division* using personnel mainly from the civilian *Ordnungspolizei* ('Order Police') with detachments from the regular army filling specialist roles such as artillery and signals. It first saw action in the invasion of France, after which it was formally adopted into the SS. It entered the Soviet Union in June 1941 as part of Army Group North and took part in the advance to Leningrad, suffering heavy casualties – the first ten weeks of the campaign cost it about 3,000 dead and wounded. As was the case with many SS formations, this was partly due to the appointment of many officers purely because of their status within the SS rather than their military training or aptitude. Casualties continued to mount through 1942, requiring regular substantial replacement drafts, and on 3 January 1943 Hitler issued orders for several divisions on the Eastern Front that were regarded as critically depleted – including *SS-Polizei* – to be withdrawn to the west for major replenishment. Rumours of the impending move spread rapidly through the division, but were dashed as quickly as they had arisen. The intention had been to dispatch replacement units to Army Group North in order to allow for the withdrawal of *SS-Polizei*, but this proved impossible. Firstly, the catastrophic deterioration of the situation around Stalingrad made it almost impossible to spare troops for other sectors; secondly, the replacements originally earmarked for the north were not ready. During 1942, there had been calls for the lavishly manned Luftwaffe to release personnel to try to bring army infantry divisions back to strength, but instead Hermann Goering, head of the Luftwaffe, persuaded Hitler that it would be better to use these men to create Luftwaffe field divisions – he argued successfully that the Luftwaffe was ideologically closer to the mindset of the Nazi Party than the regular army, and that it would therefore be better to keep these men in new formations. The Luftwaffe field divisions performed badly when deployed on the Eastern Front; like the early SS units, too many of their officers had little or no experience of modern ground warfare. Two such divisions, 19th and 20th Luftwaffe Field Divisions, had been intended to replace *SS-Polizei* but were nowhere near ready for deployment, and the SS division would have to remain in the front line.[1]

To the east of LIV Corps, the front line along the Neva to the shore of Lake Ladoga and also the east-facing front line from Lake Ladoga to the village of Lodva was under the control of General Ernst von Leyser's XXVI Corps – in many respects, the key sector for the coming battle. On the Neva, facing Leningrad Front, was 170th Infantry Division and a regiment of 227th Infantry Division. The rest of 227th Infantry Division was at the northern end of the east-facing front line, with 1st and 223rd Infantry Divisions to its south. The soldiers of 1st Infantry Division had only just arrived in their positions, replacing 24th Infantry Division in the first week of January 1943. Beyond Leyser's southern flank was XXVIII Corps.

Leyser was, like almost all senior Wehrmacht officers, a veteran of the First World War and came from a family with a strong military background – his father was Generalleutnant Hans von Leyser, who had commanded an infantry division on the Western Front with distinction in the last two years of the war. When the First World War began, both Ernst and his younger brother Fritz were serving officers, and Ernst held various posts as a junior officer in 1st Guards Reserve Regiment. Thereafter, he remained in the Reichswehr during the inter-war years and commanded an infantry regiment in the western campaign of 1940; at the beginning of *Barbarossa*, he was commander of 269th Infantry Division and led it across the Baltic region towards Leningrad. He inherited command of XXVI Corps from General Albert Wodrig in October 1942 and spent the following weeks adding to strong positions occupied by his men. Whilst Leyser wasn't a member of the Nazi Party – for many years before the war, senior personnel were officially forbidden from being members of political parties, and even by 1941 only about 29 per cent of the Wehrmacht's senior figures were Nazi Party members – he showed little inclination to reject the extreme policies of Germany's leadership.[2] During his time as commander of 269th Infantry Division and then XXVI Corps, he passed on instructions such as the infamous *Richtlinien für die Behandlung Politischer Kommissare* ('Guidelines for the Treatment of Political Commissars', usually known as the 'Commissar Order'), which ordered German soldiers to segregate the Red Army's political officers from other prisoners. Commissars were not to be regarded as entitled to any of the protection due to prisoners of war; although the order stated that commissars who were not guilty of any enemy action should simply be detained, it added: 'In judging the question "guilty or not guilty", the personal impression of the attitude and bearing of the commissar should as a matter of principle count for more than the facts of the case, which it may not be possible to prove.'[3]

After the war, Leyser was detained and prosecuted in 1947 for passing on the Commissar Order, for the illegal execution of hostages during his time as commander of 269th Infantry Division, and for forcible deportation of Croatian workers to Germany. He was sentenced to ten years' imprisonment but this was revised in 1951 to time served and he was released from captivity.[4]

As was usual practice in the Wehrmacht, Eighteenth Army had assigned additional units to XXVI Corps. Nine independent artillery battalions (including four heavy battalions which included 300mm mortars in their equipment list) provided considerable firepower beyond the normal divisional artillery complement, and armoured support came in the form of an assault gun battalion and some of the Tiger tanks of Carius' *Schwere Panzer Abteilung 502.* In addition to these units, Lindemann had 96th Infantry Division in reserve, in a holding area in and to the south of Mga. But one critical change compared with the fighting of September was the absence of any panzer divisions – 12th Panzer Division, the last such formation in Army Group North, had been transferred to the central sector, where it would play a part in the German counterattacks that crushed the Red Army's winter assault on the Rzhev salient. If Army Group North had to mount any major counterattacks, it would do so without the help of any panzer divisions. Whilst the terrain was not suited to armoured operations, the firepower of the absent panzer division – and especially in this setting, the mobility of its artillery regiment – would be sorely missed.

Despite the heavy fighting of late 1942, most of the German divisions were in good shape, with between 10,000 and 12,000 men each, and they occupied positions that had been constructed and strengthened during 1942. The first obstacle that faced any attack by Leningrad Front towards Volkhov Front was the Neva River, which in most areas was about 550 yards wide. Although the river was frozen, the ice would not be strong enough to support heavy vehicles and the Germans could break the ice using artillery and demolition charges. The riverbank facing the Neva was heavily fortified and the entire sector, along the Neva to Lake Ladoga and then running from the lake towards the south, was protected by three distinct defensive lines. Each of these consisted of three trench systems, and the defences were further strengthened by several fortified positions. The stone buildings of several villages had been carefully reinforced and turned into miniature fortresses, often with interlocking fields of fire. On the western side of the salient, facing Leningrad Front, were Gorodok 1 and Gorodok 2, workers' settlements built in the 1930s. Further south were Arbutsovo and Annenskoye, and Shlisselburg on the shore of Lake Ladoga was also heavily fortified, effectively anchoring the northern part of the defensive line. On the eastern side of the German salient were further fortified villages: Lipka in the north, close to Lake Ladoga, with Gorodok 8, Gontovaia Lipka, Tortolovo, Mishino, and Poreche strengthening the line to the south. On the east-facing side of the salient, the modest Zvankovsky Hill, rising just 130 feet above sea level, was particularly heavily fortified with numerous ramparts of soil and compacted ice, and high wicker fencing had been erected at various locations to obscure positions from Soviet observers.[5]

Within the salient were further areas of fortification. Sinyavino had seen bitter fighting around its outskirts the previous autumn and its buildings had been further strengthened during the weeks that followed. Several more settlements known purely by their numbers lay between Sinyavino and Lake Ladoga. The entire salient was thus almost continuously fortified. In combination with the swamps, waterways, and woodland, this represented one of the most difficult areas imaginable through which to conduct offensive operations. But it remained the shortest distance between the Leningrad siege perimeter and the outside world, and even if the Red Army was prepared to accept the disadvantage of advancing across a greater distance by attacking with Volkhov Front from further south and then attempting to push northwest to Leningrad, the terrain remained just as unsuited.

The German military doctrine of mounting counterattacks against enemy assaults was so deeply established that it was almost universally expected by friend and foe alike. The use of such counterattacks to restore the defensive line developed in the 19th century in the Prussian Army and was continued through the years that followed German unification; it was generally regarded as a very effective way of eliminating any gains made by the enemy, and to be most effective these counterattacks were best mounted as soon as such gains had been made by the attackers, while they were still off-balance. If there were delays, there was increasing likelihood that the enemy would be able to dig in and consolidate their gains, making restoration of the former front line far more difficult. For such counterattacks to succeed, it was essential for reserves to be available at every level. Local commanders in regiments and divisions had to have some of their men held behind the front line in anticipation of such a requirement, and corps commanders also had to have reserves available, either to shore up defences or to mount large-scale counterattacks. At the beginning of 1943, German infantry divisions were holding the same length of front line as they had done in the past, but with fewer men. Commanders thus had a difficult problem: they could either man the line with fewer soldiers than before; or they could reduce the reserves that they held in readiness for use as reinforcements or for counterattacks. This problem would grow steadily worse as the war progressed, rendering the German defensive line ever more brittle. For the moment, though, the infantry divisions of the German Eighteenth Army were in fairly good shape. Although they were below establishment strength, they were still sufficiently strong for a resolute defensive effort and their reserves would suffice for at least one round of counterattacks. However, it was the arrival of divisions transferred from Crimea that made a difference in the fighting of late summer and autumn 1942. Given the continuing crisis in eastern Ukraine, there was no prospect of such reinforcements being available if Army Group North should find itself in serious difficulties. But by positioning 96th Infantry Division in reserve near Mga,

Lindemann ensured that it was available to reinforce either front line. Given the limitations on his resources, he had deployed his troops judiciously.

There were some in German circles who felt that a continued presence in the salient stretching to the shore of Lake Ladoga was too risky. In a report sent to Lindemann's headquarters in November, Leyser asked whether it might be better to pull back from the lake to the Sinyavino area, from where it would be possible to continue to interdict the ground with artillery fire but without risking units being cut off by any new Soviet offensive. Lindemann dismissed the proposal out of hand. All attempts by the Red Army to break through had failed, and there was nothing to suggest that the situation was about to change. In any event, Lindemann knew he would have to obtain Hitler's permission for such a withdrawal, and such permission was not going to be granted – the only outcome would be that Lindemann would have earned the Führer's disapproval by making such a suggestion.[6]

In short, even though the Red Army enjoyed a considerable numerical advantage, the armies earmarked by Govorov and Meretskov for the forthcoming operation faced daunting challenges. The density of the defence lines; the firepower available to the defenders; the predictability of the likely avenues of attack; and the difficulty of advancing through such terrain – particularly in winter conditions – meant that breaking the siege ring would be a tough task. To make matters worse, even before they attacked the German front line, Leningrad Front's troops would have to cross the frozen Neva River. Thereafter, all their supplies and reinforcements would have to be brought across the river.

Plans for a renewed offensive in the Sinyavino area were first drawn up in November, while the units that had fought for this sector in preceding weeks were still recovering from their losses. From the headquarters of Leningrad Front, Govorov submitted a proposal on the eve of the great Red Army counteroffensive outside Stalingrad for a winter campaign that would come in two phases. The first was described as the Shlisselburg Operation and was intended to break the siege ring by recapturing Shlisselburg and establishing contact with Volkhov Front along the shore of Lake Ladoga. This operation would see Leningrad Front's Sixty-Seventh Army attacking across the frozen Neva River, while Volkhov Front would attack from the east with Eighth and Second Shock Armies, and the two forces would meet somewhere near Sinyavino. The second phase was the Uritsk Offensive. This would see Leningrad Front attacking between Uritsk and Pushkin, further to the west, with Forty-Second Army. At the same time, the Coastal Operational Group would break out of the Oranienbaum bridgehead, and the two forces would unite, this driving the Germans away from the southern outskirts of Leningrad. This would prevent the Germans from continuing their artillery attacks on the city and reduce their ability to interfere in the movement of Soviet warships in the Gulf of Finland. Aware that he lacked the resources to mount both operations simultaneously, Govorov requested that the attack to link up with Volkhov Front should proceed first, in mid-December, with the attack to link up with the Oranienbaum bridgehead following about two months later.[7]

In the previous attempt to break the siege ring, most of the burden was borne by Volkhov Front and the modest contributions of Leningrad Front across the Neva achieved little; although Govorov's troops managed to secure a few small bridgeheads, they were unable to expand them and were rapidly forced to abandon their positions and withdraw back across the river. By attacking in winter, Govorov planned to take advantage of thick river ice to support at least light vehicles. This added another dimension to the planning of the operation: it would have to take place during a sufficiently cold spell to guarantee that the ice was thick enough. The Red Army had dedicated bridging units, but although Sixty-Seventh Army had engineer battalions, none of these were specialist bridging formations with the appropriate equipment and training to construct crossings. Indeed, bridging resources were limited within the Leningrad perimeter and would have to be improvised and the first wave to cross the river would be accompanied by only light armour.[8]

The winter of 1942–43 was milder than the bitterly cold winter of the previous year, and the ice on the Neva River did not thicken as rapidly as expected. Within days of his first submission, Govorov drafted new timings. He now suggested that the attack to link up with Volkhov Front should commence in mid-January. At the beginning of December, he received approval from *Stavka*, and the attack was given the codename *Iskra* ('Spark'). At the time, most Soviet operations were given codenames related to objects in the sky – *Uranus*, *Mars* etc, but this operation was treated differently:

> When the plan for the operation was being discussed at *Stavka*, Stalin stunned everyone with the question: 'What shall we call the operation?' After a moment's silence, he himself answered: '*Iskra*.' The Supreme Commander went on to explain why he had selected the name: all previous attempts to break the blockade of the city on the Neva had ended in failure, and now the 'spark' would ignite the 'flame' that would bring success.[9]

As Govorov had suggested, the main effort of Leningrad Front would be made by Sixty-Seventh Army attacking across the Neva between Shlisselburg in the north and Gorodok 2 in the south; at the same time, Volkhov Front's Second Shock Army, which had been reconstituted for the third time, would attack from the east. The proposed operation to link up with the Coastal Operational Group in Oranienbaum was for the moment shelved; instead, a second phase of the main attack was envisaged, which would see the forces that had linked up turning south to attack and capture Sinyavino and Mga.

There were attempts to learn from the failures of 1942; indeed, such learning was explicit in the planning of the new operation, in that Govorov expected the units that had struggled in vain in earlier operations to have learned from their errors. The attacks of August and September had been intended to see both Leningrad and Volkhov Fronts advancing so that they could meet somewhere near Shlisselburg; but Leningrad Front's contribution proved to be minimal and was not coordinated with that of Volkhov Front. On many occasions in the war, operations involving multiple Soviet Fronts resulted in each Front attacking on a different day. This could be a valuable stratagem, as the Germans were likely to commit their reserves to whichever attack took place first and would thus have less available to deal with subsequent attacks. However, for this stratagem to work, the Front that attacked first had to sustain its pressure. Otherwise, the Germans would be able to extract their reserves and dispatch them to deal with the second attack. Whatever the intentions might have been, the Sinyavino attacks of August and September saw Leningrad Front attacking first but not sustaining its attacks. Any benefit from drawing in German reserves was therefore lost. For *Iskra*, the two Fronts were ordered to ensure that their attacks took place on the same day. Perhaps mindful of Meretskov's chequered past, *Stavka* ordered that Lieutenant General Ivan Ivanovich Fedyuninsky, deputy commander of Volkhov Front, should oversee the preparations of Second Shock Army. In order to try to improve cooperation and coordination between different Fronts, *Stavka* often sent a representative to be present on the ground and to travel between the different headquarters, and on this occasion Marshal Kliment Yefremovich Voroshilov was dispatched to the north. Voroshilov was not a man who was held in high regard by other senior officers; it was common knowledge that he owed his high rank and status almost entirely to his long personal friendship and association with Stalin, and his rigid adherence to the wishes and views of the Soviet leader. Nonetheless, he was to ensure that the two Fronts coordinated their efforts.

Other improvements were also included in the plans. The use of massive artillery bombardments to pave the way for an assault was well established, but Soviet bombardments – in the northern sector and elsewhere – often failed to achieve their purpose in 1942. There were many reasons for this, but chiefly the failure was due to poor reconnaissance. German field positions were often inadequately identified and bombardment often failed to strike known positions sufficiently heavily. Moreover, once the advancing infantry ran into difficulties, coordination with artillery support was often poor. This resulted in the infantry suffering increasingly heavy losses as they repeatedly attacked intact German positions.

In order to address these problems, Govorov took several steps. His Front was to attack on a frontage of six miles and he intended to deploy a total of about 700 guns and mortars in support of the initial attack. As plans were drawn up in detail at the end of November, Meretskov's Volkhov Front also massed its artillery to provide a higher concentration of fire than had previously been the case. Ammunition was stockpiled in advance to ensure that the gun batteries would have sufficient shells for several days, and attention was paid to improving the pace at which guns could be moved forward. This had repeatedly been a problem, particularly when the initial penetration was too narrow or the advance was on ground that made movement difficult. In an attempt to prevent a repeat of these setbacks, Govorov and Meretskov assigned engineer battalions to their attacking armies to improve and if necessary construct roads so that supplies and reinforcements as well as artillery could move forward as quickly as possible.

There was a further reason why soldiers failed to follow the artillery bombardment as it progressed into the depths of the German position, a continuing legacy of the privations of the long siege, as Iosif Mikhailovich Dushevsky, an infantry company commander, described:

> We were not trained to advance behind the curtain of fire … Neither tanks nor infantry moved forward quickly. Shortly before the blockade of Leningrad was broken [by *Iskra*], a commission from Leningrad District headquarters visited us. It concluded that the men were physically weak. They couldn't run continuously for 300m. It was decided to feed us more. We began to receive 700g of black bread, 300g of white bread, and some added butter.[10]

At the headquarters of Volkhov Front, Meretskov was looking at how best to overcome the strong defences that lay in the path of Second Shock Army, as he later recalled:

> We transferred a significant amount of artillery from other armies to [Second Shock] Army, as well as the Front reserve and everything that *Stavka* could give us.

The density of German troops in this area was almost twice as high as stipulated by their normal practice. But we were also able to provide an average of 160 guns and mortars for every kilometre of the front line. This made it possible to create an unusually high density of fire. The mistakes made in the Sinyavino Operation [in August and September of 1942] were not in vain. In general, special attention was paid to the artillery strike. In addition, first in the preliminary discussions and then during special exercises, we rehearsed the efficient combination of artillery bombardment with aerial attacks.

It would be a foolish waste of energy to attack enemy nodes of resistance head-on. But nor was it possible to bypass them completely, due to the specific conditions of the area. My chief of staff [Lieutenant General Mikhail Nikolayevich] Sharokhin and his subordinates had to study the enemy positions carefully in order to organise the offensive operation to maximise its efficacy and to ensure that our troops suffered the least possible losses. That is military reality. When a military commander plans an operation, he not only understands that there will be human losses, but also attempts to have a realistic estimate of losses, because he doesn't want to miscalculate and later suffer even greater losses as a result of underestimating a number of factors ... Unfortunately, we have to take into account the upcoming losses. But this doesn't make a person a kind of soulless machine. I have always fretted greatly about losses ...

Throughout December, the troops underwent intensive training for the forthcoming operation. Command staff meetings were held. Team rehearsals took place. Units and subunits trained in special camps with models of the centres of defence that they would have to overcome. Aerial photography provided a wealth of material and our military engineers rapidly erected simulated enemy ramparts, pillboxes in swamps, and various field fortifications. The commanders of our formations worked out thoroughly the issues of interaction between the combat arms. Several times, I assessed their readiness for the task. We all studied the lessons of the Sinyavino Operation [of September 1942].[11]

Meretskov's performance in the war to date had been variable at best, and he may have had mixed feelings when Fedyuninsky was appointed as his deputy commander in October 1942. On the one hand, Fedyuninsky had extensive experience of fighting in this sector. He had been commander of Northern Front a year earlier before briefly becoming commander of Leningrad Front, and had then led Fifty-Fourth Army in the failed offensive that led to the first encirclement of Second Shock Army. That prior experience and knowledge was a great benefit, but on the other hand there was perhaps an implication that *Stavka* continued to have doubts about Meretskov's abilities and was thus sending a highly capable deputy to the region – if he should fail to deliver, Fedyuninsky would be able to step in to replace him. Nonetheless, it seems that Meretskov tried to make the best of the situation, as Fedyuninsky later described:

> Meretskov said that I would be more than his deputy. *Stavka* had placed personal responsibility on me to oversee the breaking of the blockade of Leningrad using the right wing of Volkhov Front. 'You will have a great deal of work on important matters,' said the Front commander. 'The region is well known to you, Ivan Ivanovich, which means that you hold all the cards.'
>
> I replied that I intended to spend most of the time not at Front headquarters but with the troops, personally supervising and organising preparations for the upcoming operation. The Front commander expressed his approval.[12]

The attitude of Soviet commanders at senior levels to the casualties their units suffered varied. Many, including Zhukov, showed little or no apparent regard for the lives of ordinary soldiers and threw units into assaults with brutal determination, even when such assaults were doomed to fail, but some officers took what measures they could to avoid casualties. The fundamental problem that the Red Army faced was that its troops were relatively unskilled compared to those of other armies in the Second World War, and the existential nature of the conflict meant that there was little opportunity for proper, lengthy training. The same policies that had weakened the Red Army before the onset of the war with Germany – the flawed doctrine of basic training being completed at unit level, and the absence of any culture of career NCOs with the institutional knowledge that was such a strong feature of the Wehrmacht and of western armies – greatly hindered the speed at which the Red Army could make improvements as the war continued. Lacking the training to improvise and think for themselves and constantly in fear of criticism or arrest for failing to carry out their orders, junior commanders often felt they had no choice but to obey the instructions issued from above, however futile they were in reality. The measures that Meretskov could take to minimise casualties were at a large scale, trying to avoid mass assaults on the strongest parts of the German line; there was little or nothing he could do to reduce losses at the detailed level.

Lieutenant General Vladimir Zakharovich Romanovsky, whose rebuilt Second Shock Army would lead the assault, knew he was facing a tough challenge, attacking over ground where the Red Army had previously been defeated:

> The axis of advance for the troops was obstructed by strong bunkers and peat bogs, and deep ditches protected by ramparts made of timber and earth. There had been heavy fighting here in September 1942. Many of our tanks that had broken into the German defences had been hit and knocked out. The Hitlerites now put them to use, turning them into stationary firing points. Lieutenant General [Arkady Fedorovich] Khrenov, the head of the engineering section [of Volkhov Front] and his scouts reported the precise locations of these tanks. On the approaches to the Sinyavino Heights and on Roshu Hill in the breakthrough zone of the army there were about 40 of these, hard to destroy even with artillery.
>
> We did not expect a high rate of advance but prepared consistently to gnaw our way through the deeply echeloned enemy defences. Each division created assault groups to face and destroy the enemy's strengthened firing points. These groups were to cooperate closely with tanks and artillery.[13]

A significant failing of the previous attack on Sinyavino was the manner in which the initial penetration of the German defences had run out of momentum. Once it had come to a halt, restarting it proved almost impossible. In anticipation of similar setbacks, Govorov's original plan specified that the attacks by the two Fronts should consist of two echelons. Sufficient troops should be available in the second echelon to overcome any new German defensive positions that they might encounter, and *Stavka* responded to his plans by providing additional reinforcements. Leningrad Front was assigned an extra rifle division, five independent rifle brigades, and three ski brigades; and additional artillery formations were assigned to both Fronts so that they could achieve the desired density of fire support. As the plans matured, Govorov and *Stavka* agreed that Sixty-Seventh Army's first echelon would be sufficiently strong to break through to meet the advancing units of Volkhov Front; the second echelon would then be committed to widen the breach in the siege ring by driving the Germans south through and beyond Sinyavino. The first phase – to link up with Volkhov Front's Second Shock Army – was expected to be complete within four days. Similarly, Second Shock Army was to attack in two echelons, aiming to link up with Sixty-Seventh Army north of Sinyavino while the southern flank of Second Shock Army pressed into Sinyavino itself.[14] To the south of Second Shock Army, Eighth Army would cover the southern flank of the drive from any German counterattack.

The assembled force was formidable in numbers: Sixty-Seventh Army fielded 130,000 men and 222 tanks; Second Shock Army had been replenished after its brutal mauling in the autumn and now possessed 165,000 men and 230 tanks, of which 38 were heavy KV-1s, 131 were the ubiquitous T-34s, and 61 were light T-70s; and on its southern flank, Eighth Army had 52,000 men and 92 tanks.[15]

There were also some wide-reaching changes in the Red Army that were intended to learn from past failures. Marshal Aleksandr Mikhailovich Vasilevsky, chief of the Soviet general staff, described these in his memoirs:

> The draft Field Regulations [of the infantry] of 1943 summed up the best experience of the army and helped to turn it to good effect widely in practice. New recommendations were made in the regulations to commanding officers … Up until then, commanders of rifle units normally advanced ahead of their men when an offensive was being made. As a result, the army suffered heavy casualties among the middle-level commanders. Moreover, the desire of commanders to be always in the vanguard extremely hampered their control of the fighting … [The new regulations] prescribed that all commanding officers (with the exception of squad commanders) should choose themselves a place in the fighting where they could most conveniently organise their men, observe the field of battle and maintain contact with their superiors and neighbouring officers. According to the new regulations, when advancing against an enemy on the defensive one should avoid a routine echelonment of attacking infantry; instead, one should mass forces and equipment of units and sub-units at the point of the main attack, narrowing the width of sector for their breakthrough and offensive, and increasing the tactical density per unit of area occupied by them.
>
> The numerical strength of personnel in rifle units was reduced, while their firepower was substantially increased … the light machine-guns in the full-strength rifle division increased by more than an extra 150, and 45mm guns increased by an extra 18. Submachine-guns markedly increased …
>
> The number of types of artillery diminished from 21 to eight, which made it easier for the defence industry to fulfil the front orders.[16]

It seems likely that experienced field commanders already knew that positioning themselves at the forefront of an attack was likely to result in them becoming casualties with resultant disruption of command, but prior to these new regulations, many officers would have felt they had no choice but to take such risks – the alternative was just as risky, with superior officers and the ever-present commissars able to blame any shortcomings of the attack on the failure of the local commanders to show sufficient leadership. The change in regulations for officers was important in that it effectively gave permission to them to behave in a more sensible manner. However, whilst the insistence on massing troops for an attack was intended to avoid dissipation of effort, it also increased the risk of heavy casualties from defensive fire.

Amongst the units of Eighth Army, preparing to attack on the southern flank of Second Shock Army, was Morozov's artillery brigade. The gunners were tasked with paving the way for the Soviet attack on Tortolovo, and Morozov's commander sent him to ask for additional guns:

> I argued with the army's chief of artillery, [Major General Semen Fedorovich] Bezruk, to give us more guns. The general agreed with all my points, but couldn't help: he had no additional resources. Bezruk advised that we allocate only two batteries to suppress the enemies on the high ground on the flank, on the grounds that these heights were outside the actual offensive zone …
>
> Throughout the last week before the offensive, the chief of staff of the artillery brigade, Major Kapustin, and I refined the fire plan of the artillery bombardment, setting specific missions for the battery commanders. There were so many targets in our sector that there weren't enough batteries to suppress them. Information received from 265th Rifle Division and from the army's artillery headquarters didn't differ in terms of reliability or accuracy. We were sent a large-scale map. Enemy defences spotted by aerial photography were drawn on it. Here was everything that could be spotted through the lens of an aircraft camera: fighting trenches, communications trenches, artillery firing positions, etc. These maps were only just beginning to come into general use and were of great help in planning our bombardment. But they still had many shortcomings: detection of positions wasn't always successful, and it was often difficult to determine which trenches and positions were occupied by the enemy and which were not, and which of the structures were decoys.[17]

The commanders of the two armies earmarked for the main assault would play leading roles in the fighting. Sixty-Seventh Army had been created from a conglomerate of units deployed along the Neva and previously known as the Neva Operational Group, and was under the command of Major General Mikhail Pavlovich Dukhanov. He had commanded the Soviet Ninth Army during the war with Finland in 1939–40 and later the Neva Operational Group. He was respected by many of his peers and subordinates for his calm manner;

Vasily Ivanovich Chuikov, who was at this time commanding Sixty-Second Army in the battles for the ruins of Stalingrad, described him:

His abilities as a military commander showed themselves in a very positive manner in many operations. He knew how always to be in a place where most difficulties would arise. He was calm and reasonable and inspired confidence in the behaviour of his troops.[18]

His opposite number on the other side of the salient was Lieutenant General Vladimir Zakharovich Romanovsky, who had inherited command of Second Shock Army as planning began for *Iskra* in early December. Prior to this, he commanded First Shock Army in the fighting around Demyansk in 1942, and was in most respects an unremarkable though competent officer. Few if any of his contemporaries had much to say about him in their memoirs and it seems that this unassuming man survived the fear-filled days of Stalin's purges of the Red Army largely by being relatively anonymous and no threat to anyone. That was insufficient for many others, but perhaps due to his past record of quiet, unspectacular work, he wasn't a natural candidate for denunciations by men attempting to escape further punishment. It was a challenging task for a new army commander to settle in and become sufficiently knowledgeable about his subordinate commanders in such a short time before a major offensive, and he was aided in this considerably by Fedyuninsky, whose extensive prior experience in this sector was now of crucial importance.

The level of detail both in the planning carried out by Govorov and Meretskov and in the instructions they received from *Stavka* was impressive, and was a further indication of attempts to learn from the errors of the past. In addition to carrying out a preparatory bombardment of German positions, the Red Army's artillery units that were equipped with long-range guns were to strike far in the rear of the German positions, aiming to hit German artillery positions, headquarters, supply dumps, and other targets. Additionally, the areas immediately adjacent to the troops of Volkhov Front and facing the east bank of the Neva opposite Leningrad Front would be hit by batteries of medium and heavy guns using direct fire; in the case of Leningrad Front, this was due to concerns that heavy shelling of the German-held bank might result in the ice sheet over the Neva being destroyed. To prevent problems caused by ammunition shortages, it was stipulated that up to five full loads of ammunition per gun were to be stockpiled, with transports on skis and sleighs made available to move both weapons and ammunition.

One of the great advantages enjoyed by the Wehrmacht over the Red Army was the close cooperation between Luftwaffe units and ground forces. Repeatedly, German troops were able to call upon air strikes to help them advance or to break up Soviet attacks, and despite the presence of increasing numbers of fighters and bombers, Soviet aviation fell far short of the performance of its opponent. The two Fronts were supported by their integrated air armies – Thirteenth Air Army in Leningrad Front, Fourteenth Air Army in Volkhov Front, each fielding about 400 planes – and their units were allocated specific missions for the coming operation. Thirteenth Air Army lacked bombers, as it had mainly been concerned with disrupting Luftwaffe attacks on Leningrad, and its fighters were ordered to secure the airspace over the battlefield so that German bombers and particularly dive-bombers would not be able to interfere with the Soviet attack. By contrast, Fourteenth Air Army had rather more by way of bombers and ground attack aircraft and in order to make maximum use of these, Meretskov ordered the construction of forward airfields where fuel and munitions were stockpiled. Flying from their main bases, his bombers were to attack the Germans and then land at the forward airfields where they would be refuelled and rearmed, and would be allocated new targets. After completing this second attack, they would return to their main bases. By putting in place communications systems between the headquarters of Volkhov Front and Second Shock Army on the one hand and the forward airfields on the other, Meretskov hoped Fourteenth Air Army would be able to provide timely tactical support.[19] This fell far short of the almost routine manner in which German *Fliegerverbindungsoffiziere* ('Air Liaison Officers', often abbreviated to *Flivo*) were positioned with ground units and were able to communicate directly with aircraft, but it was nonetheless a step forward. At the beginning of the war, many Soviet aircraft either had no radios at all or were equipped only with receivers, i.e. they could receive instructions but couldn't reply or even communicate with each other. Although two-way radios were generally available by the beginning of 1943, the degree of close cooperation routinely expected by the Germans was still a long way from Soviet capabilities.

Unlike the battles around Stalingrad, the terrain in the far north was unsuitable for the operation of massed armour. Recognising this, the plans for *Iskra* dictated that the tanks deployed for the operation should be used as infantry support rather than en masse. Just as Soviet use of air support lagged far behind the abilities of the Wehrmacht, a recurring problem throughout the war was a lack of coordination between tanks and infantry. At the start of the conflict, only commanders' tanks had radios, and the intention to communicate between tanks by waving flags from the turret hatch was a complete failure. By the end of 1942, all new tanks had radios, resulting in better command and control of tank formations, but few units trained assiduously in close cooperation with accompanying infantry. There was certainly no equivalent of the German panzergrenadiers, and even the soldiers of ordinary German infantry divisions were better trained in combined arms warfare than their Soviet counterparts. At the suggestion of field commanders, T-34s now had handles welded to their hulls and turrets, allowing a handful of soldiers to ride on the vehicles as they moved into battle, but this was no substitute for proper training in all-arms warfare. Many soldiers in both tank and infantry units might have learned from past mistakes how to improve matters, but training of new recruits remained relatively basic.

Aware that the troops of Leningrad Front had less experience than the men of Volkhov Front in conducting offensive operations, Govorov attempted to improve their training. Replicas of German positions were constructed in the rear area and troops earmarked for the attack underwent detailed training on how to approach and overcome these defences. The men were also taught how to move through forested terrain and deep snow. Alongside this physical training, the Red Army carried out its usual policy of political preparation of the soldiers. Commissars and Communist Party officials from Leningrad addressed gatherings of men, impressing upon them the importance of the operation and stressing that the citizens of Leningrad were relying on them to succeed where the previous attempts had failed. As was the case everywhere along the Eastern Front, unit commissars found plenty of material to build up a strong desire for vengeance against the Germans. Many units kept diaries in which soldiers could record atrocities they had experienced, or could write about the fate of their family members who lived in the German-occupied zone. Some reports from these civilians reached the Soviet lines via the partisan network, others when desperate civilians who had often been deprived of their homes and were finding it increasingly difficult to get adequate food took the considerable risk of crossing the front line.

In mid-December, Govorov conducted a paper exercise in the Smolny Institute in Leningrad, the headquarters of the city administration and the historic base from which the Bolsheviks had seized power in 1917. The purpose was to simulate the planned operation. The commanders of the first-echelon divisions were put through their paces in detail, a task made easier by a concerted reconnaissance effort in the first fortnight of the month. One of those involved in the exercise was Major General Nikolai Pavlovich Simoniak, commander of Sixty-Seventh Army's 136th Rifle Division, which would be in the forefront of the coming assault across the Neva. Formerly a cavalryman, he commanded an independent rifle brigade at the start of the war, stationed on the island of Hanko on the northern side of the Gulf of Finland. The small island came under repeated attack by Finnish forces but Simoniak conducted an energetic defence until he and his men were evacuated by sea. His brigade was enlarged into the new 136th Rifle Division and fought in the failed attempt to link up with Volkhov Front at Sinyavino in the autumn of 1942. During the rehearsal for *Iskra*, the staff of each division was put in a separate room and Govorov and his team visited them from time to time to discuss details of their plans. When working with his division staff, Simoniak had a relaxed, almost friendly relationship with his subordinates, built on months of hard fighting side by side. He rapidly discovered that Govorov expected a far more serious tone. When Simoniak described the German defences he would have to overcome, Govorov noted some omissions:

'You haven't studied the enemy's defences enough,' said Govorov.

'I can't report every detail, Comrade Commander. In any case, my chief of staff must be left with something or he'll have nothing to report.'

Govorov failed to adopt the same jocular tone. 'I'm interested in the entire defensive system of the enemy. You know the details well, but the enemy can use their strongholds and strike your combat units from the left from Pilni-Melnitsa, or from the right from the Belyaevsky swamp. You didn't think of this.'

'I did think of this, Comrade Commander.'

'Well not enough, apparently, or you would have included this in your report.'[20]

The exercise lasted seven days, and when Simoniak presented his final report, Govorov was rather more satisfied that there had been adequate attention to detail. Perhaps in response to Govorov's criticism, Simoniak personally oversaw the allocation of targets to the guns that would bring direct fire onto the German positions along the Neva embankment. His assault teams would cross the Neva ice in groups of 24 men, with each group having a small team of sappers and at least one flamethrower. Some of Leningrad Front's artillery would be used to try to destroy obstacles that the Germans had erected on the Neva ice, and once they reached the east bank the sappers would use explosive charges to create further breaches if the direct fire of the divisional artillery had failed to create sufficient openings. Ignoring normal practice, Simoniak had his headquarters dugout constructed just 300 yards from the Neva – standard practice would have placed it further back, but that would have resulted in him being in a position where the dense forests prevented him from seeing how the attack was proceeding.[21]

There were also extensive dress rehearsals by the units of Second Shock Army, overseen personally in many cases by Fedyuninsky:

> Remembering the lessons of the Lyuban Operation, I demanded during all the exercises that the commanders clearly work out issues of cooperation and control during the offensive. I well remember one of these exercises by 18th Rifle Division, which had just arrived from near Stalingrad. Together with the army commander, General Romanovsky, we arrived at the training field where the exercise was in full swing. The division commander, [Major] General [Mikhail Nikolayevich] Ovchinnikov, was a rather elderly man [he was actually 46, only four years older than Fedyuninsky] and he had been replaced by Colonel [Nikolai Georgiyevich] Lyashchenko, who later formally took command of the unit.
>
> On the training area, ice ramparts 2m high had been built. They were made by heaping up snow and then pouring water over it. From the edge of the forest we could see clearly how the infantry and tanks moved forward in their attack. Everything seemed to be going well: the infantrymen were moving without losing contact with the tanks. But then the fighting vehicles reached the ice barrier and confusion arose. The tanks were unable to break through the ice wall and got stuck, and the rifle spearheads also stopped, not knowing how to overcome the obstacle. None of the infantrymen had assault ladders, grapples, fascines, or demolition charges. In short, the attack failed.
>
> 'The exercise should be organised differently,' I told Colonel Lyashchenko. 'The tanks should attack at top speed. Only then will they be able to break through the ramparts. We will issue orders to the commanders of tank units and of the army. And let the riflemen practice for now in overcoming the ice rampart and other obstacles.'
>
> The repeated attack was more successful. But when we analysed the exercise, I advised Colonel Lyashchenko to reduce the height and width of the snow rampart a little. 'Difficulties shouldn't be underestimated, but neither should they be exaggerated. You have built ramparts here that are different from those of the Nazis. Theirs are lower and narrower. Why dishearten the soldiers and give them the wrong idea about the strength of the enemy's defences?'[22]

Whilst the tanks may have needed to move faster in order to overcome the ice barrier, such a policy immediately increased the risk of riflemen becoming separated from the tanks, a recurring problem in Red Army operations. Unlike their German counterparts, Soviet tank crews routinely fought with all hatches closed, reducing the ability of tank commanders to retain 'situational awareness', particularly in relation to whether accompanying infantry were keeping up with the advance.

As preparations continued, Fedyuninsky travelled to Leningrad to a meeting that discussed coordination of the efforts of the two Fronts. He noted many changes during the journey; when he had visited the besieged city during the first winter of the siege, there had been considerable disarray:

> To organise interaction between the Fronts, General Meretskov and I had to go to Leningrad, to the Smolny Institute. We drove at night along the ice road across Lake Ladoga. The exceptional degree of order on the track was noteworthy. The route was cleared of snowdrifts. Vehicles travelled to Leningrad without any delays and on the entire journey we didn't encounter a single 'traffic jam'. On both sides of the road, one here and another there, one could see the firing positions of anti-aircraft gunners. It seemed that the units protecting the track were making use of their solid experience.[23]

Although the Soviet Union lacked the dedicated reconnaissance aircraft used by the Luftwaffe, there had been considerable improvements throughout the preceding year regarding the use of aerial photography; prior to this, aerial reconnaissance had largely consisted of verbal reports from the crews of combat aircraft that passed over the front line. In addition, the German preparations in the immediate front line were carefully studied and frequent patrols attempted to infiltrate deeper into the German positions to determine the layout of the entire German defensive system. These patrols were also tasked with capturing 'tongues' – prisoners who could be interrogated about the German dispositions.

Another source of information about German preparations and troop movements came from the network of partisan units operating behind German lines. At regular intervals, the Wehrmacht mounted anti-partisan sweeps that involved entire divisions of troops and after each sweep there was a reduction in partisan activity, but these lulls proved to be only temporary. There was little opportunity for partisans in the northern sector to operate in the area where the Red Army was attacking – the Germans had systematically removed all civilians from the salient stretching to the shore of Lake Ladoga, and the density of German positions was so great that partisan movement would have been very difficult. Although the area was forested, these areas of woodland were heavily mined. But operating further to the southwest, partisans were able to inform both Leningrad and Volkhov Fronts about German troop and logistic movements, and as the moment for the attack approached, they increased their disruptive activities, attacking road convoys and sabotaging railway lines. In order to aid the activities of the partisans, Soviet aircraft parachuted about 2,600 rifles and machine-guns and 16,500 pounds of explosives into the German rear areas.[24]

These plans were drawn up against the background of ongoing operations elsewhere. Stalingrad was encircled in November, but the German Sixth Army continued to fight on in the ruins and by doing so tied down considerable numbers of Red Army units. The suffering of the troops of Sixth Army worsened steadily as the winter progressed, but their continued resistance performed a vital task. The rest of the Soviet forces in the southern sector were increasingly threatening to collapse the entire German position in Ukraine; if Sixth Army ceased to fight, the Soviet units that would be released would overwhelm the threadbare German defensive lines. Further north, the Soviet forces in the central sector were drawing to the end of the disastrous Operation *Mars*, yet another attempt to destroy the German-held Rzhev salient; the bitter fighting had left their units badly depleted. In this context, it is a measure of the scale of the Soviet Union's military, human, and industrial resources that it was possible to mount such a major operation to break through to Leningrad. It is certainly arguable that this profusion of major operations was contrary to what *Stavka* had decided in 1942, that such a policy represented a dilution of effort, but there were many conflicting priorities facing Stalin and his senior commanders. The successes in the south were impressive and promised even greater victories in the coming days and weeks, and just as the initial successes of the Soviet counteroffensive outside Moscow in late 1941 led to an over-optimistic assessment of the Red Army's capabilities and the weakness of the Wehrmacht, a similar trend was developing in late 1942 and early 1943 in the southern sector. After suffering such a catastrophic setback and with so many German troops surrounded in Stalingrad, surely it would be impossible for the Germans to recover their balance; consequently, *Stavka* felt that it was possible to send additional resources to the north, as the defeat of the Germans in the south was increasingly seen as inevitable. The failure to crush the Rzhev salient was a disappointment, to be sure, but already a degree of self-deception was developing, which would continue after the end of the war. The bloody fighting around Rzhev was increasingly being portrayed as an essential adjunct of the successes further south: by attacking so hard in the central sector, the Red Army tied down German units and prevented their transfer to the critical southern sector. Such an interpretation of events is difficult to sustain given the timings of operations and the resources that were committed – and wasted – in Operation *Mars*.

But despite the setbacks around Rzhev, lifting the siege of Leningrad remained a high priority for *Stavka*. The breaking of the siege ring was anticipated to have numerous benefits. By restoring land contact, many of the hardships of the civilians and soldiers in and around Leningrad could be alleviated. It would also be possible to organise better cooperation between Leningrad and Volkhov Fronts if they had physical contact with each other, and the northern sector of the long German defensive lines could thus be put under greater pressure. And a victory outside Leningrad, the city that Hitler had vowed to capture and wipe from the surface of the earth, would have huge propaganda value both within the Soviet Union and across the world.

By the first day of 1943, preparations were complete. Although both Leningrad Front and Volkhov Front were ready to start their offensives, the weather turned unexpectedly mild, weakening the ice on the Neva, and the engineers of Leningrad Front warned that it would not be possible for any vehicles to cross. Numerous experiments had been conducted to determine the best way of creating a crossing for tanks. The outcome was a plan to use wooden beams that would be placed in grooves on the ice to reinforce it, but if this method was to be effective, the weather had to be cold enough to create new ice that would hold the beams in place – the current conditions were too warm. After a brief discussion, Meretskov and Govorov asked *Stavka* for a delay. Permission was granted and a start date of 12 January was set. Artillery units moved forward into their firing positions in the first week of the month, and infantry and tanks began to deploy a week later. The soldiers of Sixty-Seventh Army were now in trenches on the Soviet-held bank of the Neva; the first assault troops of Second Shock Army were deployed in trenches and bunkers 300–500 yards behind the front line.

In addition to Voroshilov, *Stavka* sent Zhukov to oversee the coming operation on 10 January. The fighting around Stalingrad was still continuing, and was largely being coordinated by General Aleksandr Mikhailovich Vasilevsky, chief of the Soviet general staff, and General Nikolai Nikolayevich Voronov, the deputy defence minister; Zhukov had been overseeing *Mars*, but the abandonment of further attacks against the Rzhev salient made him available for a new assignment and he was sent south to oversee the operations that were steadily destroying the German positions along the Don. In the years after the war, Soviet historiography would largely ignore the disastrous failure of *Mars* and the appalling casualties suffered by the Red Army; although his involvement was largely peripheral,

Zhukov would be given great credit for *Uranus* and the defeat of the German forces in and around Stalingrad, with the reticent and self-effacing Vasilevsky making little attempt to assert his own prominent role. The decision to send Zhukov to the Leningrad sector was curious, given that Voroshilov had already been sent there. It is possible that despite his personal friendship, Stalin had doubts about Voroshilov's abilities and wished to add a further tier of oversight. Zhukov was with Voronezh Front at the beginning of 1943 for the Ostrogozhsk–Rossosh Operation, which would tear apart the German Second Army, when he received a telephone call from Stalin:

> 'Voroshilov is in Leningrad as a representative of *Stavka*. The State Defence Committee believes that you should also go there. We need to have a report from on the spot whether everything has been done to ensure that *Iskra* is a success. You still have time to make a stop in Moscow on your way. We need to discuss something.'
>
> Since the Ostrogozhsk–Rossosh Operation was also a very important link in the strategic plan of *Stavka*, I asked what I should do with respect to the preparations for the offensive of Voronezh Front.
>
> 'What do you suggest?' Stalin asked in turn.
>
> 'Vasilevsky knows what's going on, let him complete the work he has started here, and Voronov can complete matters in the Stalingrad region.'
>
> 'I agree. Fly to Moscow immediately.'[25]

As with so many conversations between senior officers on both sides of the front line and their supreme leaders, the only account of this discussion that has survived is Zhukov's memoir, which is markedly unreliable in various aspects with regard to his involvement in and responsibility for *Mars*. Zhukov was deputy supreme commander at the time, but it would be reasonable to assume that his personal reputation had taken a beating given the disastrous failure of *Mars*, and Stalin may simply have ordered him to hand over affairs in the south to Vasilevsky rather than seeking Zhukov's advice. Vasilevsky's account of the rearrangement of command responsibilities is somewhat different, in that he implies that he was ordered to proceed to the Voronezh sector at the very beginning of the year:

> I returned to my command post at Verkhne–Tsaritsynskoye on the morning of 1 January 1943. Here there awaited me a message from Moscow that I was to telephone Stalin ...

In the conversation that shortly followed Stalin told me that *Stavka* ... was instructing me to leave at once for Voronezh Front where, as the *Stavka* representative, I was to take part in preparing and implementing the offensive operations planned on the upper Don; I was also responsible for the organisation of joint action between Voronezh, Bryansk and Southwest Fronts.[26]

In Moscow, Stalin suggested that Zhukov stop off in the Velikiye Luki sector on his way north; here, Third Shock Army was conducting an offensive that Stalin felt could only contribute to the success of *Iskra*, by tying down German units that might otherwise be sent north. Travelling north by train from the headquarters of Third Shock Army on his way to Volkhov Front, Zhukov was joined by Zhdanov and Voroshilov, who had travelled down from Leningrad to meet him. The three men immediately began to discuss plans for the imminent offensive.

As already described, the Germans recognised the importance of their narrow corridor to Lake Ladoga – known to German soldiers as the *Flaschenhals* ('bottleneck'), and it was impossible for the Red Army to hide its preparations from the Luftwaffe reconnaissance aircraft that were overhead whenever the weather permitted, despite the assiduous efforts of Soviet fighter squadrons. In an attempt to draw attention away from the critical sector, Leningrad Front's Fifty-Fifth Army, on the southern flank of Sixty-Seventh Army, simulated preparations for a major attack in the sector defended by the German LIV Corps. But however much the Red Army might try, its attempts at *Maskirovka* (literally 'disguise') or deception were of limited value in a theatre where the likely attack sectors were so obvious. Preparations on the German side continued throughout the weeks that Govorov and Meretskov were drawing up plans and concentrating their resources, with engineer battalions working constantly on improving obstacles and laying minefields that grew ever denser. On 11 January, the day before the offensive was due to begin, German artillery subjected Leningrad to a bombardment that was the heaviest for many days. Whilst the shelling of the city was unwelcome, there was some satisfaction in the headquarters of Leningrad and Volkhov Fronts: the German guns were firing at the city, not at the troops preparing for the attack. However, for the German soldiers in the front line, signs of preparation were unmistakeable, as a veteran of 1st Infantry Division late wrote:

Since the beginning of January 1943 there were clear signs of a forthcoming enemy offensive against the division's front line. By day and night, the enemy carried out movements from the rear up to their front line. The strength of these movements increased markedly from 9 January and escalated still further during the days up to 11 January. By that afternoon, these movements had taken on the character of formal preparations.[27]

Others, too, noticed unmistakeable signs that the Red Army was preparing to attack, though the lack of precise details made reacting to the observed preparations very difficult. Oberstleutnant German Kleinhenz was commander of 401st Grenadier Regiment, part of 170th Infantry Division on the Neva sector. He was summoned to division headquarters on the evening of 11 January:

> [Generalleutnant Erwin] Zander was alarmed. Intelligence reports indicated that there was increased activity in the forests on the right bank of the Neva. The Russians were moving troops and preparing for something. Zander had reported this personally [by field telephone] to the commander of Eighteenth Army, Lindemann.
>
> 'The Neva is not the Volga,' replied Lindemann reassuringly. 'We will be able to hold the bottleneck. The Russians have repeatedly tried to expand their foothold at the power plant. You know how that turned out.'
>
> Zander acquiesced and was silent ... nevertheless, he decided to summon his regiment commanders. But he couldn't add anything to what Kleinhenz already knew. Yes, the Russians were becoming more active again, but what they were preparing, where they wanted to strike, when, and with what forces – none of this was clear. There had been attempts to find out with intelligence operations on the right bank but the patrols had been destroyed.[28]

Whilst the disastrous developments in Stalingrad were still officially secret, officers like Lindemann would have been aware of the predicament of the German Sixth Army and the extreme peril that confronted the Wehrmacht in Ukraine, and some of these details would have permeated down to officers like Zander. But even if Lindemann had wished to do something, his hands were tied. He had no more troops to offer, and Hitler refused to countenance any withdrawal. All that the commander of Army Group North could do was trust in the strength of the defences that had been established.

On the eve of the offensive, Soviet preparations moved into a new phase with increased bombing of German positions on the night before the attack. In a final attempt to maintain their attempts to prevent the Germans from guessing where the attack would fall, the Soviet commanders also directed heavy air attacks on neighbouring sectors to the south. There were other measures taken that night too, as Oberleutnant Winacker, a German engineer officer with 170th Infantry Division, defending the Neva Line near Shlisselburg, discovered at dawn on 12 January. It was bitterly cold, and Winacker joined one of his men in a trench overlooking the river. As he surveyed the tangle of obstacles positioned by the Germans along the embankment, he remarked to the soldier that it was exceptionally quiet; everyone in the German positions knew an attack was coming, and only the precise timing remained to be determined. Then, as it grew a little lighter and he studied the river ice, he noticed something: there were numerous fresh footprints in the snow that lay on the ice sheet. Soviet soldiers had crossed the river under cover of darkness, and as he studied the bank in front of him, he could see signs of digging. They had been removing landmines and other obstacles. Even as he turned to the soldier, the silence was broken by the roar of Leningrad Front's artillery. *Iskra* had begun.[29]

CHAPTER 3

ISKRA – EXECUTION

Accounts written by both German and Soviet soldiers of the Red Army's offensive operations during the Second World War often describe the ferocity of the artillery bombardment that preceded the initial attacks. As the war progressed, these bombardments grew heavier and more destructive, but even in the early years of the conflict they were awe-inspiring spectacles for those who watched from a distance. For the soldiers who had to endure the bombardments, they were utterly terrifying. But however devastating the appearances of the bombardment, the key issue was whether they achieved their purpose of suppressing the defences and blasting gaps in the obstacles with which the Germans had fortified their positions. This efficacy could only be judged when the attacking troops moved forward.

On either side of the German 'bottleneck', a hurricane of fire descended upon the German positions. The trenches and bunkers in the front line were hit both by indirect shelling and by guns using direct fire, particularly on the west-facing side of the bottleneck where the Soviet artillery planners had been concerned about the possible effect of shelling on the Neva ice sheet. Long-range guns, many of them provided by the Baltic Fleet, were directed against German artillery positions, headquarters and supply dumps to the rear of the front line and almost the entire depth of the 'bottleneck' was soon shrouded in smoke. The bombardment commenced at 0930 local time, but as was commonly the case throughout the Second World War, German units continued to operate on Berlin time regardless of where they were deployed, and German accounts therefore describe the shelling as commencing at 0730:

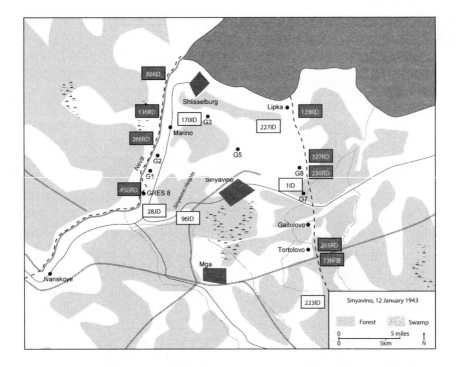

For two hours and 20 minutes the hurricane of steel howled, flashed, and crashed down on the Neva front, and for an hour and 45 minutes it swept the eastern side of the bottleneck.

'They aren't joking this time,' the men said in their dugouts, their strongpoints, their foxholes, and their trenches. Many of them were in solid bunkers deep below ground. Veritable subterranean towns had been built facing the Leningrad and Volkhov Fronts during the long wait. The strongpoints were linked by a cunning system of trenches.

The Russians were aware of this. That was why they were hitting these positions with such concentrated fire. That was why they were pounding the machine-gun posts, the approach roads, the gun emplacements, the command posts, the approach roads, the lateral communications and the camps in the woods. They smashed bridges, buildings, trenches, and all telephone wires.[1]

In every German sector, the reports were of an exceptionally heavy bombardment. In the first four days of the operation, Second Shock Army's gunners fired a staggering 600,000 rounds of all calibres.[2] A German soldier in 170th Infantry

Division later wrote: 'I still can't forget the impression from the destructive fire of the Russian artillery. As I remember all the infernal rumble of shells and bombs, it makes me shudder over and over again.'[3]

Zhukov had positioned himself with Romanovsky in a forward observation post in Second Shock Army's sector. He described the morning of the assault:

[The observation post] was located very close to the front line, and from here the first lines of the enemy's defences were clearly visible. Hazy smoke rose high above the positions of the Nazi troops. The soldiers who had been on duty at night, when our reconnaissance was usually active, were now preparing for rest and warming their stoves.

Silence reigned over the entire front line for the moment. It was a special silence – the silence before the onset of a great historical effort.

In this battle, we managed to achieve tactical surprise though the enemy knew that we were preparing to break the blockade. It is possible that he even foresaw exactly where the Soviet troops would strike – the very configuration of the front line spoke of this. Day after day, in the presumed area of our breakthrough, the Germans erected more and more defensive structures, moved their best units here, and repeatedly increased their weaponry in the defensive strongpoints that had been enhanced in more than 16 months of the blockade. But exactly when, on what day and hour, and with what forces we would begin the operation – the German command didn't know …

At 0930, the morning's frosty silence was broken by the first volley of artillery preparation. On the western and eastern sides of the Shlisselburg–Mga corridor of the enemy, thousands of guns and mortars from both fronts fired simultaneously.

For two hours a fiery hurricane raged over enemy positions along the axes of the main and auxiliary attacks of the Soviet troops. The artillery bombardment of Leningrad and Volkhov Fronts merged into a single powerful roar, and it was difficult to make out who was firing and from where. Black fountains of explosions rose up, trees swayed and fell, logs flew upwards from the enemy's dugouts. Above the ground, here and there, grey clouds appeared and quickly froze in a severe frost – evaporation from swamps that were thawed by the fire. For every square metre of the breakthrough area, two or three artillery and mortar shells fell.[4]

In the positions facing the Neva, Oberstleutnant Kleinhenz was woken by the shelling and within moments he and his adjutant were both wounded. When he tried to contact his battalions in order to determine how badly they had been hit, Kleinhenz found that all his telephone cables, both to subordinate units and back to division headquarters, had been cut by the shelling. Above the bombardment, Soviet aircraft joined the attack and struck at targets further back from the front line. The Soviet soldiers waiting to attack must have been awestruck by the inferno that erupted on the German positions. The value of impressive artillery preparation on the morale of both defenders and attackers was in many respects an important additional contribution to its overall efficacy and, as was increasingly the case, the bombardment ended with a final crescendo of shelling and the howling salvoes of *Katyusha* rockets slamming into the German lines. As the longer ranged Soviet guns switched their fire to targets deep within the bottleneck, green flares rose above the Red Army's lines and, with a ragged cheer, the infantry advanced. It was time to test just how effective the bombardment had been.

Whilst the screech of the rockets may have had an impact on the morale of both attackers and defenders alike, the noise was also a clear indicator to the Germans that a ground attack was now imminent. Like soldiers in every bombardment since the advent of artillery, the German infantrymen had spent most of the shelling in their hardened bunkers; despite the huge weight of shellfire, these shelters survived largely intact. The soldiers now hurried to man their defensive positions, bringing forth their machine-guns and clearing away debris that might obscure their field of fire.

On the Neva front, the assault of Sixty-Seventh Army was led by 86th Rifle Division in the north, near Shlisselburg, and by 136th and 268th Rifle Divisions further south. On the very southern flank of Dukhanov's attack was a small toehold on the east bank of the frozen river, the Neva bridgehead. This had originally been captured at great cost by the Red Army in the opening weeks of the siege and after heavy fighting was eventually abandoned during the summer of 1942. In September, the soldiers of 70th Rifle Division were ordered to re-establish the bridgehead as part of the September Sinyavino Operation. The division had served in the Leningrad sector since the beginning of the war – after taking part in the Winter War against Finland in 1939–40, it was involved in the defensive fighting along the Luga River and thereafter fought in the repeated attempts to break the siege ring. When the order came for it to attack in the September operation, many of its officers felt that it was too weak – it fielded barely 8,000 men and had not had sufficient time to recover its strength and to bring new drafts up to the level of training required for a major assault. Nonetheless, Colonel Anatoly Andreyevich Krasnov, the division commander, insisted that the attack proceed as ordered. The commander and commissar of one of his infantry regiments refused flatly to carry out their orders. They were arrested and executed by firing squad in front of their men. When the division crossed the river, it suffered heavy losses and by the end of the operation had been reduced to barely half its starting strength.[5] Despite its failure to achieve a breakthrough, the division was now renamed 45th Guards Rifle Division and once more replenished with fresh drafts, and found itself back in the front line in the Neva bridgehead. The bridgehead was so small that there was insufficient space for both 46th Rifle Division, which was occupying the Red Army's defensive perimeter around the bridgehead, and the assault forces of 45th Guards Rifle Division, with the consequence that much of the attacking division had to wait on the west bank and was only able to cross into the bridgehead once *Iskra* commenced and the first wave of troops attempted to break out.

The Germans had long anticipated that the Red Army would attempt to use the Neva bridgehead as a starting point for an offensive and had ensured that their defensive lines were especially strong in this sector. As soon as the Soviet artillery bombardment lifted from the front line, German guns began to shell the bridgehead and the area immediately behind it, both the frozen Neva and the far west bank, and German machine-guns swept the river with a lethal hail of fire. The initial assault on the German lines degenerated rapidly into bitter hand-to-hand fighting, and Krasnov – now promoted to major general – dispatched his second wave across the Neva. Some of these men were fed into the bridgehead while others attempted to widen the bridgehead. Tamara Rodionovna Ovsyannikova was a signaller in the division, having volunteered to serve in one of its regiments during the fighting of 1941. She was waiting to cross the river and later described how the fighting unfolded:

It was still dark. Low clouds … Our regiment faced the widest section of the Neva. The enemy riverbank was also the highest along the entire length of the breakthrough sector … The artillery preparation was so powerful that standing nearby, even if I screamed, I couldn't be heard. So we sat tensely in silence and waited. Suddenly the noise stopped. Imagine, just a deathly silence. It lasted for 20 seconds. And then the *Katyushas* fired, all along the river from Shlisselburg to us. Such a fiery blast! The rockets fired for five minutes. While they were still firing, Sinyakov's battalion – followed by the entire regiment – rolled off our riverbank onto the ice with loud shouts of 'Urrah!' … Nobody waited for the green flares. Imagine a mass of people in white camouflage suits, all crossing the Neva, a continuous line of white figures. Our 947th Rifle Regiment attacked directly against 8th GRES [*Gosudarstvennaya Rayonnaya Elektrostantsiya* or 'State District Power Plant']. The regiment came under heavy fire in the middle of the Neva. The power plant had a water intake on the riverbank at the very edge of the water ... with three windows. The Germans had walled them up so it seemed as if there was nobody there, and a blank wall faced the river. Govorov [the Front commander] ordered the regimental commanders to observe the enemy and spot his firing positions over two or three weeks ... but there wasn't a single shot from this water intake. And therefore, during the artillery preparation, machine-guns hidden there weren't suppressed. Our right-flank battalion now came under fire from these machine-guns ...

They didn't even make it to the far bank. A hurricane of fire fell on them and many were left lying on the ice. We could see them all lying there. I remember one could see the black jackets of sailors amongst the fallen soldiers in their camouflage suits.[6]

Some of the soldiers of 46th Rifle Division joined the attack by 45th Guards Rifle Division. Lieutenant Valentin Grigoryevich Arsenin, who commanded one of 46th Rifle Division's companies, had been withdrawn to the west bank of the Neva to make more room for the assault troops, but led his men forward over the ice:

The artillery preparation was concluded by the *Katyushas*. But before they had time to finish, the assault groups rushed forward and we followed them ... All the assault groups were followed by companies in line, separated by 200–300m. It was amazing. We advanced under fire like in the movies or field exercises, such was the mood of the attackers.

Unfortunately, not all enemy firing points were suppressed. The Nazis opened machine-gun fire from the front and from the right flank, from 8th GRES. I managed to overtake my company and catch up with the assault group near the riverbank. We began to climb the 12m slope of the left bank. Near me was a platoon led by Senior Sergeant Osadchy. He was a tall man and encouraged his men, helping them clamber up. Grenades were falling on us from above. Osadchy, a few other soldiers, and I were already half way up the slope, but not even a formidably strong man like Osadchy could throw grenades far enough to reach the enemy trenches.

We struggled to the top of the riverbank. Not long after, I saw a 50mm mortar team and thought, 'Those heroes are what we need!' I ordered them to fire on the trench. After several shots, the Nazis stopped throwing grenades. Taking advantage of being in dead space where the enemy's machine-guns couldn't reach us, we broke into the first trench ... We began to clear the Nazis from the trench. Many of them were already dead, but plenty were alive.

I shouted orders, 'Forward! Keep up with the artillery barrage!' …

The Nazis continued with machine-gun and artillery fire from 8th GRES. The enemy fired especially heavily from a small grove. After ordering my deputy Lieutenant Shapovalenko to establish contact with the battalion, I decided to advance a little to the right of the grove and sent a covering group to the edge of the forest. The company moved forward in line meeting little resistance. We passed piles of cut peat. The leading elements began to enter the undergrowth of another grove. From the trees, the Nazis opened up with machine-guns. The company lay down in ditches. It was already getting dark. The signals cable had run out and I made my way back to the phone to report the situation to the battalion commander and to request artillery support. As soon as I picked up the phone, a bright flash blinded me. When I regained consciousness, I saw that Masha Fridman was bandaging me.[7]

The attack by 45th Guards Rifle Division made pitiful progress on the first day, but Ovsyannikova's regiment commander ordered his headquarters to move to the west bank as the day progressed. The river was still under constant German gunfire:

The regiment commander gave the command: 'Follow me.' It was about an hour after the attack began. We moved onto the Neva and ran across the ice with the commander. We hoped that the Germans had been pushed back, but it turned out they were still there. They fired along the riverbank and across the Neva. As we ran we had to detour around numerous gaps in the ice … many of our dead lay there with their weapons. Nurses were running around looking for the wounded. They put them on special sleds and dragged them to our shore … the steep [east] bank was strewn with barbed wire. We had to climb it and go down into a small hollow … I was dressed in a short fur coat, padded trousers and a camouflage jacket. I was carrying a portable switchboard and a telephone, a heavy load. I tried to pull myself up a rope with my fur mittens … Ivan Ivanovich [Osipov, the headquarters platoon commander] later told me I looked both comical and pitiful. Together with the signaller Fedya Kokshin, he pushed me up the bank. We went into a ravine with a frozen stream and climbed into the German trenches. There were lots of German corpses there.[8]

For the second time in a few months, Krasnov's division was being eviscerated for minimal gains. Ovsyannikova's regiment was across the Neva and had widened the bridgehead a small amount, and other attacks elsewhere in the bridgehead had made almost no headway. Despite its ferocity, the Soviet bombardment had failed to suppress most of the German defensive positions, particularly beyond the immediate front line. Much of the first line of German trenches was now in Soviet hands, but even as the decimated riflemen attempted to press on they ran into inevitable German counterattacks. Whilst the Germans lacked the substantial reserves that they would have preferred to have for a deliberate defence, General Johann Sinnhuber, commander of 28th Jäger Division, had about a battalion available and threw these men into the battle at just the right moment, catching the Soviet forces while they were still heavily disorganised from their losses and the fighting in the German trenches. Combat continued at close quarters for the rest of the day; 45th Guards Rifle Division couldn't make any further headway, but nor could 28th Jäger Division. Losses accumulated steadily on both sides and the tangled front line made it impossible for either the Red Army or the Wehrmacht to use artillery to try to tip the balance. The fighting was more like the bloody struggles of the First World War than mechanised warfare; the Germans had no tanks available, and the few Soviet tanks that crossed the river were light vehicles that were quickly knocked out – in any case, the terrain was completely unsuitable for the use of armour and many tanks failed to ascend the steep east bank.

Immediately to the north of this sector, the main Soviet attack was made by 268th Rifle Division with 136th Rifle Division to its north. The German 170th Infantry Division was defending this stretch of the Neva riverbank, and as they manned their positions at the end of the Soviet bombardment, the German soldiers looked in amazement at ranks of Red Army riflemen running towards them across the Neva ice in dense lines – the Soviet troops clearly believed that the German defences could not have survived such heavy shelling. The Germans waited until the first line had almost reached the west bank before opening fire and called in artillery fire at the same moment to lay a curtain of shells on the ice and across the far Soviet-held bank. One of the shells landed right next to the command post of Simoniak, commander of 136th Rifle Division, briefly entombing the headquarters staff when the bunker entrance collapsed but causing no casualties. After his men had cleared the ice and earth, Simoniak emerged and watched as first a few men, then entire rifle companies, began to cross the ice even before the artillery bombardment had been completed. Several were caught in the explosions of the *Katyusha* salvoes. The final explosions of the bombardment faded away as the Soviet gunners switched to deeper targets, and as the Soviet riflemen surged forward, they and the German defenders suddenly became aware of a new, almost surreal sound: in order to boost the morale of the attackers, Simoniak had arranged for the *Internationale* – at that time, the national anthem of the Soviet Union – to be played by military musicians, who had gathered in the trenches immediately behind the assault troops:

> Across the Neva, as far as could be seen through the periscope, riflemen, machine-gunners, sappers and signalmen were running forward. They leaped over ice hummocks and smoking craters. The pressed on swiftly without looking back. Some fell on the ice long before they reached the bank, their blood soaking into the silvery, sparkling snow. Wave after wave of men rolled forward to the sounds of the melody of the *Internationale*, which rang out at the signal of an invisible conductor with the last volley of *Katyushas*.[9]

An officer of 170th Infantry Division later described the fighting that followed:

> Between Marino and Gorodok 2, on the seam between 2nd Battalion, 401st Infantry Regiment and 240th Reconnaissance Battalion, both of which were defending extremely wide sectors on the right flank of the division, the Russians made their main effort. After Oberstleutnant Kleinhenz, commander of 401st Infantry Regiment, and his adjutant were wounded, ten Russian battalions achieved a breakthrough against a combat strength of just 300 men ... At the same time, attacks against 1st Battalion, 401st Infantry Regiment on the division's right flank, against the bicycle battalion near the hospital [immediately behind Gorodok 1 and Gorodok 2], and against the front of 399th Infantry Regiment ... were all repulsed. After the commander of the reconnaissance battalion was killed, a thin line of strongpoints was established east of the enemy's breakthrough on either side of the road, and it was occupied by a battalion from 96th Infantry Division. But the losses suffered by the enemy between the power station and the paper factory were shockingly high, about 3,000 dead. Entire rows of fallen Russians lay on the Neva ice.[10]

Red Army losses were so heavy that a report from German 399th Infantry Regiment recorded that Soviet corpses repeatedly had to be dragged aside from in front of the machine-gun positions to allow a clear line of fire. There were repeated attacks by 136th Rifle Division on the German positions but it wasn't until the fifth assault that the German lines were overrun to the north of Gorodok 1 and Gorodok 2. Heavy snow began to fall as the day progressed, limiting the ability of Soviet aircraft to support the attack, but despite their losses the Soviet units began to gain ground. Compared to the sector further south around the Neva bridgehead, the German defences had been partly suppressed by the preliminary artillery bombardment and once the west bank had been secured, T-60 tanks began to drive cautiously across the frozen river to support the attack; sappers began work to strengthen the ice so that heavier tanks and supplies could follow. The ruins of the village of Marino, heavily fortified by the Germans, were taken and the depleted rifle companies pressed on towards the east.

The neighbouring 268th Rifle Division also came under heavy fire as it attempted to cross the ice opposite Gorodok 1 and Gorodok 2. At first, the division struggled to gain a toehold on the west bank, but after Simoniak's men had captured Marino the German defences came under heavy fire from the north and were forced back. Initially, every Soviet attempt to storm the ruins of the hospital foundered in the face of heavy defensive fire, but German casualties were also mounting steadily. The pioneer battalion of 170th Infantry Division arrived just in time to shore up the German defences and despite the appearance of a few T-34s amongst the attacking Soviet infantry, the position continued to hold as darkness fell. Nonetheless, the main assault of the Soviet Sixty-Seventh Army had secured a substantial bridgehead across the Neva, about three miles wide and perhaps half as deep, though the German strongpoints at the hospital and Gorodok 1 and Gorodok 2 continued to hold out. Under cover of darkness, the engineers of Leningrad Front began to construct wooden bridges across the Neva on either side of Marino, constantly shelled by German artillery.

At the very northern side of Sixty-Seventh Army's attack was 86th Rifle Division, tasked with penetrating into Shlisselburg with support from an independent tank battalion and substantial additional artillery. The first wave of the attack involved two rifle battalions; only one was able to seize a small area of the west bank. Colonel Vasily Alekseyevich Trubachev, the commander of 86th Rifle Division, soon realised the futility of further assaults across the Neva and with the approval of Dukhanov he instead moved his division to the south to take advantage of the crossings seized by Simoniak's 136th Rifle Division. From here, his riflemen and tanks began to press north into the woodland immediately south of Shlisselburg. Even if the original intention to penetrate into the town on the first day failed, at least the northern flank of the main advance was now protected from a German counterattack.

On the other side of the German-held bottleneck, Volkhov Front was also moving forward. At the southern edge of the offensive was Eighth Army's 73rd

Naval Rifle Brigade, with Morozov's artillery joining the bombardment. He gave a detailed description of the initial bombardment:

Watches were checked, last orders were given. Everyone waited for the signal *Beter* ['Wind'], on which the artillery [of the entire Front] would open fire. Five minutes remained, then three minutes. Commands came down the telephone wire: 'Prepare for *Beter*. Ready!' Thousands of men stood by their guns and mortars, in trenches, and in observation posts.

'*Beter!*'

The earth trembled. Thousands of guns fired. A sheaf of flaming arrows soared into the sky. The low-pitched rumble of the explosions on the enemy locations drowned out all other sounds. Fire raged along the front, 16km long. And the same distance in front of us, 1,700 guns of the Sixty-Seventh Army of Leningrad Front, advancing towards us, began to destroy the enemy's defences.

Colonel [Ivan Nikolayevich] Burakovsky [commander of 73rd Naval Rifle Brigade], a group of staff officers, and I were at an observation post dug into the railway embankment. There were a dozen telephones and radios in the trench, connecting us to the units. Nailed to pieces of plywood were a coded map, the artillery fire plan, diagrams of the targets, signals diagrams, and tables of codewords and call-signs – everything we needed for quick and accurate fire control. The observation post received a continuous stream of reports from the artillery group commanders. Orders were sent back constantly.

Everything had been planned thoroughly. All that remained for us was to monitor how the task was carried out. It was impossible to observe the enemy and our own side – everything was smothered in smoke.

The first fire attack was over. The signal *Sneg* ['Snow'] was sent, marking the beginning of a period of suppression and destruction of specific targets. The fire of the main mass of guns and mortars was transferred into the depth of the enemy positions while the remainder destroyed individual targets in the front line. Direct fire guns engaged the embrasures of bunkers and destroyed wire entanglements. Our 120mm mortars and howitzers fired on trenches, observation posts and dugouts. Heavy guns shelled the strongest bunkers and shelters …

A new signal – and again there was a general bombardment by all artillery on the first trenches of the enemy. The preparation had been under way for an hour already. It was hard work in the firing positions. Despite the January frost, the gun crews were working without their coats. It was warm work, and the barrels of the cannons and howitzers grew hotter. Then the hum of engines was heard overhead. Our planes were approaching the enemy positions in several waves. They bombed artillery batteries, headquarters and enemy reserves … 15 minutes before the end of the artillery preparation, the rate of fire increased sharply. The last barrage was the heaviest. The guns fired at the utmost rate achievable. Again, fiery arrows of rockets soared into the sky as the *Katyushas* fired a salvo five minutes before the attack.

Burakovsky shouted into the phone, warning the battalion commanders to be ready to advance quickly. I ordered the artillery group commanders to shift their fire to the first line. Without a pause, the gunners struck the enemy's first trench. We waited for a signal to move the fire to the next line – that would mean the infantry was moving forward for the assault.

But for ten minutes we held the barrage of fire on the first trench and there was still no attack. What was holding up our infantrymen? Finally, green flares rose into the sky. 'Fire on the *Panther* line!' I shouted down the phone with relief. The fire screen moved in three stages, each of 100m, to the new firing line.[11]

To the frustration of Burakovsky, his men failed to rush the German trenches and were driven to shelter by withering defensive fire. When he demanded that the men move forward, the leading battalion commander replied that his soldiers – mainly fresh recruits in their first battle – were terrified of advancing so close to the artillery bombardment. Morozov was ordered to shift fire further into the depths of the German position and two of the naval brigade's three battalions succeeded in breaking into the German lines, but the southern flank battalion – effectively the southern flank of the entire Volkhov Front advance – was hit by heavy defensive fire from German mortars and machine-guns, many firing from the high ground that Morozov had wanted to bombard. Throughout the day, the naval brigade made only minimal progress at a disproportionate cost:

> The infantry was unable to move forward and capture the full length of the enemy's trench. The soldiers were driven to ground by mortar fire and when they tried to attack, the Nazis opened up with their machine-guns.
>
> Burakovsky spoke to Major Biryukov, the battalion commander. 'Stop these pointless attacks! All you're doing is killing our men! We have to start again. We will continue the offensive in the morning.'
>
> The short winter's day ended and the fighting subsided. Both sides re-ordered their ranks.[12]

Much of the German defensive line here was held by 1st Infantry Division and the commander of one of its grenadier regiments later described the day's fighting:

Early on the morning of 12 January, the regiment was made aware by a report from a [Soviet] deserter that an attack would be made on that day. The alarm was therefore raised and preparations made. In the early morning hours there were reports from both battalions that the enemy had marked lanes through their minefields up to 10m wide with small black flags. Heavy fire from all weapons, including salvo rocket launchers, commenced at 0730 on the regiment's positions. The bombardment escalated to unimaginable and unprecedented weight, taking on the character of unbroken drumfire with no gap between one explosion and the next.

In the meantime, energetic preparations in the Russian positions could be seen. Our artillery and heavy infantry weapons opened up with disruptive fire on any spotted movements and preparations with good effect.

At 0930 the enemy commenced an attack reinforced by 20 tanks on the regiment's positions. In short order, 12 tanks moved into the 'pear trees' while the remaining eight attacked the seam between I and II Battalions. At first they were not accompanied by infantry. Shortly before reaching our trenches the tanks turned to the north and firing energetically, drove along the trench about 2–10m away. They clearly had the mission of suppressing the units in the trench in order to facilitate the advance of the infantry.

At 0940 the infantry attacked, one wave behind another. In addition, a further six tanks moved up against the left flank of the regiment at Gaitolovo, this time with mounted infantry.

During the infantry attack the bombardment on the main front line eased somewhat but continued with unabated intensity in the depths of the battlefield and further to the rear. As soon as the enemy infantry appeared, defensive fire commenced. Our blocking fire was very effective and tore bloody gaps in the ranks of the advancing Russians. In the right hand sector, where several fighting positions had been destroyed by artillery direct hits, the enemy achieved a penetration. This was immediately screened off and the enemy who had broken in was destroyed when reserves moved up with the result that by 1045 the main battle line was once more in our hands.

Meanwhile the attack against II Battalion came to a halt with heavy losses as a result of our defensive fire. The 12 tanks that had moved up against the battalion were driven off by gunfire. Nine tanks drove north and joined the six tanks moving from the left flank. The infantry weapons deployed here succeeded in separating the enemy infantry from the tanks and then destroyed them. Of the tanks, 12 were left immobile in front of the left flank.

The enemy tanks in the 'pear trees' also moved against the left flank of the regiment. They drove the Russian infantry that had gone to ground forward, but they were all gunned down. The tanks opened concentrated fire on the fighting positions in front of the left flank, which fell back as ordered to the main position. During this heavy fighting the enemy moved fresh forces against the regiment's positions. Numerous further attacks were defeated. Until midday the main battle line remained in our hands.[13]

Further north, Romanovsky was joined in his headquarters by his Front commander Meretskov and the two envoys from *Stavka*, Voroshilov and Zhukov, and they waited for news of the advance of Second Shock Army. The most northern part of the attack was carried out by 128th Rifle Division and as its soldiers overran the first line of German trenches, it seemed as if the artillery preparation had been highly effective. Several German soldiers surrendered to the attacking infantrymen; one, a Feldwebel from 227th Infantry Division, told his captors:

The [Soviet] shells struck exactly where our bunkers were located. Even before the Russians attacked, many were killed and wounded in my company. Leutnant Dehl, the company commander, his senior sergeant, and another sergeant were killed. The soldiers were overwhelmed by panic. The Russians had only just approached when the survivors in the trench greeted them with hands raised.[14]

Despite its initial success, 128th Rifle Division was unable to penetrate into Lipka at the northern edge of the advance. Here, a battalion from the German 96th Infantry Division had been attached to 227th Infantry Division as reinforcements and held a series of well-constructed bunkers both in Lipka and in an adjacent cemetery; heavy snow had covered the bunkers and had prevented Soviet observers from spotting them, and they were almost untouched in the initial bombardment. To make matters worse, the Soviet troops showed that despite the training that was organised prior to *Iskra*, coordination between infantry and armour remained poor and it proved impossible to launch a concerted attack against the bunker line.

In the centre of Second Shock Army's advance, the men of the Soviet 256th Rifle Division faced the German strongpoint of Gorodok 8. The defences both in the settlement and on either side were manned by the German 227th Infantry

Division and the Soviet riflemen were able to bypass the southern edge of the fortified buildings of the settlement, penetrating up to about a mile. The main assault on Gorodok 8 was the task of 327th Rifle Division from the northeast and its men soon discovered that the German defences had survived the Soviet bombardment with little damage. Five attacks through the day left the rifle regiments decimated, but the stubborn German defences continued to hold and the Germans in the settlement were able to direct artillery fire onto the elements of 256th Rifle Division to the south. A little to the south of the settlement was what had once been a small area of woodland known as Kruglaya Grove, now little more than a blasted array of tree-stumps, barbed wire, minefields, and trenches. Previous attacks in this area in 1942 had resulted in bitter fighting and Meretskov had specified that the area should undergo particularly heavy artillery bombardment. Despite this, the area of the grove was another hotly contested area of fighting and any attempt to penetrate between the grove and Gorodok 8 perished in withering crossfire. Many of the German bunkers in the grove area were particularly tough and proved to be impervious to both artillery and aerial bombardment; to make matters worse, the first Soviet units to advance into the area erroneously reported that they had captured the grove, and when other units moved forward in support they suddenly came under concentrated fire from the German positions and took heavy losses. After several attacks foundered, the Soviet 327th Rifle Division finally cleared the Germans out of their strongpoint in Kruglaya Grove but the depleted remnants of the German force – mainly the survivors of 227th Infantry Division's 366th Grenadier Regiment – pulled back to Gorodok 7 to the south.

The commander of 366th Grenadier Regiment was Oberstleutnant Maximilian Wengler, a Wehrmacht reservist who had held the post since September 1941 when the unit was known as 366th Infantry Regiment. In the September Sinyavino Operation, his troops found themselves on the northern side of the breach in the German lines that was created by the advance of Volkhov Front and resolutely defeated every attempt by the Red Army to widen the penetration. This proved to be of critical importance and the exposed German position – which became known as the *Wengler-Nase* ('Wengler Nose') in German reports and maps – was used as the starting point for the counterattack that eliminated the Soviet penetration and resulted in the encirclement of Second Shock Army.[15] For his part in this battle, Wengler was awarded the Knight's Cross and he now found himself once more having to hold the flank of a Soviet penetration, this time with pressure from the north. Despite their previous successes, Wengler's men might have been overrun without the timely arrival of reinforcements in the shape of a battalion from 28th Jäger Division; the combined German force held its north-facing positions stretching from Gorodok 7 towards the east despite everything that was thrown at it for the rest of the day.

As darkness fell on 12 January, there was feverish activity on both sides. Fighting continued into the night but the main effort was to prepare for the following day. In the west, Leningrad Front's engineers completed their first timber bridges across the Neva, allowing tanks and supplies to cross to the hard-won bridgehead, and wounded men were evacuated. Scouts ventured out to monitor the German positions and if possible to capture 'tongues' for interrogation. Simoniak had spent the entire day in the headquarters dugout of his 136th Rifle Division and he now made his way to the riverbank:

> Voices could be heard from the Neva and the sound of axes – the sappers, making crossings for tanks and guns. Sleds moved past to the shore, their runners creaking, carrying food for the men. Field kitchens rumbled past over the potholes. Vehicles and cars were being pushed up the left [east] bank, up the steep slope. The wounded were lying and sitting on broad sleds.[16]

At the southern edge of Leningrad Front's advance, signaller Ovsyannikova and the rest of her regiment's headquarters staff had occupied a captured German bunker directly on the west bank of the Neva:

> Some of the trenches around the dugout had been levelled, but their remains still stretched along the bank. The dugout was really good and roomy. It had two parts. The main room was about 8m in length. To the left was a stove and to the right a large table, big enough for 12 people. Beyond this it was narrower. There were two rows of bunks – two sets on the left and two on the right. The walls were covered with maps. There were mattresses on the bunks and all manner of other stuff. We threw most of it out, and our officers put their maps on the table.[17]

It was clear to both Leningrad and Volkhov Fronts that, despite all their preparations, the artillery bombardment had not been as effective as they had hoped – although several German trenches had collapsed, bunkers like the one now occupied by Ovsyannikova and her comrades were largely intact in many places. Soviet aviation had been used in far greater numbers than in previous operations in this sector, but the evidence for its efficacy was poor – perhaps the best that could be said was that the Germans had not been able to strike at the advancing Soviet units with dive-bombers and other aircraft. Ammunition for the gunners was plentiful and the advance was sufficiently modest that there would not be lengthy disruption while guns were moved forward – in the main, the artillery of both Fronts would be able to fire on the second day from their original positions. Nonetheless, the gap between the two Soviet assault groups was a mere five miles. It seemed that one more decisive push would break the siege ring.

The exhausted soldiers who had fought their way across the Neva into the German positions dug in as best they could in the frozen ground – if the Germans responded as they had done on countless previous occasions, there would be a counterattack in the next day or two to try to restore the original line. Dukhanov, commander of Sixty-Seventh Army, was also aware that it was vital to keep up whatever momentum his troops had gained – the Germans had to be prevented from re-establishing a continuous defensive line. To the east, Meretskov's Volkhov Front was also making preparations for the following day. Having suffered heavy losses in its initial attacks, Romanovsky's leading divisions were unlikely to prevail against the stubborn German strongpoints that had been the focus of such heavy fighting and Second Shock Army's commander asked for permission to move 18th Rifle Division and a tank brigade forward from his second echelon in an attempt to widen the penetration to the south of Gorodok 8. It was not how Meretskov and Romanovsky had originally envisaged deploying the second echelon – they had intended it to enter the battle en masse to break into the depths of the German position and then exploit towards the south to widen whatever corridor was created to the siege perimeter. But without reinforcements, the first echelon was highly unlikely to be able to achieve success and Meretskov gave permission, hoping that the rest of the second echelon could still be deployed as planned.

The Germans too were taking what steps they could. By early 1943 few German infantry divisions had sufficient men for adequate tactical reserves; despite almost every division being far below full strength, the length of front line held by each division remained substantial and instead of having up to a third of their men available as reinforcements, the divisions on either side of the bottleneck had perhaps a single battalion. By the end of 12 January, these reserves were fully committed. Leyser, commander of XXVI Corps, was now receiving requests from both his east and west flanks for further reinforcements and he had little to offer – although 96th Infantry Division had been deployed as a reserve formation in the middle of the bottleneck, Leyser now had to make a choice between using it as a single unit for a decisive counterattack or allowing it to be deployed piecemeal to reinforce the front line. The day's losses and the Soviet advances – particularly across the Neva in the west – left him with no real choice, and he ordered about half the division to move up to reinforce 170th Infantry Division at Gorodok 2. In addition to the infantrymen, he was able to send two batteries of guns and howitzers and a company of four Tiger tanks under the command of Leutnant Bodo von Gerdtell.[18] The Soviet advance was serious, but the situation was not yet critical. Leyser – and Lindemann at the headquarters of Eighteenth Army – knew that the Red Army had come even closer to breaking the siege ring in September, but the battle had eventually turned in favour of the Wehrmacht. However, that had only been possible due to the arrival of reinforcements from the south. Now, the entire southern sector across eastern Ukraine was in turmoil with Soviet forces advancing towards Rostov and Kharkov. Although the true plight of the German Sixth Army in Stalingrad remained a secret, Küchler at Army Group North and Lindemann at Eighteenth Army would probably have been aware at least of the overall situation and Lindemann would have shared such information with his corps commanders. There was no prospect of reinforcements arriving from elsewhere. Army Group North would have to deal with this new situation on its own and Leyser and Lindemann had to hope that the forces they were committing would be sufficient to drive the forces of Leningrad Front back across the Neva. Once that had been accomplished, Wehrmacht resources would have to be reshuffled to free up sufficient combat power to mount a counterattack against Volkhov Front. In the meantime, 1st Infantry Division was ordered to deploy whatever it could scrape together for a counterattack to try to recapture Kruglaya Grove.

At first light, the guns of Leningrad Front commenced a new bombardment, concentrating on the German positions immediately in front of Sixty-Seventh Army. This time, the shelling lasted just 30 minutes before the infantry moved forward. The main effort was made by Simoniak's 136th Rifle Division, supported by 61st Tank Brigade. A small hillock – known to the attacking Soviet soldiers as Snowdrop Hill – became the focus of fighting and the first attacks were beaten off by machine-gun fire from hitherto undetected German bunkers; the German infantry were also able to call in highly effective artillery fire. Attempts to move forward infantry support guns foundered under accurate German shelling but the machine-guns were eventually silenced and the hill captured. On the northern flank, sufficient men of 86th Rifle Division had crossed the Neva to push through the woodland south of Shlisselburg but the advance ground to a halt in front of the fortified ruins of Gorodok 3. Between this and Shlisselburg was a small elevation, Preobrazhenskoe Hill, and after its losses of the first day the Soviet division lacked the strength to break through this new line.

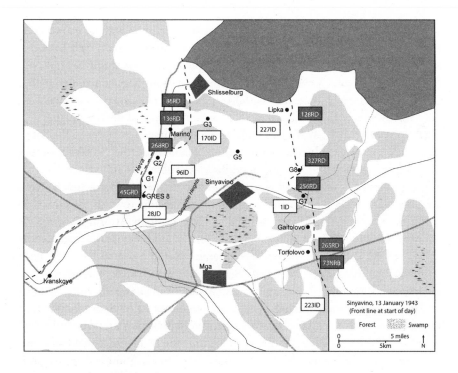

On the southern side of Sixty-Seventh Army, 268th Rifle Division was also ordered to attack with the intention of pushing through the German positions at Gorodok 1 and Gorodok 2. Despite the second bombardment, the German positions held firm and repulsed the first assault. As the Soviet troops gathered their strength to try again, tanks were reported approaching from the east and thinking that these were the leading elements of Volkhov Front advancing to meet them, the anti-tank gunners of 268th Rifle Division held their fire for the moment. They then realised their mistake: it was the counterattack by the five battalions of the German 96th Infantry Division, reinforced by the Tiger company from *Schwere Panzer Abteilung 502*.

The Tigers had already encountered and dealt with a group of Red Army T-34s and took full advantage of the uncertainty of the Soviet gunners. The lines of 268th Rifle Division were breached and two battalions found themselves surrounded as the Germans pushed home their attack. Gerdtell, the Tiger company commander, was an early casualty. It was normal German doctrine for tank commanders to go into action with the commander's head exposed in his hatch, as the benefit of being able to see the battlefield clearly outweighed the risk, but on this occasion a Soviet sniper exploited the opportunity and killed Gerdtell. Nonetheless, 268th Rifle Division fell back in disarray, conceding nearly a mile of ground.[19] But although the thick frontal armour of the Tiger was impervious to most Soviet guns, the huge tanks were still vulnerable at close range – like all tanks, their tracks could be damaged rendering them immobile, and the upper decking and rear armour were thin enough to be penetrated in close-quarter fighting. Two Tiger tanks had pressed into the depths of the Soviet positions and one was hit repeatedly and set ablaze. The crew abandoned it and boarded the second tank, making good their escape.

The German counterattack ran out of momentum as it approached the Neva and was halted just a quarter of a mile from the riverbank.[20] Another German thrust managed to reach the 'hospital' behind Gorodok 1 and Gorodok 2, strengthening the German positions there, but a Soviet air raid on the headquarters of one of 96th Infantry Division's regiments inflicted heavy losses and caused considerable disruption. German shelling succeeded in knocking out the southern of three bridges over the Neva that had been constructed overnight and the northern bridge also became temporarily unusable after it was damaged by a T-34 attempting to cross. The five German battalions in the counterattack suffered considerable losses, as did the units of 268th Rifle Division in their path – by the end of the day's fighting, the Soviet division had just one usable anti-tank gun left.[21]

Nonetheless, the leading elements of 136th Rifle Division, advancing to the north of Gorodok 1 and Gorodok 2, continued to infiltrate their way through the German positions, methodically clearing each one albeit at considerable cost. The leading unit of Simoniak's division, 269th Rifle Regiment, reported during the afternoon that it had been halted by particularly stubborn resistance at a grove codenamed *Liliya* ('Lily') towards the end of the brief hours of daylight, and Major Aleksandr Ivanovich Sherstnev, commander of 269th Rifle Regiment, reported that he was halted by heavy German shelling just short of the important Sinyavino–Shlisselburg road. Simoniak dispatched a rifle battalion that he had held back as a local reserve together with a battalion of light tanks and *Liliya* was captured. But attempts to push on to cut the vital road failed and Sherstnev had to content himself with interdicting it with gunfire.[22] By the end of the day Simoniak's leading elements were just three miles from Gorodok 5, where Second Shock Army was trying to advance towards the west.

Like Dukhanov's Sixty-Seventh Army in the west, Second Shock Army in the east commenced operations on 13 January with a heavy artillery bombardment. The weather had deteriorated with heavy snowstorms, preventing Volkhov Front's air assets from being deployed; with fighting now moving into dense woodland, artillery fire was also less precise for both sides. Gorodok 8 became a small German island, cut off from other German forces but still able to disrupt Red Army attempts to bypass it and push on to the east; anticipating that this and other strongpoints of the German defensive line might become isolated, Leyser had ensured that local stockpiles of ammunition were in place to allow prolonged defence. The soldiers in the defences of the settlement consisted of a battalion from the independent 374th Grenadier Regiment, which had been assigned to 227th Infantry Division as reinforcements; its commander, Major Gerhard Ziegler, continued to direct his men throughout the day, regularly calling in artillery fire from 96th Infantry Division's artillery regiment, which had been assigned to support him.[23]

The counterattack by 1st Infantry Division in the south of Second Shock Army's advance made no progress, but nor did Red Army attacks attempting to widen the breach in the main German line. Renewed attacks by Burakovsky's 73rd Naval Rifle Brigade further south against Tortolovo also failed – a detailed fire plan had been drawn up overnight to deal with the German defences in the village, but when the infantry advanced, most of the German bunkers were still intact. After further heavy losses, Burakovsky called a halt but then attacked again late on 13 January, this time without any artillery preparation and supported by the neighbouring 265th Rifle Division. The advancing Soviet riflemen were able to break into the village, taking the defenders by surprise, and managed to overrun perhaps half the German positions.[24]

As the second day of *Iskra* drew to a close, there was a further lull in the fighting. Govorov continued to be frustrated by German resistance at Gorodok 1 and 2, and with Shlisselburg in the north still in German hands, the flanks of his advance were still not entirely secure. But the leading elements from Simoniak's 136th Rifle Division were now almost within touching range of the forces of Volkhov Front and it seemed as if a link-up was imminent. To date, Govorov had managed to hold back his second echelon, intending to wait until he had broken the siege perimeter before using the reserves to drive the Germans back to the south, but reports from the front line suggested that the first echelon divisions were running out of men. If he was to complete the rupture of the siege ring, he would have to send forward the troops he had been holding back.

Accordingly, he issued instructions overnight for Dukhanov to commit his second echelon. The fresh 123rd Rifle Division, reinforced by a rifle brigade and a tank brigade, would enter the battle on the flanks of the successful advance of 136th Rifle Division. Additional reinforcements were sent to 268th Rifle Division in the south, where they were to be used to overwhelm the defences of

Gorodok 1 and 2. Finally, a ski brigade was deployed with 86th Rifle Division in the north in an attempt to force the German line on the edge of Shlisselburg.[25] Sending the second echelon into action before Leningrad and Volkhov Fronts had linked up was in many ways an admission that the initial plans for breaking through the German lines had failed; using the second echelon along the entire front of the offensive was a further setback, in that it effectively ensured that nowhere did the fresh troops deploy en masse. Consequently, their impact was modest and at first their deployment merely added to the problems of the units already on the ground. In particular, using 123rd Rifle Division to reinforce both flanks of 136th Rifle Division resulted in a tangle of supply and communications lines behind the front line. But the reality was that Dukhanov and Govorov had little choice. They were unsure of what resources remained available to the Germans and they knew just how effectively their enemies had counterattacked in the past. It was important to prevent such counterattacks from isolating the most advanced units as had happened twice to Second Shock Army during 1942.

Whatever the problems being experienced by higher commanders, Simoniak had reason to be pleased with the performance of his division. It had overcome tough defences and advanced more or less at the rate that had been specified at the beginning of the operation – the inability of flanking units to keep up was beyond Simoniak's control. He watched as German soldiers captured in the attack were led to the rear after night fell on 13 January:

> The prisoners made a pitiful impression. Previously, Simoniak thought, the Germans who had been captured were rude and full of confidence, repeatedly parroting 'We will win. We will defeat Russia.' Now the situation was very different. The German soldier-conquerors had far weaker spirits …
>
> Looking at the prisoners, the division commander asked [Colonel Ivan Ilyich] Trusov [Simoniak's chief of staff] what units they were from.
>
> 'Most are from 170th Infantry Division, but there are some from 96th Infantry Division.'
>
> 'Where were they captured?'
>
> 'On our right flank [i.e. to the south]. Lindemann's reserve was 96th Infantry Division. It was transferred here to plug the gap and throw us back across the river.'
>
> … Returning to his bunker, Simoniak slowly passed his tired eyes over the map. He took a ruler to measure accurately the strip that separated the Leningraders from the Volkhovites. 'Five kilometres left. We need to press harder from both sides tomorrow.'[26]

To the east of the German bottleneck, Meretskov at the headquarters of Volkhov Front faced much the same problems as Govorov: the divisions of the first echelon had chewed their way into the German lines but had been badly degraded in the process. The continued defiance of Ziegler's little garrison in Gorodok 8 was badly disrupting attempts to move forces forward and although Soviet troops in the south had overrun most of Kruglaya Grove, they had failed to dislodge Wengler's group from the shoulder of the attack. And although the late attack on Tortolovo had captured much of the village, the success there was hardly sufficient to disrupt the German positions to the south. Like Govorov, Meretskov felt that he had no choice but to release his second echelon sooner than he would have preferred and 191st Rifle Division was dispatched to complete the capture of Kruglaya Grove. The units in the main axis of Volkhov Front's attack were ordered to destroy the German battalion in Gorodok 8 and to push on and link up with Leningrad Front.

Meretskov's deputy, Fedyuninsky, went forward to the headquarters of 239th Rifle Division to see personally how the battle was progressing:

I went to [Major] General [Petr Nikolayevich] Chernyshev's division to find out the situation on the spot. I had a liaison officer and adjutant with me. The liaison officer confidently led us through the snow-covered forest, guided by landmarks known only to him. We reached the edge. From here, the path stretched across a field pitted with shell craters. At first we followed the path and then we turned off and made straight for a large fir tree with a broken top, silhouetted against the darkening sky.

Suddenly I saw a peg sticking out of the snow with a small plank nailed to it. Shining my flashlight on it, I read: 'Caution! Mines!' I felt alarmed – we were in a minefield!

But without slowing down his pace, the liaison officer replied indifferently, 'It's nothing, Comrade General. In winter, these mines won't explode – they're frozen into the ground.'

The liaison officer was right – we crossed the minefield safely.

In Chernyshev's hut, built from frozen chunks of peat, a stove provided heat. The general was wearing a heavily soiled white camouflage coat. On his lap was an unfolded map. Chernyshev was busy measuring something on it.

Glancing at the map, I saw immediately that the division's observation post was too far from the regiments' combat formations. 'Do you have secure contact with your units?' I asked Chernyshev.

Hesitantly, he replied, 'Not with everyone. I can't get in touch with the regiment that advanced beyond the railway embankment.'

'What are you going to do?'

'I'll send a liaison officer there now.'

'What's happening with the other regiments?'

'They're digging in,' said Chernyshev, not very confidently.

'Give me two men with submachine-guns, I'll go personally to the regiment that's out of contact.'

General Cheryshev began to try to reassure me that contact would be re-established soon, but I didn't wait. Coming out of the division commander's hut, I stopped for a moment. It was completely dark. Dry snow blew across the land. Sharp snowflakes, driven by the wind, struck my face. Two submachine-gunners approached me, puffing on cigarettes. 'Do you know the way?' I asked.

'We know, Comrade General. We go through the forest here, then through an embankment, it's not far.'[27]

Accompanied by the two guides, Fedyuninsky ventured forth and found that the route was longer than expected. He was surprised to find that there was no firing in the front line – the men were gathered around small fires trying to warm themselves, and similar fires were visible on the German side of no-man's land. Fedyuninsky issued orders for aggressive patrolling and returned to Chernyshev's headquarters where he admonished the division commander for poor discipline and lax communications. Suspecting that other divisions might be in a similar state, he visited two more headquarters before returning to the rear area.

Leyser was also taking stock. On the one hand, the majority of important strongpoints – Gorodok 1 and 2 in the west and Gorodok 8 in the east – remained in German hands. The counterattack against Leningrad Front had achieved some success in the south but had then come to a standstill; half the Tiger tanks that had been sent into action were either immobilised or destroyed. The Tiger had been deployed – prematurely – in the Leningrad sector the preceding summer and immediately the Red Army's specialists began to study the new vehicle to determine how best to oppose it. Their tentative conclusions were that whilst its frontal armour and its 88mm gun made it a formidable opponent, it was not without weaknesses, and tactics in Soviet anti-tank units evolved rapidly to try to come to terms with the new German tanks. Consequently, the Tigers had succeeded in helping the battalions of 96th Infantry Division to overcome the first line of Soviet resistance but had then faced concentrated anti-tank and artillery fire. Leyser's meagre reserves were now exhausted and he discussed the matter with Lindemann and Küchler. Agreeing that it was essential to strengthen the defensive line, Küchler ordered the neighbouring LIV Corps to send help: it was to release parts of *SS-Polizei* and 5th Mountain Division, which were to concentrate in Sinyavino as a new reserve for XXVI Corps. In addition, 61st Infantry Division was to be moved from its positions facing east near Kirishi to shore up the defensive line running through Gorodok 1 and 2. However, this would take time. The divisions currently holding the front line either side of Kirishi would have to extend their frontage in order to allow 61st Infantry Division to be extracted. Had these divisions been at full strength, this would have been a difficult enough task in view of the considerable sectors that they already held; given that none of the infantry divisions in Army Group North were at full strength, it would involve careful but nonetheless risky juggling of resources.

The following days were full of bitter combat at close quarters. Soldiers of both sides struggled through the snow, frozen swamps, and shattered forests, fighting and dying in a manner that was little different from the terrible attritional battles of the First World War. The front lines were now so entangled that heavy artillery bombardment of the fighting positions was often impossible; instead, the gunners shelled rear areas, approach routes, and enemy artillery positions. Meanwhile, the Red Army enjoyed a moment of good fortune. One of the Tiger tanks committed to the counterattacks against Leningrad Front was immobilised by anti-tank guns on 14 January and Soviet troops reported that the Germans had made repeated attempts to tow it to safety. Zhukov was still overseeing affairs in Meretskov's headquarters:

> We ordered the creation of a special group consisting of a rifle platoon and four tanks, which was tasked with capturing the enemy tank and towing it back to our lines where it could be examined carefully. The group was supported by powerful artillery and mortar fire.
>
> Late on 17 January, the group, led by Senior Lieutenant Kesarev, began its mission. The area where the wrecked tank was located was under constant enemy fire. Nevertheless, the vehicle was captured and towed away. They even picked up a tank manual lying in the snow …
>
> The captured tank was handed over for comprehensive study. Experts rapidly established its weaknesses. The results were immediately reported to all Soviet troops.[28]

Instead of marching forward swiftly over the narrow distance that separated him from Volkhov Front, Simoniak had to deal with a determined German counterattack early on 14 January; the units allocated to protect the flanks of his

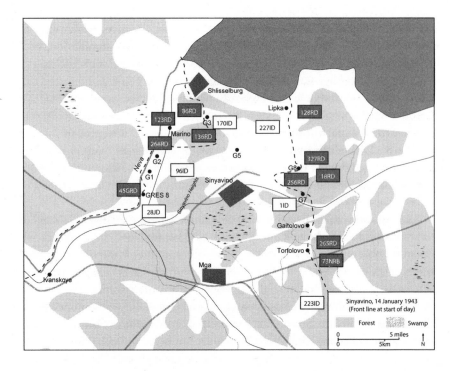

Sinyavino, 14 January 1943
(Front line at start of day)

Forest   Swamp

0   5 miles
0   5km   N

advance had not yet arrived and his southern flank in particular came under
heavy pressure. The German troops were the first elements of 61st Infantry
Division, rushed to the area by train and thrown into battle immediately. Whilst
the division commander, Generalleutnant Werner Hühner, would have preferred
to wait until all of his units were present, the urgency of the situation required
immediate action.

After a brief telephone conversation, Dukhanov directed his army's artillery
assets to bombard the German units on the flank of 268th Rifle Division and
slowly the leading Soviet regiment began to probe forward. Despite its combat
strength diminishing at an alarming rate, it managed to advance another half
mile through almost continuous German defensive positions. The counterattack
by 61st Infantry Division made little progress into the southern flank of
Simoniak's advance, and Hühner's men found themselves intermingled with the
other German soldiers who were attempting to hold back Leningrad Front's
attack.

Conditions were desperately bad for the soldiers on both sides of the front
line. For those who had only recently arrived from training depots, it must have

been a horrifying period of transition. Hasso Stachow was a young soldier who served in the Leningrad sector and he later described the fighting in terms that bring home its brutal horror:

> Many of the young men from the replacement drafts now experienced the war in a manner that none of their trainers, none of the film reports on German newsreels, and no newspaper reporters had described or were permitted to describe. They watched their friends die, had to see how they were mutilated repeatedly and reduced to something that barely looked human, covered by the ubiquitous earth and perishing in what propagandists described as heroic deaths. They stared into the muzzles of submachine-guns that were aimed at them, could barely comprehend the frenzy of redemptive anger that gripped them when Red Army soldiers fell to the ground before their bayonets, the blows of their shovels, and the blast of their hand grenades – those on whom they desperately blamed their anguish. There was nobody to help them endure the vision of bloody remains, nobody to comfort them when they heard the cries of the dying. And nobody had the strength or time to consider that the young men with Soviet stars, who were termed their enemies, experienced exactly the same things, with the same sense of horror.[29]

Leonid Nikitich Motorin was a soldier in the ski brigade that had been sent to reinforce the northern side of Leningrad Front's advance, and his experience of the fighting was typical of men on both sides:

> We were lying in low-lying ground in a ravine. Bullets struck the rucksacks on men's backs and we took them off and lay on the ground. On the first day we couldn't do anything. At night we remained in the ravine, five men on watch while five went to a dugout to warm themselves.
>
> At dawn, first light, we moved through the ravine. There was no artillery preparation as we were too close [to the German lines]. But our aircraft dominated. Whenever a German plane took off, it was attacked immediately. We found ourselves in hand-to-hand combat in the ravine ...
>
> The commander of the second squad led us towards the dugout from where the Germans were firing. He said, 'Tear open the door and drop to the ground, I'll throw in a grenade.' We did so, but when we went in there was no one there. We climbed out, I helped the commander up, and he gave me a machine-gun, and then there was an explosion next to us. The commander was wounded and I was thrown back into the dugout. My legs were trapped by a log and a huge

mound of earth. Somehow I pulled my right leg free, but my boot remained there. I had to put a mitten on my foot and wrap it tightly with a footcloth. I began to dig away the earth with my bayonet to try to see what was going on. A dead German slid down, the snow around him falling in a heap right on top of me. I pushed him away with my rifle ... I cleared a small hole with my bayonet. I could see a German machine-gun firing, but couldn't see the operator. I dug a little more and saw that the Germans had positioned themselves between two trees to fire their machine-gun. I fired twice, then loaded a fresh clip and fired again. After the third shot, the machine-gun fell silent. I'd damaged it. I began to widen my embrasure. The Germans began to fire mortars, not light company weapons but larger, regimental mortars. After my third shot [at the mortar crew], the mortar tube exploded.

The machine-gunner noticed me and fired a burst at my embrasure. I immediately dropped down, my helmet falling forward over my face. After two bursts, the Germans stopped firing. From my widened embrasure I could see a lot. I raised my head slowly, no one was in sight. Suddenly another German machine-gun started firing. I looked behind a log and saw a German nearby, he hadn't seen me. I removed the bayonet from my rifle, pointed it at his head and fired ...

And then I heard voices. It was our guys, coming back for ammunition. I shouted to them, 'Get me out of here, I've been crushed!'

... By then, I couldn't feel my crushed leg at all. I was getting very cold. Again I heard Russian voices. It was my platoon, moving into better firing positions. They lifted the log, pulled me out, rubbed warmth back into my legs, and then said, 'You sit here while we fire back [at the Germans].'[30]

Motorin found an abandoned German machine-gun and joined the firefight. It was nearly a disastrous decision – later that evening another group of Red Army infantry moved towards their position and hearing the distinctive high-speed firing of the captured German machine-gun, they were about to throw hand grenades into the dugout when they realised that Motorin and his comrades were Soviet soldiers. But in the midst of the bitter fighting on the northern flank of Leningrad Front's attack, there was one notable success for the Red Army: the German positions on Preobrazhenskoe Hill were overrun by 330th Rifle Regiment, part of 86th Rifle Division. From here, the exhausted Soviet soldiers were able to fire into Shlisselburg and preparations began for an attempt to break into the town. All along the battle line immediately east of the Neva, units from the two sides fought against their opponents in ferocious, often isolated and disconnected battles. Neither side had an accurate picture of the overall situation, but by the end of 14 January large parts of the German 227th Infantry Division in the Shlisselburg sector had effectively lost contact with the rest of XXVI Corps. At great cost, the Red Army was gaining the upper hand.

There was a similar pattern to the fighting on the eastern side of the German bottleneck. In Gorodok 8, Ziegler and his diminishing battalion continued to hold out through 14 and 15 January, but the Soviet 256th Rifle Division managed to push forward towards the edge of Sinyavino. The highly congested battlespace, the difficult terrain, the lack of roads, and the widespread German minefields made it difficult for Second Shock Army to concentrate the units of its second echelon to maximum effect and instead Romanovsky was forced to watch impotently as companies and battalions were frittered away piecemeal; despite an improvement in the weather, allowing Soviet air assets to make repeated attacks, progress remained painfully slow throughout 14 and 15 January. Immediately behind the front line, rear area units struggled to move ammunition and food forward and to evacuate the wounded. The terrain was badly chewed up by the Soviet artillery bombardments, the German counter-bombardments, and the passage of advancing Red Army units, and the widespread German minefields added greatly to the risks of moving off the few clearly marked routes. Even after they were removed from the battlefield, wounded men faced long journeys – as was the case in the fighting in the First World War on the Western Front, the flood of casualties overwhelmed hospitals close to the front line and it became necessary to move wounded men further and further to the rear. Zalman Matusovich Krichevskiy was an artilleryman involved in the fighting for Kruglaya Grove, and received a head wound from shrapnel:

> The wounded were taken to the rear on a train of sleds, which came under heavy bombardment. Many were killed or wounded a second time, and a large piece of shrapnel shattered my shoulder and penetrated through to my back, breaking my right shoulder blade. Small fragments from this wound are still in my lung today. I don't know what happened to me in the first two weeks after being wounded, I can't remember, I only woke up on 31 January when I reached the hospital in Vologda [295 miles to the east]. I remember that when they tried to remove the bandage from my head, I shuddered and opened my eyes, because the bandage was soaked with dried blood and it wasn't easy to remove it. All the hospitals were already full to overflowing and nobody knew what to do with us, where to put us or where we could be sent further back. And then began a nomadic life in hospitals: Kirov, Molotov, and Alma Ata.[31]

Lieutenant Arsenin, who had been wounded in the crossing of the Neva near 8th GRES, was evacuated first to the rear area of Leningrad Front and then across Lake Ladoga. The medical facilities around Volkhov were already overflowing and he was sent all the way to the Soviet capital:

> I ended up in a hospital in a Moscow hotel. There were 50 seriously wounded men there. The chief surgeon of the hospital began his rounds. He approached me and examined my wound, and asked if I could hear after my concussion. I nodded my head. He said I could be given alcohol and moved on.
>
> A minute later I heard a conversation between a female doctor and the chief surgeon. The woman asked to be permitted to perform surgery on a young officer. The chief surgeon said it was pointless as he already had gangrene. The woman insisted. Finally, still saying it was pointless, the chief surgeon gave her permission. The woman came up to me and asked if I had heard her conversation with the chief surgeon. I replied that I had. She said that if I agreed, she would start the operation, but it would be without any anaesthesia. I agreed. The operation seemed to take forever. I was given two glasses of alcohol, but it wasn't enough to put me out. Only the rubber bar I was biting saved my teeth. The operation was successful.[32]

The soldiers in the front line were enduring horrific conditions – the weather was bitterly cold, moving food and other supplies to the front line was often impossible, and the corpses of men killed in the battle lay everywhere. Sergei Vasilyevich Yegorov was sent forward to take command of a mortar observation post:

> With an orderly, I went to the observation post, which was in a trench about 1.5km ahead of our battery. When I approached the ridge along which our front line ran, I saw it was covered by shell craters. I reached a communications trench along which the wounded were moving towards me if they were still able to move somehow. Those who didn't have the strength to move sat or lay at the bottom of the trench. As I came closer to the front line, there were more and more people sitting or lying in the trench, many of them dead. A signaller with a telephone was running ahead of me. Near a turn in the trench he ran around the corner and there was the sound of a shell exploding. I was thrown back by the blast and fell on my back. When I jumped up, I saw blood on my coat and under my feet lay a piece of a coat's sleeve from which a hand with two black pieces of telephone cable protruded. I ran forward and turned the corner of the trench but couldn't see the

signaller. When I turned my head, I saw a disfigured corpse sprawled on the parapet with its belly torn and entrails falling out, and steam rising from them. It was a bright, sunny, frosty day.

... The junction of the communications trench and the front line, where the observation post was located, was partly covered ... The infantry in the trench tried to get under this cover, thinking it was the safest spot. In fact, it was well targeted by the enemy and fire was particularly heavy here. Soldiers who gathered under this cover were killed sooner than those spread out in the trench ... In order to get through the trench to the observation post, I had to crawl over the corpses. Finally, I reached the observation post and saw the enemy's fighting positions through the stereoscope, firing at our lines, but I couldn't direct fire because I had no communications with the battery. The commanders of neighbouring batteries were in the same predicament. The infantry demanded that we fire, cursing us, but we were powerless. In desperation, I tried to draft an initial fire plan for individual targets and sent it to the battery by messenger. Such firing without being able to adjust the fire was ineffective and the messenger often didn't reach the battery. We were protected from shrapnel in the observation post but not from a direct hit by an artillery shell or mortar bomb. The awareness of our hopelessness and the constant shelling, with explosions now on the right, then on the left, now closer, then further away, added to our extreme anxiety.

With the onset of darkness, when the enemy fire was sharply reduced and only a few shots were fired at our front line, the nervous tension was replaced by apathy and a sense of hopelessness ... An unbelievable image remained in my memory for the rest of my life – a clear and frosty night with moonlight illuminating a huge number of dead, frozen in different poses.[33]

In such a battle of attrition, the issue would ultimately be decided by which side ran out of men first. The assault groups of both Sixty-Seventh and Second Shock Armies were greatly diminished, but so too were the ranks of their opponents. After its failure to defeat the German defences on the southern flank of Leningrad Front's attacks and then enduring the powerful German counterattack supported by Tiger tanks, 268th Rifle Division had reached the end of its strength. The reinforcements that Dukhanov assigned to it made little difference and despite furious assaults, Gorodok 1 and 2 remained in German hands over the following days. On 18 January, when the division was pulled back from the front line, most of its rifle companies had lost 90 per cent of their personnel, and one battalion had been wiped out completely.[34] But elsewhere, it was the Germans who realised that they were running out of men. By the end of 15 January,

Ziegler's isolated garrison in Gorodok 8 was almost out of ammunition and no longer had sufficient men to hold out. Radio contact with other German forces had been lost and Ziegler decided that the only option left was to try to break out towards Sinyavino.

It was a daunting prospect. Ziegler had only a rough idea of where the German front line was and his men would have to drag their wounded with them on small sleds. They left their positions late on 15 January, with Ziegler at the head of the column; he was accompanied by a fluent Russian speaker who had donned a jacket taken from a dead Soviet officer. Whilst the Germans were quick to condemn Soviet attempts to adopt such measures, they showed little hesitation in using them when the situation demanded it. Behind them, the rear party detonated their last stockpile of ammunition. The small column managed to bluff its way past the encircling Soviet forces, and then encountered a Red Army mortar position and overwhelmed it, taking several prisoners. Before dawn, Ziegler reached the German positions at Gorodok 5, where he was able to link up with friendly forces.[35]

The abandonment of Gorodok 8 was just one of a series of events, each fairly small, that demonstrated the gradual advantage being gained by the Red Army. Many Soviet rifle companies had been reduced to no more than a dozen men, but the slow advance by both Leningrad and Volkhov Fronts continued. From their positions on Preobrazhenskoe Hill, Soviet troops advanced into the edge of Shlisselburg on 16 January and bitter fighting began along the fortified southwest edge of the town. At Gorodok 5, the two advances were now just half a mile apart and Leyser and Lindemann were aware that the German troops – a mixture of men from 227th and 96th Infantry Divisions and 5th Mountain Division – holding positions in Shlisselburg, along the coast of Lake Ladoga, and facing the northern parts of Volkhov Front were in serious danger of being cut off. Even if the two Soviet pincers hadn't yet met, it was now almost impossible to move supplies to Shlisselburg. During the afternoon of 17 January, after further discussions between Küchler and Lindemann, Leyser was granted permission to organise a breakout by the forces in Shlisselburg to the south before the two Soviet advances met.

Another of the units sent north by Lindemann and Leyser was a battalion from the 250th Infantry Division, the Spanish Blue Division. In addition, the rest of the Blue Division had to take over a longer stretch of front line in order to release *SS-Polizei*. The Spanish infantrymen trudged through the snow, aware that the Germans had a low opinion of their martial abilities, yet were now depending on them to reinforce the vital corridor to Shlisselburg. The German mindset, dominated by a mixture of social Darwinism and racial ideology, characterised the Spanish soldiers as being better suited to guerrilla or anti-partisan warfare on the dubious grounds that close-quarter or hand-to-hand combat was more in keeping with Spanish character and behaviour.[36] The battalion sent into the corridor found itself on the northern side of Gorodok 5. The main German force that lay between Leningrad and Volkhov Fronts consisted of two battlegroups from 61st Infantry Division, operating under the name of *Gruppe Hühner*, and it was necessary for this force to try to move north in order to hold open the withdrawal route from Shlisselburg while the Spanish battalion secured their starting positions around Gorodok 5. The losses that these battlegroups had suffered in their tenacious defence were considerable and when Hühner attacked towards the north in order to establish better contact with the Shlisselburg forces, there was the risk that not only would the Spanish battalion prove to be unable to hold back the Red Army, but that there might be further Soviet attacks to the south. It was therefore necessary to take steps to keep open the line of retreat of *Gruppe Hühner* between Gorodok 5 and Sinyavino as well as securing Gorodok 5 itself. By now, a substantial part of *SS-Polizei* had gathered in Sinyavino and Lindemann ordered it to attack north at the same time that Hühner tried to establish better contact with the Shlisselburg garrison, in order to hold open the retreat corridor.

At almost any other phase of the war, permission to abandon a position like Shlisselburg and the nearby coast of Lake Ladoga would have involved frustrating and time-consuming negotiations with Hitler's distant headquarters – the fighting outside Moscow in late 1941 had demonstrated the Führer's extreme unwillingness to give up any territory, even when it was of little or no importance. The withdrawal of the northern parts of XXVI Corps would be a very significant setback for Germany in both military and political terms. By establishing land contact between Leningrad and Volkhov Fronts, the Soviet Union would not only be in a position to coordinate its future actions more effectively, but would also be able to alleviate the terrible siege conditions in the Soviet Union's second largest city. The breaking of the siege ring would send a strong political and propaganda message to the world, particularly coming on the heels of the encirclement of the German Sixth Army in Stalingrad, and Hitler could have been expected to demand that Leyser's corps continue to hold firm. But the ordeal of Sixth Army in the ruins of Stalingrad was slowly drawing to its painful end, demonstrating in the most graphic manner the folly of clinging to exposed positions. Consequently, there was almost no delay before Army Group North received permission from *Oberkommando des Heeres* ('Army High Command' or

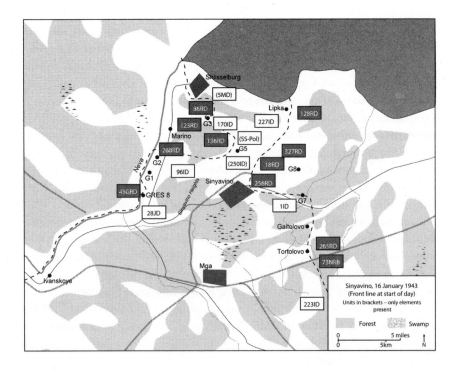

Sinyavino, 16 January 1943
(Front line at start of day)
Units in brackets – only elements present

Forest   Swamp

OKH) for the abandonment of Shlisselburg. Because the Red Army's pressure was so intense and perhaps wishing to act before Hitler changed his mind, Küchler and Lindemann ordered an immediate breakout of the troops still in and around Shlisselburg towards *Gruppe Hühner*.

These German operations coincided with ongoing Soviet attempts to break the siege ring. On 17 January, Red Army troops moving past the southern edge of Shlisselburg turned north and overran the eastern part of the town while 86th Rifle Division gathered its strength and broke into the western parts. From his command post just outside Gorodok 5, Hühner issued orders for the German units to his north to fight their way through to him. His two regimental battlegroups were fully committed to holding off the Soviet attacks on the ruins of the settlement, with Red Army units from Leningrad Front attacking on the western side and those from Volkhov Front attacking from the east; there had been three major assaults during the night of 16–17 January by Second Shock Army's 18th Rifle Division, but all had been repulsed. Nevertheless, there was little possibility of Hühner pushing north to the troops in Shlisselburg – they would have to come to him. The Soviet attack from the west consisted largely of

Simoniak's hard-fighting 136th Rifle Division, which penetrated into the edge of Gorodok 5 early on 17 January but was almost immediately driven back. At the same time, Volkhov Front's 18th Rifle Division attacked towards the settlement from the southeast and managed to come within a mile of its edge before being brought to a standstill in the middle of a peat bog. Colonel Nikolai Georgiyevich Lyashchenko, deputy commander of the division, informed Romanovsky that his men were in urgent need of food and ammunition if they were to continue their attack.[37] In the shattered forests and snow-covered minefields, coordination of forces became almost impossible. Further south, the German forces concentrating in Sinyavino moved north, trying to keep open the withdrawal route for the units further north. All would depend upon the following day's fighting.

Early on 18 January, Sergeant Aleksei Brovkin led a platoon of 136 Rifle Division forward around the southern edge of Gorodok 5. He had been briefed by his company commander that the troops of Volkhov Front were close, and his mission was to establish contact with them. He and his men groped their way forward through the gloomy dawn light of a midwinter morning:

After bypassing the village through the bushes, the scouting party crossed the narrow gauge railway and moved on … hearing the crunch of snow ahead, one of them signalled: 'Alert!'

The scouts stopped, their white jackets merging with the snowdrifts. About 30m further along a barely noticeable road, a group of Germans was hurrying along. 'Let them go,' Brovkin told the scouts. 'We have our mission.'

The scouts waited until the group of Nazis had passed. But as soon as they got up, they heard once more voices from the left, and the creak of a sled.

'What should we do?' Brovkin's assistant, Aleksander Redin, asked. 'Do we let them go past again?'

Brovkin was in no hurry to reply. 'We need to find out how many Nazis are on the road, otherwise we could end up in a right mess.'

The Nazis were getting closer. Their dark silhouettes stood out distinctly against the white background. They were approaching the [Soviet] platoon.

'Attack!' shouted Brovkin. The scouts suddenly opened fire with their submachine-guns. The Nazis rushed across the clearing. A handful remained lying in the snow while the rest fled in panic. Several scouts chased after them.

'Leave them!' shouted Brovkin. 'Stop that! We must complete our mission!'

Beyond the clearing was a thick screen of young birch trees. The scouts moved up to it. They could hear the distinct sound of Russian Maxim guns, staccato bursts of machine-guns firing. It had to be the Volkhovites, somewhere very close.

'Look!' Redin nudged Brovkin. About 200m away, across the clearing, which was cut by a deep ditch, three men in white jackets were walking cautiously. Were they moving towards Gorodok 5? The scouts crouched down, not sure who they were. They didn't look like Germans.

When the strangers were close, Brovkin shouted, 'Stop! Who are you?'

'We're on your side!' came the answer, but then all three dropped onto the snow.

'Why are you hiding? Come closer! Do you know the codeword?'

'You give the password!'

Brovkin rose to his full height, and shouted loudly the syllables, '*Po-be-da!*' ['Victory!']

'Death to Fascism!' the answer followed immediately, and the soldiers joyfully rushed towards each other.[38]

Soviet-era accounts of the encirclement of the German Sixth Army in Stalingrad described how the advancing Soviet forces were guided towards each other by flares soaring over the snowy fields and how the two columns met joyfully near the town of Kalach, but the reality was that the two forces had a brisk exchange of fire before they realised that they hadn't encountered German units. Leningrad and Volkhov Fronts had agreed a system of codewords to avoid such a clash, but the tension experienced by soldiers probing forward in the half-light, surrounded by enemy troops and unsure of the precise location of friendly forces, must have been immense and it would have been all too easy for any such encounter to end with casualties. On this occasion, matters unfolded in a fairly orderly manner and by mid-morning the leading battalions of the two Fronts had established firm contact. For the exhausted soldiers, it was a moment of huge significance. After over a year of encirclement, the siege ring around Leningrad was broken. However, contact between Leningrad and Volkhov Fronts was tenuous, and fighting flared immediately to the north as the morning grew brighter and Soviet forces attempted to secure Gorodok 5.

The infantrymen of Simoniak's 136th Rifle Division had been involved in some of the toughest fighting during Leningrad Front's advance and had been in the forefront of the drive to link up with Volkhov Front. In recognition of its achievement, the unit was renamed 63rd Guards Rifle Division and all of its regiments received the honorary title of 'Leningrad' in addition to their numbers. Two of its soldiers – Sergeant Ivan Antonovich Lapshov and Signaller Dmitry Semenovich Molodtsov – were awarded the title Hero of the Soviet Union; in the case of the latter, this was a posthumous award. Dushevsky, whose company was part of Simoniak's division, later recalled that their new status as Guards came with a welcome bonus, at least for the men who had survived the terrible fighting: as Guards, they received 1.5 times their normal salary. But, like the rest of the division, Dushevsky's company had been reduced from its original strength of 126 men to just 38 as a result of the fighting; only 50 of those casualties recovered sufficiently from their wounds to return to the ranks.[39]

In addition to the award of Guards status to Simoniak's division, there was another announcement: Zhukov was promoted to Marshal of the Soviet Union on 18 January. In some respects, it was merely recognition of his prominent role as deputy supreme commander, but whilst the timing clearly reflected the success of *Iskra* in breaking the siege ring, it was nonetheless a slightly curious promotion. Just a few weeks before, Zhukov had presided over the bloody failure of Operation *Mars* around the German-held Rzhev salient, a prolonged and costly series of attacks that cost the Red Army over 300,000 casualties for no gain. An adjective that was frequently used to describe Zhukov during his career was 'stubborn' and this trait was shown in excess in his repeated assaults against the Rzhev salient through 1942, throwing men and tanks against strong German defences over terrain that was hugely difficult for any army attempting to mount offensive operations. He showed similar stubbornness blended with equally characteristic ruthlessness and brutality during *Iskra*, angrily berating Simoniak on 18 January for not attacking more strongly and in particular for not moving against the German positions on the Sinyavino Heights. Zhukov must have known that the high ground lay outside 136th Rifle Division's sector, and in any case the division was fully committed in its attack towards Gorodok 5 and linking up with Volkhov Front. Simoniak replied over the field telephone that he had not attacked the heights for the same reason that Second Shock Army had not done so: the approaches to the heights from the start lines of Sixty-Seventh and Second Shock Armies ran across peat bogs and any attempt to advance over that ground was likely to be both slow and highly costly. Zhukov apparently raged as Simoniak, accusing him of being a 'Trotskyite' and a 'passive resister' and added, 'Who are those cowards of yours? Who doesn't want to fight? Who needs to be ousted?'

It was an accusation that Simoniak could not accept. His men had been struggling forward at great cost since 12 January and he angrily rejected Zhukov's accusations. Zhukov then gave him a direct order to storm the heights. Simoniak replied that his army was under the command of Dukhanov at Sixty-Seventh Army headquarters, and above him Govorov at Leningrad Front – any such order had to come through the proper chain of command. Zhukov hung up. No order for 136th Rifle Division to turn towards the Sinyavino Heights was issued either by Dukhanov or Govorov.[40] This was undoubtedly the correct decision – had Zhukov's orders been enforced, 136th Rifle Division would have been forced to divert units at the very moment that it was linking up with Volkhov Front. The consequence would have been that the Germans in and around Shlisselburg would have been able to break out with fewer casualties, and the modest forces that would have been available to send south would probably have made little impact on the German defences on the heights. There had been similar diversion of effort during the costly failure of *Mars* around the Rzhev salient, and it seems that Zhukov had yet to learn any lessons from his recent setback.

With Soviet tanks now amongst the ruins of the settlement and infantry engaged in hand-to-hand fighting, time was rapidly running out for the German forces in Shlisselburg. Hühner and his battered garrison continued to hold on despite now being under attack from both east and west and the leading unit from Shlisselburg – 151st Grenadier Regiment, part of 61st Infantry Division – reached them mid-morning. But in order to prevent total collapse, they had to hold off the pursuing forces, and fighting raged in both Shlisselburg in the west and Lipka in the east. Both towns fell to the Red Army during the afternoon of 18 January as Hühner ordered his men to head south towards the Sinyavino Heights. The link-up that Brodkin had made with Volkhov Front to the south of Gorodok 5 was broken in close-quarter combat and, under constant fire, the German column struggled on through the maze of shattered trees, deep snow and Soviet patrols. It took two days for the retreating force to reach the safety of the positions held by *SS-Polizei* and 96th Infantry Division:

> On 20 January Hühner's men reeled into the intercepting line. The companies of his 151st and 162nd Regiments now numbered 30–40 men each. One company of 162nd Grenadier Regiment, which had gone into battle with 128 men on 15 January, was by now reduced to a mere 44.
>
> Leutnant Dressel, wounded and supporting himself on an improvised crutch, trudged past the first German pickets ahead of his men. The pickets were sappers from 96th Infantry Division who were already busy mining the ground in front of the new main defensive line on the northern flank of the Sinyavino Heights. They welcomed Dressel and the men of 5th Company, 287th Grenadier Regiment, who were coming from Lipka …
>
> When Dressel reported at the temporary battalion headquarters he found only Hauptmann Albrecht, the regimental adjutant, there. The battalion commander?

Missing. The battalion adjutant? Killed. Most of the company commanders were dead, missing, or wounded. The battalion was down to 80 men.

'It's no use, Dressel – anyone still able to hold a rifle must go straight into the new line,' Albrecht said.[41]

As Soviet units broke into Gorodok 5, the single battalion from the Spanish Blue Division found itself in the middle of the bitter fighting. As the German units pulled back towards the Sinyavino Heights, the Spanish soldiers tried to extricate themselves from the ruins and a company was cut off. Further south in the Soviet Union, the Germans showed extraordinary disregard for their Hungarian and Italian allies when the front line along the Don River collapsed, often pulling out without informing the units of other nationalities on their flanks; it isn't clear whether something similar happened in Gorodok 5. Regardless of the reason, much of the isolated company was destroyed before a counterattack by the rest of the battalion succeeded in linking up with the survivors. In two desperate days of combat, the Spanish battalion lost 124 men killed, and a further 400 wounded, sick, disabled by frostbite, or missing.[42]

One of the Spanish soldiers taken prisoner was taken to the headquarters of Simoniak's division. With the help of an interpreter, the intelligence officer conducted an interrogation. The soldier told his captors that he had deserted rather than simply surrendering, adding that he had been looking for such an opportunity for some time:

'I don't follow the same path as the Nazis. What am I to them? They hate everyone, both Russians and Spaniards.'

'You realised that a little late,' remarked Romanov [the intelligence officer].

The defector looked back at him. 'I'm not a Fascist,' he said. When Romanov offered him the opportunity to speak on the radio, to tell his comrades how the Russians had treated him, the Spaniard agreed immediately. 'I will. I'll tell everyone else to come over.'

[Simoniak joined the interrogation and Romanov updated him.] 'They are all strong in hindsight,' said Simoniak disbelievingly. 'They come over and begin to mutter "*Hitler kaput*" or "It wasn't me, nothing to do with me."'

'This one seems genuine. Perhaps he's also telling the truth that many soldiers of the Blue Division aren't averse to sticking their bayonets into the ground.'[43]

The account of this meeting, written by two Soviet authors after the war to describe (and eulogise) the exploits of Simoniak, is of questionable accuracy; the description of the Spanish deserter says that he brought with him a guitar with which he serenaded his captors, and it seems highly unlikely that a man caught up in the fighting in Gorodok 5 and then risking his life by crossing the devastation of no-man's land would have something as cumbersome as a guitar with him. However, there were undoubtedly many soldiers from both the Wehrmacht and the Red Army who attempted to desert. Some did it out of political conviction, others because of disillusionment with their own side, perhaps triggered by some recent event; and many – particularly new arrivals in the front line – did it in an attempt to escape the slaughter around them. Both sides made extensive use of deserters to make broadcasts, either by radio or loudspeakers, to encourage other men to cross the front line. This would take place on a far more systematic basis after the final surrender of the German Sixth Army in Stalingrad. Captured German officers were often 'asked' to write personal letters to other officers they knew, urging them to give up the fight. This may have had some impact on a few individuals, but there is little to suggest that it resulted in large-scale defections.

The news of the link-up by Leningrad and Volkhov Fronts and the German withdrawal from Shlisselburg and Lake Ladoga was greeted with jubilation in Moscow. There were immediate press and radio announcements, and President Roosevelt sent a letter to the citizens of Leningrad, recognising their ordeal during the siege. The official announcement from *Sovinformburo* rather overstated what had been achieved. For most civilians in the cities of the Soviet Union, the name of Yuri Borisovich Levitan was a familiar one, though few would have been able to identify him from a photograph. Born near the city of Vladimir some 120 miles east of Moscow, he was nicknamed *Truboi* ('Trumpet') by his school-friends on account of his deep voice. Levitan travelled to the capital aged 17 hoping to become an actor but failed to secure any roles because of his strong regional accent. Instead, he started working in a radio station as a cleaner, but rapidly progressed to becoming a trainee announcer. In 1934, having ironed out some of the oddities of his accent, he was making regular announcements on the radio and was surprised when he was told that Stalin had listened to his broadcast and had decided that Levitan was to read all of the Soviet leader's pronouncements in future.[44] As a consequence, his deep, sonorous voice – still with his Vladimir accent – became well known, and he was a natural choice to read *Sovinformburo* announcements once the war with Germany began. After the successful link-up between Leningrad and Volkhov Fronts, he delivered the news to listeners of Radio Moscow, starting with his customary announcement of '*Vnimanie, govorit Moskva!*' ('Attention, this is Moscow speaking!'). There was an element of irony in this: in order to protect Radio Moscow, Levitan and his colleagues had actually been moved from Moscow to Sverdlovsk (now reverted to its pre-Soviet name of Ekaterinburg) in the Ural Mountains.

> In recent days our troops south of Lake Ladoga commenced an offensive against the German Fascist troops blockading the city of Leningrad.
>
> Our troops were given the task of destroying the opposing defences and penetrating the ring around Leningrad.
>
> It should be remembered that the enemy spent the many months of their blockade of Leningrad turning their positions on the outskirts of the city into a powerful fortified network with an interlinked system of permanent concrete fortifications and other structures with numerous anti-tank and anti-infantry obstacles.
>
> After seven days of intense fighting, having broken through the enemy's long-established fortified zone, which was up to 14km deep, and crossing the Neva River our troops overcame exceptionally stubborn enemy resistance and occupied the town of Shlisselburg, the fortified strongpoints of Marino, Dubrovka, Lipka, Gorodoks 1, 2, 3, 4, 5, 6, 7, and 8, Sinyavino station, and Podgornaya station …
>
> During the offensive, our army destroyed the German 227th, 96th, 170th Infantry Divisions, 374th Regiment of 207th Infantry Division, 85th Infantry Regiment, 5th Motorised Division, 223rd Motorcycle Battalion, and part of 1st Infantry Division.
>
> According to incomplete data, our soldiers also took 1,261 officers and men prisoner …
>
> More than 13,000 German soldiers were left dead on the battlefield.[45]

None of the divisions listed had actually been destroyed, though they had suffered substantial losses of men and equipment. Nor had all of the listed Gorodoks and other positions been captured.

The city of Leningrad had been cut off from land contact with the rest of the Soviet Union since 8 September 1941, a period of 497 days. Millions had died in the fighting and of cold and hunger. Immediately, orders were sent to establish an all-weather road from Volkhov to Leningrad via Lipka and Shlisselburg and to lay railway tracks. By contrast to the jubilation in the Soviet Union, the German high command seemed barely to notice; the diary of *Oberkommando der Wehrmacht* ('Armed Forces High Command' or *OKW*) merely recorded that 'the enemy drove our line back in the Shlisselburg area'.[46] Far to the south, Generalfeldmarschall Friedrich Paulus' Sixth Army was entering its death throes in Stalingrad, and that sector remained the focus of German attention.

CHAPTER 4

POLYARNAYA ZVEZDA

Whilst the siege ring had been broken, *Iskra* had not achieved all of its objectives. The original concept of the operation included the capture of Sinyavino and perhaps more importantly the adjacent high ground, from where the Germans could continue to interdict the narrow connection that had been achieved by Leningrad and Volkhov Fronts. Govorov and Meretskov had intended the southern flanks of their forces to meet in the Sinyavino area but the failure of the Red Army to break the German defences to the east and west of Sinyavino had prevented this. With the Germans retreating in some disarray from Shlisselburg, there seemed to be an opportunity for the Red Army to drive south on a broad front in order to overcome resistance around Gorodok 1 and 2 in the west, Sinyavino in the centre, and the *Wengler-Nase* in the east. Along the Sinyavino Heights, German infantry tried to dig in and prepare a new defensive line, hacking at the frozen ground with whatever implements they had available, but they now had to deal with a fresh onslaught from the Soviet forces to the north. The German line now consisted of *SS-Polizei*, 21st Infantry Division, and over the following days 11th Infantry Division and 28th Jäger Division. A few battered groups of survivors from the divisions chewed up trying to hold back the Soviet attacks around Sinyavino were also still in the front-line trenches.

Turning their forces to face south and to launch fresh attacks was no easy task for Govorov and Meretskov. Much of their artillery was still in its original positions and would have to be redeployed, and moving the guns forward through the difficult terrain – where there were still numerous unmarked German minefields and other hazards, including booby traps left by the retreating Germans – was a hugely difficult task. Even if the guns could be moved, supplying their ammunition was just as difficult. Nevertheless, Zhukov urged both Front commanders to make haste. Any delay gave the Germans more time to dig in and fortify their positions. The staff officers in the headquarters of both Fronts laboured to draw up plans, aware that the assault units of Dukhanov's Sixty-Seventh Army and Romanovsky's Second Shock Army were badly weakened after the recent fighting; neither army had much left by way of its second echelon.

Dukhanov's Sixty-Seventh Army concentrated most of its strength on its western flank, intending to drive through Gorodok 1 and 2 before outflanking the German positions at Sinyavino. Thereafter, the intention was to cut road and rail links between Sinyavino and Mga; at the same time, a second assault group would attempt to push into Sinyavino from the north. Romanovsky's Second Shock Army also attempted to outflank the new German defensive line by attacking through Gorodok 7 to the east. The new phase of *Iskra* began on 20 January, and the Germans had just sufficient time to set up strong defences. The attack on Gorodok 1 and 2 made almost no headway, while the attack towards Sinyavino from the north – hitting the newest and therefore least well-established part of the German line – slowly pushed forward about a mile over several days before grinding to a halt along the northwest side of the town, where German defensive fortifications proved too strong for the depleted divisions of Sixty-Seventh Army. Second Shock Army failed to make even this much progress and secured only a modest wedge in the German defences at huge additional cost.

Fedyuninsky had positioned himself on the left flank of Second Shock Army for this new attack, in the region of the Kruglaya Grove:

Not far from the edge of the grove, the enemy noticed our vehicles and carried out a short but rather heavy artillery strike along the road. Over the noise of our engine, we didn't hear the whistle of the incoming shells and to our complete surprise they began to explode very close to us. Shrapnel damaged the engine and the car stopped.

We got out of the car. Aleksandrov, the driver, lifted the hood. The fresh, shallow craters smelled of explosives. Clods of earth thrown up by the explosions blackened the snow.

Enemy mortars then started to fire. I fell on the left side of the car, Aleksandrov on the right, and Colonel Moskovsky [one of Fedyuninsky's staff officers] ran back, his shoulders hunched and stooping low.

There were several explosions. Something hit me hard on the right thigh. At first, as almost always happens with wounds, I felt no pain, but when I tried to get up I almost lost consciousness. 'Aleksandrov, are you alive?' I called out to the driver.

'I'm wounded, Comrade General,' the driver replied, 'I can't get up.'

So we lay on the snow near the car until a medic, the adjutant, and officers from operational headquarters, who were driving behind us, arrived. They also brought Colonel Moskovsky whom they encountered on the road. The colonel was safe and sound. The driver and I were hastily bandaged and taken to the command post of Colonel [Viktor Antonovich] Verzhbitsky's [294th Rifle] division. This was just in time, because the enemy began to fire on the road once more.[1]

It was the third time that Fedyuninsky had suffered a wound in his right leg, as his long-suffering wife patiently reminded him. The first occasion was in 1920 during the Russian Civil War, and the second was in August 1939 at Khalkin Gol when fighting against the Japanese. In addition to his thigh wound, Fedyuninsky also had lacerations to his head from the shelling. He underwent surgery almost immediately, and his surgeon presented him with a jagged chunk of shrapnel, about half a square inch in area, that had been removed from his thigh. Fedyuninsky was delighted when he learned that he was being awarded the Order of Kutuzov, 1st Class, for his role in *Iskra*, but this was tempered by news of other casualties. A close friend, Lieutenant General Grigory Panteleyevich Kravchenko, was commander of 215th Fighter Division at the age of 29. His aircraft was shot down in combat and although he was seen to bale out, his parachute failed to open. Major General Nikolai Antonovich Bolotnikov, commander of Volkhov Front's tank and mechanised forces, was killed on 26 January, even as the offensive was petering out; he was discussing plans with a group of other officers when their dugout was hit by German bombs.

In addition to these senior officers, there were many others who were killed and wounded. Soviet casualties came to about 115,000 – this represented about 38 per cent of all the forces committed into the operation. German losses were far lower, with estimates ranging from 12,000 to 22,000.[2] Whilst these casualties were more than Lindemann's Eighteenth Army could afford, they were of course a fraction of the losses suffered by the Red Army. And although the siege ring was broken, the German presence in Sinyavino meant that the narrow corridor that had been secured at such a high cost could come under German bombardment at any time. If the siege of Leningrad was to be lifted in full, the Germans had to be driven away from Sinyavino as a prelude to being forced back along the entire siege front line.

As was consistently the case with Red Army operations, there was an attempt to analyse the manner in which *Iskra* unfolded, to try to learn from the recent battle. The overall conclusions were clear. Although the siege ring had been broken, it had been at huge cost in terms of men and materiel. Moreover, the operation was an incomplete success: the continued presence of the Germans on the Sinyavino Heights threatened the limited corridor along the shore of Lake Ladoga through Shlisselburg with artillery fire, and there was always a possibility that the Wehrmacht might try to restore its positions by a thrust towards the north from Sinyavino.

There were several positive aspects of the operation. The assault had been made through dense German defences, and in the case of Leningrad Front had been further complicated by the requirement to cross the frozen Neva River. In some sectors at least, the massive use of artillery was effective, at least in allowing the assault troops to penetrate the first line of German defences. The volume of ammunition used by the gunners was immense: Second Shock Army recorded that its batteries used up 630,000 artillery and mortar rounds in the first week of the operation. But in other sectors, the visually impressive bombardment had comparatively little effect. Sometimes, the German bunkers and fortifications were too strongly built to suffer serious damage, and in other cases they simply hadn't been identified with sufficient accuracy. This was especially true once the Soviet troops penetrated the first German line, suggesting that identification of German positions had been primarily based upon direct observation. Secondary defensive positions, hidden from direct line of sight when the operation began, were harder to detect, and although Soviet accounts repeatedly mention the abundance of aerial reconnaissance photographs, these were almost certainly inferior in terms of quality to the images routinely gathered by the Luftwaffe.

The use of tanks was also of variable quality. Simoniak's rifle division was given exemplary support by 61st Tank Brigade in the slow grind through the German defences to Gorodok 5, but most Soviet tank units rigidly adhered to their orders and pressed on into the German positions without any regard for whether the accompanying infantry was able to keep up. Skilful use of machine-guns and mortars by the German defenders often succeeded in driving the Red Army's riflemen to cover, and the tank crews were usually unaware that this was happening as they almost always went into combat with all their hatches closed. Once they were without their infantry support, the tanks – forced to move slowly through the tangle of obstacles in the German defences, or immobilised on the numerous minefields – became easy prey for German infantrymen with demolition charges.

Compared to earlier operations, one aspect of *Iskra* performed very effectively: the Luftwaffe was unable to make any major intervention in the fighting.

Deployment of Stuka squadrons close to the front line had often resulted in timely intervention in earlier Soviet offensives. But during *Iskra*, the weather was often too poor for either side to fly many missions, and on the few clear days the Soviet fighter units were able to ensure local air superiority most of the time. This exposed a particular weakness: many German bombers, particularly the Stuka but also some of the twin-engined bombers, were obsolescent and were vulnerable in air-to-air combat. Their continued usefulness on the Eastern Front was to a large extent a reflection of the sheer scale of the front line, permitting the Germans to fly operations with little risk of interception, and the relatively poor performance of Soviet fighter units. As the war progressed, these fighters began to perform more effectively, though they continued to fall far short of the standard set by Luftwaffe fighter pilots and those of the Western Powers.

In addition to looking at how the Red Army had performed, analysts also gave recommendations about changes in equipment. On many occasions in 1942 and early 1943, including the successful encirclement of the German Sixth Army at Stalingrad, Soviet infantrymen had been used in initial attacks with the expectation that they would be able to breach enemy defences, after which tanks would be let loose to advance deep into the rear. However, the infantry attacks repeatedly stalled and at least a portion of the tanks being held back as exploitation forces had to be committed to assist the initial breakthrough. Drawing on observations of the German use of assault guns – tank chassis with guns housed in a turretless body and deployed to give infantry units mobile armoured support – the Red Army had already started to field similar weapons and there was now a decision to increase the provision of assault guns, as Meretskov described:

> By the beginning of the second winter campaign, there was already a positive experience of using experimental self-propelled guns and a decision was made to try their use on a mass scale. And at the end of January 1943, Volkhov Front was one of the first to use a new weapon on a large scale: two regiments of self-propelled guns assisted the infantry and tanks in attacks on complex enemy positions that were difficult to penetrate.[3]

The first self-propelled or assault guns in the Red Army's arsenal were rushed into production when war with Germany broke out, but were built in limited numbers partly due to the dislocation of Soviet industry while factories were relocated to the east and partly because of the need to produce other vehicles. For example, the ZiS-30, weighing just four tons, was an effective vehicle with a 57mm gun but only 100 were produced. As the relocated factories began to increase their output during 1942, it became possible to start the construction of newer assault guns. After some initial experimental vehicles, the SU-122 – a T-34 chassis with a 122mm howitzer in an enclosed hull – began trials in November and entered production a month later. It was a big vehicle, weighing 30 tons, but the lighter SU-76 made its appearance in the same month. It was built on an extended version of the chassis of the light T-70 tank and armed with a 76mm gun in an open housing. This made it vulnerable to mortar fire, but weighing a little over ten tons, it was a highly mobile vehicle and would ultimately be produced in larger numbers than any Soviet armoured vehicle other than the T-34. Both of these assault guns began to appear in increasing numbers in the front line in early 1943, but their deployment continued to be plagued by a recurring theme with Soviet combined arms warfare: there was poor coordination between vehicles and infantry, often resulting in them becoming separated during attacks.

The breaking of the siege ring around Leningrad was a great achievement, but potentially war-winning battles were being fought at the other end of the Eastern Front. On 26 January, the Soviet units attacking the besieged German Sixth Army in Stalingrad broke the German units into two pockets. A further splitting took place two days later. With tens of thousands of sick and wounded men and almost all remaining soldiers suffering from the effects of starvation and exposure to the weather, Friedrich Paulus – commander of Sixth Army – notified the German high command that his men were at the end of their strength. Hitler's response was to promote him to Generalfeldmarschall, in the expectation that he would thus feel unable to surrender and would either continue fighting or would commit suicide. The southern and central of the three pockets were overrun by Soviet troops on 31 January and Paulus and his staff went into captivity, and the northern pocket finally succumbed on 4 February.

The commander of the last units to lay down their arms in Stalingrad was General Karl Strecker. During the early years of the rise of the Nazis, he was a supporter of Hitler, but privately expressed grave reservations about the anti-Jewish policies of the new regime. Despite this he commanded numerous formations before finally leading XI Corps in Stalingrad. When his men laid down their weapons, a final signal was sent to the distant headquarters from where Hitler attempted to run the war. The official diary of *OKW* recorded the text of the message:

> With its six divisions, XI Corps has fulfilled its duties in the heaviest fighting to the very last. Long live the Führer! Long Live Germany! [Signed] Strecker.[4]

This was inaccurate. Almost certainly as a deliberate act, Strecker left out the expected words *Es lebe der Führer!* This sentence was added by staff at *OKW* in order to appease Hitler.

Meanwhile, the German defensive line stretching north towards Army Group Centre had collapsed entirely. The Romanian armies on either side of Stalingrad were effectively broken by *Uranus*, the initial Soviet encirclement operation; the Italians a little to the north were smashed first by *Malyi Saturn* ('Little Saturn'), the downsized follow-on operation in December, and then by the Ostrogozhsk–Rossosh Operation in mid-January, which also destroyed the Hungarian forces a little further north. In the last week of January, the German Second Army, immediately to the north of the sector that had collapsed during the Ostrogozhsk–Rossosh Operation, was also overwhelmed and driven back in disarray near Voronezh, and by the end of the month the Red Army was planning further attacks. *Skachok* ('Gallop') followed on in the last two days of the month from the Ostrogozhsk–Rossosh Operation without a break and was intended to overrun the northern parts of Donbas, while *Svezda* ('Star') would see the Red Army advance to and beyond Kharkov.[5] Ultimately, both of these operations were brought to an end by a highly effective German counteroffensive that restored the front line along the Northern Donets River, but as *Iskra* drew to a close this stabilisation was still in the future, and there was every expectation in Soviet circles that the comprehensive defeat of the Wehrmacht was imminent. If any of the advancing Red Army units could break through to the Sea of Azov, the Black Sea, or the lower Dnepr, German forces in southeast Ukraine would be cut off in an encirclement just as great as Stalingrad. Recovery from one such disaster was possible; two such catastrophes would leave Germany unable to continue the war. A sentence began to be repeated frequently amongst Soviet commanders: 'You cannot stop an army that achieved Stalingrad.'[6]

It was against this background that the Soviet armies in the far north began their preparations for further operations. The bitter fighting in and around Shlisselburg and the surrounding strongpoints might have resulted in terrible Soviet casualties but it had also weakened the divisions of the German Eighteenth Army; moreover, the need to move troops to Sinyavino to create a new front line and to permit the extraction of *Gruppe Hühner* meant that the other sectors covered by Lindemann's army were now relatively thinly manned. The transfer of an entire regiment of the Spanish Blue Division, for example, resulted in the other two regiments being left to hold a sector of 13 miles. The situation on the eastern flank was even worse, with three understrength infantry divisions each occupying about 33 miles of front line. Finally, there was recognition that

Eighteenth Army had used up almost all of the reserve units available to all of Army Group North. With its strength now concentrated in its central sector, it seemed to Soviet planners that it was ripe for attacks on its flanks. Just as there had been repeated encirclements in the far south, Zhukov, Meretskov, and Govorov now began to contemplate achieving a similar outcome in the north.

The German forces concentrated in the Sinyavino area became known to Soviet commanders as the Mga–Sinyavino Grouping. Govorov and Meretskov had already informed *Stavka* of their preliminary thoughts about attempting to pinch off this German concentration, and in mid-January – when *Iskra* had only just commenced and success was no means guaranteed – there was a proposal for an additional offensive, this time from immediately to the south of Lake Ilmen. Here, to the south of Meretskov's armies, the Soviet line was under the control of Northwest Front under the command of Marshal Semen Konstantinovich Timoshenko, an old Civil War crony of Stalin. To date, his performance during the current war had been at best variable and he was largely responsible for the disaster that overtook the Red Army near Kharkov in the summer of 1942. He had been in command of Northwest Front since October 1942; his northern boundary was Lake Ilmen, and the southern limit was the city of Kholm. Between these, the Germans held a prominent salient projecting to the east around the city of Demyansk. This had been the scene of bitter fighting in the first half of 1942, when two German corps were encircled until late April. Even after contact with the encircled units was restored, Hitler refused to evacuate the salient, stating that it was too valuable as a springboard for future offensive operations.

In mid-January, as *Iskra* was beginning, Timoshenko submitted plans for an offensive operation by his forces. After all, if the Germans were heavily committed in the Leningrad sector and struggling to rebuild their lines in eastern Ukraine, surely there existed an opportunity to eliminate the Demyansk salient by pinching it off at its neck – a region known to the Red Army as the 'Rumashevo corridor' – and then launch a powerful thrust towards the northwest. Northwest Front had substantial forces at its disposal; it possessed five combined arms armies and an air army, and in addition a separate group – 'Special Group of Colonel-General Khozin' – was available consisting of a combined arms army and First Tank Army, the latter led by Major General (about to be promoted to Lieutenant General) Mikhail Yefimovich Katukov. With a long history of serving in the Soviet Union's armoured forces, the redoubtable Katukov was one of the very few senior officers to emerge from Zhukov's catastrophically costly Operation *Mars* around the Rzhev salient; commanding III Mechanised Corps, he managed

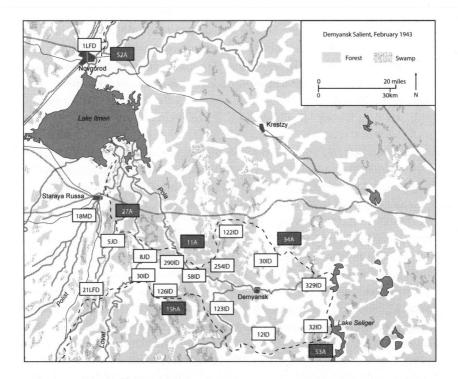

to penetrate the salient's northwest area, advancing through a near-impossible landscape of dense forests and frozen swamps around the Luchesa River. In the process, he inflicted substantial casualties on the *Grossdeutschland* Division and the ground he gained was the only area that the Germans didn't recapture in their counterattacks at the end of the battle. He was about to be promoted to lieutenant general and was highly respected by both his subordinates and his contemporaries. Sergei Matveyevich Shtemenko, who served as a senior staff officer in *Stavka* for most of the war, wrote after the end of hostilities:

> [Katukov] is a real soldier and a great expert on the combat training and tactics of armoured forces. The tank brigade which he commanded in the Battle of Moscow was the first in the Soviet Army to receive the Guards title. Katukov was on the battlefield from the first to the last day of the Great Patriotic War.[7]

The commander of the other formation – Sixty-Eighth Army – in Special Group Khozin was also a rising star of the Red Army. Major General (imminently to be promoted to Lieutenant General) Fedor Ivanovich Tolbukhin was at first sight an unlikely figure; he was a tall, slightly overweight man with heavy jowls and a substantial double chin. Born in 1894, he was rather older than many other army commanders, and his temperament was also rather different from the ruthless bullying of Zhukov or the sharp, confident assertiveness of Katukov. Sergei Semenovich Biriuzov, who would later serve as Tolbukhin's chief of staff at the headquarters of Fourth Ukrainian Front, wrote after the war:

> [Tolbukhin] gave the impression of being a very kind person. Subsequently, I had the opportunity to discover this for myself, as well as another quality that was very characteristic of Tolbukhin – his outward equanimity and calmness. I don't remember a single occasion when he lost his temper.[8]

Others remarked that unlike men like Zhukov, Tolbukhin repeatedly showed great concern for the lives of his men, urging all his subordinates not to waste lives in mass attacks.

The commander of the Special Group was in most respects far less illustrious and highly regarded than his two impressive subordinate commanders. Mikhail Semenovich Khozin, promoted to colonel general in mid-January, was the son of a railway worker and was apprenticed as a railwayman after he left school. After serving as a junior officer in the First World War he returned to railway work but then joined the Red Army and was involved in fighting against anti-Bolshevik 'bandits' in the Caucasus region. He survived Stalin's purges of the Red Army unscathed and became commander of Fifty-Fourth Army in Leningrad in September 1941. At the time, Fedyuninsky had been appointed commander of Leningrad Front but managed to persuade *Stavka* that he should swap roles with Khozin, citing the latter's greater experience of high-level command. This new appointment was a difficult enough task but was made even more complex when Leningrad and Volkhov Fronts were briefly combined in early 1942. After the disaster of the Lyuban Offensive, which resulted in the encirclement and destruction of Second Shock Army, Khozin was dismissed as commander of Leningrad Front. The order removing him from his post stated:

> [He is dismissed] for failure to comply with the orders of *Stavka* for the timely and rapid withdrawal of the troops of Second Shock Army, for his overly bureaucratic methods of command and control of his troops, [and] for allowing his troops to become separated as a result of which the enemy cut the communications of Second Shock Army and put it in an exceptionally difficult situation.[9]

There were multiple errors that led to the encirclement of Second Shock Army, and singling out Khozin in this manner was unjust. But to make matters worse, he was then sent to Western Front where he commanded Thirty-Third Army before becoming deputy commander of the Front in October 1942. In this role he was one of the main commanders in the disastrous Operation *Mars*, and although blame for the bloody failure rested fair and square on the shoulders of Zhukov, Khozin was one of those punished. On this occasion, his dismissal stated that he had an overly passive and 'frivolous' attitude to his role. Such repeated failures might have ended his career, but two factors worked in his favour. Firstly, the Red Army's successes around Stalingrad created a widespread impression in higher Soviet circles that the tide had turned and Germany would soon be defeated; and secondly, Stalin seems to have become increasingly aware that the Soviet Union would have to fight the war with the personnel it had, regardless of their strengths and weaknesses. Despite the criticism directed at Khozin, he was promoted in January and given a new command.

Timoshenko thus had substantial forces at his disposal, and at least at army level they were well led. Over the following days, Timoshenko's proposal evolved into a detailed plan. The first phase would see an attack against the base of the Demyansk salient by First Shock Army from the south and Twenty-Seventh Army from the north. Special Group Khozin would then be inserted into the battle, exploiting towards the northwest. After the southwest corner of Lake Ilmen was reached, Volkhov Front's most southern formation, Fifty-Second Army, would join the offensive by advancing past the northern edge of Novgorod while Group Khozin pressed on towards Luga. The directive issued by *Stavka* in early February went on to describe ongoing operations:

> After capturing Luga and Strugi Krasnye [41 miles to the southwest of Luga], part of the group's forces will secure the area of Kingisepp and Narva, cutting the enemy's line of retreat to Estonia.
>
> In cooperation with Volkhov and Leningrad Fronts, the main forces will encircle and destroy the enemy's Volkhov and Leningrad groupings.[10]

The cutting of the narrow neck of the Demyansk salient would require the Red Army's pincers collectively to cover a distance of just 15 miles, but the advance by Group Khozin was on an entirely different scale. Luga, the first objective, was 95 miles away, and continuing to Narva meant a further march of 75 miles. There were few good roads through this relatively flat region, which like so much of the general area was covered in dense forests and crisscrossed by numerous small waterways, many with surrounding swamps. In order to be in a position to assist Special Group Khozin with its advance, Leningrad and Volkhov Fronts were to conduct a pincer attack to meet at Tosno, isolating the central concentration of the German Eighteenth Army in Mga and Sinyavino. Thereafter, the two Fronts would attack towards the southwest where they would meet up with the advancing units of Northwest Front. The convergent attack against the Mga–Sinyavino concentration of Lindemann's Eighteenth Army would commence before Timoshenko's operation; it was expected that this would draw in whatever modest reserves remained in Army Group North, leaving the German Sixteenth Army further south to fend for itself.

As planning developed, the inclusion of Volkhov and Leningrad Fronts in the operation – now codenamed *Polyarnaya Zvezda* ('Pole Star') – meant that as was often the case with such major undertakings, a representative of *Stavka* was appointed to oversee all aspects of the coming battle. Zhukov, who had been breathing down the necks of army and even division commanders during *Iskra*, was given the task of managing what – if it was successful – would be the destruction of the entire German Army Group North. There would also be major attacks by Red Army forces in the central sector, towards Smolensk, largely growing out of the belief that the disastrous situation for the Wehrmacht in the far south would result in a rapid collapse of its positions elsewhere. There also seems to have been a large degree of 'planning by map' without much regard for the realities of the terrain where the operation would unfold, especially with the additional problems caused by attempting such a major advance in midwinter. Sustaining logistic operations for the first phase, the advance to Luga, would be a huge challenge for the Red Army; to expect it to continue operations all the way to the Narva River and the Baltic coast was optimism bordering on fantasy. Zhukov's repeated failed attacks against the Rzhev salient in 1942 showed a similar belief that the relatively modest distances indicated on maps could be covered without difficulty; it seems that he had learned little from those mistakes. As was the case with his involvement in *Mars*, Zhukov's memoirs are highly misleading in connection with *Polyarnaya Zvezda*, giving only a brief mention of how the offensive finally came to a halt. There is certainly no acknowledgement of his prolonged presence in the region and his instrumental role in planning and overseeing the operation.

In Leningrad, there continued to be intermittent artillery and air attacks by the Germans. A year before, the population had been in the grip of devastating and lethal food shortages as well as suffering one of the coldest winters on record with little or no fuel to heat their homes. Although food remained tightly rationed in early 1943, the situation was very different. Running water had been restored to much of the city, greatly improving sanitation, and sufficient stockpiles of firewood and coal had been built up before the winter to prevent some of the problems endured in early 1942. The weather was also less inclement and rarely reached the lows of 1941–42, and morale was greatly boosted by the news from Stalingrad. The two cities had become inextricably associated with each other in the minds of the population of the Soviet Union, and Leningraders had watched the defiant resistance of the Soviet Sixty-Second Army in the ruins of the city on the Volga with anxiety and hope – if the Red Army could hold onto its diminished positions in Stalingrad while Leningrad held out in the north, the Germans would be defied at either extreme of the long front line. The surrender of German forces in Stalingrad in late January and early February 1943 led to widespread celebration and jubilation across the Soviet Union, but perhaps especially in Leningrad. This news coincided with a further welcome development: the hard-working engineers of the army and railways opened a small rail link along the southern shore of Lake Ladoga, through the area recently captured in *Iskra*. The railway was in easy artillery range of German guns, but on 2 February the first train, driven by Aleksandr Mikhailov, ventured forth at walking pace. Much of the new railway ran along an elevated section stretching for about three-quarters of a mile and Mikhailov edged forward across the wooden bridge; although the structure creaked under the weight of the train, it remained intact. The following day, there was further good news as the city authorities announced a modest increase in the daily rations.[11] The first train bringing freight into Leningrad made a perilous journey on 7 February, coming under artillery fire but getting through unscathed. As if to remind the citizens of Leningrad that the Wehrmacht remained at their gates, there was particularly heavy shelling on 9 February. The German ring around Leningrad might have been broken, but the siege was by no means over.

The naval rifle brigade in which Morozov was serving as an artillery officer had been ordered to attack the Sinyavino Heights on 7 February but the assault was called off due to blizzard conditions. An attack the following day was rapidly stopped by heavy defensive fire; a frustrated Morozov could only record that the recent heavy snowfall had made it impossible to identify the German positions properly for his gunners to be assigned targets. To add insult to injury, the Germans now identified the positions of Morozov's guns and subjected his batteries to a heavy counter-bombardment, resulting in many casualties. As a result of its losses, the naval brigade was unable to join the main attack when *Polarnaya Zvezda* began.

The northern part of the new operation commenced on 10 February, with Major General Vladimir Petrovich Sviridov's Fifty-Fifth Army making an attack from the most southerly sector of Leningrad Front, between Pushkin and Kolpino. As had been the case with *Iskra*, the assault was preceded by heavy artillery fire, which continued for two hours. The Spanish soldiers of the Blue Division endured much of the initial assault. In anticipation of a Soviet attack, they had prepared three distinct defensive lines and the most northern set of trenches was rapidly overwhelmed. But sufficient numbers of men managed to pull back to the second line; although they weren't able to set up a continuous defensive line, they stubbornly held onto their strongpoints and prevented the main thrust of Sviridov's army from penetrating further. On this occasion as on many others, the Blue Division defied German stereotypical views on the reliability of Spanish troops in such warfare. But there were cases of Spanish soldiers taking the opportunity to surrender when it arose, as the company commander Dushevsky later recalled:

About 70–80m ahead of us there were, it seemed, six horses, a haystack, a sled, and three guns hidden in the bushes. Not in firing positions, but simply camouflaged. And there were no sentries. We could see closer to the embankment, about 10–15m from us, a pipe sticking out with smoke rising from it. It was a dugout. Although it was large, its roof wasn't reinforced. So if a shell had hit it, it would have broken right through. I took out a grenade, removed the protective cover from another pipe from which no smoke was emerging, and dropped the grenade down it. There was an explosion inside [the dugout], some noise and movement. But they didn't come out. I threw down a second. Smoke came out. We began to move on, leaving two men. You never knew whether there was another exit. Then a rifle with a bayonet was stuck out of the door, with a white rag attached …

We didn't know that we were facing the Spaniards. There was a rumour that Franco had given Hitler his best division. It wasn't there in its entirety. Perhaps a regiment or two, who knows?

Well, here they were, wearing a mixture of caps and jackets, with shoes on their feet. We were in short fur coats, quilted trousers and felt boots. We had hats with earflaps, and mittens. As they emerged I asked, 'How many of you are there?' They showed eight fingers. They began to line up in twos, their rifles stacked to one side.

Then one came up to me with a scrap of paper. '*Rus, Rus*, Communist!' I pushed him and he fell down. Others helped him up and shouted, 'Communist, Communist! Two years Communist!'

I asked: 'Are there any Fascists?' They pointed at three men. I ordered my messengers to take them to the Special Department [i.e. the NKVD] ...

We took 71 prisoners in that dugout. Among them were infantrymen and artillerymen.[12]

As the day progressed, German aircraft were able to intervene and provided valuable support for the men of the Blue Division, and elements of the German 212th and 215th Infantry Divisions arrived as reinforcements.

Simoniak's 63rd Guards Rifle Division, partially replenished with fresh drafts, was in the forefront of the attack on its eastern flank. The original plan for the attack involved most of the tanks assigned to support Simoniak's riflemen being deployed on his right flank, as the ground was a little more open in this area, but the Germans too had anticipated this and had positioned strong anti-tank defences to cover the open ground. Somewhat to Simoniak's surprise, it was his left flank to the east that made better progress and rapidly approached the eastern edge of Krasnyi Bor. By the end of the day, the village was in Soviet hands. Progress was limited to less than two miles, but in the context of the recent fighting a little to the north this represented an encouraging gain on the first day. As darkness fell across the battlefield, Simoniak received a welcome message: along with several other soldiers, he had been awarded the title Hero of the Soviet Union. In view of the gains, Sviridov ordered his mobile exploitation forces – mainly a modest number of ski battalions supported by a few tanks – to move forward.

Further to the east, Volkhov Front also commenced its attack with a view to linking up with Leningrad Front behind the German concentration in Sinyavino. The German lines were held by 69th Infantry Division, part of XXVIII Corps, and it came under attack from four Soviet rifle divisions supported by a tank brigade and two independent rifle brigades from Lieutenant General Aleksandr Vasilyevich Sukhomlin's Fifty-Fourth Army. Numerically, the Red Army had a huge advantage, but the Germans were occupying well-constructed defences. The heavy snowfall of the previous week made conditions even more difficult than they had been during *Iskra* – the attacking infantry had to struggle through deep drifts, which often hid barbed wire and other German obstacles, and the tanks accompanying the attack were often left stranded when they blundered into hidden trenches. Volkhov Front's four attacking divisions laboured forward,

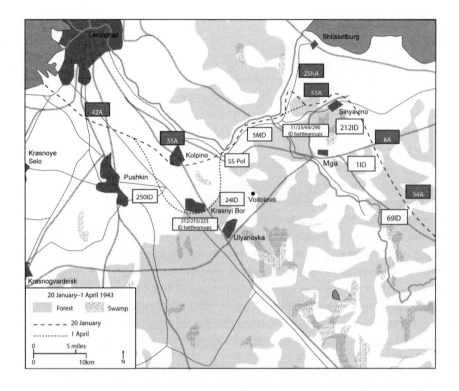

losing men as accurate German artillery fire fell on their ranks – the likely routes by which the Soviet troops would advance had been anticipated and carefully mapped out. A few modest gains were made, but the German lines remained largely intact.

By early 1943, the partisan movement was active across almost all of the occupied regions of the Soviet Union. In some areas – particularly the Baltic States, the eastern parts of Poland that had been occupied by the Red Army in 1939, and parts of Ukraine – there were complicating factors caused by the presence of significant anti-Bolshevik groups, but there was growing resistance to German occupation everywhere. Even in Ukraine, where memories of the terrible famine of the 1930s – deliberately worsened by Stalin's orders – were widespread, the partisans were becoming more assertive. A grim joke circulated in the cities and towns of Ukraine. Hitler was evidently stronger than Stalin, people told each other. Stalin had tried in vain for a decade to persuade Ukrainians to love him by killing them, but after a year of Hitler trying to kill them, the Ukrainians now loved Stalin. In addition to irregular warfare against German rear area units and acts of sabotage, blowing up railway lines and bridges, cutting telephone lines, etc, the partisans also served a valuable role gathering intelligence about German troop movements. There had been little opportunity for the partisans in the Leningrad sector to engage in open warfare against the Germans during *Iskra* due to the sheer density of Wehrmacht positions and massive repression during 1942, but intelligence gathering remained a valuable activity and Meretskov later described that the local partisan strength around Mga amounted to four brigades.[13] In order to support the new operation, there was an increase in partisan activity – south of Mga, there was more space in which the partisans could operate. Inevitably, this increased activity resulted in further reprisals by the Germans. Even as Leningrad Front's troops seized Krasnyi Bor, German troops entered a village not far from the front line where they suspected that the partisans had received help. On some occasions, these suspicions were based upon observation of partisan movements or reports from collaborators, but on others the reprisals against local people were arbitrary. The population of the village was rounded up and stood helplessly as their homes were set ablaze. Soviet accounts describe how 61 villagers were shot and a further 25 were locked in buildings that were then set alight. Inevitably, with so many men either serving in the Red Army or taken away by the Germans as forced labourers, most of the victims were women and children.[14]

The recent fighting during *Iskra* had effectively used up all of the reserves available to the German Eighteenth Army, and Küchler at Army Group North had no additional troops to spare. The commander of LIV Corps, facing Leningrad Front, was Hilpert, and he was now given control not only of the hard-pressed divisions in the front line, but also the various battlegroups that Lindemann and Küchler were able to scrape together. These were to be used to strengthen the defences on both sides of the salient stretching north to Sinyavino and consisted of a variety of units. Several infantry divisions along the Volkhov River were required to release up to a third of their strength to create these new battlegroups, while others were formed around the fragmented formations that were extracted from Shlisselburg. Since the end of January, the cluster of fragmented units in the region – a mixture of the remnants of units that had been in combat throughout *Iskra* and improvised formations scraped together from rear area personnel – had been under Hilpert's supervision and was known as *Gruppe Hilpert*. The ability of the Wehrmacht both to improvise battlegroups and then to organise corps-level command and control was a feature that would be seen repeatedly in the months that lay ahead, and is indicative of the expertise and training of German staff officers who organised these groups and the junior officers who led them with energy and skill. These skills were now vital for the survival of the German forces all along the Eastern Front. But the necessity for such improvisation also underlined the growing difficulty faced by the Wehrmacht in defending its long front line in the face of constant casualties and inadequate replacements.

Over the next two days, both Leningrad and Volkhov Fronts attempted to move forward, largely in vain. The steady trickle of battlegroups arriving for use by *Gruppe Hilpert* allowed the Germans to shore up their defences wherever they came under serious pressure and Leningrad Front made almost no further headway. The long-range artillery of the Wehrmacht also intervened in the fighting, turning its fire from bombardments of Leningrad to shelling the Soviet units struggling to advance; with the shells following a trajectory that carried them from the German gun batteries facing the southern outskirts of Leningrad towards the southeast, many Red Army soldiers feared that these rounds were actually being fired by their own guns and were erroneously falling short. Major General Georgy Pavlovich Romanov, a member of the military council of Fifty-Fifth Army, dismissed Krasnov, the commander of 45th Guards Rifle Division, which was operating on the eastern flank of Simoniak's 63rd Guards Rifle Division – although Krasnov's men had captured the village of Mishino on the first day, they made no further progress and Romanov accused him of being insufficiently forceful. Krasnov was unwell at the time and the criticism was unreasonable in view of Krasnov's previously brutal implementation of orders to attack, not least in that Romanov had enjoyed a political career and had no personal experience of commanding large numbers of troops in combat. Krasnov's replacement was Major General Savely Mikhailovich Putilov. The change in command personnel made little difference and the division remained unable to advance.

Until the days immediately preceding the new offensive operation, the weather had been less cold than the preceding winter, but temperatures plummeted for several days, with heavy fresh snowfall. Then, on 11 February, there was an unexpected warmer spell and much of the new snow melted. Terrain that had been difficult for combat now became impossible as everything disappeared into a morass of mud and slush. After three days of heavy fighting, Sviridov's Fifty-Fifth Army had advanced no more than three miles and had suffered more than 10,000 casualties. Almost all of its tanks had also been destroyed. On the other side of the German salient that projected north to Sinyavino, Sukhomlin's Fifty-Fourth Army was also approaching exhaustion. Its maximum advance was also just three miles, far short of the distance required to meet up with Leningrad Front.

Despite its tenacious defence, the Spanish Blue Division was once more the target of German criticism. On 11 February there were unfounded reports that the Spaniards had abandoned their positions when they came under artillery fire and Lindemann considered pulling the division out of the front line and replacing it with German troops; however, there were few troops to hand. Only a single weak Luftwaffe field division was available, and after its first appearance on the front line in late 1942 it had already demonstrated its weakness and unsuitability for front-line combat. The Spanish division was left in place and Lindemann was grudgingly forced to revise his assessment, writing in a report that the division had fought 'heroically'.[15]

Hoping that the assaults on the flank of the German salient would force the defenders to draw off some of the forces concentrated around Sinyavino, Sixty-Seventh and Second Shock Armies attacked from the north on 12 February, concentrating their forces on their western and eastern flanks respectively. This led Sixty-Seventh Army's forces to try once again to overrun Gorodok 1 and 2, where so many men had died in the preceding weeks. Over the following week, the ruins once more saw scenes of combat in appalling conditions as the Red Army edged forward. The two villages were finally secured by the Red Army on 17 February and the front line reached Arbuzovo. A little to the east, the northern slope of the Sinyavino Heights was held by *Gruppe Hühner*, the battered remnants of the two battlegroups that had extracted the German forces from Shlisselburg; despite their substantial losses, the Germans continued to beat off every attack, not least because the main Soviet effort was on the flanks of the Sinyavino position.

Morozov's gunners joined the bombardment of German positions on the Sinyavino Heights, hoping that the arrival of fresh mortar regiments would help tip the balance in their favour, but when the naval rifle brigade attacked it enjoyed no more success than before. It seemed that here at least, artillery – the Soviet 'god of war' – was unable to achieve much success. Even where units had sufficient guns and mortars, shortages of ammunition were now having a limiting effect. By contrast, German artillery seemed to be more effective. In addition to using their firepower to smash Soviet attacks, the Germans were also achieving considerable success in their bombardment of Soviet positions that had been identified by reconnaissance flights, radio intercepts, and visual reconnaissance, as Morozov grimly recorded:

The firepower [of the new mortar regiments] was considerable. At first we were delighted, but our hopes were immediately crushed. On the day of battle, these regiments received only a meagre supply of ammunition: eight to twelve mortar bombs per mortar.

'We'll have to try to take Sinyavino with our bare hands again,' said Major [Sergei Nikolayevich] Kapustin [chief of staff of the naval rifle brigade's artillery] in an unhappy voice when the officers dispersed from our command dugout.

On the morning of 13 February, after a short artillery preparation, two battalions of our brigade attacked Sinyavino. The planned air attacks didn't take place due to non-flying weather. The companies were driven to ground by a strong enemy barrage and after taking losses began to crawl back. The same fate befell our neighbours. This failure discouraged us.

'The infantry suffers heavy losses and we, the gods of war, can't suppress the enemy in any way whatever,' said Kapustin angrily.

'Since we didn't take Sinyavino, we'll have a reputation as poor gods,' I replied.

The next day we repeated the attack – and again without success. The enemy held fast to his key positions. I was summoned to report to the army's chief of artillery, Major General [Dmitry Dmitriyevich] Kalashnikov. We drove up to the artillery headquarters, located in a series of dugouts made in the embankment of a canal. The sudden whistle of heavy shells drove my driver and me to take cover. When the roar of explosions ceased, I saw a heap of shattered logs: it was Kalashnikov's dugout. A great officer had been killed.

The counter-battery group attacked the enemy batteries with fire raids, seeking to avenge the death of the general. After these raids, the enemy guns seemed to fall silent for a day.

Throughout the next week, units of the brigade acted only in small groups, attacking individual firing points.[16]

At the eastern end of the German line around Sinyavino was the *Wengler-Nase*, and here too the defences held out against the renewed attacks. The brief thaw was replaced by plunging temperatures that brought further snowstorms, adding to the difficulties and misery of both sides. The attacks by Sixty-Seventh Army might have succeeded in overrunning the German defences at Gorodok 1 and 2, the nearby hospital, and 8th GRES, thus eliminating the small neck of ground held by the Germans to the north of the old Neva bridgehead, but their counterparts in Second Shock Army made no progress whatsoever; Wengler's defiant infantry continued to hold their positions amidst the tree-stumps, peat bogs, and frozen swamps.

Elsewhere, greatly diminished German units were grouped together to try to create formations strong enough to mount meaningful counterattacks. One such battlegroup was nominally part of 121st Infantry Division's 405th Grenadier Regiment, but included men from several units. Its commander, Hauptmann Löffelholz, wrote an account of a typical counterattack:

> At 0840 the attack spearhead reached the bed of the stream against the strongest and most bitterly defending enemy … [There was] an attack against our right flank from the east at 0830. The enemy kept pressing on. My 2nd Squadron was penetrated at two points and cut off from the spearhead. Contact was restored with a counterthrust. 0845: the enemy attacked Jänisch's position in the spearhead from the left with numerous waves [of infantry] and three tanks. The squadron managed to hold on. Jänisch was wounded twice. But he stayed in post, and was killed later. The enemy overran the remnants of the squadron and pushed on … Losses were at least 50 per cent. The sapper platoon had six survivors out of 35 men. Individual units no longer existed. Our weapons in the spearhead had to be abandoned when they failed. The ammunition situation was very tight. Every man had to be used in repeated close-quarter combat. All communications were destroyed or unusable due to casualties.[17]

Preparations began for a further attempt by Colonel Nikolai Vasilyevich Simonov's naval rifle brigade to storm the Sinyavino Heights from the east. Reinforcements arrived for the assault troops including additional artillery formations, but ammunition remained in short supply. In an attempt to improve fire support, Morozov organised some of his howitzers into a *Gruppoy Divizionnoy Podderzhki Pekhoty* ('Infantry Division Support Group' or *DPP* group) under the command of Captain Zhitnik, who had formerly commanded the brigade's anti-tank guns:

> When drawing up the fire plan, we again had to wrestle with two insoluble problems: the limited number of shells and the paucity of intelligence on the enemy, especially about his main positions in Sinyavino itself and on the heights. We also had to consider how to suppress the enemy artillery, although this task was assigned to the army's counter-battery group. Our concern was that according to our limited intelligence reports, a significant part of the enemy artillery had changed their positions. The enemy was also making widespread use of so-called sighting guns [to allow gunners to calculate the correct range], placed at some distance from the rest of the guns of their batteries. This of course made the task of our sound and optical locating equipment much more difficult. Aerial reconnaissance of enemy batteries was not carried out – heavy leaden clouds and snowfall constantly interfered with flights.

In the morning of 22 February, the cannonade thundered once more – a two-hour artillery preparation began. The entire plain as far as the shore of Lake Ladoga was covered with haze and the flashes of gun barrels. A veil of smoke hung over the Sinyavino Heights.

'There's a lot of artillery, maybe 150 guns, but the fire is still rather weak,' said Simonov unhappily without lowering his binoculars. 'It's always bad when there aren't enough shells. And we don't have any *Katyushas* or aviation. It's going to be difficult for the infantry. Tanks can't move up there and without them there won't be any success – just casualties!'

Green flares soared towards the clouds and slowly descended, being extinguished in the grey smoke. The artillery fire moved on [into the depths of the German positions] freeing the infantry to move against the nearest objectives. Our soldiers appeared near the trenches as white shapes, merging with the snow. Slowly, extended lines of attacking infantry moved up the slope of the heights, overcoming barbed wire and minefields. In places, the ice crust broke and men disappeared into deep snow. To make matters worse, enemy guns and mortars opened up with a barrage. From the left, the high ground came to life with machine-guns hitting the flank of the advance. The infantry lines immediately thinned out.

Kapustin gave a command to our new creation, the *DPP* group. 'It's a good thing we created it,' I said with satisfaction as I saw heavy howitzer shells exploding on the high ground. The infantry rushed to the crest of the heights and broke into the trenches. Two battalions had a toehold in the enemy's front line.

'Zhitnik! Raise your fire quickly! Set up a barrier!' I ordered.

'Battery commanders, elevate!' shouted Kapustin into the phone. 'Keep up with the infantry!'

But having seized the enemy trenches located on almost the very crest of the Sinyavino Heights in the former parkland outside Sinyavino, the battalions couldn't advance further. We had gained another narrow strip of land. The enemy artillery's fire prevented our infantry from moving forward. The fighting began to subside during the afternoon. Simonov contacted the neighbouring divisions and inquired about progress. The responses were disappointing.[18]

After further attacks, Simonov was forced to call a halt on 27 February. Exhaustion was rapidly setting in, not least because none of the formations involved in the battle on either side had been remotely near full strength at the outset of *Polarnaya Zvezda*. The news from elsewhere on the Eastern Front showed spectacular changes of fortune; on 16 February, Radio Moscow jubilantly reported that the Germans had been driven out of Kharkov, and elsewhere across eastern Ukraine the Red Army continued to make substantial gains; but in the north, progress was measured in yards, with a disproportionate price being paid in blood. The assault gun brigades in which Meretskov had placed so much hope were steadily whittled away by the German anti-tank guns or left stranded in the difficult terrain and the ranks of the rifle companies and battalions grew weaker with every attack. As February entered its last week, orders were issued by *Stavka* to cease the increasingly pointless attacks. All the divisions of Leningrad and Volkhov Fronts that had been involved in the operation needed a prolonged period of rest and replenishment before further operations could be expected to succeed.

The attacks on the Sinyavino Heights and the attempts to reach Mga from east and west were intended to be the prelude to the major attack from south of Lake Ilmen, where Northwest Front was preparing its forces. As if to underline the risks involved in attempting such an operation in winter in a region with a poor road and rail network, the weather intervened suddenly on 17 February. Katukov's First Tank Army had been assembling over the preceding days and as it began to move to its final preparation area, the temperature rose above freezing and the fresh snow that had fallen over the last week turned to slush. Movement became impossible for men and machines alike, and Khozin and Timoshenko had no option but to wait to see if conditions would improve. However, the Germans had no intention of waiting for a fresh Soviet attack in this area. At the headquarters of Army Group North, Küchler was of course acutely aware of how vulnerable his positions around Demyansk were and had long been preparing for a withdrawal towards the west.

The German forces in the salient were under the command of II Corps, a total of 12 divisions. In late November 1942, there had been an attempt by the Red Army to pinch off the salient which was beaten off, but only at the cost of weakening the defending formations. In all, there were about 100,000 German troops in the salient in early 1943 – undoubtedly a large number, but allowing for many of them being in rear area units behind the front line, this total shows that none of the front-line divisions was remotely near full strength. The commander of II Corps, General Walter Graf von Brockdorff-Ahlefeldt, had been seriously ill since before the Soviet attack of November 1942 and had returned to Germany; he would die in hospital in May 1943. In his absence, his corps had been commanded first by General Otto von Knobelsdorff and then by General Paul Laux, who was alarmed by the almost complete absence of any reserves behind the front line – all available units had been deployed to defeat the Soviet attack in November. The neighbouring formation, General Christian Hansen's X Corps around Staraya Russa, was in little better shape, and when Laux contacted Sixteenth Army to request reinforcements, he was told that none were available. The army had relied upon the solitary 203rd Panzer Regiment – two battalions of tanks – for much of 1942 as its 'fire brigade' to deal with whatever crises might arise, but the regiment was withdrawn in late 1942 and sent to France, handing over its vehicles to 8th Panzer Division; early in 1943, the regiment was disbanded and its personnel transferred to 1st Panzer Division, which had also been sent to France for recuperation and replenishment. Without this small but useful group of tanks, Busch had nothing that he could offer to his subordinates.

As was increasingly the case, Laux organised his rear area units into ad hoc battlegroups and did what he could to prepare for what he feared would be a hopeless defence. Throughout the winter, the front line around the Demyansk salient was rarely quiet, with probing attacks being made on most days. A trickle of units released by Army Group North, by weakening the lines further north in the sector of Eighteenth Army, and judicious local withdrawals permitted Laux to hold his positions, but it seemed only a matter of time before the salient either collapsed or was cut off. During 1942, there had been a prolonged siege in Demyansk after the German forces there were cut off, and they survived long enough for a relief column to link up with them only through the efforts of the Luftwaffe. Indeed, the air bridge that saved the Demyansk encirclement in 1942 was the basis of Goering's pledge to keep Sixth Army alive in Stalingrad after it was encircled, and with so much of Germany's air transport capacity now committed elsewhere – either in the south to the west of Stalingrad, or in the attempts to build up the strength of German forces in North Africa – it was inconceivable that an air bridge to save Demyansk could be attempted, particularly given the heavy losses suffered by Luftwaffe transport aircraft during the failed Stalingrad airlift.

In these circumstances, Küchler contacted *OKH* to seek permission for a withdrawal. By doing so, he would extract the 12 divisions of II Corps from what seemed like inevitable encirclement, thus releasing forces for deployment elsewhere. Küchler was in a sufficiently elevated post to be aware of the disaster that was unfolding on the banks of the Volga and deliberately worded his requests in a manner that made clear the risk of another catastrophic encirclement developing around Demyansk.

The chief of the general staff, Generaloberst Kurt Zeitzler, was sympathetic to Küchler's point of view and could see the inevitable outcome of continuing to cling to the salient, but both he and Küchler can't have been surprised when Hitler refused permission for a withdrawal. Consistently, Hitler rejected such withdrawals on the grounds that the positions in question might be the starting point for future offensive operations. It was only when the Stalingrad pocket began to collapse in late January that there was a change of mind, but even this was very gradual; instead of rejecting the requests for withdrawal, Hitler resorted to another tactic that caused endless frustration amongst his subordinates. He simply prevaricated, promising a decision at some undefined moment in the next few days. On 30 January, Helmuth Greiner, who was in charge of the team that maintained the German general staff war diaries, recorded:

> Yesterday, the Führer requested a report about supplies in the Demyansk area so that he could come to a decision about evacuating the pocket. In connection with this, the Führer added in passing that he found it difficult to make a decision about evacuation as he still intended to mount an operation towards Ostashkov to close the gap in the front, even though he saw the capture of Leningrad as the greater priority.[19]

The 'gap in the front' was the poorly covered sector stretching from the tip of the Demyansk salient to the northwest corner of the Rzhev salient. Even if Army Group Centre were to contribute to this by attacking north, the operation that Hitler suggested would require the German forces to cover a distance of about 90 miles across terrain that was heavily forested, with few decent roads. In many respects, the terrain was similar to the ground between Lake Ilmen and Lake Ladoga to the north, with an additional factor that made offensive operations even more difficult: the salient itself lay in the Valdai Hills, and the ground to the east and southeast – over which Hitler's proposed operation would have to advance – was also hilly, with numerous steep-sided gullies carved by rivers. Moreover, the offensive would start from the exposed Demyansk salient, hardly a secure point of origin. It seems that Zhukov's obsession with the Rzhev salient and considering the feasibility of operations purely by looking at maps was replicated in the highest German circles, with the added nuance of Hitler's profound reluctance to abandon any territory that the Wehrmacht had gained.

Generalleutnant Walter Warlimont, deputy chief of the operations staff of *OKW*, later added an explanatory note to Greiner's diary entry:

> This was further evidence that Hitler's military thinking was becoming increasingly unrealistic at this time. Neither the closure of the open space between Demyansk

and Rzhev nor the capture of Leningrad, both of which had already been attempted on numerous occasions in the past, but also in view of the overall situation that prevailed at that time, could be considered as at all achievable.[20]

Zeitzler persisted in making the case for Küchler's plan and just two days later, the chief of the general staff was able to inform the headquarters of Sixteenth Army that he had secured permission for a withdrawal. Hitler had finally conceded, and Busch was ordered to abandon the salient over the following ten weeks. Such a timetable was absurdly slow given the pressing need to release troops, and in any event Laux and his staff had anticipated events and had been drawing up evacuation plans for the past few weeks. The operations officer with 225th Infantry Division, Major Wilfried von Rosenthal, had been given the task of overseeing planning, using the cover of a plan entitled *Müllabfuhr* ('Rubbish Clearance') to avoid the wrath of higher authorities before permission was secured. Once *OKH* gave its approval for a withdrawal, the codename *Ziethen* was adopted for the final evacuation of the salient: on receipt of this codeword, units would begin their phased withdrawal.

Rosenthal's task was not an easy one, because of the few roads available. To make matters worse, the salient was narrowest at its neck, so all evacuation routes would have to converge at the point of maximum vulnerability. The first necessity was the creation of new roads and work teams were rapidly organised to create a small network of routes that would allow the main body of the salient to be evacuated. Any equipment that could legitimately be repositioned outside the salient before specific permission was given was sent to the rear via a narrow gauge railway that ran through the salient neck, and where such repositioning might attract attention, Rosenthal ordered that it should be moved to locations within the salient as close to the railway as possible.

It was widely expected in local German headquarters that the Red Army would detect the withdrawal immediately and would then place it under immense pressure, particularly as the tip of the Demyansk salient was about 60 miles from the narrow neck. It was therefore necessary to organise a withdrawal that could be carried out in a sequential but swift manner. The task of constructing adequate roads for this orderly and speedy withdrawal faced numerous difficulties: the shortage of proper building material; labour difficulties; and the heavy snow that alternately fell, thawed, and then froze once more. Work parties were drawn from troops in the salient, particularly rear area units, and construction battalions from the Todt Organisation that often worked close to the front-line building fortifications and airfields; but many were Soviet prisoners of war, contrary to any conventions about the use of such labour. There were few civilians left in the salient after a year of heavy fighting but they too were rounded up and forced to work. Trees were felled and laid side by side to create a 'corduroy road', as was common practice in so many of the remote areas through which the Eastern Front ran. In addition, other roads were created and given names by their construction teams – 'Highway One', *'Schlesische Promenade'* ('Silesian Promenade') and *'Kurfürstendamm'* (named after the famous central road in Berlin).[21]

Rosenthal and his team also drew up a detailed list of all the means of transport that were available, ranging from tracked fighting vehicles and bulldozers to horse-drawn carts and sleds. Their careful planning was a tribute to the professionalism of the German staff officer system and Laux was able to order immediate implementation of the phased withdrawal as soon as Zeitzler gave him the go-ahead. In the two weeks that followed, the weather turned wintry once more with blizzards sweeping across the Vaidai Hills. Nonetheless, Rosenthal was able to report that 8,000 tons of equipment, 1,500 motor vehicles, and 5,000 horse-drawn sleds and wagons had been evacuated; a team of bulldozers worked constantly to shift snowdrifts and the labour teams continued to toil in bitterly cold temperatures. For the German workers, there was at least the relief of shelter in the evenings and the provision of adequate food; the press-ganged civilians and Red Army prisoners of war were often put in utterly inadequate accommodation and received rations far below what was necessary for health in such a harsh climate, let alone when demands on the body were exacerbated by daily hard labour.

It isn't clear at what stage the Red Army became aware of the German withdrawal. Whilst the blizzards of early February created additional problems for the evacuation, they also prevented Soviet reconnaissance flights from getting a detailed picture of events, and it seems that most information about what was happening around Demyansk came from Red Army patrols that infiltrated through the lines; sometimes, these patrols were carrying out specific reconnaissance tasks, and on other occasions they were sent to try to capture German soldiers for interrogation. In the meantime, Laux did what he could to deceive the Soviet forces around the salient, adopting measures that were worthy of the increasingly detailed and sophisticated Soviet practice of *Maskirovka*. The Red Army was by now aware of the fragility of Luftwaffe field divisions and began a policy of deliberately targeting them during offensives, and to turn this weakness to his advantage, Laux created fictitious 'advance parties' of Luftwaffe field divisions and had them visit the front line around the salient to create the impression that several of the regular formations were about to be replaced by these Luftwaffe divisions. Radio messages were also sent with poor levels of coding and security to reinforce this impression. This served two purposes. Firstly, it made the withdrawal of elements of the regular divisions seem less suspicious; and secondly, it encouraged the Red Army to believe that by waiting until the Luftwaffe divisions had arrived, it would have a better chance of success in what was likely to be a difficult attack across unfavourable terrain.

The German units defending the Demyansk salient were far from their establishment strength, and as was the case in large areas of the Eastern Front there was insufficient manpower to create a continuous front line. The Soviet units in the area took advantage of this, sending patrols forward at night to bypass the German defences; once they had done so, they attempted to locate and cut telephone cables from the front line to the rear area, often calling in a brief mortar bombardment. The German response was often to send a small team of signallers – usually no more than a couple of men – along the route of the line in order to locate the break and repair it, assuming that the damage was the result of the Soviet shelling; the Soviet patrol would then overwhelm the signallers and attempt to take them prisoner. There were also attempts to capture prisoners from the front line, as a document written for the US Army after the war described:

> Another incident occurred on a particularly dark night, when one of two German infantrymen manning a machine-gun momentarily left his post to investigate a suspicious noise. Five Russians belonging to a reconnaissance patrol jumped at the soldier who had remained at the machine-gun, threw ground pepper into his face, pulled a bag over his head, and disappeared with him into the night. When he heard the noise, the other man ran back to the machine-gun and fired several bursts in the direction in which the Russian patrol had vanished. On the following morning the bodies of a Russian officer and two Russian enlisted men were found in the immediate vicinity of the outpost, as was the body of the abducted German machine-gunner. Two severely wounded Russians were discovered a few yards away. Among the Russian officer's papers the Germans found an elaborate plan of attack based on preliminary reconnaissance information, indicating that during the four preceding nights the officer had observed the German outpost area from behind a disabled tank at only 30 yards distance from the German machine-gun crew.[22]

Delayed in its preparations for *Polarnaya Zvezda* by the same blizzards that hindered aerial reconnaissance over the Demyansk Salient, Timoshenko's Northwest Front was unable to be ready for its scheduled start date of 14 February.

By the middle of the month, it became clear to the Red Army that the German movements – both real and simulated – in the salient were part of an organised withdrawal and Zhukov urged Timoshenko to commence his assault before the opportunity to destroy the German II Corps slipped away. The consequence was that without having fully concentrated its resources, Northwest Front was forced to commit units as they became available rather than in a single concentrated attack. On 15 February, the German lines were hit by a heavy artillery bombardment and the Soviet Eleventh and Fifty-Third Armies moved against the neck of the salient from north and south respectively while Thirty-Fourth Army attacked from the northeast, seeking to fix the German forces within the salient and to prevent their withdrawal.

The attack on the southern side of the salient made the most progress in the sector defended by the German 126th Infantry Division. During the winter, the division had been part of a substantial German assault codenamed *Michael* to widen the neck of the salient. As a result of this operation, some ground was gained but at a considerable cost, and those losses had not been made good when the new Soviet offensive broke on 15 February. It was only with difficulty that the penetrations were sealed off, consuming what few local reserves were available. During the evening, Laux spoke to Busch, his army commander, and outlined the urgency of the situation. The Germans were aware of the strength of Soviet units massing around the salient and feared that this first attack was merely the prelude for far heavier assaults in the coming days. To remain in the salient in such an exposed position was folly, and after a brief discussion Busch gave Laux permission to commence the withdrawal of combat units towards the west.

Rosenthal's earlier implementation of *Müllabfuhr* had already removed all of the 'unnecessary' rear area formations and equipment out of the salient; evacuating troops in the front line, whilst under pressure from the Red Army, was an altogether more difficult proposition. The first units to receive instructions to pull back were those furthest to the east, and they abandoned the very tip of the salient towards the end of 17 February, withdrawing from the shore of Lake Seliger to their first stop line about four miles closer to Demyansk. Rosenthal's team had been working closely with staff officers in every division, ensuring that they had made detailed plans for traffic control behind the immediate front line and had positioned tractors at key locations so that any vehicle that broke down or became stuck in snow could be dragged away quickly. At the moment, this sector was relatively quiet and over the following day the two German divisions in the tip withdrew unmolested; several vehicles were left by the roadside, but everything proceeded more or less as planned.

The weather remained cold with frequent heavy snow showers, limiting visibility for both sides. On this occasion, this worked mainly to the advantage of the Germans, concealing their abandonment of the old front line. When the Red Army became aware of the German withdrawal, an immediate pursuit began. A Soviet ski battalion managed to slip past the rearguard screen and clashed with the main column of men pulling back; it was fought off at close range, but when the bulk of the Soviet forces facing the eastern part of the salient attempted to intervene, German artillery fired heavy blocking barrages. Large stocks of artillery ammunition had been held in and around Demyansk and there was now no time to evacuate them, so the gunners had plentiful supplies of shells and, moreover, permission to use them. As soon as they reached the first stop line, the divisions were ordered to continue their withdrawal. By the end of 19 February they were drawn up in new positions immediately to the east of Demyansk and received further orders to give up the city and pull back further to the west. Until now, the withdrawal had been highly disciplined, but one regiment found a supply warehouse in Demyansk as it moved past. Within the building were stocks of food – and perhaps more significantly, alcohol – that the soldiers hadn't seen for months. The well-meaning officer who had been left in charge of the dump, with instructions to destroy anything that couldn't be evacuated, distributed what he could to the soldiers, including generous amounts of brandy which, he reasoned, would help in the snowstorm that was currently raging. For men who hadn't drunk any alcohol for several weeks, even modest amounts were likely to have a significant effect and the regiment rapidly degenerated into a drunken mob. Some buildings were set ablaze and the fierce wind rapidly blew sparks to neighbouring structures, which in turn went up in flames. The Red Army would later claim that the near-complete destruction of the city was a deliberate act committed by the withdrawing Germans, and there were certainly many occasions when both sides carried out such large-scale destruction in order to deny their opponents any cover; on this occasion, at least some of the devastation of the city seems to have been accidental, though it is quite likely that had such fires not broken out, the German rearguard would have set the city ablaze anyway.[23]

The Red Army was by now fully aware that the Demyansk salient was being evacuated, but the constant snow showers continued to impede Northwest Front's preparations for *Polarnaya Zvezda*. The troops that were already in the front line were thrown at the withdrawing Germans, but to little avail. On 27 February, the salient effectively ceased to exist with the last German troops pulling back over the Lovat River. Originally, *OKH* had expected that the evacuation would take ten weeks, and Rosenthal had warned that he might be able to achieve it in four weeks at best. Due to the preparations that he had made, the actual abandonment of the salient took just 11 days from when the codeword *Ziethen* was issued. It was a triumph of planning and staff-work.

In the weeks that followed, the Wehrmacht would withdraw from the even bigger salient around Rzhev, again maintaining good order and falling back from one interim position to the next. In neither case was the Red Army able to interfere with the German withdrawal in any meaningful way, and whilst both withdrawals effectively conceded territory to the Soviet Union, these operations were unquestionably major successes for the Germans. Characteristically, Zhukov was furious that the Germans were escaping and urged Timoshenko to make greater efforts. Even as German troops escaped across the Lovat, the weather continued to be capricious, with frequent warmer spells melting the fresh snowfalls. It was impossible for Katukov's First Tank Army to be committed and the new attack was made by Twenty-Seventh and First Shock Armies. Due to the German withdrawal, the new front line ran through the heavily fortified neck of the old salient, almost invulnerable to the Soviet preliminary bombardment. In addition, German artillery fired its plentiful stocks of ammunition and broke up the Soviet assault without conceding any ground. In any event, even if Zhukov was still determined to press on with his plans, Stalin had run out of patience. Even as the new attack broke down with further heavy losses, *Stavka* issued instructions for *Polarnaya Zvezda* to be abandoned.

Writing after the war, Katukov had mixed feelings about what had been intended:

My units made their way to the forming up areas for the new formation [First Tank Army] with great difficulty. In the remote snowbound village of Zaitsev they found the headquarters of Twenty-Ninth Army, which according to orders from above was to be turned into the headquarters of our tank army.

Other units slowly laboured forward through almost impassable snow. In addition, there was a new problem: there was no fuel, or ammunition, or food, or fodder in the forming up areas. From here to the nearest supply base it was no less than 250km along country roads, which were also constantly blocked by snowdrifts.

It wasn't possible to move around on horseback. Moreover, using horse-drawn carts used up all the fodder. The only way was for the tanks to go into action. They drove in stages, clearing the snow for wheeled and horse-drawn vehicles.

By 17 February, as stated in the original directive, we had completed the physical formation of First Tank Army. However, concerns about organisation and logistics consumed a lot of my energy and that of my staff. We were already short of rest and sleep and we still had to draw up plans for the upcoming operation which, according to the directive, was highly complex ...

[The overall plan for *Polarnaya Zvezda*] was magnificent. It seemed that if we implemented it, we would certainly write a glorious page in the history of the Great Patriotic War. I should add that the plan really inspired us all and we prepared for military operations to the Pskov-Luga region with great enthusiasm ...

But unfortunately, not everything was going smoothly at my army headquarters. The chief of staff, [Major] General [Nikolai Sergeyevich] Dronov, and his immediate subordinates were poorly versed in the specifics of tank formations, resulting in many difficulties. Furthermore, Dronov knew he was out of his depth. I had to recall urgently my old comrade-in-arms Matvey Timofeyevich Nikitin from III Mechanised Corps and appoint him head of the army's operational department.[24]

After Katukov brought his problems to the attention of Zhukov, Dronov was removed and replaced by Major General Mikhail Alekseyevich Shalin and the tank army finally got into battle on 1 March, failing to make any impression. Towards the end of the day, new orders arrived from *Stavka*. Katukov and his tank army were ordered to move to the nearest railheads from where they were transported to the south, taking up new positions in what was becoming the large Soviet-held salient around the city of Kursk; German counterattacks were taking place with increasing frequency and efficacy all along the southern half of the Eastern Front, rapidly dispelling the belief in Moscow that the final collapse of the Wehrmacht was imminent. In the north, the grandiose dream of *Polarnaya Zvezda*, a swift advance to Lake Peipus and the Narva River, was rapidly being recognised as just that – a dream. On 1 March, the *Sovinformburo* released a statement about fighting in the Demyansk region, attempting to make the best of what must have been a sense of disappointment:

In September 1941, the Fascist German troops broke through southeast of Lake Ilmen and occupied the Zaluchye–Lychkovo–Demyansk region with the forces of the German Sixteenth Army, as far east as the shores of Lakes Velie and Seliger. Over the next 17 months, the enemy strove with persistence and stubbornness to retain the captured bridgehead and turned it into a strongly fortified zone, referring to it as 'Fortress Demyansk'. The Germans intended to use this fortified zone as the start point for an attack on the vital communications lines of the northern group of our armies. At the same time, the area was the scene of repeated fierce fighting, in which the German divisions were ground down.

Recently, the troops of Northwest Front under the command of Marshal Timoshenko went onto the offensive against the German Sixteenth Army. In the course of the fighting, after breaking through a heavily fortified enemy line in several sectors, our troops threatened to create a double encirclement of the Nazi forces. Sensing the danger of encirclement, the enemy began a hasty retreat to the west while fending off the blows inflicted by our troops.

In eight days of combat while pursuing the enemy relentlessly, our troops liberated 302 settlements including the city of Demyansk and the regional centres of Lychkovo and Zalucha. An area of 2,350 square kilometres has been cleared of the enemy.

During the eight days of combat, our troops captured 3,000 German officers and men.

During this time, the following items were also captured: 78 aircraft; 97 tanks; 289 guns of various calibres; 711 machine-guns; and a large quantity of ammunition and other military equipment.

The enemy left more than 8,000 dead on the battlefield.[25]

As with so many official announcements by all the nations involved in the Second World War, this bulletin was disingenuous. The German withdrawal from the salient wasn't precipitated by threatening Red Army attacks; whilst the Germans clearly feared another encirclement, they had initiated *Ziethen* before *Polarnaya Zvezda* commenced. The figures for German losses and the amount of captured material are also suspect. There were few German tanks in the salient, and any captured aircraft would have been machines that were too badly damaged to be evacuated. A more realistic estimate of German losses from all causes is a figure of just under 7,000, compared with Red Army losses of about 34,000.[26]

The official communiqués of the era and the cold accounts written by senior officers after the war often fail to acknowledge the appalling reality of the battlefield. Stachow drew on his personal experiences in the front line to try to paint a picture of what these battles really meant for the men who had to fight them:

What does a word like 'penetration' actually mean? The frozen marshes and meadows, the snow-covered fields, the tangle of branches and undergrowth suddenly come alive with figures leaping, stomping, crawling towards them, sending gunshots or stabbing with their bayonets into every bit of cover, every hole in the ground, every crater, behind every earthen wall, into every bunker entrance. What is actually meant by 'defence' and 'counterattack'? The hoarse screams, the gasps and groans of men in close combat all mixed together, the crackle of gunfire, the pop of mortar tubes and the bright bursts of their projectiles, the '*uff*' when shells are sucked up by the snow or swamps, the clatter of shrapnel on wood and earth, the endless, frenzied succession of impressions of violence. Above everything else, the rumbling, roaring sound of artillery barrages sealing off the battle area and pounding it, the howling engines of ground attack planes that slash like shadows over clearings and tear at defensive positions. Everyone remembers moments: the gesture of a gunner towards his machine-gun before he curls his index finger around the trigger, the tired movement as someone pushes up his helmet to wipe the sweat from his eyes, the pounding of reinforcements rushing up over the still warm bodies of the fallen, the timber planks of the trench wall which suddenly become bright red as if painted. The furious expression of the soldier trying to place a 'sticky charge' over the engine compartment of a T-34, the way he has his tongue between his teeth as the turret hatch opens over the tank commander's head and the muzzle of his pistol slowly points at the soldier. It isn't remarkable that veterans stay silent when they could describe things. They lack the words, and all superlatives are soon exhausted.[27]

The great war of movement in Ukraine was brought to an end by a combination of exhaustion, crippling casualties, depletion of supplies, and perhaps most of all the arrival of the spring thaw. The *rasputitsa* or 'muddy season' transformed the poor roads of the Soviet Union to rivers of mud and almost all movement became impossible, forcing both sides to pause and catch their breath. In the northern sector, the thaw always arrived a little later than in the south. Here, there was still time for one more round of attacks, and many of the Red Army's units remained relatively strong. The threat to the narrow corridor to Leningrad remained and the German artillery massed to the south of the city was still able to bombard factories and other key locations in Leningrad at will – on 21 February alone, 106 shells were recorded as landing within the city itself.[28] Moreover, Zhukov continued to seek a final victory to erase the bitter memory of *Mars*. Even as the evacuation of the Demyansk salient was completed, the deputy supreme commander of the Red Army began once more to consider how he could mount a major offensive operation in territory that had proved so unsuitable to such operations in recent weeks.

CHAPTER 5

THE LAST BATTLES BEFORE SPRING

On 23 February, there were commemorations across the Soviet Union to mark an important day: *Den' Zashchitnika Otechestva*, or 'Defender of the Fatherland Day'. It was the 25th anniversary of the creation of the Red Army. Govorov, commander of Leningrad Front, gave a speech on Leningrad Radio, followed by further messages from Vice Admiral Vladimir Filippovich Tributs, commander of the Baltic Fleet, and lower ranking soldiers who had been recognised for their courage in defending Leningrad. The Germans were of course aware of the significance of the date and marked it with their own contribution: the Luftwaffe carried out an air raid shortly after midday, followed by shelling that lasted for several hours.[1] It was a timely reminder to Leningraders that their city remained in a vulnerable position.

Zhukov discussed the shape of further operations with Stalin during the German withdrawal from Demyansk. The ambitious advance originally planned for *Polarnaya Zvezda* was based on the expectation that substantial German forces would be destroyed in the Demyansk salient, thus weakening German defences in the same manner that the Stalingrad encirclement left the Wehrmacht unable to shore up its defences along the Don and the partial encirclement of the German Second Army resulted in a precipitate withdrawal towards the west. With this possibility now removed, Stalin wanted to know what further offensive options remained to the Red Army. Still under the codename of *Polarnaya Zvezda*, a new offensive was launched to try to catch the Germans before they had completed their redeployment after the evacuation of the Demyansk salient. The original intention was for the fighting ultimately to involve the forces of Northwest, Volkhov, and Leningrad Fronts. In order to give the northern Fronts more time to recover their strength after the bloodletting around Sinyavino, Zhukov planned for Timoshenko's Northwest Front to start the offensive with an attack on 23 February. The initial objective of Twenty-Seventh and First Shock Armies was the city of Staraya Russa and the line of the Polist River; still hankering after a greater success to match the huge advances in the south, Zhukov then added an unrealistic order that following such a success, Special Group Khozin – now consisting of Thirty-Fourth, Fifty-Third, and Sixty-Eighth Armies – was to be inserted into any gap that opened in the German lines with a view to advancing as far as the original intentions of *Polarnaya Zvezda*.

Ten days after this attack began, the northern two Fronts were to resume offensive operations. There were some reports reaching the Red Army that the Germans were stockpiling ammunition in Sinyavino and bringing up reinforcements, and this was interpreted as preparations for an attack towards the north to restore the blockade ring around Leningrad. The two Red Army Fronts were ordered to try once more to reach Mga with pincers from the northwest and northeast, a little to the north of the failed attacks of February and without any forces being thrown against Sinyavino. Leningrad Front's attack would be in the region of Krasnyi Bor with eight rifle divisions towards the village of Ulyanovka and Voitolovo, while Volkhov Front attacked between Voronovo and Lodva with ten rifle divisions; Second Shock Army was transferred to the control of Leningrad Front. The entire operation was expected to be completed in just 15 days, and Voroshilov was sent to oversee Leningrad Front's part of the assault.[2]

The city of Staraya Russa, immediately to the south of Lake Ilmen, was a typical provincial centre in the Soviet Union before the war, mainly on the east bank of the sluggish Polist River; amongst its very few claims to fame was that it was the birthplace of the composer Sergei Rachmaninov. Much of the city had been destroyed when the Wehrmacht seized it in late 1941 and constant air attacks in the months that followed inflicted further damage. With the withdrawal of the German II Corps from the Demyansk salient, the defences to the east of Staraya Russa, between the city and the Lovat River, came under the control of X Corps, and the northern divisions of the corps were under the command of Generalmajor Werner von Erdmannsdorff; in addition to his own 18th Motorised Infantry Division, he had elements of four infantry divisions with which to hold a front line of about 18 miles. In many respects, this represented a greater concentration of defenders than the Germans could deploy in other sectors, especially as X Corps had substantial artillery assets available with which to support Erdmannsdorff. Breaking this defensive line would be a tough task for the Red Army.

Wilhelm Lubbeck's division was one of the German units holding open the neck of the Demyansk salient, and he later recalled the positions that he and his comrades occupied when they were sent into the front line as artillery spotters:

> Reaching our newly assigned post on a low ridge along this corridor, my communications specialist and I joined a group of other soldiers in a large bunker near the front that served as the living quarters. Because it was impossible to dig out an underground bunker or trenches in the frozen, rock-hard earth, it had been constructed above ground with snow camouflaging the log walls. A snow wall facing the Russian lines offered additional protection. Nearby, there was also a small observation tower.
>
> In spite of our efforts to create a secure position, we soon began to be plagued by sniper fire from a Soviet sharpshooter. Fearful of getting hit, we were forced to remain inside the confined space of the bunker during the daylight hours. After this situation had persisted for several days, I finally grew frustrated and decided to do something about it.
>
> Grabbing a Mauser rifle, I made my way from our bunker to the snow rampart. Crouching down on my knees, I carved out a small aperture through the wall with my hands. Scrutinising the winter landscape, there was nothing that gave away the location of the enemy sharpshooter.
>
> Suddenly, a shot burst through the snow wall, passing just over the top of my helmet. Accepting my defeat in our brief duel, I pulled my rifle from the hole and quickly ducked back into our bunker. As far as I was concerned, we would have to learn to live with the threat of the sniper.[3]

Successful snipers were treated almost as celebrities by the Soviet Union, perhaps because their role in warfare could so easily be imagined by almost anyone. There were constant stories in newspapers of their exploits, listing the numbers of men they had killed; like all such reports, their scores were almost certainly exaggerated, not least because it was difficult for a sniper to be certain whether he had killed the target, wounded it, or simply driven it to cover.

Although German accounts repeatedly describe the intensity and weight of Soviet artillery bombardments, German artillery seems often to have achieved better results through precision rather than volume of fire. Lubbeck deployed forward shortly before the Soviet offensive, taking with him a field telephone one morning after a fresh fall of snow:

Concealed by my white camouflage, I remained standing in order to better survey the surrounding terrain.

Without even lifting my binoculars, a quick scan of the enemy position immediately revealed a couple of Red Army bunkers. Protruding six feet above ground, the structures were plainly visible from my position less than 100m away. Though fresh snow now partially covered the layer of protective earth piled onto the bunkers, they appeared to be of recent construction and clearly posed a direct challenge to our control of the area.

Selecting the closer and larger of the two, I called back firing coordinates to one of our 150mm howitzers, requesting a single round on the target. In a couple of minutes, an explosion threw up a cloud of snow about 20m to the left of the bunker. After adjusting the distance and direction, the second round landed 10m to the right. Advancing a little closer to better observe the target, I made a further correction and requested a delayed fuse.

This round found its mark. Just after it smashed through the roof of the bunker, there was a loud whoosh of air as the shell with the delayed fuse detonated inside the structure a second later. The only thing observable externally was a little white smoke that drifted out through the roof.[4]

Almost immediately, Lubbeck had to scramble for cover as Soviet mortar rounds began to fall around him. He was lucky to escape with superficial wounds from a near miss; the fresh snow had absorbed much of the blast.

When the Soviet attack began, it was – as usual – preceded by a fierce bombardment. Major Dedo von Krosigk, a battalion commander of the German 18th Motorised Infantry Division, described the fighting:

The only supply road available for replenishment between Staraya Russa and the divisions deployed near the Lovat ... ran within 300m of the front line in places. This was the most dangerous sector between Staraya Russa and the Lovat. If the enemy could seize the road at this point, they would cut off the divisions in the front line ... I Battalion was on the left from the edge of the swamp, II Battalion in the centre along the deep gully of the Redya stream, and my III Battalion on the right either side of Yasvy. The neighbouring unit to the right [the south] was 5th Jäger Division. There was a 300m open space between II and III Battalions, a swampy area that was impassable during the summer but during the winter months had been assessed as passable for armoured vehicles. The sector of III Battalion was a little over 3km wide, running from 11 Company in the north, through a pine forest held by 10 Company, and 9 Company on the right in mixed deciduous and pine woodland.

The main point of effort in this sector was on the left by 11 Company, due to the open ground on the left flank that was passable by tanks when frozen …

So 23 February, 'Red Army Day', dawned. The incessant movement of trains, the roar of tanks moving up, and the rumble of trucks had been audible for several days and nights. Artillery batteries had fired in their ranging shots and mortars and Stalin Organs [*Katyushas*] had been spotted. Low-flying aircraft were often seen over our positions. But the night of 22–23 February was marked by the deepest silence; not a shot or a sound. A high level of alert was ordered at 0400 after a deserter reported an attack would take place on 23 February. At 0555, several flares rose from the enemy lines into the dawn sky and abruptly hundreds of guns, mortars and Stalin Organs opened fire. In a few minutes the telephone cables were destroyed. Despite the rising sun, the sky grew darker. The earth trembled, bunkers rocked like ships on the high seas. The devastating fire continued for two hours. Just before 0800 several enemy bomber squadrons dropped their loads on the positions of 11 Company, and the open ground between II and III Battalions, with several rows of minefields, was particularly heavily hit. Several Stalin Organs directed their fire at the unfortunate 11 Company and then, while the bombardment still continued inexorably, creating a barrier, 30 enemy tanks thrust deep into our battalion, several turning south towards the Redya bridge while others attacked towards the supply road. Our anti-tank gun shot up three tanks but the fourth overran it and mowed down the brave gun-crew. Contact with regimental headquarters was lost. It was only possible to send the first radio message at 0930. Enemy riflemen now attacked. The shattered 11 Company was thrown back and its remnants fought at the eastern edge of the battalion headquarters. The line of 10 Company continued to hold but bunker after bunker was destroyed by direct fire from the tanks. The fighting raged on to 1300. Meanwhile the reserve company arrived and was deployed for a counterattack to outflank the attacking enemy, but it was too late.

While the company moved off on its counterattack, the enemy made a concentrated attack on battalion headquarters, which was only beaten off at 1600 with heavy losses on our side. III Battalion was pulled out during the evening; the enemy penetration was sealed off by the reserves that had been mustered. The leading Red Army units were only 30m from the supply road. It was a substantial initial success for the Soviets. What would the next day bring? But in heavy fighting, it was possible to prevent further advances by the Russians. Their assault troops suffered terrible losses when they made repeated attacks over the next days and were smashed by concentrated artillery fire.[5]

To the immediate north of Krosigk's troops, the neighbouring II Battalion had taken over its sector during a partial thaw, which made it impossible to dig proper trenches and bunkers. Instead, most of the defensive line consisted of stacks of felled trees, and the men had to endure the initial bombardment as best they could. Whilst this account is characteristic of many such recollections written by both sides in terms of emphasising the heroic behaviour of the soldiers, it gives a flavour of the conditions they endured:

> Then tanks rolled forward! The cold was forgotten, and everyone made preparations in their burrows in the snow until the Russians arrived.
>
> We had survived the firestorm and from our foxholes we were able to mount one counterattack after another to seal off the penetrations achieved by the T-34s. These weren't always successful, but in any event they were prevented from widening their penetration towards Penna and the road.
>
> Heavy fighting raged. Our II/51 stood unshaken as the cornerstone of the defences. Its commander used every pause in fighting to run from foxhole to foxhole to speak to his men about the need to hold on and how much depended on them doing so.
>
> The soldiers of II/51 held on like this for several days in their foxholes in the snow, literally clinging on and only emerging to fight tanks and infantry. They stayed there even when the icy walls began to thaw …
>
> The artillery of the corps and *Gruppe Erdmannsdorff* concentrated ever-greater fire against the enemy's points of effort, including in front of our sector.[6]

There was an additional threat to 18th Motorised Infantry Division from Soviet infantry that took advantage of the frozen surface of Lake Ilmen to try to outflank positions from the north, and some of the division's artillery was forced to relocate further west. Arno Pentzien, a junior NCO who had recently returned from three precious weeks of home leave, described the situation:

> Fortunately, there was plenty of ammunition available. Our B-position was in Bolshoy Ushin. Our radio set was set up in the square church tower of Penykovo and soon gave us useful information.

Towards midday infantry arrived in trucks, to our relief. That evening I went up the church tower in Bolshoy Ushin as an observer. I had a good view from there. In the evening I could clearly see the dark shape of a column making its way over the ice of the lake towards Ushin. Throughout the day, our aircraft had been attacking this column.

The following morning was foggy. The enemy attacked from Ushin towards Bolshoy Ushin in the early hours. The fog greatly hindered the control of defensive fire. Fortunately an entire infantry regiment was now deployed with us.

At the same time, fighting began around the strongpoints northeast of Staraya Russa. The villages of Otvidino, Mirogoshchka, Chertitslo, and Vsad went up in flames. How fortunate that I was no longer a forward observer over there!

Our gun crews soon set off further west over the ice of Tulebiya Bay. Towards evening they reached and strengthened the 'Thule Line'. Meanwhile, despite the fog, we smashed the attack from Ushin.

During the morning our infantry attacked Ushin and recaptured it by mid-afternoon, driving the enemy back onto the ice. Happily, our losses were light …

In their attempt to cross the ice along the southern edge of Lake Ilmen in their attack, the enemy ski troops lost 215 prisoners and an estimated 1,660 dead, not including the casualties when the Luftwaffe attacked them on the ice. We captured 25 anti-tank guns, 43 anti-tank rifles, 158 machine-guns, 23 mortars, 422 submachine-guns, seven motorised sleds, and numerous other sleds and equipment. This included about 1,800 pairs of skis, which our infantry could put to good use.[7]

The German defence of Staraya Russa was crucial in order to give the troops in the Demyansk salient the time that they needed to complete their withdrawal. If the Soviet attack was to succeed, it was essential to silence the German artillery, but this required detailed knowledge of the positions of the German guns. In two days of fighting, the artillery regiment of 18th Motorised Infantry Division – two light battalions, each with 12 105mm howitzers, and a medium battalion with 12 150mm howitzers – reported that just three of its 36 guns were knocked out. Over 8,000 rounds were fired against the Soviet troops, contributing significantly to the defensive effort.[8] Unlike the Soviet guns, the German artillery proved to be very effective in its counter-battery fire, as an artillery officer later recalled:

The tactical use of our artillery featured a notable addition, with massed fire from all the guns of the regiment on suspected enemy forming up areas and artillery positions. The use of these concentrated fire strikes had good results. The firing teams worked with unparalleled precision: 'Mass fire on target – five minutes – ready – mark!' Stopwatches were set. At the precise ordered moment (the flight time of the shells had been deducted) there were shouts of 'Fire!' in our positions. The salvoes thus fell together at precisely the same time on their target areas ...

I still have notes from prisoner interrogations from those days. They all reported the fearful effect of our massed fire. One example can speak for many: '111th Rifle Battalion, deployed on 23 February with 1,000 men, was reduced to just 100 men by 10 March. The German artillery fire swept devastatingly over the Red Army troops who were mostly crouching under cover and suffering tremendous casualties. The German guns fired mostly in mass salvoes. We were helplessly at its mercy.'[9]

The Luftwaffe also provided valuable support – in addition to its attacks on the Soviet troops attempting to cross the ice of Lake Ilmen, it was able to provide close support with its Stukas. The Red Army attacks gradually lessened in intensity until it was necessary to call a halt so that they could regroup. The renewed attack by Northwest Front, scheduled for 4 March, commenced a day late due to difficulties in getting all the units involved into position. When they moved forward, the riflemen of Twenty-Seventh and First Shock Armies ran into German defences that were far more robust than the improvised line that Zhukov had expected or hoped for and the assault gained no ground. On one occasion, German reports from the front line described how fresh waves of Soviet soldiers seemed to go into battle with few weapons and were seen to pick up rifles and machine-guns from their comrades who had been killed in earlier attacks.[10]

Zhukov remained confident that he could achieve a substantial success, but the ambitions of the original operation were scaled down, as he outlined in a message sent to *Stavka* on 8 March:

I have decided ... to launch a wedge attack against the enemy ... to cut off Staraya Russa from the west.

Four days are required to regroup and prepare the offensive. Consequently, we can attack on the morning of 13 March.[11]

Stalin replied the same day, giving his approval. Full orders followed shortly after and a renewed assault began on 14 March against the defences of Staraya Russa along the line of the Lovat River. Immediately to the south, divisions from three further armies threw themselves at the German 329th Infantry Division. Covering a hopelessly large sector of the front line, the German division was unable to prevent Northwest Front from crossing the river and fell back first to the Redia River, then the Porusye River, about six miles to the west of its original positions. Here it was able to bring the Red Army's advance to a halt with the help of whatever reinforcements could be dispatched to its aid; significantly, these included considerable corps-level artillery assets, which once more intervened with decisive effect. The Soviet units had suffered disproportionately heavy losses for their modest gain and the assault on Staraya Russa failed to make any progress at all. The battles of March cost Northwest Front a staggering 103,100 casualties; the daily loss rate was one of the highest suffered by the Red Army in the entire war.[12] Total German casualties suffered by Sixteenth Army through this period came to fewer than 14,000.[13]

Since the beginning of the winter, Zhukov had personally overseen several operations: *Mars*, the disastrous failure to break up the Rzhev salient; *Iskra*, the partially successful but costly breaking of the siege ring around Leningrad; and *Polarnaya Zvezda*. In total, these battles cost the Red Army more than half a million casualties. The only success that he could show for this dreadful butcher's bill was a narrow strip of land on the southern shore of Lake Ladoga where a narrow gauge railway had been constructed, constantly swept by German artillery fire. The fact that he remained in post throughout this period is remarkable, but both the casualties suffered and Zhukov's survival are perhaps reflections of an underlying reality. Just as Stalin seems to have accepted that he did not have the luxury of dismissing senior commanders and would have to make do with what he had, Zhukov similarly was brutal in the manner in which he threw men at the Germans as he too knew that the Red Army had to win the war with what it had in terms of equipment, resources, and men. In the midst of a fight for its very survival, the Soviet Union had no opportunity to train soldiers and officers to the high levels of expertise and initiative that the Wehrmacht had enjoyed at the start of the war in the east. In any event, whilst it is arguable that basic training of soldiers could and should have been improved, the basic skill-set required for skilful officers would have required a degree of flexibility that was completely contrary to the Soviet system. Any army reflects the society from which it is recruited, and despite the considerable improvements that had occurred across the Soviet Union in the years before the war in terms of literacy, most of the Soviet Union remained comparatively primitive compared to Germany and other European nations. It should also be borne in mind that the Red Army wasn't the only force to suffer terrible casualties in offensive operations. During the Normandy campaign, the Western Allies suffered an average of 6,674 casualties per day, a figure that actually exceeded the loss rate of many of the terrible battles of the First World War.[14] The figure for this latest battle at Staraya Russa came to 6,444 per day. The Western Allies could at least justify their losses by their eventual victory in the Normandy campaign and even higher German losses. Zhukov had no such consolation.

Events further south were now intervening and Zhukov was dispatched to reorganise the Red Army's lines as the German counterattacks in the central and southern sectors came to an end with the spring thaw. The forces that had been built up in Khozin's group were dispersed, many of them also heading for the Kursk region, and all that was left of the planned operations in the north was the attempt by Leningrad and Volkhov Fronts to reach Mga. This fresh attack was preceded by an attack near Novgorod by the Soviet Fifty-Second Army in an attempt to draw German reserves away from the north. To maximise the chances of success, Lieutenant General Vsevolod Fedorovich Iakovlev's army chose the sector defended by 1st Luftwaffe Field Division for its attack, which commenced on 14 March. Whilst these divisions were repeatedly shown to be too weak to stand up to major assaults, this occasion was an exception and the lines of the Luftwaffe division held firm in fighting that continued until 27 March. However, there was a price for this successful defence: the resilience of 1st Luftwaffe Field Division was because it was reinforced by significant elements of 217th Infantry Division transferred from Kirishi in the north, and much of 58th Infantry Division, which was one of the units withdrawn from the Demyansk salient. Even if neither of these units was withdrawn from the Sinyavino–Mga sector, they would not be available as reinforcements for the northern sector when the main attack commenced.

As with so many operations during the winter, Leningrad Front needed an additional two days to complete its preparations and Fifty-Fifth Army didn't commence its attempt to break through the German defences to the south of Krasnyi until 19 March. Hilpert, who had commanded the disparate battlegroups of reinforcements and units extracted from Shlisselburg, was now commanding LIV Corps in this sector. *SS-Polizei* had been extracted from its positions on the Sinyavino Heights and was the central formation of Hilpert's corps, with the Spanish Blue Division on its left flank to the west and 24th Infantry Division on its right flank to the east. Although it had suffered heavy casualties during the closing phases of *Iskra*, *SS-Polizei* received welcome reinforcements in the shape of the *SS-Freiwilligen-Legion Flandern*, one of an increasing number of pro-German units that were being raised across Europe by the Germans. These 'international volunteers', as they were characterised by German propaganda, would play a significant part in the last battles around Leningrad.

There were several political parties and movements in Belgium and the Netherlands that espoused views and policies that were similar to those of the Nazi Party; one of these was the *Vlaamsch Nationaal Verbond* ('Flemish National League', usually abbreviated to *VNV*), which opposed the existence of an independent Belgium and wished for the creation of a larger Dutch state. In competition with other pro-Fascist groups, the *VNV* recruited volunteers after the German occupation of the region for a new SS unit on the understanding that it would not be deployed in combat roles and would be used only for security purposes. After the beginning of the German invasion of the Soviet Union, intentions changed, but it was only when the volunteers reached their training area in the east that they realised that contrary to what they had been told, they were going to be used as a combat unit and would be commanded by German officers.[15] When they learned that they were to be assigned to the *SS-Wiking* division, many of the Flemish volunteers refused and were instead organised into the Flemish Legion, which was in theory at least not part of the SS but merely attached to it. Despite this, its full name included the letters 'SS' from the outset.

The Flemish Legion was first sent to the front line in November 1941, joining the 2nd SS Motorised Infantry Brigade, with which it was involved in defending the line of the Volkhov River. It was sent to the rear area to recuperate in June 1942 after suffering heavy losses during its involvement in the fierce battles that led to the encirclement of the Soviet Second Shock Army and returned to action after a break of two months. When it was assigned to *SS-Polizei*, it had once more lost much of its strength in recent fighting, but nonetheless was received by its new parent unit as a valuable additional asset.

The first attack by the Red Army succeeded in overrunning the forward positions of *SS-Polizei* and by the end of 19 March, Fifty-Fifth Army had advanced a little over a mile in heavy fighting. On the same day, Volkhov Front's Eighth Army attacked with nine rifle divisions with tank support from the east, aiming for the junction of the German 1st and 223rd Infantry Divisions. As was the case with the western attack, progress was slow, with matters worsened by warming temperatures. Heavy rain fell all day, turning the snow to slush and softening the ground and preventing intervention by aircraft from either side.

Over the following days, there was almost no further progress by Leningrad Front. Volkhov Front's painfully slow and costly advance eventually reached the railway line running from Mga to Kirishi. Generalleutnant Christian Usinger, commander of 223rd Infantry Division, reported that his division was close to collapse and would be unable to hold back the Red Army without reinforcements. Improvising as best he could, Lindemann managed to release three battlegroups from separate infantry divisions and sent them to shore up the defensive line. Further attacks by the Soviet Eighth Army failed to make any progress and its commander, Lieutenant General Filipp Nikanorovich Starikov, advised *Stavka* that he could do no more. Nevertheless, he was ordered to make one more assault.

At the end of March the Flanders Legion, supported by a handful of Tiger tanks, mounted a counterattack in strength. The assault fell on the exhausted Soviet units that had suffered further major casualties for no gains in the preceding day and in a day of heavy fighting, the Red Army was driven back to its start line. But if the Red Army suffered heavy losses, the same was true for the Germans. The Flanders Legion, which had started the battle with about 500 men, lost more than half of its personnel as dead, wounded, or missing. On the eastern side of the salient that extended to Sinyavino, one of the battlegroups sent by Lindemann as reinforcements – from the German 121st Infantry Division – bore the brunt of Starikov's final attack on 1 April. With the spring thaw now beginning in earnest, the Red Army infantrymen struggled through the mud and heavy defensive fire and failed to make any progress. Despite being sent to the Kursk area, Zhukov continued to urge the northern Fronts to resume their attacks, but Stalin intervened on 2 April, sending directives to both Leningrad and Volkhov Fronts that they were to switch to a defensive posture and were not to undertake any further offensive operations without the specific permission of *Stavka*.[16]

The warmer weather brought operations to a halt all along the Eastern Front. Both sides desperately needed the break in order to recover from the ordeals of recent months. In the far south, the Wehrmacht suffered the disastrous loss of Sixth Army in Stalingrad and was forced to abandon all the gains made east of the Northern Donets and Mius Rivers in the preceding year, but then launched a counteroffensive that not only prevented complete collapse but also inflicted a chastening defeat on the Red Army; if there was any doubt, the battles showed the continuing advantage that the Wehrmacht held over its opponent when battles were fluid and the expertise and initiative of officers at lower levels was crucial. In the central sector, the Germans spent the winter defending the Rzhev salient and bleeding the opposing forces white in the process before conducting a skilful and professional withdrawal from the salient. In the north, the Red Army finally succeeded in breaking the siege ring around Leningrad, but it proved to be a partial success at best. All attempts to complete the operation by capturing Sinyavino failed with heavy losses, and the absurdly ambitious objectives of *Polarnaya Zvezda* at no stage looked like being achieved. The weather-imposed pause in operations gave both sides a much-needed opportunity to regroup and reorganise. For the Red Army, it was also a chance to start analysis of its recent operations.

Some senior officers expressed their dissatisfaction with how the Red Army had performed even before the spring thaw halted combat. One such individual was Voronov, who was born in 1899 in the city that would become Leningrad and after brief service in the Imperial Russian Army became a mortarman in the Red Army. He continued to serve in artillery units through the Civil War and was wounded and captured during the Soviet–Polish War in 1920. After his release a year later, he continued a steady rise as an artillery officer, serving with the Soviet military mission in Spain during the Spanish Civil War. The purges of the Red Army that took place in the late 1930s worked to his advantage, creating high-profile vacancies, and he became chief of artillery of the Red Army in 1937 after the previous incumbent, Nikolai Mikhailovich Rogovsky, was arrested and shot. After a spell in which he helped draft new regulations for the Red Army's artillery and initiated projects to modernise the equipment used by gunners – particularly anti-tank guns, anti-aircraft weapons and devices to locate enemy guns by calculating their direction from the sound of firing – Voronov took part in the Battle of Khalkin Gol against the Japanese in 1939.

Voronov travelled north and oversaw the use of artillery in the Winter War against Finland. During this operation he was critical of many features of Soviet artillery use, particularly the haphazard manner in which artillery commanders reported the results of their shelling, usually exaggerating its efficacy. He also criticised the quality of aerial reconnaissance photographs and introduced a new camera, but blamed inertia amongst Air Force reconnaissance officers for the failure to adopt it widely. The successful assault by the Red Army on the Finnish defences of the Mannerheim Line in February 1940 owed much to Voronov's careful preparations.

When war broke out with Germany in 1941, Voronov once more became head of the artillery of the Red Army and became one of the small group of men sent to different sectors by *Stavka* to oversee operations and to provide specialist advice. Perhaps because of his lifelong service with artillery units, which were (and remain) heavily dependent upon logistic support for their effective functioning, he showed an awareness of logistics that was generally far greater than that of most of his peers. Writing after the war about *Polarnaya Zvezda*, he was scathing in his criticisms of the failures of Northwest Front, drawing attention to his attempts at the time to make *Stavka* and Stalin aware of the problems. His retrospective analysis, based upon a visit to the area before the German evacuation of the Demyansk salient was spotted, is worth considering in full, as the problems he identified were widespread in the Red Army:

The more I delved into the details of the plan, the more I became convinced of the truth of the saying that 'It looked good on paper, but only if you forgot about the ravines or actually walking among them.' It would have been difficult to choose a less favourable axis for the use of artillery, tanks, and other military equipment than what was planned for this sector. The area of forthcoming operations had numerous swamps and everywhere else the water table was not far below the surface. Construction of roads took a great deal of effort here. The artillerymen were especially handicapped. For most firing positions, strong wooden decking had to be constructed so that the guns wouldn't sink into the quagmire when firing. This took a lot of time.

I remember the dugout in which I lived: there was constantly running water under the wooden floor and it was pumped out daily, with up to 80 buckets being scooped out at a time.

It was difficult to carry out reconnaissance of the enemy's defences for artillery. Visibility was very poor due to falling snow or dense fog. There were numerous small forests. In addition, the enemy camouflaged his heavy weapons with great skill. Even when we moved our forward artillery observation posts to extremely short distances from the enemy, their positions amongst the trees made it impossible to get tangible results.

Of course, the Rumashevo corridor was a tough nut to crack. Our aviators had been photographing this area for a year and a half, but there was still no clear picture of the enemy's defences. But for artillery, we needed the exact coordinates of all their firing positions. It's not surprising that the artillery of the Tsarist army had a motto: 'I can't see – I can't shoot.'

In addition, ground conditions greatly reduced the effectiveness of artillery fire; shells and mortar bombs with high explosive fuse settings penetrated deep into the soft ground and failed almost completely to hit enemy personnel with shrapnel. This was one of the reasons for the failure of our previous offensive operations.

We travelled to General Khozin's special group and there we discovered major shortcomings in preparation for combat in several units and subunits, though everything was recorded beautifully and correctly on maps. I was most surprised that the unit commanders barely considered the difficulties arising from impassable or difficult ground conditions. When I asked about this, they promised to conduct urgent reconnaissance of the routes they would cover and of their starting positions. It was clear that this strong group with several airborne divisions, ski brigades, mechanised and tank corps, anti-tank artillery regiments and numerous other units, was not ready for combat operations. It hadn't even finished being hammered and polished into shape, and hadn't completed essential training.[17]

Given that the Red Army had been holding positions around the Demyansk salient for as long as the Germans had held the salient itself, the soldiers and officers of the various Soviet units must have been aware of the difficulties of operating in this terrain, but it seems that no senior officers raised concerns about this. In addition to the problems identified by Voronov with regard to the need to construct wooden platforms for artillery, it should be added that the same terrain problems would hinder the movement of artillery once the advance began – not only would the guns have to be brought forward over soft ground, but new firing platforms would then have to be constructed after the redeployment was complete.

The failure of reconnaissance to identify German positions was a recurring problem. Simply increasing the number of guns and the duration of the barrage was little substitute for precise targeting, and although Voronov recorded that reconnaissance flights had photographed the area repeatedly for over a year, Soviet aerial reconnaissance was not of the same standard as seen elsewhere. There were no aircraft that had been designed specifically for the task, unlike several planes operating in the Luftwaffe, and the quality of cameras and film consistently fell short of what was available both to the Luftwaffe and the Western Allies despite Voronov's previous efforts to improve matters. Other measures were adopted to try to improve the Red Army's knowledge of German positions. Patrols were sent out regularly, especially when an offensive operation was being planned, to capture 'tongues' for interrogation, but the longer the interval between the capture of the 'tongues' and the actual offensive, the greater the chance that the Germans would reposition some or all of their weapons.

Another method used to try to determine the nature and detail of German defences was reconnaissance in force, with battalion-sized attacks on the German lines in an attempt to force the Germans to open fire with their support weapons. Many senior officers – particularly those who ordered such missions – later described the extensive training of battalions selected for these tasks, but the accounts of soldiers who were in these battalions are very different. It seems that on many and probably most occasions, there was little or no preliminary mission-specific training and a battalion in the front line was simply selected and ordered to carry out the mission.[18] Even if reconnaissance in force actually succeeded in provoking the Germans to use their concealed defensive weapons, the price in terms of casualties was usually high, and there remained the same disadvantage that the longer the interval between the reconnaissance in force and the actual attack, the more time there was for the Germans to redeploy, while a very short interval left little time to inform artillery units of the precise locations of German defences.

The poor training of Soviet units was another recurring feature of the Second World War, and recent fighting in Ukraine has shown that these problems persist into the modern era in the Russian Army. The practice of troops completing only rudimentary training before being sent to their units where they were meant to complete their training was and remains unsuitable for men about to enter intense combat, and even the basic training the soldiers had before being sent to the front line was often truncated in order to get men to combat units more quickly so that they could replace the ongoing heavy losses. Soviet analyses of operations frequently bemoaned the lack of close cooperation between different arms, but unless carefully planned changes were made to training, this was always going to be a recurring problem. The sheer scale of the Red Army and its enormous casualties meant that there were few officers with the time or resources to carry out the necessary training. Although training manuals were rewritten, recruits continued to arrive at the front line with poor preparation for what lay ahead.

Voronov continued in his account:

[Despite all of these shortcomings] the attack began. On 15 February, Eleventh and Fifty-Third Armies, after artillery preparation, broke into the front line of the enemy's defences and advanced a little, but then failed to capitalise on their success. But this gave the enemy good advance warning. Apparently, the Nazis knew in advance about our preparations for an offensive in this sector and, learning from their bitter experiences on the Volga and Don, began to strengthen the defence of the Rumashevo corridor. Our subsequent attacks were also unsuccessful ...

The artillery commanders who were with the forward units sent back very pessimistic reports. Colonel Afanasyev reported, 'The infantry were not prepared properly for the attack. The suppression of enemy defensive fire by the artillery preparation was not used to full effect. Rifle and machine-gun fire, and company and battalion mortars were all used very poorly. Management of the dynamics of the battle by the infantry commanders was bad.'

I received such reports constantly and demanded that the relevant commanders eliminate these shortcomings, and tried to provide practical assistance. My closest subordinates, all experienced officers, were with the leading units of the advancing infantry but despite all efforts they could not achieve the elimination of shortcomings in the activity of our troops.

After the brilliant victories on the Don and Volga, failures on this Front were depressing. It was clear that there was no need to start a major operation here. Our powerful technology needed open spaces, but here it was bogged down in swamps. Again, I was filled with irritation at those who drew up beautiful plans for the operation without bothering to study the conditions of the area, the routes of communication, and the climate.[19]

These are damning criticisms of Timoshenko and Zhukov, who were largely responsible for the planning of *Polarnaya Zvezda*. Timoshenko owed his high position entirely to his Civil War service alongside Stalin, and throughout his time in power the Soviet ruler showed a deep-seated loyalty to an inner circle of men who had fought with him against the White Russian armies, and particularly those who served him with ruthless and unquestioning brutality in the years that followed. But if Stalin remained convinced of Timoshenko's value, this wasn't a view that was shared by many senior personnel, particularly when it came to command of combat formations. After the poor performance of the Red Army in the war against Finland in 1939–40, he was appointed People's Commissar of Defence – effectively the defence minister – and showed considerable ability in drawing up plans to modernise the Soviet Union's forces, but the manner in which he passed down instructions with little regard for how effectively they could be implemented was perhaps typical of much of the functioning of the Soviet Union. When war with Germany broke out, he became chairman of *Stavka*, but his performance was uneven. Admiral Nikolai Gerasimovich Kuznetsov attended a meeting chaired by Timoshenko shortly after the conflict began and was unimpressed:

The chairmanship of the People's Commissar of Defence, Marshal Timoshenko, was only nominally in charge. I had to attend only one of these meetings but it wasn't difficult to see that [he] was unprepared for the position that he held. Nor were other members of *Stavka*. Their individual functions were unclear – there were no regulations covering this. The members of the group were unwilling to obey [Timoshenko].[20]

Shortly after, Timoshenko took command of Western Front after its initial defeat by the Wehrmacht close to the western frontier of the Soviet Union and was then sent to Kiev in an attempt to salvage the disaster that was unfolding around the city in September, where another of Stalin's Civil War cronies – Marshal Semen Mikhailovich Budennyi – had presided over a rapidly deteriorating situation. Timoshenko then commanded Southwest Front during the Battle of Moscow and performed well, or at least no worse than other Front commanders; his troops achieved considerable initial successes, but were then squandered in futile frontal attacks on the rapidly hardening German front line. However, his most disastrous performance came when he directed his troops to try to retake Kharkov in May 1942, resulting in the almost complete destruction of his Front. Despite this, he was then sent to Northwest Front where, as Voronov described, he drew up plans with no regard for the realities on the ground.

Voronov attempted to make *Stavka* and Stalin aware of the problems that were unfolding:

> I could not be silent. I decided: come what may, I will say everything that I think about the hasty and ill-considered plans for an offensive in this area. We were ensuring the loss of a great deal of equipment, the loss of many men, and the use of an incalculable amount of ammunition on clearly unpromising axes.
>
> On 8 March I sent a report to *Stavka* in which I tried to enumerate the reasons for the failures of Northwest Front. The first of these I categorised as poor study of the enemy. We had not taken into account that the enemy had experienced divisions here, well equipped and comprehensively prepared for a stubborn defence. Their battle zones were well provided for in terms of engineering, skilfully camouflaged and covered by natural features such as dense forests and lower vegetation.
>
> The faults of Northwest Front's command lay in that it was not familiar with the area of forthcoming operations. The units were in defensive positions at least 2km from the enemy without having constant contact with him. This was in the area designated for the breakthrough. Without constant observation, without good ground for positions rather than swamps or waterlogged ground covered with snow, with almost no roads, our powerful artillery equipment found itself in very unfavourable conditions. Our troops were often not able to use the artillery's firepower. Battalion mortars and heavy machine-guns lagged behind during an advance, not to mention the 45mm guns and even more so the 76mm regimental guns – they had to be pulled by up to 30 men, taking losses from

enemy fire, and still lagged behind the advance. The terrain was completely unsuitable for the use of tanks.

The troops of Northwest Front spent almost a year and a half in defensive positions, never really preparing for an offensive. The newly formed units that arrived here, hastily assembled and inadequately trained, immediately found themselves in very difficult conditions. Consequently, many commanders at all levels were unable to organise and conduct battle.

The rear areas of the Front and the advancing armies were very poorly prepared for the operation. In my opinion, this was because preparations for operations were kept secret in all our units for a long period with transport restricted to the combat units, with supplies, fuel, ammunition, and food being delivered far later. Consequently, we often found ourselves with shortages of certain supplies needed to commence operations.

When planning an operation both centrally [i.e. at *Stavka*] and in the field, we didn't always take into account the element of time. The dates for commencing operations were set without regard to realities. This created progressively greater problems at lower levels from Fronts to armies, divisions, and their subunits. Those who would be directly involved in fighting – company and battalion commanders – usually had very little time for preparation, adversely affecting their readiness and organisation in battle.

At present our tactics resulted in protracted fighting with infantry being effective only when our artillery, mortars and rocket launchers completely cleared the enemy positions. Undoubtedly the enemy suffered heavy losses from this fire but we too lost large quantities of men and materiel. The infantry suffered significant losses from enemy fire when it lay in its starting positions, only moving forward reluctantly towards the artillery bombardment from where it was meant to make a swift attack on enemy positions when artillery fire was transferred to the depths of the enemy position. Consumption of artillery ammunition was exorbitant whereas the ground gained in a day's fighting was a few hundred metres. Infantry weapons were used very poorly, even when repelling enemy counterattacks.

'On the Northwest Front,' I wrote in my report, 'of course we had partial success in that we created a threat of encircling the Demyansk group, degraded it, and forced the enemy to retreat and thereby abandon active operations here in future. At the same time, we failed in that the enemy released reserves by the withdrawal of his troops from the Demyansk salient for covering the major operation we had planned.

'In my opinion, large-scale operations with major objectives should not be planned in sectors such as Govorov's left wing, [and] the Fronts of Meretskov and

Voroshilov ... In their previous operations, they have already consumed much manpower and resources and the results are far from justifying the cost. I believe that we need to seek large solutions where we can most productively use our vast wealth of military equipment. Thus the forests and marshes can be bypassed and will be captured by the mere threat of encirclement on a large operational scale ...'

Sending the report, I hoped that in Moscow they would take my thoughts into account. However, apart from a positive decision to restore corps headquarters [these had been largely discontinued earlier in the war because of irreplaceable casualties amongst staff officers], nothing was done by *Stavka*.[21]

The general reintroduction of corps headquarters – not all had been abolished during 1942 – was an important step for Voronov, because it provided for improved flexibility at a level above division commanders, without adding to the burden of army commanders. In particular, corps commanders could now use the artillery and other support assets of more than one division to support an attack by just part of their corps. But in his account, Voronov indirectly highlighted another important problem for the Red Army. The road and railway network of the Soviet Union was far poorer than that of countries to the west, and the problem was exacerbated by the sheer scale of the landscape. In order to achieve some degree of operational surprise, timescales for preparations were deliberately kept as short as possible, but this placed impossible burdens upon logistic services. If they were to be given the time that they required, then it would be impossible to hide preparations from the Germans, particularly if preparations included the construction of new roads and railway lines. Voronov had overseen operations further south during the winter of 1942–43, where Operation *Saturn* – the follow-up to the encirclement of Stalingrad – had to be scaled down to *Malyi Saturn* ('Little Saturn') because an unexpectedly large number of Soviet units was required to maintain the ring around the German Sixth Army. Had some of the considerable resources wasted in the north been made available, it seems possible that the original plan for *Saturn* might have been possible. Whilst it was ambitious in terms of scale, the attack would have unfolded over terrain that was far more suitable for mechanised offensive operations, with the likelihood that the German position in the south would have become even more precarious. Voronov's criticism of the wasteful attacks in the north is therefore perhaps a reflection of his feeling that the 'opportunity cost' was the dilution of Red Army operations in sectors where they might have achieved much greater success.

As Voronov implied, one of the reasons why Soviet operations in the southern sector were so effective, while those elsewhere faced failure, was simply that the terrain was far more open and therefore more suitable for major operations. As is often the case, the railways of the region tended to follow the main rivers with crossing points at major cities; thus, the Red Army's positions along the Don River could be reinforced with relative ease, without the necessity for construction of large numbers of roads and railway lines. The failure of senior planners in the Red Army to recognise this fundamental factor is striking. In his book comparing and contrasting the lives of Field Marshals Montgomery and Rommel, Peter Caddick-Adams repeatedly highlights one crucial difference between the two men: Montgomery benefited from extensive experience and training as a staff officer and thus was always cognizant of the absolute importance of logistics; Rommel, by contrast, was prone to overstretching his logistic support, at least partially because he had no experience in organising and overseeing such matters and therefore often made unjustified assumptions about what would be possible. What is remarkable is that senior Soviet commanders who had benefited from the Red Army's staff officer training placed so little importance on this fundamental aspect of military operations.

In many respects, neglect of logistics was an issue that predated the Soviet Union and continues to be a major deficiency in the Russian Army in the modern era. As the Great Powers mobilised for war in 1914, the armies of Russia were severely handicapped by priority being given to combat formations, with men for support services languishing behind, and this resulted in many newly mobilised units being left stranded due to a lack of railway workers, rolling stock, or supplies.[22] To make matters worse, few Russian senior commanders had any understanding of logistics. During paper and field exercises prior to the First World War, there was a deliberate policy of not bothering with any considerations of logistics and conducting the exercises as if all units were fully supplied at all times. This was partly to spare the blushes of senior figures in the army who were both ignorant and disdainful of the importance of lowly logistics, and partly because those organising the exercises were themselves unaware of the complexity of such matters, especially once fighting began. This neglect of logistics seems to have been carried forward into the Bolshevik and Soviet era, and many aspects of it can be seen clearly in the recent fighting in Ukraine. This weakness, combined with a tendency to plan exercises on maps without any regard to the realities on the ground, repeatedly resulted in operational plans that were simply impossible to achieve.

171

However, Voronov's criticisms of operations in the northern sector miss an important point. Lifting the siege of Leningrad was of huge political and symbolic significance to the Soviet Union. Hitler had ordered the complete destruction of the city and had come terrifyingly close to starving it to death in the winter of 1941–42. There could be no doubt that if the opportunity were to arise again, the Germans would try to repeat their efforts. Conversely, lifting the siege would be of great political value to the Soviet Union and German setbacks in this region were likely to have serious consequences for the willingness of Finland to continue in the war alongside Germany. This accounts for the high strategic priority given to breaking the siege, even though the terrain was deeply unfavourable for such an operation. There simply wasn't any realistic hope of bypassing the forests and swamps via better ground for mechanised operations – any attack to relieve the city would have to be delivered over ground that greatly favoured the defenders.

The failure of *Polarnaya Zvezda* was due to several factors. Voronov correctly identified several of these, but he missed out many more. The German use of artillery was significantly more effective than that of the Red Army, as was their air support when the weather permitted air operations. Moreover, the Soviet formations thrown at the Mga–Sinyavino salient were still badly weakened by the costly fighting of *Iskra* and were far below the strength required to achieve success.

After the war, Soviet historiography of *Polarnaya Zvezda* struggled to cope with the failure of the operation and the huge losses suffered. Many accounts barely mentioned the operation by name and the heavy fighting was interpreted as an essential part of tying down German forces that might have been able to intervene elsewhere, much the same justification that was used to explain the huge casualties incurred around the Rzhev salient. Whilst this interpretation is in some respects correct in terms of what effect the operations had on the course of the war, the implication of these post-war accounts was that the attacks were always intended purely with this outcome in mind, which is manifestly not true. Zhukov made no mention of *Polarnaya Zvezda* in his memoirs, and his accounts of his activities in the winter of 1942–43 are misleading and inaccurate, attempting to downplay his critical role in overseeing the slaughter of so many Soviet soldiers in the central and northern sectors. Meretskov described the fighting of *Iskra* and the subsequent attacks against Sinyavino and Mga, but failed to add that these subsequent attacks were meant to be part of the much larger *Polarnaya Zvezda*, preferring to categorise them as purely local follow-on operations after the partial success of *Iskra*. Such was the cult of infallibility amongst senior office holders in the Soviet Union that the distorted narrative survived almost unscathed until the fall of the Soviet Union. The futile assaults on Staraya Russa were only properly recognised in Russian accounts after 1991; for those who lost family members in the futile attacks, the battles were just part of a large list of such bloody failures, best forgotten or deliberately misinterpreted. Even today, the status of figures like Zhukov is so great that criticism remains muted. Only someone with the status of Voronov was able to speak any words of criticism about these battles.

The territorial gains of the winter attacks in the Leningrad area were modest at best, but the battles had a significant impact on the Wehrmacht. Although German losses were far lighter than those of the Red Army, they were still substantial. Every formation in Army Group North was now significantly below establishment strength, with some reduced to near-catastrophic levels – in the first three months of 1943, the army group recorded a total of over 78,000 casualties.[23] In order to survive, Küchler had been forced to rotate almost every division through the bitter fighting around Sinyavino, Mga, and Staraya Russa and the modest and inadequate reserves held at army and army group level were utterly exhausted. Nor was there any serious prospect of these being replaced; even as the fighting died down, Hitler was implementing a policy of re-creating the divisions that had been lost in Stalingrad, and this meant that there were fewer replacement drafts for units still in the front line. Army Group North would have to juggle what few resources it had to deal with the attacks by the Red Army, and one miscalculation might result in a major breakthrough. If that were to happen, Küchler would have nothing left with which to restore the situation. In some respects, this was the brutal reality that the Soviet Union faced. The poor infrastructure of so much of the country, the sheer scale of the landscape, and the huge territorial gains made by the Germans in 1941 meant that any offensive to recover ground would involve operations on unfavourable terms with regard to both territory and opposition, and final success needed the Wehrmacht to be ground down and weakened so that despite its many shortcomings and all the obstacles of terrain, weather and poor road and rail networks, the Red Army was able to prevail. The only alternative would have been to try to freeze this sector of the front line while attempting to secure victory elsewhere, but even if that had been politically acceptable, it would have necessitated pinning attacks to prevent the Germans from transferring troops to more critical sectors. For a few heady weeks during the winter of 1942–43, Stalin and many others believed that the moment that Germany's resources were stretched beyond breaking point had indeed arrived, but the mirage of victory vanished as quickly as it had appeared.

As the landscape slowly turned to mud, soldiers of both sides did what they could to improve their positions and continued to mount patrols. Occasionally, these encountered groups of men from the other side; usually this resulted in sharp firefights and close-quarter combat, with a few more corpses left to sink into the swampy ground, but sometimes the outcome was rather different:

> Russian and German reconnaissance parties suddenly came across each other by surprise in a fold of ground by the edge of the forest, and each group tried to take cover in the ditches that ran on either side of the track. That was fine – but a young German soldier jumped into the wrong side. Unintentionally, he found himself shoulder to shoulder with Red Army troops. Everyone held their breath. The young man realised his mistake. Like a frog, he hopped over the road and in a flash hid amongst his own side. The Russians and Germans now stared at each other, tense, ready, fearing the worst. But then grins broke out on their faces. This was followed by a minute of loud laughter. The men wiped tears of mirth from their eyes and crept back to their own lines.[24]

In Leningrad, there were still almost daily German artillery or air attacks, but the city authorities were determined to demonstrate to Leningraders – and to the world in general – that normal life was resuming and that conditions were improving. On 24 March, a group of 60 performers from the Bolshoi Dramatic Theatre performed in the city for the first time since the beginning of the siege. Most of the actors had been evacuated in the first winter of the war to the city of Kirov, 490 miles east of Moscow, but had returned in the last few weeks; a few had remained in Leningrad, working in the city's factories. The programme for their first performance was selected with care and its symbolism was obvious to all: *Davnyim-Davno* ('A Long Time Ago'), a series of poems about the great war of 1812 which saw Russia defeat Napoleon's invasion, the original 'Patriotic War' of Russian history. Unfortunately, the Germans spoiled the performance. An air raid commenced shortly after the performance had started, forcing its abandonment.[25] There were further air attacks the following day. Official reports described how the great majority of these raids were broken up by Leningrad's anti-aircraft guns or were intercepted by fighter aircraft, and improbable numbers of destroyed German bombers were claimed, but even if the reports of successful defence were true, the raids – and particularly the artillery attacks – demonstrated the underlying truth: the Germans were still close enough to the city to cause serious harm. Until they were driven back further, Leningrad remained under constant threat.

CHAPTER 6

A TENSE SUMMER

Human nature often seeks to ascribe causality to a single factor or moment – the human brain instinctively tries to identify one moment, a specific decision or event, that is the cause of all that followed. Reality is usually far more complex and messy, with a multitude of factors contributing to the course of events, and the manner in which repeated attempts to find a decisive turning point for the Second World War identify different moments is a case in point. Some suggest that the encirclement of Stalingrad tipped the balance against Germany, while others choose other moments such as the Red Army's failed counteroffensive at Smolensk in 1941, which resulted in fatal delays to the German attempts to reach Moscow before the first winter of the war in the east. The delay in commencing *Barbarossa* is another potential moment, as is the actual decision to invade the Soviet Union at all. In truth, all of these contributed to a steady shift in the balance of the conflict. This shift was clearly visible to most observers in the summer of 1943, but the momentum behind the change had been building for some considerable time.

Moreover, as Robert Kee wrote in his account of the history of Irish independence: 'It is easy to see turning points in history where turning points later turned out to have been; but to do so often misrepresents the way things looked at the time.'[1]

As the spring thaw imposed a much-needed pause on both sides, it seemed at least superficially as if the outcome of the war was still uncertain and few would have been bold enough to declare that a decisive moment in the course of the war had occurred, and that Germany was doomed to defeat. Germany had suffered a huge setback in the destruction of its Sixth Army in Stalingrad, but the Soviet Union's casualties in the battles in and around the city actually exceeded

German losses. Moreover, the Red Army's casualties in the central sector around the Rzhev salient and in the northern sector at Shlisselburg, Sinyavino, Mga, and Staraya Russa were also far greater than those of the Wehrmacht. Stability was restored to the front line by Manstein's decisive counteroffensive that drove the Red Army back to the Mius and Northern Donets Rivers, and all that remained of the high hopes of Stalin and others was a large west-facing bulge around the city of Kursk, about 160 miles from its northern boundary to the southern edge and extending west for about 100 miles. As confidence rose in German circles with Manstein's successes, there were inevitable discussions about what offensive operations might be possible once the ground hardened and dried out, and this bulge rapidly became the centre of attention.

As a result of battle losses along the Eastern Front and inadequate replacements, the Wehrmacht was in poor shape. In terms of manpower alone, the divisions on the Eastern Front were estimated to be about 470,000 men below establishment strength.[2] The collapse of so much of the southern sector in the winter fighting and the precipitate retreat of German units resulted in many abandoning their heavy equipment, with the consequence that they were now short of artillery, with the loss of guns exacerbated by German dependence on draft horses to tow guns and other equipment. While divisions were in stationary defensive positions, this deficiency was of little importance and was given a low priority, but the sudden imposition by the Red Army of a war of movement across so much of the southern sector exposed this weakness. The panzer divisions were also in far from ideal shape, with many reduced to just a handful of tanks. German tank production was dwarfed by the number of armoured vehicles being produced by the Soviet Union, and although Albert Speer, who had become armaments minister in early 1942, had streamlined the manufacture of many weapons and had eliminated a great deal of inefficiency, it would take time to bring the cutting edge of the Wehrmacht back to a level where it could be used effectively. And of course, during that time the enemies of Germany would also be increasing their strength.

In some respects, the most serious German losses were not in terms of sheer numbers of troops or equipment, but in terms of reduced expertise. With its system of delegated command, which encouraged commanders at every level to show initiative and personal leadership, casualties amongst officers and NCOs in the front line were particularly heavy in the Wehrmacht. These men represented invaluable experience and knowledge, and their replacement was almost impossible. In a similar manner, replacement drafts of ordinary soldiers were poor substitutes for the battle-hardened veterans who were killed in the battles of

1942 and early 1943. This was a problem that would worsen steadily as the war progressed, and German armies increasingly adopted a policy of establishing *Kriegsschulen* – 'war schools' – close to the front line where new drafts could be given additional training. In particular, these recruits needed to learn how to use heavy weapons that were actually in use, rather than the older, obsolete weaponry that they had used in their training depots.

To make matters even more difficult, there was a growing threat of landings on the European mainland by the Western Allies. The Germans knew that Stalin had been demanding such landings for some considerable time, and there was plenty of intelligence about the arrival of US forces in Britain. At some stage, these forces would attempt to seize a toehold on continental Europe and it was necessary to hold back substantial forces – particularly mobile panzer formations – in anticipation of an invasion. The German forces in the east could not expect major reinforcements from France and elsewhere, and any major developments in the west might actually result in the diversion of units from the Eastern Front to wherever the new crisis had arisen.

As a consequence of these limitations, German ambitions for future offensive operations had to be scaled down from the plans of earlier years. Nonetheless, if there was any recognition within Germany that the disasters of the winter in and around Stalingrad – and the disaster that was still unfolding in North Africa, which would precipitate the collapse of Fascist Italy – represented a fundamental shift in the likely outcome of the war, this view was very much restricted to those who were already opposed to Hitler's regime. Manstein and most of the senior figures in the military continued to believe that it was at least possible to avoid defeat, and that by doing so Germany would be able to position itself to achieve final victory at some point in the future or would at least be able to negotiate a favourable peace.

The roots of what was proposed for a summer offensive lay in the dark days of January 1943 when the entire southern sector was in flux with the very real danger of further encirclements of German forces; in particular, the Red Army was striving to reach the shores of the Sea of Azov or the lower Dnepr in order to cut off German units attempting to withdraw from the Caucasus region. Manstein outlined to Hitler a potential pincer operation in which the Red Army would be permitted to enter the Donbas region and would then be attacked on both flanks in convergent attacks. Hitler rejected such a voluntary withdrawal outright, but as the subsequent campaign unfolded much of Manstein's plan became reality: the Red Army pressed on over the Northern Donets and captured Kharkov while German panzer forces retreating from the Caucasus region in the south concentrated their reduced but still considerable strength and then struck into the deep flank of the Soviet advance.

During a visit to the Eastern Front in mid-March, Hitler visited Manstein's headquarters in Zaporozhye. The Führer discussed options in full and rejected Manstein's initial suggestion that the best policy for the future was to wait for the Red Army to attack after the spring thaw, and then to counterattack in strength. This plan – often described as the 'backhand blow' – was based upon the justified belief that in mobile warfare, the tactical skill of German units was still far greater than that of their Soviet opponents and would go a considerable distance towards compensating for Soviet numerical superiority. Manstein summarised this thinking in his memoirs, believing that the limited resources available meant that for the moment, Germany should adopt a strategic defensive posture, intended to bleed the Red Army of resources:

> Army Group South had on a number of occasions brought these considerations [the likelihood of further Soviet operations to capture the valuable resources of eastern Ukraine] to the notice of *OKH* and Hitler. What the latter ultimately had to decide was whether the overall situation allowed us to wait for the Russians to start an offensive and then to hit them hard *'on the backhand'* [emphasis in original text] at the first good opportunity, or whether we should attack as early as possible ourselves and – still within the framework of a strategic defensive – strike a limited blow *'on the forehand'*.
>
> The army group preferred the former solution as one offering better prospects operationally and had already submitted a tentative plan to Hitler in February. It envisaged that if the Russians did as we anticipated and launched a pincer attack on the Donets area from the north and south – an offensive which could sooner or later be supplemented by an offensive around Kharkov – our arc of front along the Donets and Mius should be given up in accordance with an agreed timetable in order to draw the enemy westwards towards the lower Dnepr. Simultaneously all the reserves that could possibly be released – in particular the bulk of the armour – were to assemble in the area west of Kharkov, first to smash the enemy assault forces which we expected to find there and then to drive into the flank of those advancing in the direction of the lower Dnepr. In this way the enemy would be doomed to suffer the same fate on the coast of the Sea of Azov as he had in store for us on the Black Sea.[3]

Manstein's suggestion for his preferred plan – *Schlagen aus der Nachhand* ('the backhand blow') – was deliberately to create the circumstances that led to the

German counteroffensive at the end of winter 1942–43, but on a far greater scale. The operation would have carried considerable risks: the Soviet forces would have to attack as Manstein expected; territory would have to be conceded; and the armoured counteroffensive would then have to smash the Red Army's units as he anticipated. The first of these couldn't be guaranteed, and the second went against Hitler's deep-seated reluctance to give up any territory, even if only on a temporary basis. The third element was also problematic.

There were already some signs that the ability of panzer divisions to impose themselves almost at will on the Red Army was not as great as it had been in earlier times. During the failed attempt to rescue Sixth Army after its encirclement, 6th Panzer Division fought a prolonged battle to overcome Soviet anti-tank defences around Verkhne Kumsky, and the use of massed anti-tank guns was an increasing feature of Red Army defensive doctrine. The Germans had altered their use of anti-tank guns in 1941 when they encountered large numbers of Soviet tanks on the battlefield, with battery commanders using the massed fire of guns in a more organised manner – rather than each gun selecting its target, the officer commanding the guns allocated targets to each gun so that the number of enemy vehicles hit by the first salvo was maximised. This concept, known to the Germans as the *Pakfront*, was rapidly adopted by the Red Army too, with additional modifications. Soviet anti-tank gunners became increasingly adept at identifying German command tanks and attempted to target them preferentially; for heavily armoured targets like Tiger tanks, several guns were assigned to the same target to maximise the chances of success; and anti-tank units soon acquired attached sappers who rapidly laid anti-tank mines to try to channel German tanks into the field of fire of the guns themselves or to immobilise tanks by damaging their tracks, leaving them at the mercy of the Soviet anti-tank gunners.

Hitler's mood was becoming more confident after the disaster of Stalingrad, which he had no choice but to acknowledge was his responsibility. Now, Manstein's remarkable achievement in restoring the situation and in particular the success of his beloved SS Panzer Corps in retaking Kharkov left the Führer with the view that Germany was still in a position to assume major offensive operations, and his persistent refusal to give up territory unless absolutely necessary prevailed. Manstein was asked to offer a more positive option – 'on the forehand'. In discussions that looked at the entire sector, including the Soviet-held Kursk salient, Manstein suggested the possibility of an early attack against the salient before the Red Army had recovered from the mauling he had inflicted. The attack would shorten the German front line, thus releasing valuable reserves, and seemed proportionate to the resources available. Hitler left the meeting without making a clear decision, apart from reiterating his insistence that the Donbas region could not be given up in a voluntary withdrawal, even temporarily.

From Zaporozhye, Hitler travelled to the headquarters of Army Group Centre near Smolensk where he met the army group commander, Generalfeldmarschall Günther von Kluge, and the commanders of the group's armies, including one of his favourites, Generaloberst Walter Model – increasingly known as *der Löwe der Abwehr* ('The Lion of Defence') for his unbroken line of successes in defending the Rzhev salient against the Red Army.[4] Here, Hitler outlined proposals for a convergent attack on the Kursk salient by Army Group Centre and Army Group South – there was no mention of it having originated with Manstein. If he expected enthusiasm, Hitler was disappointed. Although Army Group Centre had beaten off the assaults both at Rzhev and further south, it was badly weakened by its losses and both Kluge and Model expressed doubts about whether their units were strong enough for any sort of offensive operation. There was also plenty of evidence that the Soviet forces in the Kursk salient weren't waiting passively – aerial reconnaissance showed that their positions were already heavily fortified and work was continuing steadily.

Kluge, Model, and the other senior officers of Army Group Centre might have been decidedly lukewarm about an offensive operation, but there were others in Kluge's headquarters who had even greater misgivings about the future of Germany. There was a particularly energetic group of anti-Hitler conspirators in Smolensk who decided that the moment was ripe to take action if Germany was to be saved from disaster. They had repeatedly approached Kluge to get his support, but their commander vacillated, refusing to commit himself but also taking no action against the conspirators. When they learned of the imminent visit, the conspirators made plans to arrest Hitler on arrival. Major Georg von Boeselager was to lead the arrest party but the plan was abandoned when it became clear that Hitler's SS escort was too strong. Instead, they decided to attempt an assassination during a formal lunch – at an agreed moment, Boeselager and others would draw their pistols and shoot Hitler. But Hitler decided not to attend the lunch and Kluge then intervened, forbidding any attack for fear of precipitating wider unrest. Finally, Oberstleutnant Fabian von Schlabrendorff constructed a time bomb using explosives that were of British origin, so that if the bomb was discovered, suspicion would fall elsewhere. The bomb was put in a box with two bottles of Cointreau and Schlabrendorff handed it to Oberstleutnant Heinz Brandt, a member of Hitler's staff, asking him to take it back to Berlin as a present for Schlabrendorff's friend Oberst Hellmuth Steiff.

The bomb was timed to detonate somewhere over Belarus in the hope that the loss of the plane might be blamed on an accident or perhaps interception by Soviet fighters, and the conspirators waited anxiously for news. When they received a report that Hitler had landed safely in Berlin, Schlabrendorff decided to fly to Germany to recover the bomb. When he did so, he discovered that the timer had worked perfectly, but the explosives had failed to detonate – due to the plane being crowded, Brandt had placed it in the cargo hold, where it was too cold for the explosives to ignite.[5]

Despite the lack of enthusiasm from Kluge and his army commanders for a summer offensive, Hitler issued his Directive No. 5 when he returned to his main headquarters in East Prussia. This summarised both the views of the high command about the probable outcome of events and Hitler's plans:

It is expected that after the end of the winter and the spring thaw, after creating stockpiles of material resources and partly replenishing their formations with personnel, the Russians will resume their offensives.

Therefore, our task is to pre-empt the enemy as much as possible in offensive operations at certain locations in order to impose our will upon them at least in one of the sectors of the front, as is already the case at present in Army Group South's sector.

In the remaining sectors of the front, the task is limited to bleeding the attacking enemy. We must create a particularly strong defensive line here in advance using heavy weapons, improving positions by the use of engineers, installing minefields in appropriate areas, forming strongpoints in depth, creating mobile reserves, etc ...

On the northern flank of [Army Group South, the task is] to begin immediately the formation of a sufficiently combat-ready armoured force, to be completed by mid-April in order to go onto the offensive against the Russians after the end of the spring thaw ...

[Army Group Centre is to] create a strike force for use in an offensive in cooperation with the troops of the northern wing of Army Group South ...

Since no offensive is planned on Army Group North's front in the first half of the summer, all efforts should be concentrated on maximising the strength of the defensive positions along the entire front ...

The divisions released as a result of giving up the Demyansk salient should be used to strengthen defences and to create the necessary operational reserves ...

In the second half of the summer (early July) it is planned to conduct an operation against Leningrad. The operation will be carried out with the maximum concentration of available artillery, using the latest offensive weapons. To do this, it is necessary to commence in advance the deployment of artillery and the creation of stockpiles of ammunition.[6]

The German units tasked with the attacks by the adjacent flanks of Army Groups Centre and South against the Kursk salient were too weak to undertake such an operation as early as Manstein had intended. The operation that would be given the name *Zitadelle* ('Citadel') resulted in repeated delays in the hope that additional new tanks and drafts of soldiers would restore the divisions to combat strength. Ultimately, these delays turned Manstein's original proposal for an early attack against the Red Army before it could recover from its losses into a doomed operation that handed the operational and strategic initiative to the Soviet Union for the rest of the war. Throughout the planning of *Zitadelle*, the Soviet Union received a steady flow of intelligence about German intentions from a variety of sources. The partisan movement was now far more organised and efficient, and aerial reconnaissance was steadily improving, but much of the intelligence came from spy networks within Nazi Germany.[7] At some stages of the planning for the summer, Stalin expressed concerns that the Red Army wouldn't be able to halt the new German offensive when it began, but his subordinates were far more confident. The defensive lines around the Kursk salient developed into a dense network of positions, with a completely separate line across the base of the salient – even if the Germans succeeded in breaking through the lines that faced north and south, they would then be faced by an entirely new set of defences. By the time that *Zitadelle* commenced, there was no longer the slightest prospect of Manstein's original vision – of trapping significant Soviet armoured formations that had not fully recovered from the winter fighting within the salient and then destroying them – from being realised.

The planned operation by the Wehrmacht against Leningrad in the second half of 1943 – to commence after the successful completion of *Zitadelle* – was never described in detail. The original advance to Leningrad in 1941 had been curtailed to avoid costly street-fighting and after the failed attempt to starve the city to death in the winter of 1941–42, plans were drawn up for an operation codenamed *Nordlicht* ('Northern Light'); Manstein's Eleventh Army, transferred to the north after its successful capture of the fortress of Sevastopol in Crimea, was to lead an attack intended to link up with the Finns between Leningrad and Lake Ladoga, thus preventing any supplies from reaching the city. This was abandoned as a consequence of the Soviet Sinyavino Offensive of the late summer and autumn, and it is likely that the plans for 1943 would have envisaged a drive both to recover the ground lost during *Iskra* and to carry out the intentions of *Nordlicht*.

Despite several armoured formations being badly beaten by the Wehrmacht in its counteroffensive along the Donets River in March, the Red Army remained confident that it could now win the war. Memoirs of senior and junior figures alike are full of comments that they never doubted their final victory, even during the dark days of 1941; whilst this may or may not have been true, the stunning success at Stalingrad showed beyond doubt that the Germans could be beaten. Nevertheless, the confident mood was strongly flavoured with caution. Success at Stalingrad had been achieved because the Germans had exhausted their strength in their increasingly futile attacks on the last Soviet defenders clinging to the ruins along the west bank of the Volga River, and the Red Army's counteroffensive had then taken advantage of relatively weak Romanian units deployed to defend the flanks of the Stalingrad salient. There was no guarantee that the Germans would leave their flanks so vulnerable in future, and in any case it was necessary to weaken the Wehrmacht as much as possible before launching fresh offensives. The strategy adopted by the Red Army – in full awareness of the intentions of the Wehrmacht – was to remain on the defensive until the German attack on the Kursk salient was exhausted. This would then be followed by offensive operations against the German forces on either flank of the salient – *Kutuzov* in the north and *Rumyantsev* in the south. In order to bolster the forces available both to defend the Kursk salient and to commence preparations for the counteroffensives, several major formations were withdrawn from the Leningrad sector, particularly from Northwest Front. With these units withdrawing, there was no possibility of major offensive operations and, secure in the knowledge that the Germans were also planning no major attacks, Govorov and Meretskov took the opportunity to replenish many of their units. Leningrad Front pulled most of Sixty-Seventh Army out of the front line for a prolonged period of rest as its Front reserve, and Meretskov withdrew several of his depleted units. In addition, he ordered his other armies to organise local reserves, which were then given an opportunity to absorb fresh drafts and carry out extensive training. This was essential in order to prepare new recruits for the likely ordeals that lay ahead, and Meretskov was already contemplating the orders that he was likely to receive:

> Every day I thought more and more about the nature of the forthcoming summer campaign. It was clear to me that the Red Army would launch a powerful offensive and that the Germans would now have to defend themselves not only in winter but also in summer. What role would be assigned to Volkhov Front? As often

happened, the supreme commander might ask for my opinion before making a final decision. My point of view was determined by a number of attendant circumstances that had to be taken into account.

Firstly, what was the intelligence picture? In the first half of May, intelligence reports repeatedly stated that the enemy was sending reinforcements of men and equipment towards Mga, concentrating short-range aviation in forward airfields, and carrying out extensive work in his defensive zone. This might mean that the Nazis were building up forces to attempt to restore the ring around Leningrad, or to repel our attacks on Mga, which they feared. In either case, we had to reckon with the strengthening of Army Group North.

And what were the options for Volkhov Front? We repaired the damage we had suffered during the busy winter campaign but that was about all we had done. To date, we had not created the superiority of forces necessary for an offensive in the prevailing conditions. After determining what *Stavka* and the general staff might send us in the near future, it seemed that we would not get many men … Things were better with industrial production. The hardest years were already past and I was given firm assurances that worn-out equipment, especially artillery and mortars, would be replaced and ammunition supplied in sufficient quantities to my satisfaction.

At the same time, *Stavka* assigned the following task to Volkhov Front: to prepare carefully for an assault and breakthrough with a subsequent advance towards the Baltic; to thwart any attempts by the enemy to restore the ring around Leningrad; and to tie down as many units as possible to prevent their transfer to the south …

Bearing in mind these circumstances, I came up with an idea, the essence of which was to forestall an enemy attack near Lake Ladoga. In order to prepare for this, we needed to weaken the enemy's defences. In order to draw his attention away from the left flank of my Front, we needed to make him concentrate on our right flank. And the only way for the Volkhovites to prevent Nazi divisions being sent to other sectors was to inflict casualties in our sector. Finally, to preserve the strength of our troops, we had to do all of this through the massive use of aircraft and artillery.[8]

This account is slightly at odds with the *Stavka* directives of the era, which suggest that the decision to use the northern sector to pin down German forces instead of mounting major operations originated from the centre. Meretskov went on to explain that because it was now known that the Germans had evacuated all civilians from a broad area behind their front line, Red Army gunners felt able to fire without fear of hitting innocent people; there is little evidence that such concerns ever limited their activity to any significant extent, either before this date or in the months and years that followed.

It seems therefore that the tumultuous campaigns of the winter left the senior figures on both sides cautiously optimistic that they would be able to win the war, but it is much harder to assess the mood of soldiers on both sides of the front line. Letters were heavily censored and the information that soldiers received was so restricted that few would have had any concept of overall events outside their personal experience. The destruction of the German Sixth Army was now widespread knowledge in the Wehrmacht, but the official story was that the entire army had perished, either in heroic fighting or massacred by the Red Army after Soviet forces seized the ruins of Stalingrad and captured the makeshift hospitals. There was some truth to this latter point: there were numerous cases of Soviet troops simply burning down hospitals with flamethrowers, but in 1943 the German soldiers who had witnessed these events were in prison camps in the Soviet Union. Perhaps more worrying for many German soldiers was news from home of increasingly heavy air raids on German cities, and the modest numbers of men who returned to Germany on leave often brought back terrible tales of devastated urban landscapes; some even discouraged their comrades from returning home on leave. When German soldiers were captured by the constant patrols and local raids to capture 'tongues', any signs of despondency or low morale were amplified in Soviet reports to boost morale amongst both Soviet soldiers and civilians, so the reports that were sent up the Soviet chain of command need to be treated with caution. Nevertheless, the contents of these reports were used to discourage the Germans still further by dropping leaflets on German lines with often exaggerated versions of the reports of prisoners. On 1 April, newspapers in Leningrad described how a raid on German positions seized a bag of letters. One letter was from the German province of Brandenburg to a soldier in the front line:

> I'm being called up to join the army. Russia swallows our divisions one by one, and an infinite number of march battalions [i.e. replacement drafts]. Eventually, Russia will swallow all those who are still far from the front.[9]

Another letter from the same batch was from a man named Fritz Starbeck, writing from Germany to his brother in the front line:

> Karl will be called up soon too as an anti-aircraft gunner. Students in their sixth and seventh years were called up on Monday. They're treated like soldiers and put

in uniform. Just think – our lives entrusted to children. They have to protect us from British air raids. Older, more experienced anti-aircraft gunners are being sent to Russia where they will fight as infantry.[10]

It isn't possible to say whether these were genuine quotes from letters, exaggerations, or simply fabricated. Although at first glance it seems unlikely that such comments would have been permitted by censors, the sheer volume of mail meant that censorship was rarely as comprehensive as the authorities might have wished, and in any case it was targeted more at letters being sent from the front line to the homeland than at letters sent to soldiers. It's also relevant that the use of teenagers in anti-aircraft batteries was commonplace on the Soviet side during the defences of Leningrad; the comments of the fighting on the front line devouring divisions and replacement drafts with an insatiable appetite was equally applicable to the Red Army as it was to the Wehrmacht.

Despite their terrible losses and the worrying news of bombing raids on German cities, most German soldiers seem to have remained confident that they would still win the war. Now deployed to the north of Lake Ilmen, Wilhelm Lubbeck and his comrades received news of setbacks at Stalingrad and elsewhere with a degree of stoicism:

After two years of war, we remained deep inside enemy territory and maintained faith in Germany's ultimate triumph. Our expertise at the front left us wholly convinced that our army was still superior in terms of both our troops and equipment. Our generals and other officers also retained our full confidence to give us a tactical advantage on the battlefield. Furthermore, we believed that German industry would continue to supply us with qualitatively better weapons than those of the enemy.

Even after Stalingrad, we believed that we could win a defensive struggle by not losing. The Red Army would gradually exhaust itself in its bloody assaults against us that produced only minor gains or no advantage at all. It seemed to me that the Soviet Union would eventually have to accept a negotiated peace or would leave Germany with much of its territorial gains ...

Unaware of Hitler's bungling and the political conflicts at the top, we never questioned the military decision-making until late in the war. Witnessing the skilled leadership exercised in the field, German troops at the front held the officer corps in high esteem.[11]

Despite this confidence, there was also growing recognition of the determination of the enemy:

> At the start of the war, we often viewed and treated the Soviet soldier as a primitive brute. As we came to know the enemy however, the natural courage and toughness of the Red Army soldier won him our respect. Whatever their views on Communism, it soon became clear to us that the Russian troops were willing to sacrifice their lives to repel the German invaders who had occupied their motherland.[12]

But if men in the front line had a grudging respect for their opponents, those in higher positions continued to believe in the innate superiority of Germans over their Bolshevik Slav foes.

In the city that had been the objective of Army Group North in its advance in 1941, life continued to improve slowly. The winter of 1941–42 had been exceptionally severe, but the following winter was much milder. The ice on Lake Ladoga became too fragile for traffic at the beginning of April and until it dispersed completely, thus permitting ships and barges to bring in supplies, Leningrad was dependent upon the tenuous link established along the southern shore of Lake Ladoga by *Iskra*. In anticipation of this period when the delivery of supplies would be exceeded by consumption, stockpiles of food, fuel, and ammunition had been built up in Leningrad, and there was additional good news on 3 April when a steel bridge was established over the Neva River at Shlisselburg. The final components were lifted into place under shellfire from the German positions around Sinyavino, a further reminder if any was needed that the city effectively remained under siege. The first barges bringing supplies over the lake itself reached the port that had been established at Osinovets the following day, but a cold spell resulted in more ice forming, disrupting communications once more. Nevertheless, rations were increased on 24 April to their highest level since the beginning of the siege, but four days later there was especially heavy shelling with 26 civilians killed and 62 wounded when they were caught in the bombardment of Gostinny Dvor and the Grand Hotel Europe on Nevsky Prospekt, close to the centre of the city. The main power station in the city, damaged by earlier shelling, was being repaired as a priority; there were several casualties amongst the engineers over the following days as German gunners attempted to disrupt their work.

Partisan activity behind German lines had been episodic in the first 18 months of the war. Although there had been plans made for a partisan movement in the event of war, these were often contradictory and poorly thought out, and many of the plans were deliberately destroyed during Stalin's purges immediately before the war out of fear that a dissenting movement might make use of the preparations to oppose Stalin's rule.[13] Further problems arose due to parallel and sometimes competing chains of command. As the war progressed, the partisans became better organised and more effective, not least because large numbers of Soviet troops who had been left behind during the first months of the war – not always deliberately – joined the partisan groups. Radio contact was established between the groups and partisan headquarters units, which were attached to each Front, and there were regular supply drops as well as large-scale infiltration of the front line by groups of partisans. In response to this activity, the Germans carried out regular anti-partisan operations, sometimes on a considerable scale. The Wehrmacht had anticipated problems with partisans and each army that invaded the Soviet Union included one or more security divisions, whose primary task was meant to be rear area security including dealing with partisans. Additional support came from the *Einsatzgruppen* of the SS, who were heavily involved in anti-partisan warfare as well as the wholesale slaughter of Jews, Roma, suspected Communists, the physically and mentally infirm, and any other group deemed by the Germans to be 'undesirable'. In their efforts to root out partisans, there were mass punishments of locals – sometimes these were limited to civilians who were suspected of aiding partisans, but in most cases the German reprisals were indiscriminate. The brutality with which the *Einsatzgruppen* – often aided by detachments from security divisions or even regular units, and making considerable use of locally raised paramilitary groups – carried out their tasks inevitably resulted in more people joining the partisans, which in turn triggered repeated sweeps to try to eliminate partisan activity. These sweeps grew steadily in scale during 1942, often involving several front-line divisions. Entire villages were routinely put to the torch, and their occupants were often lucky just to be driven away; rarely was there any attempt to distinguish between partisans, their suspected supporters, and local people who happened to be caught up in the fighting.

Most of the partisan activity in the rear area of Army Group North was to the south of the sector, in the forests between Lake Pskov and Lake Ilmen. Several partisan brigades had been active here since late 1941, frequently interdicting the vital roads and railways running through the region. In an attempt to reduce the risk of ambushes, the Germans cleared trees in some forests up to 100 yards on either side of roads and placed landmines in the cleared strips; in less densely forested areas, German units garrisoned important road junctions and constantly pressured the civilian population to provide information about partisan activity. Although Soviet-era accounts almost always describe most of the population as resisting such pressure, the reality for most civilians was that the struggle for survival often necessitated them cooperating with whoever applied pressure to them. Many civilians acted as informers, largely in return for rewards, though undoubtedly there were some who were motivated by anti-Communist views; these views tended to be far more widespread in the Baltic States, Belarus, and Ukraine than in Russia itself. On occasion, German forces captured partisans and successfully 'turned' them, setting them loose again to disrupt the activities of pro-Soviet groups; but many of those who had agreed to serve the Germans simply took the opportunity to rejoin their own side.

In May 1943, orders were sent from Volkhov and Northwest Fronts for the partisans to increase their level of activity. Attacks on railway line and bridges, destruction of telegraph wires and poles, mining of roads, and ambushes became more frequent, and the Wehrmacht was forced to respond. The standard policy was for German infantry units to establish a perimeter around a region where partisan activity was suspected, and for a motorised or mounted unit then to sweep through the region. The increasingly experienced partisans often slipped away before they could be caught, leaving local villagers to their fate. A report earlier in 1943 from one partisan unit described the outcome of such a sweep:

16 February 1943

Compiled in the presence of Aleksandr Ivanovich Ivanov and Vasily Kirillovich Yakushev, citizens from the village of Sevo, Pozherevitsky district:

On 10 February 1943, a German punitive detachment broke into the village of Sevo … and immediately began to massacre civilians. Hitler's executioners burned down 16 out of 17 houses and all their outbuildings. All the property of the collective farmers perished in the fire. Civilians who attempted to leave the burning houses were shot down at point-blank range regardless of gender or age, or were thrown into the fire while still alive. As a result of the savage massacre, 86 civilians were shot or burned to death, of whom 78 were from the village of Sevo and eight were from other villages. Of the dead, 61 were shot and 25 were burned alive. There were 14 men, 27 women, and 45 children ranging in age from eight months to 15 years. Only 19 people were saved from the massacre, managing to escape from the village under cover of the smoke from the burning buildings.[14]

In addition to attacks on German lines of communication, the partisans were sometimes tasked with gathering intelligence. One group of partisans operating in the northern half of the region received orders to capture a 'tongue', ideally an officer, for interrogation. Their first captive was named Anton Renke, a member of the Todt Organisation that was responsible for construction of roads, railways, airfields, and even fortifications. The group was ordered to try again, this time targeting military personnel, and succeeded perhaps better than they had expected: they managed to replace the driver of a bus carrying several officers with a partisan, who then drove at breakneck speed to a point where the partisans were able to overcome the Germans, who included the commandant of a small town. The Germans were flown out in small aircraft that made regular flights to improvised airstrips, and when news of the capture spread, there was a surge in morale amongst both partisans and their local civilian supporters.[15] Inevitably, this was followed by another anti-partisan sweep.

In the front line, combat continued at a far lower tempo than the first weeks of the year, with intermittent artillery bombardments, trench raids, and constant sniper activity. As was the case on all sectors of the Eastern Front, Soviet media and propaganda constantly reported on kill scores of snipers, encouraging them to set new records with Stakhanovite vigour. Many of the Red Army's snipers were women, as were many aircrew, another feature that was constantly highlighted by Soviet propaganda. One of the female snipers in the Leningrad sector was Nina Pavlovna Petrova, who had volunteered to serve in the army as a nurse. Even though she was 48 years old, she opted to train as a sniper in the second half of 1942 and was sent into the front line in December. She shot her first German on her second day. She continued to work as a nurse but requested permanent transfer to her regiment's sniper detachment in the second half of January. She rapidly became both a skilled sniper and responsible for training new sniper recruits. The snipers often operated in pairs, creeping into no-man's land and trying to identify high-value targets such as officers. Accompanied by Georgy Daudov, a trainee sniper, Petrova ventured out on a typical mission during the summer of 1943:

> As soon as it got dark, they made their way to a predetermined spot. They looked around: swamps on all sides, with milky fog forming. Like a great blanket, it covered the nearby shrubs and stunted birches, with pines and spruces rising above like black silhouettes.
>
> From time to time, flares rose over the enemy trenches and no-man's land, brightly illuminating the area. When they went out, the darkness seemed even denser for a time. They took turns to scrape out a foxhole ...

The weather was warm, dry and windless. They waited for dawn and in the east, the sky began to redden. 'The Fascists will appear soon, they follow a rigid routine,' whispered Georgy to Petrova. After some time, they heard the low ringing of kettles from the direction of the enemy trenches. At that moment, a Nazi stripped to the waist jumped out of the dugout. His tanned chest gleamed in the sun. He stretched and hung a towel on a nearby stake.

Daudov looked at Nina Pavlova, but she shook her head. The German took a mug, scooped water into it and yawned happily. A second German appeared from the dugout, this time wearing a tight-fitting shirt and suspenders with clasps that glinted in the sun. 'Let's get them both,' suggested Daudov impatiently. If he was alone, he would have opened fire long ago.

Petrova decided that the one with suspenders was probably an officer. She was tempted to take a shot, but decided on restraint. The orderly gave the officer some soap and poured water over his hands with the mug; the officer began to lather his face …

When he had covered his face with lather, Petrova ordered: 'Take the batman! The officer can't see anything!' A shot cracked out. The orderly collapsed silently. The officer held out his cupped hands to the batman, and swore. Another shot rang out …

Soon, the Germans realised what was happening. A characteristic, well-known unpleasant whistle was heard from their side. Daudov and Petrova drew their heads deeply into their shoulder. At its highest note, the whistle suddenly ceased and was followed immediately by a deafening explosion, then a second, a third … the mortar shells fell in a cluster. With each blast, huge columns of dry brown earth rose up, mixed with tree branches, old half-rotted stumps, and grass. The firing ended quickly, but then our artillery 'took the floor' …

Our shells damaged one bunker, and then there was silence. The snipers lay there for a long time. The day began to draw to a close. Soon it would be time to return to their own lines. Suddenly, Petrova saw two Fascists carrying a log.

'Looks like they're going to repair the bunker,' suggested Daudov.

'So, what do you think, which one do we shoot first?'

'The front one.'

'The rear one will immediately realise there's a sniper nearby and will take cover in the trench.'

'So the rear one first?'

'It's easier that way. The front one won't understand that his partner's been shot. He may think he's just stumbled, and he'll definitely stop to look around.'

'And he'll probably take a second or two to think about it,' Daudov noted.

The Germans were now approaching the bunker. 'Hit the rear one! I'll take the front one,' Nina Pavlovna commanded.

Daudov fired. The second Fascist staggered from side to side and began to sink to the ground slowly. Petrova was in no hurry with her shot. The front one now stopped and without dropping the log from his shoulder, tried to look around. Nina Pavlovna gently pulled her trigger. The Nazi fell, crushed by the log.[16]

Shortly after, the account continued, a plane flew overhead. The waiting snipers saw a German officer emerge from the bunker to try to spot the plane, and they killed him too. Whilst this account is full of the characteristic literary flourishes of so many such memoirs, it gives a good impression of the war waged by snipers on both sides. The casualties they inflicted were not huge, but the uncertainty and fear that they created was considerable.

Another 'celebrity sniper' was Iosif Iosifovich Pilyushin, who was drafted into the army in 1926. He soon became a proficient marksman, taking part in numerous shooting competitions. In 1941, he saw action on the Narva River before being wounded near Kingisepp. Such was the pressure of the German advance towards Leningrad that he was back in the front line within days. He later wrote that at first, he felt little hostility towards individual Germans, and it was only as the war progressed and several of his comrades were killed, and stories circulated about the atrocities committed by the Germans, that he became ruthlessly determined to kill as many Germans as possible. He remained in the front line throughout 1942 and rejoiced with his comrades when they learned of the breaking of the siege ring at the beginning of 1943; if they were aware that *Iskra* had only been partly successful, Pilyushin made no mention of it:

On this day [18 January] the soldiers and their officers were drunk with happiness. On 20 January I was granted leave to go to Leningrad to visit my son. What rejoicing there was on the streets of the city during these days! Literally at every step, people stopped me to congratulate me on our victory, hugged me, pressed tobacco and vodka into my hands.

One old woman stopped me and shaking my hand, said, 'Thank you, son, for clearing the path to the mainland. It's a little easier to breathe now, my dear.'

Finding no words with which to answer the Leningrad lady, I put my arms around her narrow shoulder and, in the Russian custom, kissed her withered, wrinkled face.[17]

Pilyushin was back in the front line within days, engaged in cat-and-mouse warfare against German positions. He described how he and his fellow snipers tried to spot German tracer fire in order to identify the location of machine-guns, but after they scored a few successes the Germans stopped using tracer rounds. Instead, the snipers had to rely on muzzle flashes, peering through narrow slits in small portable armoured shields. The Germans responded by constantly changing firing position. Any change in the appearance of no-man's land might represent danger; when a sheet of plywood appeared overnight, the Soviet marksmen were worried that the Germans had dug a firing position under cover of darkness, and were relieved when it disappeared the following night without any apparent sign of a new bunker or foxhole. Several days later, two prisoners were captured – one had a bullet wound in his hand, an attempt to escape from the front line. He told his captors that whilst such wounds might have earned him several months of respite in the past, he was now more likely to be sent to a penal battalion, and hence he had allowed himself to be captured easily. He also explained about the plywood sheet: an officer had wanted to erect a sign in no-man's land taunting the Soviet soldiers, but he had been shot by his own side.[18] The truth of this is hard to ascertain. There were numerous occasions when unpopular officers were shot by their own men on both sides, and such activity was easy in the confusion of fighting during the night. Not long after this incident, Pilyushin was wounded a second time, struck by a bullet in his abdomen. Just three weeks later, he was back with his comrades.

The Germans who had to face attacks by snipers often found it a deeply unsettling experience. Stachow wrote after the war about the psychological difference of coming under attack by different means:

Whoever ducks down under artillery or mortar fire feels as if they are lying under a huge hammering mechanism that is madly beating down on them. It's like a lottery: does this hammer blow hit, does the next one hit, or do none of them hit? When machine-guns chatter, it's the same as the crack of rifle fire: will one of the bullets get you? You are always at the mercy of chance or destiny. It's different for someone who is the target of a sniper. If you don't become the victim of the first shot, then he will try again – he's after you! Of course, in close combat too, your opponent personally means you harm, but at least you know who threatens you, from where, and with what. As the target of a sniper, you know only this: take cover, keep your head down, flatten yourself against the ground. But what if the sniper is in the trees? He could be anywhere or nowhere, and when the sounds of rifles, submachine-guns, and machine-guns multiply, when you don't know if the muzzle of a rifle with telescopic sights is aiming at you from above, or below, from the left or the right? Whoever jumps up in panic is finished. You have to say calm, even if your nerves are shredded.

There is just one terrible consolation for you: before you can get really scared, the sniper will have already hit you and you'll have kicked the bucket. But you can take precautions: be as imaginative and cunning and cautious as the sniper; always think – what would you do in his place? From where would you get a good field of fire?[19]

The German preparations for *Zitadelle* continued to impose delays on the operation. On the northern flank, Model was still highly doubtful about the plan and was aware of Soviet forces massing to the east; if his forces advanced south into the Kursk salient, they risked a Soviet counteroffensive against their left flank and rear. But Manstein's original plan for an offensive as soon as possible after the spring thaw was replaced by Hitler's growing belief that the newer German tanks – the Panthers and Tigers – would give the Wehrmacht a decisive advantage. The Tigers had demonstrated their effectiveness in the fighting in Ukraine earlier in the year as well as less impressively outside Leningrad, but the Panthers were a different matter entirely; they were plagued by reliability issues, and although later models would be far more dependable, they were not ready for mass deployment in the summer of 1943. In any event, production was slow, and the delay worked to the advantage of the Soviet Union: German armoured vehicle production was utterly dwarfed by the numbers of tanks and assault guns reaching the ranks of the Red Army. Despite the increasing signs of a huge and growing advantage for the Red Army, there remained an almost mystical belief in Hitler's higher circles about the qualitative advantage of German troops and equipment. Even if the Soviet Union could build two or more tanks for every German tank, the German vehicles were superior and would prevail. All that was needed was a belief in victory and the iron will to achieve it.

Numbers of men and tanks, quantities of equipment and ammunition, the nature of the terrain of the battlefield – these were the normal measures by which the ability of forces in the field to attack or defend were normally assessed. But during the Red Army's counteroffensive outside Moscow in late 1941, a new factor began to appear in German orders and diary entries. When he assumed command of the army in mid-December after the resignation of Generalfeldmarschall Walther von Brauchitsch, Hitler issued orders that the troops facing the Soviet assaults were to hold their positions with fanatical determination: retreat was out of the question. Both at the time and in the months and years that followed, many believed that this was the correct decision, as Oberst Günther von Blumentritt, who was chief of staff of Fourth Army outside Moscow, later wrote:

> Hitler believed that he personally could ward off the catastrophe which was impending before Moscow. And it must be stated quite frankly that he did in fact succeed in doing so. His fanatical order that the troops must hold fast regardless in every position, and in the most impossible circumstances, was undoubtedly correct ... Hitler realised instinctively that any retreat across the snow and ice must, within a few days, lead to the dissolution of the front.[20]

This assessment is at best partial and at worst misleading, as the orders were more nuanced and withdrawals were essential if the Wehrmacht was to switch from an offensive posture to a defensive line, but Hitler's orders and decisions thereafter made repeated mention of the importance of a 'fanatical will' to win as being an important factor in the ability of the Wehrmacht to triumph. Morale and determination are of course important, but the manner in which Hitler used such unquantifiable factors to argue against numerical disadvantages, even after the disaster at Stalingrad, continued to contribute to the setbacks suffered by German forces. Also, although officers and soldiers in the front line frequently commented on the 'fanatical' determination of Soviet combatants, this was given no value whatever in Hitler's thinking.

Throughout the relatively quiet months of the thaw and muddy season on the Eastern Front, worldwide events continued to slip inexorably against Germany and its allies. Reinforcements from Germany and Italy were rushed to Tunisia during the winter of 1942–43 after the defeat of Rommel's forces at El Alamein and the landing by the Western Allies in Northwest Africa. Had these reinforcements and supplies been made available to Rommel at an earlier stage, he might have accomplished far more, but although the Germans enjoyed a brief moment of victory at the Battle of Kasserine Pass in February 1943, the remorseless advance of British forces from El Alamein to Tunisia left the German and Italian forces facing a two-front battle for which they had completely inadequate resources. Supply difficulties were now adding greatly to the difficulties of the German forces – on 10 April, a single ship reached Tunisia, the first shipment to arrive since the beginning of the month.[21] A few days later, *Heeresgruppe Afrika* reported that it barely had sufficient ammunition for defensive fighting, and there was no prospect of mounting any major counteroffensive. Despite this, local counterattacks continued in increasingly desperate attempts to hold the front line. On 22 April, a report stressed how bad the situation now was:

> The fuel situation is extremely difficult. Essential redeployments, attacks, and counterattacks can no longer be carried out, and even local redeployments of the troops are carried out only with substantial difficulties. The limited use of ammunition on the southern sector was offset by heavy consumption in the west resulting in the same overall consumption as on previous days. The renewal of strong enemy attacks in the south is anticipated to result in still higher ammunition consumption in the coming days. The shipment of food supplies from Europe has been dispensed with in view of the priority of other supplies.[22]

A week later, the supply situation was characterised as 'catastrophic', and a report at the beginning of May showed just how effectively the Western Allies were choking German and Italian supply lines. During the whole of April, it had been possible to transport a little under 19,000 tons of supplies to Tunisia, but 14 freighters, one tanker, one destroyer, 12 smaller vessels, and over 15,000 tons of supplies had been lost at sea. The entries in the *OKW* war diary struggled to find suitable adjectives to describe how bad the supply situation was; the arrival of a ship might result in a temporary improvement, but the pressure from British, American, and Free French forces was unrelenting. The final ammunition stockpiles were distributed to combat units – with considerable difficulty – on 6 May and the front line began to break up over the next few days. A final radio message from the once-victorious *Afrika Korps* was received early on 12 May: 'Ammunition expended. Weapons and equipment destroyed. The *Afrika Korps* has fought on as ordered until it can fight no more. The *Afrika Korps* must rise again.'[23]

In Hitler's headquarters, this message – and a similar signal from the headquarters of Fifth Panzer Army in Tunisia two days earlier – must have brought back bad memories of the last radio transmissions from the encircled troops in Stalingrad. On 13 May the remaining Axis forces were forced to lay down their arms. A total of 275,000 irreplaceable veteran soldiers became prisoners, and Allied plans for an invasion of Sicily – already approved before the final German and Italian surrender in Tunisia – were accelerated. Operation *Husky*, which saw landings on 26 beaches on the Sicilian coast as well as airborne forces being dropped on the island, would commence on the night of 9–10 July, shortly after the Germans launched *Zitadelle*.

In the Atlantic Ocean, the U-boat war was coming to a climax. In addition to operating in convoys, British and American shipping was now supported by groups of escort vessels that could move at speed to give additional protection to convoys that were under attack, and the increasing number of available escorts permitted them to linger where a U-boat was known to have dived, patrolling back and forth until the German vessel ran out of air and was forced to surface. Although British code-breakers at Bletchley Park had mastered the encryption of German Enigma apparatus, new refinements such as a modification introduced in March 1943 occasionally disrupted code breaking, but only for a matter of days. During April 1943, the losses at sea began to tilt against the Germans, with 15 U-boats being destroyed for the destruction of 39 British and American ships, and the following month became known as 'Black May' amongst the men of the U-boat service. A total of 34 German submarines were destroyed in the Atlantic for only 34 ships sunk, and Admiral Karl Dönitz, commander of the U-boat arm, declared that the Battle of the Atlantic had been lost.[24] Although Hitler continued to believe – characteristically putting his faith in superior German technology – that newer U-boats would permit a resumption of the battle at a later date, convoys carried huge quantities of equipment, supplies, and personnel across the Atlantic in the months that followed almost without interruption.

The German homeland also experienced increasing consequences of the war turning against Germany. After the Casablanca Conference of January 1943, the Combined Chiefs of Staff, representing USA and UK, issued the Casablanca directive:

> [The objective is] the progressive destruction and dislocation of the German military, industrial and economic systems and the undermining of the morale of the German people to a point where their capacity for armed resistance is fatally weakened. Every opportunity [is] to be taken to attack Germany by day to destroy objectives that are unsuitable for night attack, to sustain continuous pressure on German morale, to impose heavy losses on the German day fighter force and to conserve [i.e. divert] the German fighter force away from the Russian and Mediterranean theatres of war.[25]

British bombers had been attacking German cities since early in the war, with the first 'thousand bomber raid' hitting Cologne in June 1942. The American Eighth Air Force's B-17 and B-24 fleets made their first major attack in October against targets in northern France and attacked U-boat pens in Wilhelmshaven immediately before the Casablanca directive. Thereafter, bombardment increased steadily, both by day and by night. At first, the raids often experienced substantial losses from fighter defences, but as expertise increased and longer-range fighters escorted daylight raids deeper into German airspace, the advantage began to turn in favour of the bomber fleets. In the last week of July, as fighting raged in the Kursk salient, US and British bombers conducted Operation *Gomorrah* against Hamburg over eight days and seven nights. Nearly 40,000 people perished in the firestorms that devastated the city.

Germany's allies were faring no better. Italy had entered the war in the expectation of gaining from Germany's successes, but suffered heavy losses in the fighting in North Africa and during a poorly planned invasion of Greece. The Italian Eighth Army was almost destroyed on the Don River front in the last weeks of 1942 and its remnants retreated towards the west in conditions of biting cold, constant Soviet attacks, and callous indifference from the Germans – on several occasions, retreating German columns seized motor transport from Italians, even throwing wounded men from ambulances.[26] Even when the small numbers of men who managed to escape death or capture reached German lines, they usually faced a further long march to railheads from where they were ultimately evacuated to Italy, but even at this stage their ordeal was not over. When trainloads of frostbitten, wounded, and exhausted soldiers arrived in Italy, they swamped the medical services and many died in the weeks that followed. Support for Italy's continued involvement in the war was weakening steadily through the first months of 1943, and it would take little by way of further setbacks for it to collapse entirely. Similarly, Romania had sent two armies into the Soviet Union and both had been torn apart during the Soviet encirclement of Stalingrad. For the moment, Romanian troops remained in the Soviet Union, primarily as occupation forces in Crimea, but there had already been air raids on Romania by bombers of the Western Allies, mainly targeting the oil facilities at Ploieşti. To make matters worse, there was growing dissatisfaction in government circles at the manner in which Germany was treating Romania; oil, food, and other items were routinely requisitioned for German use, but the payments that had been negotiated seldom appeared. Like the Italians, Romanians at every level were coming to question their involvement in a war in which their ally treated them with disdain and almost undisguised contempt.

In the Far East too, events were moving in favour of the Allied Powers. The early momentum of the Japanese entry into the war was dissipating. At the Battle of the Coral Sea in May, the US Navy suffered the loss of USS *Lexington*, one of a very small number of aircraft carriers that it had in the Pacific Ocean, but inflicted sufficient damage on the Japanese fleet to force abandonment of a planned capture of Port Moresby; in June, there was a further clash at Midway, which saw the destruction of four Japanese aircraft carriers for the loss of USS *Yorktown*. It was a catastrophic defeat for Japan, handing the initiative to the US forces for the rest of the Pacific war.

Meanwhile, the Red Army began its own preparations for offensive operations to commence once the German *Zitadelle* had been defeated. In order to maximise the chances of success on either side of the Kursk salient, it was essential to tie down as many German soldiers in the north as possible, as Meretskov described:

> As Karelian Front [stretching from north of Leningrad to Murmansk] couldn't yet participate actively in this plan, its implementation fell on the personnel of Leningrad and Volkhov Fronts. And the magnet to attract enemy troops was again supposed to be the Mga sector.
>
> 'What are the chances of success?' Stalin asked me. Later, I learned that he also asked Govorov the same question and received from him an answer similar to mine: if the necessary superiority of forces was created, the operation would end successfully. But *Stavka* couldn't provide troops to create such an advantageous position from its reserves that were held for the development of a breakthrough in the central sector of the Soviet-German front. And in parting, the supreme commander emphasised one point in conversation with me:
>
> 'The most important thing for you is not the capture of territory, but the destruction of German divisions!'[27]

Finally, *Zitadelle* commenced on 5 July. Repeated delays had resulted in the deployment of the much-vaunted Panthers and Tigers as well as large numbers of the older Pz.IVs and assault guns, supported by the new giant Ferdinand, a tank destroyer built on a Porsche chassis originally intended for a heavy tank that had been abandoned in favour of the Tiger; but despite the presence of these vehicles progress was slow. After the war, Soviet accounts successfully portrayed the Battle of Kursk — and specifically its climax around Prokhorovka — as a huge clash of armour in which the power of the panzer divisions was dealt an irreparable blow, but the reality was somewhat different. Although German losses were heavy, Soviet casualties were far greater. In total, the Germans lost about 54,000 men in the assault on the salient and between 250 and 330 tanks and assault guns, with a further 1,600 damaged; Red Army losses came to about 178,000 men and nearly 2,000 tanks and assault guns destroyed or damaged.[28] The battle was discontinued because of the landings in Sicily by the Western

Allies, necessitating the urgent transfer of troops to Italy and Sicily, rather than because the Wehrmacht had been decisively defeated. But the Red Army was better positioned to absorb these losses, particularly as once more, the bulk of the Wehrmacht's casualties was borne by the irreplaceable experienced core of German veterans. When the Red Army transitioned to the offensive, it began a domination of the course of events on the Eastern Front that would last until the final defeat of Nazi Germany.

CHAPTER 7

THE SUMMER OFFENSIVE: SINYAVINO

The last great attempt by the Wehrmacht to mount a major offensive in the east ended at Prokhorovka, in what Soviet historiography attempted to portray as the greatest tank battle in history. The original aim of the offensive – to draw the weakened Red Army tank units into battle as soon as possible after the spring thaw and degrade their ability to mount any offensive operations – was long forgotten, and in many respects *Zitadelle* had become a pointless operation. There were no vital assets in the Kursk salient, and the best that could be expected was a shortening of the front line by eliminating the large bulge.

Already, the Soviet counteroffensives intended to take advantage of the end of the German offensive were beginning. Operation *Kutuzov* was unleashed against the German Army Group Centre on 12 July with the customary heavy artillery bombardment, targeted against the flank of the German Second Panzer Army. This was a sector where a Soviet attack had long been anticipated and the Germans constructed defensive positions in depth, but the assault by Bryansk Front's Eleventh Guards Army overwhelmed the German troops by sheer weight of numbers. Other sectors held firm and Model, ever sceptical about *Zitadelle*, responded quickly to the crisis, releasing substantial armoured forces that he had deliberately held back with the intention of committing them only when the Red Army's defences north of Kursk had been pierced. Fighting continued for a month, costing the Germans over 86,000 men; Red Army losses were shockingly high, exceeding 420,000.[1] But the Germans were driven back a considerable distance, culminating in the Red Army retaking Oryol.

Kutuzov would play a significant role in shaping future Soviet operations. General Konstantin Konstantinovich Rokossovsky, commander of Central Front, was critical about what amounted to a bloody frontal assault on the German positions:

> The overall object of this operation was … to split the enemy group and destroy the scattered forces. The plan, however, failed to take into account that our own forces would be thinly stretched. I think it would have been simpler and surer to deliver two main powerful strikes from the north and south at Bryansk, at the base of the Oryol salient. This would have required time for Western and Central Fronts to regroup. But once again undue haste was displayed – haste, moreover, completely unjustified by the situation. As a result, the attack on the decisive sectors was launched without adequate preparation. Instead of a swift thrust the offensive deteriorated into protracted fighting, and instead of surrounding and destroying the enemy we were, in effect, pushing and jostling him out of the Oryol salient. It could have been quite a story had we begun the operation a little later, concentrating our forces in two powerful pincer movements closing at Bryansk.
>
> I also think that little or no account had been taken of the fact that the Germans had been digging in around Oryol for over a year and had built a strong, deeply echeloned system of fortifications.[2]

As had been the case on so many occasions, it seems that too little attention was paid to the reality of the German positions around Oryol. A year later, when discussing plans for Operation *Bagration*, the great summer offensive that tore apart the German Army Group Centre, Rokossovsky successfully argued against Stalin's plans for a frontal attack by his Front to capture Bobruisk; instead, he doggedly insisted on a pincer operation to avoid precisely the situation that arose in *Kutuzov*. When his Front attacked, the two-pronged attack was a complete success, swiftly encircling the German units in Bobruisk.

Manstein, whose original proposals had slowly transformed into *Zitadelle*, abandoned his attempts to continue the operation a little later than Model on the northern flank. At first, he hoped that the Wehrmacht might still benefit from the fighting – the losses inflicted upon the Red Army were surely sufficient to force a pause before further major operations. But like so many in the German higher commands, he completely underestimated the resources available to the Soviet Union. An entire Front had been held in reserve in positions across the base of the Kursk salient and this was now used as a source of reinforcements for the Red Army's units facing Army Group South. On 3 August, a new offensive – codenamed *Rumyantsev* – erupted in the Belgorod–Kharkov–Akhtyrka sector. It would prove to be one of the bloodiest battles fought by the Red Army in terms of daily casualties, but the outcome was that Manstein's armies were levered out of their positions and forced to commence a retreat that continued for several months. Manstein's constant fear had been that the Red Army would strike towards the south, attempting to pin his forces against the Sea of Azov, and he argued repeatedly for permission to pull back to the line of the Dnepr River; permission was eventually granted, but the pursuing Soviet forces raced the Germans to the river, often securing bridgeheads before the Germans had pulled back completely. By the end of the year, much of the west bank of the river and the city of Kiev were in Soviet hands.[3]

The attritional advance of the Red Army across central Ukraine failed to achieve any spectacular encirclements, but it created the circumstances in which such outcomes could be pursued. Although the great bulk of German forces managed to retreat back across the Dnepr, much of their heavy equipment had to be abandoned and once they moved out of their fortified defensive positions, many German infantry divisions proved to be no more robust and resilient in the face of heavy assaults than the Romanian, Italian, and Hungarian divisions that had collapsed along the Don front in late 1942, earning them the contempt of their German allies. In particular, the anti-tank firepower of infantry divisions was shown to be completely inadequate. Light anti-tank weapons such as the *Panzerschrek* and *Panzerfaust* were in development, but were not yet available. The *Panzerschrek* was essentially a German version of the American bazooka, first encountered by the Germans in North Africa after the commencement of Operation *Torch*, and was a highly effective weapon when it entered service, as was the single-shot *Panzerfaust*. However, neither reached the front line in large numbers until the second half of 1943. Moreover, the retreat to and over the Dnepr required the panzer divisions of Manstein's Army Group South to be in almost constant action as 'fire brigades', intercepting Red Army attempts to outflank or bypass infantry units. Most of these divisions were already weakened by their involvement in *Zitadelle* and were further handicapped by the requirement in many cases for them to send one of their two panzer battalions back to Germany to be re-equipped and re-trained with the new Panther tanks. On some occasions, those battalions were never reunited with the rest of their division, being rushed to the front line to deal with the crises that were constantly erupting. By the end of 1943, these panzer divisions were almost completely burned out. They may have prevented the retreat to the Dnepr turning into a catastrophic rout, but the price they paid was that their ability to continue intervening against the Red Army's armoured forces was effectively exhausted. Writing at the end of 1943, the senior medical officer of 8th Panzer Division reported on the poor state of his division's panzergrenadiers:

> Almost 100 per cent of the panzergrenadiers have foot problems. These are mainly due to over-exertions of the joints, muscles, and ligaments resulting in swelling ...
>
> In addition, due to the universal infestation with lice, particularly amongst the replacement drafts who arrived earlier, there are numerous infections from scratching skin. These are often a consequence of the contamination of other skin conditions ...
>
> About 80 per cent of the combat strength are suffering from illnesses related to the cold. These include respiratory infections, rheumatic complaints, stomach and intestinal disorders, with many having severe diarrhoea, as well as bladder infections resulting in frequent incontinence ...
>
> In summary, it is necessary to report that from a medical perspective, no marching or related combat can be expected of the panzergrenadiers now or in the near future.[4]

It should be remembered that panzergrenadiers – at least in theory – were mounted in trucks or half-tracks. The conditions described in this report would have been widespread or even worse amongst ordinary infantry divisions, which were still almost completely dependent on marching everywhere on foot.

The aftermath of the Kursk offensive thus saw a huge weakening of Army Group South and further heavy casualties for Army Group Centre. In the north, the intention of the Red Army was, as Stalin had told Meretskov, to destroy German divisions rather than recapture large areas of ground. Both sides marked 22 June, the second anniversary of the German invasion of the Soviet Union; Soviet aircraft from Leningrad Front carried out a series of attacks on German airfields, claiming the destruction of 20 German bombers on the ground; German artillery shelled Leningrad, randomly bombarding various parts of the city. The following day, newspapers in Leningrad reported the discovery of the mutilated corpses of Soviet soldiers and civilians in the small stretch of land south of Lake Ladoga that had been recaptured during *Iskra*:

> On the western outskirts of Gorodok 6, not far from the cemetery, there was a former Fascist prison. In three dugouts surrounded by barbed wire, the Hitlerites kept Soviet civilians and soldiers prisoner. Before fleeing from the area, the

Germans sealed the dugouts and set them ablaze. Under the remnants of the scorched logs we found 53 corpses. On examination, it was found that the Nazis brutally tortured their victims: some had crushed hands, broken legs, eyes gouged out, and broken teeth. In many cases there were signs of knife wounds on the corpses.[5]

It is impossible to know how well preserved the corpses were after the fire, or whether any of their injuries were from Soviet artillery fire, but there were so many confirmed cases of atrocities that were reported by partisans and survivors that any such story easily gained credence amongst the population of Leningrad. The message from the Soviet authorities to the population was clear: if the Germans ever succeeded in capturing the city, atrocities on a huge scale could be expected. Indeed, the Germans had made no secret of their intention to starve the city to death. The manner in which they appropriated food supplies in occupied regions without any regard for the survival of the civilian population – or even the need to leave sufficient seed corn for the following year's harvest – was widely known. German shelling continued at irregular intervals, and the city authorities became concerned that many of the people in Leningrad, soldiers and civilians alike, were no longer taking the threat as seriously as they had in earlier months; in early July, fresh edicts were circulated, threatening anyone who didn't take shelter when the alarm was raised with severe punishment.[6]

In anticipation of a renewal of heavy fighting, Leningrad Front started moving its artillery assets into position on 1 July. The operation that unfolded in the summer of 1943 has several names. For the Germans, it was the Third Battle of Lake Ladoga – the first had been the German advance to the lake in late 1941, and the second was *Iskra* in early 1943. Some western accounts list it as one of the many Sinyavino Operations, but in Soviet and Russian accounts it is usually known as the *Mginskaya Nastupatelnaya Operatsiya* or 'Mga Offensive Operation'. The shortcomings of earlier operations had been analysed and attempts were made to improve performance, and Govorov's armies planned to start their artillery preparation several days before the offensive, concentrating on more accurate demolition of German fieldworks and careful bombardment of known and suspected artillery and mortar positions. Detailed plans were sent from *Stavka* to both Govorov and Meretskov, and inevitably attention was concentrated on Sinyavino – if the Germans could be driven from the ruins of the town and particularly from the adjacent Sinyavino Heights, their ability to carry out accurate artillery interdiction of the narrow corridor along the southern shore of Lake Ladoga would be reduced. For the latest operation, Leningrad Front would use two of its armies. Fifty-Fifth Army was to attack across the Neva River towards Ulyanovka with the intention of threatening Mga from the southwest, while Sixty-Seventh Army assaulted the German positions in and immediately west of Sinyavino from the north. Volkhov Front's Eighth Army was to attack towards Mga from the east. This would achieve more than simply tying down German divisions and inflicting further losses on them; in addition to widening the corridor near Lake Ladoga, it would potentially open the way for a larger operation against the German Eighteenth Army.

In addition to trying to improve artillery preparation, there were attempts by the Red Army to organise its attacking units in a more effective manner. Starikov's Eighth Army, for example, was organised as two shock groups, each with two echelons. They would attack either side of the railway line running to Mga with two rifle divisions in the first echelon and two held back in reserve; in order to improve the odds of success, the first echelon divisions each had a tank regiment in support, with two tank brigades held back to exploit any breaks that might develop in the German lines.[7] By concentrating his resources in this manner, Starikov was able to achieve a significant advantage purely in terms of numbers over the German units in his path.

The German units in the salient extending to Sinyavino consisted of seven infantry divisions, under the control of XXVI Corps. On 1 July, General Gustav Fehn temporarily replaced Leyser as its commander; the German divisions were in heavily fortified positions and at least some of their losses earlier in the year had been made good, but none were at anything approaching full strength. The northern attack by Starikov's Eighth Army would fall on 5th Mountain Division; the southern attack would strike at the boundary between 5th Mountain Division and 69th Infantry Division. On the left flank of XXVI Corps was Hilpert's LIV Corps with four infantry divisions and *SS-Polizei*. It would be in the path of the assault by Fifty-Fifth Army. Everyone knew where the attacks would fall. The nature of the front line left little room for imaginative manoeuvre or deception.

One of Hilpert's units was the Spanish Blue Division. Although the Spanish soldiers had performed no better or worse than most of the German units around them, Lindemann continued to doubt their abilities and ordered that a German regiment be deployed immediately behind their lines. Other measures were perhaps rather more constructive. During the lull in fighting, Generalleutnant Emilio Esteban-Infantes was ordered to rotate one of his regiments out of the front line every month so that it could undergo intensive training. A battalion of replacements arrived from Spain as the spring thaw began and the Germans also delivered more anti-tank guns to the division, though this still left it with less anti-tank firepower than German divisions. This was characteristic of the manner in which Germany treated the armies of its allies. Anti-tank weapons were promised to Romanian, Hungarian, and Italian divisions throughout 1942, but rarely appeared in the quantities that had been described and ammunition for the guns was always in very short supply, making meaningful training almost impossible. In May, the Red Army made an aggressive probe into the positions of the Blue Division and there were some anxious moments at Hilpert's headquarters before reports arrived that the Spaniards had successfully sealed off the attack and then cleared it. But despite the reinforcements and additional training, morale in the division declined throughout the first half of 1943. Many of the division's soldiers came to the end of their tour of duty and returned to Spain, and the fresh troops who arrived had to begin the learning experience of how to survive on the Eastern Front all over again. As was the case with many German replacement drafts, the new soldiers arriving from Spain – either to take the place of those returning home or as reinforcements to replenish the division after its winter losses – were of poorer quality than the men who had first deployed to the Soviet Union.[8]

But in many respects, the same was true of many of the fresh recruits in the Red Army, rushed through training and dispatched to their divisions with only the most rudimentary understanding of how to fight. Just as the Blue Division organised intensive training both for troops already in the front line and for the replacements from Spain, the Soviet units on the other side of the front line had to complete the training of their new drafts. All of the criticism about earlier Soviet attacks – particularly the poor interaction of infantry, armour, and artillery – needed to be addressed if the performance of the Red Army was to improve. But despite the issue of new manuals for all parts of the Red Army, there was little concerted effort to ensure that training changed to reflect this.

Prior to the commencement of the summer attack, Soviet artillery conducted a series of sudden, heavy bombardments of key positions. One of these struck the headquarters of the Spanish Blue Division on 18 July; to add to the discomfiture of senior German officers, the strike took place on an evening when several senior German figures had joined the Spanish officers for dinner. Two days later, raiding parties ventured into the German lines during the night to capture 'tongues'. There were also several powerful probes of the defences, correctly identified by the Germans as attempts at reconnaissance in force. On this occasion, one of the groups sent forward was 14th Separate Penal Battalion, which had previously been known as the

'Special Penal Battalion of Leningrad Front'. It had been formed originally in the summer of 1942, using personnel from various sources:

> It proved difficult to establish the penal battalion with the [first] contingent ... those who had left their positions without orders, cowards and alarmists. On all Fronts – and Leningrad is no exception – they began to send convicts for any crimes to penal units with the execution of their sentence delayed until the end of hostilities. But these were not enough.[9]

If soldiers in the penal battalion distinguished themselves, their sentences might be reduced or even dismissed, a process known in the Soviet Union as 'redemption through blood' after an essay of that title written by David Iosifovich Ortenberg, editor of the Red Army newspaper *Krasnaya Zvezda*. The units were created after Stalin became aware of the German system that pre-dated the war; Wehrmacht conscripts who were deemed to be unfit for military service due to prior 'subversive activity', such as involvement in Communist demonstrations, or who repeatedly committed disciplinary offences, were sent to *Sonderabteilungen* ('Special Battalions') for corrective training, and those who failed to show the required improvement were then transferred to the concentration camp at Sachsenhausen. After the outbreak of war in 1939, these *Sonderabteilungen* were disbanded and replaced by *Feld-Sonderbataillone* ('Special Field Battalions') which in turn led to the creation of *Bewährungsbataillone* ('Probation Battalions'), via which convicted soldiers could earn the right to return to their original units.[10] The first Soviet equivalents, known as *Shtrafnoi Batalyony* or *Shtrafbat* and run by the NKVD, appeared in August 1942 near Stalingrad, and a total of over 400,000 men served in these units before the end of the war; most didn't survive.[11]

Staffing the Leningrad penal battalion with sufficient officers proved difficult, and in early 1943 Soviet officers who had been captured by the Germans but had then managed to return to their own side were brought before a tribunal, which almost invariably decided to send them to the penal battalion. The attack on the night of 19–20 July cost the battalion 31 dead and an unknown number of wounded. One of those killed was Lieutenant Vladimir Ivanovich Yermak, who had been sent to the penal battalion after his gun went off while he was cleaning it and a passing soldier was killed. According to the official after-action report, Yermak reached a German bunker and physically blocked the embrasure with his body while his platoon worked forwards. He was awarded the Order of the Red Banner posthumously.[12]

The story of brave Soviet soldiers – in regular units as well as penal battalions – giving their lives by blocking the firing ports of German bunkers with their bodies recurs in several Soviet accounts. Whilst it is possible that reports of such deeds inspired other men to emulate them, it seems improbable that these episodes happened as regularly as described, if at all. There are no German accounts that corroborate such acts, and in any event the rate of fire of the German MG-42, in widespread use by 1943, was so high that it would cut a corpse to pieces, making any such attempt futile. These stories are little different in character from the descriptions of heroic Soviet soldiers rolling under German tanks and detonating bundles of grenades, or anti-tank mines, in order to destroy the Fascist machines: they were intended to create an image of heroism to inspire others and to raise morale. In the case of penal battalions, the stories also helped legitimise the entire basis of such units, showing how men could redeem themselves through self-sacrifice. But life for most men in penal battalions was short. They were often sent into battle without weapons, being told to pick them up on the battlefield or to wait until one of their armed comrades was hit, and in some sectors – though not on Leningrad Front – they were issued dark uniforms that stood out prominently against the snow, so that they would draw fire away from regular troops.[13]

Early on 22 July, the Soviet artillery batteries on the northern side of the Sinyavino sector commenced a heavy bombardment that continued for over two hours, and Dukhanov's Sixty-Seventh Army then moved forward with two assault groups. Following his successes during *Iskra*, Simoniak was appointed commander of XXX Guards Rifle Corps, which formed one of the groups and his former division was in the first wave. Dushevsky and his rifle company, who had taken part in *Iskra*, would be involved in the main attack, and he described another innovation that was used on this occasion:

Some soldiers were given steel breastplates, which consisted of two parts. One covered the chest, hooking over the left shoulder. The second covered the stomach and groin. They were connected with what was effectively a door hinge …

They were quite heavy and the soldiers didn't like them. The stronger men wore them. Some threw away the lower shield and wore only the upper one. They often used them when going on reconnaissance raids. Sometimes, an order would be given: 'Put on the breastplates.' We would move forward about 300–400m. When we looked around, there would be breastplates lying on the ground. Nobody knew who had discarded them. I didn't wear one myself.[14]

The Soviet gunners paid particular attention to improving the efficacy of their bombardment of the German forward positions, and it seems that in many cases this was more effective than had been the case with earlier bombardments. When the Soviet infantry moved forward, they swiftly overran the first defensive line and a prisoner from the German 11th Infantry Division later described the effectiveness of the artillery fire:

'The Russian artillery,' one [prisoner] said, 'destroyed everything in the defence sector of I Battalion and reduced it to powder. Almost everyone there was killed. The trench was demolished by the artillery preparation. In places, it was difficult to make out that there had been a trench here at all. I didn't see anyone else from my company. Some were buried in their dugouts or killed by direct hits from shells.'[15]

Despite the initial success, the Soviet troops found that the positions they had overrun were covered by well-positioned guns in the second line and the attackers were swiftly brought to a halt. What followed was a repetition of the futile attacks and counterattacks of earlier battles. Dushevsky was in an attack near 8th GRES, the power station that had been the scene of such bitter fighting during *Iskra*:

We didn't know the overall plan, but there was talk in general terms about an advance to Mga. The ground was swampy. There was nowhere to take cover. When we dug small trenches, they immediately filled with water. We tried throwing bundles of branches into them and looked for drier spots. The Germans had circular defensive positions reinforced with logs. Their defences stretched along our 2km sector and were probably more than a kilometre deep. They had reinforced them with sand. Apparently they made prisoners carry the sand. Losses were very heavy on both sides. We would push forward, and then they would push back. We managed to take one fortification from the Germans, but then I was wounded. I was hit in the thigh by shrapnel. One piece left a wound 15–20cm long. Another wound was smaller, and a third was small but deep. I remember that four women carried me back on a cape.[16]

The assaults on the Sinyavino Heights resulted in little change in the front line. Hill 43.3 became a bitterly contested position, changing hands several times. The Tiger tanks of *Schwere Panzer Abteilung 502* were used to support several counterattacks but even these heavyweight vehicles proved to be vulnerable to the massive weight of artillery fire that was directed against them. As 11th

Infantry Division's ranks melted away in the fighting, reinforcements were brought into the front line from several other divisions. These included Wilhelm Lubbeck's 58th Infantry Division, and he later described the fighting as some of the heaviest experienced by his division in the entire war. The intensity of battle reached a peak in early August, after which there was a brief lull as both sides licked their wounds, but Lubbeck then had a strange encounter:

> I was tramping along a dirt road on the way from my front line position to my rear bunker about a mile behind the front. As I approached the area just behind our howitzers, a young German second lieutenant wearing an unsoiled uniform came strolling up the road toward me ...
>
> While I was baffled by his presence in the area, the officer did not appear nervous or exhibit any suspicious behaviour. As we passed one another he cordially returned my salute and I dismissed my apprehensions.
>
> Two hours later, Soviet heavy artillery slammed 50 or 60 shells into our position with pinpoint accuracy. Only our deeply dug set of entrenchments prevented the bombardment from causing any casualties or damage to the howitzers.
>
> Instantly, my mind flashed back to the mysterious German officer. In retrospect, I concluded that he must indeed have been a Russian agent gathering intelligence. His close-up scouting of our position would explain the enemy's ability to target our camouflaged position so precisely.[17]

Large numbers of German soldiers were now prisoners of war, and extensive efforts were made by their captors to persuade them to change their allegiance. During the summer of 1943, there were the first reports of unexplained 'visitors' in the German lines such as that described by Lubbeck, and this activity would increase steadily as the war progressed. In June, shortly before the latest offensive against Sinyavino began, a committee of German political exiles and four captured soldiers – two officers, a sergeant, and a private – formed the *Nationalkomitee Freies Deutschland* ('National Committee for a Free Germany'). At first, it gained little support from other German prisoners of war, and a group of 95 officers in a prison camp near Moscow formed the *Bund Deutscher Offiziere* ('League of German Officers' or *BDO*) a few weeks later. This rapidly merged with the committee that had preceded it and became involved in radio transmissions to German soldiers calling on them to surrender; many of the senior officers who joined the group also wrote personal letters to former colleagues on the Eastern Front, urging them to prevent further loss of life by laying down their weapons. The efficacy of these attempts, and the use of infiltrators to carry out reconnaissance and other activities, was limited at best, but perhaps one of its greatest impacts was the widespread increase in suspicion in German units, where rumours of *Seydlitz-Truppen* (named after General Walther von Seydlitz-Kurzbach, one of the senior officers who surrendered in Stalingrad and an early member of the *BDO*) became commonplace.[18]

The incident described by Lubbeck was not unique. Similar episodes were described by German soldiers elsewhere on the front line, but Soviet troops also had similar experiences. On 6 August, a man in the uniform of a Red Army officer, carrying documentation in the name of Davidov, crossed the front line into the Soviet-held bridgehead at Oranienbaum, to the west of Leningrad. He was promptly detained and admitted that his true name was Karashchenko; he had been badly wounded earlier in the war and captured, and had been sent back by the Germans as a spy. He apparently told his captors that he had agreed to do this not to conduct any spying but as a means of returning to the Red Army. According to the account of the incident, he was promptly sent back to the German lines to pass false information to his controllers. This may have been the case, but many men captured by either side in such circumstances faced a decidedly uncertain future at the hands of their captors.[19] Even Red Army soldiers who escaped from prisoner of war camps and made their way back to Soviet lines faced suspicion – most were arrested and interrogated by NKVD officers and were then frequently sent to prison camps in Siberia or penal battalions. At an early stage in the war, Stalin had decreed that he expected Red Army soldiers to fight to the death. Those who surrendered without suffering wounds that made them incapable of fighting on had to demonstrate to the satisfaction of their NKVD interrogators that further resistance had been impossible. Even aircrew who were shot down behind German lines, taken prisoner, and who then escaped were treated with suspicion. The issue wasn't purely concern that these men may be German collaborators; Stalin believed that they were 'contaminated' by their exposure to non-Soviet life and might corrupt the political beliefs of others.

In most battles to date, German ground forces had not been greatly bothered by Soviet air attacks. Although Soviet aviation was steadily increasing both its activity and its expertise, Luftwaffe fighters continued to be able to achieve local air superiority for long periods. But during the fighting in August on the hills near Sinyavino, Soviet ground attack aircraft began to make a greater impression than before, as Lubbeck described:

> Over the course of the war, most of the casualties in our regiment resulted from
> Russian artillery and mortars, and to a lesser extent from small-arms fire. About

this time however, we also began to endure our first bombing and strafing attacks by Soviet aircraft.

During the daytime, we occasionally faced a threat from Soviet ground-attack planes like the Ilyushin Il-2 'Sturmovik'. At night, we confronted the menace of the Polykarpov Po-2, nicknamed the *Nähmaschine* (sewing machine) for the loud rhythmic clattering of its engine.

The noisy approach of the *Nähmaschine* was audible at a great distance, but it was virtually impossible to target them in the darkness. Flying a couple of hundred feet overhead, the pilot and co-pilot would search for any flicker of light that would reveal the location of our lines or rear camps.

Despite efforts to black-out everything on the ground, there was bound to be someone who would light a cigarette or use a flashlight that the enemy could spot. Once locating a potential target, the Soviet pilots often cut their engines in order to glide silently over the spot before dropping their bombs on the unsuspecting targets below.[20]

The Polykarpov Po-2 first entered service in 1929 and would remain in production until 1978, the longest period of production of any aircraft in history; it also has the distinction of being credited with the destruction of a Lockheed F-9 fighter in the Korean War, which stalled whilst trying to intercept a slow-moving Po-2, the only occasion that a biplane had a documented air victory over a jet aircraft. It was powered by a 99-HP engine and was known as the U-2 until the death of its designer Polykarpov in 1944, after which it was renamed the Po-2 in his honour. Its bomb-load was a maximum of 770 pounds, but its real impact was in the disruption that it caused in night attacks. It had a maximum range of only 340 miles and usually operated from cleared ground very close to the front line, permitting its crews to carry out several attacks in a single night. It was heartily detested by German soldiers for its nuisance value and was so effective that the Germans deployed several squadrons of obsolete biplanes to carry out similar raids.

Wave after wave of attacks by Sixty-Seventh Army failed to make any major impression on the German defences on the Sinyavino Heights. The only moment of success for the Soviet troops finally came on 12 August when 128th Rifle Division was thrown into an assault on the high ground. Attached to the division was a battalion of engineers, commanded by Major Ivan Ivanovich Solomakhin, which was to attack on a position known to the Soviet soldiers as *Chertovoy Vysoty* ('Devil's Hill'). Unlike many of the Red Army units involved, Solomakhin had the advantage of having spent a brief time training his men on a similar ridge behind the Soviet front line and he later described the assault, a snapshot of the brutal fighting that raged throughout this latest offensive:

The commander [of 128th Rifle Division], Colonel [Pavel Andreyevich] Potapov and especially the chief of staff … were very attentive to the needs of the battalion. To reinforce it, they allocated two heavy machine-gun platoons, a signals platoon and a battery of regimental artillery.

The battalion had already redeployed to Gorodok 2. There was a thorough inspection of equipment and weapons in all companies. The soldiers were in good spirits. Over the previous three days, all officers and senior NCOs had been in the front-line trench and knew exactly the route they would follow to the enemy's front line, and where all the landmarks were. After an excellent meal the companies began to move up to the start line. The Nazis were only 400m away across a shell-pitted no-man's land. The craters were filled with stinking peat slurry. Ahead, against the skyline, the highest and most formidable ridge of Hill 45.0 stood out clearly. At midnight, the scouts left the front line and moved forward into the darkness. The headquarters group followed them. The silence of the night was broken by occasional explosions of shells and mortar bombs, and short bursts of fire from machine-guns. Bullets whistled over the crawling sappers. Every now and then the area was lit up by flares. It was only possible to move during the pauses between their illumination. The most unpleasant were the 'lanterns', as the parachute flares were known – they gave a bright light for several minutes. The headquarters group and the line of scouts ahead of it reached the foot of the heights at 0200 and settled down in deep craters that had been selected in advance by Sergei Ulyanov's scouts.

We looked around. There was no sign of our 300 men. In the night sky were our famous biplanes, the 'heavenly sluggards', their engines chattering. They passed over the Sinyavino Heights in accordance with our battle plan, dropping small bombs on enemy positions and diverting the attention of guard posts from no-man's land. Regimental mortars also fired at the heights. Finally, as it approached 0300, there were the first signs of dawn over the swamps. I glanced at my watch and whispered uneasily, 'Where are all the men? They should be here by now.'

'I'll scout for them,' replied Tarasov. Before I could say a word he jumped out of the crater – and was spotted immediately. Hand grenades rained down the slope of the hill and a swarm of tracer bullets raced over our heads. I was forced to give the signal to attack – a series of green flares.

'For the Motherland! For Leningrad! Forward, brothers! Kill the bastards!'
The battalion officers were the first to break into the trenches. The sappers were
close behind them. It's difficult to describe the panic that gripped the Nazis; with
faces twisted by fear, many in their underwear (even in the front line, the invaders
slept in comfort), they tried to flee. In the trenches they were beaten down with
shovels and in the open they were cut down by bursts of automatic gunfire. Many
of them found their end in dugouts and foxholes. Even in such an extremely
unfavourable situation, small groups of the enemy defended themselves
desperately. Two hefty Nazis attacked Senior Sergeant Viktor Feofanov and tried
to throttle him. Viktor managed to knock down one with a blow to the stomach
and the second was finished off by Corporal Aleksandr Martyanov, who came to
the rescue. Toporkov, a soldier in the first company, was knocked to the ground.
The Fascist who fell on him struck Toporkov with a knife – fortunately, the knife
was deflected by his shoulder blade. Senior Sergeant Solovyov (who later became
a colonel) ran past the company commissar, finished off the Fritz, and sent
Toporkov to the dressing station. Sapper Petr Foroshchenko, who was accepted
into the [Communist] Party before the battle, saw a Fascist lying behind a rock,
aiming at an officer moving along the trench. Abruptly he pushed the commander
into a crater and threw a grenade towards the Nazi. The enemy stronghold on
Devil's Hill was taken by the sappers in just 12 minutes. At the same time, a
network of trenches about 400m wide and 250m in depth was overrun ... The
engineer battalion lost 16 men killed and 26 men wounded.[21]

It seems that by attacking at first light without massive artillery preparation,
Solomakhin's sappers achieved something that was vanishingly rare in the
fighting around Leningrad: tactical surprise. What was needed now was the
use of artillery as blocking fire, suppression of German artillery, and to disrupt
the German defences further to the rear, together with swift reinforcements to
exploit the success, but the Germans reacted first. Their response was a heavy
bombardment of the trenches that had been captured, followed by an
immediate counterattack. Solomakhin's sappers managed to hold their
positions but found themselves isolated – it was the Wehrmacht rather than
the Red Army that used its guns to create a blocking barrage. Losses rose
steadily, both from German shelling and from counterattacks, and Solomakhin
was incapacitated by wounds to his head and leg. But the diminishing ranks
of the Red Army sappers managed to hold their position until the evening
when a rifle battalion managed to reach them. However, further advances into
the German positions proved to be impossible. A veteran from one of the rifle

divisions later remembered the desperate measures taken to try to keep the combat formations functioning:

> In these battles between 22 July and 4 August 1943, we lost half the personnel in total, and in the combat formations of the infantry up to 80 per cent of their men. Cooks, clerks, and mechanics from the artillery were rounded up – everyone was sent to the infantry. It was the cruellest, bloodiest of operations. Our infantry perished and the German infantry was destroyed too, only the artillery fired continuously. One of our battalions there moved forward but was pushed back by German counterattacks, as a result of which the battalion headquarters and the division observation post were surrounded. Major Syroedov, who was in charge, called in fire from the entire artillery regiment on his position. The regiment fired en masse on the observation post area for 40 minutes. The Germans who had broken through couldn't endure and retreated to their original positions. Of the entire headquarters, only three wounded survived: the battalion commander, a reconnaissance officer and a radio operator.[22]

The depleted subunits of 11th Infantry Division were so weak that they had to be withdrawn, leaving 21st Infantry Division in its place; it was in a weakened state too, having spent most of the previous year in defending the German bridgehead over the Volkhov River at Kirishi in a series of battles every bit as bloody and futile as the struggles for the Sinyavino Heights. Indeed, 11th Infantry Division had also been rotated through the Kirishi bridgehead during 1942, suffering heavy losses that had only been partially replaced in the months that followed. For all the divisions that were involved, the replacement drafts from Germany were far too small to compensate for the high casualty rate in Kirishi and elsewhere, with the consequence that each of the three regiments of both 11th and 21st Infantry Divisions had been reduced from the normal three battalions to just two. Despite this increasingly common practice, 21st Infantry Division – as with almost all German formations – was treated by Hitler and *OKH* as if it was at full strength. The only way that the division could survive was through the intensive use of its support weapons, and in the fighting for the Sinyavino Heights its artillery regiment repeatedly proved its worth, intervening regularly with heavy defensive bombardments. In three weeks of combat, the gunners recorded that they used up 2,315 tons of artillery ammunition.[23] Such consumption of shells may seem huge, but the division's artillery was augmented by many of the guns of 11th Infantry Division, which were left in support when the rest of the division withdrew. However, such a high rate of fire had an additional detrimental effect – gun barrels burned out, reducing the accuracy of guns and eventually requiring their replacement.

On the same day that Sixty-Seventh Army made its first assault from the north, Starikov's Eighth Army also moved forward; here, the guns of Volkhov Front had been carrying out increasingly heavy bombardments over several days and under cover of this fire, sappers cleared paths through minefields and dug trenches into no-man's land to give the attacking infantry a better starting point for their assault. Meretskov described this phase of the battle as part of his plan to wear down the German forces in the area but despite the extensive artillery preparation, the German positions proved to be almost completely intact. Earlier attacks had demonstrated the unsuitability of the terrain for major attacks and Starikov's tanks struggled to move forward in support of the riflemen. Morozov, whose artillery prepared the way for the attack, described how the attack began, highlighting weaknesses both in the strategy of heavy bombardments and the manner in which infantry training remained far below the required standard:

The morning [of 22 July] was sunny and warm with almost no wind, but an hour after the start of the artillery preparation a thick veil of smoke and dust shrouded the landscape. When the artillery fire lifted from the enemy's first trench and moved to a depth of 300-400m, it seemed even to experienced officers that the barrage of fire was still falling on its original targets. As for the young infantrymen who had not yet received a baptism of fire, they were completely at a loss and were afraid to raise their heads from the trench. On this occasion we, the gunners, overdid things. After 20 minutes, the infantry still hadn't moved. I was at the observation post of the commander of 256th Rifle Division, about a kilometre from the front line. The division commander, Major General [Fedor Kuzmich] Fetisov, was anxious, as was his artillery commander, Lieutenant Colonel Keremetsky. How could anyone keep calm in such a situation? And the infantry, stunned by the thunder of the cannonade, couldn't understand at all that the artillery fire had long moved on from their attack objectives. After all, in the smoke ahead of them, explosions continued to rumble.

We had to move the artillery fire even deeper and sharply reduce its intensity. Then the tanks arrived. Together with them, the infantry finally moved forward. The first enemy position was penetrated at several points. When the smoke cleared, the area was hard to recognise. The land was ploughed up and only burned stumps remained of the forest. Instead of the even green background, there were huge areas of black and brown. Where the rockets had exploded, smoke swirled for a long time as fires devoured everything that could burn.

The second position, about 2km deeper than the first, was not captured in the assault. The infantry delayed its attack too long and the moment was lost. Recovering from the first blow, the enemy began to put up stubborn resistance, mounting counterattacks in some areas.

Over two years, the Germans created a powerful defensive line here with many trenches, machine-gun and field gun bunkers and pillboxes with shelters, minefields and other obstacles. In order to destroy everything capable of resisting our advancing infantry, it was necessary to pound the enemy defences with heavy and rocket artillery for many hours. But ultimately, such lengthy artillery preparations didn't always justify themselves: the element of surprise was lost and the over-consumption of material resources was too great.

During the First World War, the French carried out artillery preparations that lasted up to several days, as a result of which the first German position was levelled to the ground. The French infantry captured these positions but advanced no further. Moreover, it transpired that the Germans were withdrawing their troops to the depths of their defence, in the second line, and the French artillery was hitting empty targets.

We were in favour of sudden, short, and powerful artillery preparations. The main hope was placed in clear interaction of combat arms, and the rapid attack of infantry and tanks, which made their advance as soon as the artillery preparation ended and the shelling shifted forward. Relentlessly following the curtain of fire, the infantry was meant to attack one enemy trench after another. But on this occasion our infantry was late in attacking. Taking advantage of this, the Nazis moved the first echelons of their reserves into their secondary positions. From there they not only strengthened the defences, but were also able to begin inflicting powerful counterattacks.[24]

The tactic from the First World War of moving troops out of the foremost defensive line immediately before artillery preparation began was to become a recurring feature of German defensive doctrine on the Eastern Front. In many sectors, the apparent front line was deliberately intended to be abandoned, with its positions exposed to fire from the second German line. The key was knowing when a Soviet attack was imminent, so that troops could be moved out at the last possible moment.

Morozov's account revealed no hitherto unknown failings in the performance of the Red Army's infantry. Similar problems had been described in the past, and there were repeated exhortations from *Stavka* to Front and army commanders to improve training and preparation, but little had changed. There was still no systematic attempt to define a structure for the training needs that had been repeatedly identified, and it was often left in the hands of men who had little or no experience in the very special demands of organising and managing training programmes. The huge losses suffered in earlier battles meant that there were fewer men available to undertake the task of supervising training. In many cases, the task was assigned to men who were regarded as unsuitable for further combat service. Some of these men were wounded veterans, but others were sent to oversee training as a means of removing incompetent junior officers from the front line. The value of the training that was thus provided by front-line units was therefore variable in quality. Finally, even though units that had been in the thick of previous battles were rotated out of the front line for rest and recuperation, there was often little opportunity for the men to undergo systematic and rigorous additional training to remedy problems that had been identified. There might be rehearsals for specific tasks – on occasion, replicas of known German positions that were about to be assaulted were built and units were made to practice how they would attack them, or they were taken to a river to practice how to carry out an assault crossing – but these were rarely of the standard seen in other armies and were often little more than walk-through exercises, with little attempt to simulate the chaos of real battle and the need to improvise under pressure.

Casualties accumulated in Volkhov Front's attack at an alarming rate for only modest gains and it soon became clear that the second echelon would have to be committed to replace the first wave, which was almost completely exhausted. However much Meretskov attempted to portray the attack in the best possible terms, it was a poor outcome:

> Our observations showed that the German Eighteenth Army had no more reserves left in the Poreche region … Having broken through the first line of defence and gnawed into the second, the Soviet soldiers moved forward metre by metre. A little more and the breakthrough sector could be expanded. But reports began to arrive from unit commanders that suddenly the resistance of the Nazis had increased dramatically. It turned out that the Nazi command moved two complete divisions from near Leningrad that had been intended to storm the city, and used them to plug the gap in order to seal off our breakthrough and prevent it turning into a wide gap. The Volkhovites rejoiced at this and were proud: it wasn't trivial, because the plan of the Nazis to break through again from the south to Lake Ladoga was frustrated and the instructions of *Stavka* to maximise the destruction of Nazi troops were carried out.[25]

219

In reality, there was no 'breakthrough', just a small toehold in the German positions. Nor had there been any serious plans for German offensive operations – whilst this may have been intended for a future date, it had always been the intention of Hitler and *OKH* that any attack to restore the siege perimeter would have to await the successful outcome of *Zitadelle*. But the intention to pin down and degrade German units was certainly achieved. Having anticipated the Sinyavino sector as a potential area that the Red Army would attack, Hilpert quickly dispatched reinforcements to the battle; over the days that followed, battlegroups from 58th Infantry Division, 28th Jäger Division, and finally 126th Infantry Division, supported by a handful of tanks, went into action as fighting raged for the same ground that had cost so many thousands of lives in previous months.

As had been the case with *Iskra*, the fighting degenerated into a daily cycle of attacks and counterattacks over small areas of ground. By rotating his first and second echelons, Starikov managed to keep Eighth Army inching forward and on 9 August the leading units pressed elements of the German 5th Mountain Division into a small bridgehead on the east bank of the Naziya River. From prisoner interrogations, Starikov knew that this German unit had suffered heavy losses over the preceding two weeks and, calculating that it must be approaching the end of its strength, he threw more troops into the battle, finally seizing Poreche. Although a penetration deeper into the lines of the exhausted German division was also achieved, the cost was enormous and the attackers lacked the strength to exploit their advantage. When the inevitable German counterattack came, it too failed in the face of swampy terrain and heavy defensive fire. It was only when a battlegroup from 132nd Infantry Division arrived as reinforcements that the Germans were able to shore up their defences.

Like 5th Mountain Division, the units of Starikov's Eighth Army were also running out of men. In desperation, Meretskov threw in a further rifle division and a tank battalion, held back as Front reserves, on 13 August. Writing after the war, Meretskov described how documents captured later revealed that the German lines had come close to collapse because they had run out of reserves, but the same applied to his entire Front. In mid-August, the toehold on the east bank of the Naziya River was abandoned by the remnants of 5th Mountain Division, but aside from a small area of ground around Poreche – perhaps two miles deep and three miles wide – the Soviet Eighth Army had little to show for its massive losses. A senior engineer officer later recalled the terrible conditions in which the soldiers fought and died:

> Which of the soldiers who fought in the summer of 1943 near Leningrad doesn't remember the Sinyavino swamps! Even at night the fetid fumes were nauseating,

the stench of constantly smouldering peat. After a week, the soldiers' combat tunics were saturated. The narrow paths between the rectangles where peat had been cut were targeted by enemy mortars. The orderlies who tried to carry out the wounded here were often killed – they couldn't run fast with their burdens. The gunners had to drag their weapons by hand. I saw one of them sink into the swamp to a depth of 4m. The tanks could achieve nothing here, even though they were sent forward into battle.[26]

None of the problems experienced by the Red Army in this offensive should have come as a surprise – the terrain was painfully familiar from previous offensives. The hope and expectation that German units would be badly degraded in the fighting even if it proved impossible to make major territorial gains was, to an extent, achieved. It was certainly impossible for the Germans to extract any formations for use as reinforcements elsewhere. Army Group North reported that it suffered a total of 48,400 casualties in July and August, and the need to rotate units so that burned-out formations could be given a respite meant that more and more divisions suffered losses and were left in a degraded state. But the Red Army paid a huge price for this. Leningrad and Volkhov Fronts deployed over 253,000 men in this latest offensive, and casualties amounted to nearly 80,000 men.[27]

Govorov submitted a detailed report on the operation on 21 August, and the details are very illuminating:

The course of the development of the offensive operation … took a completely distinct character in terms of the stubbornness of the fighting …

The main reason that determined the unique nature of the operation was the enemy's ability to restore his defences continuously by successive replacement as the divisions of one defensive echelon were destroyed by divisions of the second, then the third echelon …

Of the ten [German] divisions committed to battle, five divisions … were withdrawn completely from battle for replenishment, having lost their combat capability …

The second circumstance that determined the unique nature of the operation was the exceptional defensive density of infantry and firepower. In the breakthrough sector along a frontage of 10km, the enemy maintained three infantry divisions throughout the operation, i.e. one infantry division for every 3–4km of front line. The fire density of the defence was characterised by the presence of 108 artillery batteries and 80 mortar batteries in the breakthrough sector …

Finally, the third circumstance that characterises the operation is the especially difficult terrain conditions and the highly developed defensive positions, both of which have already been described in previous reports. But equally, the second and third circumstances are not the main reasons that determined the nature of the operation, as they were completely surmountable as the battle showed and did not preclude the possibility of a breakthrough and only slowed its pace, allowing the enemy to bring up operational reserves and to restore broken defensive lines …

The actions of Volkhov Front did not tie down the enemy's operational reserves, allowing him to withdraw part of the forces from Volkhov Front and send them to Leningrad Front's sector. Thus, out of seven divisions introduced in the Sinyavino area, two were from Volkhov Front's sector, one from Northwest Front's sector, two from Eighteenth Army's reserves and two from other passive sectors of Leningrad Front.

The plan of the operation assumed that the enemy reserves would be dispersed between the sectors of [Leningrad and Volkhov] Fronts. In fact, all seven infantry divisions ended up in front of Leningrad Front. As a result, the 11 rifle divisions in Leningrad Front's strike force sequentially clashed with ten enemy infantry divisions. The deployment of ten divisions by the enemy instead of six or seven as envisaged by the operational plan, and actually destroyed during the battle, allowed the enemy to prevent the inevitable breakthrough on the Sinyavino axis and changed the course of the operation, forcing us to use the forces intended in the plan for exploitation of the breakthrough to continue the destruction of the additional four infantry divisions that appeared in the front line in addition to the [pre-existing] six infantry divisions.

During the fighting, the [enemy] force of essentially ten infantry divisions and 200 tanks, supported by 108 artillery batteries and 80 mortar batteries, suffered huge losses. Five enemy infantry divisions have already been withdrawn from combat for recovery, about 100 tanks have been destroyed, and three enemy divisions from the third echelon are suffering heavy losses and the enemy is already starting to replace them as they have lost their capability for combat.

The further course of development of the operation will be of the same character until the enemy exhausts his reserves. The enemy's plan is clear. Considering that the Sinyavino axis is the main theatre as a breakthrough here decides the fate of the Mga communications junction, by shielding against Volkhov Front with weak forces the enemy continues to strengthen this main axis, weakening the passive sectors in front of his Eighteenth Army. Continuing this plan, the enemy will be able to send three more divisions to the Sinyavino axis …

It would be expedient to continue operations, seeking the destruction of the last enemy defence echelon and consequently achieving a breakthrough on the Sinyavino axis in conjunction with operations against one of the flanks of the enemy Eighteenth Army. However, without reinforcements of personnel and replenishment of ammunition, Leningrad Front alone does not have the capability to carry out this plan.[28]

The following day, a signal was received from *Stavka*: the attack was to be halted with immediate effect. It isn't clear whether this decision had already been made when Govorov's report arrived, but *Stavka* expressed satisfaction that the operation had tied down considerable German reserves and had thus achieved at least part of its purpose.

Meretskov also dispatched a report, and described the point of view of Volkhov Front in his memoirs:

Units from 11 different Fascist divisions from other sectors, ten divisions that were already in the locality, many artillery units, and several independent units were badly degraded. Küchler's remaining formations were firmly pinned down by Volkhov and Leningrad Fronts. Having committed 68 divisions and six brigades here, the Nazi command did not dare withdraw any of them for transfer to the central or southern regions.

During the battle, enemy staff documents fell into our hands. The headquarters of Volkhov Front did not have a chance to familiarise themselves fully with them during those intense days and the material, recognised as being of great interest, was forwarded in its entirety to *Stavka* ...

On 22 August, Eighth Army went onto the defensive. On the same day, the Leningraders also stopped their attacks. If I had only known what I would learn a month later! We discovered a few weeks later from captured German officers that by the last ten days of August they had no reserves left ... One more powerful push and the Nazi front near Mga could have collapsed.[29]

The accounts of both Govorov and Meretskov are interesting in terms of the detail contained in them, but are also somewhat misleading, and in the case of Leningrad Front this is probably deliberate. Govorov's task would unquestionably have been made easier if the Germans had not deployed fresh troops to replace the worn-out units on the Sinyavino Heights, but to blame this on lack of effort by Volkhov Front is incorrect. The soldiers of Eighth Army were fighting and dying in large numbers in their attempts to penetrate to Mga, and this assault used up all the resources available to Meretskov. If divisions were to be pinned down elsewhere in Volkhov Front's sector, Meretskov would have required further reinforcements and supplies, which would probably have reduced the quantities that could be sent to Leningrad Front. Leaving aside Govorov's questionable arithmetic about the precise number of German divisions rotated through his sector from other areas, the figure of 100 German tanks being destroyed is a huge overstatement, as the total tank strength deployed by the Wehrmacht in the battles for the Sinyavino Heights was far less than this. Tank kills were often inflated in reports by both sides, and several factors made this inevitable. Firstly, unless the enemy was driven from the battlefield and it was possible to count wrecked vehicles, a precise assessment was always almost impossible. From the start of the war, the Germans had included vehicle recovery teams in the establishment of panzer divisions and other mechanised units, and it was impossible for Soviet gunners to know whether the damaged tank they saw being dragged from the battlefield was going to be repaired and returned to service, or would be stripped down to provide replacement parts for other damaged vehicles. Soviet units too had recovery teams, and their numbers increased steadily throughout the war as the Red Army became aware of just how rapidly their tank units lost strength as a consequence of breakdowns and vehicles stranded by terrain difficulties and repairable damage. Secondly, it was common practice for Soviet gunners to be awarded 'kills' if they shared in the destruction of a German tank. This was particularly relevant when they were in combat against the heavy Tiger tanks, which often required several hits before they were immobilised or destroyed. Finally, as these reports of observed or claimed kills were passed up the chain of command, there was a tendency – on both sides – for the numbers to be inflated.

Although Army Group North was unquestionably put under great pressure during this latest assault on the Mga–Sinyavino sector, there is little in German reports and accounts to suggest that Eighteenth Army was approaching the end of its strength. The situation was difficult but manageable, particularly given the huge losses being inflicted on the Red Army. There is therefore little to justify Govorov's belief that if he continued the operation, he could grind his way to and beyond Sinyavino. Similarly, Meretskov's assertion that the German forces facing his Front had run out of reserves is incorrect. An account of the fighting in the German 1st Infantry Division's sector shows that despite the undoubted pressure that the Red Army brought to bear, further attacks would almost certainly have failed to achieve any decisive breakthrough:

Day after day the massed attacks of infantry and tank forces of the Soviet Eighth Army crashed against the positions of the division. Despite the heaviest and most

'Come on, let's dig a trench!' This photograph is part of a
collection showing daily life in Leningrad during the siege,
and was published in a USSR Information Bulletin in 1943.
(Merrill C. Berman Collection)

'The city has carefully covered and camouflaged the statue of Lenin.'
Until the Germans were driven back, Leningrad remained under constant threat.
(Merrill C. Berman Collection)

Leningrad. The flood of casualties overwhelmed hospitals close to the front line, and the
wounded were often moved further to the rear. (Getty Images)

A trio of Soviet infantrymen in position, armed with the PPSh-41. It was much-loved due to its reliability even in sub-zero temperatures. (Courtesy of the Central Museum of the Armed Forces, Moscow via Stavka)

Above An artillery position of the Spanish Blue Division in front of Leningrad during the winter of 1942/43. Although the Germans had a low opinion of their martial abilities, the Spanish soldiers generally performed well. (Getty Images)

January 1943: Overcome with emotion, soldiers from Leningrad and Volkhov fronts cheer, wave their hats and embrace heartily. After over a year of encirclement, the siege ring around Leningrad was broken during *Iskra*. (Getty Images)

German grenadiers taking positions in the trenches south of Lake Ladoga, February 1943. In the winter, frostbite regularly caused more casualties than enemy action. (Getty Images)

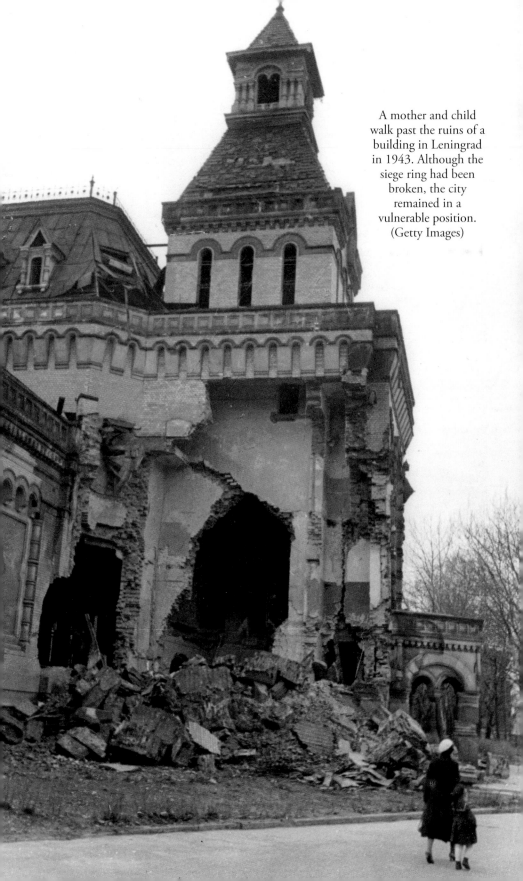

A mother and child walk past the ruins of a building in Leningrad in 1943. Although the siege ring had been broken, the city remained in a vulnerable position. (Getty Images)

Battle break: German soldiers standing next to a Tiger and a destroyed Soviet KV-1 in September 1943. Much of the terrain in the battles in this region was unsuited to the massed use of tanks. (Getty Images)

A German sign indicates a mine-free path in a minefield near Leningrad. Both sides made use of minefields, making the dense forested country even more difficult to navigate. (Alamy)

Two German infantrymen during a snow storm in their trench position, December 1943. Soldiers of both sides struggled through the snow, frozen swamps, and shattered forests of the region. (Getty Images)

A Guards artillery forward observation team calls in target coordinates to its commander. The Red Army placed great expectations on the efficacy of artillery, its 'god of war', but these were rarely met. (From the fonds of the RGAKFD in Krasnogorsk via Stavka)

Keeping watch in a front-line position, this German soldier has grenades to hand and photos of loved ones pinned to the tree. In wooded countryside such as this, men had be constantly alert for enemy patrols. (Nik Cornish)

C. Bykova (left) and R. Skrypnikova, two Soviet snipers, are shown in camouflage battle garb, returning from a combat assignment. Successful snipers were treated almost as celebrities by the Soviet Union, with constant newspaper stories about their exploits. (Getty Images)

Soviet troops on a reconnaissance mission on the Leningrad front, January 1944. Such patrols were also tasked with capturing 'tongues' – prisoners who could be interrogated about the German dispositions. (Bridgeman Images)

Latvian SS volunteers being briefed. Latvian soldiers fought in the Leningrad sector and the battles that followed the end of the siege, as the Red Army pressed into the Baltic States. (Nik Cornish)

Soviet troops from the 110th Rifle Corps rush into the Catherine Palace in Pushkin on 24 January 1944. The liberation of Pushkin, Krasnoye Selo and the Peterhof effectively marked the end of the siege of Leningrad. (Robert Forczyk collection)

Major General Nikolai Pavlovich Simoniak, the officer who succeeded in breaking the blockade of Leningrad and leading the breakout from Oranienbaum. Simoniak was arguably the best Soviet tactical commander in the siege. (Robert Forczyk collection)

Red Army soldiers lead German prisoners of war through the streets of Leningrad, a city they failed to capture despite a siege lasting 900 days, from 1941 to 1944. (Getty Images)

The Piskarevskoye Cemetery became the site of mass graves during the siege.
As Zhdanovism and Stalin's long-standing hostility to Leningrad began to take hold
after the war, the site lay neglected until the mid-1950s.
(Flickr, Alexey Ivanov, CC BY-SA 2.0)

The long-delayed plans for a formal memorial to the siege of Leningrad were resurrected in the 1960s. The bronze figures of the Monument to the Heroic Defenders of Leningrad (left and below) depict both soldiers and civilians. (Author's collection)

These poignant figures are intended to portray the suffering of ordinary people, although it is clear that there was an unwillingness to portray the true emaciated state of Leningraders during the first winter. (Author's collection)

The museum beneath the monument contains mosaics showing various aspects of the siege. This example shows victory celebrations in 1944. (Author's collection)

The sign on Nevsky Prospekt that reads: 'Citizens! During artillery fire this side of the street is more dangerous'. The notice by the flowers reads: 'This inscription was saved in memory of the heroism and courage of Leningraders during the 900-day blockade of the city'. This is not actually true, as it was erased and later re-created.
(Author's collection)

Memorials to historic events reflect the society in which they are created. It is best to see both Piskarevskoye Cemetery and the Monument to the Heroic Defenders of Leningrad in this light. (Author's collection)

determined attacks of the enemy, the front line held. All attacks collapsed in front of the main battle line. Under the command of Oberst Nagel, 1st Artillery Regiment played a considerable role in this defensive success.

The organisation of anti-tank defence by *Panzerjäger Abteilung 1* was in experienced hands (its commander was Hauptmann Siegfried). Up to 25 July, 65 enemy tanks were shot up.

After a temporary lull in attacks, the Russians tried again with support from numerous bomber attacks from 2 to 4 August, directed against the positions of 5th Mountain Division and 1st Infantry Division between Voronovo and Gaitolovo, seeking to strike into the rear of the German defensive positions on the Sinyavino Heights by a thrust towards Mga. The enemy tried in vain with superior forces to overcome our position at Poreche (432rd Grenadier Regiment). Our 22nd Fusilier Regiment fought successful defensive battles either side of the Kirov railway line. In 1st Grenadier Regiment's zone, the enemy's main point of attack was on the left flank against the strongpoints *Dorit* and *Birne*, which were temporarily lost after heavy fighting. The main difficulty in these battles of 1st Grenadier Regiment was due to the dense undergrowth, which the Russians used to achieve a penetration and further thrusts ... Through a carefully prepared counterattack these strongpoints were recovered. The intended Russian thrust was frustrated by the successful defence by 5th Mountain Division and 1st Infantry Division.

On 12 August the Russians brought fresh forces into battle and after several hours of artillery bombardment and the heaviest nightly air raids ... there was a new phase of attacks on the Sinyavino front from the east and north, which continued until 23 August. In this phase too the enemy achieved no successes in the division's sector. Our grenadiers and fusiliers, supported by sappers and anti-tank units, held their positions in the spirit of the words that stood over our cemetery in Mikhailovski: 'Here we stand, here we die.' ... After the end of the fighting the division commander reported to the army commander with pride that the division stood unshaken in the same positions as before the battle, ready for further action.[30]

There is not the slightest hint in this account to corroborate Meretskov's assertion that the Germans facing him were in danger of cracking.

The large numbers of heavy artillery batteries that had been assembled by the Germans for bombardment of Leningrad proved to be valuable assets in the fighting, and a large proportion of Red Army losses was as a consequence of artillery bombardment. Wilhelm Lubbeck had a satisfying day directing his division's artillery against an attack by a group of T-34s, and succeeded in hitting at least two tanks; others were left stranded on the battlefield due to the utterly unsuitable terrain. The predictability of the Soviet attack greatly benefited the Germans, but although the German lines held firm, the cost was considerable. Govorov's estimates of how much damage his Front had inflicted were optimistic at best, but nonetheless the resistance of XXVI Corps was sustained only at the cost of rotating a large number of divisions through the blood-soaked battlefield. Despite these casualties, morale in the German front line seems to have remained high. Lubbeck and his comrades were aware of the huge damage inflicted on Hamburg by the Western Allies, but they remained confident they would still win the war, as Lubbeck wrote to his sweetheart: 'Despite the hardships in Russia, I still expressed an abiding optimism about the outcome of the conflict. "We don't have very much of our younger years, but this will change when the war is finished. We here on the front are very positive that we will win the war."'[31]

Men like Lubbeck might still believe in their eventual triumph, but for those who could see the bigger picture, the anxious wait for the summer fighting season was being replaced by grim realisation that the ability of the Wehrmacht to impose its will on the enemy was rapidly disappearing. Defensive actions like the battles of July and August around Sinyavino were in some senses gratifying, but the Soviet Union seemed to possess endless resources. How much longer could the defences hold firm with such resolution?

CHAPTER 8

AN AUTUMN OF BLOOD
AND ATTRITION

The definition of madness, it is often said, is to do the same thing again and again in the expectation of a different outcome. By that standard, the Red Army's persistent attacks in the Sinyavino sector appear to be eccentric, to say the least. The first two attempts to break through in this sector came in the first winter of the war, and were followed by a major assault in the second half of 1942. The Soviet Second Shock Army, which was effectively destroyed in the summer when it was encircled to the west of the Volkhov River, was once more isolated and badly mauled; only a proportion of its personnel escaped, leaving most of their equipment and many of their comrades in the forests and peat bogs to the east of Sinyavino. Whilst *Iskra* in early 1943 succeeded in establishing a narrow corridor along the southern shore of Lake Ladoga between Leningrad and the rest of the Soviet Union, every attempt to widen this by attacking towards Sinyavino resulted in heavy losses for almost no gain. Despite the lengthy pause that followed the spring thaw prior to the resumption of major operations in July, the next attempt to storm the modest hills and ridges near Sinyavino also ended with the armies effectively where they had started.

The cost of these repeated battles for the same modest patch of ground was immense. Whilst different sources give somewhat different numbers, the total Red Army losses suffered in the operations in the Sinyavino sector exceeded 410,000 killed, wounded, or missing by the end of the summer of 1943; the Lyuban Operation, which saw the first encirclement and destruction of Second Shock Army, accounted for a further 308,000.[1] Clearly, this was singularly difficult terrain over which to conduct an offensive and the Germans had fortified the entire sector to such a degree that there was no question of an orthodox breakthrough followed by exploitation – the defensive belt effectively extended through the entire position. And yet, despite the repeated failures and the huge cost of earlier battles, *Stavka* issued fresh orders even as the operation of July and August came to a halt. Leningrad and Volkhov Fronts were required to launch a fresh series of attacks to capture the Sinyavino Heights.

The logic of the *Stavka* orders was dictated by the continued threat to the narrow land corridor to Leningrad along the southern shore of Lake Ladoga. While the Germans remained on the heights, they could disrupt road and rail transport at will, effectively continuing the siege that the Red Army was determined to lift. Therefore, however predictable the attack – and however bloody it was likely to be – there seemed little option other than to make another attempt to overcome the German defences. Perhaps in recognition of the state of exhaustion that prevailed and the weakened state of the two Soviet Fronts, the new operation had somewhat limited objectives. Leningrad Front would attack once more from the north while Volkhov Front attacked from the east, but there was no longer any intention to reach Mga. Instead, the intention was to capture the vital high ground and Sinyavino itself, and the eastern side of the German-held salient. The capture of Mga would have to wait for a future operation.

Given the repeated failures of the Red Army to capture Sinyavino and the heights, the question must be asked: was there any alternative? Could *Stavka* and the Red Army have attempted anything different? The terrain was difficult almost everywhere in the region, with few good roads and widespread forests and peat bogs, and the Germans had fortified their positions on all possible axes of Soviet attack. But Stalin and his advisers must have looked at the communications corridor that ran southeast from Leningrad, passing through Krasnyi Bor and then on through Ulyanovka and Tosno to Lyuban. This was the axis that had been intended for the Lyuban Operation of the first half of 1942, and there had been no attempt to repeat that operation. Advancing along this corridor, either from the Leningrad direction or from the southeast, would have left all of the German Eighteenth Army in a potentially vulnerable salient, and would have precipitated a withdrawal that would have forced the Germans to abandon the Sinyavino–Mga sector. Would this have been an alternative to a further assault on Sinyavino itself?

The answer, given the losses suffered in the failed summer attack, must be that such an operation was beyond the strength of Leningrad and Volkhov Fronts without substantial reinforcements. Arguably, such an attack might have made better use of the men and tanks squandered in July and August, but there are three factors that should be borne in mind. Firstly, just as the Wehrmacht shuffled its forces skilfully to defeat the Red Army in the Sinyavino–Mga sector, it would have been able to do much the same against an operation aimed at the Volkhov–Tosno–Krasnyi Bor axis. Secondly, both Govorov and Meretskov had believed that better use of artillery and air power would allow them to break the defences that had defied them in the past and despite the apparent futility of further attacks in this area, they still thought that success was possible. And thirdly, a battle that involved exploitation after breaking through the German defensive line ran the risk of playing to the strengths of the Wehrmacht. In the fluid situation that would then arise, the Germans repeatedly showed that their tactical superiority was as great as ever, and a repeat of the Lyuban Operation would run the risk of inviting the Germans to demonstrate once more their ability to improvise. Whilst Army Group North no longer had the motorised assets needed to conduct mobile warfare, Soviet planners had no means of knowing whether such forces would be transferred to the area if required. In any case, when *Stavka* ordered a fresh effort for September, the forces in the area didn't have the strength for anything more than a limited operation, and the only meaningful objective that could be reached lay in the north, around Sinyavino. Once again, the Red Army would throw its men against the German positions on the heights in what can be seen – with hindsight, and perhaps even at the time – as repetition in the hope of a different outcome. The terrible fighting around the Rzhev salient to the west of Moscow in 1942 earned the sector the grim nickname of the 'Meat Grinder'; the repeated battles for Sinyavino were surely worthy of a similar title.

Leningrad Front's contribution to the operation would be Simoniak's XXX Guards Rifle Corps, which was resting after its losses in the fighting of August. Simoniak now had three rifle divisions and three tank brigades, and they began to move into the sector held by Dukhanov's Sixty-Seventh Army in preparation for the new attack. At the same time, two rifle divisions would support Simoniak on his left flank to the east and three on his right flank, towards the west. Despite the pause in operations, none of these divisions had remotely restored their ranks to full strength. Dukhanov had to hope that the Germans were also still badly weakened. From the east, Starikov's Eighth Army would make a fresh attempt to force its way west between Gaitolovo and Voronovo. Starikov concentrated his forces into two shock groups, with three rifle divisions attacking the seam between the German 290th and 254th Infantry Divisions near Gaitolovo, while four further rifle divisions attacked 5th Mountain Division south of the railway line near Voronovo.

When Govorov informed him that his army was to make a fresh assault, Dukhanov – according to some sources – expressed serious doubts about the wisdom of the proposal. He argued that his army was effectively bled white by the summer fighting and there was little point in further pointless attacks.[2] Dushevsky, who was recovering from the wounds in his thigh and had been told that – at least temporarily – he was to take command of a battalion, heard about the discussions from other officers:

> Dukhanov, the commander of Sixty-Seventh Army, refused to take the heights. He said that he lacked the manpower. After the summer battles, three divisions had only the personnel of two, and even then not at full strength. Govorov was patient and understanding but [Zhdanov] the secretary of the Regional Committee [of the Communist Party] demanded that he was removed from command.
>
> At that time, Simoniak was also at the Smolny Institute [where Govorov's headquarters was co-located with the civil authorities in Leningrad]. Govorov told him, 'You will have to deal with this business. What do you need?'
>
> Simoniak replied, 'I need two heavy artillery divisions. And two aviation divisions, with bombers and fighters.' Govorov said he would provide them.[3]

For the moment, Dukhanov remained in post, despite the demands of Zhdanov. He was clearly a capable commander and his assessment of his army's weakness may have played a large part in the deliberately modest plans for the new offensive. He later served as deputy commander of Eighth Guards Army, commanded by the redoubtable Vasily Ivanovich Chuikov whose defence of Stalingrad played such a crucial part in the fighting of 1942, and Chuikov had a high opinion of him: 'A lot could be said in praise of him. His abilities as a military commander were displayed in full in several operations. He knew how to position himself in the most difficult spot. He was calm and reasonable, and brought confidence to the troops, and turned out to be an essential person both for the [army] commander and the soldiers.'[4]

Govorov had tasked his Front's artillery commander, Lieutenant General Georgy Fedorovich Odintsov, with analysing the failure of the bombardments that had preceded the summer attacks. Assisted by Colonel Grigory Mikhailovich Brusser, simultaneously commander of the artillery of Fifty-Fifth Army and chief of staff of artillery for all of Leningrad Front, Odintsov carried out a swift series of inspections and offered his preliminary conclusions to his Front commander:

> The earlier battles in this sector showed that suppression and destruction of the enemy's firing points and achieving superiority of artillery fire was insufficient

for the attack to succeed. It was necessary to destroy the combat and communications trenches completely to deprive the enemy of the ability to use them for movement. The method of artillery preparation had to be changed from what had become stereotypical and predictable. The enemy's soldiers usually waited in foxholes and other shelters and when the fire shifted into the depth of the defensive lines, they rushed back to the forward trenches in order to greet the attackers with massed fire.[5]

This was a reasonable, if incomplete, assessment. Whilst German accounts repeatedly described the weight of shellfire, the manner in which shelling was organised was indeed very formulaic, with the final salvoes of *Katyusha* rockets almost announcing the imminent attack. To make matters worse, as has already been described there were many occasions when the attacking infantry failed to move forward as soon as the barrage lifted to targets further to the rear, thus giving the Germans more time to man their main defences. There was also the continuing problem of adequately detailed reconnaissance. Unless targets could be better identified before the bombardment, there was little prospect of major success, and Odintsov took measures in an attempt to improve this factor too. One of the means used to identify the locations of German heavy weapons was to observe their firing from two different points in the Red Army's front line. Soviet gunnery observers took accurate bearings of the direction of the German weapons and compared the bearings from the two observation points, attempting to correlate them with better quality reconnaissance photographs. It was only when new more accurate compasses were distributed that an issue came to light: the old compasses were far too imprecise, resulting in triangulation of German targets usually being completely inadequate.

The solution devised by Odintsov and Brusser to improve the efficacy of artillery preparation was to alter the way that the artillery preparation was conducted. The first phase would remain the same with heavy shelling of known and presumed German positions. When this was complete and guns began to strike at positions further back, shelling of specific points in the German front line would continue while the attacking infantry moved forward. It was hoped that this would give the Germans who were sheltering in their hardened bunkers the impression that the bombardment was continuing, and would at least permit the attackers to get closer before the defences reacted.

Little had changed in the command arrangements on the German side of the front line; the critical sector remained the responsibility of Hilpert's XXVI Corps, though the rotation of divisions during the summer fighting had resulted in a slightly different line-up. But although the German lines had held firm throughout the Soviet summer offensive, the losses suffered risked reducing the tactical advantage that the Wehrmacht had always enjoyed over its opponent in the east. Steps had already been taken in late June even before the Soviet summer offensive on the Sinyavino Heights commenced, with instructions from *OKH* for further improvements in local training activity at division, battalion, and artillery battery level. Particular attention was to be paid to identifying and training suitable men as platoon commanders, with all ranks being made familiar with the latest weaponry.[6]

Hilpert and his superiors both at Eighteenth Army and Army Group North headquarters knew that the stubborn defence of the Sinyavino salient could not be sustained indefinitely. The purpose of holding it was to use it as a springboard for restoring the encirclement of Leningrad. As any such operation was now very unlikely to take place, given the manner in which events were unfolding across Ukraine, it was surely time to consider whether there was any point in exposing Army Group North's infantry divisions to further bloodletting. Indeed, given that Hitler's original plan for 1943 – a successful blow against the Kursk salient to seize the strategic initiative, and an attack against Leningrad later in the year – was now in ruins, it was time to consider what alternatives were available to Germany at every level.

Plans for a strategic defensive posture had been suggested even before the Battle of Kursk, and such a change of emphasis became increasingly urgent as a consequence of the failure of the Wehrmacht to prevail in *Zitadelle* and the landings by the Western Allies in Sicily and Italy. In mid-August, orders were issued for the widespread construction of fortifications in the east. These new defensive lines, which became known as the *Panther–Wotan Stellungen* ('Panther–Wotan Lines') were intended to form the *Ostwall*, a defensive system to parallel the *Westwall* or 'Siegfried Line' that had been built in the west before the war. As had repeatedly been the case around the Rzhev salient in 1942 and the northern sector since the siege of Leningrad began, the assumption was that the Germans would then be able to inflict further massive losses on their opponents while preserving their strength as much as possible without conceding any further territory. In the meantime, reserves would be established in the west in anticipation of a future invasion of the European mainland by the Western Allies. Once this had been crushed, these reserves would be transferred east so that offensive operations could be resumed.

As a strategy, it was perhaps the only real option left for Germany if it was to seek a successful outcome to the war. However, there were serious problems with implementing the plan. The original proposals for fortifications in the east had been rejected by Hitler, and time was now very short if such defences were to be built as Hitler was insisting that they should be as far to the east as possible. In the northern sector, the Panther Line was intended to be constructed roughly along the old western frontier of the Soviet Union, taking in Lakes Pskov and Peipus and then extending along the Narva River to the Baltic Sea. This would require a substantial withdrawal from the edge of Leningrad, and despite giving permission for the construction of the line Hitler continued to be hugely resistant to such a withdrawal. His natural unwillingness to give up any ground that had been won by the Wehrmacht was reinforced by other arguments. The Germans were extracting fuel from Estonian oil shale deposits on the Baltic coast a little to the west of Narva, and there were concerns that this area would be in the immediate rear area if Army Group North pulled back to the Narva River; and the Luftwaffe expressed concern at abandoning airfields to the east of the river on the grounds that these were essential if air attacks on targets like weapons and munitions factories to the east were to be continued. Although most of the Luftwaffe's objections related to the withdrawal of Army Group South in Ukraine, Hitler rapidly seized upon them as justification to object to withdrawals elsewhere, citing the necessity of continuing air attacks against industrial targets in Leningrad. In reality, these attacks had achieved little to date, and increasingly tough air defence systems around Leningrad were further reducing the ability of the Luftwaffe to carry out any meaningful attacks on the city, but Hitler was quick to grasp at any justification for refusing to give up ground. An additional factor that made Hitler unwilling to withdraw from the Leningrad sector was the impact that this would have on Finland. There were growing signs that Finland might seek a way out of the war, and if this resulted in the Soviet Baltic Fleet being able to operate in the Baltic Sea, it would jeopardise German U-boat training.

There was a further issue with the concept of an *Ostwall*. Even if shortages of resources and manpower could be addressed for the construction of the defences, it was doubtful that the Wehrmacht had the strength to hold such a line. Many infantry divisions had never been restored to their establishment strength after their losses in the first six months of the war in the east and the Stalingrad campaign added further to shortages – not only were several German divisions lost, many divisions deployed in the east by Germany's allies had also either been destroyed or withdrawn from the front line. There were no quiet sectors of the front from which reinforcements could be drawn, and without units held behind a defensive line, ready to respond to any Red Army penetration, an attempt to hold such a static position ran a great risk of the entire German front line becoming very brittle.

For the moment, many of these arguments were, in the case of Army Group North, merely academic. Hitler had no intention of authorising a withdrawal that would hand the Soviet Union such a huge propaganda triumph. The siege of Leningrad was to be maintained. The Wehrmacht had successfully held its positions in the face of almost every Soviet attack, with the exception of *Iskra*; it would have to continue to do so. Küchler's opinion about this is not recorded, but it is significant that he issued fresh instructions for Russian civilians in the rear area near the Leningrad perimeter to be evacuated; they were to be transported further west, where they would be used as labourers to construct defensive positions. Even if he didn't have permission to withdraw to the proposed *Ostwall*, Küchler clearly intended to ensure that the fortifications would be ready when he needed them. There was a further benefit for the Germans from this forced evacuation: there would be fewer civilians left to offer aid to partisan groups, which had resumed their attacks on road and rail movements.

Partisan activity was becoming an increasingly important problem for the German occupation forces. A report in July had highlighted the increase in attacks: in January 1943, there had been a total of 307 partisan attacks against railway lines and trains, but by June this had increased to 1,092 and there was a fourfold increase in the number of locomotives damaged. The number of bridges destroyed or damaged had more than doubled. The report concluded with an appropriately pessimistic message:

> Since ... substantial further strengthening of the anti-partisan combat forces can no longer be expected, and because the manner in which we have chosen to treat the people of the east means that we have to rely on our own strength, one must be aware that pacification of the eastern territories by our further measures cannot be expected. Rather, we will have to content ourselves with the implementation of only those measures vital to our war effort.[7]

Many of the security divisions that had originally been intended for anti-partisan warfare were now either committed to the front line or being held as army-level reserves, and similarly units such as SS cavalry formations that had been widely used in anti-partisan sweeps earlier in the war – in reality, often little more than exercises in indiscriminate killing – had now been incorporated into units that were directly engaged with the Red Army. At the same time, the Soviet Union was steadily increasing its support for the partisan movement, regularly dropping supplies and officers behind German lines. Increasingly, the Germans were forced to prioritise the defence of the most vital parts of the rear area, such as railway lines. Large swathes of territory behind the front line were controlled by the partisans, and there was little the Germans could do about it.

The partisan movement was most active in the central region of the Eastern Front, but there was also increasing activity to the north and south. On 7 August, partisans from 2nd Leningrad Brigade attacked the railway line running northeast from Pskov, one of the vital arteries that supplied Army Group North; it took four days for the Germans to repair the damage and restore rail traffic.[8] There was further disruption by increased Soviet air activity. For the first year or more of the conflict in the east, Soviet aviation was rarely able to muster sufficient aircraft for large-scale raids, but there was a steady increase in the number of aircraft available for such operations as the war progressed. The Soviet aircraft industry was now producing large numbers of suitable aircraft, with a large proportion of the bomber fleet being the Petlyakov Pe-2. This twin-engined plane entered service in early 1941 and by the end of the war formed about 75 per cent of the Soviet twin-engined bomber force; ultimately, over 11,000 were built.[9] It was originally intended as a high-altitude interceptor until Soviet experts who visited German aircraft factories in 1940 reported that the Germans were not developing or building any high-altitude bombers; thereafter, the design was modified so that the Pe-2 could be used as a medium bomber with dive-bomber capabilities. It had a maximum bomb load of 2,200 pounds. In the opening phases of the war units equipped with the Pe-2 suffered heavy losses in low level attacks, but as the experience of aircrews increased and the plane was steadily modified after analysis of aircrew reports, the Pe-2 became a capable bomber. In addition to the Pe-2, Soviet bomber formations fielded several other aircraft such as the older Tupolev SB and Tu-2, as well as steadily increasing numbers of aircraft provided by the USA. By the end of the war, 1,362 Douglas A-10s and 733 North American B-25s had been supplied; although the Soviet Union requested heavy bombers in addition to these twin-engined planes, the Western Allies declined to deliver any.[10] On the same day that the partisans mounted their attacks on the railway lines from Pskov, a mixed force of Soviet bombers, mainly Pe-2s, struck the railway junction at Mga, the objective of so many ground offensives in preceding months. The site was an obvious target and German air defences put up a fierce barrage, downing several planes. But despite these losses, such air raids became an increasingly frequent problem with which the Germans had to contend. Both air attacks and partisan operations systematically targeted the railways for about a week, causing considerable disruption.

In an attempt to reduce partisan activity, German forces were gathered over several days – a mixture of security units, a few companies detached from front-line divisions, and improvised combat groups from rear area units – and deployed in a significant anti-partisan operation on 5 September. The sweep was preceded by aircraft dropping leaflets over the area of partisan activity: 'Partisans! You are surrounded by 6,000 regular troops. Your position is hopeless. Do not resist, or you will perish under the fire of German machine-guns and artillery. Surrender!'[11]

Knowing that they faced a high risk of summary execution if they were captured, few if any partisans heeded this proclamation. Most of the partisans succeeded in evading the German sweep, disappearing into the forests and swamps of the region, but the commander of 3rd Leningrad Brigade, Aleksandr Viktorovich German, was killed. He had been a captain in the Red Army before joining the partisans, and his group was credited with over 40 successful attacks on railways and trains. He had already survived a determined anti-partisan sweep in May 1943, but his luck ran out in this latest attempt to suppress partisan activity. For a short while, partisan activity decreased, but rapidly resumed at a similar intensity to before. Support for the partisans was now far more organised and effective than it had been in the past, with regular supply drops by parachute or aircraft landing behind German lines; and the number of civilians willing to take up arms against the Germans was also increasing as the tide of war turned inexorably in favour of the Soviet Union. On 15 September, the creation of two new partisan brigades in the Leningrad region was authorised.

Early on the same day, the moment came to put Odintsov's new artillery plan to the test. The bombardment of the German front-line positions along the Sinyavino Heights continued while some gun batteries shifted their fire to targets further to the rear and Simoniak's soldiers began to edge forward. As was often the case, German soldiers who endured the bombardment later described its ferocity, describing how in at least some areas the Soviet gunners achieved their objectives. A soldier from 21st Infantry Division later wrote about how thinly manned some of the front line was:

The positions ... had repeatedly been pounded by artillery fire. The trenches were very thinly manned, with one of the battalions holding a sector of 800m with just 21 men. There was no suspicion about enemy intentions until observers became certain that new [artillery] batteries were firing 'from Ivan's side'. Was an attack by the Guards Riflemen imminent? The division staff were notified. The Ic [intelligence officer] dismissed it as nothing but pessimism. The headquarters of XXVI Corps knew no better and reported to Eighteenth Army headquarters:

'Plenty of activity in 21st Infantry Division's sector on the Sinyavino Heights.' And the artillery was advised that an enemy attack was not expected ...

What happened the following morning was what the infantrymen cynically called 'the usual catastrophe'. About 70 Russian artillery batteries and 40 'Stalin Organ' rocket launchers began their terrifying bombardment. The advance companies of 21st Infantry Division were overwhelmed in the very first minutes and all our communications systems were disrupted. Artillery batteries and command posts came under bombing and strafing attack from *Sturmoviks* [Ilyushin Il-2 ground attack aircraft] ... The forward artillery observers were almost all killed in this first fire strike and none remained in contact with their batteries. Thick clouds of dirt hindered vision. Men returning from leave or hospitals, the lightly wounded, and kitchen and supply personnel were gathered and sent forward under the command of an officer who had just reported back from leave. There were wide gaps in the front line. Groups of defenders and stragglers found themselves behind the attacking Russians. They gathered their wounded, took up hedgehog positions and engaged in combat.[12]

The attacking Soviet infantrymen were within 150 yards of the German trenches when the bombardment of forward positions ceased and they rushed forward as fast as they could. On this occasion, there was no lag as had often been the case in earlier attacks, not least because Simoniak's divisions were largely made up of experienced soldiers. The accounts of the battle that followed are contradictory; some Soviet histories state that the German front line along the heights was captured in its entirety, but others – probably accurately – suggest that only Hill 43.3 was captured.[13] German accounts appear to confirm that Simoniak's XXX Guards Rifle Corps enjoyed only modest success and captured just part of the ridge. It is also perhaps relevant that this success came very quickly, just 30 minutes after the assault began – thereafter, the Germans recovered their balance and resistance stiffened. But despite every attempt to renew the attack, including the commitment of additional divisions either side of Simoniak's corps, the advance stalled.

At the same time, Starikov's Eighth Army began its attack from the east. Here too there was an attempt to avoid the failures of the past through innovation. The German 254th Infantry Division was in the path of the planned Soviet offensive, having recently taken up front-line positions in the area in late August after the end of the summer offensive. A battalion of 474th Grenadier Regiment inherited a sector near Gaitolovo where the front line had moved back and forth over a relatively small distance in the numerous offensives in the region; as a consequence, the defensive line consisted of trenches, dugouts, and bunkers that had been constructed by both sides at various times. Although there were no hills that dominated the area, there were numerous minor gullies and intervening ridges, with several streams and rivers running from the swamps towards Lake Ladoga in the north. Much of the region had originally been forested, but few trees had survived the repeated artillery bombardments intact. Nonetheless, the summer vegetation created a degree of cover that made it difficult for either side to get a clear field of view.

One of the positions inherited by the newly arrived German regiment was known as *Olga* and was positioned on a small ridge overlooking a swampy area to the east. The Red Army's front line ran through this swamp at the bottom of a relatively steep slope; the two sides were perhaps 50 yards apart at the closest point, separated by the slope of the ridge across which ran partially demolished trenches from previous offensives. As signs of a new Soviet attack appeared, the Germans carried out regular patrols through these trenches to detect and deter any attempt by the Red Army to edge forward.

These patrols were only partially effective. Whilst German reconnaissance had spotted the build-up of Eighth Army, there were other preparations that went undetected. For several weeks, drawing on experiences from the First World War, sappers had slowly dug a tunnel under no-man's land, running from just in front of their front line and extending up the slope towards *Olga*. When they calculated they had extended their tunnel far enough, the sappers dug sideways, creating a tunnel that they hoped ran parallel and underneath the German positions for about 30 yards. They then placed about three tons of explosives in this secondary tunnel. They went to elaborate lengths to avoid detection, carrying away the excavated earth and dumping it some distance to the rear of their front line.

On 15 September, as the newly devised artillery plan for Simoniak's attack was being put into effect, the guns of Volkhov Front struck at the German defences that lay in the path of Eighth Army. By the standards of earlier attacks, it was a relatively short preparatory bombardment, lasting for perhaps 20 minutes; during this time, Soviet troops began to edge forward into the ruined trenches on the slope leading up to *Olga*, taking advantage of mist and a smoke screen. As the artillery fire lifted, the Germans began to emerge from their shelters, confident that, just as they had done before, they would be able to slaughter the attacking Red Army infantry with massed fire, but as they reached their firing points there was a huge explosion. *Olga* was literally blown to pieces, almost completely destroying the German infantry company defending this sector.

In addition, about 100 Soviet soldiers who were now just a few yards from the German front line were caught in the blast and were killed or wounded.

The losses suffered by the first wave of Soviet troops as a result of the explosion proved crucial. By the time the second wave had climbed up the slope to where *Olga* had been, German troops from either side had rushed into the sector. A hastily organised defensive line immediately opened fire and called in artillery support, crushing the Soviet attack and forcing it back to its starting positions at the bottom of the slope. Hoping to repeat their success, the Red Army sappers who had dug the tunnel that demolished *Olga* attempted to dig a second tunnel, but perhaps predictably the Germans had no intention of being caught in the same manner. Several listening posts were now in place in the German trenches and German sappers detected the sounds of excavation on 19 September. Alerted by this, German troops kept the Soviet front line under close observation and spotted suspicious movements of men carrying digging tools and coils of cable. A raid was mounted to try to reach the bunker from where the new tunnel was being dug but failed to reach its objective, and the Germans resorted to the sort of response familiar to soldiers involved in siege warfare throughout history – they dug a vertical shaft of their own to intercept the Red Army's excavations. At the same time, the front line was thinned out as a precautionary measure, with most of the men being deployed a little to the rear so that if there was a further explosion followed by a Soviet attack, they would be able to counterattack swiftly.

Digging continued for several days until the Germans broke into the Soviet tunnel on 30 September. At first they weren't detected by the Red Army sappers and a combat patrol was sent down the German shaft. Taking their opponents by surprise, the Germans rapidly cleared the tunnel and then blocked it close to its eastern end, recovering about 20 tons of explosives that had already been placed under the German positions.[14]

This attempt to emulate the endeavours of sappers in the past proved to be a failure. Perhaps the most successful such case had been at Messines Ridge in 1917, when British engineers placed over 450 tons of explosives below German positions. The resultant blast was so loud that it was heard in London, and killed or wounded an estimated 10,000 German soldiers.[15] By comparison, the Soviet efforts were modest and were spoiled by the manner in which the troops moving forward to take advantage of the explosion beneath *Olga* were caught in the blast, delaying the actual attack just enough for the Germans to recover. There were also severe constraints imposed by the terrain. There were few areas in the region where the water table was sufficiently far beneath the surface for such tunnelling to be carried out. In any event, the assaults by Eighth Army proved to be as ineffectual as those on the Sinyavino Heights. A few small patches of land changed hands once more, and Soviet soldiers wearily dug themselves shelters in trenches that had been occupied by both sides at various points in the past. This latest attempt to clear the Germans from their dominating positions near Sinyavino resulted in additional losses for no significant gain – Simoniak's corps alone lost over 3,000 men, with total Red Army losses probably exceeding 16,000 in just three days of fighting.[16] Aware that the attack had failed to make any significant progress and that the attacking forces had very limited capabilities in view of their earlier casualties, *Stavka* rapidly called a halt. Simoniak's corps was extracted from the front line and was replaced by 11th Rifle Division, which made a small number of attempts to extend the Red Army's positions on the Sinyavino Heights; the only outcome was further addition to the death toll.

Although the Soviet attacks achieved only minimal success, the capture of a section of the Sinyavino Heights reduced (but did not eliminate) the ability of the Germans to direct artillery fire against the narrow communications corridor along the southern shore of Lake Ladoga. It was now clear beyond any doubt to Küchler and his staff that there would be no offensive towards the north as Hitler had originally intended, and thoughts turned to preparations for the inevitability of further Red Army offensive operations. Although Eighteenth Army had successfully fended off almost every attack since *Iskra*, reserves at every level were at dangerously low levels. Anticipating that once its ranks had been replenished and strengthened, the Red Army would make another major attack, Küchler's assessment was that in its current configuration, his army group would not be able to withstand such an assault. It was therefore essential for sufficient reserves to be gathered behind the front line. If it wasn't possible for such reserves to be sent to Army Group North from other sectors, the only alternative was to shorten the front line within the sectors of Sixteenth and Eighteenth Armies in order to release such reserves.

During the Lyuban Operation in the first half of 1942, Volkhov Front mounted a major advance across the Volkhov River, leading ultimately to German counterattacks that brought about the encirclement and destruction of Second Shock Army. In addition, one of Meretskov's armies carried out an attack west of the river, striking from the northeast. This resulted in a Soviet-held salient projecting towards the southwest, about 12 miles wide and deep, with a slightly smaller German-held salient to its east. At the most eastern point of this salient was Kirishi, where the Wehrmacht held a bridgehead over the Volkhov River. This city was the scene of repeated bloody assaults by the Red Army, all of which were beaten off, though the price for the Wehrmacht was that several divisions had to be rotated through the sector as casualties thinned their ranks. Aware that Hitler would almost certainly object to the withdrawal of German forces from the only position that they held on the east bank of the Volkhov River, Küchler began the long and wearing process of attempting to secure permission to abandon Kirishi, thus releasing sufficient forces for him to create the reserves that he saw as essential.

Regardless of the problems of Army Group North, Hitler had other pressing concerns. Mussolini was summoned to Rome by King Victor Emmanuel III at the end of July; he was dismissed as prime minister and placed under arrest. Assurances were sent to Berlin that Italy would remain loyal to the Axis, but secret negotiations commenced immediately for an armistice with the Western Allies. An agreement was signed on 3 September, and on the same day British troops crossed from Sicily to southern Italy, followed by further landings at Salerno and Taranto on 9 September. There had been growing signs of unrest in Italy for some considerable time with industrial strikes in the northern cities, and Hitler and his advisers anticipated that Italy would seek an exit from the war or might even switch sides. There was good precedent for this – Italy had been part of an alliance with Germany and the Austro-Hungarian Empire in 1914 but had refused to enter the First World War on the side of its allies on the grounds that it had only joined the alliance for mutual defence and would not take part in a war that saw offensive operations against France, Belgium, Russia, and Serbia. In 1916, Italy was persuaded by the Western Powers to enter the conflict against the Central Powers, resulting in a long and hugely costly series of battles on the frontier with the Austro-Hungarian Empire. In order to reduce the impact of what was feared to be another probable defection, Hitler authorised the transfer of additional troops to Italy, where they reinforced the units that were evacuated from Sicily. All British and American prisoners of war being held by the Italians had already been taken into German custody, and their transfer out of Italy was now accelerated.

An armistice between Italy and the Western Powers came into force on 8 September and the Germans moved quickly to disarm Italian units. In some areas, this led to fierce fighting, both in Italy and in Sardinia and the Greek islands, where Italian forces had been occupying Cephalonia. Ultimately, the Germans were able to prevail against often determined Italian resistance and established a defensive line across the Italian peninsula, but it was another drain on German resources at a time when all the army group commanders on the Eastern Front were making requests for reinforcements.

There was a darker side to the German occupation of Italy. Many of the brutal practices of the Eastern Front were put into effect in attempts to suppress the rapidly developing Italian partisan movement, resulting in several episodes of indiscriminate killing. Many of the units in Italy were part of the Waffen-SS, partly by chance and partly because several new SS divisions were being raised and this region was chosen as suitable for these formations to work up to full combat readiness. Almost all German units were involved in crimes against civilians in their attempts to overcome partisan activity in the occupied parts of Europe, but the SS often showed a greater level of ruthlessness.

Although Mussolini's government enacted racial laws that discriminated against Jews in 1938, there was very little active persecution and large numbers of Jews were able to leave the country before the outbreak of the Second World War. In June 1940, the situation began to deteriorate with the creation of about 50 concentration camps, but these were used mainly for the detention of political prisoners and conditions were far better than in German camps for most prisoners. There were no killings of Jews (though the Roma population in the camps had to endure harsher conditions with lower rations than others) and after the arrest of Mussolini the inmates of the concentration camps began to be released. When the Germans seized control on 8 September, matters changed. About 45,000 Jews lived in the German-controlled regions of Italy and a campaign of detention and killing commenced immediately.[17]

Even before the latest attack on the Sinyavino Heights, the *Wehrmachtführungsstab* ('Wehrmacht Command Staff', often abbreviated to *WFSt*, effectively the operations staff of the Wehrmacht) had drawn up a report assessing the military needs of each theatre and the forces actually available, largely to provide definitive information on whether further forces could be sent to the east. This report was completed on 6 September by Generaloberst Alfred Jodl, chief of *WFSt*, and made sobering reading for senior German officials. The northern part of Europe was no longer an area from which reserves could be withdrawn – on the long Finnish front, there were no significant tactical reserves and a renewed Soviet offensive was expected imminently. In Norway, the withdrawal of 25th Panzer Division to France (from where it was about to be dispatched to the Eastern Front) left the country with only a single infantry division in reserve, and there were concerns that if the Western Allies were to carry out a successful landing, they might be able to overrun Norway swiftly and then put pressure upon Sweden to enter the war against Germany. Similarly, Denmark – the essential bridge between Germany and Scandinavia – was defended by only a single division. In the west, the requirement of reserves for defending France against an invasion by the Western Allies was put at seven or eight mechanised or panzer divisions and four to six infantry divisions, all at full strength; the assessment was that when current formations in France completed their assembly training, this number could be achieved, but there would be nothing to spare for operations elsewhere. Similarly, the German forces in Italy and the Balkan region could spare nothing for deployment elsewhere and were deemed to be insufficient to hold off a determined enemy assault. As was the case across so much of occupied Europe, the partisan movement in the Balkans, particularly in Yugoslavia, was tying down large numbers of German units in fighting that was highly unlikely to be conclusive but prevented the transfer of troops to other regions.

The conclusion was that the only way that troops could be released to create the reserves necessary for prolonged defence was by shortening the front line. There was no possibility of such measures in the north or west, and in the south there was potentially an option to give up the Greek islands, including Crete, and Greece itself; although this would obviate the need to defend the long Greek coastline, the price would probably be the loss of much of the heavy equipment currently on the islands. Jodl looked at the Italian situation – at time of completion of the report, the defection of Italy was expected but had not yet occurred – and suggested that it was necessary to take the initiative by issuing the Italians with an ultimatum. In the absence of any appropriate assurances that Italy would continue to resist, plans should be made for the abandonment of southern Italy and Sardinia and the adoption of a defensive line across the Apennines. It was estimated that this measure could release up to four divisions. Even these, Jodl suggested, might not be available for the Eastern Front, as he wished to use them to strengthen German positions in the Balkans.[18]

Even if Jodl's wish to use the divisions in the Balkans was ignored and they were sent instead to the Eastern Front, this was a modest force given the pressing needs. Manstein had for some considerable time been demanding the creation of a new army at the northern end of his sector with which he could conduct counterattacks against the Soviet forces threatening to pin his army group against the Sea of Azov and the Black Sea, and although some of the forces that were needed for such an army could be extracted from the German Seventeenth Army, still holding a small bridgehead in Kuban to the east of Crimea, Manstein's requirement would absorb all four of the divisions that Jodl proposed to release from Italy. Army Group Centre too was desperate for reinforcements; although it had stopped the Soviet *Kutuzov* offensive, its infantry divisions were badly weakened and there were concerns about just how robust they would prove to be in the face of a major renewed Red Army assault. And as already described, the northern sector was almost completely denuded of meaningful reserves.

As the fighting around the Sinyavino Heights raged in the third week of September, Jodl held further discussions with Hitler and suggested the possibility of a major withdrawal in the north to the proposed Panther Line positions along the Narva River and Lakes Peipus and Pskov. As was often the case when faced with a difficult decision that he didn't want to make, Hitler prevaricated and attempted to justify delay however he could. On this occasion, he placed great weight on the continued involvement of Finland in the war, without which it would prove impossible to prevent the Soviet Baltic Fleet from breaking out into the training waters that were vital for the U-boat force. On 20 September, Jodl acquiesced to Hitler's reasoning and agreed that for the moment, Army Group North should continue to hold its positions near Leningrad and the long Finnish front to the north should also not pull back to the west. Jodl suggested that at least three further divisions be sent to Finland and that sufficient Luftwaffe capacity for the complete destruction of Leningrad and the Soviet Baltic Fleet should be assembled.[19] Given his report on the overstretched state of German armed forces, he must have known that these suggestions amounted to fantasy. Even at the height of its power, the Luftwaffe lacked the heavy bomber fleet required for the destruction of large cities, and just like Germany's ground forces, its resources were hugely overstretched. Where the extra divisions for Finland were to be found was not made clear. It is likely that Jodl was using this suggestion as a means of demonstrating to Hitler that continuing to hold the current positions was not a cost-free option, and that Germany lacked the resources to pay this cost.

As if to emphasise how precarious German control of conquered territories in the east actually was, there was a significant event on 22 September. Wilhelm Kube was the Nazi Party *Gebietskommissar* ('District Commissar') for *Weissruthenien*, the German name for the occupied territory broadly equivalent to modern Belarus. In the early stages of his tenure of this post, he forwarded to Himmler a letter from one of his subordinates, the administrator of Slutsk, to protest about the manner in which Jews and others were indiscriminately killed:

> With indescribable brutality on the part of both the German police officers and particularly the Lithuanian partisans, the Jewish people and also among them Belarusians were taken out of their dwellings and herded together. Everywhere in the town shots were to be heard and in different streets the corpses of shot Jews accumulated. The Belarusians were in greatest distress to free themselves from the encirclement. Regardless of the fact that the Jewish people, among whom were also tradesmen, were mistreated in a terribly barbarous way ... the Belarusians themselves were also worked over with rubber clubs and rifle butts.[20]

The protests of Kube and his subordinate were on two counts. Firstly, the Jews were killed indiscriminately, ignoring the fact that many were deemed 'essential workers'; and secondly, Belarusians were caught up in the violence. There was no rejection of the killing of Jews *per se*. Not long after, Kube was present when a group of Jewish children were thrown into a pit near the Minsk ghetto and executed – on this occasion, the victims were deemed to be 'non-productive' Jews and their deaths were therefore simply a matter of necessity. Before dawn on 22 September 1943, a bomb placed in Kube's mattress by Yelena Grigoryevna Mazanik, a Belarusian woman who worked for Kube as a maid, exploded and killed the *Gebietskommissar*. The SS slaughtered over 1,000 civilians in reprisals, but it demonstrated beyond doubt that even high-ranking officials could not regard the occupied territories of the east as remotely safe.

Jodl's careful staffwork of the summer was an attempt to force a major strategic re-evaluation of the war, but Hitler continued to make decisions only when he was left with no alternative. For the moment, he continued to cling to his hope and belief that the Red Army could be held back long enough for the Western Allies to be defeated in a failed invasion. Every request submitted by commanders like Manstein for timely withdrawals was declined until such withdrawals were essential to avoid catastrophe, and this policy created an increasingly circular argument. Manstein and others often wished to withdraw in order to create reserves for counterattacks; by the time Hitler gave permission, the forces involved were often too weak to be able to make such counterattacks, and in any case the overall situation had usually deteriorated to the point where these counterattacks were now pointless. Hitler then used this outcome to justify rejection of further requests for withdrawals, on the grounds that the promised counterattacks never materialised.

It was in this context that Küchler conducted his negotiations for a withdrawal from Kirishi. Part of the decision-making process resulted from further new proposals from Jodl. Explicitly recognising that his suggestions created a significant risk but also acknowledging both the continuing demand for troops on the Eastern Front and the growing unlikelihood of an invasion of Western Europe in what remained of 1943 given the deteriorating weather, Jodl suggested a series of troop movements, with the net effect of several more divisions being sent to the east. Most would go to Army Group South, where the Red Army had pursued the Wehrmacht back to the Dnepr and in places had crossed to the west bank, threatening to derail the German plans to use the river as a defensive line even before most German units had reached it. Unable to secure any of these reinforcements for Army Group North, Küchler requested once more that he be given permission to evacuate XXVIII Corps from the Kirishi bridgehead and the area immediately to the west of the Volkhov River near Kirishi. Hitler was forced to agree, given that without such a withdrawal it was impossible for Army Group North to have sufficient reserves to deal with future Soviet offensive operations.

Orders had been prepared in anticipation of this and the withdrawal, codenamed *Hubertusjagd*, began almost immediately. Rear area units had already begun an unobtrusive withdrawal and large quantities of supplies had also been moved to the west. In a series of phased withdrawals, General Herbert Loch's corps began to move its combat forces out at the beginning of October almost unmolested by the Red Army. On 2 October, 132nd Infantry Division's last soldiers quietly slipped across the Volkhov via the railway bridge that had been the lifeline for the German bridgehead – despite several major assaults on the German positions in 1942, the Soviet forces repeatedly failed to destroy the bridge. Finally, Gusev's Fourth Army became aware of the German withdrawal and hastily organised a pursuit. It was too late. The salient held by XXVIII Corps was known to the Germans as the *Sekttropfen* ('Champagne Cork') on account of its shape, and Loch's withdrawal conceded the entire area. When the Soviet Fourth Army caught up with the retreating Germans and threw its forces at the German 96th Infantry Division, it was unable to achieve anything other than further casualties.

The immediate result of the withdrawal was the release of just one division, but even this represented a substantial improvement of the reserves available to Army Group North. It proved to be a timely move. Even as *Hubertusjagd* was coming to a successful conclusion, the Red Army threw substantial forces at the southern flank of Küchler's army group, attempting to break open the boundary between Sixteenth Army and Third Panzer Army – the most northern formation of Army Group Centre – near the city of Nevel. The purpose of the attack was to capture Nevel as a preliminary step for future operations, as the city would be a good starting point for a larger attack towards the west.

The Nevel Operation, as it was known to the Red Army, commenced on 6 October with reconnaissance in force at several points of the front line, in an attempt not to reveal to the Germans the precise location of the main attack. Immediately after, the massed Soviet artillery opened fire, using a similar fire plan to that devised for the latest attack on the Sinyavino Heights – when the *Katyusha* rocket batteries joined the bombardment, other Soviet guns switched to deeper targets before suddenly returning their fire to the German front line in an attempt to catch any defenders who had ventured out from their shelters in anticipation of a Soviet assault. The northern Soviet force – Third Shock Army – was held up by determined resistance from the Germans but a gap rapidly opened between the German Sixteenth and Third Panzer Armies. Swiftly, a tank brigade and a rifle division moved forward and were inserted into the breach where they struggled to advance through uncharted German minefields. Recovering their balance, the Germans began to subject the area to heavy artillery fire. Lieutenant General Kuzma Nikitovich Galitsky, commander of Third Shock Army, ordered the exploitation group to press on and avoid becoming entangled with fighting on the flanks of the breach and during the afternoon of the first day of the assault, the leading elements reached Nevel. By nightfall, the city was in Soviet hands. The rapidity of the success was so great that General Andrei Ivanovich Eremenko, commander of Kalinin Front, at first doubted the accuracy of the reports.

The reserves that Küchler had intended to hold in preparation of fresh Soviet attacks in the Leningrad sector were now urgently required in the south. A reinforced infantry division and the bulk of the Tiger tanks of *Schwere Panzer Abteilung 502* headed south to launch a counterattack from the north to close the gap with Army Group Centre. Fighting continued for several days but there was little change in the front line, even when there were larger attacks later in 1943. Nevel was in Soviet hands and a gap remained between Army Group North and Army Group South, but due to the unavailability of sufficient troops and unfavourable terrain, the Red Army was unable to take advantage of it. Nevertheless, some of Küchler's precious reserves had been drawn away to the far south of his long sector of the front line. There was also growing evidence that despite a year of dreadful bloodletting around Sinyavino, the Soviet forces in the north greatly outnumbered the Germans. By mid-October, Army Group North reported that its strength had sunk from 760,000 men in midsummer to 601,000. Accurate figures for the Red Army weren't available to Küchler and his staff, but the information that they had led them to believe that their opponents were undiminished in strength. They were broadly correct. The strength of Leningrad and Volkhov Fronts in mid-October stood at about 890,000 men, with a further 66,000 in reserve.[21]

In this situation, the rational conclusion was that further withdrawals were required and the obvious line for Army Group North was the Panther Line being constructed along the Narva River and to the south of Lake Pskov. Given the extreme reluctance of Hitler to countenance even the abandonment of the Kirishi bridgehead, Küchler knew that there was no possibility of securing permission for such a major withdrawal. Instead, he ordered preparations of the Panther Line to continue, but also organised the construction of intermediate defensive lines. If his army group came under intolerable pressure, he needed positions to which he could safely pull back, retreating in stages to the main Panther Line. By the end of 1943, a workforce of 50,000, most of them forced labourers rounded up from the local countryside and towns, or prisoners held in prisoner of war camps and the concentration camps of northern Estonia, had completed or were building an impressive 6,000 bunkers and many miles of trenches and anti-tank ditches.[22]

The intermediate positions were based upon a series of strongpoints. These were centred on Krasnogvardeisk, Chudovo, Novgorod, Luga, Kingisepp, and Narva. As had been the case with the withdrawal from Kirishi, the staff of Army Group North carefully drew up plans for a phased withdrawal under the unfortunate codename *Blau* – this had been the codename for the German advance that ended in disaster in the ruins of Stalingrad. These plans were then submitted to *OKH*, and outlined an orderly withdrawal that would commence in mid-January. By the spring of 1944, Army Group North would be safe in its fortified positions on a shorter front line, with sufficient reserves available to deal with any Soviet attacks. Küchler therefore had a few weeks in which he could secure permission for execution of the plan.

Reports from areas further south in the Soviet Union that had been overrun by the advancing Red Army showed that Soviet forces rapidly conscripted civilians of military age into their ranks as they advanced, and were just as ruthless as the Germans when it came to forcing civilians to work as labourers. Soviet-era accounts often describe how local people enthusiastically contributed to the efforts of Red Army sappers to rebuild roads and railways, or to build fortifications, but although many Soviet civilians undoubtedly welcomed the return of the Red Army, it might be more accurate to say that their greatest satisfaction was in the departure of the Germans rather than the return of Soviet rule. Undoubtedly, many civilians willingly helped in all manner of ways; equally undoubtedly, others did so because the Red Army gave them little or no choice. In order to minimise the potential for Leningrad and Volkhov Fronts to take advantage of the local population if Army Group North pulled back to the Panther Line, plans were drawn up for the forcible evacuation of all civilians in the area that was to be given up. The estimated civilian population was about 900,000, and even if they had been willing to be relocated, this would have been a major undertaking. Inevitably, most were reluctant to leave their homes and attempts to move them by force led to clashes. In one such incident in mid-October, German security troops encircled a village in preparation for a forced evacuation but were then attacked by a local partisan group. When the German soldiers withdrew to reorganise before moving forward against the partisans, the population of the village fled into the nearby forest, followed by the partisans. The cautiously advancing Germans found only deserted buildings.[23]

To add to the problems of Küchler and the staff of Army Group North, the tangle of German authorities operating in the rear area proved impossible to sort out. When the first columns of forcibly evacuated civilians reached Estonia and Latvia, they found that there was no provision for housing them. This resulted in rolling stock being left stranded at railway stations loaded with displaced civilians with nowhere to go, and this in turn prevented further evacuations from proceeding. Many of these civilians were employed by a variety of authorities behind the German front line, working as labourers, cleaners, and a hundred other roles, and protests from these authorities added to the confusion. Attempts to force-march civilians from the area were also ineffective. As the columns of wretched civilians trudged along the increasingly muddy roads in the cold autumn rain, dozens slipped away whenever the opportunity arose and Küchler ordered a pause.[24] Instead of the original mass deportation of all civilians, selected groups – mainly the men who might be conscripted by the Red Army – were to be rounded up and evacuated by train. Even this proved to be difficult. On 14 October, partisans blew up a section of track and derailed a train carrying male civilians; about 1,200 Soviet men disappeared into the forest with the partisans.[25]

For the civilians who were shipped out by the Germans, the process was one of great anxiety and misery. They were separated from their families and used as forced labour, either on the fortifications of the Panther Line or in factories in Germany. The conditions in which they were held were poor, with many forced to sleep in unheated buildings and risking severe punishments for minor infringements of regulations that they lacked the language skills to understand. Thousands of such forced labourers died through a mixture of dangerous working conditions, malnutrition, illness, mistreatment, or arbitrary executions. After the war, those who tried to return home faced an additional problem: the Soviet authorities regarded anyone who had been outside the Soviet Union as potentially contaminated by political views that were unacceptable to the Communist system and as was the case with released prisoners of war, many civilian returnees were shipped off to camps in Siberia. But however grim and difficult their time under German control and after their return to the Soviet Union was, matters were often worse for those who managed to remain near their homes until the arrival of the Red Army. Desperately short of personnel as a consequence of their terrible casualties, Soviet units routinely rounded up men of military service age and dispatched them to front-line units with only the most rudimentary training, far short of even the inadequate standard of basic training undergone by men conscripted under more normal circumstances. Whatever expectation there might have been that the front-line units would remedy any training deficiencies, these conscripts were simply thrown into combat, often in 'human wave' attacks as they lacked the training or skill for any other form of combat. Casualties amongst these conscripts were appallingly high, with most dying in their first few battles. The minority who survived did so through a combination of extreme good fortune and rapidly learning the skills that they needed from their more experienced comrades.

In addition to the civilians that Küchler wished to evacuate, there was the question of moving other resources that might potentially be of use to the Red Army. In other areas, this involved the removal or destruction of industrial equipment, electricity generation facilities, etc, but such items were scarce in the region between the Estonian frontier and Leningrad – the only such item was the modest railway network, which was to be dismantled. The main resource that would need to be moved was food, and the staff of Army Group North estimated that approximately 1 million tons of grain and potatoes and half a million cattle, sheep, and pigs would have to be moved. This created further problems. Aside from the volume of rail transport required to move such quantities, the transfer of food and livestock from the region would leave the remaining civilians with nothing to eat. Humanitarian issues were far from the forefront of German calculations, but as already mentioned many of these civilians were regarded as essential workers, creating the requirement for complex arrangements to ensure that these workers received adequate food supplies. Furthermore, such a major movement would be heavily dependent upon the railways. These were already disrupted fairly regularly by partisan attacks, and the planned dismantlement and destruction of railway lines as the Wehrmacht withdrew would have to be sequenced carefully so that it took place after the grain and livestock had been moved.

The tide of the war might have turned against Germany, but sporadic shelling of Leningrad continued on most days. The bombardments were often little more than harassment, lasting just a few minutes, and often caused no casualties; occasionally, a shell struck a target by chance that resulted in civilian deaths. On 11 October, in one such bombardment, 137 shells were fired into the city in the middle of the day, resulting in 63 casualties; one shell struck a tramcar, killing 11 people and wounding 11 more.[26] The following day, 21 were killed and 28 wounded in an almost identical incident. Soviet gunners retaliated to such attacks, and increasingly Soviet bombers also attempted to suppress the German guns, but the frequency and duration of German bombardments actually increased during October, largely because there was less need for the long-range German batteries to provide fire support for the units defending Sinyavino and other key locations.

The Soviet air attacks on railway junctions in Mga and other key locations became steadily heavier and more frequent, adding to the difficulties faced by Army Group North with its plans for mass evacuation. By contrast, German air attacks on Leningrad diminished steadily – there were no raids recorded throughout September, but in mid-October a solitary bomber appeared one night, dropping a number of incendiaries. It was a huge contrast with earlier times during the siege. In 1941, dozens of aircraft had attacked the city almost every day and night. A combination of better air defences and fewer German aircraft was having an increasing impact. With so much pressure on German front lines all along the front, the priority for the Luftwaffe was the pursuance of the mission for which it had originally been intended and to which its aircraft were most suited: tactical air support of ground forces. Even in this role, Soviet fighter pilots were growing increasingly skilful and often broke up German bomber groups before they could reach their targets. Matters were worsened for the German bombers by the need for increasing numbers of German fighters to be held in Germany to defend against the growing power of daylight bombing by the USAAF, meaning that the Luftwaffe had less ability to protect its bombers in the east from Soviet fighters.

The casualties suffered by both sides in the northern sector forced a prolonged lull in major ground operations around Leningrad. But whilst the Germans were busy planning for possible withdrawal to the Panther Line and were making appropriate arrangements, Soviet planners were also hard at work. It would soon be time for the Red Army to try once more to drive the Germans out of their positions all around the city and to lift the siege once and for all.

CHAPTER 9

WINTER PLANNING

The end of 1943 saw plenty of activity in Army Group North's sector, but it was mainly behind the front line. The partisan movement remained active and caused considerable disruption, and on 1 November Generalmajor Hans Boeck-Behrens, chief of staff of Sixteenth Army, wrote in his diary about a series of coordinated attacks by 3rd Leningrad Partisan Brigade on the vital railway line from Pskov to Staraya Russa: 'About 400 explosive charges were laid. Of these, 100 were safely defused. The rest caused great damage to the tracks and considerable disruption.'[1]

As the new year approached, Küchler's staff were able to report that they had evacuated 250,000 civilians from the region but had been forced to call a halt due to there being no further accommodation available in Estonia, Latvia, or Lithuania. Substantial quantities of agricultural produce had also been removed, and work was progressing smoothly to prepare much of the siege artillery that had been assembled outside Leningrad for transfer to the west. Just as the withdrawal of the German Ninth Army from the Rzhev salient in early 1943 was accompanied by systematic destruction of anything that might be of use to the Soviet forces following closely behind, the planners of Army Group North intended to implement a similar plan as they fell back sequentially to the intermediate defence lines between Leningrad and the Panther Line. Work on the defensive positions along the Narva River, around the town of Ivangorod on the east bank of the Narva where the Germans intended to hold onto a small bridgehead, and to the south of Lakes Peipus and Pskov was reported to be largely complete. What was now required was permission from Hitler for the withdrawal to commence in mid-January as the planners described in their documents.

Some of the formations that had been in the thick of the bitter trench warfare had already departed. For several months, the Western Allies had been applying increasing pressure on the Spanish government over the continued presence of the Blue Division, and the Catholic Church was also increasingly vocal in its opposition to the deployment. In the last week of September, even as the fighting on the Sinyavino Heights was coming to a conclusion, Franco and his Council of Ministers agreed to recall the Blue Division. A 'legion' would be permitted to stay, roughly the strength of a single regiment or a third of the original Blue Division. When the plans were presented to Hitler, the Führer rejected them, but ultimately he had no choice: the Spaniards were not citizens of Germany or an occupied country, and they could only remain on the Eastern Front voluntarily or through the cooperation of the Madrid government.

The Spanish troops in the front line had little idea that a withdrawal was coming, and even at the level of the headquarters of Army Group North and Eighteenth Army there was little more than rumour. In early October, firm information finally arrived from Madrid and Berlin. Generalleutnant Esteban-Infantes, the commander of the division, learned about the withdrawal from Lindemann at the headquarters of Eighteenth Army rather than directly from his government. Units began to entrain for Spain almost immediately and the rest of the division, pulled out of the front line, gathered in the rear area. Here, volunteers who wished to serve in the new Spanish Legion were asked to come forward. The division was formally disbanded on 16 November. The original intention to have an all-volunteer legion was altered to ensure that it remained at full strength, with all Blue Division soldiers being informed that they might have to serve. Eventually, this proved to be unnecessary, though the last replacement draft to arrive from Spain formed a substantial part of the new legion.

Many of the soldiers of the Blue Division were desperate to return home. Although officers had been instructed to identify volunteers to remain in the Soviet Union, the unwillingness of the officers to stay in the cold, muddy trenches around the Leningrad perimeter meant that they did little to encourage their men to join the legion. Plans had to be revised several times and when the Spanish Legion came into existence it consisted of two grenadier battalions and a mixed support battalion, a reconnaissance unit of less than battalion strength, and the usual logistic and support units for such a formation. The commander of the legion was Colonel Antonio García-Navarro and he gathered his men in Kingisepp, some distance from the units that were being disbanded before their personnel returned to Spain. The intention of the Germans was to rotate the three battalions into the front line with only one in the trenches at any time;

continuing to have a low opinion of the fighting prowess of their allies, the Germans intended to place the 'active' battalion in a relatively quiet sector so that German troops could then be released.

García-Navarro organised intensive training for his new command, as so many of its personnel were recently arrived drafts and he recognised the importance of integrating his modest number of veterans with the new men so that the latter could learn from the former. As had been the case with the Blue Division, there were numerous episodes of poor discipline, with complaints from neighbouring German units around Kingisepp and from the local population about incidents of theft and occasional violence. Given the ever-escalating level of partisan activity, it was inevitable that the Spaniards would be pressed into service in the rear area before their training was complete, and one battalion was used in an operation to secure the road between Narva and Kingisepp and to oversee the forcible evacuation of several villages along the road. When it had completed its training programme, the Spanish Legion was assigned to the German 121st Infantry Division and sent to the front line to the southeast of Leningrad, on the western side of the area near Kirishi that had recently been evacuated.[2]

During its time on the Eastern Front in 1942 and 1943, the Blue Division was frequently involved in fighting to hold back various Soviet offensives. Despite the repeated disparaging comments made by so many German officers, it performed competently and any shortcomings were due to its relatively poor level of modern equipment and the absence of training in close cooperation with tanks. There were 14 documented desertions from its ranks and six men were found to have self-inflicted wounds in attempts to avoid service – unremarkable totals for the Eastern Front and not dissimilar to the numbers seen in German divisions. But whilst the division performed adequately, over the two years of deployment many of its veterans noticed a decline in the quality of replacement personnel. It should be noted that a similar reduction in the quality of German replacement drafts was the subject of repeated comment by Wehrmacht officers. But if much of the criticism of the Blue Division by the Germans was largely unwarranted, the same could not be said about its successor. The Spanish Legion rarely performed as well as the Blue Division. The attitude of the Soviet side to the Spaniards varied. There were numerous occasions where Spanish prisoners were ill treated or summarily executed, but probably no more than was the case with German prisoners. The Spaniards also killed many of the men they took prisoner, but many officers and men of the Blue Division and the Spanish Legion rejected the German attitude towards the enemy. There was little of the German tendency to label all Soviet soldiers automatically as 'Bolshevik' or 'Asiatic', though some accounts written by veterans described their foes as 'Mongols, the worst scum of Asia' or 'monstrous and filthy ghosts who throw themselves to the floor like beasts to fight, biting and punching, for a fruit peel or a bare bone.'[3] As was often the case, it was easier to treat the enemy as something other than human if there was limited personal contact and whenever prisoners were held by the Spanish for any length of time, it became much more difficult to sustain such attitudes. New recruits arriving on the Eastern Front were often surprised by the number of Red Army prisoners who were working in a variety of roles for the Blue Division, often with little or no supervision.[4] The Germans repeatedly issued orders that there was to be no excessive fraternisation with prisoners; it seems that many of the Spaniards simply ignored such instructions, though others showed as little hesitation as the Germans to mistreat their captives.

Whatever opinion the Germans may have had of their Spanish allies, the withdrawal of the division reduced the manpower available to Army Group North. Although much of the strength of the army group remained concentrated in the trench lines around Leningrad and the Oranienbaum bridgehead, a further threat lay at the southern end of the front line, where the Red Army had captured Nevel in its latest offensive. The road network in this region was a little better than further north, and if the Red Army was to resume its offensive towards the west there was a danger that it would swiftly penetrate to Latvia, endangering Army Group North's lines of communication. The only practical solution was a withdrawal to the Panther Line, which would shorten the frontage held by Eighteenth and Sixteenth Armies by a quarter and would thus release substantial forces as reserves, either for use in Eighteenth Army's sector in the north or for use as reinforcements for the endangered southern flank of the army group. Küchler had ordered his staff to prepare for *Blau* in the confident expectation that, as Hitler had ordered the construction of the Panther Line as part of the *Ostwall*, permission would be given swiftly for the plan to be implemented. The plan was detailed and thorough, with artillery ammunition carefully stockpiled at each intermediate position so that the withdrawing German forces would be able to repulse any attempt by the Red Army to interfere, and given the success of a similar plan the previous year in the Rzhev salient, all of Army Group North's headquarters staff were confident that they would soon be safely installed in their new positions. Instead, on 22 December, Küchler received a telephone call from Zeitzler, the chief of the general staff. For the moment, Hitler refused to give permission for any such withdrawal. The front line had been relatively quiet and Army Group North had generally been able to beat off Soviet attacks throughout 1943. The current positions were to be held unless they came under serious pressure.

Küchler expected such pressure to come early in 1944. For several weeks, ships of the Soviet Baltic Fleet had been conducting minesweeping operations in the Gulf of Finland, removing hundreds of German mines – known to the Soviet sailors as 'sea urchins'. Later, Luftwaffe reconnaissance flights reported increased Soviet shipping between Leningrad and the Oranienbaum bridgehead, and it was assumed that the Soviet forces in the bridgehead were being strengthened. To date, this had been a quiet sector, but it seemed that this would change soon. Despite this unwelcome development, Hitler's refusal to permit a withdrawal to the Panther Line didn't cause too much alarm at Army Group North's headquarters. After the Red Army's attacks around Nevel petered out towards the end of December, Küchler concluded that for the moment, his forces would be able to hold their positions – provided that he wasn't required to release any major units for deployment elsewhere. He was therefore alarmed when orders arrived almost immediately from *OKH*. After the withdrawal from Kirishi, 1st Infantry Division had been released from the front line and was being held in reserve, allowing the veteran formation to recover its strength and absorb replacement drafts. Its personnel enjoyed Christmas in comfort. *OKH* now ordered that the division was to be released and sent to Army Group South to reinforce the fragmented front line to the west of Kiev, where there was a gap almost 48 miles wide.

This was an unwelcome development for Küchler. The division was one of his best and had repeatedly demonstrated its resilience in battle; moreover, it represented a major part of what few reserves he had been able to release. He promptly telephoned Zeitzler to protest. To his surprise, Zeitzler replied that it was of little importance, as permission to execute *Blau* was imminent. Once Army Group North was safely in its new positions on the Panther line, there would be more than enough troops freed up to permit the transfer of 1st Infantry Division. Feeling somewhat reassured, Küchler travelled to East Prussia for a conference with Hitler the following day, 30 December, attended by all the army group commanders on the Eastern Front. He confidently expected that he would be given permission to commence the withdrawal. When he presented his army group's situation, he reported on the near-completion of all fortifications on the Panther Line and outlined the time that would be required for the execution of *Blau*. When the discussion moved on to the state of the armies of Army Group North, Küchler said – almost as an aside – that Lindemann was happy for his Eighteenth Army to stay in its current positions, even without 1st Infantry Division.

Hitler asked him about these current positions, and Küchler replied that they were thoroughly fortified – indeed, the fortifications were so numerous that Eighteenth Army lacked the manpower to occupy them fully.[5]

To Küchler's surprise and concern, the meeting broke up without any permission being granted for *Blau* to proceed. The following day, after he had returned to his headquarters, he was dismayed when another order arrived from *OKH*: in addition to 1st Infantry Division, he was to release a second division. Once more, Küchler contacted Zeitzler to request an explanation. Zietzler told him that Hitler had decided not to authorise *Blau* for the moment, seizing upon Küchler's account of Lindemann's opinion of the strength of his current positions as an excuse. The two men discussed the issue at length, but unless Hitler could be persuaded to change his mind, there was no prospect of a withdrawal being authorised; such a change of mind was only likely if Lindemann could be induced to alter his previous opinion, and even then it was quite possible that Hitler's deep-seated reluctance to countenance any abandonment of territory would prevail.

For Küchler, the situation was going from bad to worse. Holding his positions with his current strength was perhaps possible. The transfer of a single division would make this task almost unachievable, and the loss of two divisions was inviting disaster. His staff drew up a detailed letter to be sent to Hitler spelling out the necessity for an early authorisation of *Blau*, and the army group commander travelled to Lindemann's headquarters to ask him to add a personal statement that it would be better for Eighteenth Army to withdraw to the Panther Line. To his irritation, Lindemann refused. He told Küchler that all his corps and division commanders were confident that despite the withdrawal of two divisions (in the meantime, the transfer of a third had been ordered and was imminent) the current positions could be held. After all, the troops in the front line had resolutely repulsed almost every Soviet effort in 1943, and Lindemann believed that there was little prospect of any different outcome in the foreseeable future. The frustrated Küchler sent his letter anyway, but can't have been surprised when Zeitzler telephoned him to tell him that Hitler remained adamantly opposed to a withdrawal, repeatedly saying that Küchler had assured him – on the basis of Lindemann's comments – that Eighteenth Army was confident it could hold its positions.

Lindemann's intransigence was probably based upon several factors. It is certainly true that his army had largely triumphed in its battles with the Red Army over the previous year; the only significant setback had been *Iskra*, and even after this battle the narrow corridor along the shore of Lake Ladoga remained very vulnerable to interdiction by German artillery. Soviet casualties had been appalling, and there was a widespread belief in the Wehrmacht that if they could continue to inflict such losses upon the Red Army, it would sooner or later run out of resources. But the successful defence of the front line along the Sinyavino Heights and facing Volkhov Front was achieved by timely rotation of relatively fresh divisions into the battle. The ongoing crisis in Ukraine necessitated the constant transfer of men to the south, and given the limited Soviet success around Nevel in recent weeks, it was questionable whether the rotation policy could be carried out in future, particularly as the divisions that were to be rotated into the battle sector would be starting in a poor state.

There was also a problem with compartmentalised thinking. In 1942, a German officer was shot down while flying over Ukraine and Soviet forces captured a complete set of plans for the coming offensive towards Stalingrad. At the time, Stalin was so convinced that the Germans intended a fresh attack on Moscow that he dismissed this windfall as a deliberate attempt by the Germans to mislead him, and an opportunity to use the intelligence information to maximum effect was lost. But dismayed by this potentially disastrous event, Hitler's reaction was to order that units were not to communicate such information to their neighbours. The result was that at every level – army group, army, corps, and division – commanding officers had few official channels of communication with the units on their flanks. Inevitably, a variety of informal arrangements existed, but it was difficult in these circumstances for any commander to have a clear overall view of the situation. This was completely contrary to the German general staff doctrine of officers being aware of the overall situation and therefore being in a better position to improvise and innovate as required.

Consequently, whilst Lindemann's subordinates might have had a fairly accurate picture of the state of their immediate neighbours, they would have had no means of being able to assess the ability of other units to release forces that could then be rotated through hotspots once battle commenced. Lindemann would have had a clear idea of his own army's capabilities and to a limited extent the capabilities of the neighbouring Sixteenth Army to the south, but he would have had little reliable information on what might be expected by way of reinforcements from elsewhere in a crisis. In the competitive world of Nazi Germany, he perhaps saw the current situation as an opportunity to catch Hitler's eye and to enhance his own reputation.

The staff officers at Army Group North didn't share Lindemann's confidence. In a discussion with Jodl, Generalleutnant Wilhelm Hasse,

Küchler's chief of staff, said glumly that by leaving its forces in positions that could not be sustained, the army group was marching to disaster with open eyes.[6] All that remained was to see if the next Soviet offensive was strong enough to overwhelm the very limited resources available to Army Group North. But Küchler and his army group had spent two years fighting a largely static war, and this was the first occasion that they had attempted – unsuccessfully – to secure permission for a substantial withdrawal. Further south, the experience of senior commanders and their staff officers was very different. Throughout the second half of 1943, Manstein's Army Group South had gone through the cycle of requesting a withdrawal, apparently getting permission for it, discovering that Hitler had changed his mind, and then having to persuade him to concede, on several occasions. In almost every case, final grudging permission to withdraw was only obtained when the benefits of such a withdrawal – the release of much-needed reserves, for example – were greatly reduced. Had they had the opportunity to discuss their experiences, Manstein would have found Küchler's frustration depressingly familiar and might have urged him to continue applying pressure upon Hitler.

For the moment, Army Group North fielded about 500,000 men. Due to the enforced transfer of several divisions to other sectors, all of Küchler's primary divisions were in his front line, with three security divisions and a training division available as reserves; and the security divisions were actively engaged in attempts to suppress the partisans, reducing the available reserves still further. Although Küchler and Lindemann remained as commanders of the army group and Eighteenth Army respectively, there had been a change elsewhere. In October 1943, Field Marshal Gunther von Kluge, commander of Army Group Centre, was injured in a car crash. Busch, who had commanded Sixteenth Army since the invasion of France in 1940, was nominated as his successor. His replacement was General Christian Hansen, the former commander of X Corps.

On paper, some of the units Army Group North received as replacements for the larger number of units sent elsewhere looked impressive. In March 1943, even as some of the first SS divisions, grouped together in a panzer corps, were fighting around Kharkov – initially earning Hitler's wrath by retreating from the city without permission, then recapturing it during Manstein's counteroffensive – Himmler decided on a further expansion of the Waffen-SS. A new corps – *III (germanisches) SS-Panzer-Korps* – was authorised, explicitly with the intention of raising several new divisions from *Volksdeutsch* (ethnic Germans living outside Germany) populations and volunteers from occupied countries. Originally, the intention was to use one existing division – *SS-Wiking* – and one new formation.

The latter was *SS-Panzergrenadier-Division Nordland*, which was created in March using volunteers from Denmark and Norway and *Volksdeutsche* from Romania. Volunteer 'legions' were originally raised in Denmark and Norway in the summer of 1941; the Norwegians saw action on the Eastern Front near Leningrad and were withdrawn back to Germany in March 1943 for expansion into a full panzergrenadier regiment. The Danish legion was originally raised when the Danish king gave permission for volunteers to join a body originally known as *SS-Freikorps Danmark*; most of its personnel were former members of the Danish armed forces. It fought on the Eastern Front as part of the *SS-Totenkopf* division and suffered heavy losses in the battles around Velikiye Luki before being sent to Germany, where it was upgraded to a full panzergrenadier regiment. Despite assurances that had been given to the Danish authorities that it would remain an exclusively Danish formation, drafts of German and *Volksdeutsche* were now added to the unit and a German – Obersturmbannführer Hermenegild Graf von Westphalen zu Fürstenberg – was appointed as its commander. In protest, many of its Danish personnel demanded immediate discharge and return to Denmark. Despite repeated assurances from both German and Danish figures, some of the officers refused to serve in a mixed unit under German command. The last Danish commander of the unit, Obersturmbannführer Knud Børge Martinsen, returned to Denmark at this time and according to some accounts he was one of those who refused to serve under German command.

The rationale for Danish personnel being permitted to join the Waffen-SS was complex. Prior to the war, Denmark had signed up to many of the provisions of the Anti-Comintern Pact. This was an agreement instigated by the Germans and Japanese in 1937 to oppose the growing influence of the *Kommunisticheskiy Internatsional* ('Communist International', usually abbreviated to 'Comintern'), a Soviet body that was actively promoting Communist values. Italy rapidly joined the new pact, followed by Hungary and Spain in 1939 and what remained of Czechoslovakia following the German annexation of Sudetenland. After its occupation in 1940, Denmark signed an agreement with Germany that included strict limits on Danish cooperation, but these clauses were moved to a secret addendum to the agreement and to all external appearances Denmark became a full member of the Anti-Comintern Pact. The clauses that remained secret included clear statements that Denmark had no military obligations to Germany and would remain neutral, but voluntary recruitment was permitted.[7]

The former commander of the Danish Legion, Martinsen, may not have been willing to serve under German command, but he remained committed to much of the ideology of Nazi Germany and the SS. He created the *Germansk Korpset* ('Germanic Corps') which was then renamed the *SS-Schalburgkorps*, a paramilitary group that persecuted and murdered members of the Danish opposition. Towards the end of the war Martinsen fell out of favour with the Germans and was arrested in October 1944 and taken to Berlin; he succeeded in escaping and returned to Denmark, where he was arrested again, this time by Danish authorities, as the war came to an end. He was charged with two counts of murder, including the killing of a fellow *Schalburgkorps* member who Martinsen believed was having an affair with his wife; he was executed by firing squad in 1949.

Martinsen was not the only former Danish SS figure to face arrest. Many of the Danes who volunteered for service faced a difficult time both during and after the war – there was widespread civilian hostility towards the Germans and the Danish volunteers faced much opposition from their fellow Danes, ranging from cold contempt to scuffles outside recruitment centres. After the war, there was pressure from many bodies within Denmark for prosecution of the volunteers and proceedings duly commenced. The defence argued that the Danish government – albeit operating under German occupation – had expressed its consent in writing to Danes serving in the SS but although some were acquitted at the first hearing, most were convicted. The sentences were modest and most were freed within two years.[8]

The commander of the new panzer corps was Obergruppenführer Felix Steiner. After serving in the *Freikorps* after the First World War, he left the peacetime army of Germany in 1933 with the rank of major and immediately joined the Nazi Party. Within two years, he commanded a battalion of SS *Verfügungstruppen*, the precursors of the Waffen-SS, and took part in the invasion of Poland as commander of the regiment *SS-Deutschland*. Shortly after the fall of France, having caught Himmler's eye through his aggressive leadership, he oversaw the creation of the division *SS-Wiking*. Unlike many senior figures in the Waffen-SS, Steiner was a highly capable officer of great personal courage; his experiences close to the front line with his troops led him to modify training constantly to take account of the evolving nature of the battlefield, and he placed great emphasis on physical fitness amongst his officers and men at a time when such attributes were not given the same value as they would be today. He was therefore an ideal candidate not only to command the new corps, but also to oversee its creation and training.

Plans for III SS-Panzer Corps changed swiftly and *SS-Wiking* was assigned to a different formation. Instead, the *SS-Freiwilligen-Legion Nederland* formed part of the new corps. In October 1943 this 'legion' was reorganised and expanded slightly to form SS-*Panzergrenadier-Brigade Nederland*. Despite its name, it was recruited from a variety of populations; when it reached the Eastern Front as part of III SS-Panzer Corps, it had 5,400 men, of whom only 2,200 were Dutch. The rest were a mixture of Germans and *Volksdeutsche*. The first combat assignment of the new corps saw it deployed to Croatia in August 1943. The following month, when Italy left the Axis, its personnel moved swiftly to disarm the Italian *Lombardi* Division. In the process, it acquired a number of Italian tanks, which were swiftly incorporated into the panzer regiment of *SS-Nordland* – although these vehicles were obsolete, the recently formed panzer regiment had not yet received any armoured vehicles and at least these captured tanks permitted training to progress. Over the next few weeks, a number of Pz.IV tanks and assault guns arrived to bring the regiment up towards strength, and the mixture of German and Italian vehicles were promptly put to use in support of the infantry of III SS-Panzer Corps in operations against partisans. A number of major raids were carried out and fighting continued into the early winter.[9] In early December, all the units of the corps began to move to Army Group North as part of the overall reorganisation that Jodl had suggested earlier in the year. Almost immediately after it arrived near Leningrad, Steiner redesignated the unit *SS-Panzergrenadier-Division Nederland* in an attempt to mislead the Red Army. On paper at least, the SS units looked formidable, particularly as they included the new panzer regiment and at least some of the panzergrenadier formations were mounted in half-tracks. Other units in Army Group North were far less impressive. The front line facing the Oranienbaum bridgehead contained two Luftwaffe field divisions, whose ability to resist a major offensive was generally regarded as very poor.

During earlier Soviet offensives, a major factor in favour of the Germans was their extensive system of fortified defences, and this would now have to compensate for weaknesses in overall manpower and the combat ability of inexperienced units. The strongest defensive lines were, as before, to the south and east of Leningrad, where there had been heavy fighting in 1942 and 1943. Here, there were multiple belts of bunkers and trenches with anti-tank obstacles, forests and swamps greatly reducing the options for the Red Army to use armoured formations. The lines facing the junction of Leningrad and Volkhov Fronts were particularly strongly fortified. The main position stretched to a depth of over three miles in places, and was further backed by a secondary defensive zone a few miles further to the rear. Every village and town was extensively fortified and minefields were laid densely everywhere. A further advantage lay in the comparatively mild winter. Whilst the first winter of 1941–42 had been bitterly cold, the following two years saw milder weather and as Küchler and his subordinates awaited a new offensive at the end of 1943, there were frequent spells of thawing temperatures, softening the ground and greatly weakening the ice on lakes and rivers. It was only around the Oranienbaum perimeter that the German defences were relatively weak, with just a single relatively shallow defensive belt. There had been almost no heavy fighting here since late 1941, and the Germans had used this part of the line as a 'quiet sector' for inexperienced units to gain some front-line experience, or for badly degraded units to recover their strength.

Almost as soon as he arrived in the Oranienbaum area, Steiner noted the build-up of Red Army units opposite his formations. He ordered the engineers of III SS-Panzer Corps to begin work on strengthening and deepening the German defensive lines. At the same time, a number of raids were mounted on the Soviet positions to capture prisoners for interrogation. Most of these miscarried; on at least one occasion, the entire raiding party was ambushed and captured.[10]

Steiner's III SS-Panzer Corps wasn't the only foreign unit in SS uniform serving with Army Group North. As the Wehrmacht moved into Latvia and the Red Army left in 1941, many Latvians took up arms against the Soviet authorities. Many of the groups that formed in the first days of the invasion were then reorganised into paramilitary police battalions; although their role was primarily declared to be for the maintenance of law and order, and for the protection of important facilities such as railways and ports, some of these battalions were used in implementing the massacres of Jews and others in the weeks that followed. From October 1941 small contingents of Latvians – usually platoon or company strength – joined German units in the front line in the northern sector and in July 1942 a full battalion of Latvians fought alongside the Germans to defeat a Red Army attack on Krasnoye Selo.

In November 1942, Alfreds Valdmanis, the Latvian Director General of Justice, produced a memorandum outlining the creation of a sovereign Latvian state (though of course under German protection), and followed this with a further suggestion that Latvia would in return raise a substantial army that could be deployed in defence of the boundaries of Latvia against the Red Army – this implicitly accepted that such a deployment might be within the territory of Russia in order to prevent the Soviet forces from reaching Latvia. The granting of such sovereignty was contrary to German occupation policies for the Baltic region and Obergruppenführer Gottlob Berger, the head of the *SS-Hauptamt* ('SS Main Headquarters') suggested to Himmler that the Latvians should first be required to prove themselves as being willing to fight against Bolshevism.

By now, two Latvian police battalions were serving in the front line near Leningrad and after visiting these units, Himmler ordered the creation of a full Latvian Legion. But whilst senior Nazi figures like Rosenberg and to an extent Himmler may have been inclined to reward the Latvians with some limited measures of autonomy, Hitler flatly refused to consider such changes.

The order to create a Latvian Legion without any accompanying political changes caused considerable resentment in Latvia. Reluctantly, the officials of the puppet Self Administration agreed to permit the creation of the legion. By now, it was anticipated that the legion would be at least the size of a division and there was considerable friction over whether the commander would be Latvian or German, but in March 1943 the Germans announced that the Latvian General Rūdolfs Bangerskis would be in command. Almost immediately, the Germans began to ignore many of the terms of their agreement with the Latvians; for example, at the end of March 1943 about 1,000 recruits were dispatched to the Eastern Front as reinforcements for Latvian units already in the front line without having completed proper training and without Latvian NCOs and officers. It was then announced that the appointment of Bangerskis as commander had been announced in error, and that German law required the division to be led by a German officer. In a token gesture to try to placate the Latvians, Bangerskis was retained as 'Inspector General of the Latvian Legion', and a new post of *Infanteriefürher* ('infantry commander'), effectively the division second-in-command, was created. This post would be held by a Latvian; the new commander of the division was Brigadefürher Peter Hansen, who was replaced within a few weeks by Gruppenführer Carl Graf von Pückler-Burghauss.[11]

Three Latvian battalions were gathered near Krasnoye Selo to create the core of the Latvian Legion and saw action in the fighting of March 1943. This legion was converted into a regiment shortly after and a second regiment was formed in the early summer. Combined as a brigade, these units were deployed on the Volkhov River near Myasnoi Bor, the scene of bitter fighting a year earlier when the Soviet Second Shock Army forced its way into the German rear zone before being cut off and destroyed. As they took up positions in the mosquito-infested swamps, the Latvians found – like the Germans and Spaniards who had preceded them – that they had to construct positions above ground level using logs. Any attempt to dig trenches or bunkers resulted in almost instant flooding, but the Latvians set about improving their positions with energy. Logs had to be laid to create roads and a railway with an improvised locomotive made from a truck – nicknamed 'Oskar' by the soldiers – was built to permit the speedy movement of supplies. Despite their industry and efforts, conditions remained grim and the area became known to the Latvian soldiers as *Pasaules gals* ('End of the World'). In October 1943, the legion was renamed 15th *Lettischen SS-Freiwilligen* Division ('15th Latvian SS Volunteer Division'). By the end of the year it was part of Sixteenth Army's XLIII Corps to the north of Nevel.

In October 1943, a new Latvian 'volunteer brigade' was created under the command of Oberführer Hinrich Schuldt. This too was steadily enlarged and on 7 January 1944 was renamed 19th *Lettischen SS-Freiwilligen* Division. When 15th *Lettischen SS-Freiwilligen* Division moved south to the Nevel sector, this new division replaced it in the trench lines north of Novgorod as part of XXXVIII Corps. Both Latvian divisions would play major roles in the winter fighting.

German intelligence about Red Army strength, capabilities, and intentions was provided by *Fremde Heere Ost* ('Foreign Armies East' or *FHO*), a department of *OKH*. From April 1942, its head was Oberst Reinhard Gehlen. Like his predecessor Eberhard Kinzel, he had no formal training in intelligence matters, but he at least attempted to collect and analyse information from a variety of sources – signals intelligence, prisoner interrogations, aerial reconnaissance, and to a very limited extent from German spies, many of whom it later transpired were either double-agents or working primarily for the Soviet Union – in a more organised manner than his predecessor. Nonetheless, the quality of information at his disposal was poor and as the war progressed his reports became increasingly ambiguous and Delphic, covering almost all eventualities and often based upon little more than educated guesswork. In late 1943, *FHO* correctly identified the increased strength of the Soviet Fronts in the northern sector and concluded that attempts would be made to break up Army Group North, with convergent attacks from the north (Leningrad), northwest (Oranienbaum), east (the Volkhov River), and the southeast (from near Lake Ilmen). These would be aimed at separating Eighteenth Army from Sixteenth Army and then encircling and destroying Eighteenth Army. Few of the reports produced by *FHO* had been particularly accurate in the past and Küchler chose to interpret this newest prediction with a degree of caution, adding it to what he and his staff already knew about the opposing forces. The conclusions of those in Army Group North's headquarters were that although there had clearly been a substantial transfer of Soviet forces to the Oranienbaum bridgehead, most of the apparent increase in Leningrad Front's strength was from local recruitment within Leningrad. They were aware of the huge losses suffered by the Red Army and in view of ongoing Soviet offensive operations further south, they persuaded themselves that neither Leningrad nor Volkhov Front would be able to mount and sustain a particularly strong offensive operation.

It seems that confidence in this prediction was stronger in some quarters than others. Lindemann in particular remained bullish about the ability of Eighteenth Army to repel all attacks, but Küchler remained concerned, particularly after the transfer of some of his divisions to the south, and constantly returned to the question of a possible withdrawal to the Panther Line positions to the east. Denied formal permission by Hitler, the best he could do was authorise the movement of some rear area formations to Estonia and the continued preparations for *Blau*. But Lindemann's optimism appears to have mollified many of Küchler's doubts. Additionally, the intelligence officers at his headquarters assessed that the Red Army units in the Oranienbaum bridgehead and on the Volkhov River lacked adequate reserves for a sustained assault. For the moment, he believed that his army group would be able to hold firm. The tendency of people towards confirmation bias – to give greater value to information that confirms pre-existing points of view and to downplay contradictory information – probably played a large part in Lindemann's thinking, and this in turn led Küchler to believe that despite his misgivings, it might be possible to weather the coming storm.

One of the German units that would face whatever new offensive was thrown at Army Group North was *Grenadier-Bataillon zur besonderen Verwendung 540* ('540th Special Deployment Grenadier Battalion'), one of the 'penal battalions' established to give soldiers guilty of various offences an opportunity to redeem themselves. In February 1943, these offences included: unauthorised absence from the front line (20 men); cowardice in the face of the enemy (four men); destruction of military equipment (eight men); attacking a superior (13 men); refusal to obey orders (five men); guard offences (usually falling asleep while on guard – eight men); abuse of rank (three men); theft (54 men); homosexuality (five men); other 'morality offences' (six men); drunkenness (one man); and other offences (ten men). Personnel came from the navy and Luftwaffe as well as the army. One of its officers later wrote about the battalion's move to the Sinyavino sector along a raised road through the marshes:

> I was sitting in the driver's cab of the leading truck so I could see ahead. Thank God, the soldiers couldn't see much. Anyone who ever drove along the embankment to the front there would never forget it: on either side of the embankment lay military cemetery after military cemetery, row after row of wooden crosses! Nothing was left to the imagination.[12]

As 1943 drew towards a close, the Wehrmacht was badly overstretched. It was clear that an invasion of mainland Europe by the Western Allies would take place in the coming months. With few good options left, Hitler further clarified what he saw as the only path to final victory for Germany to follow when he issued his *Führerbefehl 51* in November:

> For the last two and a half years, the bitter and costly struggle against Bolshevism has made the utmost demands upon the bulk of our military resources and energies. This commitment was in keeping with the seriousness of the danger and the overall situation. The situation has since changed. The threat from the east remains, but an even greater danger looms in the west: the Anglo-American invasion. In the east, the vastness of the space will, as a last resort, permit a loss of territory even on a major scale, without suffering a mortal blow to Germany's chance for survival.
>
> Not so in the west! If the enemy succeeds here in penetrating our defences on a wide front, consequences of staggering proportions will follow within a short time. All signs point to an offensive against the western front of Europe no later than spring, perhaps earlier.
>
> For that reason, I can no longer justify the further weakening of the west in favour of other theatres of war. I have therefore decided to strengthen the defences in the west.[13]

Given the increasing superiority of the forces that threatened Germany, it was only in the west that an opportunity might exist for a victory of strategic proportions: if an attempted invasion could be crushed before it succeeded in breaking out of the landing areas, and if the Battle of the Atlantic could be resumed with success using the new U-boats that were being prepared, it would then be possible for Germany's forces to turn east in strength to defeat the Soviet Union. Until then, obdurate defence in the east combined with – as a last resort, in the words of the *Führerbefehl* – conceding territory would have to suffice. But as the officers on the Eastern Front repeatedly discovered, Hitler's willingness to consider this 'last resort' involved lengthy negotiations and repeated refusals before the Führer gave permission, and inevitably these delays eroded any benefit that might have accrued from a timely withdrawal. Hitler then used this as justification for refusing further requests, telling his close associates that too many generals simply wanted to retreat but never delivered the promised benefits. At no stage did he ever acknowledge that his delay in granting permission was the main cause for those expected benefits evaporating.

Preparations for the next attempt by the Red Army to drive the Wehrmacht away from Leningrad had actually commenced before the winter of 1943–44.

Stavka could look back over the events along the Eastern Front since the previous winter with a degree of satisfaction. The siege ring around Leningrad had been broken by *Iskra*, albeit only in a very limited fashion; the attempt by the Wehrmacht to seize the strategic initiative at Kursk had been defeated; operations in the central sector, whilst very costly, had driven the Germans back a considerable distance and created favourable conditions for further attacks; and most of central Ukraine was back in Soviet hands. Despite its heavy casualties, the Red Army outnumbered the Germans significantly and by imposing its initiative at every level, it could exploit this numerical advantage still further by concentrating its resources at key positions. It was in this context that each sector prepared plans for offensives to inflict even greater damage upon the Germans.

Govorov submitted his first opinion on future operations on 9 September 1943, even before the last assault of the year on the Sinyavino Heights. His proposals were that after reinforcements and replenishment, Leningrad Front would attack from south of Leningrad and from the Oranienbaum bridgehead to link up the two forces and capture Krasnoye Selo. Thereafter, there would be a further advance towards Krasnogvardeisk and Kingisepp. A few days later, on the eve of the September attack on the Sinyavino Heights, Meretskov added his thoughts. In addition to Govorov's attacks, he proposed an attack by his Front towards Luga, aiming to prevent the general withdrawal of Army Group North towards the west.[14] From a number of sources, the Red Army was fully aware of the German construction of the Panther Line and wished to try to intercept the Germans before they could retreat to the new positions.

These proposals had a mixed reception. On the one hand, the information regarding the Panther Line suggested that it would be a formidable obstacle and after the successful German withdrawal from the Rzhev salient in early 1943, *Stavka* was anxious to prevent a repetition in the north. It was essential to apply sufficient pressure to hinder any German withdrawal, and ideally to use it as an opportunity to inflict a major setback on the Wehrmacht. But on the other hand, neither Leningrad nor Volkhov Fronts had demonstrated the technical ability to carry out such a wide-ranging and ambitious series of offensive operations; in any case, they would require substantial reinforcements before any such attempt could be made. At the end of September, orders were sent to both Fronts to intensify reconnaissance efforts and to create a mixture of shock groups and pursuit groups so that if the Germans began a withdrawal, the Red Army would be in a better position to deal with it than had been the case around Rzhev.

On 6 October, Meretskov and Govorov received general instructions from *Stavka* to prepare a new operation for the winter, intended to commence early in 1944. Operations were continuing in Ukraine on the west bank of the Dnepr where a limited German counteroffensive had stabilised the front line to the west of Kiev, and Stalin and his inner circle became increasingly confident that the constant transfer of German troops to the south would leave other sectors too weak to resist a prolonged attack. Consequently, despite their previous misgivings about the capabilities of Leningrad and Volkhov Fronts, they were now prepared to consider a major operation. In mid-October, Govorov's proposal was adopted as the basis for the coming assault. In keeping with this and the previous orders, Govorov developed two plans in parallel. *Neva 1* was to be implemented in the event of the Germans commencing a withdrawal towards the Panther Line; if the Wehrmacht showed no signs of such a withdrawal, *Neva 2*, the major operation that Govorov had outlined in September, would be put into action.

In November, Govorov began to transfer Second Shock Army into the Oranienbaum bridgehead with the intention of including this sector in the coming offensive. This was expected to reduce the ability of the Germans to reshuffle their forces once fighting commenced and recognised that, despite Steiner's preparations, the German defences around the bridgehead were less well developed than elsewhere. To the south of Leningrad were two further armies earmarked for the offensive. Forty-Second Army under Lieutenant General Ivan Ivanovich Maslennikov occupied the lines to the southwest of the city, with Sviridov's Sixty-Seventh Army to the east; this was the former Fifty-Fifth Army, now combined with the earlier incarnation of Sixty-Seventh Army. These were the three armies with which Govorov planned his contribution to what was hoped would be the decisive and definitive attack to drive the enemy away from the gates of Leningrad.

To the east, Meretskov's Volkhov Front had three armies north of Lake Ilmen. From north to south, these were Starikov's Eighth Army and Lieutenant General Sergei Vasilyevich Roginsky's Fifty-Fourth Army, both on the west bank of the lower Volkhov as far as the junction with Leningrad Front; and further south, along the Volkhov River, Lieutenant General Ivan Terentyevich Korovnikov's Fifty-Ninth Army. Further south, there had been a reorganisation of the Red Army in October in the wake of the Nevel Operation. The old Kalinin Front was now known as 1st Baltic Front, still commanded by Eremenko. The former Bryansk Front headquarters was transferred north, taking command of forces between Eremenko's 1st Baltic Front and Meretskov's southern wing; originally, Bryansk Front was renamed Baltic Front, but with the renaming of Eremenko's Front, it was now given the title of 2nd Baltic Front. Its commander was the rather colourful General Markian Mikhailovich Popov, who had been chief of staff of Leningrad Front in the first autumn of the war with Germany. He was younger than many of his contemporaries, with no history of service in the First World War; as a teenager, he lied about his age in order to join the Red Army and rose steadily in rank in the years after the Russian Civil War. He was generally viewed by his contemporaries in a positive light; Pavel Alekseyevich Rotmistrov, who commanded Fifth Guards Tank Army for much of the Second World War, remembered him with approval from the pre-war years: 'Back in the 1920s, we had the opportunity to command companies in the same division. I knew him as an excellent tactical commander, a proficient sportsman, witty and unfailingly cheerful.'[15]

During the war with Germany, Popov held a number of different commands. During the Soviet offensives that followed the encirclement of Stalingrad, he led an eponymous mobile group into Donbas and was amongst the first to feel the force of Manstein's counteroffensive, resulting in the almost complete destruction of his group. Despite this severe setback he remained in favour and was given command of first Reserve Front, then Bryansk Front. But despite the positive description of Popov by Rotmistrov, he was a man who had other problems. He was a heavy drinker, not unusual per se in the Soviet Union, but drunkenness on duty would eventually lead to his demotion in April 1944.

After being wounded in early 1943, Fedyuninsky spent a few weeks in hospital before returning to Volkhov Front and was then sent to the central sector of the Eastern Front where he became deputy commander of Bryansk Front under Popov's predecessor, Colonel General Maks Andreyevich Reiter. In this role, he was involved in the offensives mounted towards Oryol and Gomel after the end of the Battle of Kursk. In the late autumn of 1943 he was summoned back to Moscow: he was being sent back to the north, where he would take command of Second Shock Army in the Oranienbaum bridgehead. There was a moment of unpleasantness when he reached his new command: Romanovsky, who had commanded Second Shock Army since December 1942, had not been told that he was being replaced and was displeased to learn this from Fedyuninsky rather than via the chain of command. Despite this inauspicious start, Fedyuninsky rapidly started work on developing plans for coming operations.[16]

As had been the case prior to *Iskra*, Fedyuninsky organised training areas behind the front line where replicas of German positions were built, so that units could rehearse how to overrun them. Given the heavy losses suffered throughout 1943, the value of these earlier exercises is questionable, but nonetheless it was an improvement on simply ordering men to move forward without any preparation at all. In order to get new recruits accustomed to battlefield conditions and to

overcome 'tank fear', Fedyuninsky asked for a volunteer to sit in a trench while a
T-34 drove over the top; when the soldier emerged unscathed, doubtless with a
degree of relief, Fedyuninsky presented him with his own wristwatch as a reward.
In addition to the artillery of his army, Fedyuninsky would be supported by
several long-range naval guns that had been dismounted from warships and
installed in the forts of Krasnaya Gorka and Seraya Loshad, but possession of
artillery was only half of the issue: the other half was having meaningful
information on targets. It was clear that the Germans were strengthening their
defences, and in order to discover the details of new positions, several raids were
organised to capture 'tongues'.[17]

Simoniak's XXX Guards Rifle Corps would once more be in the front rank of
the assault, as part of Forty-Second Army. At this stage of the war Simoniak's
divisions had a mixture of battle-hardened veterans and new drafts, and during
preparations for the battle there was particular attention to training the new
recruits in the importance of following the artillery barrage as closely as possible.
After his success in the last attack on the Sinyavino Heights, Odintsov once more
made careful preparations for the offensive. In the paths of the two armies that
would be carrying out the assault, his reconnaissance and intelligence officers
identified a large number of German positions: over a hundred artillery and
mortar batteries; 19 forward observation posts; 185 bunkers and pillboxes, many
reinforced with concrete; and hundreds of other dugouts and entrenchments. In
order to suppress as many of these as possible, Odintsov and Govorov concentrated
a huge number of guns from the armies of Leningrad Front, additional units
directly controlled by Front headquarters, and the firepower of the Baltic Fleet.
Odintsov estimated that the combined firepower would deliver 44 tons in a
single salvo, giving the bombardment twice as much weight as had been used by
Leningrad Front during *Iskra*.[18] But as the Red Army had discovered repeatedly
to its great cost, having huge numbers of guns was not the complete answer: the
success or failure of the infantry assault would depend on the accuracy and
comprehensive nature of the bombardment.

The forces available to the Red Army for the new offensive were impressive,
at least numerically. The total strength of Govorov's Leningrad Front amounted
to a little over 417,000 men, with a further 89,000 serving in the Baltic Fleet.
Another 260,000 men waited in the east under Volkhov Front. Further south,
2nd Baltic Front's First Shock Army, which was expected to take part in the
assault, added another 55,000, and an estimated 35,000 partisans were operating
in the German rear areas.[19] The total was therefore in the region of 858,000. By
concentrating forces at the chosen points for the offensive, the Red Army could

accentuate its numerical advantage considerably. Fedyuninsky calculated that by regrouping his forces for the attack, he could expect an advantage of 3:1 in terms of infantry and 4:1 in terms of tanks. But similar concentrations had been achieved before without any major benefit. The traditional heavy use of massed artillery required the stockpiling of large volumes of ammunition, and most of the artillery assets of Leningrad Front were either concentrated under Fedyuninsky's control in the Oranienbaum bridgehead or assigned to Forty-Second Army, the two forces that would converge to end the isolation of the Oranienbaum troops. The commander of this unit, Maslennikov, had enjoyed mixed fortunes in the war to date. He commanded Thirty-Ninth Army during the battles outside Moscow at the end of 1941, advancing deep into the flank of the German Army Group Centre to the west of Rzhev. His army ended up in a large salient bulging into the German positions, in an area of forest and marshes with few good roads, and in the summer of 1942 the Germans moved against this salient. Almost all of Thirty-Ninth Army was destroyed and the men who escaped the resultant encirclement were forced to abandon their heavy equipment. Despite this, Maslennikov – a former NKVD officer with longstanding connections to senior figures in the Soviet Union's security apparatus – remained in favour. He held a number of posts before being appointed commander of Forty-Second Army in December 1943, and he now found himself preparing for the new offensive.

Leningrad Front's offensive was expected to create an early encirclement, with the assault groups of Second Shock Army and Forty-Second Army meeting near Krasnoye Selo. Thereafter, Fedyuninsky was to thrust towards the southwest in order to reach Kingisepp and the line of the lower Luga River, while Maslennikov attacked south towards Luga. As usual, the instructions from *Stavka* to Front headquarters and from the latter to individual armies stressed the need for keeping up momentum so that the Germans had no opportunity to regain their balance. Additional engineer assets were made available to try to ensure that supplies and reinforcements were brought forward in a timely manner once the advance began, but there was widespread recognition that the campaign would be difficult and costly. There was confidence that there would be success, but how great would this success be?

After the terrible bloodshed of the battles to break into the Sinyavino salient from the east, Meretskov opted for a different approach for the coming offensive with his main effort being made further to the south. Here, at the southern end of Volkhov Front, Fifty-Ninth Army was to encircle and capture the city of Novgorod, immediately to the north of Lake Ilmen. It would then advance west, with forces from 2nd Baltic Front clearing the southern shore of Lake Ilmen. This latter attack was also expected to tie down elements of the German Sixteenth Army, to prevent the rotation of divisions that had been such a major part of the Germans' successful defence in the battles of 1943. The northern pincer of the attack on Novgorod would be undertaken by the bulk of Fifty-Ninth Army, and the southern pincer consisted of a specially constituted Southern Operational Group. It was led by the deputy commander of Fifty-Ninth Army, Major General Teodor-Verner Andreyevich Sviklin; he had formerly been chief of staff of Second Shock Army during the failed attacks on Sinyavino in September 1942 and as commander of 311th Rifle Division he was badly wounded in February 1943 and was unable to return to duty until December. His special group would have to cross the ice of Lake Ilmen to complete the southern pincer of the encirclement operation, and was assigned special units to help it with this. In addition to an independent rifle brigade and a rifle regiment, Sviklin had a ski battalion and two aerosled battalions. The aerosleds consisted of lightly armoured sleds with a large fan at the rear; some were armed with machine-guns, while others carried anti-tank rifles or light anti-tank guns. Their use in the previous two winters was rarely successful, especially when the Germans realised that their armour was easily penetrated even by light anti-tank guns, and their mobility over snowy terrain was limited by even modest slopes. However, on the frozen surface of Lake Ilmen, they offered the potential to move support weapons forward far faster than would otherwise be the case.

After capturing Novgorod, Fifty-Ninth Army was to move against the city of Luga to the west. As it would carry the main burden of Volkhov Front's contribution to the coming offensive, it was assigned the great bulk of Meretskov's artillery and air assets. To aid the initial advance, engineers were assigned to the assault formations to secure crossings over the frozen Volkhov and to assist in destroying German obstacles to the west of the river. The encirclement and capture of Novgorod was anticipated to take no more than five days. Further north, Fifty-Fourth and Eighth Armies would also attack, aiming to capture Chudovo and Tosno respectively. If all operations proceeded according to plan, Leningrad, Volkhov, and 2nd Baltic Fronts were then to continue their attacks towards the west with the intention of reaching and ideally penetrating the Panther Line before German troops could retreat and occupy the positions.

Like Fedyuninsky, Meretskov tried to improve on the preparations for earlier offensives. He held a Front-level paper exercise in November 1943 in which the staff officers of his armies rehearsed command and control and attempted to improve the standard of communications at every level, so that attacking units could better coordinate their activities and would be able to send clearer information to artillery and logistic units further to the rear. This was followed by lower level 'tactical review exercises' in December, particularly for the formations of Fifty-Ninth Army. There were live firing exercises with artillery, tanks and infantry working together in an attempt to acclimatise new recruits to the noise and confusion of battle and to try to improve cooperation between these elements. Officers from company commanders to senior Front officers were ordered to make personal reconnaissance of the front line and to familiarise themselves with the terrain and their objectives.[20]

Morozov was one of the artillery officers who took part in these exercises, which were also used as opportunities for further training and education:

The gathering of artillery officers took place in a village near the front line that had been abandoned by its inhabitants. All around was deciduous forest, peppered with snow. Everything was conducive to quiet study. The main points of our programme were the generalisation of the experiences of organising and planning an artillery offensive, the development of common views, and the elimination of different practices ... Particular attention was paid to the suppression of enemy personnel and weapons in trenches, since the Nazis didn't use a focal defensive system and had trenches everywhere ...

There were ten hours of classes every day and four hours of private study ... The exchange of combat experiences and the development of common procedures brought significant benefits in the preparation of the new offensive operation.

At the same time, the Front artillery headquarters' reconnaissance department also conducted training. Intelligence officers from the artillery headquarters of armies, divisions and other units took part.[21]

Although Soviet aerial units still lacked specialist photo-reconnaissance aircraft, their ability to carry out such tasks was improving steadily. Meretskov overruled the reluctance of air force commanders to commit so many planes to such a task and huge numbers of images were taken, allowing for detailed maps to be drawn up for gunners and front line commanders alike. By taking repeated photographs of the same locations and comparing the images, intelligence officers tried to identify German movements and alternative positions; there were also attempts to take photographs at different times of the day, in the hope that shadows might reveal further German fortifications.

By early 1944, there were estimated to be 35,000 partisans active in the sector of Army Group North.[22] Orders were sent to them as early as November 1943 to increase their activity. This was initially to involve the instigation of popular uprisings and unrest in towns across the area and to interfere with the forced deportation of civilians; once the offensive began, the partisans were to strike against German occupation units and escalate attacks on lines of communication. Attacks on railways were regarded as particularly important, as the Germans would be heavily dependent upon rail traffic to evacuate their heavy artillery from the Leningrad siege perimeter.[23] Attacks on railway lines and on trains were now an established part of partisan operations, and had the additional benefit of forcing the Germans to deploy precious troops in defensive roles purely to deter such attacks.

The overall scale of the operation was ambitious and much greater than what had been attempted in the previous year around Sinyavino, but the intervening months had seen major changes. German losses elsewhere reduced the forces available to the Wehrmacht in the north – in the front line, as local and regional reserves, and as reinforcements that might be sent to the area from other sectors. There was no longer the option of abandoning salients like the one around Demyansk or Kirishi to free up troops – all such measures had been taken already. If the German lines could be penetrated, the complete lifting of the siege might finally be achieved.

The city that had been the objective of Army Group North endured a mixed winter. The weather was far less severe than the bitterly cold conditions of 1941–42 when so many people perished from a mixture of starvation and exposure, and was even milder than the winter of 1942–43. There were sufficient stockpiles of food and fuel in Leningrad for most life in the city to continue almost unaltered from the summer months – there was no necessity to concentrate activity on only the most essential tasks. In mid-November, for example, ice-skating lessons were conducted by a former champion skater. Such activity was widely publicised by the city authorities to give a strong message to the citizens of Leningrad and to the outside world: despite the efforts of the Germans to destroy the city, it continued to function. In time, the memories of such moments would feed into the mythology of the siege and the sense amongst Leningraders that they had survived unique hardships through their own resilience and determination. A few days later, a formal decision was made to cease the evacuation of industrial equipment from Leningrad as the city was now deemed to be sufficiently safe. In practice, this had little impact as all the industrial assets that could sensibly be evacuated had already been removed, but the announcement was a further demonstration of 'normality'.

Although the breaking of the siege ring during *Iskra* was hailed as a great success, the vulnerability of the railway line to German interdiction meant that for the moment, Leningrad continued to rely on food and supplies brought over Lake Ladoga. Shipping continued until 22 November when sufficient ice had accumulated to prevent barges from being towed to the port facilities on the western side of the lake. There would now be a hiatus until the ice was firm enough for roads to be established across it, but everyone in Leningrad could sense the preparations being made for a new offensive and the population hoped that soon – very soon – the rail link along the southern shore of Lake Ladoga would be safe from artillery fire, and that other routes would be opened up. The steady thickening of the ice on Lake Ladoga and elsewhere was not without its problems: it disrupted shipping from Leningrad to the Oranienbaum bridgehead, delaying the build-up of Fedyuninsky's Second Shock Army and the stockpiling of ammunition and other supplies for the coming offensive. While the city awaited what everyone hoped would be the definitive lifting of the siege, the siege conditions continued with shelling of either the artillery positions of Leningrad Front or the city itself on most days.

As the day of the offensive approached, Fedyuninsky became increasingly concerned that the Germans would detect the planned axis of advance of Second Shock Army and would take appropriate steps to smash his shock group. In an attempt to mislead the Germans, he took elaborate steps to create the impression that his forces would make their main effort to the west, aiming to push towards the Narva River and thus cutting the lines of communication between Estonia and the German forces around Leningrad:

> For three days in early January, infantry, artillery, and tanks appeared to concentrate on our right flank. Wooden models were widely used for this, as well as powerful loudspeaker installations [to give the impression of heavy vehicle movements at night] …
>
> Artillery and tank units' radio stations were positioned on the right flank. Reconnaissance in force was carried out along the entire front, with the most active operations again being on the right. Aviation repeatedly conducted heavy reconnaissance on that axis, bombed enemy strongpoints every night, and simulated fighter cover for the concentration of our forces.[24]

It wasn't his only concern. Despite the best efforts of the Baltic Fleet, some elements of Second Shock Army were still in Leningrad, their transfer to the Oranienbaum bridgehead delayed by the unpredictable ice conditions that warships, tugboats, and barges had to navigate. Almost all of the army's combat elements were in place, but several logistic and support units would arrive over the next few days. Their timely arrival was vital. As the Red Army had repeatedly learned, offensive operations consumed huge amounts of ammunition and other supplies. Sustaining an offensive would require all support elements to be functioning as effectively as possible.

On 12 and 13 January, Red Army sappers all along the front line began the careful work of lifting mines and digging forward trenches. Explosive charges were laid amongst the barbed wire entanglements and minefields, and were to be triggered when the artillery preparation began. To date, with the exception of the partial success of *Iskra*, German defensive measures had proved to be superior to the Red Army's attack plans and abilities. Which side would prevail in this latest offensive?

CHAPTER 10

YANVARSKIIY GROM

Heavily fortified defensive positions have existed almost as long as there has been armed conflict. They have repeatedly been shown to be a mixed blessing. On the one hand, their intention is to provide protection for defending forces so that they can inflict disproportionate losses on their enemies and can hold a key location, often despite being heavily outnumbered, and in this role fortifications are often highly effective. But this defensive advantage comes at a considerable cost.

Firstly, there is the cost in terms of both resources and effort in constructing defensive positions. On some occasions, defences constructed at huge cost are never put to the test – a good example is the Maginot Line built by the French in the 1930s to defend against an attack by the Germans. There is also an issue of wasted resources if the defences are poorly designed. In late 1944, as the Red Army approached and penetrated into the fringes of Germany in East Prussia, a senior Nazi Party official was awarded a substantial contract for the construction of one-man anti-tank fortifications, consisting of a buried vertical concrete cylinder, just large enough to accommodate a single person, with a folding lid. The intention was to position these along the German frontier, so that infantry manned with weapons like the *Panzerfaust* and *Panzerschrek* could then destroy Red Army tanks at close range. These cylinders became known as *Kochtöpfe* ('Koch pots', named after Erich Koch, Gauleiter of East Prussia) and proved to be almost useless. Men who used them felt isolated and alone and the field of view from them was very limited. The concrete that was used was also prone to fragmentation, with the consequence that whenever one of the cylinders was hit by a shell, the result was a rain of concrete shrapnel.[1]

The example of the Maginot Line reveals another major weakness of fortifications. By occupying such positions, an army effectively concedes the initiative to the enemy. The decision of when and often where to attack lies entirely with the force that is about to attack the fortifications, and in the case of the Maginot Line, the consequence was that the Wehrmacht chose simply to sidestep the entire line of defences. This option isn't always available; however much the Red Army might have wished to avoid a frontal assault on the German fortified positions around Leningrad, the constraints of terrain and geography left no real alternative. But the ability to choose when to attack, and how to concentrate resources at a selected point, always lies with the attacker.

There is a further disadvantage to defensive positions. For soldiers enduring the rigours of warfare, the lure of a fortified line of defences often seems irresistible, representing a possibility of shelter from inclement weather, and fighting positions from where a superior enemy can be repulsed. For commanders too, these positions can be a great temptation, an opportunity to pull back to a firm line that can then be held while exhausted units catch their breath and reinforcements are brought up. This factor was one that Hitler used repeatedly to justify his reluctance to prepare positions behind the existing front line: the very existence of such fortifications, he argued, acted as a lure for soldiers who would then show less resolve to hold their current positions. Although permission to construct the Panther Line was given in good time and most of the fortifications were meant to have been completed by early 1944, construction of the intended defensive line along the Dnepr River in Ukraine was barely started by the time that the retreating units of Army Group South reached it. Even if it had been a good defensive position – and the ability of the Wehrmacht to find sufficient men to hold such a long line was doubtful – it existed largely on paper rather than reality. Nonetheless it became an almost irresistible object in the minds of German soldiers struggling back across Central Ukraine in the hope of finding safety on the Dnepr.

The history of fortified lines in the 20th century is generally one of failure. With the possible exception of Verdun – and it was held only at a huge cost to the French Army – none of the much-vaunted and expensive fortified systems intended to hinder an enemy advance achieved very much. In Eastern Europe, there were several such fortresses, built in the 19th century and then modernised at huge cost as artillery performance steadily improved, and their only impact in military terms was a negative one. The Russian line of fortresses intended to channel a German or Austro-Hungarian attack on Imperial Russia into areas where Russian field armies could concentrate their strength had almost no impact on operations, and it was only at Przemyśl in what is now southeast Poland that there was a protracted siege. This fortress was deliberately intended by the Austro-Hungarian Empire to be besieged in the belief that it would be an impregnable point of resistance behind any Russian advance and the substantial garrison would be able to mount widespread raids against Russian lines of communication. As the Russian Army advanced in 1914 it was encircled and the siege was briefly lifted during an Austro-Hungarian counteroffensive late in the year; however, this proved to be detrimental, as the relieving forces helped themselves to the stockpiles in Przemyśl so that when the siege resumed a few days later, the garrison lacked the resources to hold out for long. The shortages of food were so great that most of the garrison's horses were soon butchered and consumed, effectively eliminating any positive raiding role for the garrison. During the winter of 1914–15, tens of thousands of Austro-Hungarian soldiers died in the Carpathians in futile attempts to break through to the city and to lift the siege, and finally the Russians carried out a successful attack and overran the much-vaunted fortress. Including the loss of the garrison and the failed relief attempts, Przemyśl cost the Austro-Hungarians about a quarter of a million casualties, for almost no detrimental impact on the Russians.[2]

For Küchler and his subordinates in Army Group North, there was no possibility of controlling the initiative or tempo of operations outside Leningrad. The soldiers in the front line had done all they could to strengthen their positions; Küchler's staff had drawn up detailed plans both for the defence of this fortified line and for a phased withdrawal to the Panther Line along the Estonian frontier; and for the first few days of January, the troops and their officers awaited what was inevitable. Everyone knew that a new Soviet assault was coming. All that remained to be revealed was its precise timing and location. Any possibility of withdrawing in a timely manner to the Panther Line before such an assault took place was lost when Lindemann refused to withdraw his optimistic assessment that his units would be able to hold their positions. That optimism would now be put to the test. For the Red Army, there was tense expectation. The resources available were greater than had been deployed in earlier offensives in this sector, but so too was the ambitious scale of the operation. But before a major advance across the region could be attempted, the German lines outside Leningrad would have to be overcome.

By the first week of January, it was clear to Govorov and Meretskov that the Germans intended to stand and fight. The plan that they had drawn up for pursuing a retreating Army Group North – *Neva 1* – was put to one side. *Neva 2*, the full-blooded assault on the German fortifications, also became known as the Krasnoye Selo–Ropsha Operation and in some documents was referred to as

Yanvarskiiy Grom ('Winter Thunder'). The operation actually began on 12 January when 2nd Baltic Front attacked far to the south, whereas the forces further north were to attack the following day; as usual, the intention of this was to try to draw German reserves away to the south in order to improve the chances of success around the Leningrad perimeter. The forces in the Oranienbaum bridgehead were to attack on 14 January, with Forty-Second Army joining the operation a day later to the south of Leningrad. The two forces were separated by just 20 miles, but almost the entire distance consisted of German defensive positions.

After the customary bombardment, Popov's 2nd Baltic Front began its assault with Tenth Guards Army. Popov and his subordinates had hoped for surprise, but it seems that the Germans were alerted by a variety of sources – aerial reconnaissance, prisoner interrogations, and reports from a few deserters who crossed the front line at the last moment – and were ready. The leading Soviet soldiers managed to break into the first line of German trenches, but then came under heavy artillery fire. German shelling also created a barrier for the movement of Tenth Guards Army's second echelon into the battle and by the end of the day the leading units had penetrated no more than a mile into the German positions and at the cost of about 9,000 men.[3] Realising the futility of continuing with the planned attack, Popov called a halt and notified *Stavka*, proposing that instead of trying to attack directly west towards Pskov, he might enjoy more success if he angled his attack further south towards Opochka. In his report, Popov criticised the leadership of Tenth Guards Army, stating that Lieutenant General Aleksandr Vasilyevich Sukhomlin, the army commander, had failed to show sufficient tactical control of his subordinate units. The response from *Stavka* was almost immediate. Sukhomlin was removed from his post and permission was granted for the change of emphasis of the operation. The new commander of Tenth Guards Army was Lieutenant General Mikhail Ilyich Kazakov, who had been Popov's deputy commander both in Bryansk Front and in 2nd Baltic Front. It was the end of Sukhomlin's time as a front-line commander; his career to date had been unspectacular, and he spent the rest of the war in charge of the Frunze Military Academy. The only tangible territorial gain by 2nd Baltic Front was that by the time the offensive fizzled out on 20 January, it had cut the Leningrad–Nevel railway line, but the more important impact was that Hansen, Sixteenth Army's commander, was forced to commit all of his reserves to the battle. There could be no prospect of him releasing forces for use by Army Group North in Eighteenth Army's sector.

It was an inauspicious start to what was hoped to be a major Soviet victory. Late on 13 January, Soviet riflemen in the Oranienbaum bridgehead began to move forward into the new trenches that had been prepared as jumping-off points, often no more than 100 yards from German positions. Behind them, gunners completed their preparations and awaited the order to open fire. Snow fell heavily all night; despite this, over 100 Soviet bombers swept over the German positions and attacked a variety of targets.

By dawn on 14 January, the snow had stopped and heavy mist covered the entire Leningrad sector as temperatures climbed above freezing, turning much of the new snowfall to slush. The massed artillery that Odintsov had carefully prepared began its bombardment at first light and continued firing for about an hour. As the longer range guns switched to targets further to the rear, there was the almost inevitable final salvo of *Katyusha* rockets followed by a further bombardment of the German front line, much as had been the case in the final attack on the Sinyavino Heights. Behind this barrage, the Soviet troops began to move forward. There were surreal echoes of earlier eras of warfare. Some of the attacking soldiers were accompanied by a brass band and at least one unit – 286th Rifle Regiment, part of 90th Rifle Division – had its regimental flag in the leading wave. Aware that it would be impossible for tanks to operate in large groups, Fedyuninsky had dispersed his armour amongst the rifle units to provide close support and he and Govorov watched with nervous anticipation as the tanks struggled forward over the rapidly softening ground past Second Shock Army's command post. Slowly, reports began to come back from the attacking divisions. The first German lines had been overrun, and as the short winter day drew to an end, the leading units were up to two miles into the German positions on a broad front of about six miles. Two of the fortified villages that formed part of the German defensive network – Porozhki and Gostilitsy – had been captured. Although the leading rifle divisions had taken substantial casualties, their losses fell short of the slaughter of earlier campaigns and there was every prospect that further successes lay ahead. The artillery fire plan, too, had largely succeeded in its tasks. It was an encouraging start.

As was so often the case, the Red Army chose to throw the main weight of its attack at units that were thought to be weak – in this case, two Luftwaffe field divisions that had been part of L Corps but came under the control of Steiner's III SS-Panzer Corps at the beginning of 1944. After their dismal performance in late 1942 and 1943, the divisions had been transferred from Luftwaffe control to the German Army in November, but they still retained their earlier personnel. The total infantry strength of 9th Field Division was just seven battalions – six organised in two regiments, and a single 'fusilier battalion' as a local reserve. One of its two regiments performed relatively well, holding onto many of its positions despite heavy casualties. The division commander was Oberst Heinrich Geerkens,

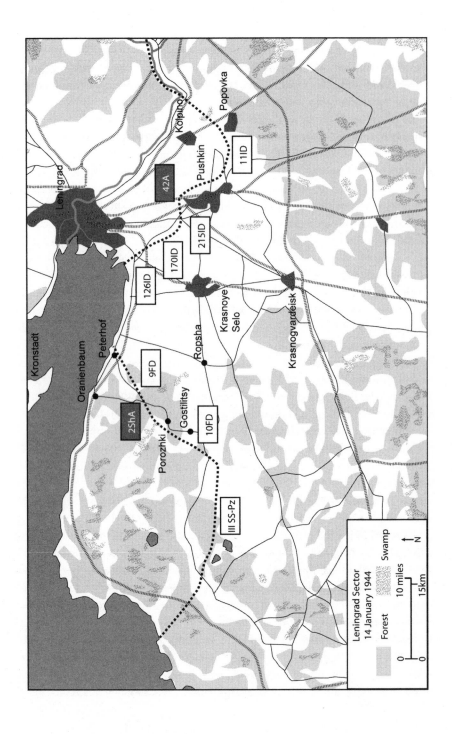

Leningrad Sector
14 January 1944

Forest

Swamp

N

0   10 miles
0   15km

who had formerly commanded one of the two regiments in the division and had just taken up his new post. Like so many of the Luftwaffe officers in these divisions, he had very limited experience of ground warfare – most of his career had been spent commanding Luftwaffe training formations for aircrew.

A company of SS combat engineers happened to be precisely between the two Luftwaffe field divisions, tasked with constructing new positions. Most of its personnel were new recruits with no experience of front-line warfare, and suddenly found themselves caught in the initial Soviet artillery barrage:

> The front line positions and the forest line presented a gruesome picture. Bunkers had been shot to pieces by the naval guns and the earth ploughed up. The woods had been cut down to a height of 2m. Dead and wounded were everywhere. For many soldiers, the first great baptism of fire was too much for their nerves. Obersturmführer Knepel [the battalion commander] hurried with his headquarters section leader from one man to the next. They energised the totally apathetic-looking men. Severely wounded men were placed on *Akyas* (boat-shaped light sleds) and pulled or carried to the rally point.[4]

On the evening of 14 January, Geerkens was able to send a cautious signal to Steiner's headquarters: for the moment at least, 9th Field Division was still intact, but it had no reserves and it was highly questionable whether it would be able to hold on if the Red Army attacked once more in strength. But the soldiers of the field division owed much of their survival to the determined resistance of the SS combat engineers. Recovering from their initial shock, they fell back to higher ground where they succeeded in stopping the Red Army's advance, albeit at the cost of over half their men killed or wounded.

The neighbouring 10th Field Division fared worse. It had only six battalions organised in two regiments. It was fortunate in that its commander, Generalmajor Hermann von Wedel, was an army officer who had won the Knight's Cross in 1943 for personally leading a group of 25 infantrymen in a desperate counterattack to restore the front line.[5] But however personally brave he might be, he couldn't compensate for the weakness of his division, which largely disintegrated in the face of Fedyuninsky's attack. As darkness fell, the division was in tatters and Wedel was desperately struggling to retain contact with the various units that continued to fight on, often completely isolated. Odintsov's gunners continued to pound German positions throughout the night, concentrating on routes that had been identified as likely paths for German reinforcements and forming up areas from where these reinforcements might launch counterattacks. At the same time, guns all along the front shelled a variety of locations to prevent the Germans from being able to predict precisely where the next blow would fall. Fedyuninsky also took further precautions to defeat any German counterthrust: an independent battalion equipped with numerous machine-guns and light field guns deployed rapidly on the right flank of the penetration, digging in and preparing to meet any counterattack.

The following morning, Forty-Second Army joined the offensive, and at the same time Second Shock Army resumed its attacks. The remnants of the German 10th Field Division disintegrated completely, just as a panzergrenadier battalion from *SS-Nordland* and three construction battalions were thrown into the battle in a counterattack. Heavy fighting continued all day and Fedyuninsky's troops edged closer to Ropsha, but were held just short of their objective by heavy defensive fire. Further to the east, the artillery bombardment that preceded Forty-Second Army's attack was even heavier than had been the case with the breakout from the Oranienbaum bridgehead. Simoniak's XXX Guards Rifle Corps waited to commence its attack, a thrust towards the west to link up with Second Shock Army:

The earth trembled and seemed to shake. The god of war was speaking. The guns fired from everywhere: direct fire from the front line, from hidden positions on reverse slopes, from the outskirts of the city, from armoured trains, and from the Baltic Fleet's warships on the Neva. Wave after wave of bombers flew past, hunchbacked attack aircraft sweeping by at low level.

The enemy positions were shredded by shells and bombs. Observation posts, dugouts and bunkers, firing positions, all were destroyed, trenches were torn up and barbed wire ripped away.

For an hour and 40 minutes the artillery rumbled. About 220,000 shells exploded on the enemy positions. The volleys of the *Katyushas* were still firing, columns of earth and smoke were still rising on the enemy's front line, when our infantry rose from the trenches as the signal flares were fired.

Turning his periscope, Simoniak could see men running everywhere across the snow-covered slope. 'The Guards are up!' The leading line was already clearing the first enemy trench. 'Faster! Faster!' Simoniak urged the soldiers, as if they could hear him in the furious hail of metal and fire. 'Faster! Faster!'[6]

The attack by XXX Guards Rifle Corps rapidly overcame the first German defensive line with only modest losses, but the units on either flank – CIX and CX Rifle Corps – both struggled in the face of tough resistance. The German line in this sector was held by L Corps with three infantry divisions and despite Simoniak's initial success, the advance soon came to a halt. A substantial anti-tank ditch and minefields held up most of the supporting tanks and losses now mounted steadily. Despite the ferocity of the Soviet barrage, the 'god of war' failed to suppress the German divisions' artillery positions fully and the intensity of defensive fire increased, preventing reinforcements from moving forward. Despite their best efforts, the reconnaissance flights over the German lines had failed to identify all of the positions that needed to be destroyed in the initial bombardment.

Govorov urged both armies to renew their attacks. On 15 January there was a further heavy artillery bombardment by Forty-Second Army and the three leading rifle corps attacked once more. As had been the case on the first day of their offensive, Simoniak's troops led the way and gained further ground. To their left, there was also some progress, but the right flank continued to be held up by strong German defences. Further to the west, Fedyuninsky's early successes had degenerated into a repetition of earlier operations, with attack and counterattack following each other and resulting in escalating losses, but by the end of the day much of the German first defensive belt had been overrun by Second Shock Army. The two Soviet armies were edging ever closer to each other.

Both sides attempted to gather their resources for a further effort. In increasingly costly fighting, Fedyuninsky's troops managed to clear the remaining German positions in the first defensive line but there was little progress at the key position of Ropsha. In order to try to break the German line, Fedyuninsky brought forward some reserves and created a new group consisting of a tank brigade, a regiment of self-propelled artillery, a light artillery regiment, and a motorised rifle battalion reinforced by two sapper companies. In addition, the entire second echelon of Second Shock Army was committed to put pressure upon the German line while the new group attempted to break through at Ropsha.

At the same time, Maslennikov brought forward a rifle corps from the second echelon of Forty-Second Army to try to break resistance on XXX Guards Rifle Corps' right flank. Within a few hours, its troops found themselves stranded in the tangle of smashed trenches and bunkers, unable to push forward. When Fedyuninsky's mobile group attacked, it ran into fierce resistance and made little impression, and two tank brigades committed by Forty-Second Army also failed to penetrate the bitterly contested front line; by the end of the day, Maslennikov had to order the brigades back to their start lines to regroup. Nonetheless, the infantry forces of both Second Shock Army and Forty-Second Army were edging closer to each other in fighting rightly described in memoirs as 'gnawing' through the German defences, and by the end of 16 January they had covered roughly half the distance between their start lines.

In Leningrad, the population had long grown used to the thunder of artillery around the siege perimeter, but Leningraders were aware of the different character of the latest fighting. Yevgeniya Vadimovna Shavrova was a schoolgirl who lived in the city throughout the siege. On 16 January, she wrote in her diary:

> Soon, soon we will be free, the siege will be over. Yesterday morning in thick, frosty clouds of smoke we saw bolts of fire: we could hear from far away an unusually loud roar of cannonades. Everyone was saying: 'It's begun!' Now everyone knows that our forces are approaching all along the Leningrad front. But how many shellings have there been only recently, just this month, how many victims? Our classmate Rita Vinogradova's father was killed, Lena Pezner's mother was wounded. A shell that landed in the courtyard of 27 Nevsky [Prospekt] killed Sima Pavlova's father and mother.[7]

For ordinary Leningraders, their mental picture of what was happening was of relief columns battering their way through the German siege lines towards the city; but the reality was the reverse, with the forces within the siege perimeter attempting to push back the Wehrmacht. The German defences were still holding on, but the fierce fighting continued to inflict heavy losses and the defenders were running out of men. To the north of the Soviet assaults, 9th Field Division and 126th Infantry Division were in danger of being cut off, and their commanders ordered some of their rear area units to pull out to the south, but such a move ran the risk of depriving the combat elements of support and supplies. To shore up the sagging front line, Lindemann had been forced to deploy 61st Infantry Division – his only substantial reserve – to take over much of the sector that had been held by 10th Field Division, but he continued to assure Küchler that he would be able to hold on. Küchler had severe doubts, especially given the lack of reserves at every level. Early on 17 January, he contacted Zeitzler at *OKH* and discussed the situation with him. The Red Army's attacks showed no sign of slackening and in these circumstances it was essential to create sufficient local reserves if the line was to be held. In order to release sufficient reserves, he requested permission for the units on the Sinyavino Heights to pull back to or even south of Mga. The result would only be a modest shortening of the overall front line, but it would be sufficient to stabilise the situation for at least the immediate future by releasing two infantry divisions. Holding on longer than that, he said, would depend on the arrival of additional reinforcements for his army group.

Despite Hitler's insistence on compartmentalisation of the German command system, Küchler would almost certainly have been aware of the situation elsewhere. Moreover, he knew from the text of *Führerbefehl 51* that troops would not be made available from Western Europe, where they were being held in anticipation of an invasion (this rule was actually broken by Hitler when First Panzer Army was cut off in southwest Ukraine, and two SS panzer divisions were temporarily 'loaned' to the east from France in order to extract the panzer army). Therefore, the only options were either to shorten the line sufficiently to release local reserves, or to pull back to the Panther Line where far more substantial reserves could be released. Having encountered Hitler's intransigence already, he can hardly have been surprised when his request resulted merely in Hitler's habitual prevarication. Without definitively ruling out the abandonment of the Sinyavino Heights, Hitler asked Küchler whether it might be better to withdraw the units that were at risk of being caught between the two Soviet assault groups.

Küchler could see no lasting benefit from this – the result would be that Second Shock Army in the Oranienbaum bridgehead would establish firm contact with the rest of Leningrad Front, and the retreating forces of Eighteenth Army would face continuing pressure. As the exchanges between Army Group North and *OKH* continued, Küchler ordered 21st Infantry Division – on the Volkhov River to the east of Chudovo – to send battlegroups to reinforce the weakening units facing the Soviet Forty-Second and Second Shock Armies. Although permission to pull back to Mga hadn't been given, 225th Infantry Division – defending the northwest side of the German salient around Sinyavino – was also ordered to send troops to the west. Similarly, 11th Infantry Division was ordered to start moving its forces west; at a local level, Küchler was using whatever freedom he had to make changes that he regarded as essential. Even these measures were technically going too far, as Hitler insisted that divisions could only be moved with his express permission.[8]

As was so often the case, the decision paralysis imposed by Hitler's prevarication meant that developments on the battlefield would determine matters. Throughout 17 January, Fedyuninsky kept up the pressure from the west, slowly grinding forward, while Maslennikov's Forty-Second Army also edged closer. On the southern flank of XXX Guards Rifle Corps, the German lines began to weaken, allowing Simoniak's guardsmen once more to lead the advance, and to the rear of the battles Soviet artillerymen laboured to move their guns forward so that they could continue supporting the attack. On 18 January, while Küchler continued to press Hitler to give him permission for a transfer of forces from the Sinyavino salient, Fedyuninsky launched attacks along the entire frontage of his army. As he moved forward to a new command post, Fedyuninsky had an alarming encounter with a German force of a few tanks and some infantrymen. Cursing his carelessness at exposing himself to danger in this manner, Fedyuninsky gave the order for his little group of 14 officers and men to prepare for combat. He wrote that when he and his men opened fire, the Germans promptly surrendered – they said that they had become separated from their unit and had been wandering through the forest for two days. It seems an unlikely account, especially if the group had tanks, all of which would have had radios permitting them to make contact with other units, but small groups of isolated Germans were increasingly being cut off and many were then laying down their weapons.[9]

With all his reserves now moving forward, Fedyuninsky could only await the outcome of the attack. The reports of progress continued on 18 January and the reserves went into battle the following day. Belatedly, the tone of Lindemann's reports changed dramatically: instead of expressing continuing confidence, he warned that Eighteenth Army was close to collapse. On the same day, Maslennikov – who had paused briefly on 18 January to regroup his depleted divisions – also attacked in strength. From the west, CXXII Rifle Corps forced its way into Ropsha while XLIII Rifle Corps captured Volosovo, immediately to the southwest. The German defences were finally cracking. Simoniak's corps also moved forward and captured Krasnoye Selo shortly after sunset and a battalion of combat engineers probed forward to establish tenuous contact with Second Shock Army. Küchler's fears of his forces being cut off to the north of a link-up by the two Soviet attack groups had been realised. Pushing on from Krasnoye Selo, elements of XXX Guards Corps also broke into Krasnogvardeisk.

The tenuous contact established by Second Shock Army and Forty-Second Army confirmed all of Küchler's worst fears, and for the same reasons was greeted with jubilation in the Soviet Union. There was an announcement on Radio Moscow that night with a gun salute in honour of the guardsmen who took Krasnoye Selo and Krasnogvardeisk, though at that stage the latter town was still being contested. Krasnogvardeisk had a special status in the Soviet Union on account of past events. It was known as Gatchina during the reign of the tsars and then as Trotsk in honour of Leon Trotsky's determined defence of Petrograd during the Russian Civil War before being renamed again in honour of the Red Guards after Trotsky's fall. For over two years, Krasnogvardeisk had been the location of numerous German occupation forces, including at one time *Einsatzgruppe A*, whose murderous activities accounted for the deaths of thousands of civilians – Jews, suspected partisans or sympathisers, hostages, and the physically and mentally infirm. During much of this period, it was known to the German occupiers – at least unofficially – as Lindemannstadt. Struggling with road conditions that were made worse by alternating spells of freezing weather and partial thaws, more Soviet units moved to establish firmer contact and fuel and ammunition was brought forward to the troops who had finally achieved the link-up; as they did so, they encountered the few civilians who remained in the area and learned something of the brutal years of German occupation.

Aware that time was of the essence, Küchler gave permission for any German forces north of the Soviet link-up to break out towards the south; if necessary, they were to destroy any heavy weapons that they had to leave behind. He sent a signal to *OKH* stating his intention and received formal permission a few hours after he had actually issued the order. In chaotic conditions, with the Red Army struggling to establish complete contact between the forces that had advanced from east and west, groups of soldiers clashed repeatedly in the forested landscape. Soviet armour surged west from Krasnoye Selo before dawn, surprising, overwhelming and scattering numerous German groups – either men pulling back from the north or groups of rear area personnel, many of whom were being organised hastily into combat groups. Most of the forces cut off from Eighteenth Army were from either 126th Infantry Division or 9th Luftwaffe Field Division. Even before Küchler's orders for a breakout to the south, it was clear late on 19 January that a speedy withdrawal was required:

> At 2000, it was seen from Kotselovo that the battle had spread along the road from Krasnoye Selo to Kipen. Several tanks were rolling west, their engines roaring and their guns blazing. Tracer rounds indicated their route from the east to the leading attack elements in the west and it was clear that they had closed the ring around the divisions ... Oberst [Gotthard] Fischer (commander of 126th Infantry Division) decided to regroup the division quickly and break out of the encirclement ... All who were to break out towards Telesi stood ready south of Kotselovo at midnight. The leading unit of the division was now 424th Grenadier Regiment. The attacking wedge was supported on both flanks by assault guns ... Tracer rounds and the flames from Telesi illuminated the battlefield. Nobody who experienced this would ever forget it.[10]

The breakout rapidly degenerated into confusion. Stachow's description of the conditions of the retreat gives a strong impression of the situation that developed:

> The word 'retreat' conjures up grim images: choked roads, overcrowded buildings, disrupted command and supply routes. Tangles of vehicles at every bridge,

crossing or choke point, with vehicles jammed together as advancing blocking units and reinforcements for rearguards run into rear area columns, airfield ground crews, workshop companies fleeing to the rear. Heavy artillery moving to new positions, ammunition trucks pushing forward, tanks shoving aside horse-drawn wagons, trucks with broken axles or engine problems left abandoned. And ever more crises when partisans attack roads and bridges, when ground attack aircraft leave vehicles ablaze. And the panicky reports and rumours that spread like lightning, the anxiety, cries and angry exchanges between traffic officers and column commanders. And then the fighting of the rearguards, or of nameless individual combatants, the rising fury of both sides, the dramas that have no living witnesses. The dead are buried in their foxholes if they can't be brought back, the wounded are carried out, the more severely wounded for whom there is no transport are bandaged and left to the mercy or the gunfire of the attackers. The front lines are completely entangled. On the Duderhof Heights, which were taken in a counterattack by an assault battalion from Eighteenth Army and then had to be abandoned because it was impossible to direct the fire of German artillery, there are unbelievable scenes of night-fighting in houses, with cellars and different floors changing hands between the Germans and Russians.[11]

Despite the chaos and confusion, large parts of the two encircled divisions – and many of the personnel of a naval artillery battalion that had been deployed in the area to bombard Leningrad – managed to reach safety.

Simoniak came forward to inspect the progress being made by his troops and climbed the Duderhof Heights – in reality, little more than a low ridge, but sufficiently high to dominate the surrounding flat terrain, where he met Colonel Afanasy Fedorovich Shcheglov, commander of 63rd Guards Rifle Division. The two men stood amidst the debris of battle and stared north: the island base of Kronstadt, the home of the Baltic Fleet, was clearly visible, as were the outskirts of Leningrad. This was one of the points from which the German bombardment of Leningrad had been coordinated. They could hear continuing gunfire as Soviet troops cleared the last German stragglers from Krasnoye Selo, but there was little time to celebrate. It was essential to complete the destruction of the encircled German forces to the north. By the end of 20 January, the task was complete. About 1,000 prisoners were taken, and perhaps more importantly the retreating Germans were forced to abandon most of their heavy weapons. About 265 artillery pieces, including 85 heavy weapons of up to 400mm calibre, were captured. The two Luftwaffe field divisions were left in tatters, and the commanders of both divisions were killed shortly after the breakout from the encirclement. With most

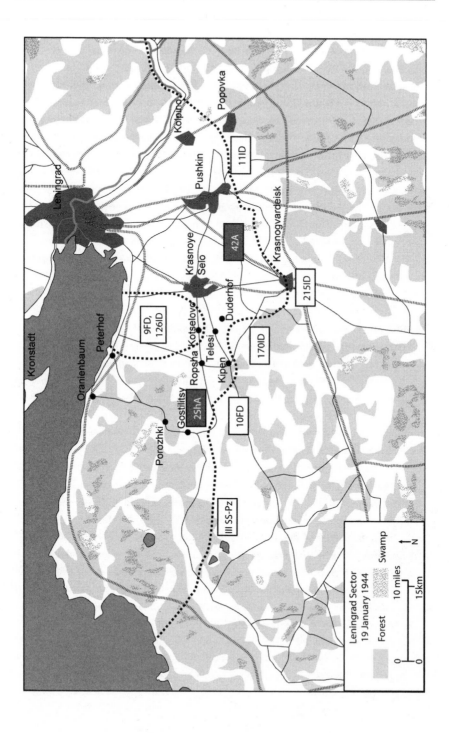

of its heavy weapons lost, 126th Infantry Division was now barely capable of combat and ultimately had to be pulled out of the front line.

Semen Nikolayevich Borshchev's 46th Rifle Division was part of Forty-Second Army's final attack and moved forward to secure the area around the Pavlovsk Palace, an imperial residence built by Catherine the Great for her son Grand Duke Paul. The Palladian buildings of the palace housed a museum after the Russian Revolution and most of the contents were hastily evacuated before the Germans occupied the area; many of the larger statues were buried in the gardens to save them from damage or theft. During the two years of German occupation, the palace was used as accommodation for German officers; their vehicles were parked in the ballroom and although many items were looted and taken back to Germany, most of the hidden treasures remained undiscovered. There had been some damage to the buildings from German artillery fire prior to occupation, but the entire palace complex was deliberately set ablaze by the retreating Germans. Borshchev reached the area late on 18 January:

At midnight, our car drove into the depleted woodland of Pavlovsk Park. Huge flames blazed and crackled as the wind blew in the darkness. The Pavlovsk Palace was on fire. Burning timbers fell, huge bursts of fire flew in different directions.

Visiting Pavlovsk now, admiring the beautiful palace, pavilions and parkland, I always remember that night when we saw the burning palace. It seemed that it had perished, that it would be impossible to restore it from the ruins and ashes. Only the statue of Paul, illuminated by the flames of the conflagration, stood untouched in its old place in front of the palace.

We were exhausted. We still had to find accommodation. We got into the car and drove out of the park, and in the glow of the flames we saw more terrible scenes of destruction. Pavlovsk was in ruins. Were the people who hid in the basements of the palace in September 1941 from shelling and bombing still alive? ...

The commander of the headquarters platoon overtook us. He said that in a large ditch between Pavlovsk and Pushkin he found former German dugouts, furnished with gilded armchairs, sofas, and mirrors, apparently taken from the palaces. We decided to spend the night in one of these dugouts.

The furniture was truly like being in a museum. According to the small inventory numbers preserved on some sofas and chairs, we established that it had come from the Catherine Palace [in Pushkin]. The upholstery was torn in several places and the gilding had been scraped off. I ordered the headquarters platoon commander to organise some soldiers the following morning to search for and to collect palace furniture.[12]

Looting of palaces was widespread during the Second World War, with both German and Soviet soldiers showing little hesitation in taking whatever they wished; on some occasions, this was purely for personal gain, but first the German authorities and then their Soviet counterparts drew up lists of treasures that were to be collected from occupied enemy territory and shipped back to their respective homelands. Many of these treasures were never returned. The Germans also carried out systematic destruction of many of the palaces that had been in their hands. When the Catherine Palace in Tsarskoye Selo was evacuated, there was widespread destruction and parts of the palace were dynamited, including a large reception hall with an ornate, gilded ceiling. Shortly after the palace was taken by the Red Army, the slow task of reconstruction began. Thousands of fragments from the ceiling were sorted by hand and painstakingly matched together, and over a third of the current ceiling is made up of recovered fragments. In their reconstruction, Soviet workers and experts were aided by an unexpected source of information: German soldiers had taken photographs of each other in various parts of the palaces in the area as souvenirs, and when they were captured, these photographs were gathered together and given to the restorers to be used as guidance on how the palaces had looked before their destruction.

Borshchev's division moved on through Gatchina in pursuit of the Germans. He described the detritus left by the retreating Wehrmacht:

When dawn broke, we saw the heavy artillery abandoned by the enemy. Many of them were so badly damaged that they were good only for scrap. Near one of these guns, on a small hill, lay the corpses of enemy artillerymen. Unbidden, a tragic episode that I had witnessed surfaced in my memory. Quite recently, before our latest offensive, an enemy shell hit a tram on Route Ten before my very eyes. It seemed that I heard again the roar of the explosion, I saw the flames, broken glass, pools of blood, the dead and wounded.

Our car couldn't drive along the highway as it was completely clogged with abandoned guns, tractors and wagons. We could barely bypass it via a clearing in the forest to get to Gatchina.[13]

At various times during the siege of the city, Army Group North had considered attacking and reducing the Oranienbaum bridgehead, but had instead pursued other options. At those moments, the bridgehead had seemed almost an irrelevance – success elsewhere was likely to result in the fall of Leningrad itself, after which the bridgehead would in any case cease to exist. But throughout the siege, several German divisions remained in this sector, reducing the forces available elsewhere. Indeed, for much of the siege, more German troops were deployed around the bridgehead than Soviet troops within it. Perhaps the best opportunity had been when the siege was first established and before the panzer divisions of Army Group North were pulled out and sent to Moscow, but at that moment it must have seemed as if such an operation would be unnecessary and would result in pointless casualties. With hindsight, it could be seen that leaving the bridgehead intact was an error, but it is by no means clear that this could have been anticipated at a time when the Germans had sufficient resources to overrun the Soviet positions without incurring too great a cost.

The losses suffered by the Soviet forces in their victory were substantial. Nonetheless, they had overcome an almost continuous network of German defensive positions, and both Forty-Second and Second Shock Armies still had considerable reserves available. With the Germans driven out of the fortifications that they had built over a period of more than two years, there was every prospect of further successes and Govorov urged his commanders to bring forward their troops so that they could continue the offensive. On the German side, staff officers struggled to sort out the tangled and disorganised remnants of units pulling back from the battlefield, aware that every man would be needed to establish a new front line. Without further reinforcements, the new positions were unlikely to be held for long. But events were unfolding further south that made the appearance of any such reinforcements impossible.

The overall Soviet operation to defeat Army Group North required a substantial attack against the southern flank of Küchler's forces at Novgorod, and this offensive began on 14 January. Korovnikov's Fifty-Ninth Army attacked after a heavy artillery barrage with two rifle corps. Heavy snow fell all day, reducing visibility for artillery observers and making air support impossible. When they moved forward, the Soviet riflemen found that many of their supporting tanks rapidly became stranded on obstacles that were buried beneath the snow. The northern attack struggled to penetrate more than about half a mile, as the artillery officer Morozov later described:

> The 110-minute artillery preparation ended and with the same rate of fire the support bombardment for the attack began. The thunder of the cannonade didn't ease for even a minute. The infantry and tanks of the two corps attacked the enemy positions but it became impossible to follow the course of the battle. Everything was covered by a veil of snow hanging over the ground, and by smoke from explosions.

It soon became clear that the battle had bogged down. The successes of our infantry at first turned out to be very insignificant. In some areas, they captured only the first trench of the enemy positions. The whole day became a fierce struggle for every bit of land. By evening, the troops had advanced only 500m to 1km, capturing one or two trenches and strongpoints located in the front line. What had gone wrong? Would the offensive stall as during the operation near Mga? Had we made mistakes? We were restless and deeply worried, from the Front commander to the ordinary soldiers.

When I reached the observation posts of 5th Mortar Brigade, there was nothing visible. The snowdrifts covered everything. The battery commanders, who were with their company commanders, could not detect enemy firing points. But as soon as the rifle companies tried to move forward, the Nazis opened fire with machine-guns and other weapons. The soldiers were driven to ground.

'I just don't know what to do,' said the brigade commander, Colonel Titar, irritably. 'The Germans have a bunker or pillbox every hundred metres or so. General shelling is pointless and just burns through our ammunition without any result. The riflemen have tried direct fire but who knows how many guns there are? They can't push forward the last 200m to the bunkers. They'll be slaughtered.'[14]

There was better progress a little to the south. Realising that the German defenders had moved out of their front-line positions to avoid being caught in the preliminary bombardment, the commander of one of 378th Rifle Division's regiments ordered his men to attack before the Germans could move back into their fortifications. The neighbouring regiment swiftly followed and much of the first German defensive line was overrun for relatively few casualties.[15] At the same time, the operational group led by Sviklin ventured out over the frozen surface of Lake Ilmen in an attempt to envelop Novgorod from the south. An artillery bombardment prior to the attack would have risked damaging the ice, and the lack of such shelling contributed considerably to the manner in which the Germans were taken by surprise. The force reached the western shore of the lake and rapidly established a substantial bridgehead about two and a half miles wide and up to four miles deep.

During the night, combat engineers laboured to set up a bridge over the Volkhov River to facilitate the movement of tanks and trucks in support of the northern group. The river was frozen, but gaps had to be created in the ice for bridging pontoons to be placed. It was difficult work, not least because of the need to restrict lighting in order to avoid drawing German attention; carrying

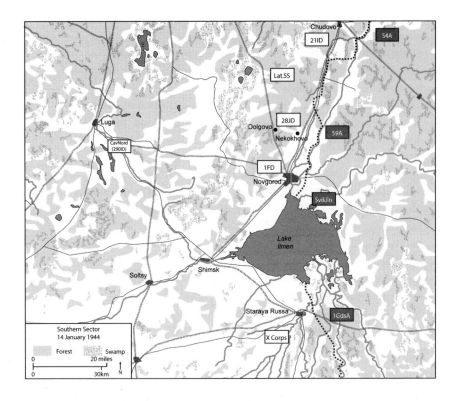

out such construction in the bitter cold in the midst of further blizzard conditions made matters even more difficult.

The commander of the German XXXVIII Corps, General Kurt Herzog, rapidly dispatched what few reinforcements that he had available – a single regiment from 290th Infantry Division and *Kavallerie-Regiment Nord*, created in 1943 from the mounted reconnaissance units of several infantry divisions. With these units he hoped to seal off the Soviet bridgehead over Lake Ilmen. But this left him with no further reserves and he immediately requested help from Lindemann. After a brief discussion with Küchler, Lindemann ordered 24th Infantry Division, deployed immediately to the northwest of Mga, to be pulled out of line and transferred to Herzog's corps. This would take time – for the moment, only a single regiment, held in reserve behind the front line, would be available – but given the constraints on resources, it was the best that could be done. The full weight of the attack north of Novgorod had fallen on 28th Jäger Division, and its local reserves were now fully committed; to its north was

2nd *Lettischen SS-Freiwilligen* Brigade and it dispatched a battlegroup consisting of two battalions under the command of Obersturmbannführer Voldemārs Veiss, the Latvian *Infanteriefūhrer* of the brigade, towards the south in order to ensure that contact was retained with its neighbouring formation.

In what rapidly became a race to reinforce their units, the Soviet commanders had the advantage of plentiful reserves located close to the battle zone. During the night of 14–15 January, a rifle division and a battalion of armoured cars crossed Lake Ilmen to reinforce Sviklin's bridgehead. This latter force faced considerable difficulties when it found that it had mistakenly ventured onto a part of the frozen lake where the ice was weaker. Several breaks in the ice sheet appeared and some horse-drawn vehicles fell into the bitingly cold water, but after a hard night of labour, the reinforcements were safely across to the west side of the lake. As soon as the exhausted combat engineers of Fifty-Ninth Army declared their new bridges across the Volkhov were open, a tank brigade and an artillery regiment equipped with self-propelled guns crossed to reinforce the northern assault; these were soon followed by a further tank brigade and a rifle division from the army's second echelon. Morozov described the labour of men trying overnight to prepare for a resumption of fighting:

In the front line, the soldiers took turns to rest for two or three hours. It wasn't bad in the captured dugouts and shelters – the blizzard couldn't reach here and it was warm in a mass of human bodies pressed against each other. It was much worse in the open trenches with the wind blowing from all sides. They huddled in their short fur coats against their comrades. Those who could cover themselves with a coat could shelter from the wind and take a nap. Those who had dry footcloths or half a pot of hot, rich cabbage soup, or could drink a mug of tea, felt they possessed luxuries. A can of food shared between three, or a piece of smoked sausage with bread – that was a typical meal. And if the logistic support worked well and didn't get stuck in the snowdrifts, there might be a thermos with porridge or tea.

They stayed awake in shifts in the front line, watching the enemy vigilantly. Both sides quieted down after the day's fighting. Only occasional firefights broke out. Flares soared over the front line now and then: the Nazis were nervous and worried about night attacks.

The counter-battery group continued to suppress the German guns, which were firing at our road junctions, crossings, and rear areas. Darkness didn't hinder our long-range guns. Sound reconnaissance worked to detect each firing battery on the Nazi side. All night long, under the very noses of the enemy, our artillerymen dug entrenchments and rolled forward guns of various calibres, from

45mm to 203mm howitzers. About 300 guns were supposed to hit the enemy with direct fire in the morning. Pickaxes, crowbars, and shovels thumped dully at the firing positions, biting into the frozen earth: the positions had to be equipped and camouflaged before dawn and the guns had to be brought forward with their ammunition, prepared for firing, the sights and recoil mechanisms checked. There was so much to do before morning.

Nobody in our department slept. Reports were drawn up, new orders were issued. Clerks bent wearily over maps. Black shadows swayed on the wet walls of the dugout. The new fire plan for the artillery, drawn up in the Front's artillery headquarters, was fleshed out overnight.[16]

The recollections of veterans of the German soldiers of 28th Jäger Division suggest that the night was rather more unsettled than portrayed by Morozov:

The night of 14–15 January was long, very long. There were shots and explosions from all directions. The burning haystacks and wooden houses of the few villages cast a ghostly light over the battlefield on the Volkhov, over which hung acrid smoke, constantly thickened by explosions; the cries of the wounded and dying mixed with the growls of confused animals. There was no possibility of resupply as the rear area units were themselves fighting for their lives.[17]

On 15 January, Korovnikov urged his subordinates to attack once more. It had stopped snowing and there was better visibility for the gunners. Even though the barrage was far shorter than on the first day – Morozov noted wryly that sufficient largesse to permit the consumption of over 150,000 shells and mortar bombs was only possible on the opening day of an offensive – the Soviet gunfire was in many respects far more effective. The guns that had been brought forward for direct fire were used against some of the German positions that had been so difficult for the Soviet riflemen to suppress as they tried to struggle forward across the snow, and Soviet aviation was also able to intervene. The reinforcements that had been brought forward overnight by Korovnikov led the way when the soldiers in the trenches commenced their attack. Within the first two hours, the lines of 28th Jäger Division were breached at several points and Soviet infantry and tanks began to move into the rear area of the German positions, albeit at a continuing high cost in casualties. By the end of the day, the advance had gained a little more than four miles in places; importantly, the Soviet armour and a rifle division – all significantly depleted by casualties and in the case of the armour by breakdowns and stranded vehicles – reached the road running from Chudovo in the north to

Novgorod in the south. It was an essential transverse line of communication for the Germans, and as soon as it arrived the first regiment from the German 24th Infantry Division was thrown into the battle in an attempt to check the Red Army's advance.

The Latvian battlegroup commanded by Veiss probed forward into what was now a confused battle zone. Instead of establishing contact with the northern flank of 28th Jäger Division, the Latvians encountered only Soviet troops and managed to reach the village of Nekokhovo. Here they were joined by a company of German infantrymen, a battery of artillery, and three assault guns and took up defensive positions around the southern perimeter.[18] But the greatest Soviet success was on the southern side of the penetration, where the lines of 28th Jäger Division were flanked by 1st Luftwaffe Field Division. Although it had performed adequately in earlier fighting, this formation proved to be as brittle as any of the Luftwaffe ground combat formations that had been created in late 1942 and rapidly disintegrated. In addition to the modest reserves that Herzog had already dispatched to the region, the commander of XXXVIII Corps had a single battlegroup from 21st Infantry Division – the rest of the division was a considerable distance to the north, defending the town of Chudovo. This battalion was now rushed to prevent a complete collapse of the German line and its commander, Major Hans von Oeynhausen, hastily established a line to intercept the fleeing Luftwaffe troops. Many were brought back into line, sometimes only when threatened with immediate execution, adding about two more battalions to Oeynhausen's command.

A substantial group of German soldiers found itself cut off by the advancing Soviet units and pulled back through dense woodland to a railway embankment, only to find that the Red Army had already reached the area and was blocking the line of retreat. The Soviet troops along the embankment opened fire and the desperate Germans immediately attacked, overcoming the blocking force. The cost in terms of dead and wounded was high and there were now more wounded men than unhurt soldiers; a medical officer in the battlegroup volunteered to remain with the wounded, accompanied by his medical personnel, while the rest of the group attempted to escape. About 80 men struggled on through deep snow and dense woodland, still dragging sleds bearing heavy weapons and some of the wounded. After two days and nights of sleepless marching, they covered about nine miles and reached safety.[19]

Although the rout of 1st Field Division was a serious setback for the Germans, the state of 28th Jäger Division was little better. Its units were now isolated from each other and Generalmajor Hubert Lamey had no means of coordinating his division. Most of the division's rear area units had been withdrawn west on the eve of the Soviet offensive and whilst this protected them, it left the combat elements with little or no access to supplies. As the remnants of the division fell back they occasionally encountered small supply units that hadn't been able to withdraw to safety; on at least one occasion, the supply officers refused to release their stockpiles on the grounds that they didn't have the proper authorisation, and the soldiers simply took what they needed at gunpoint. Whilst 28th Jäger Division fought better than its neighbouring Luftwaffe division, it ceased to be a coherent unit and in the second half of January it lost 2,500 killed, wounded, or missing. The remnants were barely sufficient to form a single battlegroup.[20]

As described above, a recurring feature of fighting on the Eastern Front was the ability of the Germans to reinforce weakened sectors of the front line either by bringing in units from other theatres or by moving units sideways; in some battles, this amounted to the wholesale rotation of relatively fresh formations to replace those that were approaching the end of their strength. By early 1944, the ability of the Wehrmacht to undertake such measures was greatly limited. The constant losses of previous years and the requirement to hold forces in reserve in France to counter any invasion by the Western Allies combined to restrict severely the options available. But to prevent even modest local transfers, Meretskov ordered Fifty-Fourth Army, facing the Germans across the middle Volkhov region, to launch attacks against the German positions with the objective of breaking through to Lyuban. Commencing on 17 January, four rifle divisions from Fifty-Fourth Army attempted to force their way through the German lines in a series of bloody assaults before coming to a halt just three miles closer to Lyuban. Reaching the city was probably never a serious objective – it would only have been possible if the Germans had already stripped the local defences of troops for use elsewhere – but the fighting eliminated any possibility of Lindemann being able to treat this sector as one from which he could transfer reinforcements to his critical flanks. The cost was high in terms of blood, as was almost every such operation attempted by the Red Army.

The situation facing Lindemann in the headquarters of Eighteenth Army was deteriorating rapidly. His earlier confidence that he would be able to withstand any Soviet attack was long gone, transformed almost instantly into the gravest concern for his army's survival, and he now saw both of his flanks under severe threat. It was clear that the attacks that had led to the Oranienbaum bridgehead merging with the Leningrad perimeter were far from finished and that the Red Army would attempt to push further south, and on the opposite flank, although heavy fighting was raging around Novgorod, the Red Army was steadily gaining the upper hand. In particular, the customary German solution to such developments – energetic counterattacks against the enemy forces, intended to catch them while they were still exhausted from their own attacks and hadn't had sufficient time to secure the ground they had captured – was impossible. Eighteenth Army had no reserves whatever, and Küchler could provide no reinforcements either.

It was Lindemann's confidence that was largely the cause of the crisis – had he not insisted that his army could defeat any Soviet offensive, Küchler might have been able to argue successfully for the implementation of *Blau* and an orderly withdrawal to the Panther Line. When he gave those assurances, Lindemann was strongly influenced by the fighting of earlier months, in which his men had weathered almost every Red Army attack and in exchange for conceding modest amounts of ground had inflicted heavy losses on the Soviet forces. How realistic was it to expect a repetition of this by the end of 1943? With hindsight, it's easy to see what had changed. The German divisions facing the Red Army around Oranienbaum and Leningrad and along the Volkhov were individually weaker than they had been, with losses usually outstripping replacement drafts – even where the divisions had been able to make good their losses in numerical terms, the fact remained that the new, inexperienced drafts were poor substitutes for the veterans who had died or been wounded in the bitter fighting of 1943. Moreover, the transfer of several experienced and battle-hardened divisions from Army Group North to other sectors weakened the army group overall, leaving it with few significant reserves. The divisions that it had been given in return for these transfers were generally far weaker. Repeatedly, the Luftwaffe field divisions showed little or no resilience when they came under sustained attack, and the SS divisions of Steiner's III SS-Panzer Corps and the Latvian formations were still relatively inexperienced. The overall impact of this was to leave Army Group North in a far more brittle state. Its units could be expected to fight fiercely in their long-established defensive positions, but it was questionable whether they would be able to sustain this for long.

The Red Army was also no longer the same force that it had been through 1942 and much of 1943. The painful process of evolution towards a more capable fighting machine continued with each cycle of offensive operation and review. To a very large extent, the Red Army would remain a blunt instrument – more of a mace or a cudgel than the sharp sword of the Wehrmacht – but it was unquestionably a more effective blunt instrument than it had been. In particular, its officers at all levels were learning how to fight and win, how to wield that blunt instrument more effectively. It is worth noting that the memoirs of German soldiers and officers make little or no mention of the improving performance of their enemies. The emphasis in these accounts is always on the great numerical superiority of the Soviet forces, with little recognition that they were operating more effectively, and that their equipment was steadily improving.

At the time, the overall picture may have seemed different to Lindemann. After several years of propaganda that treated the enemy as *Untermenschen* ('subhumans'), it is likely that Lindemann continued to believe that his soldiers were inherently superior to their foes. His refusal to accept Küchler's urging to withdraw his optimistic assessments was based on multiple factors, including a desire to impress Hitler with his willingness to satisfy the Führer's demands to hold on to territory for as long as possible. Like many people faced with conflicting evidence, his personal bias probably played a large part, allowing him to ignore or downplay factors that were contrary to what he believed and wished to do. As a consequence of this, Lindemann's army now faced the serious possibility of total defeat, and his soldiers would pay a heavy price for his mistaken opinion. If either thrust against his flanks managed to break into the rear area where partisans were already making German control tenuous, Eighteenth Army would be in a perilous situation; if both Soviet attacks were to break through, there was a threat of an encirclement to rival Stalingrad.

CHAPTER 11

RETREAT FROM LENINGRAD

After almost every military operation in the Second World War, the Red Army carried out detailed analysis in attempts to learn from what had worked and what had gone wrong. Repeatedly, the same issues were identified as being the causes of setbacks and failures, and the recurrence of these issues highlights a major problem that the Red Army – and its successors, the Soviet Army and the modern Russian Army – repeatedly failed to address. Identifying problems is of course an essential step in improving performance; but such identification without then devising solutions to those problems and then implementing these solutions is pointless.

The reports that were produced at the end of *Yanvarskiiy Grom* concluded that in the case of Korovnikov's Fifty-Ninth Army near Novgorod, the failures of the first day of the offensive and the subsequent slow development of the operation were largely due to poor command and control at every level. Korovnikov was criticised for not having adequate control of his army; his corps commanders were criticised for not coordinating their subordinate formations properly; and division commanders repeatedly failed both to manage their subordinate regiments and to cooperate with each other. None of these criticisms were new, and the fact that these issues were problematic on many occasions perhaps highlights a different, more fundamental problem. The training of Soviet commanders was flawed in a manner that hindered their ability to learn from these mistakes.

As Helmuth von Moltke the Elder, the 'father of the German general staff', wrote, 'No plan of operations extends with any certainty beyond the first contact with the main hostile force.'[1] Even when attacking a relatively static enemy position, events are likely to progress in a manner that may not have been anticipated, and the ability of an army to recognise and adapt to new circumstances is often the main factor that determines success or failure. At every level, the Soviet state stifled any sense of showing initiative in all aspects of society; the higher the position held by an individual, the greater the personal risk of acting in an individualistic manner that might attract criticism and potential punishment. It was often safer simply to follow instructions, regardless of whether changed circumstances made such instructions invalid. In these circumstances, it is hardly surprising that Korovnikov's subordinates chose to follow their orders with dogged determination. Moreover, for officers at any level to act with any degree of independence and initiative, they had to have the trust and confidence of their superiors. This was rarely the case in the Red Army. Another factor was that corps-level headquarters had been partially abolished in late 1941 because of the loss of so many staff officers during the long run of defeats suffered by the Red Army – although some units still continued to function as part of corps organisations, the universal use of corps was only reintroduced in late 1942 and early 1943. A year later, many of these corps-level headquarters were still learning how they should function.

Despite the rigid manner in which Korovnikov's army attacked the German positions around Novgorod, it slowly and steadily asserted itself on the Germans. Sviklin's Southern Operational Group used its reinforcements to good effect, rapidly overcoming the hastily erected defences in its path and advancing to cut the road and rail link running southwest from Novgorod to Shimsk. The German units that had been dispatched to the area could do little more than deploy an intermittent screen in the path of the Soviet units, and Lindemann realised that if this Soviet force should turn north, there was little to prevent it from advancing into the area to the west of Novgorod itself. At the same time, the northern attack by Korovnikov continued to batter its way forward through the German defences. A sudden rise in temperature resulted in a partial thaw, greatly complicating movement for both sides, but the immediate consequence was that with reinforcements struggling to reach the area, any advantage lay with whichever side already had the greater strength on the battlefield. For the moment, that was unquestionably the Red Army.

Although the softening ground made movement of large numbers of men and vehicles much more difficult, Korovnikov was able to throw another rifle corps and tank brigade into the battle, pushing them forward on his northern flank in order to widen the penetration. The Latvian battlegroup that had reached Nekokhovo found itself under increasing pressure and was driven away towards the west, where it took up new positions in Dolgovo. This was close to the railway line running northwest from Novgorod and it was essential that the Soviet thrust was stopped before it could cut the line; Veiss and his diminished command dug in as best they could and were relieved when a second battlegroup of Latvian troops arrived as reinforcements. But to make matters worse for the defenders, there were repeated skirmishes with partisan groups operating in the rear of the Latvian force.

Lindemann spoke to Küchler about the worsening situation. The army group commander immediately granted permission to Lindemann to commence a withdrawal from Novgorod and contacted *OKH* to secure Hitler's approval; he can't have been surprised when permission was refused. For the moment, the Soviet forces on either side of the city were able to make only slow progress towards each other, hindered by a mixture of desperate German resistance and the increasingly troublesome thaw, which turned a region where roads were always poor into a quagmire. The Soviet report after the operation would criticise these units for making poor use of reconnaissance and for attacking the German positions without any attempt to find gaps in the defensive line, but given the difficulties in moving forward, it is hardly surprising that such flexible manoeuvre was rarely attempted. But the conditions that hindered the Soviet advance also complicated matters for the Germans. Taking advantage of Küchler's order, Lindemann passed instructions to Herzog's XXXVIII Corps to commence a withdrawal to the east before the only remaining escape route was cut. Rear area units and artillery began to pull out along a road that was barely adequate in good conditions. The combination of softening ground, the passage of heavy vehicles, and intermittent attacks by Soviet aircraft and partisans resulted in a series of blockages and progress was slow at best.

Throughout 19 January, Küchler continued to exchange messages with Zeitzler and Hitler at *OKH*, trying to secure permission for Novgorod to be abandoned completely. In addition, he wanted to pull back the entire eastern line in order to shorten it, releasing sufficient troops to reinforce both flanks of Eighteenth Army. Hitler repeatedly refused, demanding that Novgorod continue to be held – he declared that its retention was of great political importance, and its propaganda value to the Red Army was great enough to justify continued defence. By now, only five German battalions – from 1st Field Division and 28th Jäger Division – remained in the city, with Soviet troops on the outskirts to the north, east and west. Late on 19 January, an exhausted Zeitzler telephoned Küchler. He informed the army group commander that Hitler had grudgingly given permission for Novgorod to be abandoned. Hitler joined the conversation and chose this moment to complain bitterly about unnecessary withdrawals and their effect on morale; Küchler, who had felt that such a withdrawal was 'necessary' for several weeks, listened in silence. But the outcome was that, at last, Army Group North could commence what its commander regarded as an essential redeployment.

A major withdrawal while facing an active enemy is a difficult undertaking. In order to prevent the enemy from taking advantage of the departure of combat units, a level of deception is at least preferable and often essential. The sequence of departing units must be strictly controlled, and whilst rear area formations should be removed first, consideration has to be given to the consequences of their departure – for example, the removal of all supply units may leave combat formations unable to be resupplied if they suddenly come under pressure. The enemy has to be held in check by a rearguard that is sufficiently strong to avoid being overwhelmed, and ideally the enemy should be disrupted by aggressive activity, such as air attacks, both as a deception measure and to hinder pursuit. Detailed planning has to take account of roads and other transport routes with strict control of traffic, especially at choke points such as bridges and important junctions, and as the rearguard shrinks there is increasing temptation for units and soldiers who feel isolated to commence unauthorised withdrawals – tight command and control is essential. The staff officers of Army Group North had drawn up orders for *Blau* – the orderly and phased withdrawal of the army group's forces to the Panther Line – in the last days of 1943, and the Wehrmacht had good experience of conducting such withdrawals, but many of the features described above were impossible to achieve in the context of the units facing encirclement in Novgorod. It is a measure of the continuing professionalism of the officers of the Wehrmacht that despite there being no possibility of achieving any level of deception, the withdrawal actually unfolded comparatively smoothly.

Although the Soviet encirclement of Novgorod was incomplete, the evacuation of the city during the night of 19–20 January was nonetheless a difficult exercise. Many wounded men had been brought to Novgorod where there were several medical facilities and those who were too badly injured to be moved easily had to be left behind. Medical personnel volunteered to stay with them as the rest of the German garrison began its withdrawal. Soviet artillery to the northeast of Novgorod bombarded both the city and the German line of retreat and there were repeated attacks by Soviet bombers. There was no longer any question of organised companies and battalions – instead, men from different units, both combatant and rear area, many of them wounded, were grouped

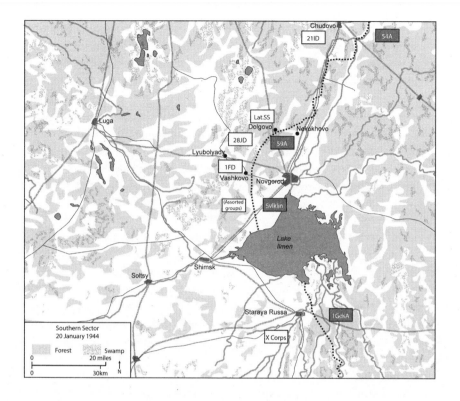

together under energetic officers who attempted to keep the withdrawal moving. The units of 1st Field Division effectively disintegrated and constant rumours swept up and down the retreating column, but most of the five battalions managed to escape, albeit abandoning any heavy equipment that they still had. At dawn on 20 January, the exhausted Germans reached Vashkovo, ten miles to the west. There was no opportunity for rest; they were ordered to prepare defensive positions immediately.[2]

Meretskov, the commander of Volkhov Front, travelled to the city as soon as it had been secured:

Dead silence reigned in the streets. There were heaps of broken masonry everywhere … The greatest historical monuments, the pride and adornment of ancient Russian architecture, had been blown up. Of the Church of the Saviour on Ilyin and the Church of Saints Peter and Paul in Kozhevniki, only the barest skeletons of walls remained. All of the Nikolsky Cathedral, the Yevfimievskaya

Tower and belfry had collapsed completely. The Cathedral of Sophia, erected in 1052, had been plundered, its glittering gilded dome torn off, and the city park had been torched. There had been a monument in Novgorod, erected in 1862 to mark the first millennium of Russia. Planning to give the Novgorod region to colonists from East Prussia, the Nazi command intended to wipe any evidence of Russian history from the face of the earth. Orders were therefore issued to melt down the millennium monument. Special detachments of soldiers had already sawn the metal statues into pieces, but didn't have sufficient time to take them away. When the Soviet soldiers broke into the city, they saw the bronze statues of Aleksandr Nevsky, Tsar Peter I, and General Suvorov lying half-buried in snowdrifts.[3]

The cross of the Sophia Cathedral, taken by soldiers of the Spanish Blue Division during their time in the area in 1942, was not returned to Russia until 2004. Most of the city's population was also gone. Some had fled before the arrival of the Germans; all but 50 of those who remained were either dead or had been shipped to Germany as forced labourers.

As they advanced to the west of Novgorod, Morozov and his men had an opportunity to see first hand the impact that the gunners had made on the retreating Germans:

When we left the ruins of the city on the road to Lyubolyady [14 miles to the west of Novgorod] I met Captain Egorov, an officer of the operations department of Front headquarters, returning from the front line. 'Don't go straight ahead, take a detour,' he advised. 'Our gunners did a lot of work there. Well, you'll see for yourself.'

Soon we saw what was left of the defeated enemy column ahead of us. The entire road was littered with burned out cars, wrecked staff vehicles, radio equipment, tanks, and abandoned guns. And around them – hundreds of corpses of Nazi soldiers. The driver Doronin and Senior Lieutenant Zhumshidov, who were travelling with me, fell silent when they saw this scene. Our car meandered for a long time along the jolting parallel road.[4]

Much of the discussions between Küchler and Zeitzler had centred on the so-called 'Rollbahn position'. The Rollbahn – a German expression used in many sectors to describe the main road along which supplies and reinforcements could move – ran parallel to the front line in the north, and Hitler insisted on defending a line that ensured the Rollbahn remained under German control. For Küchler, this raised several problems. Firstly, the resultant withdrawal might be too small to make any material difference. Secondly, the entire basis of *Blau* was that it consisted of a series of withdrawals all the way back to the Panther Line – merely to make a small initial withdrawal without any further movement was no better than staying in the front line and not withdrawing at all. Almost as soon as he had given Küchler permission to abandon Novgorod and to pull back closer to the Rollbahn, Hitler changed his mind and ordered Zeitzler to reverse the decision with regard to the northern sector. Zeitzler replied that it was too late and that it was now impossible to countermand the orders.

With the recapture of Novgorod, the Red Army essentially reached the end of *Neva 2*. Even as the last battles were being fought, *Stavka* ordered both Leningrad and Volkhov Fronts to submit detailed proposals for further operations – the overall shape of an offensive to drive the Germans back to and beyond the old frontier with Estonia and Latvia had already been agreed, and these plans were now fleshed out in detail. Leningrad Front was to advance to capture Tosno while Volkhov Front advanced on Chudovo; as a result, a large part of the German Eighteenth Army would be squeezed between these forces and either destroyed or forced to pull back a substantial distance. The result would be the complete lifting of the siege of Leningrad. Whilst this plan concentrated on events in the northern sector, Meretskov was keen to continue exploiting the costly success of Fifty-Ninth Army around Novgorod and wanted to unhinge the German positions from the south. To that end, he had already ordered 7th Guards Tank Brigade and VII Rifle Corps to form an exploitation force that could press forward before the new German defensive line could harden. Even as these units moved towards the front line, Lindemann began the general withdrawal from the Volkhov River on 21 January, releasing a few battalions for use elsewhere. The arrival of these modest reinforcements for the German lines west of Novgorod forced a re-evaluation. Meretskov now ordered his Front to commence a general offensive to pin down the Germans and prevent any further withdrawals, with the result that Fifty-Ninth Army no longer received the supply priority that it had thus far enjoyed.

At the same time, Leningrad Front resumed its attacks from the north, with Second Shock Army and Forty-Second Army advancing side by side past Gatchina while Volkhov Front's Fifty-Ninth Army threatened to advance towards Luga. On 21 January, the blood-soaked Sinyavino Heights and the remains of the town of Sinyavino were abandoned to the forces pressing from the north. In many respects, it was a quiet and uneventful end to the German possession of the modest ridge where so many men of both sides had been killed or maimed.

The same day, while the Red Army kept up its constant pressure from the north, the ruins of Mga – the objective for so many operations in the preceding two years – fell to the Soviet CXVIII Rifle Corps. There was considerable rejoicing in Leningrad when this was announced; the town had fallen to the Wehrmacht at the end of August 1941 and as a consequence the main railway line from Leningrad to Moscow had been cut, ending any hopes for most civilians of a timely evacuation. However, the success was nuanced by criticism of the timid manner in which the Red Army pursued the retreating Germans. The town's defenders had effectively been permitted to leave almost unmolested. In fact, the Red Army missed a great opportunity to inflict serious damage upon the Germans. General Martin Grase, who had inherited command of XXVI Corps at the beginning of the year from Hilpert, had been forced to hand over his 227th Infantry Division to L Corps, leaving him with just 212th Infantry Division, and to make matters worse this unit was only at half its establishment strength. Whilst the pursuing Soviet formations of Eighth Army were also far from full strength, they comfortably outnumbered the Germans but failed to make any significant impression.[5]

A little to the south, the Soviet Fifty-Fourth Army also struggled to assert itself over Loch's XXVIII Corps. As was the case with XXVI Corps, Loch had been forced to send one of his divisions – SS-Polizei – to a neighbouring formation, in this case the battered XXXVIII Corps near Novgorod. But the remaining units – two regular infantry divisions, the Spanish Legion, and two Luftwaffe field divisions – made good use of the forested terrain to hold up the Red Army. In an attempt to accelerate progress and keep up with the ambitious rate of advance that was expected by Stavka, Meretskov shuffled his forces to maintain pressure, but as had been the case in every Soviet offensive in this region, the terrain remained favourable to the defenders and almost every advance became an intermittent series of attacks followed by pauses while reinforcements, supplies, and artillery were moved forward; the Germans frequently used these pauses to continue their slow withdrawal.

For the moment, General Wilhelm Wegener's L Corps continued to cling to defensive positions close to Krasnogvardeisk, but the troops to the east once more faced the threat of being cut off. For Küchler, the implementation of the first part of Blau was meaningless unless it was followed by the subsequent phases of the planned withdrawal to the Panther Line. After the frustrating experience of having to make repeated representations to OKH by telephone and teleprinter before being permitted to commence his withdrawal, he decided that the matter had to be resolved once and for all and flew to Hitler's headquarters in East

Prussia late on 21 January. The following day, he met the Führer to discuss the matter and stated plainly that he expected the defence of Krasnogvardeisk to come to an end imminently. Furthermore, while Army Group North had started the year with sufficient men to man the Panther Line with adequate reserves behind the front line, the losses suffered during the Soviet attacks on either flank of Eighteenth Army were so great that there was now barely sufficient strength to hold the line even if an immediate withdrawal was authorised before more units were worn down.

Given his unwillingness to agree to earlier requests for modest withdrawals, the refusal of Hitler to accept Küchler's arguments must have come as no surprise. He continued to insist that every bit of ground had to be held in order to maximise the losses suffered by the Red Army:

> I am against all withdrawals. We will have crises wherever we make a stand. There is no guarantee we will not be broken through on the Panther Line. If we pull back voluntarily, [the enemy] will not get there with only half his forces. He must be bled white along the way there. The battle must be fought as far as possible from the German border.[6]

Küchler's arguments that his forces were already badly weakened and would be further degraded in any prolonged battle to the east of the Panther Line were categorically rejected. Hitler replied that Army Group North had enjoyed a privileged position with few or no serious crises for over a year, whereas other sectors of the Eastern Front had experienced far heavier fighting. After he dismissed Küchler from the meeting, the dispirited commander of Army Group North commiserated with Zeitzler and learned why Hitler was so intransigent. The Western Allies had carried out a successful landing at Anzio that morning, Zeitzler told Küchler, and the Führer was badly distracted by this development. He suggested that it might be better to wait a few days before making a further request for permission to withdraw.

A disheartened Küchler flew back to the headquarters of Army Group North, aware that the Red Army was unlikely to oblige him by giving him sufficient time for Hitler to be won over. The only small crumb of comfort he had to show for his visit to Hitler's headquarters was that Zeitzler informed him at the last moment of reinforcements: 12th Panzer Division was to be transferred from Army Group Centre's Third Panzer Army to Army Group North; at the same time, the Tiger tanks of *Schwere Panzer Abteilung 502*, technically already part of Army Group North and operating with Sixteenth Army near Nevel, were ordered to concentrate as a single battalion as part of Eighteenth Army rather than the current unsatisfactory arrangement of separate companies of Tigers being sent to different hot spots.

This latter item highlighted another area of huge frustration for senior German officers. Even when they had armoured forces under their control, the deployment of these units was often under the tight control of *OKH*, i.e. they couldn't be reassigned without Hitler's personal permission. This would have catastrophic consequences just a few weeks later in Ukraine, when the Red Army succeeded in surrounding a substantial part of the German Army Group South in what became known as the Cherkassy Pocket. Manstein, the commander of Army Group South, ordered 24th Panzer Division – originally destroyed in Stalingrad and then rebuilt around elements of the division that had been outside the encirclement of Sixth Army and had survived – to move from the Nikopol region to mount a relief operation from the south in order to rescue the encircled men. Of all the panzer divisions available to Manstein, 24th Panzer Division was arguably the strongest and the closest to full strength. Unfortunately, there was very limited railway capacity to move the division from Nikopol to the Cherkassy area and much of its wheeled transport had to make the journey across snow-covered roads, with the result that dozens of vehicles were left stranded in snowdrifts or abandoned when they broke down. When the division reached the Cherkassy area, it attacked for less than a day before Hitler abruptly intervened and ordered it to return to the Nikopol sector: the transfer had been carried out without his knowledge and approval and he resolutely refused to accept any arguments about it remaining in the Cherkassy area. The result was that the division lost a great deal of its wheeled vehicles in the two moves, and was unable to intervene either at Cherkassy or in its original deployment area, where a fresh Soviet offensive commenced almost as it was being moved north by Manstein.[7]

Otto Carius, the Tiger company commander in *Schwere Panzer Abteilung 502*, later recalled that he and his tanks arrived by rail in Krasnogvardeisk where the railway station was under heavy artillery fire. The train was backed into a siding where the tanks were unloaded with some difficulty and prepared for battle. As they worked on their tanks, the crews learned some bad news about part of the battalion that had already gone into action:

When we arrived, we discovered the sad details of the destruction of our 1st Company. It had been surrounded on the Rollbahn by Russian tanks. Leutnant Meyer's platoon was almost completely annihilated. Meyer himself put his pistol to his head when the Russians tried to take him prisoner. We were crestfallen by this news. In my mind, I faulted the commander for not delaying the employment of the men until all companies were together.[8]

This criticism of Major Willi Jähde, the commander of *Schwere Panzer Abteilung 502*, is technically correct: the battalion would undoubtedly have been able to function better if it had gathered all of its current strength of 22 Tiger tanks before going into action. But the crisis in the front line was so severe that valuable and highly effective weapons like the Tiger tanks were simply ordered into action as they became available; even if Jähde had been inclined to hold his tanks back until the rest of the battalion arrived, he would almost certainly have been overruled by Wegener, the commander of L Corps, to whom the Tigers had been assigned. Carius added that whilst his criticism might have felt appropriate at that moment, with hindsight he accepted that Jähde had been operating with very limited information about the closeness of Soviet armour. He further wrote that Jähde was the best battalion commander he had in the war, who always did his best for his men.

By this stage of the fighting, the formerly bullish Lindemann was loudly warning of impending disaster. Regardless of the arguments between Hitler and Küchler about the Rollbahn Line, the commander of Eighteenth Army signalled the headquarters of Army Group North and *OKH* on 23 January that he would have to pull back to the south or risk his men being completely overwhelmed. Informing his superiors that he was abandoning Pushkin and Slutsk, he added that if *OKH* chose to countermand his orders, then Hitler should appoint a replacement commander for Eighteenth Army.

On the same day, Moscow announced that the town of Krasnogvardeisk was to be renamed once more, this time reverting to its original name of Gatchina; this was part of a widespread policy initiated by Stalin to revert to older names for many towns, cities, and streets. Nevsky Prospekt, the great avenue through the centre of Leningrad, had been renamed several times in preceding years – in the aftermath of the October Revolution it became Ulitsa Proletkulta ('Proletkult Street', named in honour of the new 'proletarian' culture organisation) and then Prospekt 25 Oktyabrya to mark the date of the Bolshevik seizure of power. But people continued to refer to the avenue by its old name, as they did to so many renamed places. For older people, Leningrad never ceased to be 'Piter', and many continued to refer to towns like Krasnogvardeisk by their old names too. Recognising this and hoping perhaps to evoke patriotic memories, Stalin instigated his policy of renaming a modest number of locations, including Nevsky Prospekt. Almost all Leningraders greeted the restoration of the old names with satisfaction. Whatever Stalin and others might think in faraway Moscow, the city on the Neva was timeless for its residents.

Lindemann's declaration that he couldn't hold the Rollbahn Line triggered an angry exchange between Küchler and Lindemann. Knowing that his carefully drawn plans for a withdrawal to the Panther Line had effectively been undermined by Lindemann's confident assertion in December that Eighteenth Army could defeat any Soviet attack, Küchler visited his subordinate's headquarters on 24 January and bitterly berated him for overstating the defensive strength of Eighteenth Army and the number of reserves available. Lindemann had to acknowledge that his earlier assessment had been wrong, but this made little practical difference. With fighting still raging around Gatchina, Soviet units slipped past L Corps' defensive line and advanced rapidly towards the Luga River, threatening to break up the entire German line.

After failing to take advantage of his numerical superiority over the single division of XXVI Corps, Starikov handed over his units to the neighbouring Fifty-Fourth Army and moved his headquarters to the southern flank of Volkhov Front, where he was to take control of Sviklin's group, part of Fifty-Ninth Army, and then attack towards Luga from the east. Using the transferred troops as reinforcements, Korovnikov attacked once more towards Tosno and Lyuban. In order to deal with the threat to Luga, the Spanish Legion was ordered to pull out of the front line and proceed by rail to Luga where it would occupy defensive positions, but when the soldiers reached Lyuban to commence their journey, they were told that the rail line to Luga had been cut by partisans. Instead, they were to make a march of 75 miles along a badly degraded road to reach their destination. It proved to be a difficult move. Partisans took advantage of the forests to mount hit-and-run attacks along the road, blocking it in several places with felled trees to create choke points where they then carried out lethal ambushes. Morale in the Spanish Legion began to collapse, with many soldiers refusing to obey orders.[9]

Behind the Spanish troops, Korovnikov's army continued to attack. In the headquarters of Volkhov Front, Meretskov knew that he remained under close scrutiny by *Stavka* after his decidedly mixed career since the start of the war and he was acutely aware of the need to continue to deliver results. The initial phase of the winter offensive had been a success, albeit at some cost, with German lines that had resisted for two years being overrun, but greater prizes seemed within reach. He urged Korovnikov to show more energy – if Fifty-Ninth Army could press on to Luga, there was a very real possibility that it would open up such a large breach between the German XXVIII Corps to the north and XXXVIII

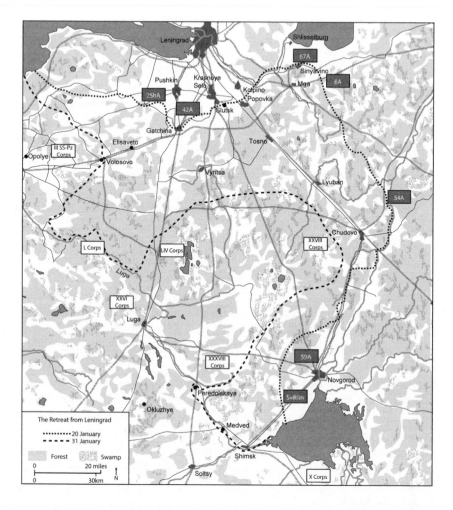

The Retreat from Leningrad

Corps to the south that both would be in danger of having their supply lines cut and would then face destruction. But Korovnikov faced considerable difficulties. The frozen Volkhov River lay across his lines of communication and engineers were struggling to construct bridges to ferry supplies and reinforcements to the west bank. Even when they succeeded in crossing the river, the Red Army's columns faced difficulties due to the very limited road network and widespread forests and marshes. The temperature continued to fluctuate, meaning that the ground was frequently too soft for rapid movement, and although Korovnikov had deployed additional engineer support with his leading troops in an attempt to keep the roads in a usable state, the scale of the task they faced was enormous.

To the north, Fedyuninsky was also unhappy with how the battle was unfolding. His forces had battered their way through multiple defensive positions to link up with Soviet forces to the east, but thereafter there had been a tendency to revert to the unsatisfactory policies of the past – when they encountered German strongpoints, they simply made repeated frontal attacks instead of attempting to bypass and isolate them. When these frontal attacks failed, Soviet units then stopped and waited for reinforcements, or for the Germans to abandon their positions. On 23 January, Fedyuninsky wrote to his subordinate commanders:

> Despite my orders, the army's units continue to wait in their positions in front of the badly degraded enemy formations, instead of inflicting further casualties or achieving a definitive success. As has repeatedly been the case, corps commanders show slowness, engaging half-heartedly in combat and not directing their corps to use manoeuvre to achieve decisive movement. The enemy, who is conducting covering operations in small groups, is exploiting our slowness and withdrawing his main forces to the south and southwest from Krasnogvardeisk and Elisaveto.[10]

Fedyuninsky's criticisms were perhaps the result of Govorov's growing dissatisfaction. The commander of Leningrad Front urged a change of tactics: for understandable reasons, the Red Army had assaulted the strong German defensive positions on a relatively broad front, having learned that isolated penetrations faced almost immediate counterattacks on their flanks. But now that the Germans had been levered out of their trenches and bunkers, there were opportunities for a greater degree of mobility. Speed was of the essence, and every opportunity to bypass points of resistance had to be taken in order to hasten the collapse of the German forces.[11]

The battle for Gatchina – still referred to by many Soviet officers at the time as Krasnogvardeisk, perhaps because the decision to rename it had not yet been fully disseminated – began to come to a climax on 22 January as Maslennikov's Forty-Second Army brought the full weight of its main force to bear. Wegener's L Corps continued to cling to its defences, primarily with 11th and 170th Infantry Divisions; there were elements of four further divisions in and around the town, the remnants of formations that had lost much or most of their artillery and heavy weapons and were now assembled into ad hoc battlegroups. Some of the siege artillery that had been gathered to destroy Leningrad had already been evacuated towards the Estonian frontier, and some had been destroyed or overrun by the Red Army, but much of it was still in action; there was a particularly heavy concentration of guns to the southeast of Gatchina and their long reach continued to limit the freedom of movement of Soviet rear area formations and reinforcements. The first elements of 12th Panzer Division were also arriving and forming up further to the southwest. But the Red Army was also concentrating its resources and even as Soviet infantry began to press into Gatchina, other units closed in on Pushkin from three sides. Elsewhere too there were further gains for the Red Army, but German units continued to cling tenaciously to their positions wherever they could, preventing the Soviet forces from achieving a broad advance.

By the end of the day, the lines of Army Group North were looking increasingly ragged. In the south, the muddled units of XXXVIII Corps were manning positions about 11 miles west of Novgorod, with a large gap to their north – the best the Germans could hope for was that the swampy and forested ground was too difficult for the Red Army to exploit. Further north, German troops continued to hold a line near Chudovo, but thereafter the Wehrmacht units were slowly pulling back as pressure grew around the 'bend' in the German lines. South of Leningrad, LIV Corps, reduced to just two divisions, continued to occupy its original fortified positions, with L Corps looking increasingly isolated in Gatchina. There was only the most tenuous contact with III SS-Panzer Corps further to the west.

There was another event on 22 January, the significance of which didn't become clear until some time later. Several German artillery shells exploded in Leningrad, killing two civilians and wounding three more.[12] It was the last time that German artillery would fire upon the city. For a total of 870 days, German guns had been able to bombard Leningrad, and Soviet estimates suggested that in the days between 4 September 1941 and 22 January 1944, a daily average of 240 shells of various calibres were fired at the city, with a total of over 148,000 projectiles. The bitter siege, which cost hundreds of thousands of lives both within and around Leningrad, was effectively over. By 24 January, even the rumble of gunfire from the front line was too distant to be heard clearly in the city streets. A few days later, Yevgeniya Shavrova wrote in her diary:

I just can't realise that the siege is over, that there are no shellings, blackouts, bombardments, that now it will always be *quiet* [emphasis in original text]. Yesterday everyone was at the Field of Mars. They watched the first Leningrad salute. Out in the frost it was actually hot. Everyone unbuttoned their coats, no one was afraid of catching cold. It was impossible, of course, to describe the joy. Mainly it is hard to believe that it is now quiet. Wasn't it not so long ago that we pressed ourselves against the walls of the buildings and couldn't lift our heads?[13]

On 24 January, the attempts by Korovnikov to break through and press on to Luga faltered as the units leading the attack – VI Rifle Corps and 29th Tank Brigade – were brought to a halt as a consequence of exhaustion and rising casualties. The rifle divisions of VI Rifle Corps had been in almost continuous action since the start of the offensive and their depleted ranks desperately needed rest; 29th Tank Brigade could field just eight tanks as a result of losses and vehicles left stranded in the swamps and forests. A brief warm spell resulted in widespread flooding, with troops on both sides often finding themselves in a metre or more of water in their trenches. Korovnikov had VII Rifle Corps in reserve and decided that instead of trying to push through the ranks of VI Rifle Corps to try to sustain the earlier attack, he would send the fresh divisions further south. This inevitably led to later criticism that he was diluting his efforts on too wide a front, but simply throwing them into the earlier sector would have resulted in even greater congestion in conditions that were already almost impossible for any sort of concentration and movement. In his reports after the battle, Meretskov wrote that Fifty-Ninth Army failed to carry out adequate reconnaissance and showed little inclination to manoeuvre past German positions, attacking them head-on instead, but this again failed to take account of the ground over which the battle was being fought.

Despite these issues, Lindemann reported tersely shortly before midnight on 24 January that he was facing disaster. The last available men from rear area units had been pressed into service as makeshift infantry and a gap was opening up between Eighteenth Army and its southern neighbour, Sixteenth Army. Moreover, the troops clinging to the ruins of Gatchina were running out of ammunition and the loss of the town was imminent. Küchler promptly telephoned *OKH* to spell out the urgent need to withdraw further; the main 'stop line' that had been considered for *Blau* was along the line of the Luga River, and attempting to defend positions further forward invited the destruction of the formations that Küchler needed to defend the Panther Line. Zeitzler bluntly told Küchler that there was no point in discussing the matter with Hitler: the Führer had already reached the frame of mind that his subordinates described as 'obdurate' and insisted that positions like Gatchina, regarded by Hitler as bulwarks on which the waves of Red Army assaults could be broken, had to be held to the last man. Unable to offer Küchler anything else, he urged the Army Group North commander to be 'a little ruthless' for the time being.[14]

The fighting slackened slightly the following day, giving the exhausted German troops the briefest of respites, but it was largely due to the Red Army reorganising its forces in preparation for further attacks. Almost immediately the attacks resumed and Fedyuninsky's Second Shock Army enjoyed particular success, advancing to capture Elisaveto to the west of Gatchina. From there, the bulk of Fedyuninsky's forces turned west, driving the badly disorganised elements of III SS-Panzer Corps towards Kingisepp and the Estonian frontier. Even if the Gatchina garrison could continue to hold its positions, it faced the increasing risk of being cut off and destroyed.

In Ukraine, far to the south, another major catastrophe was developing for the Wehrmacht. Earlier Soviet offensives had left the German Army Group South holding a large salient projecting towards the northeast, with its tip still on the Dnepr River. Within the salient was the bulk of the German Eleventh Army and two Soviet Fronts commenced attacks on the flanks of the salient on 25 January. The German infantry showed a level of brittleness that was increasingly commonplace: they put up fierce resistance at first and inflicted major casualties on their foes, but were then driven back after the Red Army succeeded in achieving a number of penetrations. The two Soviet Fronts were soon able to advance with increasing freedom and the inevitable German counterattack intended to close the breach failed to make any impression; although several panzer divisions were thrown into the battle, they were all badly worn down from almost continuous combat since the beginning of the Battle of Kursk in the summer of 1943. The consequence of this offensive was the encirclement of nearly 60,000 German troops in a large pocket around the town of Korsun-Shevchenkovsky, but in the western world the battle would always be known as the Cherkassy encirclement, even though Cherkassy lay outside the pocket. German accounts written after the war preferred this latter name, partly because Cherkassy was a larger town and easier to find on maps, and most western accounts then adopted the name. Given this crisis, it was unimaginable that further reinforcements could be spared for the Leningrad sector.

The tide of the war had turned irrevocably against Germany, and whilst it is likely that the turning point had been reached months or even years before, the reality was beyond question by January 1944. Hitler's last gamble was to await the long-expected invasion of Western Europe by Anglo-French forces and to crush it with the forces gathered in France before turning east once more, but it must have been clear to all senior German officers that whilst such a strategy might have been the 'least worst' option available, it was hardly one that had any major chance of success. In the declaration that followed the Casablanca conference of early 1943, the Allied Powers had announced that they would continue to wage war until the unconditional surrender of Germany. Almost immediately after, President Roosevelt added an explanatory note in a radio address, stressing that the declaration and indeed the war was directed against the leadership of the Axis powers, but such nuances were of little importance and – apart from within the small circle of anti-Hitler conspirators – were largely unknown or ignored.[15] Even if men like Küchler, Kluge, and Manstein could see the inevitability of defeat, they saw no alternative but to continue fighting. Only a few were prepared to consider what most found unthinkable: the removal of Hitler and other senior figures so that Germany might be spared the catastrophe of total destruction.

Gatchina was finally abandoned on 26 January, much to the joy of the Red Army. An announcement in Leningrad proclaimed the victory, claiming the complete destruction of the German 11th Infantry Division; the reality was that although the division was badly mauled, it managed to escape to the south. On the same day, restrictions on civilian movements in Leningrad to reduce the danger of injury or death from German artillery attacks were lifted, but there was a warning that the risk of air raids remained. Even as Gatchina was finally cleared, Sviridov's Sixty-Seventh Army pushed ever closer to Slutsk and Tosno. When the leading Soviet formations reached the line of the Izhora River, there was a brief opportunity for the bulk of LIV Corps (now commanded by General Otto Sponheimer) to be encircled, but Sviridov failed to recognise the moment. He granted his exhausted men a day of rest, and Sponheimer was able to extract his equally tired men and withdraw to the west. On the same day, the southern wing of Korovnikov's Fifty-Ninth Army managed to move forward and reach the outskirts of Shimsk, to the west of Lake Ilmen. Other Soviet units reached Medved, a little further to the northwest, driving the Germans away towards the southwest. In an attempt to concentrate his resources better, Korovnikov called a halt to this thrust, replacing the advancing troops with the more static units of 150th Fortified Region – a unique type of unit used in the Red Army to hold sectors where little or no movement was required. The entire sector now came under the control of the newly arrived headquarters of Starikov's Eighth Army, and prepared to concentrate on attacking towards Luga. The intention was for Fifty-Ninth Army to attack the key town from the east, while Eighth Army advanced from the southeast.

On 27 January, even as the Soviet spearheads moved closer to each other in Ukraine (the encirclement at Korsun-Shevchenkovsky would be completed on 28 January) and Govorov and Maslennikov urged their subordinates forward in the north, Hitler summoned his senior commanders to a conference in East Prussia. It must have been a surreal experience for the senior officers who were facing a growing series of crises, any one of which might leave the Wehrmacht facing total defeat in the east. Instead of being able to discuss possible operational and strategic options, or even to hear of new proposals for how Germany could continue the war, they were subjected to a series of monologues from the Führer on the importance of increasing National Socialist awareness at all levels of the army.

It was a reiteration of the attitude that had first come to prominence during the Battle of Moscow in late 1941, the view of Hitler and other senior Nazi figures that the 'fanatical will' to win was as important a factor as numbers and firepower, and by increasing and exploiting this will, Germany could deal with the consequences of being outnumbered and outgunned on the battlefield. For most of the senior officers present, Hitler's arguments failed to take account of three important factors. Firstly, there was little to suggest that the front-line soldiers and officers of the Wehrmacht lacked such a will to fight. Even as the war drew towards its inevitable conclusion, the loyalty of soldiers to Hitler remained strong, and there was widespread dismay and anger at the assassination attempt of July 1944, despite the soldiers being fully aware from their personal experiences that the war was going very badly for Germany. Secondly, despite constant reports of the stubbornness and determination of the soldiers of the Red Army, Hitler and others failed to acknowledge the simple fact that the enemy was equally determined to prevail in what had become an existential struggle between two mutually incompatible world views. And finally, there comes a point where no amount of fanaticism and determination can compensate for material disadvantages. On a global scale, Germany had passed that stage long ago, and the reality of the imbalance was becoming increasingly clear in every theatre of war.

The first part of the 'conference' ended abruptly. After Hitler had told his senior commanders that 'If the end should come one day, it should really be the field marshals and generals who stand by the flags to the last', Manstein – who must have been chafing to get back to his headquarters in order to deal with the developing crisis around Cherkassy – retorted angrily, 'And so they will, *mein Führer*!'[16] It was sufficient to break Hitler's train of thought and the commanders were dismissed. Generalfeldmarschall Wilhelm Keitel, head of *OKW*, then met privately with Manstein and warned him that such interruptions would not be tolerated in future. It should be remembered that the only account of this meeting with Keitel – and the retort that brought Hitler's speech to a premature end – was written by Manstein after the war, and therefore may not be entirely accurate. Other parts of Manstein's memoirs are demonstrably distorted to portray the field marshal in the best possible light.

After this initial monologue, Hitler held personal meetings with each commander. Küchler took this opportunity to spell out the looming disaster in the north. His army group faced several major enemy offensives, he explained, that threatened the cohesion of the entire front line. In the north, the Soviet Second Shock Army was now driving III SS-Panzer Corps towards Kingisepp and the Narva River. Luga faced attacks from the north and east, and the success of either of these would cut the supply lines – and the lines of retreat – of most of the divisions of Eighteenth Army. To stay in the current front line was to invite catastrophic losses, which would leave the army group unable to defend the Panther Line and the Baltic region. Hitler replied by reiterating his prohibition of any withdrawal without his express permission. Küchler stubbornly repeated several of his earlier points, adding that his divisions had suffered 40,000 casualties since the beginning of the year and – in view of Hitler's demands for greater National Socialist awareness and increased fanatical willingness to fight – went on to add that his men had fought as hard as anyone could expect. Hitler dismissed this, telling Küchler that this wasn't true, and that he had heard from other sources that the army group was not fighting at every point with as much determination as was needed. He declined to explain the source of this information.[17] Like every officer whose soldiers were fighting and dying in desperate battles, Küchler must have felt deeply insulted by the remarks of a man who had made so few visits to any of the army group headquarters on the Eastern Front and had never visited Army Group North, let alone going any further forward.

The rarefied atmosphere of Hitler's conference was an utterly different world from the front line. While Hitler harangued his generals and field marshals, Fedyuninsky's Second Shock Army moved closer to Volosovo, astride the road that ran west from Gatchina through Elizaveto to Kingisepp. On 28 January, Lyuban and Chudovo changed hands and in both towns the soldiers of the Red Army were greeted by the few tearful civilians who remained, who told them of tales of persecution, killings, and deportations. Events on the battlefield were rapidly slipping out of control as far as the Germans were concerned. In the north, III SS-Panzer Corps was badly disorganised and falling back towards the

Narva River, with the Red Army hindered as much by the capricious weather and logistic difficulties as it was by German resistance. A gap was opening up on the southern flank of Steiner's corps and the retreating fragments of other corps to the south were unable to establish firm contact with the SS units. There was a growing threat that Fedyuninsky's Second Shock Army would succeed in pushing a mobile force through this gap; if the Red Army was able to do this, it stood an excellent chance of reaching the Narva crossings before III SS-Panzer Corps, thus threatening the destruction of the northern wing of Eighteenth Army. It was vital that this was prevented, and the Germans were fortunate to have two particular assets available. Firstly, many of the Tiger tanks of *Schwere Panzer Abteilung 502* were operating in this area, and the difficulties that the Red Army experienced in moving its heavy artillery forward meant that the heavyweight German tanks were often almost invulnerable. With the innovative flair that was characteristic of the German way of war, a new tactic was rapidly developed, as Carius described:

> Our mission – to cover the retreat of all infantry and artillery units out of the Gatchina-Leningrad area – wasn't easy.
>
> Almost all the units had to be brought back on the single Rollbahn. At the same time, the Russians, always moving between the coast and the Rollbahn, advanced past us and cut the Rollbahn. We then had to move forward to clear the Rollbahn. Ivan was then able to attack the rearguard again. Occasionally, we advanced farther to the north to hold the enemy away from the Rollbahn and prevent his attempts to overtake us.[18]

The other great German asset in this sector was the presence of 366th Grenadier Regiment, commanded by Maximilian Wengler, now promoted to Oberst. In earlier battles to the northeast of Sinyavino, Wengler and his men had demonstrated remarkable resilience and determination, holding their exposed salient that became known as the *Wengler-Nase* in German reports. They repeatedly defied every attempt by the units of Volkhov Front to overrun the salient, earning the grudging respect of the Soviet forces in the sector.[19] The regiment now formed the most reliable component of the German rearguard, working closely with the Tiger tanks of *Schwere Panzer Abteilung 502*. Repeatedly, small groups of Wengler's grenadiers and a few Tigers would hold a position in front of the main German line, either preventing Soviet units from outflanking it or holding up the pursuit along the Rollbahn; the Tigers would then escort the infantry back to safety once the retreating German columns had pulled back further.

The ruins of the town of Volosovo became a key position during the retreat towards Kingisepp, and Wengler's regiment put up prolonged resistance here; in honour of their determined commander, the German soldiers gave the position the nickname of 'Wenglerovo'. But whilst resistance here blocked the Soviet advance along the Gatchina–Kingisepp road, there was a second road to the north to Kingisepp from Krasnoye Selo and this too had to be held to prevent 'Wenglerovo' from being outflanked. Carius was dispatched with four Tiger tanks and a battalion of infantry to secure the village of Opolye on this second road:

> The village was about 100m on the other side of the [main] road. In the morning, everything was still clear of the enemy and the rearward flood of troops rolled on past us … Because many units weren't motorised, the withdrawal proceeded in fits and starts. Except for a few stragglers, the Rollbahn was as good as empty in the afternoon. The village in front of us then came to life.
>
> We saw figures run back and forth, and we had to be on our toes. Once again, it promised to be a very pleasant night. At the onset of darkness, the infantry battalion also departed. I was alone with my four Tigers for far and wide. Fortunately, the Russians weren't in the know about our sticky situation. Perhaps they also had too much respect for us. In any case, they twice set up anti-tank guns in positions across from us, but we never let them fire more than a single round. They didn't make a third attempt.
>
> The Russian commander appeared to believe that we would also leave in the morning. In any case, he assumed that there were all sorts of infantry with us. Otherwise, he would have probably approached our tanks on foot.
>
> Shortly after midnight, vehicles appeared from the east. We were able to recognise them in time as ours. It was a fusilier battalion, which had missed its link-up and advanced to the Rollbahn late. As I later discovered, the commander sat in the only tank that formed the lead. He was completely drunk. The disaster occurred with great alacrity.
>
> The entire unit had no idea of what was going on and moved in the open into the Russian field of fire. A terrible panic followed when the machine-gun and mortar fire kicked off. Many soldiers were hit. With no one in charge, everyone ran back on the Rollbahn instead of seeking cover in the area south of it. Any form of comradeship had disappeared. The only thing that counted was: 'Every man for himself.'
>
> The vehicles drove right over the wounded, and the Rollbahn became a portrait of horror. The entire disaster would have been preventable had the

commander of this mob done his duty and led his men cross-country instead of sitting in his tank and sleeping off his drunk [sic].[20]

Carius and the other Tiger tank commanders did what they could to drive forward and rescue some of the wounded, but their position came under increasing mortar fire. Although mortar bombs couldn't be expected to destroy a Tiger tank, they were nonetheless capable of inflicting significant damage and two of the tanks were soon disabled by holes in their radiators. After securing permission to withdraw, Carius and a second Tiger commander towed the two crippled tanks to safety, narrowly avoiding injury when a German food depot was blown up by the retreating troops. Unfortunately, some of the wounded infantry that the tank crews had rescued had huddled together near the exhaust vents of the tanks for warmth; three died of carbon monoxide poisoning.

As they approached Volosovo, Carius and his fellow Tiger crewmen attempted to link up with Wengler's grenadiers who were pulling back from an exposed position in front of the town. When their position was outflanked, the Tigers were ordered to withdraw to the west, taking their two crippled vehicles with them. They decided to attempt their withdrawal under cover of darkness:

> In order to be able to use the firepower of the two towed vehicles, we had turned their turrets backward. These crews could then cover the rear. We were scarcely on the road and turning to the west when a Russian anti-tank gun started knocking on the turret from the rear. The vehicle in tow, however, soon created some breathing room for us. Despite that, we had to dismount, as the Russians had shot through a tow cable. But even that went well. We only had another 3km until the new line. Of course the Russians on both sides of the Rollbahn wanted to finish us off. A few of them jumped onto our tanks but without success. In this instance, our hand grenades did the trick. Whether the cursing of my steadfast driver Köstler also scared away Ivan could not be determined with any certainty. Shortly before our objective, we received anti-tank fire. Our comrades thought we were the enemy! Not until we shot back with the same calibre did we get any relief.[21]

Like many other German soldiers, Carius had a high opinion of the commander of the rearguard operation:

> Wengler was the model of a troop leader. He was a reservist and a bank director by profession. He had a personality that inspired complete confidence in his people. They would have gone through hell any time for their commander.

His composure was admirable, a characteristic that is priceless in critical situations. On one occasion, we had a situation briefing in a little wooden house about 100m behind the front line. The Russians were shooting from three sides and it was anything but cosy. Wengler was already briefing the situation to us, when an impacting mortar round shattered the window. One officer was grazed on the arm and sought cover under the table. Our Oberst just looked nonchalantly in his direction and said, 'Gentlemen, let's not allow ourselves to be driven crazy by this shooting. Let's stay with the subject matter in hand, so we can finish and return quickly to our posts.'[22]

The defence of 'Wenglerovo' was not a protracted battle, and the rapidly deteriorating situation forced the Germans to abandon their position. Carius and the other personnel of *Schwere Panzer Abteilung 502* were relieved when they were ordered to entrain and head back across the Narva River to relative safety, but even during this withdrawal a Tiger company commander was killed when Soviet tanks opened fire on the car in which he was travelling. As the Germans evacuated Volosovo and headed west, Fedyuninsky arrived on the heels of his troops to see the ruined town for himself:

A terrible picture presented itself here to our eyes. Previously, it had been a clean and picturesque holiday village. Now, blackened chimneys protruded from the snow-covered ashes. The surviving houses were no more than dark hollows, with shattered windows.

The Nazis carried out brutal executions of Soviet civilians in Volosovo and humiliated the local residents in every way possible. I still have a photograph of a 16-year-old Volosovo schoolgirl, Nadia Tuganova, a simple and modest girl. Nadia had been in contact with a partisan detachment. Acting for the partisans, she worked for the German post office and obtained valuable intelligence information.

Shortly before the start of our offensive, the Nazis carried out mass arrests in Volosovo. Nadia Tuganova was taken to a Gestapo dungeon. She was beaten and tortured with electric shocks, but the courageous girl didn't betray the partisans.

On 23 January, the Nazis took 14 prisoners suspected of having links with the partisans to the Terpelitsy Forest to be executed. All of them were taken in turn to pre-dug pits and shot at point-blank range. The Nazi who shot at Nadia was drunk and missed her head. The bullet struck her neck. Losing consciousness, she fell into the pit. After some time, she awoke and heard the sound of a vehicle approaching: the Nazis had brought two more girls who were to be executed ...

With great difficulty, Nadia climbed out of the grave and reached her house where her mother hid her ...

The political workers of the army ensured that the atrocities of the Nazis became known to all units. Hatred for the enemy, an ardent desire to expel the Fascist invaders from our native land carried the soldiers forward.[23]

When they reached German territory, the soldiers of the Red Army would exact a terrible revenge upon German civilians for the atrocities committed in the Soviet Union; hundreds of thousands of German women were raped and there was indiscriminate looting and killing. Just as the Germans had forcibly transported civilians to the west as labourers, the Soviet occupiers followed a similar policy, justifying it on the grounds that such labour was repayment for the destruction that the Germans had inflicted upon the Soviet Union. There were other similarities in the conduct of the two sides. Just as the accounts of German veterans almost never make any mention of the crimes that the Wehrmacht undoubtedly committed in the Soviet Union, Soviet accounts turned a blind eye to the atrocities committed by the Red Army. Even today, this remains a subject that is often ignored in Russia, or justified as a series of acts of revenge.

It seems that Küchler was badly affected by his conversations with Hitler. When he returned to his headquarters, he was very subdued and rather woodenly repeated Hitler's exhortations for greater determination to resist the Soviet attacks, and ordered counterattacks wherever possible. He was greeted on his return with the news that Lyuban, the objective of several Soviet attacks in preceding months, had fallen. Küchler mechanically ordered that it be recaptured and the old front line restored. The reaction of his headquarters staff, who knew that there were no forces available for such counterattacks, can only be imagined. The chief of staff of Army Group North was now Generalleutnant Eberhard Kinzel, who in 1941 had been head of *Fremde Heere Ost* ('Foreign Armies East'), the branch of military intelligence responsible for assessing the strength, capabilities, and intentions of potential and actual foes to the east of Germany. In this role, he had completely failed to assess the true size of the Red Army and his optimistic reports played a considerable part in the failure of Germany to realise just how great a challenge it faced when the invasion of the Soviet Union began. Since then, he had held a series of staff posts before joining the headquarters of Army Group North in early 1943, and any lingering beliefs about the inferiority of the Soviet Union and its armed forces were long gone. Whilst Hitler had forbidden Küchler from carrying out any withdrawals, Kinzel reasoned that the exigencies of the situation required immediate action and that he would simply issue instructions verbally via staff officer channels, thus leaving no written evidence of disobedience.

The chief of staff at Eighteenth Army was Oberst Albert Friedrich Foertsch, and he wasted no time in passing Kinzel's instructions to Lindemann. The degree to which Lindemann was aware of the subterfuge between the staff officers of Army Group North and Eighteenth Army isn't known, but it is inconceivable that he was unaware of Hitler's unwillingness to countenance withdrawals. Whatever doubts he might have had were put aside owing to the urgency of the moment and orders were issued for a general withdrawal. Satisfied that for the moment at least, disaster had been averted, Kinzel turned his attention to Küchler, impressing upon him the futility of relying on 'fanatical will' to hold back the Red Army. There were limits to what could be achieved through quiet disobedience, and it was vital for the army group commander to secure greater freedom of action. On 29 January, Küchler agreed to send a further report to *OKH* and Hitler: Eighteenth Army had effectively been split into three fragments. One – III SS-Panzer Corps – was retreating towards Narva; a second was in danger of being isolated close to Gatchina, even though it was falling back; and the third was to the east, with both its flanks exposed. It was inconceivable that any coherent front line could be created forward of the Luga River.[24] This was something that had been recognised by Army Group North's staff officers during the planning of *Blau*, and they had always intended for the first phase of the withdrawal to the Panther Line to be to the Luga River. Defending any sort of line forward of the river had been considered during planning but ruled out as there were no natural features that would be of benefit to the defenders, and there was too great a risk that in the dense woodland and marshy ground, the Red Army might be able to infiltrate past whatever line the Germans chose and might then be able to reach the Luga before the retreating Wehrmacht formations.

After the reorganisation of the southern flank of Volkhov Front with Eighth Army taking control of units to the southwest of Novgorod, the renewed attack on Luga had begun on 27 January, even as Hitler's conference in East Prussia was starting. The northern part of the attack was led by CXII Corps and pushed forward and crossed the Luga River at several points, but was unable to push further west and northwest; as a consequence, the German XXVIII Corps, which had been badly outflanked on its southern flank by this advance, was able to pull back almost unmolested. The brief pause in operations had given the men of the Soviet VI Rifle Corps some much-needed rest and they managed to reach the Luga River to the east of Batetskiy, but could go no further. The southern part of the attack fared little better. A complex battle developed around Peredolskaya, midway between Luga and Shimsk, as Meretskov later described:

> In accordance with the general operational plan, the partisans moved to link up with the units of Eighth Army. Major Karitsky's 5th Partisan Brigade captured Peredolskaya station on the morning of 27 January and immediately notified Volkhov Front headquarters of this by radio. I promptly ordered VI Rifle Corps to accelerate its advance and 7th Tank Brigade rushed forward to the railway line. But in the meantime the Nazis sent an armoured train carrying additional infantry from the north and attempted to recapture Peredolskaya. Despite this, the partisans managed to hold on until the units of the Red Army arrived. At that point, 372nd Rifle Division [part of VII Rifle Corps] entrenched itself firmly in Peredolskaya, releasing the tanks that were to move forward to Okluzhye, bypassing Luga to the south and linking up with more partisans who were still disrupting the German front line.[25]

The partisans were perhaps the most mobile units in the battle – they had been operating in this area for months and knew all the routes through the forests and swamps, but they lacked the heavy weaponry to overcome German units. Despite being badly overstretched, the Germans managed to hold the Red Army to the east of Luga, thus allowing the withdrawal of XXVIII Corps to the north to continue. A signal arrived at Meretskov's headquarters late on 29 January, making clear the sense of frustration and exasperation in *Stavka*:

> The enemy's grouping that is operating in front of Leningrad Front's left wing and Volkhov Front's right wing is withdrawing towards Luga and Pskov. Meanwhile, the offensive by Volkhov Front's main grouping along the Luga axis is developing slowly and *Stavka*'s demand to capture Luga no later than 29–30 January has not been met.
>
> *Stavka* now orders:
>
> The Front's main forces are to capture Luga as quickly as possible. Mobile units are to cut the road and rail links south of Luga no later than 30–31 January. The Front's left wing is to dig in firmly along the line Utogorsh–Shimsk in order to protect the main force's operations towards Luga.
>
> After occupying Luga, [Meretskov should] anticipate conducting an offensive towards Pskov from the Luga-Shimsk region.[26]

A further signal arrived from Moscow almost immediately, stressing the need to concentrate on Luga – operations towards the southwest were not to become a priority for Volkhov Front. Reinforcements of both men and tanks were promised, but it would take time for them to arrive. Such reinforcements were essential. The armoured units of Volkhov Front were badly depleted and most of the brigades and regiments fielded fewer than ten vehicles. In order to prevent the Germans from threatening the southern flank of the attack towards Luga, *Stavka* also urged Popov's 2nd Baltic Front to show more energy. Popov's formations had been regrouping for several days and a new attack was planned on the German Sixteenth Army at Novosokolniki using Sixth Army, Tenth Guards Army, and parts of Twenty-Second Army. It was hoped that this attack – aimed at the southern flank of Army Group North – would at least tie down German units, and at best would create a threat to separate Army Group North from Army Group Centre. Hansen, the commander of Sixteenth Army, was fully aware of the danger. He waited until he judged that the Soviet attack was imminent, and then ordered the abandonment of Novosokolniki. Somewhat characteristically, the Red Army's pursuit of the withdrawing Germans was too slow and cautious to achieve anything, and Hansen was even able to release substantial forces to reinforce the front line around Luga.

The first phase of the Soviet winter campaign in the Leningrad sector saw the link-up between Fedyuninsky's Second Shock Army in the Oranienbaum bridgehead with the rest of Leningrad Front, and as the last days of January dawned, the second phase was coming to an end, with Army Group North slowly forced to abandon the heavily fortified line that it had held for so long. The siege of Leningrad was now over with the Germans driven back at least 60 miles from the city perimeter. This was a considerable achievement, especially in light of the failures of 1942 and 1943, but a greater opportunity – to destroy large bodies of German troops before they could withdraw – slipped through the fingers of Govorov and Meretskov. Although there was considerable criticism of both Fronts for the manner in which their units operated, much of this was misdirected. By launching such an operation in the depths of winter, commanders at all levels took risks with the weather, which proved to be unreliable and oscillated between snowstorms that made the use of air power almost impossible and spells of warmer weather that turned the landscape into a sea of mud. The Red Army had learned, at great cost, how to pick apart German defensive positions, but found it almost impossible to move sufficient supplies and artillery forward to sustain early successes; moreover, many division and corps commanders lacked the experience and expertise to take advantage of more fluid battle conditions. Such failings had repeatedly been identified and if they persisted, this was as much a reflection on the failure of higher commands to organise appropriate training as it was the fault of the commanders themselves.

Leningrad was now safe from artillery attacks or any possibility of the Wehrmacht renewing its siege, though it remained within range of Luftwaffe raids. The German Army Group North had narrowly escaped being caught in untenable positions and was slowly withdrawing towards the Panther Line, but there remained a possibility that it might still face destruction before the withdrawal was complete.

CHAPTER 12

SCHILD UND SCHWERT

For a professional soldier like Küchler, the gradual disintegration and collapse of his army group must have been a painful and frustrating experience. If he had been permitted to execute *Blau* as he had originally planned, it is very likely that his troops would have been able to pull back from Leningrad without major losses, and the Red Army had repeatedly demonstrated that it lacked the levels of initiative and skill at middle and lower levels to react to a fast-changing situation. Army Group North could have pulled back in stages, much as Model's Ninth Army did during *Büffel*, the withdrawal from the Rzhev salient in early 1943, and sufficient reserves would have been released to ensure that future Soviet assaults could be defeated. Even if some of those reserves had then been transferred to other theatres, Sixteenth and Eighteenth Armies would still have been in far better shape, with morale intact and most of the heavy equipment – artillery, engineering equipment, supplies, etc. – stockpiled behind the Panther Line. Instead, Hitler's refusal to permit an early withdrawal, coupled with Lindemann's misplaced optimism, led to huge damage being done to the Wehrmacht. It was no longer purely a question of pulling back from one set of positions to another in an orderly fashion; the survival of the army group was now at risk. Moreover, if Army Group North collapsed completely, the entire German position on the Eastern Front would unravel. For over a year, Manstein had been warning of a similar sequence of events destroying the Eastern Front from the south; there now existed the real possibility of the same outcome being triggered from the north.

In an attempt to secure the freedom that he regarded as essential if he was to extract his armies from imminent disaster, Küchler flew back to East Prussia on 30 January. Once more, he described the looming catastrophe. Grudgingly,

Hitler agreed to pull back all units to the Luga Line, but insisted that it had to be held at all costs. All gaps in the front line were to be sealed with immediate counterattacks. Such orders might have been possible to implement if permission to pull back to the Luga Line had been given sooner, but it was now unworkable. When Küchler passed instructions to his headquarters, his staff officers reported with dismay that substantial Soviet forces had already crossed the Luga River to the northwest of the town of Luga at Staritsa. It was a recurring issue: Hitler would refuse permission for a timely withdrawal on the grounds that the benefits of such withdrawals never appeared and the only outcome was a request for further withdrawals, and he then gave permission for the withdrawal at the last possible moment, by which time events had moved on significantly and the withdrawal was no longer going to be a sufficient response to the situation, thus setting up a repeating cycle with the critical delay in granting permission effectively creating the justification used to refuse permission.

Wearily, Küchler discussed the matter with Zeitzler, who promised to inform Hitler that the Luga Line was compromised and couldn't be held. He also told the commander of Army Group North that Hitler wished to speak to him the following day, 31 January. It was customary for business to commence fairly late in the morning in Hitler's headquarters and the daily conference began at noon. Küchler was informed that he was dismissed from his post. His replacement would be Generaloberst Walter Model.

It was the end of Küchler's military career. He remained part of the 'Führer reserve' for the rest of the war and although he was approached by the anti-Hitler conspirators Carl Goerdeler and Johannes Popitz, he declined to join their movement but also remained silent about their overtures.[1] At the end of the conflict, he was arrested by US occupation forces and worked for several months with the US Army Historical Division, helping to draft a history of German military operations. He regarded it as essential that any such account should be written in a manner that praised the German Army, and wrote a directive for those working under his supervision: 'The deeds of Germans are seen from a German perspective, and are defined and form a memorial for our troops ... The achievements of our soldiers are to be duly acknowledged and highlighted. Of course, this must not result in the truth being disregarded.'[2]

When the department dealing with the German experience of the war closed in 1961, it had employed more than 300 senior German officers, including Franz Halder, former chief of the German general staff. The documents that they produced may have been – largely – correct from a strictly factual point of view, but they deliberately distorted the historical record; the truth may not have been 'disregarded', but it was far from the complete truth. Küchler and other senior officers consistently attempted to portray the Wehrmacht as fighting with honour in a crusade against Bolshevism, blaming all atrocities on organisations operating behind the front line. The attitude of Halder, who led the German team for much of its existence, was unequivocal: 'The entire Wehrmacht, but above all the army high command, were simply historical victims of Hitler, or at the very most instruments of his criminal policies.'[3]

Despite his attempts to prove his usefulness to the US military, Küchler was brought before the Nuremberg Tribunals as part of the wave of prosecutions that followed the original International Military Tribunal. Together with several other senior officers, he faced multiple charges. Many of these related to the mistreatment and deaths of Soviet prisoners of war. He had no choice but to accept that the death rate of prisoners in the first winter of the war had been shockingly high; about 2.8 million prisoners perished, through a mixture of exposure to the cold weather and starvation.[4] However, he claimed that this was due almost entirely to the exceptionally cold weather, and that the Wehrmacht deliberately exaggerated the death rate in an attempt to secure more rations. However weak this defence was, he didn't even have this level of excuse for other charges, including his willing collaboration with – and deliberate use of – *Einsatzgruppe A* to massacre innocent civilians. He was found guilty of causing the deaths of prisoners of war, the use of forced civilian labour, passing on the infamous 'Commissar Order', and involvement in the persecution and killing of Jews in areas under his control. In October 1948 he was sentenced to 20 years' imprisonment.

If he had been extradited to the Soviet Union, Küchler might have been executed for his crimes; there was a brief period when the Soviet Union suspended the death penalty, but even if he had been tried during that time the outcome would have been a long sentence of hard labour, which would probably have proved fatal for a man who was 67 years old when he faced judgement at Nuremberg. Instead, his sentence was reviewed in 1951 and reduced to 12 years, at a time when the Western Powers were increasingly minded to overlook German criminal behaviour during the war due to the growing need to integrate West Germany into the post-war world. Just two years later – having served only five years in prison – he was paroled on medical grounds. He lived for a further 18 years. Like almost all other senior Wehrmacht figures, at no stage did he ever express any remorse for the crimes that had been committed in areas under his control. Although many have argued that there was little that such men could have done, the behaviour of others – for example, Generalfeldmarschall

Ewald von Kleist, commander of First Panzer Army and Army Group A in the Caucasus region – shows that refusing to cooperate with criminal activities was perfectly possible.[5]

Küchler's replacement, Model, was at the height of his personal popularity with Hitler. Unlike so many other senior Wehrmacht officers, he didn't come from a traditional Prussian background with a long line of illustrious military ancestors; he was the son of a schoolmaster who taught in a girls' school near Magdeburg. During his service as a junior officer in the First World War, he demonstrated traits that were to characterise his military career: he was known for being determined and outspoken to the point of tactlessness, and made few friends amongst his contemporaries. During the invasion of the Soviet Union he commanded 3rd Panzer Division, a post that he had taken up in November 1940. In the months before *Barbarossa*, he demonstrated another characteristic form of behaviour, frequently ignoring normal military protocol and lines of command and dealing directly with junior figures in the division. Whilst this gained him the personal respect of those juniors, it did nothing for his relationship with his more immediate subordinates who felt that their status and authority was constantly undermined. His division led the northern pincer in the great encirclement battle near Kiev in August and September 1941 and he was then appointed to command of XLI Panzer Corps for the Battle of Moscow. His reputation preceded him – the entire staff of the panzer corps requested transfers.

As the Soviet winter counteroffensive tore huge holes in the German lines in December 1941, Model's improvisation and defensive ability both became increasingly prominent. One of his innovations was the cobbling together of battlegroups using troops from different divisions and from rear area units, and his ruthless drive and determination played a large part in helping to stabilise the German lines; on several occasions, he personally stopped retreating columns, pistol in hand.[6] At a time when Hitler was dismissing so many senior commanders who he felt had failed him, the Führer saw the prickly, fiercely determined Model – free of all the 'taints' of a conservative Prussian background – as the ideal example of a modern National Socialist commander, and appointed him to command of Ninth Army in January 1942. It was in this post that his reputation as a great defensive commander was cemented. During 1942, the Red Army made repeated attempts to destroy Ninth Army in and around Rzhev, and on every occasion Model and his men fought off the assaults, inflicting huge losses on the Soviet forces, before withdrawing from the Rzhev salient in an exemplary, orderly retreat. During the retreat, all male civilians were forcibly evacuated, water supplies were poisoned, and cities and towns were deliberately devastated in an attempt to create a barren zone from which the Red Army would struggle to operate.

To an extent, Model was fortunate in that he had several excellent corps commanders as his immediate subordinates in Ninth Army, and this was still a time when the Wehrmacht had comparatively good resources, with most divisions able to field sufficient reserves. These divisions also had good levels of manpower in their rear area formations, which Model ruthlessly combed to create ad hoc combat units; in later years of the war, attempts to repeat this were less successful because so many men had already been moved to combat units and their replacements in the rear area units were often men who had been exempted from service in the past due to age, disability, etc, and the rear area units were themselves now far from establishment strength and had barely sufficient personnel to fulfil their functions.

On many occasions, Model demanded reinforcements from *OKH*, and his high standing with Hitler resulted in these demands being treated far more sympathetically than those of less favoured commanders. Even though he ordered withdrawals that would have earned the anger of the Führer if carried out by other commanders, he was given considerable leeway because Hitler believed Model would only order such withdrawals if there was really no alternative. He was characteristically unafraid of using his privileged position, ensuring that when his Ninth Army was used to attack the northern side of the Kursk salient in the summer of 1943, he kept back sufficient reserves to be able to defend against the Soviet Operation *Kutuzov* around the city of Oryol. As fighting in that operation died down, he was granted a much-needed period of leave, and was thus available when the crises of early 1944 erupted. It seems that he was originally going to be given command of Army Group South, whose commander, Manstein, had an increasingly fractious relationship with Hitler, but the need to replace Küchler with a trusted commander who had previously demonstrated great defensive prowess took priority.

As he boarded a plane to fly to Army Group North's headquarters in Pskov, Model sent a radio signal to his new command: they were to hold firm and make no further withdrawals until he arrived. If he was aware of Lindemann's role in creating the catastrophic situation with his overly confident assertions that Eighteenth Army would be able to defeat any Soviet offensive, he gave no sign of it, adding in his signal that he had worked with Lindemann in the past and reminding the commander of Eighteenth Army of their mutual trust.[7]

Model had been in Hitler's headquarters for several days before flying north and therefore had at least some idea of what awaited him. The details were laid before him by Kinzel when he arrived in his new headquarters. At the beginning of the year, Eighteenth Army had fielded a total infantry combat strength of nearly 58,000 men, but in the heavy fighting of January this had been reduced to just 17,000. Casualties included several senior officers. There were two Luftwaffe field divisions that had been heavily involved in the attempts to prevent Fedyuninsky's Second Shock Army and Maslennikov's Forty-Second Army from linking up. Geerkens, commander of 9th Field Division, was killed on 24 January, and Wedel, commander of 10th Field Division, would be wounded almost as Model was taking up his post and would die in hospital in early February. There was no longer a coherent front line, with retreating units forced to pull in their flanks for protection and thus losing contact with their neighbours. To make matters even worse, the general faith that everyone in Army Group North placed in the safety of the Panther Line was unjustified: only about half of the planned fortifications had actually been built, not least because of the difficulties in obtaining sufficient forced labour. There was a network of slave labour camps in northeast Estonia, with a workforce made up largely of Jews from Lithuania and Latvia. These workers were used in the arduous and often dangerous work of extracting oil shale, and although some had been diverted to help with the construction of the Panther Line, the SS – who had control of these camps – was unwilling to release more than the bare minimum.

As had been the case in XLI Panzer Corps outside Moscow, Model clashed almost immediately with the staff officers in his new post. Kinzel had been chief of staff of Army Group North for a year and had established a close working relationship with Küchler, whose working practices were very different from those of Model. As was his usual practice, Model often spent prolonged periods away from his headquarters, visiting front-line units; by contrast, Küchler had been a more 'traditional' senior commander, operating via the established chains of command.

The years of the siege had been generally comfortable times for the staff of the headquarters of Army Group North; once the staff settled into their accommodation in late 1941, they stayed in the same location for over two years. The urbane Küchler had been punctiliously correct in his behaviour towards his subordinates, with everyone living in considerable comfort in Pskov. Kinzel was accustomed to working late into the night with a resultant later start in the morning, but Model insisted on seeing his chief of staff at 0730 before he set off on his tour of division and corps headquarters. This took Kinzel by surprise and on the first morning of working together, Kinzel appeared before Model still wearing pyjamas with a greatcoat thrown over his shoulders, resulting in an angry exchange. Model grumbled about Kinzel's 'inappropriate, insolent get-up', triggering an indignant response. On his flight to the front line that morning, Model ordered his personal adjutant, Hauptsturmführer Rudolph Maeker – it was highly irregular for a Wehrmacht officer to have a member of the SS in such a role – to change the sleeping arrangements in Army Group North's headquarters. Meanwhile, Kinzel unburdened himself in a telephone call to Generalleutnant Hans Krebs, chief of staff of Army Group Centre. 'He's totally mad,' he told his old friend, 'he just hasn't realised it yet.'[8] Shortly after, Kinzel contacted Zeitzler at *OKH* to request a transfer. Discussing the request with Generalleutnant Adolf Heusinger, chief of the *Operationsabteilung* ('Operations Department'), Zeitzler commented: 'Others have said the same thing before. But I can't constantly change chiefs of staff whenever Model shows up somewhere. The Führer always sends him to the hottest spots.'[9]

One of Model's first acts was to forbid anyone from talking about the Panther Line, in accordance with Hitler's opinion that the lure of a theoretically safer position to the rear would reduce the will of the troops to fight in their current lines. As he travelled from one location to another, he issued a torrent of instructions. Officers who outlined problematic situations to him were expected also to provide three possible solutions, and everyone was expected to show greater determination. When his plane landed at the airfield near Dorpat, he noticed that none of the Stuka dive-bombers were ready for action. He demanded a reason (even though control of Luftwaffe assets lay outside his command). The commander of the Stuka squadron explained that it wasn't 'Stuka weather' as it was too foggy. Model's response was typical: 'Not Stuka weather? You think so? But infantry weather – that's always the case?' The Stukas took off shortly after.

Many of the staff officers who worked with Model in his various posts criticised him for failing to grasp the difference between tactical and operational command, feeling that – like Rommel – he overly involved himself in the minutiae of individual engagements. But to a large extent, the path that his career followed prevented him from demonstrating any operational talents. In his time with 3rd Panzer Division, he showed great tactical flair and this perhaps shaped his behaviour in later years, but once he became first a corps commander, then an army commander, and finally an army group commander, he was almost always in a position where he was reacting to circumstances imposed upon him by events and an increasingly aggressive Red Army. The exception was when he carried out the attack on the northern side of the Kursk salient. Here, his operational plan proved to fall short of what was required. Worried that the Soviet defences would take too great a toll on his armour, he attempted to break the Red Army's lines with his infantry, resulting in heavy losses, and when his armour was then committed it made no real impact. But the opposing point of view is that his caution avoided a crisis when the Soviet *Kutuzov* counteroffensive began. If he had committed his forces fully in *Zitadelle*, he would not have had sufficient reserves to deal with the assault on Oryol. But now, regardless of his past record, he faced a greater challenge than before, attempting to prevent the disintegration of an entire army group.

Obdurate refusal to consider the possibility of retreat was clearly not an option, given the growing collapse of Eighteenth Army. Throughout the region, the Red Army was in positions from where it could threaten to inflict serious defeats on the Wehrmacht. In the north, the two formations that had initiated the collapse of the overall German position – Second Shock Army and Forty-Second Army – either were already on the line of the Luga River or were approaching it; in places, Soviet troops were already across the frozen river. In their path, III SS-Panzer Corps and XXVI Corps could do little more than mount delaying actions. On the eastern flank of this group, the Soviet Sixty-Seventh Army was approaching Luga from the north. Two armies from Volkhov Front – Fifty-Ninth Army and the newly re-formed Eighth Army – continued to edge closer to Luga from the east and southeast, with Fifty-Fourth Army approaching from the northeast. LIV Corps headquarters had been ordered to proceed to northern Estonia, handing over what little remained of its combat assets to other corps. The battered remnants of most of the German Eighteenth Army that remained facing the Soviet assaults – from west to east, L, XXVIII and XXXVIII Corps – faced multiple threats. If Sixty-Seventh Army and Fifty-Fourth Army managed to link up in their converging attacks, L Corps was threatened with encirclement, and if Fifty-Fourth Army and its southern neighbours, Fifty-Ninth and Eighth Armies, closed the remaining gap between them, XXVIII Corps and much of XXXVIII Corps risked being trapped and destroyed. The only German divisions available to Model that were still relatively intact and able to fight as coherent roles were 12th Panzer Division, recently arrived from the south, and 58th Infantry Division, released by Sixteenth Army.

In the past, Model had mastered defensive crises by using a combination of factors: strict enforcement of his orders forbidding retreat; the rapid organisation of local reserves and the transfer of additional reinforcements from other sectors; energetic counterattacks; and, to an extent, reliance on the relative lack of expertise in the Red Army when it came to mounting and sustaining offensive operations. In late January 1944, a new approach was needed. There were no local reserves and no prospect of reinforcements from other sectors; counterattacks

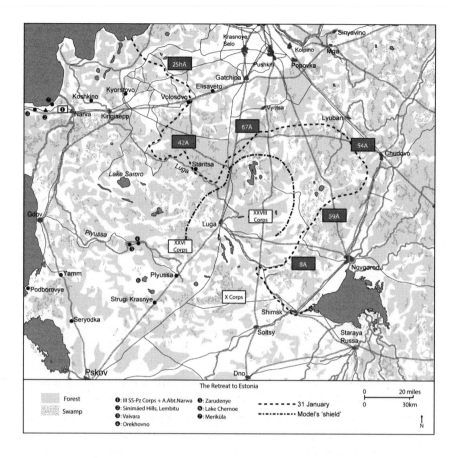

The Retreat to Estonia

Forest	❶: III SS-Pz Corps + A.Abt.Narwa	❺: Zarudenye	- - - - - 31 January
Swamp	❷: Sinimäed Hills, Lembitu	❻: Lake Chernoe	········ Model's 'shield'
	❸: Vaivara	❼: Meriküla	
	❹: Orekhovno		

0   20 miles
0   30km

were likely to be of limited efficacy due to the shattered state of Eighteenth Army's divisions; and whilst *Stavka* continued to express dissatisfaction at the manner in which the Red Army was conducting operations, the performance of Leningrad and Volkhov Fronts was nonetheless a considerable improvement on earlier offensives. Instead, Model attempted to implement a new form of defence, one that he had discussed at length with Hitler before taking up his new command. The Führer had named this *Schild und Schwert* ('shield and sword'), and the concept was a simple one: German units were to withdraw if under pressure, conducting a determined defence that eroded enemy strength, while concentrating sufficient forces to mount a counterthrust to restore the situation. There was little that was new in this, as it largely restated long-standing German military doctrine, and its efficacy in the current situation in the northern sector was doubtful. Firstly, the forests and swamps of the region and the numerous rivers and streams, combined with a poor road network, were not suited to rapid, mobile operations of the sort that would be required for successful counterattacks. Secondly, the forces required for such counterattacks were – with the exception of 12th Panzer Division – almost non-existent, and there was a limit to how much could be expected from a single division on such a large battlefield. But Model knew that even after taking into account Hitler's high opinion of his favourite defensive commander, getting permission for withdrawals would be difficult at best, and he was far more likely to secure the operational freedom he required if he described such withdrawals as precursors to counterattacks. One of his first steps was to try to sort out the tangle of units staggering back before the blows of the Red Army. LIV Corps had already handed over control of its remaining units to neighbouring corps headquarters, and Sponheimer was withdrawing his staff to northern Estonia. Here, they would form *Armee Abteilung Narwa* ('Army Detachment Narva'), taking command of a mixture of units rapidly being organised for the defence of Estonia.

In its attempts to destroy Eighteenth Army, *Stavka* issued fresh instructions at the end of January. First Shock Army was transferred from the northern wing of 2nd Baltic Front to Volkhov Front in order to give Meretskov more striking power. With these additional forces, he was to seize Luga as quickly as possible, with the expectation of then advancing rapidly towards Pskov. Leningrad Front was to continue its two major operations: its west flank was to force the lower Luga River and push on towards Narva and Estonia, while its east flank would close in on Luga. After completing the capture of Luga, Leningrad Front would be able to pull Sixty-Seventh Army out of line and place it in reserve, allowing it to recover its strength prior to deployment in an attack into Estonia. Almost immediately, there was a report of success: Second Shock Army seized Kingisepp on 1 February with one rifle corps, while other units reached and crossed the Narva River at two points between the city of Narva and the Baltic coast. It was a significant moment, because this was where the no-longer-mentioned Panther Line was meant to stop further Soviet advances. After they cautiously crossed the frozen river, the Soviet riflemen found themselves in a forested strip that ran parallel to the river. There were a few scattered positions that put up resistance, but it was far from what Küchler and others had imagined when they had talked of pulling back to this defensive line. But this was at least partly due to the losses suffered by Eighteenth Army. It now lacked the strength to man the planned line, especially as so much of Eighteenth Army was still fighting further to the southeast. The sector running from the city of Narva to the sea was of particular importance: just 14 miles to the west was the town of Vaivara, where the Germans were running their shale extraction programme. Loss of this would leave the Reich – already struggling with constant shortages of fuel – in an even more compromised state.

The bulk of Steiner's III SS-Panzer Corps was gathered immediately to the east of Narva, holding a bridgehead across the Narva River to which various units were retreating. Although the SS units had started the year with a significant number of tanks, most of these had now been lost either through being destroyed or because they were abandoned. During 1943, many panzer-equipped formations received the new Panther tank, but the first models proved to be very unreliable and it was usual for battalions to lose as many vehicles as a consequence of breakdowns as from enemy action. If these stranded tanks could be recovered, there was a reasonable chance of them being repaired, but recovery became far more difficult when the Germans were in retreat; even vehicles that had previously been dragged back to workshops had to be destroyed to prevent them falling into enemy hands. With the remaining motorised elements – primarily an armoured reconnaissance battalion – forming a rearguard, the rest of the SS formations made their way back towards Narva largely on foot. One battalion from *SS-Danmark*, in theory designated as panzergrenadiers, walked 24 miles through the snow to reach Kyorstovo, to the northeast of Kingisepp, only to find that it now faced a further long march before it could reach safety. Part of *SS-Norge* was cut off and lost contact with higher commands, and another battlegroup made up of a mixture of Norwegian SS and naval coastal defence formations found itself having to deal with a plethora of contradictory orders. In just one day, the battlegroup received no fewer than seven orders either from Steiner's headquarters or directly from Hitler's headquarters, and the frustrated battlegroup commander, Brigadeführer Christian Peder Kryssing, ordered the telephone switchboard dismantled. He had already dispatched a small force to secure the bridge over the Luga River at Koshkino, seven miles northeast of Narva, and pulled back with his men without any further contact from above.[10]

What remained of 227th Infantry Division – without Wengler's 366th Grenadier Regiment, still fighting as a rearguard – which had started the year on the Sinyavino Heights was deployed in a series of weak battlegroups along the Narva River between the city and the coast, supplemented by a few battalion-strength groups of soldiers hastily cobbled together from rear area units, occupation forces, and naval personnel. As they wearily arrived in Narva, the soldiers of Kryssing's *Kampfgruppe Küste* were directed to reinforce this line. The Narva River flows into the city from the southwest, crossing a large area of flood plain and swamps with trackless forests – much the same terrain that extends to the east, to the Volkhov River and beyond. The defenders of this part of the German line were even weaker than to the north of the city – just a single battalion of Norwegian SS and some police units. In a retreat full of a growing sense of doom, there was a brief moment for the SS to celebrate: unexpectedly, the remnants of the company of *SS-Norge* that had been cut off further to the east managed to reach the Narva bridgehead. Only 30 men remained, and even their survival was tempered by a last setback: at the very moment that they reached safety, they suffered a further loss when their commander was killed by 'friendly fire' from the German defences.[11]

Even if III SS-Panzer Corps could hold the Red Army at arm's length before Narva, it seemed as if opportunities existed for Fedyuninsky's forces to cross the river to north and south and then encircle Steiner's men. To the west of Narva, a plain stretches away to the Estonian capital, Tallinn. Near Narva are the Sinimäed Hills, three relatively small hills in an east-to-west line between the coast in the north and the swamps and forests to the south. If the Red Army could reach this area, either by forcing the Narva River north of the city or by crossing it to the southwest of the city, Narva would be cut off.

But however enticing the prospects seemed, the reality on the ground was rather different – a good example of the seductive nature of maps and how they can give misleading impressions. The lower Narva valley, between the city and the coast, has relatively high banks. Whilst the frozen river was easy for infantrymen to cross, moving vehicles across was a far more difficult exercise. Even if the ice was thick enough, the banks would require substantial modification on either side of the river to create approach and exit points, and the dense woodland on either bank was a further obstacle. To the south of Narva, the ground was soft, making the approach of vehicles to the river and their subsequent advance to the west problematic. In the city of Narva itself, the crossing point of the river is dominated even today by Hermann Castle, first established in 1256 by the Danes, and facing it on the east side of the river is the Ivangorod Fortress, built about 200 years later by the Muscovite Prince Ivan III as a barrier to incursions from the west. The truth that was easy to overlook when giving the maps a cursory glance was that the crossing at Narva, with its fortresses, had been there for centuries with no attempt made to create permanent crossings to the north or south for the simple reason that it was the only practicable point at which to create a bridge.

The bridgehead secured by the Soviet troops across the Narva River between Narva and the coast was typical of the manner in which Soviet units increasingly operated as the war progressed. The thrust across central Ukraine in 1943 resulted in several Soviet units reaching the Dnepr River either on the heels of the retreating German units or even in some cases before the Germans could pull back, and there were repeated attempts – not always successful – to secure bridgeheads before the Germans could prepare proper defensive positions. Improvised bridgeheads carry substantial risks for an army. Such operations become a race between the two sides to move troops to the area, and in the case of the Narva crossing the Red Army had a major disadvantage: the road network to the west of the river, in what had been independent Estonia until the Soviet seizure in 1940, was far better than the road network to the east in Russia itself. Consequently, even if the Soviet forces in the area outnumbered the Germans substantially, it was far easier for the Germans to move mobile forces to oppose and attack the bridgehead than for Fedyuninsky's Second Shock Army to reinforce and develop it.

Modern armies have detailed procedures for bridgehead operations. These include extensive reconnaissance; the provision of adequate artillery support, particularly long-range guns that may have to support combat on the far bank until it becomes possible to move guns across the river; special training and rehearsal to ensure that the seizure of the bridgehead proceeds as smoothly as possible; the bridging units themselves, adequately equipped and supplied to be able to perform their primary function; strict traffic control at every level, including entry to and exit from the bridgehead and traffic across the crossing point; and a clear plan to exploit the bridgehead as soon as possible and to advance decisively from it. Many of these considerations are impossible in hastily improvised bridgehead operations, and in any case the Red Army lacked the expertise for such tasks even when there was adequate time to plan and implement them. Fedyuninsky described in his memoirs how the troops designated for the task of establishing a bridgehead underwent special training, but the reality described by Karl Iuliysovich Rammus, a Leningrader who served as a scout in the Red Army, suggests that this training fell far short of what was required:

> [The scouts] were driven hard to make big jumps forward during the war. For example, we often advanced 20–30km at a time. These advances were over rough terrain with full gear. We also forced water barriers without special equipment. In other words, we had to find out for ourselves how and on what to cross the river. This happened on the Luga when I was assigned to a reconnaissance company. We practiced crossing the Luga. To do so, we had to find a log or the devil knows what else to build some kind of small raft in order to cross the water obstacle.[12]

Despite the terrain on either side of Narva favouring the defenders, the Germans were desperately in need of reinforcements if the line was to be held against even the limited forces that Fedyuninsky could project over the Narva River. Fortunately for Army Group North, a new division was available. In August 1942, an Estonian Legion had been established, which served for a while with *SS-Wiking* and ultimately formed the core of a new SS formation; in order to create a larger unit, several Estonian battalions were grouped into 20th *Estnische SS-Freiwilligen* Division ('Estonian SS Volunteer Division') without any consultation. The new division was formally created on 24 January 1944 under the command of Brigadeführer Franz Augsberger and was sent immediately to reinforce the Narva positions. In the meantime, *Kampfgruppe Küste* mounted a counterattack against the Soviet troops that had crossed the river between Narva and the coast and broke the Soviet bridgehead in two. Meanwhile, further reinforcements arrived from Army Group Centre: the Panzergrenadier Division *Feldherrnhalle* was ordered north, and its first units began to deploy to cover the stretch of the Narva River between Lake Peipus and Narva itself. Here too, the Red Army secured a large bridgehead with the intention of pushing northwest to outflank the Narva–Ivangorod bridgehead held by III SS-Panzer Corps, but it proved almost impossible to bring sufficient heavy equipment across the river and the neighbouring swamps to make a quick advance. By the time that the Soviet troops had gathered their strength, *Feldherrnhalle* and other German units were in position to hold them off. There were repeated attacks by the Red Army to reach the Sinimäed Hills from the southeast, with heavy fighting along the edge of a forest line to the south of the high ground; the German infantry, supported by *Feldherrnhalle* and the Tiger tanks of *Schwere Panzer Abteilung 502*, defeated every attempt, comfortably dealing with the few Soviet tanks that were brought across the river. But the terrain difficulties that hindered the Red Army also hindered German counterattacks, and it proved impossible to eliminate this southern bridgehead.[13]

Even as Kingisepp fell to Fedyuninsky's forces, Model set about implementing his *Schild und Schwert* policy. In order to close the gap between Eighteenth and Sixteenth Armies, he ordered Lindemann to pull back to a tighter perimeter around the city of Luga; 12th Panzer Division, acting under the direct control of Lindemann, was then to attack towards Sixteenth Army. As soon as this operation was complete, the panzer division would join the relatively fresh 58th Infantry Division to attack northwest along the Luga River in order to close the gap between the city of Luga and III SS-Panzer Corps near Narva. Whilst the first part of the operation, which concluded on 6 February, was broadly successful in restoring at least partial contact with Sixteenth Army, the gap to the Narva positions was simply too large. But the withdrawals around Luga and the need for the Red Army to have a small operational pause while it brought forward supplies and reinforcements gave Eighteenth Army a desperately needed opportunity to catch its breath. The exhausted soldiers who had struggled back from the Leningrad perimeter and the Volkhov River could reorganise and regroup, but they remained hugely outnumbered and outgunned.

In an area with poor roads, both sides were heavily reliant upon rail transport and the retreating Germans did what they could to destroy railway infrastructure to hold up the Soviet advance. Iuliyus Moiseyevich Lvovich had been drafted into the Red Army in August 1942 and was disappointed when he was sent to a railway service unit rather than a combat formation. He was sent to Leningrad in late 1943 and followed the advancing units of Maslennikov's Forty-Second Army to Elisaveto, where he and his comrades were ordered to restore the railway lines:

> We arrived at the station there in the morning into the midst of a real nightmare. It was a large railway junction. What did we see? Every rail was broken, some into several fragments, all of the joints were broken and the sidings had been blown up. Well, what were we there for? Our eyes saw and our hands went to work. It was hard physical toil, working twelve hours a day. In wet or dry weather, the work continued. Fortunately, the Germans didn't shell or bomb us as they had been driven off and they didn't fly overhead. The situation was more or less calm … Four platoons would be assigned to a kilometre of track with each platoon working on a 250m stretch. Repair work was difficult. There were no spare rails, nothing. All industrial production was for defence purposes, so where could we get replacement rails? Until the factories produced them, there was nothing … Well, we dismantled destroyed tanks, tried to melt their metal, and carved out pieces … We found some joints and laid our improvised tracks and fastened them together. As a result, the trains that ran on our restored tracks were limited to a speed of no more than 10km/hour.[14]

On the southern flank of Eighteenth Army, the demoralised and increasingly rebellious soldiers of the Spanish Legion had regrouped immediately to the west of Luga. They now formed part of Grase's XXVI Corps. He had intended to deploy the Spanish Legion to secure his rear area by protecting the railway line between Pskov and Luga, but the legion was so badly degraded that it was regarded as unreliable. Instead, it was dispatched to the northern Estonian town of Tapa with the intention of being rested and re-formed before returning to action. The reputation of the Spanish soldiers for indiscipline and looting was such that the local German rear area commander expressed severe reservations about having the Spanish Legion in his area, but in any event the appetite of the Spanish government for continued involvement in the war in the east was now at an end. Franco made a formal request for the Spanish Legion to be sent home, and despite prevaricating for several days, Hitler had no choice but to acquiesce – Spain was a source of the tungsten ore wolfram, essential for the German war effort, and it was therefore essential to ensure that good relations continued between Berlin and Madrid. It would take several weeks for all arrangements to be completed, but the great majority of the Spanish soldiers returned to their homeland in March and April 1944. Only a few chose to remain as combatants, but nonetheless, there were sufficient volunteers left to form two SS companies.[15] Their motivations to continue fighting were probably varied – some would have been diehard anti-Bolshevik crusaders, and others were too embittered or traumatised by years of war to be able to imagine any other life. They ended the war fighting in the ruins of Berlin. Most were killed in this last battle, but several were taken prisoner; together with 219 former members of the Blue Division, the 21 surviving men of the two volunteer companies were finally released by the Soviet Union in 1954.[16]

The relative lull in fighting didn't last long. German aerial reconnaissance detected the build-up of two large Soviet groups near Luga; a force supported by an estimated 200 tanks was spotted to the southwest of Novgorod and the southeast of Luga, with a second substantial group to the northwest of Luga, near Lake Samro. If these converged, there was a high likelihood that Model's *Schild* in Luga would be encircled and destroyed. At the same time, Model informed *OKH* that he had completed preparations for the *Schwert* phase of his plan. The attack by 12th Panzer Division towards the south, to restore contact with Sixteenth Army, resulted in the brief encirclement of parts of two Soviet rifle divisions and a partisan brigade, but there were too few troops available and too little time to spare to reduce the encirclement and destroy the surrounded units. Fighting continued here until the middle of the month. Soviet aircraft managed to fly about 22 tons of supplies to the encirclement, which combined with the resources of the partisan brigade proved to be sufficient to sustain the defence. On 15 February, a relief column from the Soviet Fifty-Ninth Army managed to link up with the encircled Soviet troops.

With little time for rest and replenishment, 12th Panzer Division concentrated close to Pskov, leaving the reduction of the pocket to other units, while 58th Infantry Division formed up to the east nearer Luga. There were two options,

Model informed Zeitzler and Hitler. The simpler and easier option was to push northeast from the concentration area near Luga to the northeast corner of Lake Peipus. The second more ambitious option was to attempt to advance down the Luga River in order to restore the line that had been abandoned further north during the retreat to the Narva River. It seems that Model's energy and determination had won over an unlikely ally – even Kinzel, his chief of staff, commented to Foertsch, the chief of staff at Eighteenth Army headquarters, that after the gloom and despondency of January it was refreshing even to be discussing a counteroffensive operation.[17] The more ambitious option was almost certainly beyond the ability of Eighteenth Army, given the limited resources at hand, and even the lesser option would require an advance of about 65 miles across difficult terrain. Not all of this region was in Soviet hands and the operation would perhaps be better described as a series of smaller advances to link up the disparate formations reeling back from the Leningrad siege perimeter, but with only a single panzer division supported by an infantry division, it was an extremely ambitious undertaking. Ideally, Model would have liked a stronger force – perhaps a full panzer corps with two panzer divisions and an infantry division – but the crisis in Ukraine was drawing in more and more resources on both sides. By the time the battle to extract the encircled German forces in the Korsun-Shevchenkovsky encirclement came to a climax in mid-February, it had drawn in more than half the German panzer divisions and Soviet tank formations on the entire Eastern Front. Model's operation would have to proceed with what little was available.

The *Schild und Schwert* concept had originated in conversations between Hitler and Model, but now that the moment had arrived for the operation to take place the Führer seemed to have lost his enthusiasm for counteroffensive operations. Perhaps distracted by the fighting in Ukraine, he stressed to Model the importance of preventing collapse in the Narva sector and ordered him to pull back to the Panther Line if there was any danger of the forces in Luga being driven away to the south or becoming trapped in an encirclement. The thinking behind this apparent change of heart is difficult to determine with any certainty, and it is certainly possible that Hitler had actually accepted the need for such a withdrawal several days earlier, but chose to delay implementation. There were several reasons for such a delay. Firstly, it was highly characteristic that when faced with a decision that he didn't want to make, Hitler would find reasons to prevaricate for as long as possible. Secondly, to accept a withdrawal to the Panther Line earlier would have been a vindication of Küchler's requests, and the dismissal of the commander of Army Group North meant that – in order to spare Hitler from embarrassment – there had to be at least the appearance of a gap between Küchler's departure and permission being given to retreat.

Model accepted Hitler's words as giving him freedom to carry out whatever withdrawals he felt were needed. He ordered Lindemann to ensure that the road and rail links between Luga and Pskov were kept open, and for some of the forces gathered around the city to be moved west in order to prevent the Red Army from thrusting south between Luga and Lake Peipus. The intention was to leave XXXVIII Corps and L Corps to sustain the 'shield' around Luga while XXVI Corps, to which 12th Panzer Division was now assigned, would be the 'sword', further to the west. The main strike force would now consist of 12th Panzer Division, supported by 126th Infantry Division and 12th Luftwaffe Field Division. The daily reports percolating up the German chain of command gave some much-needed relief: with men being released from hospitals and returning from home leave, or simply through the careful collection of stragglers and their return to the ranks, the numerical strength of Eighteenth Army was now significantly better than it had been when Model took command. In a characteristic move, Model took steps to boost this still further: all rear area units were ordered to assign 5 per cent of their remaining personnel to combat units.[18]

Fighting flared on 7 February as Model attempted to assert a level of control on events; at the same time, the Soviet Forty-Second Army moved south against Luga with three rifle corps. The most westerly corps reached Yamm where it ran into the German 207th Infantry Division, hastily dispatched to the area in order to protect the forming up area for XXVI Corps. Two further German divisions – 13th Luftwaffe Field Division and 58th Infantry Division – were moving into positions between Yamm and Luga, but the latter ran into two Soviet divisions attacking towards the southeast. Suffering heavy losses, 58th Infantry Division was driven back, exposing the flank of 13th Field Division. Two further German divisions were still en route, with the consequence that 58th Infantry Division, intended to attack in conjunction with XXVI Corps to the west, continued to bear the brunt of the weight of Maslennikov's Forty-Second Army. When 12th Panzer Division began its attack towards the north, it ran into three rifle divisions attempting to outflank the last German positions in Yamm; although the Soviet advance was brought to a halt, the consequence was that Model's counterthrust was also unable to make any progress. Meanwhile, Soviet troops closer to Lake Peipus reached Podborovye and the point at which Lake Peipus and Lake Pskov were connected by a small channel; a small Soviet force even crossed to the west bank of the lakes.

In terrain that – like the rest of the region – was eminently unsuitable for large formations to mount major operations, and in a capricious winter with alternating heavy snowfalls and warmer spells of partial thaw, it was inevitable that the plans of both sides degenerated into chaotic but bloody clashes. The few roads in the area wound through the forests and swamps, skirting numerous shallow lakes and minor rivers – none of these rivers was a major obstacle, but they were sufficient to hinder vehicular movement. The changeable weather also grounded aviation assets, and whilst the efficacy of Soviet air support was often very limited, the inability of the Luftwaffe to fly sustained operations had a big detrimental effect on German capabilities. Airstrikes by dive-bombers had repeatedly influenced the outcome of ground fighting all along the Eastern Front, and aerial reconnaissance assets were vital for the Germans to be able to anticipate Soviet operations.

After being mauled in the initial Soviet attack, 58th Infantry Division managed to organise some semblance of a battle line but came under renewed pressure on 10 February. It had 21st and 24th Infantry Divisions on its left and right flanks respectively, but these divisions were badly weakened and had no more than four relatively weak battalions each – less than half the combat strength of a full establishment infantry division. The three German divisions had been holding a line just to the south of the Plyussa River near Zarudenye and Orekhovno but were now forced back; in the dense woodland, communication with one of the regiments of 58th Infantry Division was lost and the regiment failed to receive the order to withdraw. It was rapidly encircled and Soviet units hurled themselves at the hastily erected perimeter in an attempt to destroy it. A counterattack by 24th Infantry Division failed to reach the encircled troops and Model's 'shield' rapidly disintegrated as Soviet troops continued to press forward, encircling a second regiment from 58th Infantry Division 11 miles further to the south.

This collapse created a major threat to the southern half of Eighteenth Army. The leading Soviet units were now within striking range of the rail and road link between Pskov and Luga, and if they severed this the German forces in Luga faced encirclement and destruction. Without those troops, Lindemann would have no resources with which to stop the Red Army advancing to and beyond Pskov. In these circumstances, Model had no choice but to abandon his planned 'sword' attack. Instead, 12th Panzer Division and 13th Luftwaffe Field Division were ordered to attack towards the east to reach the two encircled German infantry regiments. The latter unit ran into a Soviet rifle division moving in the opposite direction and was first halted, then driven back. A battlegroup from

12th Panzer Division, consisting largely of its 5th Panzergrenadier Regiment, made better progress further south and reached the southern encirclement but then came under sustained pressure. Unable to hold its positions, the combined force was driven south and rapidly disintegrated. Abandoning most of their heavy equipment, the German troops attempted to cross the frozen Lake Chernoe to reach Strugi Krasnye. Those who reached the safety of the village – astride the railway line between Pskov and Luga – were exhausted and almost weaponless.

All along Eighteenth Army's front line, crises were developing. The Soviet forces that had crossed to the western shore of Lake Peipus moved into the village of Mehikoorma almost unopposed; the only resistance came from a few companies of Estonian home guard. On the Narva Line, the Soviet forces expanded their bridgehead south of the city, edging closer to the vital Sinimäed Hills, and then attempted to bypass the German positions from the north. On the night of 13–14 February, Soviet ships approached the coastline to the west of the estuary of the Narva River and landed a force of a little over 400 men near the village of Meriküla; the intention was that they would advance inland rapidly to link up with the troops still clinging to their bridgehead north of the city of Narva, and the combined force would then push on to the Sinimäed Hills.

The concept of a 'coastal hop' – transporting troops a relatively short distance by sea in order to outflank an enemy position – was not a new one. During the Estonian War of Independence, Estonian troops had landed in almost exactly the same position, coming ashore from British warships that provided them with fire support, and the British and Americans had carried out a series of coastal hops in Sicily. Even as the Soviet troops splashed ashore, the Anzio operation, another attempt at a 'coastal hop', was raging in Italy. But although such operations look tempting when viewed from a map, they are fraught with difficulties. All coastal landings face contradictory requirements. On the one hand, a suitable beach is required for troops to come ashore without too much difficulty; but on the other hand, there needs to be a port close at hand that can be seized quickly so that reinforcements and supplies can then be landed, particularly if – as was the case in the northern Baltic region – the naval forces supporting the landing do not have dedicated landing vessels capable of bringing large numbers of men and large quantities of supplies and heavy weapons to the landing beaches. For this coastal hop, the intention was to move out of the beachhead rapidly in order to link up with the Soviet forces further east, but the mission rapidly ran into problems.

Although there is a small shingle beach near Meriküla, it is overlooked by a steep bluff up to 100 feet high, studded with trees. The area had been partly fortified by the Estonians in the 1930s in anticipation of such a landing and the

Germans had further refined these fortifications along the edge of the bluff, with the intention of manning them with sufficient troops to be able to check any landing until mobile reinforcements could arrive. This sector was defended by a battalion of Estonian paramilitary police with a naval coastal artillery battery of four 100mm guns in a fixed emplacement and six 20mm anti-aircraft guns. To the east of the Estonian police was *Marine-Bataillon Hohnschild*, made up of German naval personnel who had been deployed in the area to man the coastal artillery but were now organised into an ad hoc combat group. Barbed wire was liberally used on the beach itself and on the steep slope to the top of the bluff, and a battlegroup from 227th Infantry Division, named after the division commander, General Wilhelm Berlin, was in the village of Meriküla.

The landing fleet consisted of 12 small vessels, a mixture of armed coastal ships and trawlers, escorted by a few Soviet destroyers. The ships stopped a short distance from the beach and soldiers clambered into small boats and rowed for the shore. They were still 65–100 feet from dry land when the water became too shallow and the men disembarked, wading through the icy water. The first encounter with the defenders was when the Soviet troops encountered a company of Hohnschild's battalion, swiftly overwhelming it before pressing on towards Meriküla. Here, they encircled Berlin's headquarters, but the brief firefight on the beach had alerted the Germans and their heavy guns began to fire. Two of the Soviet landing vessels ran aground and the others withdrew a short distance. The Soviet troops who had come ashore – a little over 400 were landed before the ships were driven off – made repeated, futile attempts to fight their way up the steep slope to the German artillery emplacement but most found it impossible to find a way through the dense trees and barbed wire.

As it grew light on 14 February, the Germans gathered their forces to deal with the landing. In addition to the men already in the area, they now had an armoured reconnaissance battalion from III SS-Panzer Corps and several Tiger tanks from *Schwere Panzer Abteilung 502*. The counterattack was from the east and rapidly overcame the lightly armed Soviet soldiers who had been unable to land any heavy weapons. The only major problem experienced by the Germans was when a group of Stukas attacked and mistakenly bombed the Tiger tanks, damaging them and killing several men before signal flares made the pilots aware of their mistake. By the end of 14 February, the landing was effectively over with half the men who splashed ashore dead and most of the rest taken prisoner. About 75 managed to remain at large and desultory fighting continued for three days until they were all eliminated.[19] Not long after, the Soviet troops that had crossed the Narva River between the city and the coast were also driven back.

The northern flank of the Narva position was now secure, and fighting around the southern flank slowly settled into a stalemate. The Red Army held a tree line immediately to the south of the Sinimäed Hills, cutting the railway line between Narva and the west, but the Germans held the village of Lembitu and the hills themselves, through which the road between Narva and the west ran.

Meanwhile, the Red Army was altering its command arrangements. In order to improve cooperation between the different armies involved in the fighting, Govorov proposed that Volkhov Front be abolished and its forces assigned to his Leningrad Front. It seems that Meretskov was not consulted, and the new proposals came as a surprise to him:

> In mid-February 1944, I was urgently summoned to *Stavka*. The reason for the call was unexpected for me: Volkhov Front was being liquidated, its troops were to be transferred to Leningrad Front, and I was appointed commander of Karelian Front. This change didn't please me. I had been pressing for assignment to the western axis [i.e. the forces facing the German Army Group Centre] for a long time. And now, when our troops were close to the borders of Belarus, the territory of which was well known to me from my pre-war service, the transfer to the north seemed undesirable to me. I said this at *Stavka*, but Stalin replied to me:
>
> 'You know the north very well. In addition, you have gained experience in conducting offensive operations in difficult conditions of wooded and swampy terrain. You have all the right assets, especially since back in 1939–40 you commanded an army on the Viborg axis and broke through the Mannerheim Line. It is inappropriate to send another person who doesn't know the features of this theatre of operations and doesn't have any experience of fighting in the conditions in Karelia and the arctic, to Karelian Front, as this will result in delays in organising the defeat of the enemy. Any other commander would have to learn from scratch and that would take a long time, which we just don't have.'[20]

Meretskov wasn't alone in finding the new arrangement not to his liking. Shtemenko, head of the Operations Directorate, was not enthusiastic about so many armies coming under the control of a single Front:

> The disbanding [of Volkhov Front] had been proposed by General Govorov ... who considered that for the sake of unity of control on the Pskov line of advance the whole Pskov sector should be handed over to him. *Stavka* had agreed with him, but this turned out to have been a mistake. The realities of the battlefield soon required that a 3rd Baltic Front should be set up in almost this very sector.[21]

On the battlefield on Eighteenth Army's southern flank, events continued to run against the Germans. Remaining in Luga was impossible – it merely invited the destruction of a substantial part of Eighteenth Army, and Model gave Lindemann permission to abandon the city. The Germans pulled out late on 12 January and the Red Army took possession of the ruins. As the Red Army's soldiers landed on the Estonian coast and began their doomed attempt to establish a beachhead, Model contacted *OKH* to inform Hitler and Zeitzler that, in keeping with the instructions from Hitler, he was now ordering a withdrawal to the Panther Line positions and was abandoning all territory to the east of Pskov, Lakes Pskov and Peipus, and the Narva River. The bridgehead at Narva itself, where Fedyuninsky had been attacking in vain for several days, was also to be abandoned in order to release sufficient forces to reinforce the Narva Line. Having effectively agreed this in advance, Hitler conceded. The withdrawal was to begin on 17 February and would be completed within two weeks.

As soon as the wrecked divisions of Eighteenth Army began their retreat, the Red Army pursued aggressively. Partisan activity behind the German front line had intensified and the area close to and south of Pskov had long been a particular partisan hotspot; in addition to harassing retreating German columns, the partisans were able to alert the Red Army to the withdrawal. There were now several threats to the Germans retreating from Luga. From the north, Maslennikov's Forty-Second Army was threatening to continue its drive southwards between Lakes Peipus and Pskov with the intention of reaching Pskov or at least severing road and rail links between the city and the retreating Eighteenth Army. At the same time, an array of armies that had been converging on Luga now threatened to overwhelm the German rearguard. Sviridov's Sixty-Seventh Army had been immediately to the north of Luga, with Roginsky's Fifty-Fourth Army to the east. On the southern flank of Roginsky's troops was Korovnikov's Fifty-Ninth Army, with Starikov's Eighth Army on the very southern flank. Opposing them were several German corps: XXVI Corps was between Lake Pskov and Luga, having abandoned its role as Model's 'sword'; XXVIII Corps had been defending the northern approaches to Luga but was now pulling back to the southwest; XXXVIII Corps was alongside, after defending the eastern approaches to Luga; and finally X Corps covered the south. All but X Corps were assigned to *Armeenahtgruppe Friessner* ('Army Link Group Friessner'), under the command of General Johannes Friessner, who had been waiting to take command of Fourth Army. Nearly all units on both sides were depleted, and the Germans were reduced to a series of disparate battlegroups of varying strength. Despite suffering substantial losses in its abortive attack towards the north and then in the attempts to rescue the encircled elements of 58th Infantry Division, 12th Panzer Division remained the most mobile and formidable asset available to the Germans; together with an independent panzer battalion, it provided all of the armour available to intercept and beat back Soviet attempts to slip forward.

On 15 February, two days before the formal withdrawal to the Panther Line was meant to commence, the leading units of the Soviet Sixty-Seventh Army reached the town of Plyussa, but could go no further. Similarly, the Soviet forces that pursued the remnants of 58th Infantry Division to Strugi Krasnye came to a halt. Heavy fighting continued over the following days, but the transfer of nearly all of Volkhov Front's forces to Leningrad Front created a huge burden of work for Govorov's staff officers. In the north, Fedyuninsky's Second Shock Army failed to exploit its earlier rapid advance to the Narva River by capturing Narva itself and thus opening the traditional east–west route that armies had followed for centuries; in vain, Fedyuninsky offered the award of Hero of the Soviet Union to the first Soviet soldier who was able to cut the vital supply road running west from Narva, along which all of the supplies of *Armee Abteilung Narwa* were moved. The German bridgehead across the river was eventually abandoned, though not without incident – at the last moment, Soviet troops managed to reach the bridge over the river before it could be blown up and it was only by a desperate counterattack that the German engineers were able to secure control of it for long enough to detonate the demolition charges that they had laid. The bridgehead secured by the Red Army to the north of Narva had been eliminated and every attempt to break out of the southern bridgehead was thwarted by the Germans, but conversely when the Germans mounted counterattacks to eliminate this bridgehead, they too had only limited success. To allow Fedyuninsky to concentrate his army against Narva itself, the southern bridgehead had been passed to Korovnikov's Fifty-Ninth Army, whose headquarters was transferred to the region. The Red Army had established a bulge pointing towards the north in their attempts to push through to the Sinimäed Hills and the first German counterattack cleared the western part of this bulge, but despite repeated attacks it proved impossible to dislodge the Soviet troops in the eastern part from the forests and swamps closer to the Narva River, not least because these Soviet positions were covered by artillery on the east bank. The arrival of an infantry division transferred from Norway allowed the Germans to reshuffle their forces and strengthen their defensive lines and as the spring thaw set in, the northern sector grew quiet. Friessner, who had commanded an eponymous link group between Sixteenth and Eighteenth Armies, had by now replaced Sponheimer as commander of *Armee Abteilung Narwa*.

The repeated attempts to force the Narva River line were part of Govorov's overall plan to exploit his successes to date and to destroy the German Eighteenth Army before it could recover from its mauling. In addition to the northern attacks, he intended to mount two thrusts in the south with Forty-Second and Sixty-Seventh Armies towards Pskov and Ostrov. In this manner, he hoped to break through on both flanks of Lindemann's battered army. In the central area lay the waters of Lakes Peipus and Pskov, and although a small bridgehead had been established on the west bank, Govorov recognised that these lakes were collectively a formidable barrier. The smaller Lake Pskov flows north into Lake Peipus, and both lakes drain several rivers from the surrounding area. The Narva River leaves the northern part of Lake Peipus and flows to the Gulf of Finland via Narva itself. The two lakes have extensive regions on their east and west banks that are relatively shallow, but the central third of Lake Peipus and a somewhat smaller central portion of Lake Pskov are far deeper. Although both lakes freeze in the winter, the ice in the deeper central parts can break up relatively easily due to the faster current. Mounting and sustaining a crossing over the lakes during the winter would be a formidable undertaking. Once the ice broke up, there were further problems. Unless specialist amphibious or landing vessels were available, the different depths of the lakes meant that craft capable of crossing the shallow sectors might struggle in the deeper central channels, while vessels that could cope with the deeper water would only be able to approach the shoreline at a limited number of points. There was also the problem of fire support for a landing operation. The Soviet forces had no gunboats on the lakes and the only point at which artillery on the east bank could support operations on the west bank was at the relatively narrow channel that connected the two lakes. It was therefore far easier to defend the region of the lakes than to attack across it, and the Germans were able to concentrate their forces at the obvious landing points on the west coast where the water was deeper; the rest of the west bank was covered by a mixture of Estonian home guard reservists and motorised patrols. On 16 February, German forces counterattacked against the small bridgehead around Mehikoorma on the west bank of the lakes. Fighting continued for a week before the Soviet troops were either killed, taken prisoner, or forced to evacuate back across the lakes.

The only sector where there remained any significant movement was therefore to the south, where Govorov hoped to capture Pskov and Ostrov before bursting into Estonia to the south of the two great lakes. Progress was slow; the Germans were pulling back ever closer to their main supply points and were thus able to replenish their combat units with ease, whereas the Red Army was now operating at the end of long supply lines that ran through very difficult terrain. An increasingly impatient Stalin urged faster progress, demanding that the northern group complete its breakout via Narva before attacking southwest towards Pärnu on the Baltic coast; such an advance would leave *Armee Abteilung Narwa* isolated in northwest Estonia, entirely reliant upon maritime transport for supplies. At the same time, operating in conjunction with the northern flank of 2nd Baltic Front, the southern part of Leningrad Front was ordered to accelerate its conquest of the Pskov–Ostrov region. The fresh III Guards Tank Corps was given to Govorov as reinforcements, but it proved impossible for Leningrad Front to bring this unit into action. Taking advantage of the detailed preparations drawn up by Kinzel in anticipation of *Blau*, the original plan for a withdrawal from the Leningrad perimeter to the Panther Line, Eighteenth Army fell back slowly from one defensive position to another. Despite all the German divisions being badly degraded, they were able to retain contact with each other, denying the Red Army any chance to insert the fresh tank corps into an inviting gap.

On 24 February, the leading troops of Maslennikov's Forty-Second Army reached Seryodka, 22 miles due north of Pskov. They continued to grind their way south over the next six days, edging closer to Pskov and finally being brought to a halt by the strong defensive positions that the Germans had built immediately to the north of the city. To their east, Sviridov's Sixty-Seventh Army was meant to attack through Strugi Krasnye along the main communications axis between Luga and Pskov. In its path was the German 24th Infantry Division and two Luftwaffe field divisions, and on this occasion the field divisions managed to put up stubborn resistance. There was a three-day fight outside Plyussa, which cost the Red Army heavy losses for almost no gain, before the Germans pulled out on 18 February. Further to the southeast, Fifty-Fourth Army and 2nd Baltic Front's First Shock Army rapidly captured Staraya Russa, the objective of failed operations earlier in the war, but this too was part of the planned withdrawal of the German Sixteenth Army.

The failure of Sviridov to show more energy led to a growing sense of frustration in the headquarters of Leningrad Front. On 20 February, Govorov's impatience was clear in a signal that he sent to the commander of Sixty-Seventh Army:

The enemy forces opposing your army are only deploying covering forces in combat. Your army is advancing slowly because you have spread your forces equally across the front, and thus you have no shock 'fist' at all, and you haven't exploited the potential for CXVI Rifle Corps' right flank to envelop the enemy defences facing your army.[22]

It was an oft-repeated criticism. Sviridov was ordered to concentrate sufficient forces to cooperate with the neighbouring Fifty-Fourth Army to the southeast in order to accelerate the advance along the Luga–Pskov axis, but there was little further progress. Sviridov complained that his leading rifle divisions were too weak to sustain such an offensive; Govorov responded by transferring a relatively fresh rifle corps from Starikov's Eighth Army and pulling out one of Sviridov's badly depleted rifle corps. This finally created sufficient pressure to force Lindemann to order the abandonment of Strugi Krasnye on 23 February but Sviridov was still unable to make decisive progress; although his army managed to move forward about 40 miles in the following week, this was largely due to the orderly withdrawal of the German forces. Crucially, no German units were cut off and destroyed as Govorov had intended.

Slowly, the fighting died down as the spring thaw took hold. It was an opportunity for both sides to take stock of a month of great change. In all sectors of the long Eastern Front, the Germans had suffered setback after setback. But here in the north, where the front line had been fossilised for over two years, the change seemed the most startling. The siege of Leningrad and the long, bloody efforts to break the siege were all at an end. The final outcome of the great conflict between Germany and the Soviet Union was surely no longer in doubt; the precise nature of that end remained to be determined.

CHAPTER 13

AFTER THE SIEGE

The achievements of the Red Army in the Leningrad sector in the first two months of 1944 were remarkable. Although the siege ring around Leningrad had been broken a year before, the city remained under almost daily artillery fire and there was always a possibility, albeit a remote one, that the Wehrmacht would be able to restore its tight grip on the city. By the end of February this was an impossibility, and the only question was whether Army Group North could survive. But despite this apparently successful transformation of the battlefield, which saw the front line move from the line of the Volkhov River and the Leningrad perimeter to the Narva River and the great lakes between Estonia and Russia – a shift to the west of about 132 miles – there was considerable dissatisfaction in the Soviet high command. A great deal had undoubtedly been accomplished, but potentially war-winning opportunities had also been missed.

In addition to moving the front line far to the west and away from the Soviet Union's second city, the entire series of operations commencing with *Yanvarskiiy Grom* and then continuing until the spring thaw inflicted substantial losses on the Wehrmacht. Analysis of the returns submitted by Army Group North show that the total losses suffered by Sixteenth and Eighteenth Armies up to 1 March came to about 77,000 men.[1] Soviet estimates of the damage that they inflicted were inevitably greater. More than half of the German figures were wounded and at least some would return to the ranks, but it was nonetheless a heavy toll. But the Red Army paid a brutal price for its success. The armies of Leningrad, Volkhov, and 2nd Baltic Fronts lost over 76,000 dead or missing and a further 237,000 wounded, giving a total of nearly 314,000.[2] Given these losses, it is perhaps unsurprising that the Soviet forces were unable to sustain the high tempo of operations demanded by their Front commanders and by *Stavka*.

Almost immediately, the staff officers of Leningrad Front began their usual post-operational analysis. The main problem in the manner that the operations unfolded was that after the initial rupture of the German siege lines around Leningrad and the Oranienbaum bridgehead, the Soviet troops repeatedly failed to break through the lines of the German forces. Without such breaks, it was impossible for them to isolate and destroy the retreating Wehrmacht divisions. The commanders of the armies, corps, divisions, and brigades could all claim – with considerable justification – that they had faced serious obstacles. The terrain was, as had been the case in every operation in the region, far from ideal for attacking forces, and the changeable weather made the difficult task of attempting an advance in winter through forests and swamps with few decent roads even harder.

When the reports generated by Leningrad Front reached *Stavka*, they contained a list of defects in Red Army performance that must have seemed frustratingly familiar. There were criticisms of failings of command and control at every level resulting in forces not being coordinated effectively; as always, artillery and air support failed to be as effective as expected; and logistic and engineering support was also weak with units often unable to engage in combat due to shortages of fuel, ammunition, and food. But in all of the analysis and acknowledgement that almost every problem had occurred before, it seems that there was little attempt to consider why such flaws arose time and time again. Nobody appeared to be able to take a step back, look at the entire picture, and ask the vital question: why are these problems not being eliminated?

The issues about failures of command and control reflected the continuing weaknesses of the Soviet officer corps. Red Army doctrine from the 1930s had been based upon the concept of 'deep battle', first proposed by Marshal Mikhail Nikolayevich Tukhashevsky, and he explicitly described the importance of officers having sufficient training and confidence to act independently as circumstances dictated.[3] Such concepts are perhaps easier to describe than to implement. Officers who are able to behave in this manner require training and practice in making decisions rapidly without always having to seek the approval of their superiors, and this in turn requires their superiors to trust them to do whatever is needed to deliver the overall tactical and operational objectives. If the analysis of the situation and resultant decision-making is to occur at a sufficiently high tempo, there will be many occasions when officers have to act on incomplete information, and this increases the risk of error; therefore, in order to develop such decision-making skills, the overall system must be prepared to tolerate errors. In an authoritarian state like the Soviet Union, such independence of thought and acceptance of errors were factors that were rarely encouraged. Indeed, as the war progressed and Hitler imposed increasing levels of authoritarian National Socialist dogma on the German military, this too had a stifling effect on initiative and made the German command structure increasingly rigid and inflexible.

In its unique way, the Red Army had attempted to resolve this conundrum. Whilst commanders at the level of divisions and above were expected to show initiative and to react to a fast-changing battlefield, the expectation was that this would result in them exerting tighter and more accurate control over their subordinates. There was no recognition that this simply denied those subordinates any opportunity to develop the flexible and rapid decision-making skills that were absent in senior officers. Unless those at early stages of progressing through military careers were encouraged and trained to use independence of thought and rapid decision-making, it was unrealistic to expect these skills to appear suddenly once they had risen to higher rank.

To make matters worse, the Red Army continued to suffer from the terrible purges of the late 1930s, which resulted in the arrest and execution or imprisonment of so many officers at all levels, including Tukhashevsky. These purges had two effects. Firstly, a generation of officers was stripped of its brightest and best figures. These included men who were suggesting further innovations and improvements – for example, Nikolai Mikhailovich Sunyavsky, a senior military engineer, was a close associate of Tukhashevsky and had been working on improving and increasing the use of radios by the Red Army, but he was arrested in late 1937, forced to sign spurious confessions, and executed the following year largely because of his close relationship with Tukhashevsky.[4] Secondly, those who remained were deeply fearful of becoming victims of future waves of arrests, and in such circumstances it was almost unthinkable for them to risk showing any personal initiative or independence of thought. To expect these officers suddenly to start behaving in a different manner in the midst of the brutal war with Germany was utterly unrealistic.

The Red Army placed great emphasis and therefore expectations on the efficacy of its 'god of war', the massed artillery that was used in every offensive operation. In addition to the guns attached to every military formation from regiments to armies, there were large numbers of independent artillery, mortar, and rocket formations that were assigned as reinforcements to Fronts and armies in order to augment their initial bombardments, but as had been the case in every battle in the Leningrad sector the efficacy of this artillery remained a cause for concern. Compared to previous offensives, the bombardment that preceded the attacks by

Second Shock Army in January 1944 was relatively effective and permitted the first attacks to make significant penetrations into the main German defensive system, but one of the main requirements of the initial bombardment was the suppression of German defensive fire. For this to be effective, German artillery and other heavy weapons had to be destroyed, and despite continuing efforts, many of the positions where the Germans had deployed these heavy weapons remained unknown to the Red Army. This reflected continuing weaknesses in reconnaissance. Although the gathering of information about German deployments had improved considerably by early 1944 – through the better collection and collation of data from aerial reconnaissance, sound location of artillery, prisoner and deserter interrogations, partisan reports, and the use of reconnaissance in force to try to trigger the use of defensive fire by the Germans and thus reveal the locations of weapons – the efficacy of such activity remained variable at best. Although Fedyuninsky's forces fared relatively well in terms of reconnaissance and artillery support, the divisions of Maslennikov's Forty-Second Army struggled in the face of almost intact German positions. Perhaps the biggest weakness of the Soviet reports at the end of operations was their failure to consider what could be done to improve such matters, and to evaluate what steps had been taken in the past and why they had failed to deliver the required improvements.

The heavy reliance on sheer weight of firepower to crush German positions meant that once the Germans had been forced to start their withdrawal, the Red Army's progress would be at least partly dependent upon the ability of artillery units to move forward with advancing infantry and tanks. Any delay in forward movement carried the risk that if the Germans managed to establish any sort of defensive line, Soviet troops would have to attack without artillery support, and in such circumstances they still tended to revert to massive frontal attacks, playing to the strengths of their opponents and giving German firepower every opportunity to shred the attacking formations. Given the difficulties of movement over the forested terrain with its numerous swamps and rivers and few good roads, the movement of artillery was always going to pose severe challenges to the Red Army. But were these challenges insurmountable? In order to make artillery units more mobile, there were numerous options available. The Red Army could have used more self-propelled artillery; it could have given higher priority to procuring high-powered tractors to move artillery; and it could have put greater effort into creating and improving roads. There was some progress in all these areas, but not enough to eliminate the problem.

Engineering support was a vital part of the operations in early 1944. Govorov and Meretskov knew that their armies would have to advance through difficult terrain with poor roads and numerous rivers. Even though these rivers would be frozen, their banks still created substantial barriers to vehicles attempting to cross the frozen ice or to ford them. The Red Army had dedicated bridging units of varying sizes, classified as light, medium, and heavy bridging battalions. They were often combined to form bridging regiments so that they could construct longer bridges. But as the operations unfolded in the region between Leningrad, the Volkhov River, and the Estonian frontier, the bridging assets that both Govorov and Meretskov had assigned to their armies became increasingly ineffective. Many had started the campaign below their establishment strength and as they advanced and deployed their bridging equipment, they were often forced to leave it in place, reducing their capacity for further bridging operations. The Germans were of course aware of the value of such assets and subjected the bridges to air attacks whenever the weather and aircraft resources permitted, and the casualties suffered by the engineers in these attacks further degraded their capacity.

Logistic support was a major problem for the Red Army during these battles. Again, Govorov and Meretskov had anticipated this and had attempted to pre-position sufficient ammunition, fuel, and food to permit their combat formations to sustain a high tempo of operations. But the initial breakout in mid-January took much longer than had been anticipated, and therefore consumed far more resources than had been expected. The consequence was that after the link-up between Second Shock Army and Forty-Second Army, when there was a potential opportunity to take advantage of the chaos and confusion in the German Eighteenth Army, the Soviet units in the front line lacked the resources to act immediately. By the time further supplies were brought forward, the Germans had used the small interval to reorganise. Thereafter, the terrain and weather issues ensured that it would be increasingly difficult to move sufficient supplies forward to sustain the advancing forces. Like the declining ability of engineers to support ongoing operations, the same was to be expected of logistic support. However much the reports after the operation criticised logistic failures, there was little that could have been done differently to prevent such failures given the resources available. Even if more motorised transport had been available, the road network would have remained the limiting factor. There was a further aspect of logistic support that created problems for the Red Army. The particular reliance upon artillery created a considerable supply burden. Artillery ammunition is heavy and bulky and guns can easily exhaust what seem to be substantial quantities of shells. Whenever the German lines solidified, there would be delays while the Red Army's guns were laboriously brought forward and supplied with sufficient ammunition for new attacks to be mounted.

As had consistently been the case in the fighting in the northern sector, the Red Army suffered heavy losses in its attacks. The initial assaults on the fortified German positions around the Oranienbaum bridgehead and the siege perimeter were always going to be costly, even if Soviet artillery support was effective, and as operations unfolded the failure of Soviet artillery to keep up with advancing units meant that there was increasing reliance on infantry and armour to assault the German positions with only modest preliminary bombardments, particularly given the relentless pressure from higher commands for momentum to be sustained. As a consequence, the rifle divisions that fought the last battles of the winter were badly depleted; the average strength of each division in Leningrad Front's armies had fallen to only 3,000 men.[5]

Regardless of the shortcomings of the Soviet armies that fought in the northern sector in early 1944, the key question for senior Soviet officers was whether more might have been accomplished. On the one hand, the Germans were driven far from Leningrad, a large area of territory was recovered, and Eighteenth Army was badly mauled. There were also political repercussions that would have a major outcome on the shape of the war, as is described below. But without question, there had been moments when Eighteenth Army was at serious risk of partial or even complete destruction, and these opportunities had not been seized, even though they were clearly identified at the time.

Some of these opportunities were missed because local commanders showed too much timidity, but others seem to have been far more systemic. The various armies deployed their forces for the operation in two echelons with the clear intention of committing their second echelons as exploitation forces, but in many cases the deployment of these reserves was markedly different from what had been expected. When the first-echelon troops failed to complete their initial breakthroughs, they were often reinforced with units from the second echelons but in a piecemeal fashion. On other occasions, for example when Fifty-Ninth Army attacked north of Novgorod, second-echelon troops were sent into action on a completely new axis rather than reinforcing or exploiting the main thrust.[6] This merely resulted in dissipation of effort for minimal gain.

But in the final analysis, all of the failings to take advantage of opportunities to envelop and destroy large parts of Eighteenth Army were due to the inescapable truth that despite previous reports and orders for improvement, the Red Army – like its imperial Russian predecessor and ultimately its modern Russian descendant – was a blunt instrument. The manner in which it was wielded was unquestionably improving as the war progressed, but its fundamental character was a reflection of its ancestry and the society from which it was derived. However much Stalin and others might aspire to using it in a far more flexible and incisive manner, it would always remain a tool for bludgeoning its opponent into defeat. It was inconceivable that it could easily be made into something closer to the armies of Germany or the Western Powers without implementing reforms of a fundamental nature. The entire approach to training would have to change, and that in turn would require a body of experienced, knowledgeable NCOs and officers who could both lead more effectively in battle and ensure adequate training of new drafts.

However, even if Stalin had been willing to embark on the creation of such NCOs and officers, it was impossible in the prevailing culture of the Soviet Union. To a large extent, many large organisations – police forces as well as the military – reflect the character of the society from which they are recruited. The Soviet Union, and Russia before it, had no tradition of encouraging initiative at lower levels. Moreover, as orthodox Marxist theory teaches, it is a primary function of every organisation to reproduce itself, largely in the same shape and with the same values as before. To ask the training personnel of the Red Army to create a new organisation that behaved very differently from the manner in which current personnel behaved was to ask the impossible, particularly on the timescale that was needed in wartime.

This raises a further question. The British Army that entered both world wars evolved markedly during those conflicts and emerged in 1918 and again in 1945 in a very different shape from how it entered the wars. Why was it possible for this to occur, but by contrast the Soviet Union failed to implement such major changes? The answer is twofold. Firstly, the British Army was drawn from a very different population, in which initiative and independence of thought was normal. This meant that it contained personnel at every level who showed the same initiative and independence of thought and recognised it in others. Nor was there any political danger from encouraging such trends – by contrast, Stalin's huge paranoia created a system where any such willingness to show independent thinking attracted suspicion and risked arrest, imprisonment, and execution. Secondly, the Red Army did actually evolve and improve, and the performance of Leningrad and Volkhov Fronts in the fighting of early 1944 was a marked improvement on the repeated failures of earlier years. But the very nature of the army, and the society from which it was recruited, limited just how much it could evolve, and the directions that evolution would take. Given those constraints, the relatively modest improvements that were achieved were probably all that could be expected.

Of all the components of the Soviet advance to the edge of Estonia, it was the performance of the partisans behind German lines that came closest to what had been expected by *Stavka*. Nikolai Ivanovich Afanasyev, who had been a partisan officer in the region throughout the war, was now commander of 5th Leningrad Partisan Brigade and he later recalled that reconnaissance activity was intensified in the weeks before the offensive, with large quantities of information being passed to higher commands. On 12 January, orders from the partisan command groups at Leningrad and Volkhov Front stated that all partisan units were to increase their activity sharply on the second day of the offensive in order to maximise disruption of German communications. At first, the partisans were operating some distance from the attacking Red Army forces, but closer cooperation became possible as the Germans began to retreat. Afanasyev listed some of the achievements of the Leningrad partisans:

On the night of 14–15 January, 11th Brigade raided the station and village of Mshinskaya, on the Warsaw railway line [about 19 miles north of Luga]. The station was held by the partisans for more than six hours and was completely destroyed; about 300 rail segments, a water tower, a gas station, a railway shed with a communications centre, fuel and food depots, and two signalling towers were blown up, and a railway junction was destroyed. About 1.5km of communications lines were destroyed. After this raid, the Krasnogvardeisk–Luga road section was unusable for 13 hours.

On 15, 16, and 17 January, detachments of 5th Brigade made a series of raids on the enemy's XXXVIII Corps ... against the railway line. Together with the local population, the partisans disabled this section for a prolonged period. In addition, on 15 January alone, the local population aided by small partisan groups destroyed 28km of telegraph lines. During the first week of the offensive, 5th Brigade damaged five railway bridges, 7,000 rail segments, 18 locomotives, 160 wagons and their associated crew and equipment, and one armoured train. During the same period, 24 bridges were blown up on roads and 218 enemy vehicles and their occupants were destroyed.

On the night of 16–17 January, partisans from 12th Brigade damaged several hundred rail segments between Tikopis and Kingisepp. The following night, detachments of the same brigade raided the Veymarn station [to the east of Kingisepp] where all the track facilities were destroyed, many wagons set ablaze, and the enemy garrison was destroyed. Successful raids on the Baltic railway were carried out by 9th Brigade. As a result, in the first days of the offensive the main railway communication on the left flank of the Nazis' Eighteenth Army was completely disrupted …

During the first ten days of the offensive by Leningrad and Volkhov Fronts, the partisans destroyed 11 stations and sidings, blew up 34 railway bridges and 23,000 rail segments, derailed 36 military transports and three armoured trains, destroyed more than 300km of telegraph lines, and killed more than 3,000 Nazi soldiers.

The scope of the activity behind enemy lines was such that on 16 January, on the second day of activation of the partisans, the commander of Army Group North reported to his high command that it was impossible to ensure the security of communications with the forces available. He asked for the urgent allocation of security units from Army Group Centre.[7]

However, even these successes were two-edged. The activity of the partisans undoubtedly disrupted German rail movement, but this damage also greatly hindered the ability of the advancing Soviet forces to bring the railway network back into service in order to move their own supplies and reinforcement forward.

No analysis of the performance of any army is complete without consideration of the performance of its opponent. The divisions of Eighteenth Army had largely been successful in holding their positions throughout the siege; the only significant lasting gain made by the Red Army was the capture of the narrow strip of land on the southern bank of Lake Ladoga during *Iskra* in early 1943. But in this latest series of battles, the units that had stood so firmly were comprehensively defeated. Eighteenth Army suffered serious losses and although it inflicted even heavier losses on the attacking Soviet armies, the balance of power deteriorated badly for the Germans. In late 1943, the Red Army outnumbered the Wehrmacht by about 1.5:1 in terms of manpower; even though it lost huge numbers of men during the offensive, the arrival of replacement drafts meant that by the end of the spring thaw in 1944, this ratio was almost 3:1. There were similar increases in tank and artillery strength.

When looking at the performance of the Wehrmacht in early 1944, two questions arise. Firstly, why were the Germans so comprehensively defeated given their stubborn resistance in earlier years? And secondly, how much did the performance of German units prevent the Red Army from achieving all of its desired objectives?

The answer to the first question is complex. Throughout the war against the Soviet Union, the Wehrmacht suffered a slow and steady degradation of its fighting ability. Losses in the opening months were never fully rectified, and in particular the loss of so many horses greatly reduced the mobility of infantry divisions. Without their horses, the divisions were unable to move artillery, supply wagons etc. as fast as they might have wished, particularly if they were forced out of their fortified positions. Throughout the war, German losses of experienced officers and NCOs proved to be a critical factor in the declining performance of front-line units. These men were literally irreplaceable. Obergruppenführer Herbert Otto Gille, who would end the war as commander of IV SS-Panzer Corps, commanded *SS-Wiking* for much of the conflict, and in the closing months of the war his troops were involved in the failed attempt to lift the siege of Budapest. When the chief of the German general staff visited his headquarters to investigate why the operation had failed, Gille – a widely respected soldier in the regular army as well as the SS – responded with a phlegmatic shrug: 'We no longer have the material of 1940. I now need three men where before I could have made do with two, or even one.'[8]

The loss of these experienced leaders added to the brittleness of the German units. They would still fight to hold their initial positions with great resolution, but once they were forced out, there were fewer local commanders capable of rallying the men, organising an improvised defence, and launching the swift counterattacks that were such a hallmark of German defensive doctrine. There was also a growing sense of gloom amongst soldiers. Those who returned to the front line from leave brought reports of cities devastated by bombing and widespread shortages of basic foodstuffs. Letters from home made soldiers aware of the growing casualties and setbacks on all fronts, and although for the moment belief in Hitler remained strong, it was inevitable that soldiers began to question whether they would personally survive the conflict.

But despite this growing weakness, Eighteenth Army's divisions fought an effective rearguard action to the Estonian border and although several divisions and corps were in danger of being isolated, the only occasion that such isolation actually occurred was during the initial link-up by Fedyuninsky's Second Shock Army and Maslennikov's Forty-Second Army; and even on this occasion, the bulk of the encircled troops managed to escape, albeit losing all of their heavy weapons. Some of the failure of the Red Army to turn advantageous moments into major victories was undoubtedly due to the ongoing weaknesses of Soviet command and control, but much of it was because of timely withdrawals by the Germans, often at the very last moment. The retreating forces also benefited greatly from the preparations made by Kinzel and his staff officers for *Blau*, Küchler's planned retreat to the Panther Line, with supplies prepositioned for them and intermediate defensive lines identified in advance. When the Germans

372

fell back to these positions, the pursuing Soviet forces were unable to dislodge them until their artillery and other support services caught up with the advance.

The consequence of the fighting of early 1944 was that the Germans were now holding the Panther Line, where Küchler had hoped to be before the Soviet offensive broke. But instead of relatively intact divisions manning the positions that had been prepared – and despite Küchler's intentions, the Panther Line proved to be far less well developed and constructed than originally planned – the German units arrayed in defence of the northern Baltic region were exhausted and depleted. Just how long they would be able to hold up in the face of fresh Soviet assaults was open to question, and Govorov soon received instructions to prepare for a new offensive to advance across Estonia. When the first major attempt was made in the summer of 1944, the Germans had abandoned Narva and pulled back to the Sinimäed Hills. Here, when Fedyuninsky attacked, the formations of III SS-Panzer Corps – replenished and reinforced after their retreat from the Oranienbaum bridgehead – fought the Soviets to a bloody standstill. The Germans might have suffered major setbacks, but they were far from beaten.

By that stage, some of the figures who dominated the winter battles had moved on. Despite the failure of his *Schild und Schwert* plan, Model was lauded by Hitler for bringing the Soviet advance to a halt. The reality was that the Red Army stopped because of deteriorating weather, casualties, and impossible supply problems rather than Model's supposed skills as a defensive genius, but Model was informed that he was being promoted to Generalfeldmarschall. In the last week of March, Model and all other senior officers were asked to submit reports on what forces, if any, they could spare for use in other theatres; the near-rout of the German Army Group South across western Ukraine had left the entire southern sector of the Eastern Front badly weakened, and there was a need to free up troops as reinforcements for that sector. Model's submission was that he might be able to release two divisions now that fighting in the north was diminishing, but even this was not guaranteed. Generalleutnant Rudolf Schmundt, Hitler's adjutant, visited the headquarters of Army Group North on 28 March to inform Model of his promotion and also to tell him that he was going to be transferred to replace Manstein as commander of Army Group South. Immediately, Model redrafted his report, declaring that Army Group North would be able to release five infantry divisions and a corps headquarters immediately for transfer to the south, and that 12th Panzer Division could also be released as soon as two assault gun brigades arrived to take its place.

The following day, Model and Schmundt flew to Hitler's headquarters where Model's promotion and new appointment were confirmed. Model now telephoned Kinzel, ordering him to arrange the immediate transfer of not five but six infantry divisions to Army Group South. Zeitzler, who had been watching Model's machinations with growing alarm, intervened and ordered Kinzel to await further instructions from *OKH* before arranging the transfer of any personnel. On 31 March, after Model had departed to take up his new post, Zeitzler raised the matter with Hitler and pointed out that the transfer of so many divisions would result in a potentially catastrophic weakening of the position of Army Group North. Model's popularity with Hitler was undiminished and it took another day of careful argument and representations before the Führer agreed: only one division would be transferred, and even that would have to wait until a later date.[9]

Model arrived at the headquarters of Army Group South just as it was being reorganised: the northern part was to become Army Group North Ukraine, under Model's control, while the southern part became the separate Army Group South Ukraine. Even as Model took up his new command, fighting was dying down for much the same reasons as in the northern sector; the Soviet forces in Ukraine were at the end of an almost continuous series of offensives that had commenced shortly after the end of the Battle of Kursk and had swept the Germans from central and western Ukraine. Once more, Model was given credit for stabilising the front line and when a new crisis developed in the central sector during the summer of 1944, he was once more dispatched as Hitler's fireman to deal with the near-complete destruction of Army Group Centre. From there, he was rushed to the west where he became *Oberbefehlshaber West* ('Supreme Commander West'); his predecessor, Generalfeldmarschall Günther von Kluge, committed suicide in the aftermath of the failed July Plot to assassinate Hitler. Shortly after, Model was moved to command of Army Group B, the northern component of the German forces facing the Western Allies, but by now his personal belief in Hitler, and Hitler's belief in Model, were both declining. Having held high command in both the east and the west, Model was ideally placed to see just how hopeless the situation was for Germany. He oversaw the failed Ardennes offensive of the winter of 1944–45 and then found his army group encircled in the Ruhr region in April 1945. Despite Hitler's demands that the encirclement be treated as a fortress, to be held to the last man, Model issued instructions that Army Group B be dissolved. The older and younger soldiers in the army group were told that they were discharged from the army with immediate effect; those who were left were given the personal freedom either to surrender or to attempt to fight their way out of the encirclement. Several days later Model shot himself rather than become a prisoner.

After Model departed from Army Group North, his replacement as commander of the battered forces defending the northern Baltic region was none other than Lindemann, whose misplaced confidence had fatally undermined Küchler's patient negotiations with Hitler for a timely withdrawal to the Panther Line. His rise to high office was remarkable given the opinion that many of his contemporaries had of his limited abilities. He had commanded L Corps in the early phases of *Barbarossa* and during the German attack on Velikiye Luki at the beginning of August 1941, 251st Infantry Division – part of his corps – had to make a hasty withdrawal across the Lovat River after its artillery ran out of ammunition in heavy fighting to the west of the city. Lindemann attempted to blame the setback on the division commander and as a result of Lindemann's report Generalleutnant Hans Kratzert was removed from his post. A more thorough enquiry over the next few days showed that Kratzert was blameless and the ammunition shortage had been caused by the failure of corps-level supply arrangements, for which Lindemann had responsibility. Kratzert was exonerated and appointed artillery commander for Eighteenth Army, but many in 251st Infantry Division didn't forgive Lindemann for what they saw as a cynical attempt to pass blame to others. The chief of staff of the division wrote in a letter: 'For some time we have been under a higher command with a staff composition of such an unsatisfactory and moreover unpleasant nature, that I have never experienced before. This is very harmful to us.'[10]

During the advance towards Leningrad, Lindemann's corps was tentatively designated as the unit that would occupy the city with Lindemann acting as city commandant. When Generalfeldmarschall Wilhelm Ritter von Leeb was dismissed as commander of Army Group North and Küchler replaced him in early 1942, Lindemann in turn replaced Küchler as commander of Eighteenth Army, even though two other corps commanders in the army – General Albert Wodrig and General Kuno-Hans von Both – had greater seniority; Lindemann's leadership to date had been decidedly lacklustre and he had done nothing to justify his appointment ahead of these two figures. With the departure of Model to the southern sector, Lindemann now found himself commanding the entire army group and in the summer of 1944 he had to deal with a new crisis when the Soviet Operation *Bagration* tore huge holes in the central sector of the German front line, opening a gap of 24 miles between the southern flank of Army Group North and the northern flank of Army Group Centre. Lindemann sought permission for a withdrawal of Army Group North to the line of the Daugava River in Latvia as the only feasible way that the front line could be shortened sufficiently to release enough troops for the restoration of a continuous front. When Hitler refused, Lindemann offered his resignation, but instead was ordered to undertake a counterattack with whatever forces were available towards the city of Polotsk. In the circumstances, the forces that could be provided for such an attack were hopelessly inadequate – just eight under-strength infantry battalions and 44 assault guns – and the two Soviet armies between Lindemann's forces and Polotsk were easily able to hold them off. Lindemann cancelled the counterattack and requested permission to abandon Polotsk, and although Hitler had to agree to this, he also removed Lindemann from his post.

Thereafter, Lindemann was placed in reserve until late January 1945 when he was sent to Denmark as overall commander of the Wehrmacht in the country. His instructions were to organise forces for a final battle against the Western Allies, but most of the occupation forces had long since been transferred to other theatres as the mounting series of crises threatened to overwhelm Germany. He survived an attempt by the Danish resistance to blow up his train in February and after Hitler's death he was one of a small group of officers who advocated one final battle in an absurd belief that this would somehow be a fitting manner to uphold the honour of the Wehrmacht, but he was overruled by Dönitz, Hitler's successor as head of state.[11]

After the war, Lindemann remained a prisoner until he was released in 1947. There were attempts to prosecute him for war crimes, but he insisted that he had refused to pass on the infamous Commissar Order and had also protested about the arbitrary execution of prisoners of war by the SS. He also claimed that he had written to senior figures in the Nazi Party to inform them that whilst he had no intention of interfering in areas that were the political remit of the Party, he would not tolerate any Party interference in what he saw as military matters. There could be little doubt that his rise to command first of Eighteenth Army and then of Army Group North was at least partly because of his attempts to ingratiate himself with Hitler, for example by insisting contrary to Küchler's opinion that Eighteenth Army could successfully defend its positions in front of Leningrad in early 1944, but these were hardly sufficient grounds for prosecution and conviction. In the absence of any concrete evidence against him, the investigation was dropped. He died in 1967.

Eberhard Kinzel, the chief of staff at Army Group North, remained in post until July 1944. He was then promoted to Generalleutnant and took command of 337th Volksgrenadier Division. He and his men were caught up in the great Soviet offensive of January 1945, retreating across Poland towards the Vistula estuary, and he was transferred to the headquarters of Army Group Vistula as chief of staff. In the closing weeks of the war – now promoted to General – he became a member of Dönitz's staff and took part in the surrender negotiations with the Western Allies. He continued working as a staff officer after the cessation of hostilities until June 1945 when the British formally dissolved the remaining Wehrmacht commands. Facing imminent internment as a prisoner of war, he drove to the shore of a lake in Schleswig-Holstein with his mistress Erika von Aschhoff, and the couple committed suicide.

Maximilian Wengler, the reservist officer who impressively fought several successful defensive battles against the Red Army in the Leningrad sector and was largely responsible for the efficacy of the rearguard during the retreat of the northern wing of Eighteenth Army to the Narva River, rose to the rank of Generalmajor – one of only 15 reservists to rise to such a level. He became commander of 227th Infantry Division, of which his former command, 366th Grenadier Regiment, was a part, and was part of the German forces that were driven back to the coastal port of Pillau (now Sovetsk) in East Prussia in the closing weeks of the war. He had been informed that he was to take command of 83rd Infantry Division, an almost meaningless appointment in that all German units in the area were made up of a mixture of survivors from a multitude of original formations and none of them was remotely close to the full strength of a division. Before he could take up his new appointment, he was killed in a Soviet air raid in late April 1945, just a few days before the end of the war in Europe.

The Soviet commanders who played major roles in the fighting of 1943 and 1944 outside Leningrad followed different paths in the months and years that followed. Govorov, the commander of Leningrad Front, continued to hold his post in the months that followed the fighting of early 1944. He oversaw the Red Army's attacks against the Finns to the northwest of Leningrad, as is described below. Promoted to marshal in June, Govorov then directed his troops to storm the city of Vyborg. In the second half of 1944 he also oversaw the eventual Soviet reconquest of Estonia, despite the initial failure to penetrate III SS-Panzer Corps' positions in the Sinimäed Hills in August 1944, and he continued to command his men in their eventual advance across Latvia. After the war he held a number of posts but was troubled by failing health. He suffered a series of heart attacks in 1954 and died in March 1955.

Meretskov, who survived arrest and torture at the hands of the NKVD in 1941 to become commander of Volkhov Front, took command of Karelian Front after his command was abolished in the wake of the fighting of early 1944. He ended the war on the northern frontier with Norway and held a number of military and political posts until he retired in 1961. He died seven years later.

Despite his fall from grace in 1941 and the repeated failures suffered by the armies of Volkhov Front, many in the higher levels of the Soviet Union regarded him with approval. Vyacheslav Mikhailovich Molotov, Stalin's foreign minister, later explained Stalin's nickname for Meretskov, and in the process demonstrated the anti-Semitism that lay just below the surface of the Soviet Union at that time: 'Stalin called him "Yaroslavets" [because] in Yaroslavl, he said, the people were so resourceful that there are almost no Jews there. Russians themselves took on all functions, and Meretskov was just like that.'[12] Molotov's willingness to accept anti-Semitic comments from Stalin and others is all the more remarkable given that his wife, Polina Zhemchuzhina, was Jewish.

Fedyuninsky, the commander of Second Shock Army, was still in command when the Red Army made its bloody attempt to storm the Sinimäed Hills in August 1944, where the Germans held a position known to them as the Tannenberg Line. The bitter fighting resulted in the Soviet troops overrunning the eastern hill – known to the Germans as Orphanage Hill – but although subsequent attacks reached and captured the summit of the central Grenadier Hill, Steiner launched counterattacks with the last of his men to recapture it. One such attack was led by the Estonian Sturmbannführer Paul Maitla, who gathered together a disparate group of stragglers and walking wounded for a final desperate charge. When the fighting died down, the modest patch of ground – each hill covers an area of less than three-quarters of a square mile – was littered with corpses. German losses in the battle came to about 10,000; Soviet casualties are almost impossible to determine with any accuracy, but one estimate is that Fedyuninsky's army lost 30,000 dead and several times as many wounded.[13] In a manner that was characteristic of post-war Soviet historiography, Fedyuninsky made little mention of this failure in his memoirs:

> The enemy made skilful use of favourable terrain conditions. He had a developed network of trenches with machine-gun positions. There were numerous bunkers and fortified firing points at key locations. Barbed wire and minefields were set up on the forward edge. On the left flank [towards the Baltic coast], firing points were protected by earthworks. The enemy's dugouts and observation posts in the depths of the defensive positions were buried up to 8m underground.
>
> The terrain made it difficult for our troops to manoeuvre, and made it easy for the Nazis to manoeuvre with tanks and self-propelled artillery. Their direct fire was supported by heavy artillery and mortar fire from covered locations.
>
> In short, the enemy's defences were solid. We made several attempts to attack the Tannenberg Line in early August but to no avail.[14]

Fedyuninsky is correct in his assessment that the modest Sinimäed Hills, lying astride the relatively narrow strip of open ground between the coastline and the dense forests and swamps to the south, were a formidable position. It was perhaps inevitable that the Red Army would attempt to storm them in a frontal attack before concluding that the path to success lay in an offensive further south, bypassing the long barrier of Lakes Peipus and Pskov and then sweeping both westward to the Baltic coast and northwest towards Tallinn. Nonetheless, Fedyuninsky's repeated attempts to force the line cost his army dearly in blood. He remained a senior figure in Soviet military circles right up to his death in October 1977.

Maslennikov, whose Forty-Second Army fought a tough battle to link up with Fedyuninsky's forces in January 1944, became deputy commander of Leningrad Front after the conclusion of the advance to the Estonian frontier. He led 3rd Baltic Front in the second half of the year, and after the war he rose to become deputy minister of internal affairs. His long-term association with Lavrenty Beriya, head of the NKVD, may have protected him during the years of Stalin's purges immediately before the war but he came under suspicion following Stalin's death. Beriya was arrested and executed in 1953 and Maslennikov was also placed under arrest and interrogated at length about suspicions of a plot by Beriya to use Maslennikov's internal security troops to seize power.[15] Although he was released and no charges were brought against him, he committed suicide a year later.

The January offensive drove the Germans away from the southern outskirts of Leningrad and back towards Estonia, but an enemy remained close to the northwest of the city. The Finns had fought a war with the Soviet Union in the winter of 1939–40 when the Red Army attacked Finland in order to secure territorial gains that would protect Leningrad; when Germany invaded the Soviet Union in 1941, the Finns joined the German attack largely to recover their lost territory, in particular the city of Vyborg. At several moments of the siege, the Germans made assumptions about the degree of cooperation that they could expect from Finland that proved to be misplaced. When the Wehrmacht surged across the Volkhov River in late 1941 and advanced to Tikhvin, there was an expectation that the Finns would secure the north coast of Lake Ladoga and that the two forces would then meet to the east of the lake, thus sealing off Leningrad, but the Finns had no intention of attempting an offensive over such difficult terrain. Similarly, the Germans constantly expected the Finns to push the siege perimeter of Leningrad from the north much closer to the city, but the Finns had largely achieved all that they wished to achieve and saw little benefit in further attacks. The Finns had explicitly stated that they intended to reverse the changes imposed by the Soviet Union in 1940. There were no bombardments of Leningrad by the Finnish Army and German requests to deploy Wehrmacht units in the Finnish sector were either ignored or rejected; in the summer of 1942, Marshal Carl Mannerheim, the commander of Finland's armed forces, told Hitler explicitly that he would not order an attack on Leningrad because Finland wished to avoid provoking a strong response by the Soviet Union.[16] But as far as Hitler was concerned, the Finns were full allies of Germany and were expected to behave as such, even though the Finns repeatedly described themselves as Germany's 'co-belligerent' rather than 'ally'.

Throughout the war, Finland attempted to maintain diplomatic links with several of the Western Powers, and although there was some sympathy for Finland in the USA, this was undermined by the use of Finnish territory as a launch pad for attacks to try to capture Murmansk and the vital railway line running south from the port; the US government formally demanded in October 1941 that the Finns take no part in such attacks and although President Risto Ryti officially rejected these demands, he quietly instructed the Finnish Army to stop its advance. Even at this early stage, many in the Finnish government were expressing doubts about the final outcome of the war in the east and were anxious to secure whatever goodwill they could amongst the nations they saw as the ultimate victors.

One of the reasons that Hitler had refused Küchler's request to withdraw to the Panther Line was out of concern for the effect that this would have upon the Finnish government. There were good grounds for such concerns. Finland had been making tentative approaches to the Soviet Union since late 1941 and these gained pace after the German defeat at Stalingrad in early 1943, but Stalin refused to make any concessions. Nonetheless, Mannerheim repeatedly warned Hitler that if Germany was forced to give up Estonia – and the Soviet armed forces thus acquired bases along the southern side of the Gulf of Finland – the Helsinki government would have no choice but to accept peace on whatever terms the Soviet Union was prepared to offer.[17] At the Tehran Conference in late 1943, Roosevelt and Churchill had stressed to Stalin their requirement that Finland should be left independent at the end of the war; they accepted Stalin's counter-proposal that this would be on condition of the Soviet Union recovering the ground that it had seized in the Winter War of 1939–40 and the seizure of the municipality of Pechenga, from where attacks had been mounted towards Murmansk in the far north, together with substantial reparations. Having effectively neutralised any western support for Finland, Stalin now felt able to prosecute a campaign intended to force Finland out of the war on terms that were favourable to the Soviet Union.

On 6 February, a force of about 200 Soviet aircraft attacked targets in and around Helsinki and the US government sent a diplomatic note the following day, advising the Finnish government that the longer it stayed in the war on the side of the Germans, the worse would be the outcome for Finland. There were two further air raids, but most of the aircraft dropped their bombs at random and were driven off by fierce anti-aircraft fire. On 12 February, a Finnish delegation was dispatched to Stockholm to discuss peace terms with Soviet representatives; at the same time, the Germans made preparations to seize key Finnish islands in order to prevent the Soviet Baltic Fleet from exiting the Gulf of Finland in the event of Finland leaving the war. For Germany, the last hope of winning the war was to defeat the Western Allies on the shores of France and then resume the Battle of the Atlantic, and for the latter the Baltic Sea was regarded as a vital U-boat training area.

After two weeks of discussions in Stockholm, the Finnish delegation returned to Helsinki. The terms demanded by the Soviet side were harsh. The frontiers of 1940 were to be restored and German forces in Finland were to be interned. All Soviet prisoners of war were to be released and the Finnish Army faced at least partial demobilisation. The amount of reparations to be paid by Finland and the transfer of Pechenga were described in outline only; the official wording was that the details would be negotiated later. The Finns rejected these terms, particularly the Soviet insistence that all prisoners be released even before an armistice came into effect, but expressed a wish to continue discussions. Shortly after, Moscow published its full demands for reparations: Finland was to pay the Soviet Union $600 million (about $10.1 billion by 2022 values). The Finns rejected these demands in April 1944, at a time when the Germans seemed to be consolidating their hold on Estonia and appeared to have stopped the Red Army's advance.

Hitler had been following Finnish moves closely and began to apply pressure of his own, reducing or stopping shipments of arms and food in order to exert leverage on Helsinki. Meanwhile, the Red Army was preparing its forces. On 9 June, with fighting now raging in Normandy, Govorov's Leningrad Front began an offensive to drive the Finnish Army back from Leningrad and to recover the disputed territory that was first seized by the Red Army in 1939–40, and then by the Finnish Army in 1941. After two days of heavy fighting, the Soviet forces broke the first Finnish defensive line and then penetrated the second line four days later. Vyborg changed hands on 20 June with the Finns abandoning the city rather than engaging in prolonged fighting. Instead, they concentrated their troops to hold the Viipuri–Kuparsaari–Taipale line together with German reinforcements, and the Soviet assault here resulted in by far the heaviest fighting of the conflict between Finland and the Soviet Union. The attack by the Soviet Twenty-First Army began on 20 June and for the first six days the Red Army struggled to achieve any sustainable advances. On 27 June, an attempt by the Finns to isolate and destroy the leading four Soviet divisions also failed and after further heavy combat the exhausted Finnish units were forced to withdraw. By concentrating about half of its total artillery strength in the area, the Finnish Army was able to smash Soviet attempts to break through, and fighting died down – but didn't stop completely – in the second week of July.

By now, the Finns were effectively defending a line that approximated to their starting positions in 1941. Even though Leningrad Front's attacks had been halted, the Finnish Army was exhausted and any resumption of major fighting risked total collapse. In addition, the catastrophe that had overtaken the Wehrmacht in Belarus as the Soviet Operation *Bagration* overwhelmed the German defences was having a growing effect, as was the ongoing combat in Normandy. There was no possibility of Germany being able to spare any further reinforcements for Finland and on 1 August President Ryti resigned and was replaced by Mannerheim. He resumed negotiations with Moscow later in the month and had no choice but to accept the hard terms imposed by Stalin. A ceasefire came into effect on 4–5 September. The conflict had cost Finland over 63,000 dead and 158,000 wounded.[18] The final bill for reparations was reduced from $600 million to $300 million, but Stalin insisted that it was paid at 1938 exchange rates, which effectively doubled the value. In addition to its human and financial losses, Finland was forced to concede territory in the north and some islands in the Gulf of Finland, but unlike many nations in Eastern Europe, it succeeded in remaining independent of Moscow.

All of the soldiers who fought in the bitter, prolonged battles around Leningrad were marked for the rest of their lives by their experiences. For the Spanish soldiers of the Blue Division and the short-lived legion that succeeded it, there was the added surreal nuance of returning to a country that wasn't directly involved in the war as a belligerent. About 5,000 Spaniards died during their time on the Eastern Front and nearly half as many were left with permanent physical disabilities. The psychological scars of the war were also widespread. The first soldiers to return to Spain after their tour of duty, in 1942, received a lacklustre and ill-prepared welcome, including for the wounded. This resulted in protests by the returnees, their families, and their supporters. Although improvements were instigated almost immediately, the soldiers found that no real consideration had been given to their future life in Spain and German diplomats reported with alarm to Berlin that many Blue Division veterans were seen wandering the cities of Spain wearing their insignia and medals, seeking some form of employment and even begging.[19] Despite requests from German consuls for these veterans to be given preferential treatment in employment, there was widespread resistance in many Spanish cities, particularly where anti-Fascist support had been strong during the Spanish Civil War – the authorities were often reluctant to be seen by the public as favouring Fascists out of fear of stimulating resentment and unrest. Matters improved slowly in Spain, but many veterans volunteered to travel to Germany to seek employment in the factories of the Reich.

Many within the Spanish Fascist movement hoped and expected that the returning veterans would boost the image of Spanish Fascism, but they were largely disappointed. Some veterans, particularly senior NCOs and officers, remained in the army and eventually rose to high rank, while others used their combat record as a means of securing work in the Spanish civil service. Many benefited from other initiatives – for example, veterans were exempted from tuition and examination fees if they enrolled for study in Spain's universities. A number of 'Blue Division Brotherhoods' arose across Spain; many of these were primarily for the veterans themselves, while others focused more upon the families of men who were killed on the Eastern Front.

Leningrad, created as Peter the Great's window on the west, was already taking steps towards recovery before the end of the fighting around the city perimeter. In one of her regular radio broadcasts, the poet Olga Berggolts spoke to her fellow Leningraders in the closing minutes of 1943:

> This is the third New Year we've celebrated under siege. We won't have a fourth one like this. Enough. That's it![20]

In the days that followed the commencement of the January offensive, the citizens of Leningrad rejoiced at the steady stream of reports of towns liberated by the advancing Red Army and marvelled at how the city steadily became quieter – there was no longer the constant background rumble of artillery and explosions from the front line. For several weeks, people walking along Nevsky Prospekt continued to veer towards the south side of the street; the German shells that had repeatedly struck the city came from that direction, and consequently the buildings on the south side gave some protection, whereas pedestrians on the north side were more exposed. After the terrible starvation, cold, and the ever-present threat of sudden death from shells or bombs, there was a great sense of unreality for many. Vera Mikhailovna Inber, another Leningrad poet, wrote in her diary:

> It's the greatest event in the life of Leningrad, its complete liberation from the blockade. And here I am, a professional writer, and I simply can't find the words for it. All I can say is that Leningrad is free. And that's all.[21]

Many of the great landmarks of Leningrad had been disguised to avoid them being used as targets by the Germans. The statue of Peter the Great known as the Bronze Horseman that stands on Admiralty Embankment near St Isaac's Cathedral had been encased in padding and then enclosed in wooden walls with additional layers then added to camouflage its shape, and it was revealed once more amidst great celebration. For the moment, many of the gilded rooftops retained their grey canvas covers; it was still possible that the Luftwaffe might launch long-range raids. But before the end of the year, even these covers had disappeared.

The citizens of Leningrad began to venture out into the surrounding region, where many discovered the changes that the war had brought. Yevgeniya Shavrova and her mother went to Sestroretsk, on the northern side of the Gulf of Finland opposite the island of Kronstadt, where the family had had a dacha before the war:

> We came out onto the square by the old railway station and immediately we sensed a strange silence. Before the war this little town, no matter what time of day, was always full of people, it was all motion, alive and bustling. And now time stood still. But it wasn't just quiet all around, but some kind of ominous emptiness. We knew that everyone had been evacuated from here in 1942 because of the proximity of the Finnish front, and that only military personnel had remained. But the inhabitants apparently had not begun to return …
>
> When we turned onto our Liteinaia Street, there appeared before us an unexpected and eerie picture, as if from a book on ancient cities, destroyed and abandoned forever. The entire street was overgrown with tall weeds that reached above our heads. Wild burdock, gigantic goose-foot, nettles, and some completely unknown plants that we had never seen before the war … There was no sound from anything living – the cry of a rooster or a dog …
>
> We didn't stay there long. It was sad and simply frightening in the desert of nettles. The whole way back on the train we couldn't talk.[22]

As 1944 progressed, there were more visible reminders of the great victory as captured German tanks and other equipment were put on display. As the initial sense of unreality that the siege was finally over began to fade, thoughts turned to rebuilding the devastated city. Before the war, Leningrad had been home to about 3.1 million people; now, barely half a million remained. Many would return in the months and years that followed, but the Leningrad diaspora left its mark on the rest of the Soviet Union, with survivors of the siege scattered across its vast landscape. The Soviet authorities in Leningrad began to replace the posters exhorting the people to continue resisting and to work ever harder in war industries with new images; one new poster showed a young woman clad in a worker's smock, bearing a medal on her chest, against a background that included one of the great Rostral Columns of the city, with the caption *Mi Otstoyali Leningrad. Mi Bosstanovym Evo!* ('We defended Leningrad. We will rebuild it!')[23] But reconstruction would be a gargantuan task. Surveyors estimated that a total of over 3 million square yards of housing, more than 500 schools, about 65 per cent of the historic buildings of Leningrad, and more than 800 factories needed repairs. The infrastructure of the city was also greatly damaged: an estimated 45 miles of sewers, 27 miles of water mains, dozens of bridges large and small, and nearly 120 miles of streets would have to be repaired or replaced.[24]

The magnificent Winter Palace and Hermitage Museum on the Neva embankment had been repeatedly targeted by German shells and bombs; it was struck by 32 artillery shells and two aerial bombs during the siege. Most of its treasures had been evacuated as the Wehrmacht drew closer to Leningrad in 1941, but repairing the damage to the building itself would have to precede the return of the exhibits. Just as the destruction of the Hermitage was seen by the Germans as a useful means of undermining the morale and pride of the citizens of Leningrad, its early restoration was a useful way for the city authorities to demonstrate that Leningrad was recovering from its terrible ordeal. Iosif Abgari Orbeli, the administrator of the museum, was given the task of organising the repairs. He reported to the local Communist Party Committee that the work would require 65 tons of plaster, 80 tons of alabaster, a hundred tons of cement, two tons of glue, 40 tons of chalk plaster, 30 tons of chalk chippings, and a hundred tons of asphalt just to make the walls and ceilings sound. To complete the restoration, he added, would require even more material: 50 tons of pigments, ten tons of white lead, 20 tons of linseed oil, four tons of bronze, 13 pounds of gold, and huge amounts of glass, canvas, and decorative fabrics.[25] And this was just one building that had been hit by a relatively modest number of shells and bombs. Undaunted, Orbeli and his staff got to work, organising builders and craftsmen. The first trains bringing back the treasures of the Hermitage arrived in Leningrad in October 1945, and part of the museum re-opened a month later.

The return of the great treasures of the Hermitage Museum coincided with the appearance of other objets d'art. As the Red Army pushed into Europe and reached Germany, it was accompanied by officials who had been given a special task: they were to collect art treasures that had been identified and listed, and were to transport them to the Soviet Union. The rationale for this was stated clearly by the director of the Pushkin Museum in Moscow in 1944: 'The German-Fascist barbarians, who tried to annihilate Russian culture and destroyed many famous examples of Russian art, must be held responsible for all their crimes. The museums of the Axis countries are full of wonderful masterpieces, which must be given to the Soviet Union as compensation.'[26]

Just as Hitler had intended German cities to be adorned with looted treasures from the rest of Europe, Stalin ensured that Moscow and Leningrad in particular benefited from the enforced collection of large numbers of statues, paintings and other treasures.

As thoughts turned from survival and the war effort to reconstruction and rebuilding there were discussions – often heated – about the future of Leningrad. Many felt that the great palaces of the past were too badly damaged by the war and their reconstruction would be too expensive; there were suggestions that they should be left as permanent monuments to the barbarity of the German invasion. But this view was rapidly replaced by a desire to demonstrate that despite the immense damage inflicted upon Leningrad, the people of the Soviet Union would demonstrate to the world that they could rebuild the city, restoring all of its great buildings and creating alongside them a new Soviet Leningrad. Many great plans were drawn up for the city of the future that was to arise from the ruins, but most failed to materialise. Stalin had always been deeply suspicious of the city in the north with its tradition of independent thought and challenge to authority, and the people of Leningrad had suffered particularly badly during the era of his purges before the war. Zhdanov, the chair of the local Communist Party throughout the conflict, was a powerful figure after the war, second only to Stalin in the eyes of many, and his rigid and dogmatic vision came into conflict with the views of many of Leningrad's intellectuals as the city's population began to grow once more.

Zhdanov became the centre of what was known as *Zhdanovshchina* or 'Zhdanovism'. From 1946, his doctrine portrayed the world as being divided between the imperialistic world as exemplified by the USA and the democratic world with the Soviet Union at its head. All intellectual activity in the Soviet

Union was to conform to this view. There was no longer any room for 'apolitical' works of art or literature – everything had to be harnessed to the Zhdanovist vision of the world. For those in Leningrad, this meant deliberately turning their backs on the past. The city of St Petersburg, even of Petrograd, was to be dismissed from memory. Leningrad was to be home of a pure, anti-imperialist viewpoint. And yet, despite this, the old palaces and monuments were to be reconstructed in full.

Always careful to ensure that he retained Stalin's approval, Zhdanov moved against several prominent members of the city's intelligentsia – the poet Anna Akhmatova, the satirist Mikhail Zoschenko and the composer Dmitry Shostakovich were all condemned for decadent tendencies. As is described below, many reminders of the siege were deliberately removed. The hopes of many that Leningrad would once more be a great window to the west perished and in place of the daring architectural visions that had briefly circulated in the months after the siege, stark concrete apartment blocks rose across the city. Housing for the workers was – understandably – to take priority, and this was used as justification for the abandonment of other projects.

Zhdanov died of heart disease in 1948, but there was no question of changing direction as far as Leningrad was concerned – the principles of Zhdanovism would persist until after Stalin's death. Indeed, rebuilding the devastated city on the Neva was now assigned a far lower priority. Instead, reconstruction in other cities across the Soviet Union – Stalingrad on the lower Volga, Kiev and Odessa in Ukraine, and Minsk in Belarus, as well as Moscow itself – took precedence. Already, the creation of post-war myths was having a huge effect on what was to be remembered, and how it was to be remembered.

CHAPTER 14

MILITARY MEMORIES AND ASSESSMENTS OF THE SIEGE OF LENINGRAD

Any campaign that lasted as long as the siege of Leningrad, and that cost so many lives, was certain to be remembered in the memoirs of the people who were there at the time. Like all of the great episodes of almost any war, the manner in which it was recalled was highly selective.

There is no doubt that the Wehrmacht had an opportunity to reach and attack the city in the autumn of 1941, and many reviews of the war written by Germans saw this as a missed opportunity. On 18 July, less than a month after the Wehrmacht had entered the Soviet Union, Brigadeführer Franz Walter Stahlecker, commander of *Einsatzgruppe A*, speculated that Leningrad might fall to the rapid advance of the panzer divisions of Generaloberst Erich Hoepner's Fourth Panzer Group within a few days.[1] It is argued that had Leningrad been captured swiftly, it would not have been necessary for two German armies to remain in the northern sector, releasing forces for decisive battles elsewhere. Similarly, the failure to destroy the Oranienbaum bridgehead was seen as an error. It would surely have been easier for the Wehrmacht to concentrate resources against this modest bridgehead, which ultimately became the springboard for Fedyuninsky's Second Shock Army's successful assault of early 1944 that unlocked the German lines around Leningrad, than it would have been for the Red Army to reinforce it. But how realistic are these criticisms?

There is no question that the Soviet forces facing Army Group North as it approached Leningrad were in disarray. They had suffered heavy losses in the fighting in Lithuania and Latvia and they were badly handicapped by several factors. Their obsolescent equipment, particularly the huge tank fleet, was further weakened by major shortages of spare parts for machinery. The pre-war doctrine of the Red Army was badly out of step with the reality of modern warfare, with unit organisation, tactics, training, communications, and operational thinking all contributing to clumsiness and failure. The largest avoidable disadvantage suffered by the Red Army was the hugely disruptive effect of Stalin's paranoid purges of its officer corps, with the result that large numbers of the officers who attempted to deal with the German invasion were in posts far higher than was justified by their training or experience, and they were further inhibited from showing any initiative by continuing fear of arrest, imprisonment, and execution. In such circumstances, it was safer simply to follow orders from above. This in turn led to rigid enforcement of orders on subordinates, often backed up with the threat of punishment – hardly an environment conducive to initiative and independence of thought.

Whilst much of the Wehrmacht's equipment was also of questionable value – its tank fleet in particular included large numbers of vehicles that were too lightly armoured and carried guns that were too small for use in tank-to-tank combat – the tactical superiority of German units compensated greatly, meaning that even when Soviet units came up against German formations armed with obsolescent tanks and guns, the Germans still often prevailed. After the defeats close to the western frontiers of the Soviet Union, the divisions and armies of the Red Army desperately needed time to recover and the rapidity of the drive towards Leningrad denied them this breathing space.

The final battles of the German advance on Leningrad eventually died down on the southern outskirts of the city due to a combination of factors. The German formations were now far weaker than they had been at the beginning of the campaign. A large number of tanks had either been lost in combat or were stranded far to the rear of the front line, awaiting repairs or recovery from forests and swamps. Moving supplies forward to the front line was increasingly difficult – when they reached the Pulkovo Heights immediately south of Leningrad, the German units were over 430 miles from their start line, and the poor roads and rail links within the Soviet Union, combined with slowly growing partisan activity, made it difficult to move sufficient ammunition, fuel, and food to sustain a high tempo of operations on all fronts. There was also a significant element of over-reach. By stockpiling supplies before *Barbarossa* commenced, the Germans had been able to sustain operations by three army groups on diverging axes, consuming supplies far faster than they could be replenished. Once the initial stockpiles neared exhaustion, Germany lacked the industrial capacity to allow all sectors to continue such high-tempo operations. From the outset, *Barbarossa* had been a highly risky undertaking: if the invasion was to be a success, victory had to be achieved before the end of 1941.

As the Wehrmacht moved out of the Baltic States and into Russia proper, it ventured into territory that was increasingly unsuitable for major mechanised operations, with few roads and railways. Red Army resistance was also increasing steadily, to the growing concern of German officers who had happily accepted the wildly optimistic and inaccurate estimates of Soviet strength that had been prepared before the conflict. In addition, the Red Army was now fighting in terrain that was more suited to defensive operations, and was aided by the labour of tens of thousands of civilians who worked to dig trenches and anti-tank ditches. With so much of its strength now concentrated in overcoming the Soviet defences, Army Group North struggled to maintain a coherent front line as far as Army Group Centre. The consequence was that the latter army group was forced to pause its drive towards Moscow while it dealt with issues on both flanks. Although it is arguable that these flank operations fatally delayed the advance on Moscow, Hitler's original intention had always been to delay the capture of the Soviet capital until his goals had been achieved in the north and south: Moscow was explicitly a secondary objective in his overall plans with the capture (or at least elimination) of Leningrad and the destruction of the Soviet Baltic Fleet in the north, and the capture of the agricultural and industrial resources of Ukraine in the south, taking precedence. But although this was stated clearly by Hitler, many senior German commanders remained convinced that their ultimate success would come with the capture of Moscow. Halder, the chief of the German general staff, was not alone in hoping that the fluidity of operations would be sufficiently great for the Wehrmacht to pursue its desired objective of reaching the Soviet capital regardless of Hitler's wishes.

However, the biggest factor that stopped the Germans from advancing into and beyond Leningrad was Hitler's view on the future of the city and indeed of all Soviet urban centres. As the precise details of what would happen when Army Group North reached its objective were not defined clearly before the campaign began, many officers in the army group believed that just as was the case regarding Moscow, they would crown their campaign by seizing the city. But Hitler's intentions were different. Leningrad was an important centre for industry and military production, and the elimination of its industrial production was therefore seen as a vital war goal. However, this did not necessarily mean that the city had to be physically captured and occupied. In addition Germany would not be able simultaneously to appropriate millions of tons of grain while ensuring sufficient food for Soviet urban populations.

Consequently, as Army Group North advanced towards Leningrad in 1941 and it became ever more important to define clearly what would happen to the city, the instructions from Hitler's headquarters began to talk of isolating the city and leaving it to starve to death over the coming winter. Many German officers and soldiers later wrote of a sense of dissatisfaction or frustration that their campaign didn't culminate in the fall of Leningrad, but the physical capture of the city had effectively been ruled out even before the final push began. Specific orders for the establishment of a siege perimeter 'as close as possible' to the city were issued on the last days of August 1941; thereafter, Leningrad was to be bombarded with artillery and aircraft while starvation and the winter took their toll on the population and remaining defenders.[2] General Eduard Wagner, the quartermaster-general of the Wehrmacht, summed up the situation in a letter to his wife: 'First we will have to let them stew in Petersburg, what can we do with a city of 3.5 million who will just be a drain on our food resources? There is no room for sentimentality.'[3]

There were also concerns about the consequences of attempting to take the city. During the Russian Civil War, Leon Trotsky was sent to Petrograd as it was then known to organise its defence against approaching White Russian forces and he drew up plans for the citizens of the city to be armed and organised for urban warfare. Every city block and street was to be contested with the intention of drawing the White Russians into dozens of small but costly actions. Whilst the White Russian force was better trained and included large numbers of experienced soldiers, Trotsky calculated that this would count for little once the battle became a series of isolated engagements, with little opportunity for the enemy to coordinate actions. If the Wehrmacht had attempted to storm Leningrad in late 1941, it is highly likely that the same sort of fighting that Trotsky had intended would have taken place, and the cost to the Wehrmacht would have been high. Some in Leningrad called for Stalin to declare it an 'open city' in order to spare the population from the horrors of war, but neither Hitler nor Stalin would have considered such a proposal as acceptable.

Moreover, after their losses in the advance to Leningrad, the infantry formations of Army Group North would probably have lacked the strength to clear the entire city of resistance. Similarly, even if the final German attacks on Moscow had succeeded in reaching and even isolating the city, it is unlikely that the infantry divisions of Army Group Centre had enough strength to capture a large urban centre. Therefore, the physical capture of Leningrad in 1941 would have been highly problematic for the Wehrmacht. Even if the Germans had succeeded in taking the city, the cost would have been high.

Another factor that precluded any prolonged and costly battle for the streets of Leningrad was that according to the plans for *Barbarossa*, the Wehrmacht was to concentrate its forces for one final campaign to end the year, with a thrust to capture Moscow. The expected result would be the complete disintegration of the Soviet state, and in such circumstances the city in the north would simply die before the arrival of warm weather in 1942. In essence, Hitler's original objective in the north – the elimination of Leningrad as an industrial centre – had effectively been achieved. Similarly, with most of Ukraine now occupied, it was time to concentrate on what had Hitler had originally intended to be the culmination of the war.

The German accounts written after the war also benefit greatly from hindsight. At the time, it seemed pointless to suffer heavy losses in urban warfare when the ultimate outcome seemed almost certain. With German units on the southern shore of Lake Ladoga and artillery able to strike anywhere in the city, and with the Red Army so badly degraded and facing defeat on all fronts, it must have seemed that allowing Leningrad to face an inevitable death in a winter of hunger and bitter cold was an expedient way of avoiding German casualties. Whilst many senior figures in the Wehrmacht were beginning to doubt whether total victory over the Soviet Union could be achieved by the end of 1941, they remained broadly confident that they would still ultimately win the war. The decision not to storm the city and complete its physical capture is therefore entirely understandable. However, further German attacks near Leningrad might have achieved a more limited but vital objective. It would probably have been possible to carry out an advance along the western shore of Lake Ladoga to cut off Leningrad from the lake and to link up with Finnish forces that had advanced towards Leningrad from the northwest. Had this been achieved, the tight siege perimeter around the city would have guaranteed the death of most of its occupants during the winter that followed.

In the case of the Oranienbaum bridgehead, the issue was perhaps a little less clear. When the Wehrmacht reached the outskirts of Leningrad and succeeded in pushing through to the Gulf of Finland to the southwest of the city, thus cutting off the Oranienbaum bridgehead from the rest of the Red Army's defences, the final collapse of both Leningrad and the isolated bridgehead must have seemed inevitable. Hitler instructed Leeb, who was commander of Army Group North at the time, to draw up plans for further operations during the late autumn and winter, and Leeb and his staff offered several options. One was an attack to eliminate the Oranienbaum bridgehead, but instead Hitler opted for another option that was offered, an advance across the Volkhov River to capture the town of Tikhvin and to link up with the Finns to the east of Lake Ladoga. If such a link-up had taken place – and perhaps more importantly if the Germans and Finns had then been able to hold their positions so far to the northeast – it would have been impossible for Leningrad to survive. As it was, Leningrad narrowly avoided complete collapse due to starvation largely because Soviet engineers were able to construct the 'Road of Life' across the frozen lake, and completing the capture of the entire lake shoreline would have made this impossible.

Ultimately, the Wehrmacht was unable to hold onto Tikhvin and was forced to withdraw back to the Volkhov River, and in any case the Finns made no attempt to advance past the northern shore of Lake Ladoga. The German units that were used in the thrust to Tikhvin could have been deployed instead either to advance between Leningrad and Lake Ladoga, or to destroy the Oranienbaum bridgehead. Neither operation would have been guaranteed to be a success; in the case of Oranienbaum, the Red Army units that defended the bridgehead benefited throughout the months that followed from fire support provided by the ships of the Soviet Baltic Fleet, and any German attack would probably have required the Luftwaffe to carry out major attacks to cripple or destroy most of the Soviet warships. Similarly, an attack to isolate Leningrad from Lake Ladoga would have been resisted strenuously by the Red Army, as it would have been clear to the city's defenders that a German success would doom the city to destruction. But even with these reservations, the likelihood of success either by attacking the Oranienbaum bridgehead or by pushing north between Leningrad and Lake Ladoga was probably far higher than the ambitious thrust to Tikhvin. Choosing the latter operation in preference to the alternatives was, it seems, a major mistake. It is arguable that leaving the Oranienbaum bridgehead to wither and fall as Leningrad starved to death was a reasonable decision; but pushing on to Tikhvin rather than creating a tight siege ring around Leningrad and thus ensuring the collapse of both Leningrad and the Oranienbaum bridgehead was not.

The accounts written after the war by German veterans and officers rarely if ever interpret events in this manner. Almost all describe the failure to capture Leningrad in late 1941 as the critical error. There is little or no recognition that even as German formations entered Russia from Estonia and Latvia, Hitler had already declared that he had no intention of physically storming the city – indeed, he even ordered that if the Soviet authorities offered to surrender the city, the Wehrmacht was to refuse to accept any such offer. Instead, the impression in these accounts is of a missed opportunity that doomed Army Group North to a long, ultimately futile occupation of defensive lines around a city that refused to fall. To an extent, this may reflect the desire of Leeb and other senior officers to achieve the personal fame of being the conquerors of Leningrad. Few of Hitler's views on the destruction of the city by siege were passed down to lower levels during the last weeks of the German advance.

As with all of the so-called missed opportunities on the Eastern Front throughout the war, the failure to pursue the physical capture of Leningrad is usually attributed to Hitler. But such attribution of blame is contradictory. Many of the same authors go on to lament the failure to capture Moscow, but the scale of the Eastern Front and the challenges that faced the Wehrmacht were so great that ultimately *Barbarossa* failed because of a mismatch between the forces available to Germany and the wide-ranging and widely separated objectives. The problems confronting the Wehrmacht were compounded by the necessity to operate on diverging axes: Army Group North drove towards the northeast and Leningrad, creating a gap on its southern flank; Army Group South's advance across Ukraine, particularly after it was concentrated in a thrust south of Kiev, opened a similar gap on its northern flank; and Army Group Centre fought its way towards Moscow with both of its flanks increasingly exposed. Remedying this added to the delays that bedevilled the German advance.

The overall conclusion of the purely military side of the siege of Leningrad, from the German perspective, is that the capture of the city was a formidable task and the difficulties involved – particularly relating to logistics and communications routes – had been seriously underestimated by the German planners. Projecting force over such a great distance and over so few viable roads and railways was a difficult undertaking even without partisans operating in the huge forests that covered so much of the terrain. Despite its reputation for excellence, the German military machine repeatedly failed to take proper account of the realities of modern warfare, in which logistic constraints are paramount. Instead, there was a widely held belief that logistics should serve the needs of operational planning and should not constrain such planning.

At no stage did the Germans properly consider the lengths to which the Soviet Union in general and Leningraders in particular would go in order to prevent the fall of Leningrad. The Wehrmacht had captured major cities in earlier campaigns – Warsaw in 1939, and Paris, Copenhagen, Amsterdam, and Brussels in 1940 – but on all of these occasions the cities fell to the Germans at a time when the national armies of those nations had already been defeated. It was clearly the intention of the Wehrmacht to seek to surround and destroy most of the Red Army close to the western frontiers of the Soviet Union and major encirclements were in fact achieved, but there had been a consistent underestimation of the resources available to the Red Army. The continuing resistance of Soviet units and the constant appearance of new formations made clear to the Germans that despite their undoubted successes, the enemy was far from defeated. To attempt to storm a city as large as Leningrad in such circumstances would have been a hard task even without any recognition of the willingness of ordinary Leningraders to take up arms to defend their homes. Although Hitler and others stressed the political and psychological importance of Leningrad to the Soviet Union as the cradle of the Bolshevik Revolution, they failed to recognise that its very importance meant that both the Red Army and Soviet civilians would fight bitterly to prevent its fall. In addition, there was the special pride of Leningraders. Their city had been attacked repeatedly in living memory, with two major battles being fought on the southern outskirts against White Russian forces, and then there had been a long, brutal wave of political repression that left its scars on every part of Leningrad's population. Despite these ordeals, or perhaps more accurately at least partly because of them, Leningraders regarded themselves as a distinct group. They had endured a great deal in their city in the north, and had emerged intact. It was their tragedy that they were then tested again to a far greater extent than any of their earlier ordeals.

The memoirs of other nationalities that fought alongside the Germans outside Leningrad were also selective in their recollections. The Spanish soldiers of the Blue Division and Blue Legion who returned to their homeland brought with them memories of a terrible battle of attrition in a distant land, where freezing winters were followed by summer plagues of mosquitoes, interspersed with endless mud and misery. The generally contemptuous attitude of the Germans towards their allies added to the disillusion felt by many Spanish veterans. Inevitably, those who had fought near Leningrad wished to tell their stories after they returned home, and did so in as selective and self-promoting a manner as veterans of any conflict. The Blue Division was portrayed repeatedly in both memoirs and novels as a strongly Catholic group, leading the fight against Bolshevism in defence of old European values. Almost all of these memoirs attempted to portray the Spanish troops as purely military combatants with no involvement in the atrocities of the Eastern Front. In particular, there was a strong desire to deny any involvement in the persecution and murder of Jews, but some of the works written by veterans showed strong anti-Semitic traits. In one autobiographical novel, there were sections that could have been lifted verbatim from Nazi publications:

> Today's Jews are as they were a thousand years ago and will be the same in another
> thousand years if the world lasts that long. And if the last one is victorious, all

those who preceded him will rub their hands with glee in hell ... if the last brother of their race rips the skin off the last Christian.[4]

German memoirs and accounts, whether written by generals and officers or by ordinary men, also concentrated almost exclusively on military matters. If atrocities were ever mentioned, it was only in passing and such acts were always portrayed as being carried out by 'others' – the SS, paramilitary units, local police forces, or local people carrying out justifiable 'reprisals' against suspected Bolsheviks whom they blamed for repression before the arrival of the Germans. In some cases, such as Manstein's memoirs, there were deliberate falsehoods – Manstein claimed that he had refused to pass on the various orders regarding the illegal treatment of captured commissars and other Communist Party officials, but evidence was presented at his war crimes trial that he had clearly disseminated such instructions. German accounts made much of the endurance and suffering of German soldiers in the primitive conditions that existed on the entire Eastern Front, but there was almost no mention of the suffering of ordinary civilians as a consequence of either the fighting or the enforced seizure of houses and food. The myth of the 'clean Wehrmacht', fighting an honourable war for Germany to protect all of Europe from the scourge of Bolshevism, became the dominant narrative and even embraced the SS divisions that fought on the Eastern Front.

In reality, almost every unit on the Eastern Front was involved in atrocities against civilians, whether they were ethnic Russians or Jews. That is not to say that every member of every unit was involved; but it seems highly unlikely that the soldiers in the front line were completely unaware of what was being done in the areas immediately behind the front line. Many witnessed the mass killing of Jews and other groups deemed 'undesirable', and they would have shared their experiences with their comrades. An example of this can be seen in a well-known photograph known as 'The Last Jew of Vinnitsa'. A solitary Jew kneels at the side of a mass grave as a German prepares to execute him, while a group of uniformed men watch in the background. The uniforms of those present are almost a comprehensive list of all German authorities in the occupied territories: *Reichsarbeitsdienst* ('Reich Labour Administration'); army; SS; police; and Luftwaffe. It seems from this photograph and others that despite orders for spectators to be kept away from mass killings, large numbers of men from units in the area attended them. The 'clean Wehrmacht' myth dominated English language accounts of the Eastern Front for decades, not least because when German accounts were written and then translated into English, there was a need to rehabilitate the reputation of West Germany as part of the anti-Soviet alliance, and the Soviet Union was the new enemy. The strength of this myth is so great that in many respects it persists even today.

After the survival of Leningrad during the first winter of the siege, the sector assumed a low priority in German plans for further operations. When Sevastopol fell to the Germans, Manstein's Eleventh Army was to be moved to the northern sector so that it could repeat its storming of a fortified stronghold – by the summer of 1942, it seems, the Germans were committing themselves to the sort of urban fighting that Hitler had attempted to avoid in late 1941. But this planned offensive, codenamed *Nordlicht* ('Northern Light'), was abandoned when the Red Army struck first, attempting to break the siege by attacking towards the Sinyavino Heights from the east. It was the last time that the Wehrmacht made any serious preparations for an attack to capture Leningrad. There were tentative thoughts that if the summer operations around Kursk unfolded successfully, there might be a new northern offensive later in 1943, but such considerations didn't move beyond such broad outlines. After the failure of the German attack on the Kursk salient, there was no longer any possibility of further attacks. The role of Army Group North was now reduced to holding the Red Army as far from Germany as possible.

The accounts of the military aspects of the siege that were written in the Soviet Union after the war were in many respects even more selective and distorted than those written by German veterans. Prior to Stalin's death, the war was portrayed as a demonstration of Stalin's infallible genius and the unique strengths of the Soviet Union. There were several repeated themes in post-war Soviet writing; heroic acts of self-sacrifice featured in dozens of accounts, with brave young Komsomol members blocking German firing positions with their bodies in order to protect their comrades, or deliberately throwing themselves under German tanks in order to detonate explosive charges. Many of these accounts may have been true, but they highlighted a hidden truth: such acts were necessary because the Red Army was so badly prepared for a war against the Wehrmacht. If sufficient anti-tank weapons had been available, for example, there would have been no need for suicidal attacks on German tanks. The disasters of the fighting in 1941 were carefully described to avoid any recognition of tactical or operational errors, and the cult of Stalin's infallibility was assiduously maintained. His failure to recognise or accept the repeated warnings of German preparations receives only the most oblique references in the memoirs of men like Zhukov who witnessed the near-complete paralysis in the highest Soviet circles in the opening days of the war.

The Soviet accounts of fighting as the Wehrmacht edged closer to the city are also full of examples of individual heroism, together with examples of German atrocities as Luftwaffe aircraft attacked trains and towns, killing hundreds of civilians. There were major errors made by the Soviet civilian administration as the siege perimeter was established that resulted in exacerbation of the problems that the city faced during the winter; few serious preparations were made to ensure that there were sufficient stockpiles to feed the population, or to ensure that there would be enough coal to keep factories running, let along to provide heating for civilians. But these failings were rarely mentioned during the period between 1945 and Stalin's death in 1953. Instead, there was perhaps understandable emphasis on the ingenuity of Soviet authorities in the north who devised a multitude of solutions to the problems that they faced, such as the creation of the Road of Life across Lake Ladoga that saved the population from complete starvation. Even these incidents sought to stress the role played by individuals and organisations of the Communist Party. As with the suffering of soldiers in the front line, mention of civilian hardships in Leningrad and elsewhere was permitted in only two contexts: either to show how badly the Germans had behaved in the occupied parts of the Soviet Union, or to show that the people of the Soviet Union had been willing to make huge sacrifices to achieve victory. It was victory in particular that mattered, and everything was interpreted as a means of achieving that end. The effect that this had on the very specific memories and myths of Leningraders and *Blokadniki*, as those who had endured the siege became known, is discussed in more detail in the final chapter.

The repeated attempts made by the Red Army to lift the siege of the city resulted in huge losses of life throughout 1942. In early 1943, it was possible to create a narrow land corridor along the southern shore of Lake Ladoga, but every attempt to widen this merely increased the already terrible total of casualties. The memoirs of men like Fedyuninsky and Meretskov recognised some of the weaknesses of the Red Army, but like most Soviet writers they seized upon an opportunity to heap blame and opprobrium upon an easy target. When the Soviet forces attacked in the first half of 1942 in their attempts to reach Lyuban, Second Shock Army was commanded by Lieutenant General Andrei Andreyevich Vlasov. His army was encircled by the Germans and forced to surrender through no fault of its commander, and he became a prisoner of the Germans and subsequently cooperated with his captors. Eventually, Vlasov took command of the *Russkaya Osvoboditelnaya Armiya* ('Russian Liberation Army', often abbreviated to 'ROA'), a force made up of former Red Army personnel.[5] The ROA fought against the Red Army as an anti-Bolshevik force; although many of its personnel were volunteers, others agreed to join the ranks of the army in order to escape the harsh conditions of prisoner of war camps, or in the hope that they might be able to defect back to the Soviet side of the front line. There were many other former Soviet soldiers who aided the Germans in a variety of roles with different levels of willingness, such as the *Hilfswillige* ('voluntary helpers', often abbreviated to *Hiwi*) who acted as orderlies, cleaners, cooks, drivers, and even combatants. But whenever Soviet soldiers encountered such men in combat, they referred to them in their memoirs as 'Vlasovites', even though the men who fought for the Germans under Vlasov only saw action relatively late in the war.

The role played in the fighting near Leningrad by a man who became widely known in the Soviet Union after the war as a traitor was a great opportunity for writers in the Soviet era to highlight his treachery and thus draw attention away from the operational failures that resulted in Second Shock Army's encirclement. In this manner, the flawed overall conception of the Lyuban Operation, poor operational planning and conduct by Meretskov, and the lack of adequate support for Second Shock Army were all glossed over in the concerted attempts to blame Vlasov for the disastrous outcome.

The military accounts written in the Soviet era repeatedly failed to show proper consideration of the catalogue of setbacks and failures. In a region where the lack of roads and the widespread forests and swamps made any use of massed armour almost impossible, the Red Army came to rely heavily on artillery, and on numerous occasions when this failed, the same problems were identified. The constant criticisms of reconnaissance to identify all German fortifications and firing points; the failure of artillery to destroy those German positions that were actually identified; the difficulties in moving guns and their ammunition forward to keep up with an advance; all of these were listed almost verbatim after every operation. Broad and generalised instructions were issued for the problems to be remedied, but there was no formal assessment of what measures had been taken to put matters right, how appropriate they were, and what practical changes they brought.

One of the many lessons that the Red Army had to learn was the efficient and effective use of engineering support, but like so many other areas where its performance was found to be deficient, veterans of the war rarely described any meaningful steps that were taken to remedy the problems. This was yet another area where problems might have been identified, but detailed solutions were rarely articulated, implemented, or assessed for efficacy.

In this context, it is worth noting that the Leningrad Military District was one of the premier such military regions prior to the war. It was commanded by a long succession of leading military figures and was regarded as a prestigious posting; the units in the district regularly carried out large-scale field exercises that were often innovative and revolutionary, for example looking at the use of airborne forces. After carrying out such exercises in this region in peacetime, senior Soviet commanders must have been aware of the practical difficulties in mounting operations in the forested terrain and the limitations placed upon operations by the poor road network. But despite this, there is no indication that any such lessons were learned from the pre-war exercises, or were remembered once fighting began.

The encirclement and destruction of Second Shock Army in the failed Lyuban Operation of 1942 was followed by further attempts to lift the siege; as a consequence of the failure of the large-scale operation intended to capture Lyuban and then to break the siege ring, future attacks concentrated on a far smaller sector. This was partly a recognition of the failures of the Lyuban Operation and partly due to constraints imposed by the overall war, with other sectors jostling for resources, but by concentrating on breaking the siege ring at the shortest point – the Shlisselburg–Sinyavino–Mga corridor to the south of Lake Ladoga – the Red Army also permitted the Germans to concentrate their resources. There was a further consequence of attacking in this region. The Wehrmacht steadily increased their heavy artillery around Leningrad, particularly after the fall of Sevastopol in the summer of 1944. When the Red Army made its assaults upon the Shlisselburg–Sinyavino–Mga sector, the Germans were able to support their forces using this massed artillery, often with devastating effect. The second destruction of Second Shock Army in the autumn of 1942 was the consequence of several factors: inadequate width of the initial breakthrough; poor cooperation between Leningrad and Volkhov Fronts; continuing failures of the Soviet god of war, its artillery, both in the initial barrage and in keeping up with the advance; the difficulty of attempting an advance through what was effectively a continuous defensive zone; highly effective use of artillery by the Germans; and the continuing tactical superiority of German soldiers, whether in defensive mode or in the counterattacks that isolated the exposed Soviet units. None of these factors was new. All of them should have been anticipated.

Until the beginning of 1943, all of these attempts to break the siege ring failed, but nonetheless they had important consequences. Firstly, although the fighting resulted in disproportionately heavy Soviet casualties, the losses suffered by the Wehrmacht were also significant. Most of the tens of thousands of Red Army soldiers who were killed or wounded in these battles were relatively new recruits with little or no combat experience. By contrast, most of the Wehrmacht's losses were veterans, and this resulted in a serious degradation in the resilience and fighting power of the Wehrmacht. As the battles of 1942 and 1943 unfolded, this progressive loss of capability on the German side steadily eroded the tactical advantages that the Wehrmacht had enjoyed and had demonstrated so frequently. At the same time, the Red Army was slowly and painfully learning from its mistakes and improving its tactical performance. Despite its heavy losses, most formations now had a core of experienced veterans who knew how to fight and win; casualties were particularly heavy amongst new drafts, and the longer a soldier had been in the front line, the greater the likelihood of survival. The tactical discrepancy between the two sides therefore slowly narrowed. The Germans retained their advantage, but it was no longer as great as it had been before, and it wasn't sufficient to counterbalance the numerical advantage enjoyed by the Red Army.

The second consequence of the attempts to lift the siege, and one that featured repeatedly in Soviet-era accounts, was that the fighting around Leningrad resulted in the diversion of German resources from other sectors. The failure of Army Group North to capture Leningrad – or more accurately, the survival of Leningrad – in the first winter of the conflict ensured that the German Army had to leave substantial forces in the north. This meant that there were fewer resources available to the Wehrmacht for deployment elsewhere, particularly on the key southern axis where the tide of the war turned decisively against Germany in late 1942. One of the foremost examples of this diversion of German military assets to the north that was often cited in Soviet accounts was the decision to send Manstein's Eleventh Army to Army Group North in the late summer of 1942 after the fall of Sevastopol, in preparation for *Nordlicht*. Had these divisions been available in the south, it was argued, the outcome of the fighting around Stalingrad might have been very different. The huge sacrifice of life in repeated Soviet attacks in the north was therefore justified by the assertion that these attacks forced Hitler to try to crush Leningrad before one or other Soviet attack succeeded in breaking through the siege ring.

But how true is this assertion? For this argument to be sustained, it would be necessary to demonstrate that the retention of Eleventh Army in the south would have made a decisive difference in the Stalingrad battles. At first glance, the availability of several battle-hardened divisions would seem to be a considerable asset. However, what seems a self-evident truth becomes more complex at closer examination. As the recent conflict in Ukraine has demonstrated, the dull business of logistics is often of crucial importance in the outcome of operations. During the Stalingrad campaign, the German forces in Stalingrad and further south in the Caucasus region were operating at the end of long, very tenuous supply lines. When the Red Army withdrew across the Dnepr in 1941, most of the river crossings were destroyed; by the following summer, the Germans had restored only a single major railway bridge across the river. In an era in which the Germans (and indeed their Soviet counterparts) were heavily dependent upon railways for their logistic support, all the German units in Army Groups A and B – and also all of their Romanian, Italian, and Hungarian allies – were being supplied via this one railway bridge. If Eleventh Army had remained in the region, it would only have augmented the fighting strength of German forces if it had been possible to supply it properly. This would have been very difficult given the constraints imposed by the rail network. Moreover, in order to reduce the Soviet defences around Sevastopol, Eleventh Army possessed a disproportionately large number of heavy artillery formations. All artillery is resource-hungry in terms of logistics; shells are both bulky and heavy and are rapidly consumed once fighting commences. It is therefore by no means a certainty that had Eleventh Army been assigned to help German operations in the south, it would have made a decisive difference. At best, the defensive positions of the armies of Germany's allies – the Romanian, Italian, and Hungarian divisions – deployed either side of Stalingrad and along the Don River might have been strengthened by the presence of strong German infantry divisions, but it would have been difficult to supply them properly, even if the allied units had been withdrawn. The German divisions, with their greater firepower, required larger quantities of supplies than the allied divisions.

However, the constant threat of renewed Soviet attacks to reach Leningrad undoubtedly prevented the transfer of veteran formations to other sectors, and it can certainly be argued that in this respect, the operations of Leningrad and Volkhov Fronts succeeded in tying down German forces. Whether this could have been achieved at a lower cost in terms of Red Army casualties is a debatable point. Given the terrain and the nature of the Red Army – far more of a blunt instrument than a weapon with a cutting edge – it is difficult to see how operations sufficiently threatening to tie down German strength could have been mounted without such casualties. Simply bombarding the German lines with artillery would not have been an alternative – as already described, artillery is very resource-hungry, and it would not have been possible to furnish Leningrad and Volkhov Fronts with sufficient shells for them to have battered the German divisions with endless bombardments.

Remembrance of the role played by men from Latvia and Estonia has been difficult and complex. Soldiers from both countries were enrolled into SS divisions that fought in the Leningrad sector and the battles that followed the end of the siege, as the Red Army pressed into the Baltic States. Many of the veterans of these divisions were able to surrender to the Western Allies at the end of the conflict. The Estonian 20th *SS-Waffen-Grenadier* Division ended the war in central Germany and was able to move west in order to come under American control;

the Latvian 15th *SS-Waffen-Grenadier* Division was almost completely destroyed in Pomerania in the closing weeks of the war with a few fragmented units pulling back to northern Germany; and only its sister formation, 19th *SS-Waffen-Grenadier* Division, was forced to surrender to the Red Army, trapped in the German pocket in Courland in western Latvia. By the time of the surrender, many of the men of this latter division had already slipped away, attempting to return to their homes. The fact that so many of these men from the Baltic region who served alongside German soldiers had escaped to the west played into the Soviet post-war view that they were Nazis who were being sheltered by the imperialist bloc, thus becoming part of the Zhdanovite narrative. This was further strengthened by evidence that many of the paramilitary police units that were used to create the three Baltic SS divisions had been extensively involved in the Holocaust and in anti-partisan operations in the German-occupied areas of the Soviet Union. But if the portrayal of the Baltic soldiers by the Soviet Union was that they were war criminals and Fascists, many Latvians and Estonians saw the men differently, as soldiers who attempted to prevent the return of Soviet rule to the region.

Clearly, it was impossible to articulate such thoughts while the three Baltic States remained part of the Soviet Union, but some of the SS veterans remained at large in the forests of the region as resistance fighters known as the Forest Brothers. The movement grew rapidly in the decade after the war and caused considerable difficulties for the Soviet garrisons in all three Baltic States until roughly 1956 when through a mixture of infiltrating the groups and major military deployments, the Soviet forces were able to achieve a dominant position. Nevertheless, acts of resistance continued with individuals coming out of hiding from time to time into the 1980s. Such prolonged resistance would have been impossible without ongoing support from the local population.

Even after the end of the Soviet Union and the independence of the Baltic States, remembrance of the wartime veterans remained controversial. Many in the newly independent states on the Baltic coast saw them as men who had fought against the return of Soviet rule. Although some acknowledged the obvious truth that the veterans had been fighting for Nazi Germany and therefore had aided, even if only indirectly, the crimes of that state, the counterargument was that the Soviet Union was also guilty of terrible crimes against civilians. In addition to the deportations of tens of thousands of Baltic civilians in the year before the German invasion of the Soviet Union, there were further waves of deportations to Siberia after the triumphant return of the Red Army at the end of the war. Such was the scale of Soviet deportations from the region that it was possible to show that many – probably most – of the men who fought in the ranks of the three Baltic SS divisions had lost family members during the Soviet deportations, adding a personal element to their motivation to fight against the Soviet Union. The role that many of these men played in the perpetration of war crimes – the Holocaust, and the indiscriminate slaughter of civilians during anti-partisan operations – was often overlooked or ignored in the Baltic States.

During the Soviet era a great memorial was built in the city of Tallinn, portraying the Red Army as liberators of the Estonian people from Nazi occupation. The fact that many – perhaps most – Estonians regarded the return of Soviet rule as just a change of occupiers was ignored. Several memorial stones are displayed, bearing the names of Red Army units involved in the fighting, including a so-called Estonian rifle corps – during the Soviet advance to Tallinn, the Red Army went to considerable lengths to ensure that this corps was in the vanguard of the advance. In reality, a large proportion of its personnel were ethnic Russians. After Estonia became independent, the memorial was enlarged. There is now a long walkway within which are the names of many of the thousands of people who were deported to Siberia by the Soviet rulers. A great display on the outside of the walkway shows dozens of small metal bees, arranged to portray the numerous prison camps where these deportees were taken in the Soviet Union (and where thousands of them died, far from their homeland), and after Estonian independence a new set of military memorial stones was erected bearing the names of Estonian units that fought against the Red Army in 1944. Like many memorials, what is missing is as important as what is present. None of these memorials to Estonian soldiers who fought against the Red Army includes the fateful letters 'SS'. Nor is there any mention in this memorial of the tens of thousands of Jews from all over the region who were brought to Estonia during German rule, held under Estonian guard, and worked to death in the oil shale extraction plants on the Baltic coast and elsewhere. It wasn't until January 2022 that a memorial was created in Tallinn in memory of Estonian Jews who were killed after the arrival of the Germans in 1941.

Further east in Estonia, there is a memorial in the Sinimäed Hills, created in 2007, commemorating the great battle in the summer of 1944. Again, although many Estonian and other 'international SS' units are named, there is no mention of them being part of the SS. But not everyone in Estonia has been happy about this commemoration of the past. The memorial slabs on the Sinimäed Hills bear the scars of attempts to destroy them, and there are now surveillance cameras in place to deter any future attempts. In a similar vein, there have been protests at commemoration marches in honour of Latvian veterans who fought against the Red Army.

Attempts by the Baltic States to remove memorials erected during the era of Soviet rule have resulted in several incidents. A bronze statue of a Soviet soldier known as the 'Monument to the Liberators of Tallinn' was located in a central part of the city at the site of a small Soviet war cemetery and in 2007 the graves were exhumed and their contents were re-interred in a larger cemetery elsewhere in the city, with many Russian families being given the option to have the remains of their family members returned to Russia. The statue was also moved to the new location amidst widespread protests by ethnic Russians living in Estonia, and there then followed a sophisticated cyber-attack on Estonia resulting in widespread disruption. This was blamed on groups working either directly for the Russian government or in sympathy with it. In 2022, after the beginning of the war between Russia and Ukraine, a decision was made to move a T-34 tank from a Soviet-era memorial on the Narva River to the northwest of the city of Narva where Fedyuninsky's forces had attempted to create a bridgehead to bypass the German defences within the city. Again, there were protests by ethnic Russians, who make up a large percentage of the population of the Narva region, and there was a candlelit vigil at the site after the tank had been removed.

The great battles that swept across the central and southern parts of the Soviet Union between 1941 and 1945 shaped the Red Army, effectively dictating the nature of the forces that finally advanced into Germany to and beyond Berlin; the impact of the experiences of the campaigns in Ukraine and Belarus could still be seen in Soviet doctrine and equipment right to the end of the Cold War. By contrast, the fighting in the northern sector had far less lasting influence on the structure or function of the armies of either side. To a large extent, this is because the terrain over which the fighting took place was unusual and lessons learned here had limited applicability to fighting elsewhere. The sheer scale of the casualties suffered, both military and civilian, and the very fact that the battles were for possession of the city of Leningrad, ensured that these clashes would be the subject of copious works; but their impact on the manner in which the war was fought elsewhere was modest. Perhaps the greatest lesson for both sides from the battles was the critical importance of logistics and the need to ensure good road and rail mobility, by either rapid construction or repair of such facilities; inevitably, most accounts concentrate instead on the nuts and bolts of fighting, with little regard for a simple truth. Without adequate supplies, the best army in the world cannot function. Ultimately, the factor that prevented the Wehrmacht from achieving outright victory in 1941 and repeatedly led to the failure of Soviet operations in 1942, 1943, and 1944 was inadequate attention to logistic issues.

CHAPTER 15

THE MYTHS AND LEGENDS OF LENINGRAD

Just a few months after the end of the war, the poet Olga Berggolts encountered a soldier who had recently returned to the Soviet Union. He told her that he wanted to read about what he regarded as the 'real' war – he wished for tales of 'heroism and brave deeds'.[1] It was a sentiment shared by many, in the Soviet Union and across the world. For soldiers and civilians who had been mentally and physically scarred by the brutality, random destruction, and chaos of war, there was an almost desperate need for a narrative within which they could come to terms with their personal experiences. In the Soviet Union, this narrative would be tightly controlled by Stalin.

Almost every institution in the Soviet Union had been forced to change during the war. Much of the rigid top-down diktat of the pre-war years had been found to be too inflexible, especially in the military – in order to have any chance of tactical success, junior officers had to learn to think for themselves, and their commanders had to learn to permit this. As the war came to an end, many soldiers returning to civilian life and many of those who had endured German occupation and the privations of wartime looked forward to these reforms becoming embedded in Soviet society and taken still further. Farmers hoped for the abolition of the widely disliked collective farming system; factory workers felt that their huge efforts had been the bedrock of Soviet survival and would be rewarded with greater autonomy; prisoners in the widespread network of camps across Siberia, many of whom had been arrested in the pre-war years, looked forward to being released; and intellectuals anticipated greater freedom in their works. All were rapidly disillusioned by what followed.

Almost as soon as the guns fell silent, the orthodox Soviet view of the war years began to be imposed. In part, Stalin was determined to claim all the credit for the defeat of Nazi Germany and sidelined the great commanders of the Red Army like Zhukov and Govorov; anything that might glorify their records was either downplayed or mutated into a version of events that showed Stalin as the prime mover behind their victories. So much of the war had been a litany of setbacks for the Red Army: the opening months were disastrous, and 1942 and 1943 saw repeated offensive operations that resulted in huge losses for little gain. All of these were either deliberately forgotten or distorted almost beyond recognition. The great slaughter around the Rzhev salient, for example, was either ignored or portrayed as an essential means of weakening the Wehrmacht and tying down German reserves to prevent their deployment in critical sectors like Stalingrad. Indeed, Stalingrad became the defining battle in Soviet historiography, the triumph of the Soviet State via its instrument, the Red Army, over the Fascists in a city that coincidentally happened to be named after the man who was now claiming credit. By contrast, Leningraders saw the survival and ultimate triumph of their city in the north as a victory for ordinary people. Even in the spring of 1942, as Leningrad began the slow, painful recovery from near-collapse during the terrible winter of starvation and lethal cold, Berggolts articulated the special status of the *Blokadniki* who had endured and survived in a poem that she read on Radio Leningrad:

> By one unprecedented battle
> One unique fate,
> We are all marked.
> We are Leningraders.[2]

A year later, the British journalist and writer Alexander Werth – who was born in 1901 in what was then St Petersburg – commented from Leningrad where he was working as a BBC correspondent:

> I noticed in Leningrad a slight aloofness towards Moscow, a feeling that, although this was part of the whole show, it was also in a sense a separate show, one in which Leningrad had largely survived thanks to its own stupendous efforts and those of its local chiefs.[3]

This Leningrad-centric view concentrated on the very real struggle of ordinary citizens to survive, but ignored an important truth. Although many Leningraders had fought in the front line against the Wehrmacht during the siege, the majority of the Red Army's soldiers who struggled and perished in the terrible battles were from other parts of the Soviet Union. The great military figures who had played such prominent parts in the fighting were also not from Leningrad. Govorov was from a small village over 400 miles to the northeast of Moscow; Meretskov's family were residents of a village immediately to the west of Moscow; Fedyuninsky was born in the Ural Mountains; and Simoniak came from the Kuban region to the northwest of the Caucasus Mountains. In a military sense, the triumph of the defence of Leningrad was therefore the result of the efforts of officers and men of the entire Soviet Union, but Leningraders continued to see it as their personal triumph.

Even before the end of the war, steps were being taken to curb the individuality of Leningraders and their city and in particular any attempt by them to deviate from officially sanctioned points of view. In late 1943, the writer Vsevolod Vitalyevich Vishnevsky was informed by the city authorities that his new play *U Sten Leningrada* ('At the Walls of Leningrad') was unacceptable because some of the characters were too pessimistic and negative. His protests that this merely reflected reality were dismissed. The composer Mikhail Iosifovich Nosyrev was aged just 19 at the end of 1943 when he was suddenly arrested together with his family by the NKVD and charged with counter-revolutionary activities: the precise nature of these activities was that he had kept a diary during the siege that recorded the near-collapse of Leningrad's hospitals in February 1942. He was sentenced to death, but this was commuted to ten years' imprisonment, which he spent in a work camp in the far north near Vorkuta. Even after his release he was exiled to the town of Syktyvkar, 680 miles east of Leningrad, and wasn't exonerated until several years after his death in 1981.

The comments of Berggolts and the views noticed by Werth were entirely in character for Leningrad and its previous incarnations of Petrograd and St Petersburg, but unacceptable to Stalin. Victory had been achieved collectively and was to be celebrated as a great Soviet achievement. The emphasis was on the belief that the defeat of Nazi Germany by the Soviet Union was possible only because of the unique nature of the state: it was the great union of different nationalities, all combined and led by the Communist Party – which was, in turn, led by the infallible Stalin – that had achieved triumph, and in the absence of Stalin and the Communist Party, this triumph would have been impossible. Henceforth, it was better to concentrate on the future, on reconstruction and the growing tension with the capitalist west.[4] The undeniable suffering caused by the war was not to be forgotten, but was to be put in the context of being the price that the Soviet Union paid to achieve victory. Indeed, part of the mythology of the Great Patriotic War was that the Soviet Union had suffered more than any other nation and therefore had a right to reparations and territorial gains at the expense of Germany.

Despite increasingly authoritarian measures, many in Leningrad continued to cling to their sense that they had survived the great siege because of their special character as Leningraders, drawing an important distinction between the military defence of the city by soldiers from all over the Soviet Union and the endurance of ordinary citizens. It is difficult to know whether Leningraders were unique in their willingness to express hostility to Stalin's heavy-handed imposition of the orthodox Soviet view, or whether the evidence of their continuing resistance reflects the multitude of writers in the city who were prepared to record and comment on it. From the very start of the war, many in Leningrad had taken a markedly different attitude to the conflict. Some in Leningrad wished for the declaration of an 'open city' as had been the case when the Wehrmacht closed in on Paris; attempts by the city authorities to prepare for fighting close to and even in Leningrad by evacuating civilians were haphazard and organised far too late and on too small a scale. A second repeated criticism was the lack of preparation for a siege, by timely evacuation of as many civilians as possible and stockpiling of sufficient food and fuel to serve the needs of those who remained. Both of these are worth further consideration.

At the time, declaring Leningrad to be an open city may have seemed like a rational measure to protect the civilian population, but most people in Leningrad did not know the genocidal intentions of the Germans with regard to the urban population of the Soviet Union at the time. Hitler had already decreed that any surrender of the city was to be refused, and given his characterisation of the war with the Soviet Union as lying outside the normal rules of warfare, it seems likely that if Leningrad had been declared an open city, the consequences would almost certainly have been disastrous. The Wehrmacht would have expelled most of the population towards the east as part of the implementation of the Hunger Plan, refusing to take on the burden of feeding such a large number of people, and the release of a large proportion of the military formations of Army Group North would have been of huge value to the Germans elsewhere.

The failure to evacuate the city and lack of adequate preparation for a siege by way of food and fuel stockpiles almost brought about the outcome that Hitler wished, namely the death of the city during the winter of 1941–42. Such criticisms are at first glance reasonable. But stockpiling of food and civilian evacuation would have required intensive use of the railway system at a time when all capacity was being used to keep the Red Army alive. Finding sufficient supplies for stockpiles would have been challenging enough, and moving them to Leningrad before the siege ring closed was probably impossible. Even if sufficient railway capacity had been allocated to this – and the trains had then survived Luftwaffe interdiction – the arrival of such large stocks in Leningrad would have required preparation of adequate warehouse space, again at a time when the exigencies of the military situation were consuming all resources and capabilities. Just when the Red Army was using every ounce of strength to prevent the encirclement of Leningrad, diversion of resources as a precaution against failure would have been impossible on many levels, both military and political.

Once the siege commenced, there was a strong sense within the city that its people were defending their homes as distinct from defending the Soviet Union. Inevitably, this allowed some to express nuances in their attitude. This was demonstrated by Rimma Neratova, who was a medical student in Leningrad when the siege commenced. She described sympathetically how the old imperial palaces and mansions of the city took on a broken-down and careworn appearance, almost as if they were enduring the same suffering as the people, but by contrast the people looked at official government buildings with disdain: 'All Leningraders very much hoped that bombs would fall on the NKVD building on Liteyni [Prospekt] and destroy its archives. But the building, with its grandiose marble entryway, remained standing – enormous, terrible.'[5]

Although the Bolsheviks had moved the national capital from Petrograd to Moscow, many Leningraders – who had been born before this change took place – continued to feel that their city was the true heart of the nation, and this added both to their determination that Leningrad was to be defended at all costs and to the sense of local pride with which they looked back on their experiences in the siege. Throughout the war, the ordeal of Leningrad was portrayed both within the Soviet Union and across the world as a city of culture that stood defiantly against the barbaric Nazi invasion; when the war was over, Stalin required all of this to be changed into merely part of the overall defiance of the Soviet people.

To the surprise and dismay of many, attempts to commemorate the war faded away rapidly. Three wooden victory arches were erected around Leningrad through which the sons of the city who had been serving in the Red Army marched home; these were deliberately modelled upon the arch created in 1814 to commemorate the return of soldiers from Paris in what had been the original Patriotic War. The architect Armen Konstantinovich Barutchev noted that the 1814 arch had originally been made of wood before being replaced by a stone arch in 1829, and he confidently predicted that a similar transformation would take place in the coming years with the new arches.[6] Instead, the arches were rapidly dismantled and disappeared. In some respects, the low priority given to memorials was understandable – with so much destruction across the Soviet Union, priority was given to rebuilding factories, infrastructure, and homes. In the years that followed the end of the war, far more memorials were built under Soviet supervision in the cities of Eastern European countries than within the Soviet Union itself, driven by a perceived need to impress upon these other nations the essential role of the Soviet state in defeating Germany.

In the case of Leningrad, reconstruction also restored the old palaces and buildings of the tsarist era. After the October Revolution, many old buildings had been converted into communal housing and they remained in use even after the war; restoration was therefore not seen as an attempt to preserve the past but more as an essential requirement to provide housing for the city's population, which was now growing again as many of those who had been evacuated or mobilised into the army returned home. Even in the case of buildings that had been almost completely destroyed, plans to replace them with modern structures were widely opposed on the grounds that this would create harsh dissonance with the surrounding neo-classical buildings. The Small Philharmonic Hall on Nevsky Prospekt was a case in point and was reconstructed as an almost perfect replica of the original building to ensure that it fitted in with the adjacent Kazan Cathedral. In other cases, reconstruction was used as an opportunity to restore buildings from the era of Catherine the Great to their former appearance, removing many of the 19th-century embellishments that were now viewed as garish and unwelcome. One of the consequences of such reconstruction was that, without intending to, architects and builders actually helped embed the sense of individuality and continuity with the past amongst Leningraders that irritated Stalin so much.

Instead of memorials, Leningrad's city planners created two new victory parks. One in the south of the city in the Moskovsky district was deliberately intended to cover a large area badly scarred by defensive preparations during the siege, and the other was on Krestovsky Island where the Neva flows into the Gulf of Finland. Almost all traces of the war were removed from the parks and Leningraders turned out in large numbers to help plant trees, but although the original plans anticipated the creation of sculptures and plaques in the parks, none were placed there until 1971. The parks explicitly drew a line under the past: it was time to move forward, and remembrance that drew special attention to any one aspect of the war, particularly if it was Leningrad, was deprecated.

Wartime propaganda that attempted to give meaning to sacrifice by emphasising its local value was replaced by new propaganda that subsumed everything into universal pan-Soviet patriotism.

Almost inevitably, the continuing resentment in Leningrad at the refusal of the official viewpoint to recognise the unique character of the city and its inhabitants, and their unique suffering, resulted in a further wave of repression. In 1949, three prominent local Communist Party figures – Petr Popkov, Aleksei Kuznetsov, and Nikolai Voznesensky – organised a trade fair in Leningrad. At Stalin's instigation, state-controlled media immediately criticised the fair as an inappropriate use of state funds to boost local economic growth. This was followed by allegations that together with others, the three men responsible for the trade fair were plotting to create a Russian Communist Party as a direct competitor to the Soviet Communist Party. Such national or regional parties existed in many parts of the Soviet Union but Stalin had always resisted any attempt to create a separate party for the Russian majority in the Soviet state, seeing such a party as a major threat to centralised rule, particularly as he feared that this new Russian Communist Party would be centred on Leningrad. Whilst it is possible that there were plans afoot to create this Russian Communist Party, other allegations about election irregularities and financial misconduct were unfounded. Nonetheless, hundreds of people were arrested in what became known as the Leningrad Affair. Most faced trials behind closed doors and in 1950 six of the main figures – including Popkov, Kuznetsov, and Voznesensky – were shot. The Soviet Union had actually abolished the death penalty in 1947, but it was reinstated in early 1950; it has been suggested that this was specifically to ensure that the victims of the Leningrad Affair did not survive.[7] Large numbers were imprisoned or sentenced to internal exile and Stalinist loyalists took over all major and intermediate Party posts in Leningrad. Many of the remaining symbols of the siege of Leningrad were also effaced. All of the blue and white stencilled warnings to citizens about which side of the street was safer during German artillery bombardments were painted out. When Georgy Maksimilianovich Malenkov, the Deputy Chairman of the Council of Ministers and a Stalin loyalist, visited Leningrad, he angrily denounced the official guidebook for the Museum of the Defence of Leningrad. According to one witness, he waved it at the museum workers and shouted, 'It has created a myth of Leningrad's "special" blockade fate! It has minimised the role of the great Stalin!'[8] Shortly after, senior staff at the museum were arrested and given long prison sentences and the museum was closed while the exhibits were reorganised in order to portray the 'correct' message. In 1953, the building was handed over to the Soviet Navy and the museum collection, largely made up of weapons taken there directly from the battlefield and various exhibits of life in Leningrad during the siege, was dispersed.

The very deliberate reduction in the status of the siege of Leningrad had consequences in many fields. The Piskarevskoye Cemetery was on the northern edge of Leningrad close to the village of Piskarevka and became the site of mass graves during the siege, with over half a million bodies – 50,000 military personnel, the rest civilians who perished during the long years as a result of starvation, cold, illness, and German attacks – interred there. In February 1945, as plans for a new Leningrad were being drawn up, there was a competition to design a memorial on the site, but as Zhdanovism and Stalin's long-standing hostility to Leningrad began to take hold, these were deferred for several years and the huge cemetery gradually became a neglected and run-down location.

As Leningrad began the long, slow process of recovering from its ordeal, people began to return to the city. But many had made new lives for themselves elsewhere, and would never return; others had died whilst away from their homes. Lyubov Borisovna Beregovaya, a young girl whose father was serving in the army, had been sent far to the east with her mother, and they travelled back to Leningrad in stages in the summer of 1944. After the end of the war, they waited for news of Beregovaya's father:

> After the intoxicating joy of families returning from the front, families returned to their day-to-day lives. Those whose husbands had not returned repeated each day the legends of a miraculous return from prison, from some camps, even after completing a special mission.
>
> We had a hope that was not imaginary: a return address – 'Special Ski Battalion'. Mama was writing wherever possible; the first days after she had sent off letters, we would run to the mailbox several times a day. Then it would begin to seem to me that they had by chance printed too many of the forms 'Not included in the lists of killed, injured or missing in action.' Nevertheless, we persistently and confidently awaited a miracle.
>
> On the streets I would peer at every tall man and sometimes for a long while I would follow those who seemed familiar on the basis of particular characteristics I had chosen – a nice wide smile, broad shoulders, and tightly curled hair, but they never paid any attention to me.
>
> As for stories with another outcome – fathers who were alive but did not return to their families – I simply didn't listen. Nothing like that could ever happen with my father.

I would imagine how it would all be. He'll ring. I'll go to open and will ask, 'Who is it?' I'll recognise his voice, will throw myself on his neck and then, taking him by the hand, we'll go into the room. I would even talk to myself, telling him about school …

Then the slender envelope arrived with the death notice – died from wounds, 13 May 1942. That precise indication of time prosaically cancelled any belief in a miracle …

I don't know where my father's grave is. Every summer at the Pioneer Camp I would take flowers to place at the foot of the small tower with a star – the grave of an unknown soldier. Every 13 May I go to the Piskarevskoe Cemetery. First I put one flower on the slabs where the name 'Boris' is written, then on the slabs that show my father's year of birth. There are never enough flowers.[9]

The sheer scale of losses suffered by the Red Army was such that accurate records of deaths and wounding were almost impossible to maintain, and notification of deaths reached families many years after their loved ones had died. For some, there would always be the suspicion that the dates had been arbitrarily fabricated.

After Stalin's death in 1953, the plans for the Piskarevskoye Cemetery resurfaced. By this stage, the site was in a poor state. Wooden signs had been erected on many of the mass graves of soldiers, but these were now decaying and falling apart. There were plans to disinter many of the buried soldiers so that they could be reburied in a communal grave, but this was abandoned after protests from family members of the dead. It wasn't until 1956 that work on the cemetery finally commenced. Four years later, the project was completed. The haphazard burial mounds of the siege were now landscaped into symmetrical shapes with stone markers – these bear a star if the mound was a military grave and the hammer and sickle if it was a civilian grave. In addition, many stones bear a date, the year in which the dead were buried. There was more than an element of fiction about these stones. So long after the interment, it was impossible to know for sure which mass graves were for soldiers and which for civilians, and in any case the bodies had frequently been buried together, but it served a purpose. Like many Leningraders, Lyubov Beregovaya came to associate individual stones with specific groups of military or civilian dead and even if most people were aware that this wasn't entirely accurate, it fulfilled an emotional need, giving focus for mourning and remembrance. In the years that followed, a series of plaques appeared around the cemetery, made by Leningraders to give names to at least some of their dead, often commissioned by workers in factories to remember their former colleagues. One such plaque reads:

> To the water utility workers who died in the Siege of Leningrad
> May the earth protect you into the future
> We remember you
> We remember your names

Next to this plaque is another, inscribed with the names of 20 water utility workers. A bronze sculpture known as the Motherland Monument, nearly 20 feet tall, was designed by the Leningrader and *Blokadnik* Vera Vasilyevna Isayeva. It stands atop a rectangular block of stone and portrays a woman holding an open wreath, and an eternal flame burns at the entrance; Isayeva died of lung cancer in 1960, two months before the cemetery was formally opened. Behind the Motherland Monument is a stone wall and there was little doubt that Olga Berggolts, whose poems and broadcasts were forever associated with the siege in the minds of most *Blokadniki*, would be asked to write a poem that would then be engraved upon the wall. She described how she was taken to the site while it was being constructed:

> It was a foul, autumnal Leningrad day when we made our way to the city outskirts. We walked through still completely shapeless mounds, not graves, but already beyond them there was a huge granite wall and there stood a [sculpture of a] woman with an oak wreath in her hands. An indescribable feeling of grief, sadness, and complete isolation overwhelmed me at that moment when I walked along the planks of the footway, through that terrible ground amongst the huge hills of burial towards that blank, silent wall.[10]

Her poem is engraved on the wall:

> Here lie Leningraders
> Here are townspeople – men, women, and children.
> Next to them, Red Army soldiers.
> They defended you, Leningrad,
> The cradle of the revolution
> With all their lives.
> We cannot list their noble names here,
> There are so many of them under the eternal protection of granite.

But know this, those who look at these stones:
No one is forgotten, nothing is forgotten.

The closing words were carefully chosen. There was no doubt in the minds of Leningraders that much had deliberately been forgotten. Even in their personal accounts, many shied away from the full brutal truth of what they had endured. Accounts written by *Blokadniki* described the consequences of starvation in the first winter using the somewhat euphemistic expression 'dystrophy' in preference to 'emaciation'; some of this may have been influenced by awareness that the former would be more acceptable to orthodox state historiography. Perhaps the darkest and most distressing aspect of the first winter – the outbreak of cannibalism – was almost completely absent from the *Blokadniki* accounts. Even if the heavy hand of the state had permitted discussion of such a terrible example of how desperate people had become, Leningraders themselves found the subject too painful to articulate.

After the death of Stalin and his denunciation by Khrushchev, Soviet views of the war began to change slowly, with Khrushchev increasingly contrasting the heroic determination of ordinary Soviet citizens, military and civilian, with the crimes and errors of Stalin and his inner circle. The history of the Great Patriotic War was to be redefined as the victory of the Soviet people rather than as being due to Stalin's military genius. In the early years of the Bolshevik state, Stalin had warned about the personality cult that was developing around his rival Leon Trotsky and Khrushchev ensured that this hypocrisy was fully exposed, particularly after his denunciations of Stalin became public in 1961. Prior to 1934, Khrushchev argued, harsh measures had been largely necessary in order to eliminate any danger of counter-revolution; thereafter, they had been driven entirely by Stalin's paranoia and megalomania.[11]

Despite this, many myths that were established in the first years after the war persisted. The infallibility of Stalin and the higher Soviet leadership was so strongly engrained that it remained difficult to describe the siege of Leningrad with complete honesty – to do so would be to admit that although the Germans were unquestionably responsible for the deaths from starvation and exposure during the first winter, the failures of the Soviet administrators of the city and of the Red Army also contributed greatly to the suffering. A decade or more after the end of the war, the stories of Leningraders had become incorporated – sometimes with difficulty – into the official orthodox account, and this now became an impediment to reassessing the past: would it be possible for this official narrative to be questioned without at the same time calling into question the memories of *Blokadniki* whose personal stories were now embedded in the narrative? The answer was to make the victory the property of the Soviet people – but under the guidance of the Communist Party as a whole, not its leader.

The victims of the Leningrad Affair were rehabilitated in April 1954, even before Khrushchev made his condemnatory speech about Stalin to the Communist Party in 1956. Slowly, memories of the siege that were both personal and also recognised the special nature of Leningrad and its citizens began to appear, cautiously at first but then in growing numbers. Leonid Rakhmanov, an author and screenwriter who would oversee a uniquely Soviet interpretation of *King Lear* in 1970, told the writer Vera Ketlinskaya about a 'literary-artistic matinée' in a frozen building in Leningrad in the depths of the first winter. Lev Aleksandrovich Ilyin, the chief architect of the city, addressed those who had gathered, describing various locations in the city where slogans had spontaneously appeared, proclaiming the city's immortality. Rakhmanov recalled how the words moved him to tears:

> If there were people who, in these terrible conditions of the blockade – of cold and hunger – could still feel the beauty of Leningrad so strongly, then the city and its inhabitants really are immortal.[12]

Whilst it was now permissible to focus on individual experiences and there was no longer any requirement to ensure that all possible credit was given to Stalin, there was a new orthodoxy. If ordinary people could be heroic, then it was important to regard every ordinary person as a hero. The title 'hero city' had first been used in 1942 and just a few days before the end of the war in Europe, Stalin had called for gun salutes to be fired to the hero cities of Leningrad, Stalingrad, Sevastopol, and Odessa. In 1961, the title became official: together with Moscow, Brest, and Kiev, the original four cities were awarded the status of Hero City of the Soviet Union. For Leningraders, the recognition of their city was tempered by the fact that its ordeal was equated with that of several other cities. Stalingrad had been reduced to rubble by the fighting of 1942 and early 1943, and Radio Leningrad had made much of the solidarity of Leningrad in the north with Stalingrad in the south; but there was a degree of resentment at the inclusion of the other cities in the list.

Briefly, the optimism that had been commonplace in 1945 that better times were coming returned to the Soviet Union. Khrushchev confidently declared that full Communism would be achieved by about 1980 and all the years of building a new state would be rewarded by peace and general prosperity. Instead, the

Soviet Union entered a period of increasing stagnation and after the fall of Khrushchev there was a return of repression of those who dared to challenge official narratives. Shortages of food and consumer products became widespread and with younger people becoming increasingly disillusioned, there were attempts to use the history of the Great Patriotic War to remind this new generation of the need to emulate their forerunners. Partly because of this, the memorials that began to appear around Leningrad – one of the blue signs warning people about the safe side of the street during bombardments was repainted on Nevsky Prospekt, and plaques were put up to draw attention to bomb and artillery damage that remained visible – concentrated more on the military and quasi-military aspects of the siege, and only in passing to the heroic endurance of the *Blokadniki*. There were still no memorials to the tens of thousands who starved and froze to death in the winter of 1941–42.

The long-delayed plans for a formal memorial to the siege of Leningrad were resurrected in the 1960s and in an attempt to create a communal sense of ownership of the project, it was initially funded through public subscriptions.[13] Unlike many Soviet projects, this also involved consultation of the public, often by inviting Leningraders to write to newspapers with their suggestions, and despite Khrushchev's removal from power in 1963 the project continued more in the spirit of the relative openness of his rule than the increasingly repressive character of the Brezhnev years that followed. Many *Blokadniki* regarded the memorial as a testament to their ordeal and to the ordinary Leningraders who perished in the siege, but the usual Soviet orthodoxy remained strong with other Leningraders wanting to commemorate the heroic defence of the city by the Red Army. Consequently, even the precise location of the memorial created questions about precisely what was being commemorated. Those who wished for a memorial to the civilian dead wanted it to be in the centre of Leningrad, whereas those who wanted the military defenders of the city to be remembered preferred a location to the south of the centre, near where the front line had run for several months of the siege. Some even called for a completely different approach to commemoration: many *Blokadniki* were still living in crowded communal apartments, and there were suggestions that new housing blocks in a specially created district should be built for them as the best possible commemoration of their ordeal and survival. Some of the suggestions showed echoes of personal experiences. One writer asked for the memorial to be on the Field of Mars, near the city centre, because she remembered how people had left their dead relatives on the field during the first winter when it was impossible to dispose of the corpses by other means.

A competition was announced for the design of the memorial, and Leningraders were invited to view the first round of entries. A total of 83 were exhibited, including many designed by amateurs rather than professional architects. Most of the latter group chose locations away from the city centre, either on Vasilevsky Island to the west or the Pulkovo Heights to the south; there were many objections to these from Leningraders, perhaps best articulated by one person who warned against the memorial being too remote from areas visited by ordinary people – 'You know,' he wrote to a newspaper, 'nobody goes there.' But the nuances of remembrance that had dominated thinking in the first decade after the war persisted and others argued that the memorial should be forward-looking, perhaps surrounded by new housing and portraying a better future. The problem of incorporating a large memorial into the neo-classical centre of Leningrad without an incongruous clash with older buildings also played a part in the final decision; again, this is a mark of the special character both of the city and of its residents, as such concerns played little or no part in the creation of monuments elsewhere.

The site of the new memorial was finally settled: it was to be in the south of Leningrad on Moskovsky Prospekt, which ran through the concrete architecture created both before and after the war. About six miles south of the historic centre of Leningrad, several roads met at a major junction known as Sredney Rogatki Ploshchad; this was renamed Ploshchad Pobedy ('Victory Square') in 1962.

The next step was to decide the actual nature of the memorial, and once more a competition was organised, but no overall winner was selected. In 1970, after further submissions were invited, a total of 44 entries were received. The public was invited to comment, but the decision was made in private. Nonetheless, many ordinary Leningraders and professional architects submitted their opinions. One repeated criticism was that although many of the designs were impressive, they lacked a specific Leningrad connection – they could have been in any region of the Soviet Union, and Leningraders wanted something that reflected the unique experiences of their city. Such a view would have been unacceptable in Stalin's time, but was now openly articulated and accepted. There were also persisting questions about the precise nature of the memorial: was it a testament to the victims – both military and civilian – of the siege, or was it a celebration of Leningrad's victory? Or was it possible to create something that achieved both goals?

Finally, the city administration selected the winner for what became known as the *Monumentalno-Geroicheskim Zashchitnikam Leningrada*

('Monument to the Heroic Defenders of Leningrad'): the architect Sergei Borisovich Speransky, who had already overseen the creation of a memorial in Belarus. The project was completed in 1978, 34 years after the end of the siege of Leningrad. It is effectively a monument on several levels, each of which has a different role. In some respects, it is as bombastic and brutalist as so much Soviet-era architecture, but on other levels it is a deeply poignant and moving memorial. Given the complexity of remembering such a terrible siege in a society where almost every design decision had political dimensions, such 'compromises' were perhaps inevitable.

The first part of the memorial that is visible to visitors is a granite obelisk that rises 157 feet above the complex. Significantly, it bears the dates '1941–1945', thus referencing the entire war rather than just the siege of Leningrad. At the foot of the obelisk are two bronze figures, one of a soldier and one of a worker, intended to symbolise the unity between the combatants in the front line and the workers of the city. On two walls that flank the steps rising to the base of the obelisk are further bronze figures, rather fewer than originally proposed. These show a variety of people: soldiers with weapons; civilian figures digging trenches; a man with a sniper's rifle embracing a woman; workers carrying a piece of rail for use in a barricade; and a female medic standing with the soldiers, holding a stretcher.

Behind the obelisk are steps to a lower level, enclosed in a circular wall. The wall is incomplete, symbolising the breaking of the blockade, and in the centre of the lower space are perhaps the most poignant of all the bronze figures. One portrays a woman holding the body of a dead child; another is of a woman crouching over her child, portraying a scene that the sculptor, Mikhail Anikushin – himself a *Blokadnik* – said he had witnessed during an artillery bombardment of Leningrad. Next to them is a soldier, helping a woman to her feet. Although these figures are intended to portray the suffering of ordinary people during the siege, it is worth noting that they may have thin faces, but they are otherwise substantial figures: even in the 1970s, there was a continuing unwillingness to portray the true emaciated state of Leningraders during the first winter.

On either side of the break in the circular wall are the captions '900 days' and '900 nights'. Whilst the dates on the obelisk refer to the war in general, these captions and other writing on the walls clearly place Leningrad at the centre of the commemoration. Below this space is a museum, lit by 900 small lamps fashioned from the shell-cases of 76mm guns, one for each day of the siege. The museum is in many respects the most memorable part of the monument. A sound system plays the sound of a metronome, the beating heart of the city that was broadcast by Radio Leningrad, interspersed with the musical call-sign of Radio Moscow and excerpts from other pieces of music. The displays include some of the weapons that were originally displayed in the short-lived museum that closed in 1949; others show the portions of bread that were meant to be issued as the daily ration (though the amount actually given to *Blokadniki* often fell short of this), and a violin used in the first performance in Leningrad of Shostakovich's Leningrad Symphony. Video clips show scenes from the siege, including the joyous removal of plywood sheeting from around many of the city's statues in 1944 after the Germans were driven away. On some of the walls are mosaics showing various aspects of the siege: soldiers departing and returning, and victory celebrations.

Adding to the overall appearance of the memorial are several buildings, intended to complement it. These concrete structures have not aged well; they were intended to address the calls for new housing for the surviving *Blokadniki* and some were relocated there, but most remained in their former apartments. Partly, this was through choice. For many, their homes – some still bearing the stains and scars of the siege – had become their personal memorials to the past and to loved ones who perished.

As a further development to the Monument to the Heroic Defenders of Leningrad, a classical victory arch was constructed across the road a short distance to the south; since then, it has been replaced with a single pillar supporting a stylised portion of arch next to the new multi-lane highway that runs past the airport. It is plainly the case that contrary to the words of Olga Berggolts, the monument itself does not 'remember all'. It has been criticised for showing so few female figures, and even then mainly in supporting roles such as medics or embracing soldiers heading to the front line – some feel that there is too little recognition that with so many men mobilised into the front line or evacuated with factory equipment to the east, a very large proportion of the city's population during the first winter was made up of women who struggled to keep their children alive. The Soviet theme of ultimate victory equating to ultimate recovery is prevalent. But these criticisms highlight an underlying truth about history. What is commonly regarded as 'history' can be considered as three separate components. The first is the factual record, and the Soviet Union was certainly guilty of attempting to falsify elements of this. The second is the manner in which that record is described and interpreted, and this reflects the nature of society at the time when those interpretations are made: during the Soviet era, this changed from the Stalinist version of the leader being the infallible genius to the later portrayal of the war as the triumph of all the people, often in spite of

Stalin's errors. The third component of 'history' is how we commemorate and remember it. This too reflects the society that creates the memorials, and it is best to see both Piskarevskoye Cemetery and the Monument to the Heroic Defenders of Leningrad in this light.

The death of Leonid Brezhnev in 1982 was followed in quick succession by the deaths of his successors, Yuri Andropov (1984) and Konstantin Chernenko (1985). The new – and last – leader of the Soviet Union, Mikhail Gorbachev, initiated a policy of *Glasnost* ('openness'), and for the first time it became possible for previously taboo subjects to be discussed openly. The long-suppressed stories of cannibalism during the siege surfaced in several new accounts, and previous memoirs that had been heavily censored or edited in order to make them acceptable to the authorities were published in their full form. In Leningrad, these accounts sharpened the views both of the declining number of *Blokadniki* and of other citizens that the history of the siege had been deliberately downplayed by authorities who were hostile to Leningrad; by revealing the darkest moments of the siege, the heroic survival of the city and its inhabitants became even more prominent. The role of Zhdanov and other senior Communist Party officials in the city had survived earlier revisions of history, but now they too were seen as being at least partly responsible for the suffering of the siege and in particular for continuing to enjoy privileges and good food while so much of the population starved. In an era of ongoing shortages, economic decline, and general social and political disillusion, the heroic conduct of ordinary people during the 900-day siege became a symbol of how far the nation had fallen. And *Glasnost* touched on more than the experiences of Leningraders. The distortions in the official Soviet record about operational and strategic blunders, and about the huge – and potentially avoidable – casualties suffered by the Red Army were increasingly laid bare. For the first time, the Soviet Union officially acknowledged the 'secret protocol' to the Molotov–Ribbentrop Pact of 1939, under which Eastern Europe was divided between Nazi Germany and the Soviet Union into 'spheres of influence', and the massacre of thousands of Polish Army officers by their Soviet captors in the forests of Katyn in 1940 was also recognised.

The impact of this new openness was widespread across the Soviet Union, but nowhere more so than in Leningrad where the sense of local grievance at the official orthodox view was strongest. A particularly damaging aspect of the 'new' publications was recognition that they had been written long ago, often in the months and years immediately after the war, but either they had been deliberately banned or the authors had been too fearful of the consequences of attempting to publish them. One such work was by Olga Mikhailovna Freidenberg who died in 1955. She was a cousin of the writer Boris Pasternak of *Doctor Zhivago* fame and wrote her account in 1942, creating a retrospective diary of the siege of Leningrad. In this, she wrote openly about cannibalism during the worst moments of the siege:

> Although such things were talked about with horror, blanching, and shudders, I felt no terror. Think about it, to cut up and sell a corpse! How much more horrifying was our reality, our Russian martyrdom of the living person, our NKVD, political repression, moral scalpels and knives.[14]

Freidenberg went on to argue that the official portrayal of what she called 'beautiful patriotism' was a deliberate falsehood, a patronising attempt by the state to 'entertain' those who had suffered the most by the creation of an illusion by 'pomposity and deception'. Whilst Freidenberg's criticisms of the deceptions of the state were correct, many of her views – she was one of those who had advocated the surrender of Leningrad in 1941 to avoid bloodshed – were also flawed. But when she died in 1955, many aspects of the German intentions towards Leningrad were still not widely known, or were dismissed by critics of the Soviet Union as little more than propaganda. This was one of the lingering poisons of the manner in which Stalin had rewritten history to suit his personal agenda. With so many obvious deceptions in the official account, it was easy for critics to dismiss the elements of the account that were actually true. As the years passed and the level of criticism grew, this became an ever-larger problem, and resulted in some extraordinary moments. Iuliya Konstantinovna Zhukova served as a sniper in the Red Army during the war and attended numerous reunions as the years passed. At one such reunion, she met a man who had been a pilot during the war. He told her:

> During a meeting with high school students of one of the Moscow schools he was asked: 'Was it necessary to tear off to that war, to show mass heroism? Was it not better to surrender to the Germans? You look, today we would live like them.' This fact indicates that a generation of young people enters their lives with no idea about the past war, the striving of Hitler's fascism to destroy the Soviet Union, to enslave its peoples.[15]

In 1989, the Soviet Union experienced its first elections in which officially endorsed Communist candidates competed against non-endorsed persons; several such candidates, including Boris Yeltsin, were elected, and the 'official' nominees had their poorest results in the Leningrad region. In April 1990, the Communist Party lost control of the Leningrad Soviet with the lawyer Anatoly Aleksandrovich Sobchak becoming its chairman. In 1991, he created the post of mayor and ran successfully for election. Another prominent politician in the city was Vitaly Valeriyevich Skoybeda, who was an activist in the *Demokraticheskogo Soyuza* ('Democratic Union' or DS, the first openly declared opposition party to the Communist Party in the Soviet Union). He started to display the white-blue-red tricolour flag despite protests from other deputies on the city council and immediately before the mayoral election of 1991, he made an important announcement:

> Fellow deputies, I ask you to include on the agenda a short discussion and resolution of an important issue based upon numerous appeals from our electorate – the holding of a citywide referendum on the restoration of the historical name of the city. All of us, Democrats and Communists, promised to listen to the voters during the elections, so it is essential to ask their opinion on this issue.[16]

Restoring the old name of St Petersburg was an immensely emotive question. Newspapers took a predictably partisan line; *Leningradskaya Pravda*, which had always been a mouthpiece for the Communist Party, was uncompromising in its support for preserving the name Leningrad. Other newspapers, including *Smena* – once the official newspaper of the Komsomol youth movement, but now independent – took the opposite view. But despite their editorial allegiances, it is an indicator of the degree to which the Soviet Union had relaxed its former control of the media that newspapers from all parts of the political spectrum received and published letters from Leningraders that often expressed opinions at odds with those of the editors. One letter to *Leningradskaya Pravda* compared Lenin's impact upon Russia with that of Batu, the grandson of Genghis Khan who led the Golden Horde into the west in the 13th century: 'The scale of the October [Revolution] tragedy is equivalent to that of the Mongol invasion – are there 130 monuments to Batu in Moscow?'[17]

The arguments about the merits or crimes of Lenin were, however, something of a distraction. Sobchak was reluctant to support the suggestion when it first circulated, but later became a proponent of the change of name and stressed that Lenin's name would continue to be preserved in the names of streets and in a number of monuments around the city. He even offered to arrange for the transfer of Lenin's remains from Moscow to a cemetery in Leningrad where other members of his family were buried. The arguments about the iconic value of the name 'Leningrad' were more focussed on its resonance with the wartime generation and the epic history of the siege. Critics accused Skoybeda, Sobchak, and other proponents of attempting to achieve what Hitler had failed to implement: the elimination of the name Leningrad from the face of the earth. Ironically, given the stress placed in the Stalin years on avoiding any 'special status' for Leningrad, it was precisely that special status that was now used by many Communists to argue in favour of retaining the name under which the city had been known during most of the 20th century. To change the name would be a blasphemous insult to those who had fought and died for the city, who had perished from hunger and cold in the dreadful first winter, and who had defiantly turned the tide and driven the Fascists from the outskirts.

The counter-arguments drew on the history of the city. Whilst the siege had clearly been a hugely important episode, they reasoned, it was only one of several such episodes that stretched back over the years. So much of the identity of the city was tied up with its pre-Leningrad past, and they argued that it was precisely that unique past that had helped the city to endure the siege. There were very few people left in Leningrad or elsewhere who remembered a time when the city had been known as St Petersburg, and for many who had known it as Leningrad all their lives, the older name conjured up an almost magical past with mental images drawn from the rich literature the city had produced – a further example of the continuing effect of the city on its literature, and the effect of that literature on the city. For some, the return of this magical older name would help provide the impetus for their city to develop along new lines now that the Communist era was clearly coming to an end. Others sardonically pointed out that the restoration of an old name would not of itself result in clean streets overnight.

Support for the change of name broadly followed the age of voters, with younger adults who had not experienced the war more likely to be in favour of reverting to St Petersburg. But although support for retaining the name Leningrad was strong amongst the wartime generation, it was by no means universal. For many Leningraders, their city had always been 'Piter', regardless of its official name. Even amongst the *Blokadniki* and the soldiers who had fought on the city's outskirts, many felt that their sense of 'homeland' had been their city, the physical homes and factories and other buildings that made the place so special: the name was of less importance to many than might have been expected.

On the last day before the referendum, the two camps used newspapers to project their messages. *Leningradskaya Pravda* published an image of the female bronze statue in the Piskarevskoye Cemetery with the caption *Otstoim Leningrad!* ('We Defend Leningrad') – a deliberate echo of the posters and captions that appeared towards the end of the war. *Smena* countered with a photograph of the gilded angel atop the Alexander Column outside the Winter Palace, a memorial to the original Patriotic War against Napoleonic France. The result of the referendum was a 55 per cent majority in favour of the change, but as the referendum was advisory and had no legal status in the eyes of the national government, the change was only enacted later in 1991 after the failed coup against Gorbachev.

The modern city of St Petersburg continues to be a place of multi-layered memories and eras and openly embraces all its incarnations. The wide avenues with the buildings created by the tsars dominate the centre. On one bank of the Neva, Peter the Great sits astride his rearing horse placed upon a huge block of granite that was brought to the city at huge effort and expense in the 18th century, while not far away on the other bank Lenin stands atop a stylised armoured car outside the Finland Station where he returned to the city in 1917. On Nevsky Prospekt, the restored stencil sign warning that the other side of the street is safer during bombardments has become a minor memorial; a shelf has been placed below it, and flowers are left there every day. Visitors to the city who travel from the airport at Pulkovo pass the pillar that replaced the victory arch to the south of the Leningrad Monument, and it bears the words 'St Petersburg, Hero City of Leningrad'. The Field of Mars contains memorials to those who fell in the 1917 revolutions; the eternal flame that burns there was first lit from the furnaces of Leningrad's Kirov Factory in 1957 and then used to light the similar eternal flames in the Piskarevskoye Cemetery in 1960 and at the Tomb of the Unknown Soldier in Moscow in 1967. It has become commonplace for newlywed couples to go to the Leningrad Monument and to lay their wedding bouquets at the memorial in honour of the wartime dead. The city that exists today is self-consciously a manifestation of all its history, embracing its rich and varied past, and its long tradition of individualism and independence of thought continues. When the 2022 war with Ukraine commenced, St Petersburg saw some of the largest protests and demonstrations. Facing charges brought against him by Putin for extortion, Skoybeda left Russia in 2003 to live in Georgia; at the time of writing, he is believed to be with the Georgian Legion in Ukraine, fighting against the Russian Army.

For the Soviet soldiers who died in such large numbers to defend Leningrad and to lift the siege, there are numerous memorials on or near the battlefields. These list the various divisions, corps, and armies that fought in the costly battles, but unlike western monuments they do not give the names of the fallen. The sheer scale of losses would make such an undertaking almost impossible.

Diminishing numbers of veterans continue to gather at these memorials each year to remember their lost comrades; others make the easier journey either to the Piskarevskoye Cemetery or to the monument at Ploshchad Pobedy, where they are joined by the equally diminished ranks of the remaining *Blokadniki* and by later generations who continue to revere the memory of the siege and those who took part in it. For the tens of thousands of German soldiers who died around the outskirts of Leningrad, on the perimeter of the Oranienbaum bridgehead, or in the swamps and forests along the Volkhov River, there are no monuments. Many of the Germans who were buried by their comrades during the siege were re-interred after the end of the Soviet Union in a cemetery in Sologubovka, about 43 miles southeast of the city; at least 34,000 are buried there and, until recently, more were added almost every year as their remains were discovered. Although many former Red Army veterans and their supporters objected vociferously to this project which was overseen by the *Volksbund Deutsche Kriegsgräberfürsorge* ('German War Graves Commission'), many Russian youth groups joined their German equivalents in annual visits to the battlefields to identify the remains of the dead. In the past few years, under the increasingly authoritarian rule of Vladimir Putin, such activity has almost stopped.

The German memory of the siege has also been difficult. After the end of the war, many wished to draw a line under the past, and given the scale of involvement of Germans in so many terrible crimes, it was inevitable that only a minority would ever face justice. Even those who were convicted often received lenient sentences or had their punishment commuted. For example, in the trial of senior *Einsatzgruppen* personnel that concluded in 1948, 14 men were sentenced to death. Of these, one died before sentence could be carried out and only four were executed. Despite many being given life sentences, all were released by 1958. It was only with the trials of several SS personnel from Auschwitz in 1964 that the full horror of the Holocaust entered mainstream discussion in West Germany, and even in the years that followed there has been perhaps too little attention to the other atrocities committed by Nazi Germany, particularly of Soviet deaths through starvation.

In 1991, there was a moment that seemed to highlight the flaws in the manner in which both the Soviet Union and Germany had remembered the siege of Leningrad. Yelena Oskarovna Marttila was an artist who lived in the city during the war and kept a sketchbook of what she experienced. After the war, she hid her sketches, aware that they portrayed the siege in a manner that was frowned upon. Even in the last decade of the Soviet Union, she was forbidden from displaying most of her pictures because they were deemed to be too pessimistic and negative – indeed, any attempt to portray depression or low mood as a consequence of the suffering endured by civilians was condemned as defeatist and anti-Soviet. Finally, she received an invitation to display all her works, not in the Soviet Union or post-Soviet Russia but in Berlin. Her pictures went on display in 1991, a total of over 80 images, and she watched as many elderly German men came to see her work. She could see from their eyes: they were veterans of the German Eighteenth Army that had tried to strangle the city to death. She took a group of them on a personal tour, answering their questions about her experiences of the siege:

> They just stood there, with tears in their eyes. One of them stepped forward. 'I ask your forgiveness,' he said. 'None of this was necessary, from a military point of view. We tried to destroy you, but we destroyed ourselves as human beings. On behalf of all of us, I ask for your forgiveness.'
>
> [Marttila replied,] 'War is terrible, but my quarrel is with Fascism, not with the German people. And Fascism exists in all of us.'[18]

NOTES

INTRODUCTION

1   M. Loskutova (ed.), *Pamiat o Blokade: Svidetelstva Ochevidtsev I Istoricheskoe Soznanie Obshchestva* (Novoe Izdvo, Moscow, 2006), pp.277–84

2   Quoted in L. Kirschenbaum, *The Legacy of the Siege of Leningrad, 1941–1995* (Cambridge University Press, Cambridge, 2006), p.24

3   V. Toporov, *Mif, Ritual, Simvol, Obraz: Issledovaniia v Oblasti Mifopoeticheskogo: Izbrannoe* (Kultura, Moscow, 1995), p.282

4   V. Toporov, *Petersburgskii Tekst* (Nauka, Moscow, 2009), p.268

5   P. Buttar, *To Besiege a City: Leningrad 1941–42* (Osprey, Oxford, 2023)

CHAPTER 1: UNFINISHED BUSINESS

1   For an account of the fighting around Rzhev in 1942, see P. Buttar, *Meat Grinder: The Battles for the Rzhev Salient 1942–43* (Osprey, Oxford, 2022)

2   W. Dunn, *The Soviet Economy and the Red Army* (Greenwood, Westport CT, 2005), p.53

3   Ibid., p.226

4   F. Strauss, *Geschichte der 2. (Wiener) Panzer-Division* (Dörfler, Eggolsheim, 2005), p.132

5   *Bundesarchiv-Militärarchiv,* Freiburg, RW 19/164, f.150 'Vortrag Obstlt. Matzky, Major Knapp, Hptm. Emmerich beim Amtschef'

6   C. Gerlach, *Kalkulierte Morde: die Deutsche Wirtschafts-Vernichtungspolitik in Weissrussland 1941 bis 1944* (Hamburger, Hamburg, 1998), pp.67–68

7   *Aktennotiz über Ergebnis der heutigen Besprechung mit den Staatssekretären über Barbarossa 2/5/41,* printed in *Der Prozess gegen die Hauptskriegsverbrecher vor dem Internationalen Militärgerichtshof, Nürnberg* (Sekretariat des Gerichtshofs, Nuremberg, 1948, henceforth cited as *IMG*), Vol. 31, p.84

8   A. Kay, *Exploitation, Resettlement, Mass Murder: Political and Economic Planning for German Occupation Policy in the Soviet Union 1940–1941* (Berghahn, New York, 2006), p.134

9   P. Broucek (ed.), *Ein General im Zwielicht: Die Erinnerungen Edmund Glaisees von Horstenau* (Böhlau, Vienna, 1988, 3 volumes), Vol. III, pp.107–08

10 *IMG*, Vol. 39, p.371

11 *IMG*, Vol. 4, pp.50–51

12 *IMG*, Vol. 27, p.622

13 T. Snyder, *Bloodlands: Europe Between Hitler and Stalin* (Vintage, London, 2011), p.169

14 Snyder, *Bloodlands*, p.411

15 C. Burdick and H.-A. Jacobsen (eds), *The Halder War Diary 1939–1942* (Greenhill, London, 1988), p.346

16 W. Beorn, *The Holocaust in Eastern Europe: At the Epicenter of the Final Solution* (Bloomsbury, New York, 2018), pp.122–23

17 Quoted in S. Friedländer, *The Years of Extermination: Nazi Germany and the Jews 1939–1945* (Harper-Collins, New York, 1997), p.129

18 S. Platonov, *Bitva za Leningrad 1941–1944* (Voyenizdat, Moscow, 1964), p.216

19 A. Burov, *Blokada Den' za Den'* (Lenizdat, Leningrad, 1979), p.288

20 E. Klee, *Das Personenlexikon zum Dritten Reich. Wer war was vor und nach 1945* (Fischer-Taschenbuch-Verlag, Frankfurt, 2007), p.347

21 Quoted in L. Erickson and M. Erickson (eds), *Russia: War, Peace and Diplomacy* (Weidenfeld & Nicolson, London, 2004), p.125

22 J. Hürter, 'Die Wehrmacht vor Leningrad' in *Vierteljahrshefte für Zeitgeschichte* (Oldenbourg Wissenschaftsverlag, Munich, 2001), Vol. 3, p.436

23 K.-M. Mallmann, A. Angrick, J. Matthäus, and M. Cüppers (eds), *Die Ereignismeldungen UdSSR 1941: Dokumente der Einsatzgruppen in der Sowjetunion* (WBG, Darmstadt, 2011), p.845

24 Hürter, 'Die Wehrmacht vor Leningrad', Vol. 3, pp.435–38

25 E. Busch, 'Ist die Schlachtentscheidende Rolle der Infanterie zu Ende?' in *Jahrbuch für Wehrpolitik und Wehrwissenschaft* (Hanseatische Verlagsanstalt, Hamburg, 1937), pp.11–27

26 S. Smirnov, *Marshal Zhukov. Kakim my Yego Pomnim* (Izdatelstvo Politicheskoy Literatury, Moscow, 1989), p.169

27 D. Glantz, *The Battle for Leningrad 1941–1944* (University Press of Kansas, Lawrence KS, 2002), pp.543–44

28 See for example Y. Syakov, 'Chislennosti Poteri Germanskoy Gruppy "Sever" v Khode Bitvy za Leningrad (1941–1944gg)' in *Voprosy Istorii* (RAS, Moscow, 2008), No. 1, pp.133–36

29 W. Lubbeck, D. Hurt., *At Leningrad's Gates* (Casemate, Newbury, 2006), p.133

30 O. Carius, R. Edwards (trans.), *Tigers in the Mud: The Combat Career of German Panzer Commander Otto Carius* (Stackpole, Mechanicsburg PA, 2003), p.30

31 X. Núñez Seixas, *The Spanish Blue Division on the Eastern Front, 1941–1945: War, Occupation, Memory* (University of Toronto Press, Toronto, 2022), p.140

32 D. Morozov, *O Nikh ne Upominalos v Svodkakh* (Voyenizdat, Moscow, 1965), p.133

CHAPTER 2: *ISKRA* – PLANNING

1 P. Schramm (ed.), *Kriegstagebuch der Oberkommandos der Wehrmacht* (Bernard & Graefe, Munich, 1982, 8 volumes), Vol. 5 Part 1, p.29

2 O. Bartov, *The Eastern Front 1941–1945: German Troops and the Barbarisation of Warfare* (St Martin's Press, New York, 1986), p.49

3 H. Buchheim, M. Broszat, H.-A. Jacobsen, H. Krausnick, *Anatomie des SS-Staates* (Deutsche Taschenbuch-Verlag, Munich, 2005), p.171

4 K. Heller, *The Nuremberg Military Tribunals and the Origins of International Criminal Law* (Oxford University Press, Oxford, 2011), p.432

5 M. Telitsyn, *Marshal Govorov* (Veche, Moscow, 2013), p.118

6 V. Zolotarev (ed.), *Velikaia Otechestvennaia* (Terra, Moscow, 1996–2005, 25 volumes), Vol. 16, p.202

7 Platonov, *Bitva za Leningrad 1941–1944*, p.234

8 Zolotarev, *Velikaia Otechestvennaia*, Vol. 16, pp.563–65

9 L. Vinnitsky, *Slavnaya Pobeda pod Leningradom: Vospominaniya, Stati I Dokumenty, Posvyashchennyye Razgromu Nemetsko-Fashistskikh Voysk pod Leningradom* (Lenizdat, Leningrad, 1976), p.198

10 Interview with I. Dushevsky, available at http://iremember.ru/memoirs/pekhotintsi/dushevskiy-iosif-mikhaylovich/?sphrase_id=4656, retrieved via archive.org

11 K. Meretskov, *Na Sluzhbe Narodu* (Politizdat, Moscow, 1968), pp.321–22

12 I. Fediuninsky, *Podnyatyye po Trevoge* (Voyenizdat, Moscow, 1961), p.130

13 V. Kuznetsov, *Vtoraya Udarnaya: V Bitve za Leningrad, Vospomynanyie, Dokumenti* (Lenizdat, Leningrad, 1983), p.137

14 Platonov, *Bitva za Leningrad 1941–1944*, pp.238–39

15 T. Koptelova, *Operatsiya Iskra. Proryiv Blokadyi Leningrada* (Galart, St Petersburg, 2012), p.13

16 A. Vasilevsky, *A Lifelong Cause* (Progress, Moscow, 1973), pp.231–32

17 Morozov, *O Nikh ne Upominalos v Svodkakh*, pp.134–35

18 V. Chuikov, *Konets Tretyego Reykha* (Sovetskaya Rossiya, Moscow, 1973), pp.73–74

19 Koptelova, *Operatsiya Iskra*, p.15

20 M. Streshinskiy, I. Frantishev, *General Simoniak* (Lenizdat, Leningrad, 1971), p.137

21 Ibid., p.143

22 Fediuninsky, *Podnyatyye po Trevoge*, pp.132–33

23 Ibid., p.131

24 W. Haupt, *Army Group North: The Wehrmacht in Russia 1941–1945* (Schiffer, Atglen PA, 1997), p.160

25 G. Zhukov, *Vospomimaniya I Razmyshleniya* (Olma, Moscow, 2002, 2 volumes), Vol. I, p.406

26 Vasilevsky, *A Lifelong Cause*, p.225

27 W. Richter, *Die 1. (Ostpreussische) Infanterie-Division* (Max Schmidt & Söhne, Munich, 1975), pp.92–93

28   Streshinskiy and Frantishev, *General Simoniak*, p.150

29   P. Carrell, *Scorched Earth: The Russian-German War 1943–1944* (Schiffer, Atglen PA, 1994), p.217

CHAPTER 3: *ISKRA* – EXECUTION

1   Carrell, *Scorched Earth*, p.218

2   Telitsyn, *Marshal Govorov*, p.128

3   Zolotarev, *Velikaia Otechestvennaia*, Vol. 16, p.204

4   Zhukov, *Vospomimaniya I Razmyshleniya*, Vol. I, p.410

5   N. Volkovsky, *Blokada Leningrada v Dokumentach Rassekreennych Archivov* (Poligon, St Petersburg, 2005), p.202

6   Interview with T. Ovsyannikova, available at https://iremember.ru/memoirs/svyazisti/ovsyannikova-tamara-rodionovna/

7   Quoted in S. Borshchev, *Ot Nevy do Elby* (Lenizdat, Leningrad, 1977), pp.207–08

8   Ovsyannikova interview

9   Streshinskiy and Frantishev, *General Simoniak*, pp.153–54

10   H. Kardel, *Die Geschichte der 170. Infanterie-Division 1939–1945* (Podzun, Bad Nauheim, 1953), p.88

11   Morozov, *O Nikh ne Upominalos v Svodkakh*, pp.138–39

12   Ibid., pp.142

13   Richter, *Die 1. (Ostpreussische) Infanterie-Division*, pp.93–95

14   Platonov, *Bitva za Leningrad 1941–1944*, p.259

15   H. Pohlman, *Wolchow: 900 Tage Kampf um Leningrad 1941–1944* (Podzun-Pallas, Wölfersheim-Berstadt, 2003), p.66

16   Streshinskiy and Frantishev, *General Simoniak*, p.157

17   Ovsyannikova interview

18   Carrell, *Scorched Earth*, p.226

19   Platonov, *Bitva za Leningrad 1941–1944*, p.258

20   Koptelova, *Operatsiya Iskra*, p.30

21   Burov, *Blokada Den' za Den'*, p.298

22   Streshinskiy and Frantishev, *General Simoniak*, pp.167–68

23   Carrell, *Scorched Earth*, p.230

24   Morozov, *O Nikh ne Upominalos v Svodkakh*, pp.143–44

25   Platonov, *Bitva za Leningrad 1941–1944*, pp.263–64

26   Streshinskiy and Frantishev, *General Simoniak*, pp.172–73

27   Fediuninsky, *Podnyatyye po Trevoge*, pp.136–37

28   Zhukov, *Vospomimaniya I Razmyshleniya*, Vol. I, p.415

29   H. Stachow, *Tragödie an der Newa: Der Kampf um Leningrad 1941–1944* (Herbig, Munich, 2001), p.217

30   Interview with L. Motorin, available at iremember.ru/memoirs/pekhotintsi/motorin-leonid-nikitich-/

31 Interview with Z. Krichevskiy, available at iremember.ru/memoirs/artillerist/kr ichevskiy-zalman-matusovich/

32 Quoted in Borshchev, *Ot Nevy do Elby*, pp.208–09

33 Interview with S. Egorov, available at iremember.ru/memoirs/minometchiki/e gorov-servey-vasilevich/

34 Ovsyannikova interview

35 Carrell, *Scorched Earth*, pp.231–33

36 *Bundesarchiv-Militärarchiv*, Freiburg, *Kriegstagebuch LIV AK 31/12/1942*, RH 24-54/60

37 Vinnitsky, *Slavnaya Pobeda pod Leningradom*, p.207

38 Streshinskiy and Frantishev, *General Simoniak*, pp.185–86

39 Dushevsky interview

40 H. Salisbury, *The 900 Days: The Siege of Leningrad* (Da Capo, Cambridge MA, 2009), p.548

41 Carrell, *Scorched Earth*, p.238

42 F. Carrera Buil, A. Ferrer-Dalmau, *Batallón Román. Historia Fotográfica del 2.' Batallón del Regimiento 269 de la División Azul* (Fundación División Azul, Madrid, 2003), pp.237–38

43 Streshinskiy and Frantishev, *General Simoniak*, pp.202–03

44 E. Taranova, *Levitan: Golos Stalina* (Partner SP6, St Petersburg, 2010), p.74

45 M. Kozlov (ed.), *Velikaya Otechestvennaya Voyna 1941–1945: Entsiklopediya* (Sovetskaya Entsiklopediya, Moscow, 1985), pp.586–87

46 Schramm, *Kriegstagebuch*, Vol. 5 Part 1, p.49

CHAPTER 4: *POLYARNAYA ZVEZDA*

1 Fediuninsky, *Podnyatyye po Trevoge*, p.140

2 Glantz, *The Battle for Leningrad*, p.285; National Archives and Records Administration, Washington DC, T-311 roll 105

3 Meretskov, *Na Sluzhbe Narodu*, pp.333–34

4 Schramm, *Kriegstagebuch*, Vol. 5 Part 1, p.92

5 For an account of these battles, see P. Buttar, *On a Knife's Edge: The Ukraine, November 1942–March 1943* (Osprey, Oxford, 2018), pp.146–411

6 P. Bell, *Twelve Turning Points of the Second World War* (Yale University Press, New Haven CT, 2011), p.106

7 S. Shtemenko, *The Soviet General Staff at War 1941–1945* (Progress, Moscow, 1970), p.395

8 S. Biriuzov, *Kogda Gremelyi Pushki* (Voyenizdat, Moscow, 1961), p.121

9 V. Isaev, *Kratkiy Kurs Istorii VOV* (Eksmo, Moscow, 2005), p.360

10 *Tsentral'nyy Arkhiv Ministerstva Oborony*, Moscow F.148a Op.3763 D.103 L.253, 254

11 Burov, *Blokada Den' za Den'*, pp.308–09

12 Dushevsky interview

13 Meretskov, *Na Sluzhbe Narodu*, pp.330–31
14 Burov, *Blokada Den' za Den'*, pp.312–13
15 *Bundesarchiv-Militärarchiv*, Freiburg, *Kriegstagebuch AOK* 18 11/2/1943, RH-20-28/470
16 Morozov, *O Nikh ne Upominalos v Svodkakh*, pp.154–55
17 Stachow, *Tragödie an der Newa*, p.240
18 Morozov, *O Nikh ne Upominalos v Svodkakh*, pp.156–57
19 Schramm, *Kriegstagebuch*, Vol. 5 Part 1, p.87
20 Ibid.
21 Carrell, *Scorched Earth*, pp.258–59
22 *Small Unit Actions During the German Campaign in Russia* (Department of the Army, Washington DC, 1953), pp.260–61
23 Carrell, *Scorched Earth*, pp.263–65
24 M. Katukov, *Na Ostriye Glavnogo Udara* (Voyenizdat, Moscow, 1974), pp.192–94
25 *Soobshcheniya Sovetskogo Informbyuro* (Sovinformburo, Moscow, 1944, 9 volumes), Vol. IV, p.152
26 G. Krivosheyev (ed.), *Rossiya I SSSR v Voynakh XX Veka. Poteri Vooruzhonnykh Sil: Statisticheskoye Issledovaniye* (Olma, Moscow, 2001), p.224
27 Stachow, *Tragödie an der Newa*, pp.222–23
28 Burov, *Blokada Den' za Den'*, p.317

CHAPTER 5: THE LAST BATTLES BEFORE SPRING

1   Burov, *Blokada Den' za Den'*, p.318
2   Zolotarev, *Velikaia Otechestvennaia*, Vol. 16, pp.89–90
3   Lubbeck and Hurt, *At Leningrad's Gates*, pp.135–36
4   Ibid., pp.136–37
5   Quoted in W. Hermann, *Die Geschichte des Infanterie-Regiments 51 und in Teilen die der 18. Infanterie-Divisions* (Regiments-Kameradschaft IR-51, Kassel, 1967), pp.106–07
6   R. Frank (ed.), *Unsere Division in Sieg und Untergang: Erlebnisberichte von Angehörigen der 18. Infanterie-Division (Motorisiert)/Panzergrenadier-Division* (Self-published, Gliching, 1988), p.92
7   Ibid., p.88
8   Ibid., p.90
9   Ibid., p.93
10 Hermann, *Die Geschichte des Infanterie-Regiments 51*, p.104
11 Zolotarev, *Velikaia Otechestvennaia*, Vol. 16, pp.283–84
12 Krivosheyev, *Rossiya I SSSR*, p.320
13 *Bundesarchiv-Militärarchiv*, Freiburg, *Unfallmeldungen pro Heer/heeresgruppe* RW 6/559
14 P. Caddick-Adams, *Monty and Rommel: Parallel Lives* (Arrow, London, 2012), p.364

15   D. Littlejohn, *The Patriotic Traitors: A History of Collaboration in German-Occupied Europe 1940–1945* (Heinemann, London, 1972), p.165

16   *Tsentral'nyy Arkhiv Ministerstva Oborony*, Moscow F.148a Op.3763 D.143 L.135

17   N. Voronov, *Ha Sluzhbe Voyennoy* (Voyenizdat, Moscow, 1963), pp.354–55

18   M. Voloshin, *Razvedchiki Vsegda Vperedi* (Voyenizdat, Moscow, 1977), pp.43–44; B. Gorbachevsky, *Rzhevskaya Myasorubka. Vremya Otvagi. Zadacha – Vyzhit!* (Eksmo, Moscow, 2007), pp.135–36

19   Voronov, *Ha Sluzhbe Voyennoy*, pp.355–56

20   N. Kuznetsov, *Nakanune* (Voyenizdat, Moscow, 1969), p.312

21   Voronov, *Ha Sluzhbe Voyennoy*, pp.356–57

22   P. Buttar, *Collision of Empires: The War on the Eastern Front in 1914* (Osprey, Oxford, 2014), p.116

23   Y. Syakov, 'Chislennost'i Poteri Germanskoy Gruppy Armiy "Sever" v Khode Bitvy za Leningrad (1941–1944 gg.)' in *Voprosy Istorii* (Rossiyskaya Akademya Nauk, Moscow, 2008), No. 1, pp.133–36

24   Stachow, *Tragödie an der Newa*, p.248

25   Burov, *Blokada Den' za Den'*, p.329

CHAPTER 6: A TENSE SUMMER

1   R. Kee, *The Green Flag: A History of Irish Nationalism* (Penguin, Harmondsworth, 1972), p.149

2   S. Newton, *Kursk: The German View* (Da Capo Press, Cambridge MA, 2002), p.374

3   E. von Manstein, A. Powell (trans. and ed.), *Lost Victories: The War Memoirs of Hitler's Most Brilliant General* (Presidio, Novato CA, 1994), pp.445–46

4   M. Stein, *Generalfeldmarschall Walter Model. Legende und Wirklichkeit* (Biblio, Osnabrück, 2001), p.19

5   F. von Schlabrendorff, G. von Gaevernitz, *Offiziere Gegen Hitler* (Fischer, Frankfurt am Main, 1959), pp.116–17

6   *Bundesarchiv-Militärarchiv*, Freiburg, *OKW/WFSt/Op.Nr.66,624/43*, BArch RW 4/N1033

7   For details of the *Lucy* spy network and other intelligence operations, see Buttar, *Collision of Empires*, pp.247–49; V. Tarrant, *The Red Orchestra* (J. Wiley, London, 1995); S. Radó, *Sous la Pseudonyme Dora* (Julliard, Paris, 1972), pp.140–50; A. Foote, *Handbook for Spies* (Museum, London, 1964), pp.92–95

8   Meretskov, *Na Sluzhbe Narodu*, pp.340–41

9   Quoted in Burov, *Blokada Den' za Den'*, p.333

10   Ibid.

11   Lubbeck and Hurt, *At Leningrad's Gates*, pp.139–40

12   Ibid., p.141

13   V. Kvachkov, *Spetsnaz Rossii* (Russkaya Panorama, Moscow, 2007), p.206

14   N. Afanasyev, *Front Bez Tyla. Zapiski Partizanskogo Komandira* (Lenizdat, Leningrad, 1983), pp.81–82

15 I. Veselov, *Tri Goda v Tylu Braga: Zapiski Partizana* (Permskoye Knizhnoye Izdatelsetvo, Perm, 1961), pp.136–37

16 V. Mizin, *Snayper Petrova* (Lenizdat, Leningrad, 1988), pp.69–71

17 I. Pilyushin, *U Sten Leningrada* (Voyenizdat, Moscow, 1965), p.208

18 Ibid., p.220

19 Stachow, *Tragödie an der Newa*, p.206

20 Quoted in W. Richardson, *The Fatal Decisions: The Decisive Battles of the Second World War from the Viewpoint of the Vanquished* (Pen & Sword, Barnsley, 2012), pp.66–67

21 Schramm, *Kriegstagebuch*, Vol. 5 Part 1, p.309

22 Quoted in Ibid., p.375

23 Ibid., p.465

24 J. Costello, T. Hughes, *The Battle of the Atlantic* (Collins, London, 1977), p.281

25 A. Harris, S. Cox, *Despatch on War Operations: 23 February 1942 to 8 May 1945* (Routledge, Milton, 1995), p.196

26 E. Corti, P. Levy (trans.), *Few Returned: Twenty-Eight Days on the Russian Front, Winter 1942–1943* (University of Missouri Press, Columbia MO, 1997), pp.58–60

27 Meretskov, *Na Sluzhbe Narodu*, p.344

28 K.H. Frieser, K. Schönherr, G. Schreiber, K. Ungváry, *Die Ostfront 1943–1944 – Der Krieg im Osten und an den Nebenfronten* (Deutsche Verlags-Anstalt, Munich 2007), pp.150, 153, 200; D. Glantz, J. House, *The Battle of Kursk* (University Press of Kansas, Lawrence KS, 2004), p.276; A. Searle, *Armoured Warfare: A Military, Political and Global History* (Bloomsbury, London, 2017), p.80; Krivosheyev, *Rossiya I SSSR*, p.303

CHAPTER 7: THE SUMMER OFFENSIVE: SINYAVINO

1 Frieser et al., *Die Ostfront 1943–1944*, p.154; Krivosheyev, *Rossiya I SSSR*, p.133

2 K. Rokossovsky, *A Soldier's Duty* (Lancer International, New Delhi, 1985), p.204

3 For an account of these campaigns, see P. Buttar, *Retribution: The Soviet Reconquest of Central Ukraine, 1943* (Osprey, Oxford, 2019)

4 W. Haupt, *Die 8. Panzer-Division im Zweiten Weltkrieg* (Podzun-Pallas, Friedburg, 1987), p.323

5 Burov, *Blokada Den' za Den'*, pp.365–66

6 Ibid., p.371

7 A. Babin (ed.), *Na Volkovskom Fronte 1941–1944 gg.* (Mauka, Moscow, 1982), pp.221–22

8 Núñez Seixas, *The Spanish Blue Division*, pp.120–22

9 A. Moroz, 'Preodoleniye' in *Krasnaya Zvezda* (Ministerstva Oborony Rossiyskoy Federatsii, Moscow, 26/07/2012)

10 For a full account of one of these battalions, see H. Konsalik, O. Coburn, *Straf Bataillon 999* (Futura, London, 1980)

11 Krivosheyev, *Rossiya I SSSR*, p.92
12 A. Pyltsin, 'O Shtrafnikakh-Geroyakh' in *Sovetskaya Rossiya* (Moscow, 3/08/2017)
13 For further details of Soviet *Shtrafnoi Batalyony*, see A. Pyltsin, *Penalty Strike: The Memoirs of a Red Army Penal Company Commander 1943–1945* (Stackpole, Mechanicsburg PA, 2006)
14 Dushevsky interview
15 Quoted in Burov, *Blokada Den' za Den'*, p.377
16 Dushevsky interview
17 Lubbeck and Hurt, *At Leningrad's Gates*, p.148
18 For more information about both organisations, see G. Ueberschär (ed.), *Das Nationalkomitee 'Freies Deutschland' und der Bund Deutscher Offiziere* (Fischer Taschenbuch, Frankfurt-am-Main, 1996); B. Scheurig, *Verräter oder Patrioten: Das Nationalkomitee 'Freies Deutschland' und der Bund Deutscher Offiziere in der Sowjetunion 1943–1945* (Propyläen, Berlin, 1993)
19 Burov, *Blokada Den' za Den'*, p.385
20 Lubbeck and Hurt, *At Leningrad's Gates*, pp.150–51
21 I. Solomakhin, *Shturm 'Churtovoy Vysoty'. Inzhenernyye Voyska Goroda-Fronta* (Lenizdat, Leningrad, 1979), pp.218–22
22 Interview with N. Myasoedov, recovered from http://iremember.ru/artilleristi/myasoedov-nikolay-sergeevich/stranitsa-4.html
23 Pohlman, *Wolchow: 900 Tage Kampf um Leningrad*, p.89
24 Morozov, *O Nikh ne Upominalos v Svodkakh*, pp.183–85
25 Meretskov, *Na Sluzhbe Narodu*, p.345
26 B. Bychevsky, *Gorod – Front* (Lenizdat, Leningrad, 1967), p.121
27 Krivosheyev, *Rossiya I SSSR*, p.226
28 *Tsentral'nyy Arkhiv Ministerstva Oborony*, Moscow RF.F.217 Op.1227 D.62 L81-84
29 Meretskov, *Na Sluzhbe Narodu*, pp.345–46
30 Richter, *Die 1. (Ostpreussische) Infanterie-Division*, pp.100–01
31 Lubbeck and Hurt, *At Leningrad's Gates*, p.152

CHAPTER 8: AN AUTUMN OF BLOOD AND ATTRITION

1 Krivosheyev, *Rossiya I SSSR*, pp.142, 282–83, 310, 312; G. Sigin, *Bitva za Leningrad: Krupnyye Operatsii, Belyye Pyatna, Poteri* (Poligon, Moscow, 2005), p.320
2 Sigin, *Bitva za Leningrad*, pp.224–27
3 Dushevsky interview
4 Chuikov, *Konets Tretyego Reykha*, pp.73–74
5 A. Gribkov (ed.), *Istoriia Ordena Lenina Lengradskogo Voennogo Okruga* (Voyenizdat, Moscow, 1974), p.333
6 Schramm, *Kriegstagebuch*, Vol. 5 Part 1, pp.682–83
7 Ibid., Vol. 5 Part 2, p.775

8   Burov, *Blokada Den' za Den'*, p.385

9   P. Smith, *Petlyakov Pe-2 Peshka* (Ramsbury, Marlborough, 2003), p.155

10   A. Weeks, *Russia's Life-Saver: Lend-Lease Aid to the USSR in World War II* (Lexington, Lanham MD, 2004), p.145

11   Burov, *Blokada Den' za Den'*, p.396

12   Stachow, *Tragödie an der Newa*, pp.264–65

13   Gribkov, *Istoriia Ordena Lenina Lengradskogo Voennogo Okruga*, p.333; V. Kovalchuk, *Doroga Pobedy Osazhdennogo Leningrada* (Nauka, Moscow, 1984), pp.115–51

14   *Small Unit Actions*, pp.165–68

15   A. Turner, *Messines 1917: The Zenith of Siege Warfare* (Osprey, Oxford, 2010), p.53; A. Goodbody, 'Tunnelling in the Deep: Battle of Messines' in *Mining Magazine* (Aspermont Media, London, 2016)

16   D. Zhuravlev, 'Lechebno-Evakuatsionnoye Obespecheniye Boyevoy Operatsii 30-go Gvardeyskogo Strelkovogo Korpusa 15–19 Sentyabrya 1943g' in *Antigipertensyavnaya Liga* (St Petersburg, 2014) retrieved from http://www.ahleague .ru/index.php?option=com_content&view=article&id=530&Itemid=204&lang=ru

17   For more information on the Holocaust in Italy, see S. Klein, *Italy's Jews from Emancipation to Fascism* (Cambridge University Press, Cambridge, 2018); M. Sarfatti, *The Jews in Mussolini's Italy: From Equality to Persecution* (University of Wisconsin Press, Madison WS, 2006); S. Sullam, *The Italian Executioners: The Genocide of the Jews of Italy* (Princeton University Press, Princeton CT, 2018)

18   Schramm, *Kriegstagebuch*, Vol. 5 Part 2, pp.1074–75

19   Ibid., Vol. 5 Part 2, p.1123

20   International Military Tribunal, *Nazi Conspiracy and Aggression* (United States Government Printing Office, Washington DC 1946, 11 volumes), Vol. III, pp.783–89

21   National Archives and Records Administration, Washington DC, *Microfilm series T-78: Fremde Heere Ost (Ic) Kraftegegenüberstellung 1943*

22   E. Ziemke, *Stalingrad to Berlin: The German Defeat in the East* (Dorset, New York, 1986), p.249

23   Burov, *Blokada Den' za Den'*, p.411

24   *Bundesarchiv-Militärarchiv*, Freiburg, *Ia Heeresgruppe Nord, Evakuierung der Bevölkerung*, RH 19-II 138/43 75129/64

25   Burov, *Blokada Den' za Den'*, p.411

26   Ibid., p.410

CHAPTER 9: WINTER PLANNING

1   Quoted in Burov, *Blokada Den' za Den*, p.419

2   Núñez Seixas, *The Spanish Blue Division*, pp.122–24

3   C. Ydígoras, *Algunos no Hemos Muerto* (Cyr, Madrid, 1984), pp.52–53

4   Núñez Seixas, *The Spanish Blue Division*, p.158

5   Center for Military History, Fort McNair, Washington DC, OCMH Files: *Besprechung mit Gen Feldmarschall Kuechler vom 30.12.43*

6   *Bundesarchiv-Militärarchiv*, Freiburg, *Kriegstagebuch Ia Heeresgruppe Nord* 6/1/44, RH19/11 75128/33

7   T. Kaarsted, *De Danske Ministerier 1929–1953: et Hundredepolitisk-Historiske Biografer* (Pensionsforsikringsanstalten, Copenhagen, 1977), pp.173–80

8   H. Dahl (ed.), *Danske Tilstander, Norske Tilstander Forskjeller og Likheter Under Tysk Okkupasjon 1940–1945* (Forlaget Press, Oslo, 2010), pp.394–95

9   W. Tieke, F. Steinhardt (trans.), *Tragedy of the Faithful: A History of the III (germanisches) SS-Panzer-Korps* (Fedorowicz, Winnipeg, 2001), pp.7–12

10   Ibid., p.29

11   A. Silgailis, *Latvian Legion* (Bender, San Jose CA, 1986), pp.9–32; D. Littlejohn, *Foreign Legions of the Third Reich* (Bender, San Jose CA, 1987, 4 volumes), Vol. 4, pp.182–84

12   Quoted in Stachow, *Tragödie an der Newa*, p.273

13   D. Zabecki (ed.), *World War II in Europe* (Taylor & Francis, Milton, 2015), p.1212

14   Platonov, *Bitva za Leningrad 1941–1944*, pp.299–300

15   P. Rotmistrov, *Stalnaya Gvardiya* (Voyenizdat, Moscow, 1984), p.136

16   Fediuninsky, *Podnyatyye po Trevoge*, pp.168–69

17   Ibid., pp.173–74

18   Streshinskiy and Frantishev, *General Simoniak*, p.236

19   Krivosheyev, *Rossiya I SSSR*, p.199

20   Meretskov, *Na Sluzhbe Narodu*, pp.353–54

21   Morozov, *O Nikh ne Upominalos v Svodkakh*, p.190

22   Telitsyn, *Marshal Govorov*, p.141

23   Platonov, *Bitva za Leningrad 1941–1944*, p.304

24   Fediuninsky, *Podnyatyye po Trevoge*, p.175

CHAPTER 10: *YANVARSKIIY GROM*

1   K. Dieckert, H. Grossmann, *Die Kampf um Ostpreussen* (Motor Buch Verlag, Stuttgart, 2002), p.31

2   Buttar, *Collision of Empires*, pp.314–55; P. Buttar, *Germany Ascendant: The Eastern Front 1915* (Osprey, Oxford, 2015), pp.57–77, 132–33, 138–43

3   Kozlov, *Velikaya Otechestvennaya Voyna*, Vol. 3, p.23

4   Tieke, *Tragedy of the Faithful*, p.31

5   *Die Ordensträger der Deutschen Wehrmacht* (Verlag Media Data, Hamburg, 2000, CD-ROM)

6   Streshinskiy and Frantishev, *General Simoniak*, p.241

7   C. Simmons and N. Perlina (eds), *Writing the Siege of Leningrad: Women's Diaries, Memoirs and Documentary Prose* (University of Pittsburgh Press, Pittsburgh PA, 2002), pp.44–45

8   Glantz, *The Battle for Leningrad*, p.343

9   Fediuninsky, *Podnyatyye po Trevoge*, pp.181–82
10 G. Lohse, *Geschichte der Rheinisch-Westfälischen 126. Infanterie-Division 1940–1945* (Podzun, Bad Neuheim, 1957), p.178
11 Stachow, *Tragödie an der Newa*, pp.273–74
12 Borshchev, *Ot Nevy do Elby*, pp.201–02
13 Ibid., p.204
14 Morozov, *O Nikh ne Upominalos v Svodkakh*, pp.194–95
15 I. Korovnikov, *Novgorodsko-Luzhskaiia Operatsiia* (Voyenizdat, Moscow, 1960), pp.73–74
16 Morozov, *O Nikh ne Upominalos v Svodkakh*, pp.196–97
17 Stachow, *Tragödie an der Newa*, pp.275–76
18 Silgailis, *Latvian Legion*, p.39
19 Stachow, *Tragödie an der Newa*, pp.276–77
20 Ibid., p.277

CHAPTER 11: RETREAT FROM LENINGRAD

1   D. Hughes (ed.), *Moltke on the Art of War: Selected Writings* (Presidio, Novato CA, 1995), p.92
2   A. Seaton, *The Russo-German War 1941–1945* (Praeger, New York, 1971), p.411; Pohlman, *Wolchow: 900 Tage Kampf um Leningrad 1941–1944*, p.124
3   Meretskov, *Na Sluzhbe Narodu*, p.356
4   Morozov, *O Nikh ne Upominalos v Svodkakh*, pp.198–99
5   Platonov, *Bitva za Leningrad 1941–1944*, p.369
6   Ziemke, *Stalingrad to Berlin*, p.256
7   P. Buttar, *The Reckoning: The Defeat of Army Group South, 1944* (Osprey, Oxford, 2020), pp.126–27
8   Carius, *Tigers in the Mud*, p.43
9   Núñez Seixas, *The Spanish Blue Division*, pp.124–25
10 Platonov, *Bitva za Leningrad 1941–1944*, p.359
11 Telitsyn, *Marshal Govorov*, p.165
12 Burov, *Blokada Den' za Den'*, p.456
13 Simmons and Perlina, *Writing the Siege of Leningrad*, p.45
14 *Bundesarchiv-Militärarchiv*, Freiburg, *Kriegstagebuch Ia Heeresgruppe Nord, 24/1/44*, RH 19-III
15 F. Roosevelt, S. Rosenman (ed.), *The Public Papers and Addresses of Franklin D. Roosevelt* (Random House, New York, 1949, 13 volumes), Vol. 12, p.71
16 Manstein, *Lost Victories*, p.511
17 *Bundesarchiv-Militärarchiv*, Freiburg, *Heeresgruppe Nord Oberbefehlshaber Aktennotiz 29/1/44*, RH 19-III
18 Carius, *Tigers in the Mud*, p.44
19 R. Forczyk, *Leningrad 1941–44: The Epic Siege* (Osprey, Oxford, 2009), p.15
20 Carius, *Tigers in the Mud*, p.48

21   Ibid., pp.50–51
22   Ibid., p.51
23   Fediuninsky, *Podnyatyye po Trevoge*, pp.184–85
24   *Bundesarchiv-Militärarchiv*, Freiburg, *Heeresgruppe Nord Ia 24/44, 29/1/44*, RH
      19-III
25   Meretskov, *Na Sluzhbe Narodu*, pp.360–61
26   Zolotarev, *Velikaia Otechestvennaia*, Vol. 17, p.38

CHAPTER 12: *SCHILD UND SCHWERT*

1   S. Mitcham, *Hitler's Field Marshals and Their Battles* (Guild, London, 1988),
      p.266
2   E. Hansen, G. Schreiber, B. Wegner, *Politischer Wandel, Organiserte Gewalt und
      Nationale Sicherheit: Beitrage zur Neueren Geschichte Deutschlands und Frankreichs*
      (Oldenbourg, Munich, 1995), p.294
3   W. Wette, *Die Wehrmacht: Feindbilder, Vernichtungskrieg, Legenden* (Fischer
      Taschenbuch, Frankfurt am Main, 2013), p.227
4   D. Goldhagen, *Hitler's Willing Executioners: Ordinary Germans and the Holocaust*
      (Little, Brown & Co., London, 2014), p.290
5   C. Barnett (ed.), *Hitler's Generals* (Grove Weidenfeld, New York, 1989),
      pp.259–60
6   S. Newton, *Hitler's Commander: Field Marshal Walter Model – Hitler's Favorite
      General* (Da Capo, Cambridge MA, 2006), pp.160–67
7   *Bundesarchiv-Militärarchiv*, Freiburg, *Kriegstagebuch Ia Heeresgruppe Nord,
      31/1/44*, RH 19-III
8   W. Görlitz, *Strategie der Defensive – Model* (Limes, Wiesbaden, 1982), p.164
9   Quoted in ibid., p.165
10   Tieke, *Tragedy of the Faithful*, pp.43–44
11   Ibid., p.55
12   Interview with K. Rammus, available at iremember.ru/razvedchiki/rammus-karl
      -uliusovich/
13   For an account of these battles, see P. Buttar, *Between Giants: The Battle for the
      Baltics in World War II* (Osprey, Oxford, 2013), pp.157–83
14   Interview with I. Lvovich, available at iremember.ru/memoirs/drugie-voyska/lvovi
      ch-yuliy-evel-moiseevich/
15   Núñez Seixas, *The Spanish Blue Division*, p.125
16   Stachow, *Tragödie an der Newa*, p.279
17   Ziemke, *Stalingrad to Berlin*, pp.260
18   Glantz, *The Battle for Leningrad*, p.378
19   Tieke, *Tragedy of the Faithful*, pp.61–64
20   Meretskov, *Na Sluzhbe Narodu*, pp.365–66
21   Shtemenko, *The Soviet General Staff at War*, p.265
22   Platonov, *Bitva za Leningrad 1941–1944*, p.401

CHAPTER 13: AFTER THE SIEGE

1   *Bundesarchiv-Militärarchiv*, Freiburg, RW 6/559
2   Krivosheyev, *Rossiya I SSSR*, pp.293–94
3   M. Tukhashevsky, *Izbrannyye Proizvedeniya* (Voyenizdat, Moscow, 1964, 2 volumes), Vol. 2, pp.85–130
4   A. Pomogaybo, *Vyrvannyy Mech Imperii 1925–1940gg* (Veche, Moscow, 2006), p.35
5   Platonov, *Bitva za Leningrad 1941–1944*, p.403
6   Glantz, *The Battle for Leningrad*, p.411
7   Afanasyev, *Front Bez Tyla*, pp.112–13
8   E. Kieser, *Danziger Bucht 1945: Dokumentation einer Katastrophe* (Bechtle, Munich, 1978), p.12
9   Ziemke, *Stalingrad to Berlin*, pp.265–66
10 H. Meier-Welcker, *Aufzeichnungen eines Generalstabsoffiziers 1939–1942* (Rombach, Freiburg, 1982), p.127
11 J. Zimmermann, *Pflicht zum Untergang. Die Deutsche Kriegsführung im Westen des Reiches 1944–1945* (Schöningh, Paderborn, 2009), pp.385–93
12 F. Chuev, *Sto Sorok Besed s Molotovym: Iz Dnevnika F Cheva* (Terra, Moscow, 1991), p.623
13 M. Laar, *Sinimäed 1944; II Maailmasõja Lahingud Kirde-Eestis* (Varrak, Tallinn, 2006), p.326
14 Fediuninsky, *Podnyatyye po Trevoge*, p.200–01
15 P. Sudoplatov, *Razvedka I Kreml'* (Geya, Moscow, 1977), p.433
16 J. Clements, *Mannerheim: President, Soldier, Spy* (Haus, London, 2012), p.213
17 H. Grier, *Hitler, Dönitz, and the Baltic Sea: The Third Reich's Last Hope, 1944–1945* (US Naval Institute Press, Annapolis MD, 2007), p.121
18 T. Kinnunen and V. Kivimäki (eds), *Finland in World War II: History, Memory, Interpretation* (Brill, Boston MS, 2011), p.172
19 *Politisches Archiv des Auswärtigen Amtes*, Berlin, Rohrbach report 23/07/1942, 22/08/1942, Box 796, Geheimakten 6/9
20 O. Berggolts, *Izbrannye Proizvedenie v Dvu Tomah* (Izdatelstvo Hudozestvennaia Literatura, Leningrad, 1967), Vol. 2, p.241
21 V. Inber, *Stranitsy Dnei Perebiraia* (Sovetskaya Pisatel, Moscow, 1967), p.209
22 Simmons and Perlina, *Writing the Siege of Leningrad*, pp.45–46
23 *Tsentralnyi Gosudarstvennyi Arkhiv Kinofotofonodokumentov Leningrada*, St Petersburg
24 W. Lincoln, *Sunlight at Midnight: St Petersburg and the Rise of Modern Russia* (Basic Books, New York, 2000), p.300
25 S. Varshavsky, B. Rast, *Saved for Humanity: The Hermitage During the Siege of Leningrad* (Aurora, Leningrad, 1985), pp.253–54
26 G. Norman, *The Hermitage: The Biography of a Great Museum* (Fromm International, New York, 1998), p.265

CHAPTER 14: MILITARY MEMORIES AND ASSESSMENTS OF THE SIEGE OF LENINGRAD

1 K.-M. Mallmann et al., *Die Ereignismeldungen UdSSR 1941*, p.139
2 Schramm, *Kriegstagebuch*, Vol. 2, pp.477–79
3 *Bundesarchiv-Militärarchiv*, Freiburg, N 510/48
4 A. Hernández Navarro, *Ida y Vuelta* (Espasa-Calpe, Madrid, 1971), pp.57–60
5 For full accounts of Vlasov and the ROA, see W. Strik-Strikfeldt, *Against Stalin and Hitler: Memoir of the Russian Liberation Movement 1941–1945* (John Day & Co, New York, 1970); S. Frölich, *General Vlasov* (Markus, Cologne, 1994); J. Hoffmann, *Die Tragödie der 'Russischen Befreiungsarmee' 1944–1945: Wlassow gegen Stalin* (Herbig, Munich, 2003)

CHAPTER 15: THE MYTHS AND LEGENDS OF LENINGRAD

1 J. Garrard and C. Garrard (eds), *World War 2 and the Soviet People: Selected Papers From the Fourth World Congress For Soviet and East European Studies* (St Martin's Press, New York, 1993), p.111
2 O. Berggolts, *Govorit Leningrad: Glavy iz Knigi* (Sovetskaya Rossiya, Moscow, 1964), p.388
3 A. Werth, *Leningrad* (Hamish Hamilton, London, 1944), p.64
4 For a detailed discussion of these themes, see J. Brunstedt, *The Soviet Myth of World War II: Patriotic Memory and the Russian Question in the USSR* (Cambridge University Press, Cambridge, 2021)
5 V. Neratova, *V Dni Voiny: Semeinaya Khronika* (Zvezda, St Petersburg, 1996), p.97
6 A. Barutchev, 'Arki Pobedy' in *Arkhitektura I Stroitelstvo Leningrada* (Lenizdat, Leningrad, 1946), No. 1, p.4
7 M. Pazin, *Strasti po Vlast: Ot Lenina do Putina* (Piter, Moscow, 2012), p.202
8 Quoted in Kirschenbaum, *The Legacy of the Siege of Leningrad*, p.144
9 Simmons and Perlina, *Writing the Siege of Leningrad*, pp.205–06
10 O. Berggolts, *Sobranie Sochinenii v Trech Tomach* (Chudosesetvennaya Literatura, Leningrad, 1988, 3 volumes), Vol. 1, p.44
11 I. Erenburg, *Post-War Years* (MacGibbon & Key, London, 1966), p.321
12 V. Ketlinskaia, *Molodoi Leningrad* (Sovetskii Pisatel, Moscow, 1966), p.8
13 For details of the designing and construction of the memorial, see Kirschenbaum, *The Legacy of the Siege of Leningrad*, pp.208–27
14 Quoted in Kirschenbaum, *The Legacy of the Siege of Leningrad*, p.248
15 I. Zhukova, *Devushka so Snayperskoy Vintovkoy* (Tsentrpoligraf, Moscow, 2006), p.208
16 B. Vishnevsky, 'Legenda o Vosvrashchenyii' in *Politicheskyii Zhurnal* (Rodnaya, St Petersburg, 09/05/2013)
17 *Leningradskaya Pravda*, 29/09/1990
18 M. Jones, *Leningrad: State of Siege* (John Murray, London, 2008), p.295

BIBLIOGRAPHY

Bundesarchiv-Militärarchiv, Freiburg
Center for Military History, Fort McNair, Washington DC
National Archives and Records Administration, Washington DC
Politisches Archiv des Auswärtigen Amtes, Berlin
Tsentral'nyy Arkhiv Ministerstva Oborony, Moscow
Tsentralnyi Gosudarstvennyi Arkhiv Kinofotofonodokumentov Leningrada, St Petersburg

Antigipertensyavnaya Liga (St Petersburg)
Arkhitektura I Stroitelstvo Leningrada (Lenizdat, Leningrad)
Jahrbuch für Wehrpolitik und Wehrwissenschaft (Hanseatische Verlagsanstalt, Hamburg)
Krasnaya Zvezda (Ministerstva Oborony Rossiyskoy Federatsii, Moscow)
Leningradskaya Pravda
Mining Magazine (Aspermont Media, London)
Politicheskyii Zhurnal (Rodnaya, St Petersburg)
Sovetskaya Rossiya (Moscow)
Vierteljahrshefte für Zeitgeschichte (Oldenbourg Wissenschaftsverlag, Munich)
Voprosy Istorii (Rossiyskaya Akademiya Nauk, Moscow)

https://iremember.ru

Afanasyev, N., *Front Bez Tyla. Zapiski Partizanskogo Komandira* (Lenizdat, Leningrad, 1983)
Babin, A. (ed.), *Na Volkovskom Fronte 1941–1944 gg.* (Mauka, Moscow, 1982)
Barnett, C. (ed.), *Hitler's Generals* (Grove Weidenfeld, New York, 1989)
Bartov, O., *The Eastern Front 1941–1945: German Troops and the Barbarisation of Warfare* (St Martin's Press, New York, 1986)
Bell, P., *Twelve Turning Points of the Second World War* (Yale University Press, New Haven CT, 2011)
Beorn, W., *The Holocaust in Eastern Europe: At the Epicenter of the Final Solution* (Bloomsbury, New York, 2018)
Berggolts, O., *Govorit Leningrad: Glavy iz Knigi* (Sovetskaya Rossiya, Moscow, 1964)

Berggolts, O., *Izbrannye Proizvedenie v Dvu Tomah* (Izdatelstvo Hudozestvennaia Literatura, Leningrad, 1967)

Berggolts, O., *Sobranie Sochinenii v Trech Tomach* (Chudosesetvennaya Literatura, Leningrad, 1988, 3 volumes)

Biriuzov, S., *Kogda Gremelyi Pushki* (Voyenizdat, Moscow, 1961)

Borshchev, S., *Ot Nevy do Elby* (Lenizdat, Leningrad, 1977)

Broucek, P. (ed.), *Ein General im Zwielicht: Die Erinnerungen Edmund Glaisees von Horstenau* (Böhlau, Vienna, 1988, 3 volumes)

Brunstedt, J., *The Soviet Myth of World War II: Patriotic Memory and the Russian Question in the USSR* (Cambridge University Press, Cambridge, 2021)

Buchheim, H., Broszat, M., Jacobsen, H.-A. Krausnick, H., *Anatomie des SS-Staates* (Deutsche Taschenbuch-Verlag, Munich, 2005)

Burdick, C., Jacobsen, H.-A. (eds), *The Halder War Diary 1939–1942* (Greenhill, London, 1988)

Burov, A., *Blokada Den' za Den'* (Lenizdat, Leningrad, 1979)

Buttar, P., *Between Giants: The Battle for the Baltics in World War II* (Osprey, Oxford, 2013)

Buttar, P., *Collision of Empires: The War on the Eastern Front in 1914* (Osprey, Oxford, 2014)

Buttar, P., *Germany Ascendant: The Eastern Front 1915* (Osprey, Oxford, 2015)

Buttar, P., *On a Knife's Edge: The Ukraine, November 1942–March 1943* (Osprey, Oxford, 2018)

Buttar, P., *Retribution: The Soviet Reconquest of Central Ukraine, 1943* (Osprey, Oxford, 2019)

Buttar, P., *The Reckoning: The Defeat of Army Group South, 1944* (Osprey, Oxford, 2020)

Buttar, P., *Meat Grinder: The Battles for the Rzhev Salient 1942–43* (Osprey, Oxford, 2022)

Buttar, P., *To Besiege a City: Leningrad 1941–42* (Osprey, Oxford, 2023)

Bychevsky, B., *Gorod – Front* (Lenizdat, Leningrad, 1967)

Caddick-Adams, P., *Monty and Rommel: Parallel Lives* (Arrow, London, 2012)

Carius. O., Edwards R. (trans.), *Tigers in the Mud: The Combat Career of German Panzer Commander Otto Carius* (Stackpole, Mechanicsburg PA, 2003)

Carrell, P., *Scorched Earth: The Russian-German War 1943–1944* (Schiffer, Atglen PA, 1994)

Carrera Buil, F., Ferrer-Dalmau, A., *Batallón Román. Historia Fotográfica del 2.' Batallón del Regimiento 269 de la División Azul* (Fundación División Azul, Madrid, 2003)

Chuev, F., *Sto Sorok Besed s Molotovym: Iz Dnevnika F Cheva* (Terra, Moscow, 1991)

Chuikov, V., *Konets Tretyego Reykha* (Sovetskaya Rossiya, Moscow, 1973)

Clements, J., *Mannerheim: President, Soldier, Spy* (Haus, London, 2012)

Corti, E., Levy, P. (trans.), *Few Returned: Twenty-Eight Days on the Russian Front, Winter 1942–1943* (University of Missouri Press, Columbia MO, 1997)

Costello, J., Hughes, T., *The Battle of the Atlantic* (Collins, London, 1977)

Dahl, H. (ed.), *Danske Tilstander, Norske Tilstander Forskjeller og Likheter Under Tysk Okkupasjon 1940–1945* (Forlaget Press, Oslo, 2010)

Der Prozess gegen die Hauptkriegsverbrecher vor dem Internationalen Militärgerichtshof, Nürnberg (Sekretariat des Gerichtshofs, Nuremberg, 1948)

Die Ordensträger der Deutschen Wehrmacht (Verlag Media Data, Hamburg, 2000, CD-ROM)

Dieckert, K., Grossmann, H., *Die Kampf um Ostpreussen* (Motor Buch Verlag, Stuttgart, 2002)

Dunn, W., *The Soviet Economy and the Red Army* (Greenwood, Westport CT, 2005)

Erenburg, I. *Post-War Years* (MacGibbon & Key, London, 1966)

Erickson, L., Erickson, M. (eds), *Russia: War, Peace and Diplomacy* (Weidenfeld & Nicolson, London, 2004)

Fediuninsky, I., *Podnyatyye po Trevoge* (Voyenizdat, Moscow, 1961)

Foote, A., *Handbook for Spies* (Museum, London, 1964)

Forczyk, R., *Leningrad 1941–44: The Epic Siege* (Osprey, Oxford, 2009)

Frank, R. (ed.), *Unsere Division in Sieg und Untergang: Erlebnisberichte von Angehörigen der 18. Infanterie-Division (Motorisiert)/Panzergrenadier-Division* (Self-published, Gliching, 1988)

Friedländer, S., *The Years of Extermination: Nazi Germany and the Jews 1939–1945* (Harper-Collins, New York, 1997)

Frieser, K.-H., Schönherr, K., Schreiber, G., Ungváry, K., *Die Ostfront 1943–1944 – Der Krieg im Osten und an den Nebenfronten* (Deutsche Verlags-Anstalt, Munich, 2007)

Frölich, S., *General Vlasov* (Markus, Cologne, 1994)

Garrard, J., Garrard, C (eds), *World War 2 and the Soviet People: Selected Papers From the Fourth World Congress For Soviet and East European Studies* (St Martin's Press, New York, 1993)

Gerlach, C., *Kalkulierte Morde: Die Deutsche Wirtschafts-Vernichtungspolitik in Weissrussland 1941 bis 1944* (Hamburger, Hamburg, 1998)

Glantz, D., *The Battle for Leningrad 1941–1944* (University Press of Kansas, Lawrence KS, 2002)

Glantz, D., House, J., *The Battle of Kursk* (University Press of Kansas, Lawrence KS, 2004)

Goldhagen, D., *Hitler's Willing Executioners: Ordinary Germans and the Holocaust* (Little, Brown & Co., London, 2014)

Gorbachevsky, B., *Rzhevskaya Myasorubka. Vremya Otvagi. Zadacha – Vyzhit!* (Eksmo, Moscow, 2007)

Görlitz, W., *Strategie der Defensive – Model* (Limes, Wiesbaden, 1982)

Gribkov, A. (ed.), *Istoriia Ordena Lenina Lengradskogo Voennogo Okruga* (Voyenizdat, Moscow, 1974)

Grier, H., *Hitler, Dönitz, and the Baltic Sea: The Third Reich's Last Hope, 1944–1945* (US Naval Institute Press, Annapolis MD, 2007)

Hansen, E., Schreiber, G., Wegner, B., *Politischer Wandel, Organiserte Gewalt und Nationale Sicherheit: Beitrage zur Neueren Geschichte Deutschlands und Frankreichs* (Oldenbourg, Munich, 1995)

Harris, A., Cox, S., *Despatch on War Operations: 23 February 1942 to 8 May 1945* (Routledge, Milton, 1995)

Haupt, W., *Die 8. Panzer-Division im Zweiten Weltkrieg* (Podzun-Pallas, Friedburg, 1987)

Haupt, W., *Army Group North: The Wehrmacht in Russia 1941–1945* (Schiffer, Atglen PA, 1997)

Heller, K., *The Nuremberg Military Tribunals and the Origins of International Criminal Law* (Oxford University Press, Oxford, 2011)

Hermann, W., *Die Geschichte des Infanterie-Regiments 51 und in Teilen die der 18. Infanterie-Divisions* (Regiments-Kameradschaft IR-51, Kassel, 1967)

Hernández Navarro, A., *Ida y Vuelta* (Espasa-Calpe, Madrid, 1971)

Hoffmann, J., *Die Tragödie der 'Russischen Befreiungsarmee' 1944–1945: Wlassow gegen Stalin* (Herbig, Munich, 2003)

Hughes, D. (ed.), *Moltke on the Art of War: Selected Writings* (Presidio, Novato CA, 1995)

Inber, V., *Stranitsy Dnei Perebiraia* (Sovetskaya Pisatel, Moscow, 1967)

International Military Tribunal, *Nazi Conspiracy and Aggression* (United States Government Printing Office, Washington DC, 1946, 11 volumes)

Isaev, V., *Kratkiy Kurs Istorii VOV* (Eksmo, Moscow, 2005)

Jones, M., *Leningrad: State of Siege* (John Murray, London, 2008)

Kaarsted, T., *De Danske Ministerier 1929–1953: et Hundredepolitisk-Historiske Biografer* (Pensionsforsikringsanstalten, Copenhagen, 1977)

Kardel, H., *Die Geschichte der 170. Infanterie-Division 1939–1945* (Podzun, Bad Nauheim, 1953)

Katukov, M., *Na Ostriye Glavnogo Udara* (Voyenizdat, Moscow, 1974)

Kay, A., *Exploitation, Resettlement, Mass Murder: Political and Economic Planning for German Occupation Policy in the Soviet Union 1940–1941* (Berghahn, New York, 2006)

Kee, R., *The Green Flag: A History of Irish Nationalism* (Penguin, Harmondsworth, 1972)

Ketlinskaia, V., *Molodoi Leningrad* (Sovetskii Pisatel, Moscow, 1966)

Kieser, E., *Danziger Bucht 1945: Dokumentation einer Katastrophe* (Bechtle, Munich, 1978)

Kinnunen, T., Kivimäki, V. (eds), *Finland in World War II: History, Memory, Interpretation* (Brill, Boston MA, 2011)

Kirschenbaum, L., *The Legacy of the Siege of Leningrad, 1941–1995* (Cambridge University Press, Cambridge, 2006)

Klee, E., *Das Personenlexikon zum Dritten Reich. Wer war was vor und nach 1945* (Fischer-Taschenbuch-Verlag, Frankfurt, 2007)

Klein, S., *Italy's Jews from Emancipation to Fascism* (Cambridge University Press, Cambridge, 2018)

Konsalik, H., Coburn, O., *Straf Bataillon 999* (Futura, London, 1980)

Koptelova, T., *Operatsiya Iskra. Proryiv Blokadyi Leningrada* (Galart, St Petersburg, 2012)

Korovnikov, I., *Novgorodsko-Luzhskaiia Operatsiia* (Voyenizdat, Moscow, 1960)

Kovalchuk, V., *Doroga Pobedy Osazhdennogo Leningrada* (Nauka, Moscow, 1984)

Kozlov, M. (ed.), *Velikaya Otechestvennaya Voyna 1941–1945: Entsiklopediya* (Sovetskaya Entsiklopediya, Moscow, 1985)

Krivosheyev, G. (ed.), *Rossiya I SSSR v Voynakh XX Veka. Poteri Vooruzhonnykh Sil: Statisticheskoye Issledovaniye* (Olma, Moscow, 2001)

Kuznetsov, N., *Nakanune* (Voyenizdat, Moscow, 1969)

Kuznetsov, V., *Vtoraya Udarnaya: V Bitve za Leningrad, Vospomynanyie, Dokumenti* (Lenizdat, Leningrad, 1983)

Kvachkov, V., *Spetsnaz Rossii* (Russkaya Panorama, Moscow, 2007)

Laar, M., *Sinimäed 1944; II Maailmasõja Lahingud Kirde-Eestis* (Varrak, Tallinn, 2006)

Lincoln, W., *Sunlight at Midnight: St Petersburg and the Rise of Modern Russia* (Basic Books, New York, 2000)

Littlejohn, D., *The Patriotic Traitors: A History of Collaboration in German-Occupied Europe 1940–1945* (Heinemann, London, 1972)

Littlejohn, D., *Foreign Legions of the Third Reich* (Bender, San Jose CA, 1987, 4 volumes)

Lohse, G., *Geschichte der Rheinisch-Westfälischen 126. Infanterie-Division 1940–1945* Podzun, Bad Neuheim, 1957)

Loskutova, M (ed.) *Pamiat o Blokade: Svidetelstva Ochevidtsev I Istoricheskoe Soznanie Obshchestva* (Novoe Izdvo, Moscow, 2006)

Lubbeck, W., Hurt, D., *At Leningrad's Gates* (Casemate, Newbury, 2006), p.133

Mallmann, K.-M., Angrick, A., Matthäus, J., Cüppers, M. (eds), *Die Ereignismeldungen UdSSR 1941: Dokumente der Einsatzgruppen in der Sowjetunion* (WBG, Darmstadt, 2011)

Manstein, E. von, Powell, A. (trans. and ed.), *Lost Victories: The War Memoirs of Hitler's Most Brilliant General* (Presidio, Novato CA, 1994)

Meier-Welcker, H., *Aufzeichnungen eines Generalstabsoffiziers 1939–1942* (Rombach, Freiburg, 1982)

Meretskov, K., *Na Sluzhbe Narodu* (Politizdat, Moscow, 1968)

Mitcham, S., *Hitler's Field Marshals and Their Battles* (Guild, London, 1988)

Mizin, V., *Snayper Petrova* (Lenizdat, Leningrad, 1988)

Morozov, D., *O Nikh ne Upominalos v Svodkakh* (Voyenizdat, Moscow, 1965)

Neratova, V., *V Dni Voiny: Semeinaya Khronika* (Zvezda, St Petersburg, 1996)

Newton, S., *Kursk: The German View* (Da Capo Press, Cambridge MA, 2002)

Newton, S., *Hitler's Commander: Field Marshal Walter Model – Hitler's Favorite General* (Da Capo, Cambridge MA, 2006)

Norman, G., *The Hermitage: The Biography of a Great Museum* (Fromm International, New York, 1998)

Núñez Seixas, X., *The Spanish Blue Division on the Eastern Front, 1941–1945: War, Occupation, Memory* (University of Toronto Press, Toronto, 2022)

Pazin, M., *Strasti po Vlast: Ot Lenina do Putina* (Piter, Moscow, 2012)

Pilyushin, I., *U Sten Leningrada* (Voyenizdat, Moscow, 1965)

Platonov, S., *Bitva za Leningrad 1941–1944* (Voyenizdat, Moscow, 1964)

Pohlman, H., *Wolchow: 900 Tage Kampf um Leningrad 1941–1944* (Podzun-Pallas, Wölfersheim-Berstadt, 2003)

Pomogaybo, A., *Vyrvannyy Mech Imperii 1925–1940gg* (Veche, Moscow, 2006)

Pyltsin, A., *Penalty Strike: The Memoirs of a Red Army Penal Company Commander 1943–1945* (Stackpole, Mechanicsburg PA, 2006)

Radó, S., *Sous la Pseudonyme Dora* (Julliard, Paris, 1972)

Richardson, W., *The Fatal Decisions: The Decisive Battles of the Second World War from the Viewpoint of the Vanquished* (Pen & Sword, Barnsley, 2012)

Richter, W., *Die 1. (Ostpreussische) Infanterie-Division* (Max Schmidt & Söhne, Munich, 1975)

Rokossovsky, K., *A Soldier's Duty* (Lancer International, New Delhi, 1985)

Roosevelt, F., Rosenman, S. (ed.), *The Public Papers and Addresses of Franklin D. Roosevelt* (Random House, New York 1949, 13 volumes)

Rotmistrov, P., *Stalnaya Gvardiya* (Voyenizdat, Moscow, 1984)

Salisbury, H., *The 900 Days: The Siege of Leningrad* (Da Capo, Cambridge MA, 2009)

Sarfatti, M., *The Jews in Mussolini's Italy: From Equality to Persecution* (University of Wisconsin Press, Madison WS, 2006)

Scheurig, B., *Verräter oder Patrioten: Das Nationalkomitee 'Freies Deutschland' und der Bund Deutscher Offiziere in der Sowjetunion 1943–1945* (Propyläen, Berlin, 1993)

Schlabrendorff, F. von, Gaevernitz, G. von, *Offiziere Gegen Hitler* (Fischer, Frankfurt am Main, 1959)

Schramm, P. (ed.), *Kriegstagebuch der Oberkommandos der Wehrmacht* (Bernard & Graefe, Munich, 1982, 8 volumes)

Searle, A., *Armoured Warfare: A Military, Political and Global History* (Bloomsbury, London, 2017)

Seaton, A., *The Russo-German War 1941–1945* (Praeger, New York, 1971)

Shtemenko, S., *The Soviet General Staff at War 1941–1945* (Progress, Moscow, 1970)

Sigin, G., *Bitva za Leningrad: Krupnyye Operatsii, Belyye Pyatna, Poteri* (Poligon, Moscow, 2005)

Silgailis, A., *Latvian Legion* (Bender, San Jose CA, 1986)

Simmons, C., Perlina, N. (eds), *Writing the Siege of Leningrad: Women's Diaries, Memoirs and Documentary Prose* (University of Pittsburgh Press, Pittsburgh PA, 2002)

Small Unit Actions During the German Campaign in Russia (Department of the Army, Washington DC, 1953)

Smirnov, S., *Marshal Zhukov. Kakim my Yego Pomnim* (Izdatelstvo Politicheskoy Literatury, Moscow, 1989)

Smith, P., *Petlyakov Pe-2 Peshka* (Ramsbury, Marlborough, 2003)

Snyder, T., *Bloodlands: Europe Between Hitler and Stalin* (Vintage, London, 2011)

Solomakhin, I., *Shturm 'Churtovoy Vysoty'. Inzhenernyye Voyska Goroda-Fronta* (Lenizdat, Leningrad, 1979)

Soobshcheniya Sovetskogo Informbyuro (Sovinformburo, Moscow 1944, 9 volumes)

Stachow, H., *Tragödie an der Newa: Der Kampf um Leningrad 1941–1944* (Herbig, Munich, 2001)

Stein, M., *Generalfeldmarschall Walter Model. Legende und Wirklichkeit* (Biblio, Osnabrück, 2001)

Strauss, F., *Geschichte der 2. (Wiener) Panzer-Division* (Dörfler, Eggolsheim, 2005)

Streshinskiy, M., Frantishev, I., *General Simoniak* (Lenizdat, Leningrad, 1971)

Strik-Strikfeldt, W., *Against Stalin and Hitler: Memoir of the Russian Liberation Movement 1941–1945* (John Day & Co, New York, 1970)

Sudoplatov, P., *Razvedka I Kreml'* (Geya, Moscow, 1977)

Sullam, S., *The Italian Executioners: The Genocide of the Jews of Italy* (Princeton University Press, Princeton CT, 2018

Taranova, E., *Levitan: Golos Stalina* (Partner SP6, St Petersburg, 2010)

Tarrant, V., *The Red Orchestra* (J. Wiley, London, 1995)

Telitsyn, M., *Marshal Govorov* (Veche, Moscow, 2013)

Tieke, W., Steinhardt, F. (trans.), *Tragedy of the Faithful: A History of the III (germanisches) SS-Panzer-Korps* (Fedorowicz, Winnipeg, 2001)

Toporov, V., *Mif, Ritual, Simvol, Obraz: Issledovaniia v Oblasti Mifopoeticheskogo: Izbrannoe* (Kultura, Moscow, 1995)

Toporov, V., *Petersburgskii Tekst* (Nauka, Moscow, 2009)

Tukhashevsky, M., *Izbrannyye Proizvedeniya* (Voyenizdat, Moscow, 1964, 2 volumes)

Turner A., *Messines 1917: The Zenith of Siege Warfare* (Osprey, Oxford, 2010)

Ueberschär, G. (ed.), *Das Nationalkomitee 'Freies Deutschland' und der Bund Deutscher Offiziere* (Fischer Taschenbuch, Frankfurt-am-Main, 1996)

Varshavsky, S., Rast, B., *Saved for Humanity: The Hermitage During the Siege of Leningrad* (Aurora, Leningrad, 1985)

Vasilevsky, A., *A Lifelong Cause* (Progress, Moscow, 1973)

Veselov, I., *Tri Goda v Tylu Braga: Zapiski Partizana* (Permskoye Knizhnoye Izdatelsetvo, Perm, 1961)

Vinnitsky, L., *Slavnaya Pobeda pod Leningradom: Vospominaniya, Stati I Dokumenty, Posvyashchennyye Razgromu Nemetsko-Fashistskikh Voysk pod Leningradom* (Lenizdat, Leningrad, 1976)

Volkovsky, N., *Blokada Leningrada v Dokumentach Rassekreennych Archivov* (Poligon, St Petersburg, 2005)

Voloshin, M., *Razvedchiki Vsegda Vperedi* (Voyenizdat, Moscow, 1977)

Voronov, N., *Ha Sluzhbe Voyennoy* (Voyenizdat, Moscow, 1963)

Weeks, A., *Russia's Life-Saver: Lend-Lease Aid to the USSR in World War II* (Lexington, Lanham MD, 2004)

Werth, A., *Leningrad* (Hamish Hamilton, London, 1944)

Wette, W., *Die Wehrmacht: Feindbilder, Vernichtungskrieg, Legenden* (Fischer Taschenbuch, Frankfurt am Main, 2013)

Ydígoras, C., *Algunos no Hemos Muerto* (Cyr, Madrid, 1984)

Zabecki, D. (ed.), *World War II in Europe* (Taylor & Francis, Milton, 2015)

Zhukov, G., *Vospomimaniya I Razmyshleniya* (Olma, Moscow 2002, 2 volumes)

Zhukova, I., *Devushka so Snayperskoy Vintovkoy* (Tsentrpoligraf, Moscow, 2006)

Ziemke, E., *Stalingrad to Berlin: The German Defeat in the East* (Dorset, New York, 1986)

Zimmermann, J., *Pflicht zum Untergang. Die Deutsche Kriegsführung im Westen des Reiches 1944–1945* (Schöningh, Paderborn, 2009)

Zolotarev, V. (ed.), *Velikaia Otechestvennaia* (Terra, Moscow, 1996–2005, 25 volumes)

INDEX

Latvia 249, 253, 256, 264–66, 403–6
Laux, Gen Paul 139–40, 142, 143–44, 145
Leeb, GenFM Wilhelm Ritter von 375, 393–95
Lelyushenko, Dmitry Danilovich 38
Lenin, Vladimir 425, 427
Leningrad Affair 413–14, 418
Levitan, Yuri Borisovich 114–15
Leyser, Gen Ernst von 49–50, 53, 91–92, 98–99
Leyser, Genlt Hans von 50
Lindemann, Genob Georg 36, 53, 72, 92, 375–76
  and Küchler 257–59, 260, 267
  and withdrawal 311, 315, 316
  and *Yanvarskiiy Grom* 288, 298, 302–3, 304, 307
Lipka 88, 112
literature 17
Loch, Gen Herbert 246
Löffelholz, Hptm 137
Lubbeck, Wilhelm 42, 153–54, 186–87
  and Sinyavino offensive 211, 212–13, 225–26
Luftwaffe 48, 49, 63, 160
  and Baltic Fleet 394
  and deception 143–44
  and eastern withdrawal 233
  and *Iskra* 120–21
  and Jodl 244
  and Staraya Russa 158
  and *Yanvarskiiy Grom* 283, 285, 292, 294, 301–2
Luga 127, 316–17, 320, 330–32, 336, 350–54
Lvovich, Iuliyus Moiseyevich 349
Lyashchenko, Col Nikolai Georgiyevich 66, 109

Maeker, Hptm Rudolph 341
Maginot Line 279, 280
Maitla, Paul 378

Malenkov, Georgy Maksimilianovich 413
Mannerheim, Marshal Carl 380, 382
Manstein, GenFM Erich von 176, 177, 178–80, 243, 397
  and Hitler 323–24
  and Ukraine 314
  and Zitadelle 202–3
Martinsen, Ob Knud Børge 261–62
Marttila, Yelena Oskarovna 428–29
Maskirovka (deception) 71, 143
Maslennikov, Lt Gen Ivan Ivanovich 270, 273, 318, 366, 379
  and *Yanvarskiiy Grom* 287, 290
mass executions 35–36
Mazanik, Yelena Grigoryevna 245
memorials 405–6, 411–12, 419–23, 427–28
Meretskov, Gen Kirill Afanasyevich 39–41, 53, 56–58, 91, 377–78, 409
  and air strikes 63
  and Estonia 356
  and German withdrawal 309–10, 311, 312
  and logistics 366–67
  and Luga 316–17, 331–32
  and memoirs 399
  and Oranienbaum 269–70, 273–75
  and *Polyarnya Zvedza* 172
  and redeployment of artillery 117–18
  and reserves 183–85
  and Sinyavino offensive 205–6, 219, 223–24
  and weaponry 121
  and *Yanvarskiiy Grom* 281–82, 302
Meriküla 354–55
Mikhailov, Aleksandr 129
Model, Genob Walter 180, 194, 201, 336, 338–43, 373–74
  and *Schild und Schwert* 344, 348, 350–53, 357
Molodtsov, Sgn Dmitry Semenovich 110